Neural Networks

IEEE PRESS
445 Hoes Lane, PO Box 1331
Piscataway, NJ 08855-1331

Neural Networks

Theoretical Foundations and Analysis

Edited by

Clifford Lau
Office of Naval Research
Arlington, Virginia

IEEE
PRESS

A Selected Reprint Volume
IEEE Neural Networks Council, *Sponsor*

The Institute of Electrical and Electronics Engineers, Inc. New York

Printed in the United States of America

10 9 8 7 6 5 4 3 2

ISBN 0-87942-280-7

IEEE Order Number: PC0279-0

Library of Congress Cataloging-in-Publication Data

Neural networks: theoretical foundations and analysis / edited by Clifford G. Y. Lau.
p. cm.
"IEEE Neural Networks Council, sponsor."
Includes papers published in two IEEE proceedings special issues and in other publications, 1987-1990.
"A Selected reprint volume."
Includes bibliographical references and indexes.
IEEE order no.: PC0279-0.
ISBN 0-87942-280-7
1. Neural networks (Computer science) I. Lau, Clifford. II. IEEE Neural Networks Council.
QA76.87.N489 1992
006.3—dc20 91-39114
CIP

Contents

Preface vii

Part 1 Introduction 1

An Introduction to Computing with Neural Nets 5
R. P. Lippman (*IEEE Acoustics, Speech, and Signal Processing*, April 1987)

Part 2 Theoretical Foundations 25

30 Years of Adaptive Neural Networks: Perceptron, Madaline, and Backpropagation 27
B. Widrow and M. A. Lehr (*Proceedings of the IEEE*, September 1990)

Mathematical Foundations of Neurocomputing 54
S.-I. Amari (*Proceedings of the IEEE*, September 1990)

The Self-Organizing Map 74
T. Kohonen (*Proceedings of the IEEE*, September 1990)

Networks for Approximation and Learning 91
T. Poggio and F. Girosi (*Proceedings of the IEEE*, September 1990)

Part 3 Neural Modeling 107

Synthetic Neural Modeling: The "Darwin" Series of Recognition Automata 109
G. N. Reeke, Jr., O. Sporns, and G. M. Edelman (*Proceedings of the IEEE*, September 1990)

Neural Networks and Physical Systems with Emergent Collective Computational Abilities 142
J. J. Hopfield (*Proceedings of the National Academy of Sciences*, April 1982)

A Massively Parallel Architecture for a Self-Organizing Neural Pattern Recognition Machine 147
Gail A. Carpenter and Stephen Grossberg (*Computer Vision, Graphics, and Image Processing*, 1987)

Part 4 Analysis and Applications 209

Backpropagation Through Time: What It Does and How to Do It 211
P. J. Werbos (*Proceedings of the IEEE*, October 1990)

A Neural Network for Visual Pattern Recognition 222
K. Fukushima (*IEEE Computers*, March 1988)

CMAC: An Association Neural Network Alternative to Backpropagation 233
W. T. Miller III, F. H. Glanz, and L. G. Kraft III (*Proceedings of the IEEE*, October 1990)

A Statistical Approach to Learning and Generalization in Layered Neural Networks 240
E. Levin, N. Tishby, and S. A. Solla (*Proceedings of the IEEE*, October 1990)

On the Convergence Properties of the Hopfield Model 247
J. Bruck (*Proceedings of the IEEE*, October 1990)

Constructive Approximations for Neural Networks by Sigmoidal Functions 254
L. K. Jones (*Proceedings of the IEEE*, October 1990)

On the Decision Regions of Multilayer Perceptrons 258
G. J. Gibson and C. F. N. Cowan (*Proceedings of the IEEE*, October 1990)

Nearest Neighbor Pattern Classification Perceptrons 263
O. J. Murphy (*Proceedings of the IEEE*, October 1990)

Convergence Properties and Stationary Points of a Perceptron Learning Algorithm 267
J. J. Shynk and S. Roy (*Proceedings of the IEEE*, October 1990)

Part 5 Related Techniques 273

Entropy Nets: From Decision Trees to Neural Networks 275
I. K. Sethi (*Proceedings of the IEEE*, October 1990)

A Performance Comparison of Trained Multi-layer Perceptrons and Trained Classification Trees 284
L. Atlas, R. Cole, Y. Muthusamy, A. Lippman, J. Connor, D. Park, M. El-Sharkawi, and R. J. Marks II (*Proceedings of the IEEE*, October 1990)

Maximum A Posteriori Decision and Evaluation of Class Probabilities by Boltzmann Perceptron Classifiers 289
E. Yair and A. Gersho (*Proceedings of the IEEE*, October 1990)

Part 6 Applications 299

Radar Signal Categorization Using a Neural Network 300
J. A. Anderson, M. T. Gately, P. A. Penz, and D. R. Collins (*Proceedings of the IEEE*, October 1990)

Neural Network Models of Sensory Integration for Improved Vowel Recognition 311
B. P. Yuhas, M. H. Goldstein, Jr., T. J. Sejnowski, and R. E. Jenkins (*Proceedings of the IEEE*, October 1990)

Author Index 321

Subject Index 323

Editor's Biography 327

Preface

For any research field to have credibility, there must be a firm theoretical foundation. Neural networks research is no exception. This book is intended to provide that firm theoretical and mathematical foundation necessary for the continued growth of research and development in neural networks.

Neural networks have enjoyed a revival after some twenty years of hibernation. In the last five years, more than three thousand papers have been published on neural networks and related fields. More than twenty new books have been published in the last three years. New researchers are entering neural networks every day. There are numerous well attended international conferences on neural networks. Several new journals and transactions on neural networks have been introduced in this rapidly growing field. These journal papers are a great source of information on the latest research results; yet the need exists to place all the foundational mathematical theories on neural networks for study in one easy reference.

This book fills that need. It consists of excellent papers published in two IEEE Proceedings special issues on neural networks which are further supplemented in this book by several classic papers in neural networks. The book is divided into six sections. In the Section 1: Introduction, a very readable paper by R. Lippmann has been included for an easy introduction to neural networks and its terminologies. In Section 2, Theoretical Foundations, the papers provide the analytical foundations for the rest of the book. In Section 3: Neural Modeling, several papers of extreme significance have also been added to the paper on synthetic neural modeling. The paper by J. Hopfield is a turning point in the revival of neural networks, and has generated a large group of followers. The paper by G. Carpenter and S. Grossberg is added to lay the foundation for a popular kind of neural network called adaptive resonance theory (ART) nets. In Section 4: Mathematical Analysis, a paper by K. Fukushima on the Neocognitron has been added to the collection of papers. In Section 5: Related Techniques, comparisons are made between neural networks and traditional statistically based techniques. Finally in Section 6: Applications, two examples of how neural networks can be applied to engineering problems are presented.

This book covers all aspects of mathematical theories that are necessary to understand the many different neural network architectures. It can be used as a text book for advanced students with a certain amount of mathematical maturity, or it can be used as a reference book for scientists and engineers interested in the mathematical analysis of neural networks.

I would like to thank the many contributors of this book for their outstanding papers. I want to thank the IEEE Proceedings Executive Editor, W. Reed Crone, and his staff for putting together two excellent special issues on neural networks. Foremost, I want to thank my IEEE Press Executive Editor, Dudley Kay, for his assistance and to thank IEEE Press Associate Editor, Anne Reifsnyder, and Assistant Editor, Karen Miller for their editorial help.

Clifford G. Lau

Part 1
Introduction

The term *neural network*, or more properly *neuronal network*, originally referred to a network of interconnected neurons. The human nervous system is anatomically subdivided into the central nervous system, which comprises the brain and spinal cord, and the peripheral nervous system, which comprises the cranial and spinal nerves. The brain is subdivided into five major anatomical units called the cerebrum (or cortex), cerebellum, midbrain, pons, and medulla. Functionally, the brain can be subdivided into smaller parts, such as the motor cortex, visual cortex, auditory cortex, hippocampus, and various nuclei groups in the brain stem. The average human brain consists of 1.5×10^{10} neurons of various types, with each neuron receiving signals through as many as 10^4 synapses. With that kind of complexity, it is no wonder that the human brain is considered to be the most complex piece of biological machinery on earth. Fortunately, after years of research by neuroanatomists and neurophysiologists, the understanding of the brain has progressed to a point in which the overall organization is well understood, although many of the detailed neural mechanisms remain to be elucidated. Some parts of the brain are better understood than others. The cerebellum, for example, is better understood than the neocortex because of its isolated and identifiable input, output, and internal circuitry with climbing fibers, mossy fibers, and purkinje cells.

To try to understand brain function, various models have been proposed. Probably the best known was the work of Hodgkin and Huxley on the modeling of the giant squid axon. They methodically collected empirical data, postulated the mechanism of ion transport channels, formulated mathematical and circuit models, and then developed the voltage clamped technique to validate their models. Certainly, modeling work done by many others, such as Von Bekesy's cochlear microphonics work, can be cited as contributing to the understanding of brain function. For example, the discovery of special feature detecting cells in the visual cortex by Hubel and Wiesel has had a profound impact on the understanding of information processing in the visual system, and on the field of pattern recognition.

We are now dealing with the ultimate question: How does the brain work? Neurobiologists have taken the bottom-up approach by studying the stimulus-response characteristics of single neurons and networks of neurons. On the other hand, psychologists have taken the top-down approach by studying brain function from the cognitive and behavioral level. They are gradually and incrementally getting a better idea of how the brain works, both at the single neuron level and at the behavioral level. However, it may take another fifty years before we have a solid, complete microscopic, intermediate, and macroscopic view of how the brain works. Engineers can not wait that long. We must design computational apparatus to solve practical problems. We seek solutions to problems that are difficult with today's digital computing technology; problems that are easily solved by people and animals. Therefore, we keep one eye on the brain studies, and the other eye on making use of available models and paradigms, and possibly developing new ones. We try to build more brainlike computers out of neuronlike parts.

It was this view that led to the development of many of the earlier models of neurons and neural networks. McCullogh and Pitts in the 1940s showed that the neuron can be modeled as a simple threshold device to perform logic function. In the same time frame, relationships among engineering principles, feedback, and brain function were expounded by Wiener as the principle of cybernetics. Ashby's model of brain function and principle of homeostasis strongly influenced engineering and vice versa. By the late 1950s and early 1960s, neuron models were further refined into Rosenblatt's Perceptron, Widrow and Hoff's Adaline (ADAptive LINear Element), and Steinbuch's Learning Matrix. The Perceptron received considerable excitement when it was first introduced because of its conceptual simplicity. However, that excitement was short lived when Minsky and Papert proved mathematically that the Perceptron cannot be used for complex logic functions. On the other hand, the fate of Adaline was quite different. The Adaline is a weighted sum of the inputs, together with a least mean square (LMS) algorithm to adjust the weights to minimize the difference between the output and the desired signal. Because of its linear and adaptive nature, the technique has developed into a powerful tool for adaptive signal processing, which is used in equalization, echo and noise cancellation, adaptive beam forming, and adaptive control. The reason is primarily due to the rigorous mathematical foundation of the LMS algorithm. Because of that, it has stood the test of time.

Today the term neural network, or more properly artificial neural network, has come to mean any computing architecture that consists of massively parallel interconnections of simple "neural" processors. The motivation comes mainly from the fact that human beings are much better than digital computers at pattern recognition. The brain has taken millions of years to evolve into its present architecture, and has become the most efficient machine in vision processing and speech recognition. Therefore, there must be computational principles that the brain uses to accomplish such high speed pattern recognition. Our job is to understand these computational principles and put them to good use in the design of practical systems.

The present impetus in neural network research is due in part to the paper John Hopfield published in 1982 in the *Proceedings of the National Academy of Sciences* and which is reprinted in this book. In this paper, he presented a model of neural computation that is based on the interaction of neurons. The model consisted of a set of first order (nonlinear) differential equations that minimize a certain "energy" function. He argued that there are emergent computational capabilities at the network level that are nonexistent at the single neuron level. This kind of neural network is now known as a Hopfield net.

Certainly Hopfield was not the first to recognize the neuron's spatial and temporal integration properties, which were known in the very early days of neurophysiology. Furthermore, the idea that neurons organize themselves to perform the necessary functions was promoted by a number of researchers. During the 1970s, when no one else was working on neural networks, Steven Grossberg at Boston University and Teuvo Kohonen at Helsinki University were making significant contributions. Grossberg, together with Gail Carpenter, have developed a neural network architecture they call *adaptive resonance theory* (ART), based on the idea that the brain spontaneously organizes itself into recognition codes. The dynamics of the network were also modeled by first-order differential equations. Meanwhile, Kohonen was developing his ideas on self-organizing maps, based on the idea that neurons organize themselves to tune to various and specific patterns. In the early 1970s, Paul Werbos discovered the mathematical principles of the backpropagation algorithm while studying problems in the social sciences. In the mid 1980s, David Rumelhart and his colleagues published their landmark books on parallel distributed processing, which established the backpropagation algorithm and feedforward layered network as the major paradigm of the field. This and earlier works have finally galvanized a large segment of the scientific community into thinking in terms of collective neural computation rather than single neurons.

Although neural networks can serve to further the understanding of brain functions, engineers are interested in neural networks for problem-solving. As an engineering technique, neural networks have their own set of advantages, disadvantages, and assumptions. The natural question is: What can neural networks do that traditional signal processing techniques cannot do? Certainly speed of computation is a factor. In traditional single processor Von Neumann computers, the speed is limited by the propagation delay of the transistors. Neural networks, on the other hand, because of their massively parallel nature, can perform computations at a much higher rate. Because of their adaptive nature, neural networks can adapt to changes in the data and learn the characteristics of input signals. Furthermore, because of their nonlinear nature, neural networks can perform functional approximation and signal-filtering operations, which are beyond optimal linear techniques. Neural networks can be used in pattern classification by defining nonlinear regions in the feature space.

In the realm of engineering, no single technique is a panacea, and neural networks are no exceptions; they have their limitations. The nonlinear sigmoidal functions used in layered networks cause multiple minimums to appear during learning, and one is never sure whether the system has reached its global minimum. Stochastic techniques such as "simulated annealing," can help the situation but often require excessive computation time. As in adaptive signal processing, there is always a trade-off between the speed and the stability of convergence. Digital computer simulations of neural nets are still too slow for practical use in large-scale problems.

What are the research and development issues? Certainly there is a need to further investigate and understand brain information processing. From these investigations, many new neural network architectures will be invented. There is a need to develop techniques to extend these networks to reasonably large scale in order to solve real-world problems. Mathematically, it is necessary to understand the nonlinear dynamics of these networks and to develop new algorithms that are fast, robust in the presence of noise, stable, and that guarantee to converge to the global minimum. Certainly, there is a need to develop the analog/digital and optics technology to implement these unconventional computing architectures. In terms of applications to engineering problems, there is a need to develop good mathematical theories to explain the experimental results. In engineering, it is necessary to develop quantitative techniques to evaluate neural network's performance with real-world data. The performance of neural networks must be compared, objectively and quantitatively, with traditional signal processing techniques. Rigorous mathematical foundations must be developed to determine the characteristics of the training set, and the network's ability to generalize from the training data.

This book is expressly put together to build the foundations to address these research and development issues. It is intended for scientists and engineers with a certain level of mathematical maturity who want to make a contribution to neural network research and development. The book is organized into six sections, with emphasis on mathematical rigor and theoretical analysis. In the first section, the paper by R. Lippmann is a very readable introduction to the subject of neural networks for the beginner. It provides a brief introduction to the theory of multilayered nets and then explains some examples of applications to signal processing.

In Section 2: Theoretical Foundations, the first paper by B. Widrow and M. Lehr outlines the historical perspective of thirty years of adaptive signal processing and neural network development. It develops the basic theory of several neural network training algorithms, including the Perceptron rule, the least mean square (LMS) technique, the backpropagation algorithm, and the latest Madaline learning rule. It is a "must-read" for anyone who plans to do research in multilayered neural nets. The second paper, by S. Amari, describes the mathematical foundations for neurocomputing. It considers the capabilities and limitations in mathematical terms of the various neurocomputing architectures. It develops the general theory of transformation by layered networks, statistical neurodynamics, associative memory, and neural learning. The third paper by T. Kohonen, is a tutorial on self-organizing brain maps. The fourth paper, by T. Poggio and F. Girosi, describes the mathematical foundations of neural networks for approximation and learning. The authors review for the reader the theoretical framework for approximation based on regularization networks that are mathematically related to the well known radial basis functions.

In Section 3: Neural Modeling, the papers provide the motivation for studying neural networks, which is to develop models of the brain and to understand the computational principles of brain information processing. The paper by G. Reeke, O. Sporns, and G. Edelman provides a good description of their continuing effort to develop the "Darwin" neural networks. Their synthetic neural modeling effort is intended to aid the understanding of the neuronal basis of adaptive behavior, and it takes into account possible evolutionary origins and modes of development of the nervous system. The paper by J. Hopfield is a milestone in the annals of neural network research and motivates a new generation of researchers to look at a network of neurons in a different light. The paper by G. Carpenter and S. Grossberg, in which they model the adaptive behaviors in pattern recognition, form the basis of their Adaptive Resonance Theory neural network.

Section 4: Mathematical Analysis, contains the largest group of nine papers, which form the basis of much of the research that is going on in neural networks. The first paper, by P. Werbos, introduces the element of time into the popular backpropagation learning algorithm, which originally is static. The second paper, by K. Fukushima, explains the neocognitron model of neural networks. The third paper, by W. Miller III, F. Glanz, and L. Kraft III, describes the well known cerebellar model arithmetic computer (CMAC) as an alternative to the backpropagation algorithm. Although most of the research has been centered on deterministic networks, the next paper by E. Levin, N. Tishby, and S. Solla, describes a general statistical approach to the problem of learning from examples. By imposing the equivalence of minimum error and the maximum likelihood criteria, they arrive at the Gibbs distribution on the ensemble of networks with a fixed architecture. The next paper, by J. Bruck, is centered on the convergence properties of the popular Hopfield net. The paper by L. Jones further expands on the technique of constructive approximation by sigmoidal functions. The next two papers, one by G. J. Gibson and C. N. F. Cowan, and the other by O. J. Murphy, are centered on the analysis of multilayer perceptrons as pattern classifiers. The final paper in this group, by J. Shynk and S. Roy, demonstrates that the LMS algorithm with a momentum term is always stable if the momentum constant is chosen appropriately. However, the stationary points are not unique but are dependent on algorithm step size.

Section 5: Related Techniques, contains three papers on conventional techniques that are related to neural networks. The first paper, by I. Sethi, discusses the relationship between multilayered neural nets and decision tree classifiers. The next paper, by L. Atlas, R. Cole, D. Park, M. El-Sharkawi, and R. Marks II, presents a performance comparison of trained multilayer perceptron network and classification trees. They show that in almost all cases, the multilayer perceptron network performs as well as, or sometimes better than, the trained classification tree, even for piecewise linear trees. The third paper in this group, by E. Yair and A. Gersho, shows that maximum a posteriori classifiers are constructed as a special case of the Boltzmann perceptron classifier (BPC). The authors further show, by simulation, that the BPC is comparable in performance to the classical Bayesian classifier although no assumptions are made on the probabilistic models of the problem.

In the Section 6: Applications, two examples of neural network applications are presented. Applications in this field are beginning to emerge and are an important part of the research. The first paper, by J. Anderson, M. Gately, P. Andrew Penz, and D. Collins, shows that neural networks can be used in radar signal categorization and emitter identification. The second paper, by B. Yuhas, M. Goldstein, Jr., T. Sejnowski, and R. Jenkins, demonstrates that neural network models can be used to integrate the visual and auditory cues for improved vowel recognition. Numerous other application papers on speech recognition, image processing, and pattern recognition can be found in the new journals and transactions on neural networks. Hopefully, this book provides much of the theoretical basis so that new application areas can be formulated by the readers.

An Introduction to Computing with Neural Nets

Richard P. Lippmann

Abstract

Artificial neural net models have been studied for many years in the hope of achieving human-like performance in the fields of speech and image recognition. These models are composed of many nonlinear computational elements operating in parallel and arranged in patterns reminiscent of biological neural nets. Computational elements or nodes are connected via weights that are typically adapted during use to improve performance. There has been a recent resurgence in the field of artificial neural nets caused by new net topologies and algorithms, analog VLSI implementation techniques, and the belief that massive parallelism is essential for high performance speech and image recognition. This paper provides an introduction to the field of artificial neural nets by reviewing six important neural net models that can be used for pattern classification. These nets are highly parallel building blocks that illustrate neural- net components and design principles and can be used to construct more complex systems. In addition to describing these nets, a major emphasis is placed on exploring how some existing classification and clustering algorithms can be performed using simple neuron-like components. Single-layer nets can implement algorithms required by Gaussian maximum-likelihood classifiers and optimum minimum-error classifiers for binary patterns corrupted by noise. More generally, the decision regions required by any classification algorithm can be generated in a straightforward manner by three-layer feed-forward nets.

INTRODUCTION

Artificial neural net models or simply "neural nets" go by many names such as connectionist models, parallel distributed processing models, and neuromorphic systems. Whatever the name, all these models attempt to achieve good performance via dense interconnection of simple computational elements. In this respect, artificial neural net structure is based on our present understanding of biological nervous systems. Neural net models have greatest potential in areas such as speech and image recognition where many hypotheses are pursued in parallel, high computation rates are required, and the current best systems are far from equaling human performance. Instead of performing a program of instructions sequentially as in a von Neumann computer, neural net models explore many competing hypotheses simultaneously using massively parallel nets composed of many computational elements connected by links with variable weights.

Computational elements or nodes used in neural net models are nonlinear, are typically analog, and may be slow compared to modern digital circuitry. The simplest node sums N weighted inputs and passes the result through a nonlinearity as shown in Fig. 1. The node is characterized by an internal threshold or offset θ and by the type of nonlinearity. Figure 1 illustrates three common types of nonlinearities; hard limiters, threshold logic elements, and sigmoidal nonlinearities. More complex nodes may include temporal integration or other types of time dependencies and more complex mathematical operations than summation.

Neural net models are specified by the net topology, node characteristics, and training or learning rules. These rules specify an initial set of weights and indicate how weights should be adapted during use to improve performance. Both design procedures and training rules are the topic of much current research.

The potential benefits of neural nets extend beyond the high computation rates provided by massive parallelism. Neural nets typically provide a greater degree of robustness or fault tolerance than von Neumann sequential computers because there are many more processing nodes, each with primarily local connections. Damage to a few nodes or links thus need not impair overall performance significantly. Most neural net algorithms also adapt connection weights in time to improve performance based on current results. Adaptation or learning is a major focus of neural net research. The ability to adapt and continue learning is essential in areas such as speech recognition where training data is limited and new talkers, new words, new dialects, new phrases, and new environments are continuously encountered. Adaptation also provides a degree of robustness by compensating for minor variabilities in characteristics of processing elements. Traditional statistical techniques are not adaptive but typically process all training data simultaneously before being used with new data. Neural net classifiers are also non-parametric and make weaker assumptions concerning the shapes of underlying distributions than traditional statistical classifiers. They may thus prove to be more robust when distributions are generated by nonlinear processes and are strongly non-Gaussian. Designing artificial neural nets to solve

Reprinted from *IEEE ASSP Magazine*, April 1987, pp. 4–22.

problems and studying real biological nets may also change the way we think about problems and lead to new insights and algorithmic improvements.

Work on artificial neural net models has a long history. Development of detailed mathematical models began more than 40 years ago with the work of McCulloch and Pitts [30], Hebb [17], Rosenblatt [39], Widrow [47] and others [38]. More recent work by Hopfield [18, 19, 20], Rumelhart and McClelland [40], Sejnowski [43], Feldman [9], Grossberg [15], and others has led to a new resurgence of the field. This new interest is due to the development of new net topologies and algorithms [18, 19, 20, 41, 9], new analog VLSI implementation techniques [31], and some intriguing demonstrations [43, 20] as well as by a growing fascination with the functioning of the human brain. Recent interest is also driven by the realization that human-like performance in the areas of speech and image recognition will require enormous amounts of processing. Neural nets provide one technique for obtaining the required processing capacity using large numbers of simple processing elements operating in parallel.

This paper provides an introduction to the field of neural nets by reviewing six important neural net models that can be used for pattern classification. These massively parallel nets are important building blocks which can be used to construct more complex systems. The main purpose of this review is to describe the purpose and design of each net in detail, to relate each net to existing pattern classification and clustering algorithms that are normally implemented on sequential von Neumann computers, and to illustrate design principles used to obtain parallelism using neural-like processing elements.

Neural net and traditional classifiers

Block diagrams of traditional and neural net classifiers are presented in Fig. 2. Both types of classifiers determine which of M classes is most representative of an unknown static input pattern containing N input elements. In a speech recognizer the inputs might be the output envelope values from a filter bank spectral analyzer sampled at one time instant and the classes might represent different vowels. In an image classifier the inputs might be the gray scale level of each pixel for a picture and the classes might represent different objects.

The traditional classifier in the top of Fig. 2 contains two stages. The first computes matching scores for each class and the second selects the class with the maximum score. Inputs to the first stage are symbols representing values of the N input elements. These symbols are entered sequentially and decoded from the external symbolic form into an internal representation useful for performing arithmetic and symbolic operations. An algorithm computes a matching score for each of the M classes which indicates how closely the input matches the exemplar pattern for each class. This exemplar pattern is that pattern which is most representative of each class. In many situations a probabilistic model is used to model the generation of input patterns from exemplars and the matching score represents the likelihood or probability that the input pattern was generated from each of the M possible exemplars. In those cases, strong assumptions are typically made concerning underlying distributions of the input elements. Parameters of distributions can then be estimated using a training data as shown in Fig. 2. Multivariate Gaussian distributions are often used leading to relatively simple algorithms for computing matching scores [7]. Matching scores are coded into symbolic representations and passed sequentially to the second stage of

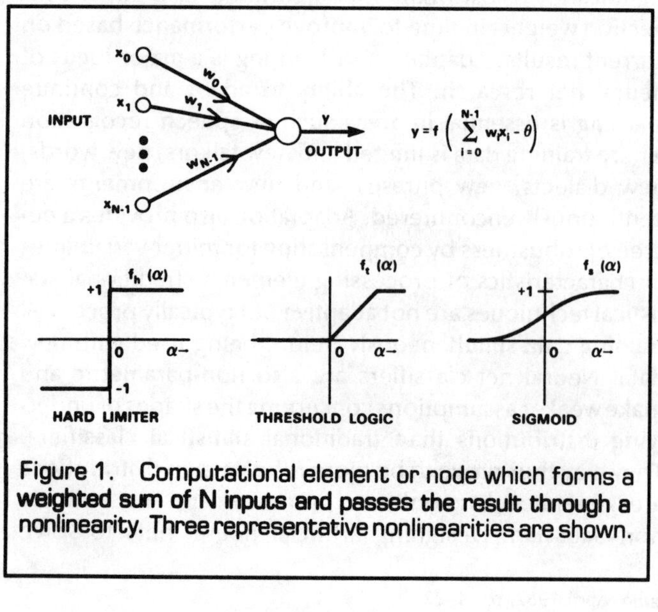

Figure 1. Computational element or node which forms a weighted sum of N inputs and passes the result through a nonlinearity. Three representative nonlinearities are shown.

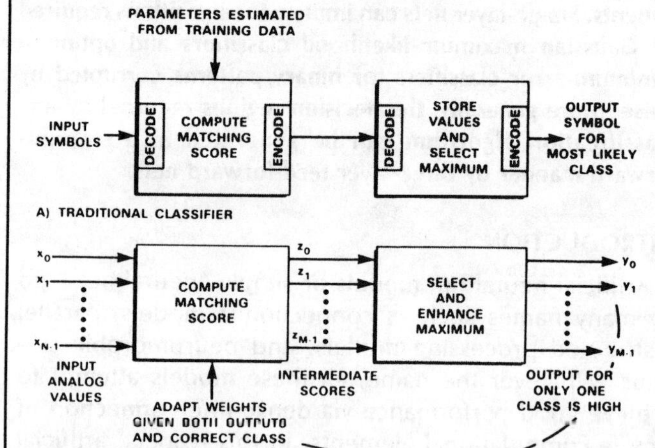

Figure 2. Block diagrams of traditional (A) and neural net (B) classifiers. Inputs and outputs of the traditional classifier are passed serially and internal computations are performed sequentially. In addition, parameters are typically estimated from training data and then held constant. Inputs and outputs to the neural net classifier are in parallel and internal computations are performed in parallel. Internal parameters or weights are typically adapted or trained during use using the output values and labels specifying the correct class.

the classifier. Here they are decoded and the class with the maximum score is selected. A symbol representing that class is then sent out to complete the classification task.

An adaptive neural net classifier is shown at the bottom of Fig. 2. Here input values are fed in parallel to the first stage via *N* input connections. Each connection carries an analog value which may take on two levels for binary inputs or may vary over a large range for continuous valued inputs. The first stage computes matching scores and outputs these scores in parallel to the next stage over *M* analog output lines. Here the maximum of these values is selected and enhanced. The second stage has one output for each of the *M* classes. After classification is complete, only that output corresponding to the most likely class will be on strongly or "high"; other outputs will be "low". Note that in this design, outputs exist for every class and that this multiplicity of outputs must be preserved in further processing stages as long as the classes are considered distinct. In the simplest classification system these output lines might go directly to lights with labels that specify class identities. In more complicated cases they may go to further stages of processing where inputs from other modalities or temporal dependencies are taken into consideration. If the correct class is provided, then this information and the classifier outputs can be fed back to the first stage of the classifier to adapt weights using a learning algorithm as shown in Fig. 2. Adaptation will make a correct response more likely for succeeding input patterns that are similar to the current pattern.

The parallel inputs required by neural net classifiers suggest that real-time hardware implementations should include special purpose pre-processors. One strategy for designing such processors is to build physiologically-based pre-processors modeled after human sensory systems. A pre-processor for image classification modeled after the retina and designed using analog VLSI circuitry is described in [31]. Pre-processor filter banks for speech recognition that are crude analogs of the cochlea have also been constructed [34, 29]. More recent physiologically-based pre-processor algorithms for speech recognition attempt to provide information similar to that available on the auditory nerve [11, 44, 27, 5]. Many of these algorithms include filter bank spectral analysis, automatic gain control, and processing which uses timing or synchrony information in addition to information from smoothed filter output envelopes.

Classifiers in Fig. 2 can perform three different tasks. First, as described above, they can identify which class best represents an input pattern, where it is assumed that inputs have been corrupted by noise or some other process. This is a classical decision theory problem. Second, the classifiers can be used as a content-addressable or associative memory, where the class exemplar is desired and the input pattern is used to determine which exemplar to produce. A content-addressable memory is useful when only part of an input pattern is available and the complete pattern is required, as in bibliographic retrieval of journal references from partial information. This normally requires the addition of a third stage in Fig. 2 to regenerate the exemplar for the most likely class. An additional stage is unnecessary for some neural nets such as the Hopfield net which are designed specifically as content-addressable memories. A third task these classifiers can perform is to vector quantize [28] or cluster [16, 7] the *N* inputs into *M* clusters. Vector quantizers are used in image and speech transmission systems to reduce the number of bits necessary to transmit analog data. In speech and image recognition applications they are used to compress the amount of data that must be processed without losing important information. In either application the number of clusters can be pre-specified or may be allowed to grow up to a limit determined by the number ber of nodes available in the first stage.

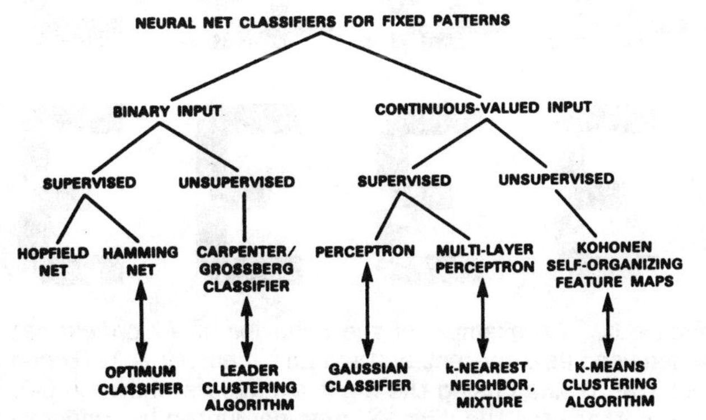

Figure 3. A taxonomy of six neural nets that can be used as classifiers. Classical algorithms which are most similar to the neural net models are listed along the bottom.

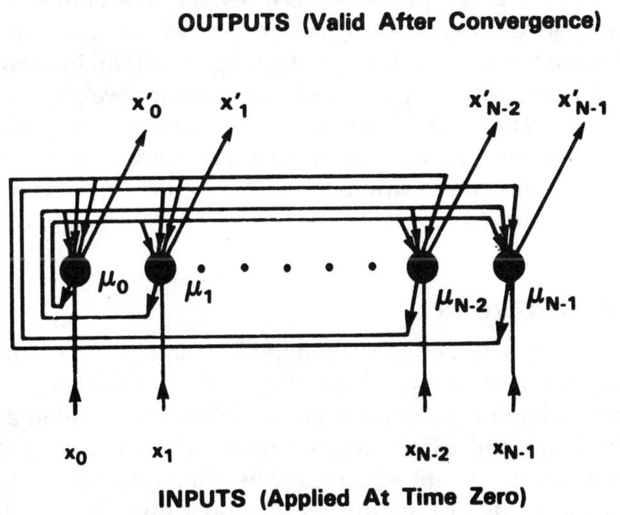

Figure 4. A Hopfield neural net that can be used as a content-addressable memory. An unknown binary input pattern is applied at time zero and the net then iterates until convergence when node outputs remain unchanged. The output is that pattern produced by node outputs after convergence.

A TAXONOMY OF NEURAL NETS

A taxonomy of six important neural nets that can be used for classification of static patterns is presented in Fig. 3. This taxonomy is first divided between nets with binary and continuous valued inputs. Below this, nets are divided between those trained with and without supervision. Nets trained with supervision such as the Hopfield net [18] and perceptrons [39] are used as associative memories or as classifiers. These nets are provided with side information or labels that specify the correct class for new input patterns during training. Most traditional statistical classifiers, such as Gaussian classifiers [7], are trained with supervision using labeled training data. Nets trained without supervision, such as the Kohonen's feature-map forming nets [22], are used as vector quantizers or to form clusters. No information concerning the correct class is provided to these nets during training. The classical K-means [7] and leader [16] clustering algorithms are trained without supervision. A further difference between nets, not indicated in Fig. 3, is whether adaptive training is supported. Although all the nets shown can be trained adaptively, the Hopfield net and the Hamming net are generally used with fixed weights.

The algorithms listed at the bottom of Fig. 3 are those classical algorithms which are most similar to or perform the same function as the corresponding neural net. In some cases a net implements a classical algorithm exactly. For example, the Hamming net [25] is a neural net implementation of the optimum classifier for binary patterns corrupted by random noise [10]. It can also be shown that the perceptron structure performs those calculations required by a Gaussian classifier [7] when weights and thresholds are selected appropriately. In other cases the neural net algorithms are different from the classical algorithms. For example, perceptrons trained with the perceptron convergence procedure [39] behave differently than Gaussian classifiers. Also, Kohonen's net [22] does not perform the iterative K-means training algorithm. Instead, each new pattern is presented only once and weights are modified after each presentation. The Kohonen net does, however, form a pre-specified number of clusters as in the K-means algorithm, where the K refers to the number of clusters formed.

THE HOPFIELD NET

The Hopfield net and two other nets in Fig. 3 are normally used with binary inputs. These nets are most appropriate when exact binary representations are possible as with black and white images where input elements are pixel values, or with ASCII text where input values could represent bits in the 8-bit ASCII representation of each character. These nets are less appropriate when input values are actually continuous, because a fundamental representation problem must be addressed to convert the analog quantities to binary values.

Hopfield rekindled interest in neural nets by his extensive work on different versions of the Hopfield net [18,19,20]. This net can be used as an associative memory or to solve optimization problems. One version of the original net [18] which can be used as a content addressable memory is described in this paper. This net, shown in Fig. 4, has N nodes containing hard limiting nonlinearities and binary inputs and outputs taking on the values +1 and −1. The output of each node is fed back to all other nodes via weights denoted t_{ij}. The operation of this net is described in Box 1. First, weights are set using the given recipe from exemplar patterns for all classes. Then an unknown pattern is imposed on the net at time zero by forcing the output of the net to match the unknown pattern. Following this initialization, the net iterates in discrete time steps using the given formula. The net is considered to have converged when outputs no longer change on successive iterations. The pattern specified by the node outputs after convergence is the net output.

Hopfield [18] and others [4] have proven that this net converges when the weights are symmetric ($t_{ij} = t_{ji}$) and

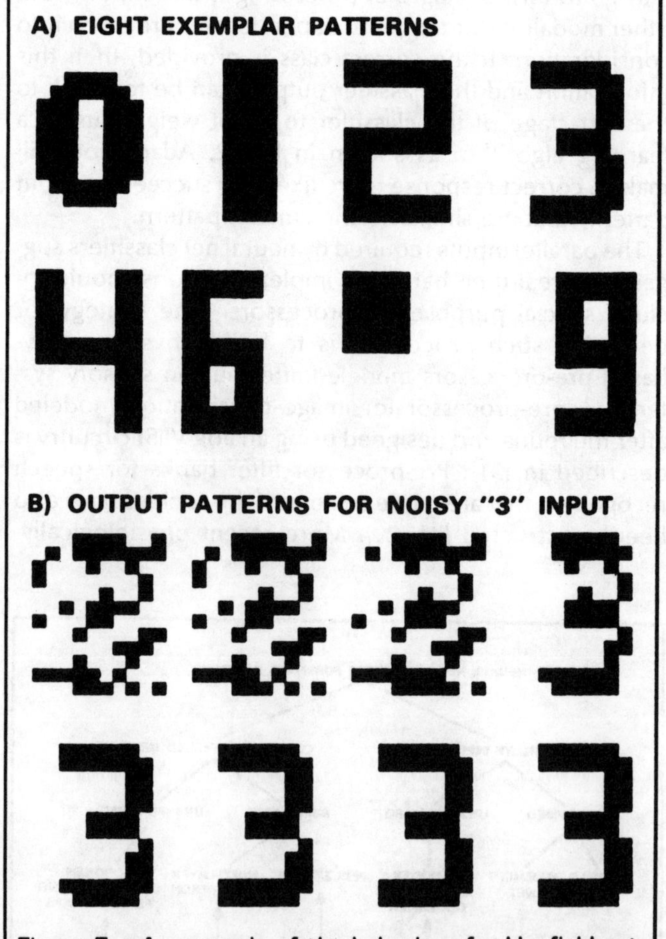

Figure 5. An example of the behavior of a Hopfield net when used as a content-addressable memory. A 120 node net was trained using the eight exemplars shown in (A). The pattern for the digit "3" was corrupted by randomly reversing each bit with a probability of .25, and then applied to the net at time zero. Outputs at time zero and after the first seven iterations are shown in (B).

node outputs are updated asynchronously using the equations in Box 1. Hopfield [19] also demonstrated that the net converges when graded nonlinearities similar to the sigmoid nonlinearity in Fig. 1 are used. When the Hopfield net is used as an associative memory, the net output after convergence is used directly as the complete restored memory. When the Hopfield net is used as a classifier, the output after convergence must be compared to the M exemplars to determine if it matches an exemplar exactly. If it does, the output is that class whose exemplar matched the output pattern. If it does not then a "no match" result occurs.

Box 1. Hopfield Net Algorithm

Step 1. Assign Connection Weights

$$t_{ij} = \begin{cases} \sum_{s=0}^{M-1} x_i^s x_j^s, & i \neq j \\ 0, \; i = j, \; 0 \leq i, \, j \leq M\text{-}1 \end{cases}$$

In this Formula t_{ij} is the connection weight from node i to node j and x_i^s which can be +1 or −1 is element i of the exemplar for class s.

Step 2. Initialize with Unknown Input Pattern

$$\mu_i(0) = x_i, \qquad 0 \leq i \leq N-1$$

In this Formula $\mu_i(t)$ is the output of node i at time t and x_i which can be +1 or −1 is element i of the input pattern.

Step 3. Iterate Until Convergence

$$\mu_j(t+1) = f_h\left[\sum_{i=0}^{N-1} t_{ij}\mu_i(t)\right], \quad 0 \leq j \leq M\text{-}1$$

The function f_h is the hard limiting nonlinearity from Fig. 1. The process is repeated until node outputs remain unchanged with further iterations. The node outputs then represent the exemplar pattern that best matches the unknown input.

Step 4. Repeat by Going to Step 2

The behavior of the Hopfield net is illustrated in Fig. 5. A Hopfield net with 120 nodes and thus 14,400 weights was trained to recall the eight exemplar patterns shown at the top of Fig. 5. These digit-like black and white patterns contain 120 pixels each and were hand crafted to provide good performance. Input elements to the net take on the value +1 for black pixels and −1 for white pixels. In the example presented, the pattern for the digit "3" was corrupted by randomly reversing each bit independently from +1 to −1 and vice versa with a probability of 0.25. This pattern was then applied to the net at time zero. Patterns produced at the output of the net on iterations zero to seven are presented at the bottom of Fig. 5. The corrupted input pattern is present unaltered at iteration zero. As the net iterates the output becomes more and more like the correct exemplar pattern until at iteration six the net has converged to the pattern for the digit three.

The Hopfield net has two major limitations when used as a content addressable memory. First, the number of patterns that can be stored and accurately recalled is severely limited. If too many patterns are stored, the net may converge to a novel spurious pattern different from all exemplar patterns. Such a spurious pattern will produce a "no match" output when the net is used as a classifier. Hopfield [18] showed that this occurs infrequently when exemplar patterns are generated randomly and the number of classes (M) is less than .15 times the number of input elements or nodes in the net (N). The number of classes is thus typically kept well below $.15N$. For example, a Hopfield net for only 10 classes might require more than 70 nodes and more than roughly 5,000 connection weights. A second limitation of the Hopfield net is that an exemplar pattern will be unstable if it shares many bits in common with another exemplar pattern. Here an exemplar is considered unstable if it is applied at time zero and the net converges to some other exemplar. This problem can be eliminated and performance can be improved by a number of orthogonalization procedures [14, 46].

THE HAMMING NET

The Hopfield net is often tested on problems where inputs are generated by selecting an exemplar and reversing bit values randomly and independently with a given probability [18, 12, 46]. This is a classic problem in communications theory that occurs when binary fixed-length signals are sent through a memoryless binary symmetric channel. The optimum minimum error classifier in this case calculates the Hamming distance to the exemplar for each class and selects that class with the minimum Hamming distance [10]. The Hamming distance is the number of bits in the input which do not match the corresponding exemplar bits. A net which will be called a Hamming net implements this algorithm using neural net components and is shown in Fig. 6.

The operation of the Hamming net is described in Box 2. Weights and thresholds are first set in the lower subnet such that the matching scores generated by the outputs of the middle nodes of Fig. 6 are equal to N minus the Hamming distances to the exemplar patterns. These matching scores will range from 0 to the number of elements in the input (N) and are highest for those nodes corresponding to classes with exemplars that best match the input. Thresholds and weights in the MAXNET subnet are fixed. All thresholds are set to zero and weights from each node to itself are 1. Weights between nodes are inhibitory with a value of $-\epsilon$ where $\epsilon < 1/M$.

After weights and thresholds have been set, a binary pattern with N elements is presented at the bottom of the Hamming net. It must be presented long enough to allow the matching score outputs of the lower subnet to settle and initialize the output values of the MAXNET. The input is then removed and the MAXNET iterates until the output of only one node is positive. Classification is then complete and the selected class is that corresponding to the node with a positive output.

The behavior of the Hamming net is illustrated in Fig. 7.

Box 2. Hamming Net Algorithm

Step 1. Assign Connection Weights and Offsets

In the lower subnet:

$$w_{ij} = \frac{x_i^j}{2}, \quad \theta_j = \frac{N}{2},$$

$$0 \le i \le N-1, \quad 0 \le j \le M-1$$

In the upper subnet:

$$t_{kl} = \begin{cases} 1, & k = l \\ -\varepsilon, & k \neq l, \quad \varepsilon < \frac{1}{M}, \end{cases}$$

$$0 \le k, l \le M-1$$

In these equations w_{ij} is the connection weight from input i to node j in the lower subnet and θ is the threshold in that node. The connection weight from node k to node l in the upper subnet is t_{kl} and all thresholds in this subnet are zero. x_i^j is element i of exemplar j as in Box 1.

Step 2. Initialize with Unknown Input Pattern

$$\mu_j(0) = f_t\left(\sum_{i=0}^{N-1} w_{ij}x_i - \theta_j\right)$$

$$0 \le j \le M-1$$

In this equation $\mu_j(t)$ is the output of node j in the upper subnet at time t, x_i is element i of the input as in Box 1, and f_t is the threshold logic nonlinearity from Fig. 1. Here and below it is assumed that the maximum input to this nonlinearity never causes the output to saturate.

Step 3. Iterate Until Convergence

$$\mu_j(t+1) = f_t\left(\mu_j(t) - \varepsilon\sum_{k\neq j}\mu_k(t)\right)$$

$$0 \le j, k \le M-1$$

This process is repeated until convergence after which the output of only one node remains positive.

Step 4. Repeat by Going to Step 2

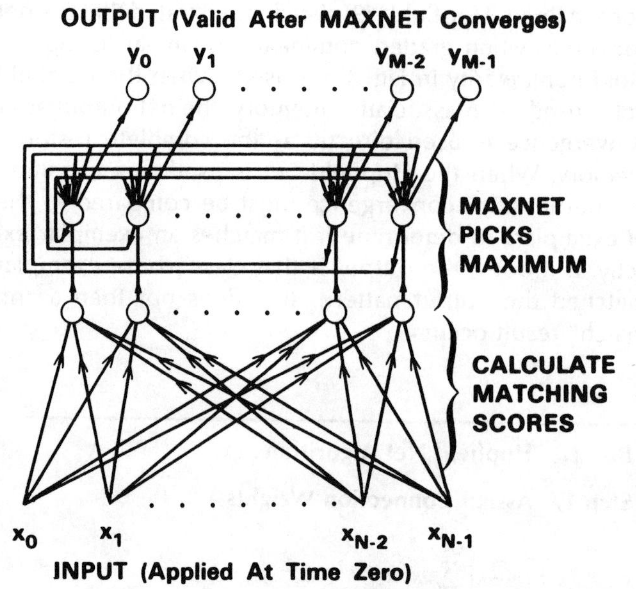

Figure 6. A feed-forward Hamming net maximum likelihood classifier for binary inputs corrupted by noise. The lower subnet calculates N minus the Hamming distance to M exemplar patterns. The upper net selects that node with the maximum output. All nodes use threshold-logic nonlinearities where it is assumed that the outputs of these nonlinearities never saturate.

The four plots in this figure show the outputs of nodes in a MAXNET with 100 nodes on iterations 0, 3, 6, and 9. These simulations were obtained using randomly selected exemplar patterns with 1000 elements each. The exemplar for class 50 was presented at time zero and then removed. The matching score at time zero is maximum (1000) for node 50 and has a random value near 500 for other nodes. After only 3 iterations, the outputs of all nodes except node 50 have been greatly reduced and after 9 iterations only the output for node 50 is non-zero. Simulations with different probabilities of reversing bits on input patterns and with different numbers of classes and elements in the input patterns have demonstrated that the MAXNET typically converges in less than 10 iterations in this application [25]. In addition, it can be proven that the MAXNET will always converge and find the node with the maximum value when $\varepsilon < 1/M$ [25].

The Hamming net has a number of obvious advantages over the Hopfield net. It implements the optimum minimum error classifier when bit errors are random and independent, and thus the performance of the Hopfield net must either be worse than or equivalent to that of the Hamming net in such situations. Comparisons between the two nets on problems such as character recognition, recognition of random patterns, and bibliographic retrieval have demonstrated this difference in performance [25]. The Hamming net also requires many fewer connections than the Hopfield net. For example, with 100 inputs and 10 classes the Hamming net requires

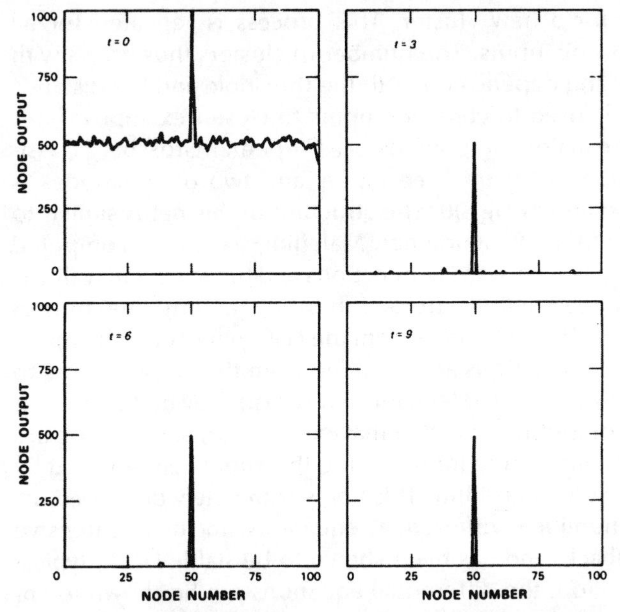

Figure 7. Node outputs for a Hamming net with 1,000 binary inputs and 100 output nodes or classes. Output values of all 100 nodes are presented at time zero and after 3, 6, and 9 iterations. The input was the exemplar pattern corresponding to output node 50.

only 1,100 connections while the Hopfield net requires almost 10,000. Furthermore, the difference in number of connections required increases as the number of inputs increases, because the number of connections in the Hopfield net grows as the square of the number of inputs while the number of connections in the Hamming net grows linearly. The Hamming net can also be modified to be a minimum error classifier when errors are generated by reversing input elements from +1 to −1 and from −1 to +1 asymmetrically with different probabilities [25] and when the values of specific input elements are unknown [2]. Finally, the Hamming net does not suffer from spurious output patterns which can produce a "no-match" result.

SELECTING OR ENHANCING THE MAXIMUM INPUT

The need to select or enhance the input with a maximum value occurs frequently in classification problems. Several different neural nets can perform this operation. The MAXNET described above uses heavy lateral inhibition similar to that used in other net designs where a maximum was desired [20, 22, 9]. These designs create a "winner-take-all" type of net whose design mimics the heavy use of lateral inhibition evident in the biological neural nets of the human brain [21]. Other techniques to pick a maximum are also possible [25]. One is illustrated in Fig. 8. This figure shows a comparator subnet which is described in [29]. It uses threshold logic nodes to pick the maximum of two inputs and then feeds this maximum value forward. This net is useful when the maximum value must be passed unaltered to the output. Comparator subnets can be layered into roughly $\log_2(M)$ layers to pick the maximum of M inputs. A net that uses these subnets to pick the maximum of 8 inputs is presented in Fig. 9.

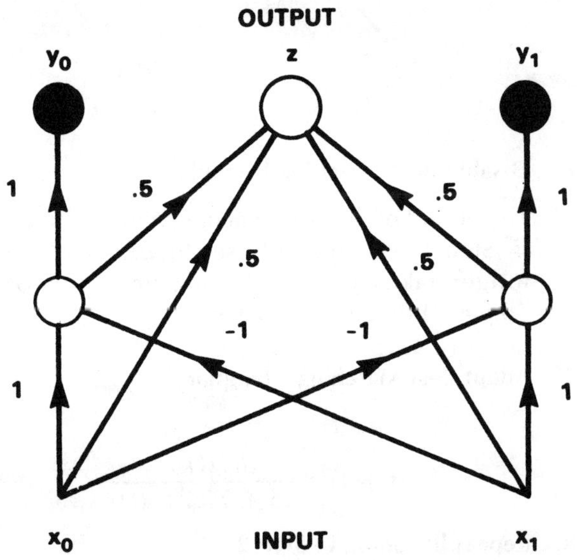

Figure 8. A comparator subnet that selects the maximum of two analog inputs. The output labeled z is the maximum value and the outputs labeled y_0 and y_1 indicate which input was maximum. Internal thresholds on threshold logic nodes (open circles) and hard limiting nodes (filled circles) are zero. Weights are as shown.

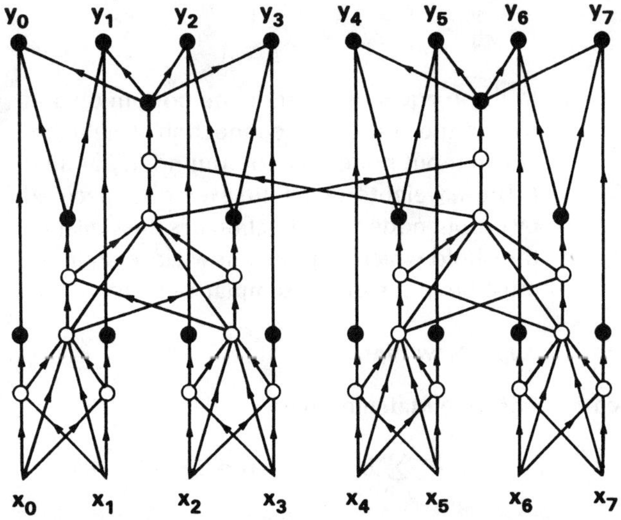

Figure 9. A feed-forward net that determines which of eight inputs is maximum using a binary tree and comparator subnets from Fig. 8. After an input vector is applied, only that output corresponding to the maximum input element will be high. Internal thresholds on threshold-logic nodes (open circles) and on hard limiting nodes (filled circles) are zero except for the output nodes. Thresholds in the output nodes are 2.5. Weights for the comparator subnets are as in Fig. 8 and all other weights are 1.

In some situations a maximum is not required and matching scores must instead be compared to a threshold. This can be done using an array of hard-limiting nodes with internal thresholds set to the desired threshold values. Outputs of these nodes will be −1 unless the inputs exceed the threshold values. Alternatively, thresholds could be set adaptively using a common inhibitory input fed to all nodes. This threshold could be ramped up or down until the output of only one node was positive.

THE CARPENTER/GROSSBERG CLASSIFIER

Carpenter and Grossberg [3], in the development of their Adaptive Resonance Theory have designed a net which forms clusters and is trained without supervision. This net implements a clustering algorithm that is very similar to the simple sequential leader clustering algorithm described in [16]. The leader algorithm selects the first input as the exemplar for the first cluster. The next input is compared to the first cluster exemplar. It "follows the leader" and is clustered with the first if the distance to the first is less than a threshold. Otherwise it is the exemplar for a new cluster. This process is repeated for all following inputs. The number of clusters thus grows with time and depends on both the threshold and the distance metric used to compare inputs to cluster exemplars.

The major components of a Carpenter/Grossberg classification net with three inputs and two output nodes is presented in Fig. 10. The structure of this net is similar to that of the Hamming net. Matching scores are computed using feed-forward connections and the maximum value is enhanced using lateral inhibition among the output nodes. This net differs from the Hamming net in that feedback connections are provided from the output nodes to the input nodes. Mechanisms are also provided to turn off that output node with a maximum value, and to compare exemplars to the input for the threshold test required by the leader algorithm. This net is completely described using nonlinear differential equations, includes extensive feedback, and has been shown to be stable [3]. In typical operation, the differential equations can be shown to implement the clustering algorithm presented in Box 3.

Box 3. Carpenter/Grossberg Net Algorithm

Step 1. Initialization

$$t_{ij}(0) = 1$$

$$b_{ij}(0) = \frac{1}{1+N}$$

$$0 \le i \le N-1,$$

$$0 \le j \le M-1$$

$$\text{Set } \rho, \quad 0 \le \rho \le 1$$

In these equations $b_{ij}(t)$ is the bottom up and $t_{ij}(t)$ is the top down connection weight between input node i and output node j at time t. These weights define the exemplar specified by output node j. The fraction ρ is the vigilance threshold which indicates how close an input must be to a stored exemplar to match.

Step 2. Apply New Input

Step 3. Compute Matching Scores

$$\mu_j = \sum_{i=0}^{N-1} b_{ij}(t)x_i \qquad 0 \le j \le M-1$$

In this equation μ_j is the output of output node j and x_i is element i of the input which can be 0 or 1.

Step 4. Select Best Matching Exemplar

$$\mu_j^* = \max_j \{\mu_j\}$$

This is performed using extensive lateral inhibition as in the maxnet.

Step 5. Vigilance Test

$$\|X\| = \sum_{i=0}^{N-1} x_i$$

$$\|T \cdot X\| = \sum_{i=0}^{N-1} t_{ij^*}x_i$$

$$\text{is } \frac{\|T \cdot X\|}{\|X\|} > \rho \text{ ?}$$

NO — GO TO STEP 6

YES — GO TO STEP 7

Step 6. Disable Best Matching Exemplar

The output of the best matching node selected in Step 4 is temporarily set to zero and no longer takes part in the maximization of Step 4. Then go to Step 3.

Step 7. Adapt Best Matching Exemplar

$$t_{ij^*}(t+1) = t_{ij^*}(t)x_i$$

$$b_{ij^*}(t+1) = \frac{t_{ij}{}^*(t)x_i}{.5 + \sum_{i=0}^{N-1} t_{ij^*}(t)x_i}$$

Step 8. Repeat by Going to Step 2

(First enable any nodes disabled in Step 6)

The algorithm presented in Box 3 assumes that "fast learning" is used as in the simulations presented in [3] and thus that elements of both inputs and stored exemplars take on only the values 0 and 1. The net is initialized by effectively setting all exemplars represented by connection weights to zero. In addition, a matching threshold called *vigilance* which ranges between 0.0 and 1.0 must be set. This threshold determines how close a new input pattern must be to a stored exemplar to be considered similar. A value near one requires a close match and smaller values accept a poorer match. New inputs are presented sequentially at the bottom of the net as in the Hamming net. After presentation, the input is compared to all stored exemplars in parallel as in the Hamming net to produce matching scores. The exemplar with the highest matching score is selected using lateral inhibition. It is then compared to the input by computing the ratio of the dot product of the input and the best matching exemplar (number of 1 bits in common) divided by the number of 1 bits in the input. If this ratio is greater than the vigilance threshold, then the input is considered to be similar to the best matching exemplar and that exemplar is updated by performing a logical AND operation between its bits and those in the input. If the ratio is less than the vigilance threshold, then the input is considered to be different from all exemplars and it is added as a new exemplar. Each additional new exemplar requires one node and 2N connections to compute matching scores.

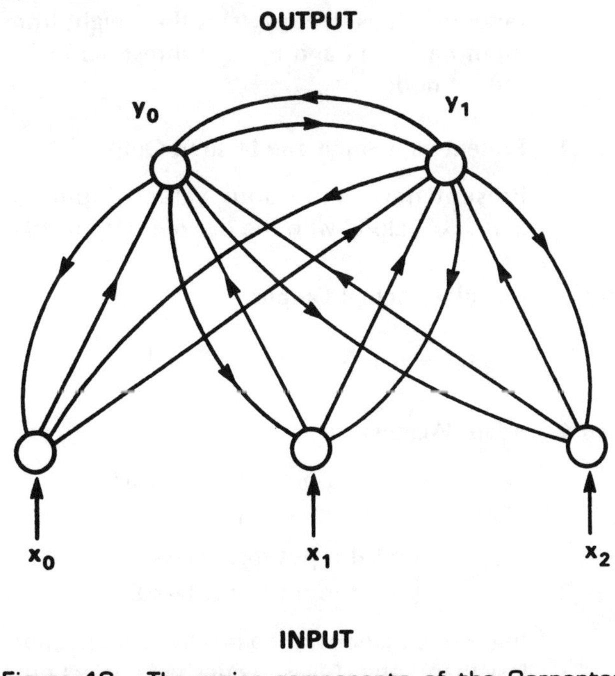

Figure 10. The major components of the Carpenter Grossberg Classification net. A binary input is presented at the bottom and when classification is complete only one output is high. Not shown are additional components required to perform the vigilance test and to disable the output node with the largest output.

The behavior of the Carpenter/Grossberg net is illustrated in Fig. 11. Here it is assumed that patterns to be recognized are the three patterns of the letters "C", "E", and "F" shown in the left side of this figure. These patterns have 64 pixels each that take on the value 1 when black and 0 when white. Results are presented when the vigilance threshold was set to 0.9. This forces separate exemplar patterns to be created for each letter.

The left side of Fig. 11 shows the input to the net on successive trials. The right side presents exemplar patterns formed after each pattern had been applied. In this example "C" was presented first followed by "E" followed by "F", etc. After the net is initialized and a "C" is applied, internal connection weights are altered to form an internal exemplar that is identical to the "C". After an "E" is then applied, a new "E" exemplar is added. Behavior is similar for a new "F" leading to three stored exemplars. If the vigilance threshold had been slightly lower, only two exemplars would have been present after the "F"; one for "F" and one for both "C" and "E" that would have been identical to "C" pattern. Now, when a noisy "F" is applied

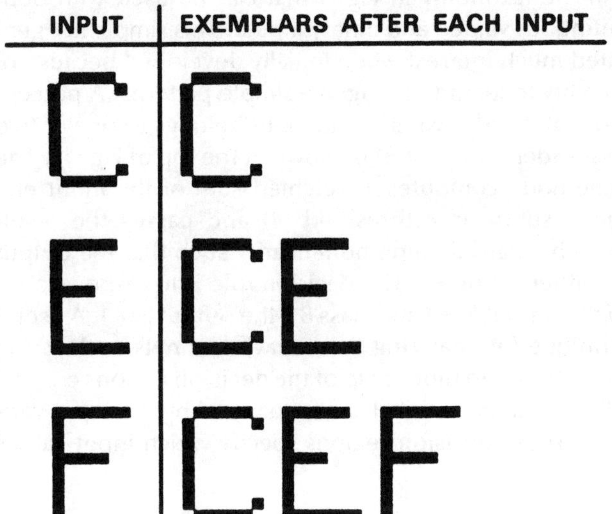

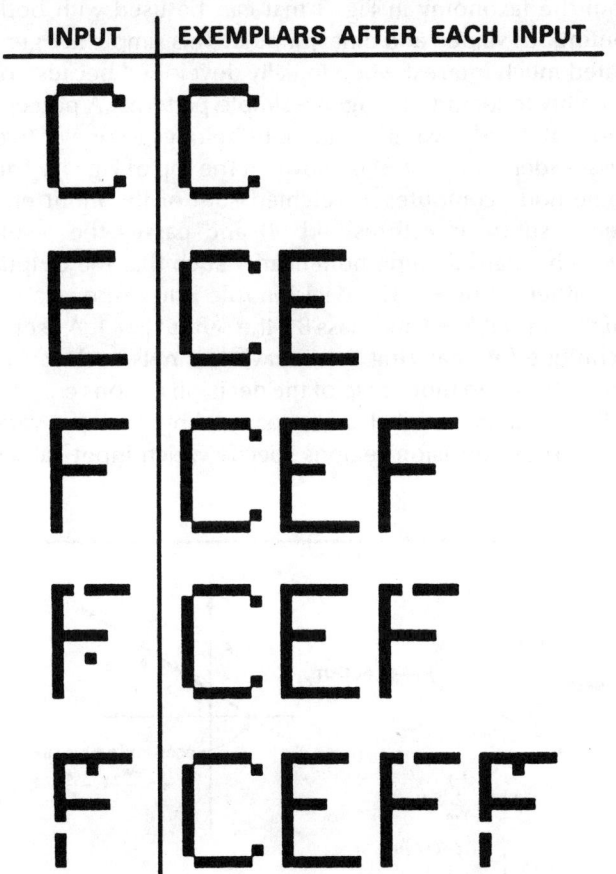

Figure 11. An example of the behavior of the Carpenter Grossberg net for letter patterns. Binary input patterns on the left were applied sequentially starting with the upper "C" pattern. Exemplars formed by top-down connection weights after each input was presented are shown at the right.

with a missing black pixel in the upper edge it is accepted as being similar to the "F" exemplar and degrades this exemplar due to the AND operation performed during updating. When another noisy "F" is applied again with only one black pixel missing, it is considered different from existing exemplars and a new noisy "F" exemplar is added. This will occur for further noisy "F" inputs leading to a growth of noisy "F" exemplars.

These results illustrate that the Carpenter/Grossberg algorithm can perform well with perfect input patterns but that even a small amount of noise can cause problems. With no noise, the vigilance threshold can be set such that the two patterns which are most similar are considered different. In noise, however, this level may be too high and the number of stored exemplars can rapidly grow until all available nodes are used up. Modifications are necessary to enhance the performance of this algorithm in noise. These could include adapting weights more slowly and changing the vigilance threshold during training and testing as suggested in [3].

SINGLE LAYER PERCEPTRON

The single layer perceptron [39] is the first of three nets from the taxonomy in Fig. 3 that can be used with both continuous valued and binary inputs. This simple net generated much interest when initially developed because of its ability to learn to recognize simple patterns. A perceptron that decides whether an input belongs to one of two classes (denoted A or B) is shown in the top of Fig. 12. The single node computes a weighted sum of the input elements, subtracts a threshold (θ) and passes the result through a hard limiting nonlinearity such that the output y is either +1 or −1. The decision rule is to respond class A if the output is +1 and class B if the output is −1. A useful technique for analyzing the behavior of nets such as the perceptron is to plot a map of the decision regions created in the multidimensional space spanned by the input variables. These decision regions specify which input values result in a class A and which result in a class B response. The perceptron forms two decision regions separated by a hyperplane. These regions are shown in the right side of Fig. 12 when there are only two inputs and the hyperplane is a line. In this case inputs above the boundary line lead to class A responses and inputs below the line lead to class B responses. As can be seen, the equation of the boundary line depends on the connection weights and the threshold.

Connection weights and the threshold in a perceptron can be fixed or adapted using a number of different algorithms. The original perceptron convergence procedure for adjusting weights was developed by Rosenblatt [39]. It is described in Box 4. First connection weights and the threshold value are initialized to small random non-zero values. Then a new input with N continuous valued elements is applied to the input and the output is computed as in Fig. 12. Connection weights are adapted only when an error occurs using the formula in step 4 of Box 4. This formula includes a gain term (η) that ranges from 0.0 to 1.0 and controls the adaptation rate. This gain term must be adjusted to satisfy the conflicting requirements of fast adaptation for real changes in the input distributions and averaging of past inputs to provide stable weight estimates.

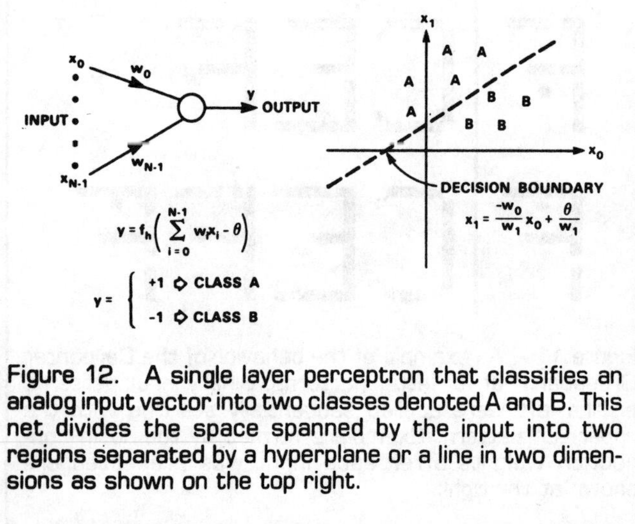

Figure 12. A single layer perceptron that classifies an analog input vector into two classes denoted A and B. This net divides the space spanned by the input into two regions separated by a hyperplane or a line in two dimensions as shown on the top right.

Box 4. The Perceptron Convergence Procedure

Step 1. Initialize Weights and Threshold

Set $w_i(0)$ $(0 \le i \le N-1)$ and θ to small random values. Here $w_i(t)$ is the weight from input i at time t and θ is the threshold in the output node.

Step 2. Present New Input and Desired Output

Present new continuous valued input $x_0, x_1 \ldots x_{N-1}$ along with the desired output $d(t)$.

Step 3. Calculate Actual Output

$$y(t) = f_h\left(\sum_{i=0}^{N-1} w_i(t)x_i(t) - \theta\right)$$

Step 4. Adapt Weights

$$w_i(t+1) = w_i(t) + \eta[d(t) - y(t)]x_i(t), \quad 0 \le i \le N-1$$

$$d(t) = \begin{cases} +1 \text{ if input from class A} \\ -1 \text{ if input from class B} \end{cases}$$

In these equations η is a positive gain fraction less than 1 and $d(t)$ is the desired correct output for the current input. Note that weights are unchanged if the correct decision is made by the net.

Step 5. Repeat by Going to Step 2

An example of the use of the perceptron convergence procedure is presented in Fig. 13. Samples from class A in this figure are represented by circles and samples from class B are represented by crosses. Samples from classes A and B were presented alternately until 80 inputs had been presented. The four lines show the four decision boundaries after weights had been adjusted following errors on trials 0, 2, 4, and 80. In this example the classes were well separated after only four trials and the gain term was .01.

Rosenblatt [39] proved that if the inputs presented from the two classes are separable (that is they fall on opposite sides of some hyperplane), then the perceptron convergence procedure converges and positions the decision hyperplane between those two classes. Such a hyperplane is illustrated in the upper right of Fig. 12. This decision boundary separates all samples from the A and B classes. One problem with the perceptron convergence procedure is that decision boundaries may oscillate continuously when inputs are not separable and distributions overlap. A modification to the perceptron convergence procedure can form the least mean square (LMS) solution in this case. This solution minimizes the mean square error between the desired output of a perceptron-like net and the actual output. The algorithm that forms the LMS solution is called the Widrow-Hoff or LMS algorithm [47,48,7].

The LMS algorithm is identical to the perceptron convergence procedure described in Box 4 except the hard limiting nonlinearity is made linear or replaced by a threshold-logic nonlinearity. Weights are thus corrected on every trial by an amount that depends on the difference between the desired and the actual input. A classifier that uses the LMS training algorithm could use desired outputs of 1 for class A and 0 for class B. During operation the input would then be assigned to class A only if the output was above 0.5.

The decision regions formed by perceptrons are similar to those formed by maximum likelihood Gaussian classifiers which assume inputs are uncorrelated and distributions for different classes differ only in mean values. This type of Gaussian classifier and the associated weighted Euclidean or straight Euclidean distance metric is often used in speech recognizers when there is limited training data and inputs have been orthogonalized by a suitable transformation [36]. Box 5 demonstrates how the weights and threshold in a perceptron can be selected such that the perceptron structure computes the difference between log likelihoods required by such a Gaussian classifier [7]. Perceptron-like structures can also be used to perform the linear computations required by a Karhunen Loeve transformation [36]. These computations can be used to transform a set of $N + K$ correlated Gaussian inputs into a reduced set of N uncorrelated inputs which can be used with the above Gaussian classifier.

It is straightforward to generalize the derivation of Box 5 to demonstrate how a Gaussian classifier for M classes can be constructed from M perceptron-like structures followed by a net that picks the maximum. The required net is identical in structure to the Hamming Net of Fig. 6. In this case, however, inputs are analog and the weights and node thresholds are calculated from terms II and III in likelihood equations similar to those for L_A in Box 5. It is likewise straightforward to generalize the Widrow-Hoff

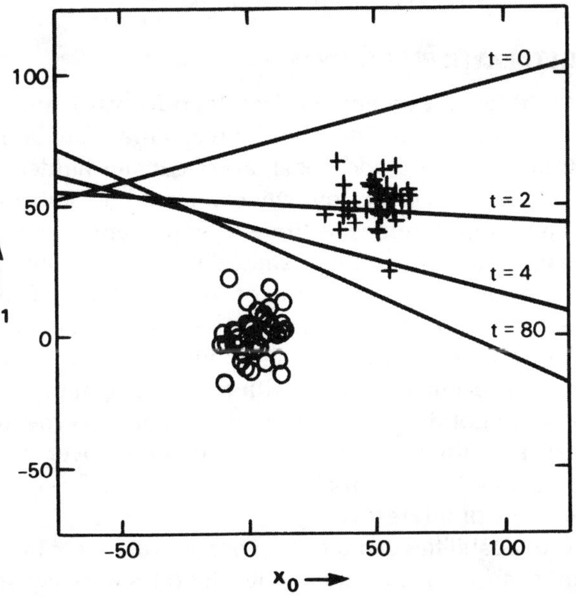

Figure 13. An example of the decision boundaries formed by the perceptron convergence procedure with two classes. Samples from class A are represented by circles and samples from class B by crosses. Lines represent decision boundaries after trials where errors occurred and weights were adapted.

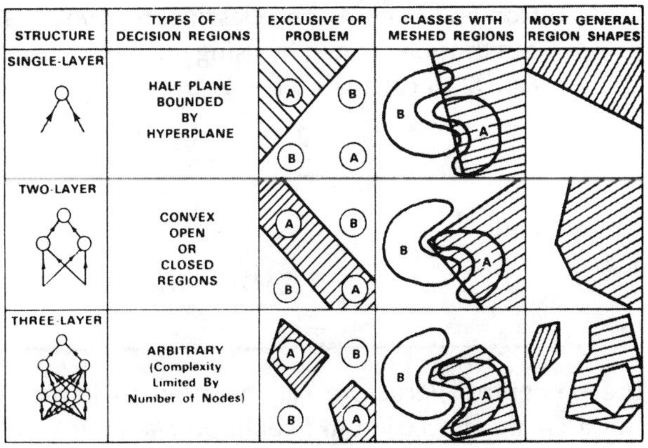

Figure 14. Types of decision regions that can be formed by single- and multi-layer perceptrons with one and two layers of hidden units and two inputs. Shading denotes decision regions for class A. Smooth closed contours bound input distributions for classes A and B. Nodes in all nets use hard limiting nonlinearities.

variant of the perceptron convergence procedure to apply for M classes. This requires a structure identical to the Hamming Net and a classification rule that selects the class corresponding to the node with the maximum output. During adaptation the desired output values can be set to 1 for the correct class and 0 for all others.

Box 5. A Gaussian Classifier Implemented Using the Perceptron Structure

If m_{Ai} and σ^2_{Ai} are the mean and variance of input x_i when the input is from class A and M_{Bi} and σ^2_{Bi} are the mean and variance of input x_i for class B and $\sigma_i^2 = \sigma^2_{Ai} = \sigma^2_{Bi}$, then the likelihood values required by a maximum likelihood classifier are monotonically related to

$$L_A = -\sum_{i=0}^{N-1} \frac{(x_i - M_{Ai})^2}{\sigma_i^2}$$

$$= -\sum \frac{x_i^2}{\sigma_i^2} + 2\sum \frac{M_{Ai} x_i}{\sigma_i^2} - \sum \frac{M^2_{Ai}}{\sigma_i^2}$$

and

$$L_B = -\sum_{i=0}^{N-1} \frac{(x_i - M_{Bi})^2}{\sigma_i^2}$$

$$= \underset{\substack{\uparrow \\ \text{Term I}}}{-\sum \frac{x_i^2}{\sigma_i^2}} + \underset{\substack{\uparrow \\ \text{Term II}}}{2\sum \frac{M_{Bi} x_i}{\sigma_i^2}} - \underset{\substack{\uparrow \\ \text{Term III}}}{\sum \frac{M^2_{Bi}}{\sigma_i^2}}.$$

A maximum likelihood classifier must calculate L_A and L_B and select the class with the highest likelihood. Since Term I in these equations is identical for L_A and L_B, it can be dropped. Term II is a product of the input times weights and can be calculated by a perception and Term III is a constant which can be obtained from the threshold in a perceptron node. A Gaussian classifier for two classes can thus be formed by using the perceptron of Fig. 12 to calculate $L_A - L_B$ by setting

$$w_i = \frac{2(M_{Ai} - M_{Bi})}{\sigma_i{}^2},$$

and

$$\theta = \sum_{i=0}^{N-1} \frac{M^2_{Ai} - M^2_{Bi}}{\sigma_i^2}.$$

The perceptron structure can be used to implement either a Gaussian maximum likelihood classifier or classifiers which use the perceptron training algorithm or one of its variants. The choice depends on the application. The perceptron training algorithm makes no assumptions concerning the shape of underlying distributions but focuses on errors that occur where distributions overlap. It may thus be more robust than classical techniques and work well when inputs are generated by nonlinear processes and are heavily skewed and non-Gaussian. The Gaussian classifier makes strong assumptions concerning underlying distributions and is more appropriate when distributions are known and match the Gaussian assumption. The adaptation algorithm defined by the perceptron convergence procedure is simple to implement and doesn't require storing any more information than is present in the weights and the threshold. The Gaussian classifier can be made adaptive [24], but extra information must be stored and the computations required are more complex.

Neither the perceptron convergence procedure nor the Gaussian classifier is appropriate when classes cannot be separated by a hyperplane. Two such situations are presented in the upper section of Fig. 14. The smooth closed contours labeled A and B in this figure are the input distributions for the two classes when there are two continuous valued inputs to the different nets. The shaded areas are the decision regions created by a single-layer perceptron and other feed-forward nets. Distributions for the two classes for the exclusive OR problem are disjoint and cannot be separated by a single straight line. This problem was used to illustrate the weakness of the perceptron by Minsky and Papert [32]. If the lower left B cluster is taken to be at the origin of this two dimensional space then the output of the classifier must be "high" only if one but not both of the inputs is "high". One possible decision region for class A which a perceptron might create is illustrated by the shaded region in the first row of Fig. 14. Input distributions for the second problem shown in this figure are meshed and also can not be separated by a single straight line. Situations similar to these may occur when parameters such as formant frequencies are used for speech recognition.

MULTI-LAYER PERCEPTRON

Multi-layer perceptrons are feed-forward nets with one or more layers of nodes between the input and output nodes. These additional layers contain hidden units or nodes that are not directly connected to both the input and output nodes. A three-layer perceptron with two layers of hidden units is shown in Fig. 15. Multi-layer perceptrons overcome many of the limitations of single-layer perceptrons, but were generally not used in the past because effective training algorithms were not available. This has recently changed with the development of new training algorithms [40]. Although it cannot be proven that these algorithms converge as with single layer perceptrons, they have been shown to be successful for many problems of interest [40].

The capabilities of multi-layer perceptrons stem from the nonlinearities used within nodes. If nodes were linear elements, then a single-layer net with appropriately chosen weights could exactly duplicate those calculations performed by any multi-layer net. The capabilities of perceptrons with one, two, and three layers that use hard-limiting nonlinearities are illustrated in Fig. 14. The second column in this figure indicates the types of decision regions that can be formed with different nets. The next two columns present examples of decision regions which could be formed for the exclusive OR problem and a problem with meshed regions. The rightmost column gives examples of the most general decision regions that can be formed.

As noted above, a single-layer perceptron forms half-plane decision regions. A two-layer perceptron can form any, possibly unbounded, convex region in the space spanned by the inputs. Such regions include convex polygons sometimes called convex hulls, and the unbounded convex regions shown in the middle row of Fig. 14. Here the term convex means that any line joining points on the border of a region goes only through points within that region. Convex regions are formed from intersections of the half-plane regions formed by each node in the first layer of the multi-layer perceptron. Each node in the first layer behaves like a single-layer perceptron and has a "high" output only for points on one side of the hyperplane formed by its weights and offset. If weights to an output node from N_1 first-layer nodes are all 1.0, and the threshold in the output node is $N_1 - \varepsilon$ where $0 < \varepsilon < 1$, then the output node will be "high" only if the outputs of all first-layer nodes are "high". This corresponds to performing a logical AND operation in the output node and results in a final decision region that is the intersection of all the half-plane regions formed in the first layer. Intersections of such half planes form convex regions as described above. These convex regions have at the most as many sides as there are nodes in the first layer.

This analysis provides some insight into the problem of selecting the number of nodes to use in a two-layer perceptron. The number of nodes must be large enough to form a decision region that is as complex as is required by a given problem. It must not, however, be so large that the many weights required can not be reliably estimated from the available training data. For example, two nodes are sufficient to solve the exclusive OR problem as shown in the second row of Fig. 14. No number of nodes, however, can separate the meshed class regions in Fig. 14 with a two-layer perceptron.

A three-layer perceptron can form arbitrarily complex decision regions and can separate the meshed classes as shown in the bottom of Fig. 14. It can form regions as complex as those formed using mixture distributions and nearest-neighbor classifiers [7]. This can be proven by construction. The proof depends on partitioning the desired decision region into small hypercubes (squares when there are two inputs). Each hypercube requires $2N$ nodes in the first layer (four nodes when there are two inputs), one for each side of the hypercube, and one node in the second layer that takes the logical AND of the outputs from the first-layer nodes. The outputs of second-layer nodes will be "high" only for inputs within each hypercube. Hypercubes are assigned to the proper decision regions by connecting the output of each second-layer node only to the output node corresponding to the decision region that node's hypercube is in and performing a logical OR operation in each output node. A logical OR operation will be performed if these connection weights from the second hidden layer to the output layer are one and thresholds in the output nodes are 0.5. This construction procedure can be generalized to use arbitrarily shaped convex regions instead of small hypercubes and is capable of generating the disconnected and non-convex regions shown at the bottom of Fig. 14.

The above analysis demonstrates that no more than three layers are required in perceptron-like feed-forward nets because a three-layer net can generate arbitrarily complex decision regions. It also provides some insight into the problem of selecting the number of nodes to use in three-layer perceptrons. The number of nodes in the second layer must be greater than one when decision regions are disconnected or meshed and cannot be formed from one convex area. The number of second layer nodes required in the worst case is equal to the number of disconnected regions in input distributions. The number of nodes in the first layer must typically be sufficient to provide three or more edges for each convex area generated by every second-layer node. There should thus typically be more than three times as many nodes in the second as in the first layer.

The above discussion centered primarily on multi-layer perceptrons with one output when hard limiting nonlinearities are used. Similar behavior is exhibited by multi-layer perceptrons with multiple output nodes when sigmoidal nonlinearities are used and the decision rule is to select the class corresponding to the output node with the largest output. The behavior of these nets is more complex because decision regions are typically bounded by smooth curves instead of by straight line segments and analysis is thus more difficult. These nets, however, can be trained with the new back-propagation training algorithm [40].

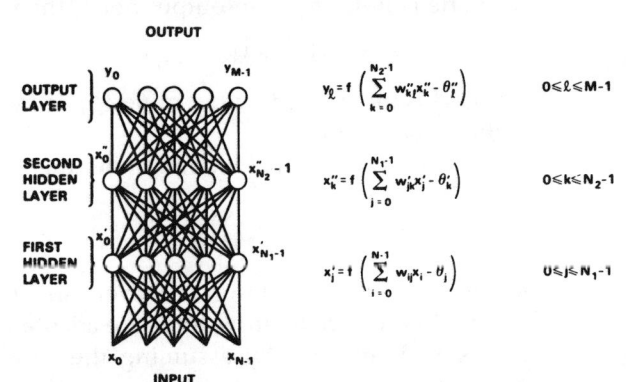

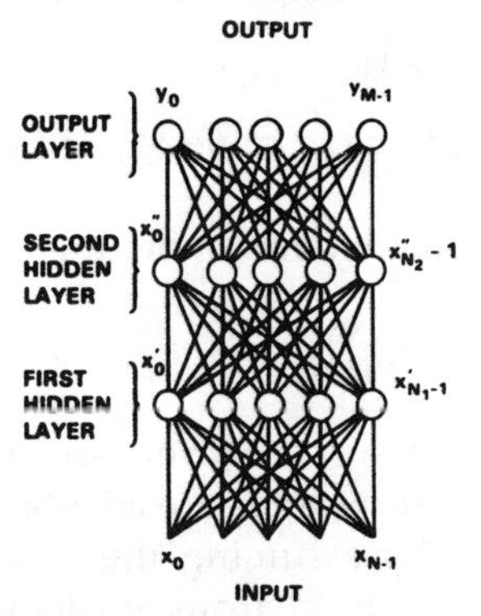

$$y_\ell = f\left(\sum_{k=0}^{N_2-1} w''_{k\ell} x''_k - \theta''_\ell\right) \qquad 0 \le \ell \le M-1$$

$$x''_k = f\left(\sum_{j=0}^{N_1-1} w'_{jk} x'_j - \theta'_k\right) \qquad 0 \le k \le N_2-1$$

$$x'_j = f\left(\sum_{i=0}^{N-1} w_{ij} x_i - \theta_j\right) \qquad 0 \le j \le N_1-1$$

Figure 15. A three-layer perceptron with N continuous valued inputs, M outputs and two layers of hidden units. The nonlinearity can be any of those shown in Fig. 1. The decision rule is to select that class corresponding to the output node with the largest output. In the formulas, x'_j and x''_k are the outputs of nodes in the first and second hidden layers, θ'_k and θ''_l are internal offsets in those nodes, w_{ij} is the connection strength from the input to the first hidden layer, and w'_{ij} and w''_{ij} are the connection strengths between the first and second and between the second and the output layers respectively.

The back-propagation algorithm described in Box 6 is a generalization of the LMS algorithm. It uses a gradient search technique to minimize a cost function equal to the mean square difference between the desired and the actual net outputs. The desired output of all nodes is typically "low" (0 or <0.1) unless that node corresponds to the class the current input is from in which case it is "high" (1.0 or >0.9). The net is trained by initially selecting small random weights and internal thresholds and then presenting all training data repeatedly. Weights are adjusted after every trial using side information specifying the correct class until weights converge and the cost function is reduced to an acceptable value. An essential component of the algorithm is the iterative method described in Box 6 that propagates error terms required to adapt weights back from nodes in the output layer to nodes in lower layers.

An example of the behavior of the back propagation algorithm is presented in Fig. 16. This figure shows decision regions formed by a two-layer perceptron with two inputs, eight nodes in the hidden layer, and two output nodes corresponding to two classes. Sigmoid nonlinearities were used as in Box 6, the gain term η was 0.3, the momentum term α was 0.7, random samples from classes A and B were presented on alternate trials, and the desired outputs were either 1 or 0. Samples from class A were distributed uniformly over a circle of radius 1 centered at the origin. Samples from class B were distributed uniformly outside this circle up to a radius of 5. The initial decision region is a slightly curved hyperplane. This gradually changes to a circular region that encloses the circular distribution of class A after 200 trails (100 samples from each class). This decision region is near that optimal region that would be produced by a Maximum Likelihood classifier.

The back propagation algorithm has been tested with a number of deterministic problems such as the exclusive OR problem [40], on problems related to speech synthesis

Box 6. The Back-Propagation Training Algorithm

The back-propagation training algorithm is an iterative gradient algorithm designed to minimize the mean square error between the actual output of a multilayer feed-forward perceptron and the desired output. It requires continuous differentiable non-linearities. The following assumes a sigmoid logistic nonlinearity is used where the function $f(\alpha)$ in Fig. 1 is

$$f(\alpha) = \frac{1}{1 + e^{-(\alpha-\theta)}}$$

Step 1. Initialize Weights and Offsets

Set all weights and node offsets to small random values.

Step 2. Present Input and Desired Outputs

Present a continuous valued input vector $x_0, x_1, \ldots x_{N-1}$ and specify the desired outputs $d_0, d_1, \ldots d_{M-1}$. If the net is used as a classifier then all desired outputs are typically set to zero except for that corresponding to the class the input is from. That desired output is 1. The input could be new on each trial or samples from a training set could be presented cyclically until weights stabilize.

Step 3. Calculate Actual Outputs

Use the sigmoid nonlinearity from above and formulas as in Fig. 15 to calculate outputs $y_0, y_1 \ldots y_{M-1}$.

Step 4. Adapt Weights

Use a recursive algorithm starting at the output nodes and working back to the first hidden layer. Adjust weights by

$$w_{ij}(t + 1) = w_{ij}(t) + \eta\delta_j x_i'$$

In this equation $w_{ij}(t)$ is the weight from hidden node i or from an input to node j at time t, x_i' is either the output of node i or is an input, η is a gain term, and δ_j is an error term for node j. If node j is an output node, then

$$\delta_j = y_j(1 - y_j)(d_j - y_j),$$

where d_j is the desired output of node j and y_j is the actual output.

If node j is an internal hidden node, then

$$\delta_j = x_j'(1 - x_j')\sum_k \delta_k w_{jk},$$

where k is over all nodes in the layers above node j. Internal node thresholds are adapted in a similar manner by assuming they are connection weights on links from auxiliary constant-valued inputs. Convergence is sometimes faster if a momentum term is added and weight changes are smoothed by

$$w_{ij}(t + 1) = w_{ij}(t) + \eta\delta_j x_i' + \alpha(w_{ij}(t) - w_{ij}(t - 1)),$$

where $0 < \alpha < 1$.

Step 5. Repeat by Going to Step 2

and recognition [43, 37, 8] and on problems related to visual pattern recognition [40]. It has been found to perform well in most cases and to find good solutions to the problems posed. A demonstration of the power of this algorithm was provided by Sejnowski [43]. He trained a two-layer perceptron with 120 hidden units and more than 20,000 weights to form letter to phoneme transcription rules. The input to this net was a binary code indicating those letters in a sliding window seven letters long that was moved over a written transcription of spoken text. The desired output was a binary code indicating the phonemic transcription of the letter at the center of the window. After 50 times through a dialog containing 1024 words, the transcription error rate was only 5%. This increased to 22% for a continuation of that dialog that was not used during training.

The generally good performance found for the back propagation algorithm is somewhat surprising considering that it is a gradient search technique that may find a local minimum in the LMS cost function instead of the desired global minimum. Suggestions to improve performance and reduce the occurrence of local minima include allowing extra hidden units, lowering the gain term used to adapt weights, and making many training runs starting with different sets of random weights. When used with classification problems, the number of nodes could be set using considerations described above. The problem of local minima in this case corresponds to clustering two or more disjoint class regions into one. This can be minimized by using multiple starts with different random weights and a low gain to adapt weights. One difficulty noted with the backward-propagation algorithm is that in many cases the number of presentations of training data required for convergence has been large (more than 100 passes through all the training data). Although a number of more complex adaptation algorithms have been proposed to speed convergence [35] it seems unlikely that the complex decision regions formed by multi-layer perceptrons can be generated in few trials when class regions are disconnected.

An interesting theorem that sheds some light on the capabilities of multi-layer perceptrons was proven by Kolmogorov and is described in [26]. This theorem states that any continuous function of N variables can be computed using only linear summations and nonlinear but continuously increasing functions of only one variable. It effectively states that a three layer perceptron with $N(2N + 1)$ nodes using continuously increasing nonlinearities can compute any continuous function of N variables. A three-layer perceptron could thus be used to create any continuous likelihood function required in a classifier. Unfortunately, the theorem does not indicate how weights or nonlinearities in the net should be selected or how sensitive the output function is to variations in the weights and internal functions.

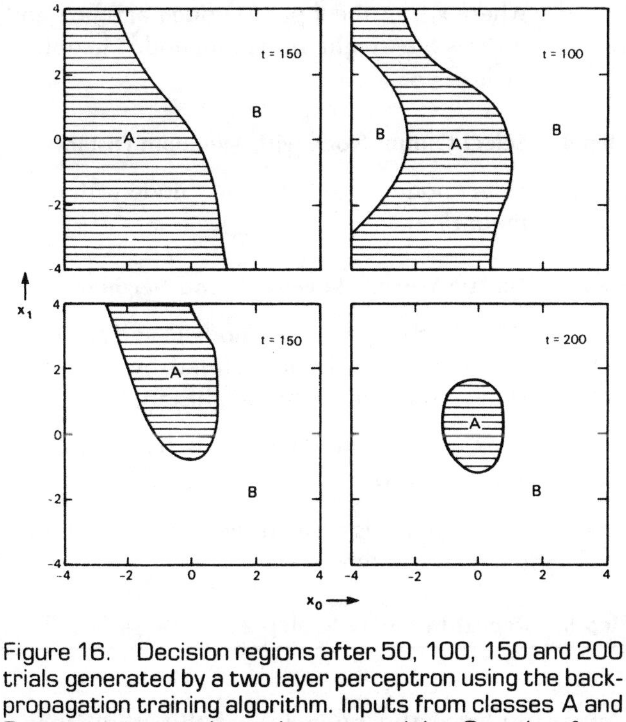

Figure 16. Decision regions after 50, 100, 150 and 200 trials generated by a two layer perceptron using the back-propagation training algorithm. Inputs from classes A and B were presented on alternate trials. Samples from class A were distributed uniformly over a circle of radius 1 centered at the origin. Samples from class B were distributed uniformly outside the circle. The shaded area denotes the decision region for class A.

KOHONEN'S SELF ORGANIZING FEATURE MAPS

One important organizing principle of sensory pathways in the brain is that the placement of neurons is orderly and often reflects some physical characteristic of the external stimulus being sensed [21]. For example, at each level of the auditory pathway, nerve cells and fibers are arranged anatomically in relation to the frequency which elicits the greatest response in each neuron. This tono-

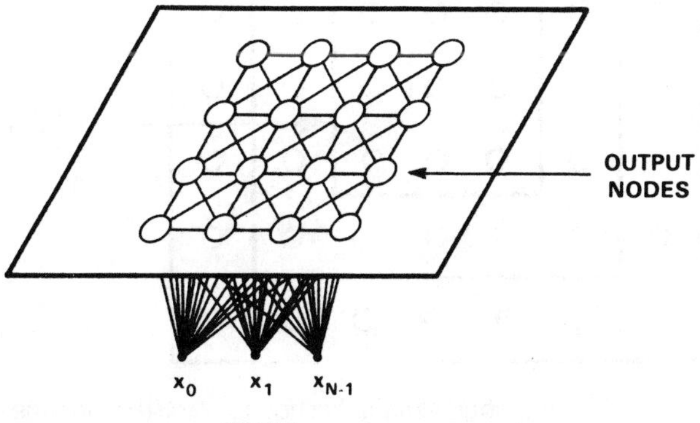

Figure 17. Two-dimensional array of output nodes used to form feature maps. Every input is connected to every output node via a variable connection weight.

topic organization in the auditory pathway extends up to the auditory cortex [33, 21]. Although much of the low-level organization is genetically pre-determined, it is likely that some of the organization at higher levels is created during learning by algorithms which promote self-organization. Kohonen [22] presents one such algorithm which produces what he calls self-organizing feature maps similar to those that occur in the brain.

Kohonen's algorithm creates a vector quantizer by adjusting weights from common input nodes to M output nodes arranged in a two dimensional grid as shown in Fig. 17. Output nodes are extensively interconnected with many local connections. Continuous-valued input vectors are presented sequentially in time without specifying the desired output. After enough input vectors have been presented, weights will specify cluster or vector centers that sample the input space such that the point density function of the vector centers tends to approximate the probability density function of the input vectors [22]. In addition, the weights will be organized such that topologically close nodes are sensitive to inputs that are physically similar. Output nodes will thus be ordered in a natural manner. This may be important in complex systems with many layers of processing because it can reduce lengths of inter-layer connections.

The algorithm that forms feature maps requires a neighborhood to be defined around each node as shown in Fig. 18. This neighborhood slowly decreases in size with time as shown. Kohonen's algorithm is described in Box 7. Weights between input and output nodes are initially set to small random values and an input is presented. The distance between the input and all nodes is computed as shown. If the weight vectors are normalized to have constant length (the sum of the squared weights from all inputs to each output are identical) then the node with the minimum Euclidean distance can be found by using the net of Fig. 17 to form the dot product of the input and the weights. The selection required in step 4 then turns into a problem of finding the node with a maximum value. This node can be selected using extensive lateral inhibition as in the MAXNET in the top of Fig. 6. Once this node is selected, weights to it and to other nodes in its neighborhood are modified to make these nodes more responsive to the current input. This process is repeated for further inputs. Weights eventually converge and are fixed after the gain term in step 5 is reduced to zero.

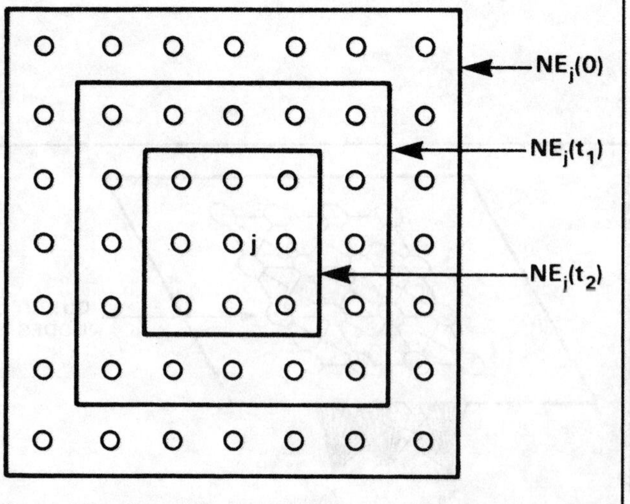

Figure 18. Topological neighborhoods at different times as feature maps are formed. $NE_j(t)$ is the set of nodes considered to be in the neighborhood of node j at time t. The neighborhood starts large and slowly decreases in size over time. In this example, $0 < t_1 < t_2$.

Box 7. An Algorithm to Produce Self-Organizing Feature Maps

Step 1. Initialize Weights

Initialize weights from N inputs to the M output nodes shown in Fig. 17 to small random values. Set the initial radius of the neighborhood shown in Fig. 18.

Step 2. Present New Input

Step 3. Compute Distance to All Nodes

Compute distances d_j between the input and each output node j using

$$d_j = \sum_{i=0}^{N-1} (x_i(t) - w_{ij}(t))^2$$

where $x_i(t)$ is the input to node i at time t and $w_{ij}(t)$ is the weight from input node i to output node j at time t.

Step 4. Select Output Node with Minimum Distance

Select node j^* as that output node with minimum d_j.

Step 5. Update Weights to Node j^* and Neighbors

Weights are updated for node j^* and all nodes in the neighborhood defined by $NE_{j^*}(t)$ as shown in Fig. 18. New weights are

$$w_{ij}(t+1) = w_{ij}(t) + \eta(t)(x_i(t) - w_{ij}(t))$$

For $j \in NE_{j^*}(t) \qquad 0 \le i \le N-1$

The term $\eta(t)$ is a gain term ($0 < \eta(t) < 1$) that decreases in time.

Step 6. Repeat by Going to Step 2

An example of the behavior of this algorithm is presented in Fig. 19. The weights for 100 output nodes are plotted in these six subplots when there are two random independent inputs uniformly distributed over the region enclosed by the boxed areas. Line intersections in these plots specify weights for one output node. Weights from

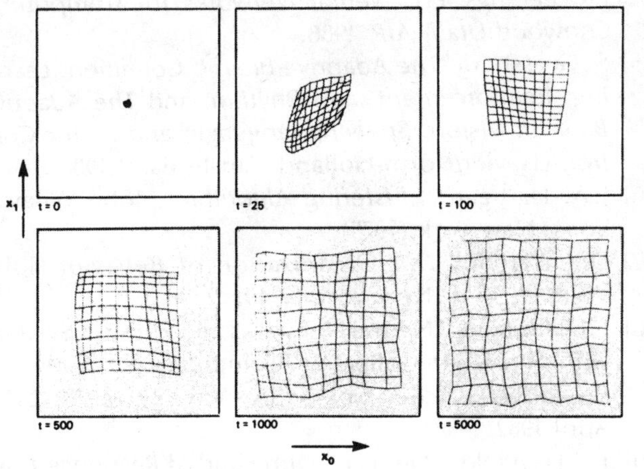

Figure 19. Weights to 100 output nodes from two input nodes as a feature map is being formed. The horizontal axis represents the value of the weight from input x_0 and the vertical axis represents the value of the weight from input x_1. Line intersections specify the two weights for each node. Lines connect weights for nodes that are nearest neighbors. An orderly grid indicates that topologically close nodes code inputs that are physically similar. Inputs were random, independent, and uniformly distributed over the area shown.

input x_0 are specified by the position along the horizontal axis and weights from input x_1 are specified by the position along the vertical axis. Lines connect weight values for nodes that are topological nearest neighbors. Weights start at time zero clustered at the center of the plot. Weights then gradually expand in an orderly way until their point density approximates the uniform distribution of the input samples. In this example, the gain term in step 5 of Box 7 was a Gaussian function of the distance to the node selected in step 4 with a width that decreased in time.

Kohonen [22] presents many other examples and proofs related to this algorithm. He also demonstrates how the algorithm can be used in a speech recognizer as a vector quantizer [23]. Unlike the Carpenter/Grossberg classifier, this algorithm can perform relatively well in noise because the number of classes is fixed, weights adapt slowly, and adaptation stops after training. This algorithm is thus a viable sequential vector quantizer when the number of clusters desired can be specified before use and the amount of training data is large relative to the number of clusters desired. It is similar to the K-means clustering algorithm in this respect. Results, however, may depend on the presentation order of input data for small amounts of training data.

INTRODUCTORY REFERENCES TO NEURAL NET LITERATURE

More detailed information concerning the six algorithms described above and other neural net algorithms can be found in [3, 7, 15, 18, 19, 20, 22, 25, 32, 39, 40]. Descriptions of many other algorithms including the Boltzmann machine and background historical information can be found in a recent book on parallel distributed processing edited by Rumelhart and McClelland [41]. Feldman [9] presents a good introduction to the connectionist philosophy that complements this book. Papers describing recent research efforts are available in the proceedings of the 1986 Conference on Neural Networks for Computing held in Snowbird, Utah [6]. Descriptions of how the Hopfield net can be used to solve a number of different optimization problems including the traveling salesman problem are presented in [20, 45]. A discussion of how content-addressable memories can be implemented using optical techniques is available in [1] and an introduction to the field of neurobiology is available in [21] and other basic texts.

In addition to the above papers and books, there are a number of neural net conferences being held in 1987. These include the "1987 Snowbird Meeting on Neural Networks for Computing" in Snowbird, Utah, April 1–5, the "IEEE First Annual International Conference on Neural Networks" in San Diego, California, June 21–24, and the "IEEE Conference on Neural Information Processing Systems—Natural and Synthetic" in Boulder, Colorado, November 8–12. This last conference is cosponsored by the IEEE Acoustics, Speech, and Signal Processing Society.

CONCLUDING REMARKS

The above review provides an introduction to an interesting field that is immature and rapidly changing. The six nets described are common components in many more complex systems that are under development. Although there have been no practical applications of neural nets yet, preliminary results such as those of Sejnowski [43] have demonstrated the potential of the newer learning algorithms. The greatest potential of neural nets remains in the high-speed processing that could be provided through massively parallel VLSI implementations. Several groups are currently exploring different VLSI implementation strategies [31, 13, 42]. Demonstrations that existing algorithms for speech and image recognition can be performed using neural nets support the potential applicability of any neural-net VLSI hardware that is developed.

The current research effort in neural nets has attracted researchers trained in engineering, physics, mathematics, neuroscience, biology, computer sciences and psychology. Current research is aimed at analyzing learning and self-organization algorithms used in multi-layer nets, at developing design principles and techniques to solve dynamic range and sensitivity problems which become important for large analog systems, at building complete systems for image and speech and recognition and obtaining experience with these systems, and at determining which current algorithms can be implemented using neuron-like components. Advances in these areas and in VLSI implementation techniques could lead to practical real-time neural-net systems.

ACKNOWLEDGMENTS

I have constantly benefited from discussions with Ben Gold and Joe Tierney. I would also like to thank Don Johnson for his encouragement, Bill Huang for his simulation studies, and Carolyn for her patience.

REFERENCES

[1] Y. S. Abu-Mostafa and D. Pslatis, "Optical Neural Computers," *Scientific American*, 256, 88–95, March 1987.

[2] E. B. Baum, J. Moody, and F. Wilczek, "Internal Representations for Associative Memory," NSF-ITP-86-138 Institute for Theoretical Physics, University of California, Santa Barbara, California, 1986.

[3] G. A. Carpenter, and S. Grossberg, "Neural Dynamics of Category Learning and Recognition: Attention, Memory Consolidation, and Amnesia," in J. Davis, R. Newburgh, and E. Wegman (Eds.) *Brain Structure, Learning, and Memory,* AAAS Symposium Series, 1986.

[4] M. A. Cohen, and S. Grossberg, "Absolute Stability of Global Pattern Formation and Parallel Memory Storage by Competitive Neural Networks," *IEEE Trans. Syst. Man Cybern.* SMC-13, 815–826, 1983.

[5] B. Delgutte, "Speech Coding in the Auditory Nerve: II. Processing Schemes for Vowel-Like Sounds," *J. Acoust. Soc. Am.* 75, 879–886, 1984.

[6] J. S. Denker, *AIP Conference Proceedings 151, Neural Networks for Computing, Snowbird Utah, AIP,* 1986.

[7] R. O. Duda and P. E. Hart, *Pattern Classification and Scene Analysis,* John Wiley & Sons, New York (1973).

[8] J. L. Elman and D. Zipser, "Learning the Hidden Structure of Speech," Institute for Cognitive Science, University of California at San Diego, *ICS Report 8701,* Feb. 1987.

[9] J. A. Feldman and D. H. Ballard, "Connectionist Models and Their Properties," *Cognitive Science, Vol. 6,* 205–254, 1982.

[10] R. G. Gallager, *Information Theory and Reliable Communication,* John Wiley & Sons, New York (1968).

[11] O. Ghitza, "Robustness Against Noise: The Role of Timing-Synchrony Measurement," in *Proceedings International Conference on Acoustics Speech and Signal Processing,* ICASSP-87, Dallas, Texas, April 1987.

[12] B. Gold, "Hopfield Model Applied to Vowel and Consonant Discrimination," *MIT Lincoln Laboratory Technical Report, TR-747, AD-A169742,* June 1986.

[13] H. P. Graf, L. D. Jackel, R. E. Howard, B. Straughn, J. S. Denker, W. Hubbard, D. M. Tennant, and D. Schwartz, "VLSI Implementation of a Neural Network Memory With Several Hundreds of Neurons," in J. S. Denker (Ed.) *AIP Conference Proceedings 151, Neural Networks for Computing, Snowbird Utah, AIP,* 1986.

[14] P. M. Grant and J. P. Sage, "A Comparison of Neural Network and Matched Filter Processing for Detecting Lines in Images," in J. S. Denker (Ed.) *AIP Conference Proceedings 151, Neural Networks for Computing, Snowbird Utah, AIP,* 1986.

[15] S. Grossberg, *The Adaptive Brain I: Cognition, Learning, Reinforcement, and Rhythm,* and *The Adaptive Brain II: Vision, Speech, Language, and Motor Control,* Elsevier/North-Holland, Amsterdam (1986).

[16] J. A. Hartigan, *Clustering Algorithms,* John Wiley & Sons, New York (1975).

[17] D. O. Hebb, *The Organization of Behavior,* John Wiley & Sons, New York (1949).

[18] J. J. Hopfield, "Neural Networks and Physical Systems with Emergent Collective Computational Abilities," *Proc. Natl. Acad. Sci.* USA, Vol. 79, 2554–2558, April 1982.

[19] J. J. Hopfield, "Neurons with Graded Response Have Collective Computational Properties Like Those of Two-State Neurons," *Proc. Natl. Acad. Sci.* USA, Vol. 81, 3088–3092, May 1984.

[20] J. J. Hopfield, and D. W. Tank, "Computing with Neural Circuits: A Model," *Science,* Vol. 233, 625–633, August 1986.

[21] E. R. Kandel and J. H. Schwartz, *Principles of Neural Science,* Elsevier, New York (1985).

[22] T. Kohonen, *Self-Organization and Associative Memory,* Springer-Verlag, Berlin (1984).

[23] T. Kohonen, K. Masisara and T. Saramaki, "Phonotopic Maps—Insightful Representation of Phonological Features for Speech Representation," *Proceedings IEEE 7th Inter. Conf. on Pattern Recognition,* Montreal, Canada, 1984.

[24] F. L. Lewis, *Optimal Estimation,* John Wiley & Sons, New York (1986).

[25] R. P. Lippmann, B. Gold, and M. L. Malpass, "A Comparison of Hamming and Hopfield Neural Nets for Pattern Classification," *MIT Lincoln Laboratory Technical Report, TR-769,* to be published.

[26] G. G. Lorentz, "The 13th Problem of Hilbert," in F. E. Browder (Ed.), *Mathematical Developments Arising from Hilbert Problems,* American Mathematical Society, Providence, R.I. (1976).

[27] R. F. Lyon and E. P. Loeb, "Isolated Digit Recognition Experiments with a Cochlear Model," in *Proceedings International Conference on Acoustics Speech and Signal Processing, ICASSP-87,* Dallas, Texas, April 1987.

[28] J. Makhoul, S. Roucos, and H. Gish, "Vector Quantization in Speech Coding," *IEEE Proceedings, 73,* 1551–1588, Nov. 1985.

[29] T. Martin, *Acoustic Recognition of a Limited Vocabulary in Continuous Speech,* Ph.D. Thesis, Dept. Electrical Engineering Univ. Pennsylvania, 1970.

[30] W. S. McCulloch, and W. Pitts, "A Logical Calculus of the Ideas Imminent in Nervous Activity," *Bulletin of Mathematical Biophysics,* 5, 115–133, 1943.

[31] C. A. Mead, *Analog VLSI and Neural Systems,* Course Notes, Computer Science Dept., California Institute of Technology, 1986.

[32] M. Minsky, and S. Papert, *Perceptrons: An Intro-*

duction to Computational Geometry, MIT Press (1969).

[33] A. R. Moller, *Auditory Physiology,* Academic Press, New York (1983).

[34] P. Mueller, and J. Lazzaro, "A Machine for Neural Computation of Acoustical Patterns with Application to Real-Time Speech Recognition," in J. S. Denker (Ed.) *AIP Conference Proceedings 151, Neural Networks for Computing, Snowbird Utah, AIP,* 1986.

[35] D. B. Parker, "A Comparison of Algorithms for Neuron-Like Cells," in J. S. Denker (Ed.) *AIP Conference Proceedings 151, Neural Networks for Computing, Snowbird Utah, AIP,* 1986.

[36] T. Parsons, *Voice and Speech Processing,* McGraw-Hill, New York (1986).

[37] S. M. Peeling, R. K. Moore, and M. J. Tomlinson, "The Multi-Layer Perceptron as a Tool for Speech Pattern Processing Research," in *Proc. IoA Autumn Conf. on Speech and Hearing,* 1986.

[38] T. E. Posch, "Models of the Generation and Processing of Signals by Nerve Cells: A Categorically Indexed Abridged Bibliography," *USCEE Report 290,* August 1968.

[39] R. Rosenblatt, *Principles of Neurodynamics,* New York, Spartan Books (1959).

[40] D. E. Rumelhart, G. E. Hinton, and R. J. Williams, "Learning Internal Representations by Error Propagation" in D. E. Rumelhart & J. L. McClelland (Eds.), *Parallel Distributed Processing: Explorations in the Microstructure of Cognition. Vol. 1: Foundations.* MIT Press (1986).

[41] D. E. Rumelhart, and J. L. McClelland, *Parallel Distributed Processing: Explorations in the Microstructure of Cognition,* MIT Press (1986).

[42] J. P. Sage, K. Thompson, and R. S. Withers, "An Artificial Neural Network Integrated Circuit Based on MNOS/CD Principles," in J. S. Denker (Ed.) *AIP Conference Proceedings 151, Neural Networks for Computing, Snowbird Utah, AIP,* 1986.

[43] T. Sejnowski and C. R. Rosenberg, "NETtalk: A Parallel Network That Learns to Read Aloud," *Johns Hopkins Univ. Technical Report JHU/EECS-86/01,* 1986.

[44] S. Seneff, "A Computational Model for the Peripheral Auditory System: Application to Speech Recognition Research," in *Proceedings International Conference on Acoustics Speech and Signal Processing, ICASSP-86,* 4, 37.8.1-37.8.4, 1986.

[45] D. W. Tank and J. J. Hopfield, "Simple 'Neural' Optimization Networks: An A/D Converter, Signal Decision Circuit, and a Linear Programming Circuit," *IEEE Trans. Circuits Systems CAS-33,* 533–541, 1986.

[46] D. J. Wallace, "Memory and Learning in a Class of Neural Models," in B. Bunk and K. H. Mutter (Eds.) *Proceedings of the Workshop on Lattice Gauge Theory, Wuppertal, 1985,* Plenum (1986).

[47] B. Widrow, and M. E. Hoff, "Adaptive Switching Circuits," *1960 IRE WESCON Conv. Record, Part 4,* 96–104, August 1960.

[48] B. Widrow and S. D. Stearns, *Adaptive Signal Processing,* Prentice-Hall, New Jersey (1985).

Part 2
Theoretical Foundations

30 Years of Adaptive Neural Networks: Perceptron, Madaline, and Backpropagation

BERNARD WIDROW, FELLOW, IEEE, AND MICHAEL A. LEHR

Fundamental developments in feedforward artificial neural networks from the past thirty years are reviewed. The central theme of this paper is a description of the history, origination, operating characteristics, and basic theory of several supervised neural network training algorithms including the Perceptron rule, the LMS algorithm, three Madaline rules, and the backpropagation technique. These methods were developed independently, but with the perspective of history they can all be related to each other. The concept underlying these algorithms is the "minimal disturbance principle," which suggests that during training it is advisable to inject new information into a network in a manner that disturbs stored information to the smallest extent possible.

I. Introduction

This year marks the 30th anniversary of the Perceptron rule and the LMS algorithm, two early rules for training adaptive elements. Both algorithms were first published in 1960. In the years following these discoveries, many new techniques have been developed in the field of neural networks, and the discipline is growing rapidly. One early development was Steinbuch's Learning Matrix [1], a pattern recognition machine based on linear discriminant functions. At the same time, Widrow and his students devised Madaline Rule I (MRI), the earliest popular learning rule for neural networks with multiple adaptive elements [2]. Other early work included the "mode-seeking" technique of Stark, Okajima, and Whipple [3]. This was probably the first example of competitive learning in the literature, though it could be argued that earlier work by Rosenblatt on "spontaneous learning" [4], [5] deserves this distinction. Further pioneering work on competitive learning and self-organization was performed in the 1970s by von der Malsburg [6] and Grossberg [7]. Fukushima explored related ideas with his biologically inspired Cognitron and Neocognitron models [8], [9].

Manuscript received September 12, 1989; revised April 13, 1990. This work was sponsored by SDIO Innovative Science and Technology office and managed by ONR under contract no. N00014-86-K-0718, by the Dept. of the Army Belvoir RD&E Center under contracts no. DAAK 70-87-P-3134 and no. DAAK-70-89-K-0001, by a grant from the Lockheed Missiles and Space Co., by NASA under contract no. NCA2-389, and by Rome Air Development Center under contract no. F30602-88-D-0025, subcontract no. E-21-T22-S1.

The authors are with the Information Systems Laboratory, Department of Electrical Engineering, Stanford University, Stanford, CA 94305-4055, USA.

IEEE Log Number 9038824.

Widrow devised a reinforcement learning algorithm called "punish/reward" or "bootstrapping" [10], [11] in the mid-1960s. This can be used to solve problems when uncertainty about the error signal causes supervised training methods to be impractical. A related reinforcement learning approach was later explored in a classic paper by Barto, Sutton, and Anderson on the "credit assignment" problem [12]. Barto *et al.*'s technique is also somewhat reminiscent of Albus's adaptive CMAC, a distributed table-look-up system based on models of human memory [13], [14].

In the 1970s Grossberg developed his Adaptive Resonance Theory (ART), a number of novel hypotheses about the underlying principles governing biological neural systems [15]. These ideas served as the basis for later work by Carpenter and Grossberg involving three classes of ART architectures: ART 1 [16], ART 2 [17], and ART 3 [18]. These are self-organizing neural implementations of pattern clustering algorithms. Other important theory on self-organizing systems was pioneered by Kohonen with his work on feature maps [19], [20].

In the early 1980s, Hopfield and others introduced outer product rules as well as equivalent approaches based on the early work of Hebb [21] for training a class of recurrent (signal feedback) networks now called Hopfield models [22], [23]. More recently, Kosko extended some of the ideas of Hopfield and Grossberg to develop his adaptive Bidirectional Associative Memory (BAM) [24], a network model employing differential as well as Hebbian and competitive learning laws. Other significant models from the past decade include probabilistic ones such as Hinton, Sejnowski, and Ackley's Boltzmann Machine [25], [26] which, to oversimplify, is a Hopfield model that settles into solutions by a simulated annealing process governed by Boltzmann statistics. The Boltzmann Machine is trained by a clever two-phase Hebbian-based technique.

While these developments were taking place, adaptive systems research at Stanford traveled an independent path. After devising their Madaline I rule, Widrow and his students developed uses for the Adaline and Madaline. Early applications included, among others, speech and pattern recognition [27], weather forecasting [28], and adaptive controls [29]. Work then switched to adaptive filtering and adaptive signal processing [30] after attempts to develop learning rules for networks with multiple adaptive layers were unsuccessful. Adaptive signal processing proved to

Reprinted from *Proc. IEEE*, vol. 78, no. 9, Sept. 1990, pp. 1415–1442.

be a fruitful avenue for research with applications involving adaptive antennas [31], adaptive inverse controls [32], adaptive noise cancelling [33], and seismic signal processing [30]. Outstanding work by Lucky and others at Bell Laboratories led to major commercial applications of adaptive filters and the LMS algorithm to adaptive equalization in high-speed modems [34], [35] and to adaptive echo cancellers for long-distance telephone and satellite circuits [36]. After 20 years of research in adaptive signal processing, the work in Widrow's laboratory has once again returned to neural networks.

The first major extension of the feedforward neural network beyond Madaline I took place in 1971 when Werbos developed a backpropagation training algorithm which, in 1974, he first published in his doctoral dissertation [37].[1] Unfortunately, Werbos's work remained almost unknown in the scientific community. In 1982, Parker rediscovered the technique [39] and in 1985, published a report on it at M.I.T. [40]. Not long after Parker published his findings, Rumelhart, Hinton, and Williams [41], [42] also rediscovered the technique and, largely as a result of the clear framework within which they presented their ideas, they finally succeeeded in making it widely known.

The elements used by Rumelhart *et al.* in the backpropagation network differ from those used in the earlier Madaline architectures. The adaptive elements in the original Madaline structure used hard-limiting quantizers (signums), while the elements in the backpropagation network use only differentiable nonlinearities, or "sigmoid" functions.[2] In digital implementations, the hard-limiting quantizer is more easily computed than any of the differentiable nonlinearities used in backpropagation networks. In 1987, Widrow, Winter, and Baxter looked back at the original Madaline I algorithm with the goal of developing a new technique that could adapt multiple layers of adaptive elements using the simpler hard-limiting quantizers. The result was Madaline Rule II [43].

David Andes of U.S. Naval Weapons Center of China Lake, CA, modified Madaline II in 1988 by replacing the hard-limiting quantizers in the Adaline and sigmoid functions, thereby inventing Madaline Rule III (MRIII). Widrow and his students were first to recognize that this rule is mathematically equivalent to backpropagation.

The outline above gives only a partial view of the discipline, and many landmark discoveries have not been mentioned. Needless to say, the field of neural networks is quickly becoming a vast one, and in one short survey we could not hope to cover the entire subject in any detail. Consequently, many significant developments, including some of those mentioned above, are not discussed in this paper. The algorithms described are limited primarily to those developed in our laboratory at Stanford, and to related techniques developed elsewhere, the most important of which is the backpropagation algorithm. Section II explores fundamental concepts, Section III discusses adaptation and the minimal disturbance principle, Sections IV and V cover error correction rules, Sections VI and VII delve into steepest-descent rules, and Section VIII provides a summary.

Information about the neural network paradigms not discussed in this paper can be obtained from a number of other sources, such as the concise survey by Lippmann [44], and the collection of classics by Anderson and Rosenfeld [45]. Much of the early work in the field from the 1960s is carefully reviewed in Nilsson's monograph [46]. A good view of some of the more recent results is presented in Rumelhart and McClelland's popular three-volume set [47]. A paper by Moore [48] presents a clear discussion about ART 1 and some of Grossberg's terminology. Another resource is the DARPA Study report [49] which gives a very comprehensive and readable "snapshot" of the field in 1988.

II. Fundamental Concepts

Today we can build computers and other machines that perform a variety of well-defined tasks with celerity and reliability unmatched by humans. No human can invert matrices or solve systems of differential equations at speeds rivaling modern workstations. Nonetheless, many problems remain to be solved to our satisfaction by any man-made machine, but are easily disentangled by the perceptual or cognitive powers of humans, and often lower mammals, or even fish and insects. No computer vision system can rival the human ability to recognize visual images formed by objects of all shapes and orientations under a wide range of conditions. Humans effortlessly recognize objects in diverse environments and lighting conditions, even when obscured by dirt, or occluded by other objects. Likewise, the performance of current speech-recognition technology pales when compared to the performance of the human adult who easily recognizes words spoken by different people, at different rates, pitches, and volumes, even in the presence of distortion or background noise.

The problems solved more effectively by the brain than by the digital computer typically have two characteristics: they are generally ill defined, and they usually require an enormous amount of processing. Recognizing the character of an object from its image on television, for instance, involves resolving ambiguities associated with distortion and lighting. It also involves filling in information about a three-dimensional scene which is missing from the two-dimensional image on the screen. An infinite number of three-dimensional scenes can be projected into a two-dimensional image. Nonetheless, the brain deals well with this ambiguity, and using learned cues usually has little difficulty correctly determining the role played by the missing dimension.

As anyone who has performed even simple filtering operations on images is aware, processing high-resolution images requires a great deal of computation. Our brains accomplish this by utilizing massive parallelism, with millions and even billions of neurons in parts of the brain working together to solve complicated problems. Because solid-state operational amplifiers and logic gates can compute

[1]We should note, however, that in the field of variational calculus the idea of error backpropagation through nonlinear systems existed centuries before Werbos first thought to apply this concept to neural networks. In the past 25 years, these methods have been used widely in the field of optimal control, as discussed by Le Cun [38].

[2]The term "sigmoid" is usually used in reference to monotonically increasing "S-shaped" functions, such as the hyperbolic tangent. In this paper, however, we generally use the term to denote any smooth nonlinear functions at the output of a linear adaptive element. In other papers, these nonlinearities go by a variety of names, such as "squashing functions," "activation functions," "transfer characteristics," or "threshold functions."

many orders of magnitude faster than current estimates of the computational speed of neurons in the brain, we may soon be able to build relatively inexpensive machines with the ability to process as much information as the human brain. This enormous processing power will do little to help us solve problems, however, unless we can utilize it effectively. For instance, coordinating many thousands of processors, which must efficiently cooperate to solve a problem, is not a simple task. If each processor must be programmed separately, and if all contingencies associated with various ambiguities must be designed into the software, even a relatively simple problem can quickly become unmanageable. The slow progress over the past 25 years or so in machine vision and other areas of artificial intelligence is testament to the difficulties associated with solving ambiguous and computationally intensive problems on von Neumann computers and related architectures.

Thus, there is some reason to consider attacking certain problems by designing naturally parallel computers, which process information and learn by principles borrowed from the nervous systems of biological creatures. This does not necessarily mean we should attempt to copy the brain part for part. Although the bird served to inspire development of the airplane, birds do not have propellers, and airplanes do not operate by flapping feathered wings. The primary parallel between biological nervous systems and artificial neural networks is that each typically consists of a large number of simple elements that learn and are able to collectively solve complicated and ambiguous problems.

Today, most artificial neural network research and application is accomplished by simulating networks on serial computers. Speed limitations keep such networks relatively small, but even with small networks some surprisingly difficult problems have been tackled. Networks with fewer than 150 neural elements have been used successfully in vehicular control simulations [50], speech generation [51], [52], and undersea mine detection [49]. Small networks have also been used successfully in airport explosive detection [53], expert systems [54], [55], and scores of other applications. Furthermore, efforts to develop parallel neural network hardware are meeting with some success, and such hardware should be available in the future for attacking more difficult problems, such as speech recognition [56], [57].

Whether implemented in parallel hardware or simulated on a computer, all neural networks consist of a collection of simple elements that work together to solve problems. A basic building block of nearly all artificial neural networks, and most other adaptive systems, is the adaptive linear combiner.

A. The Adaptive Linear Combiner

The adaptive linear combiner is diagrammed in Fig. 1. Its output is a linear combination of its inputs. In a digital implementation, this element receives at time k an input signal vector or input pattern vector $\boldsymbol{X}_k = [x_0, x_{1_k}, x_{2_k}, \cdots, x_{n_k}]^T$ and a desired response d_k, a special input used to effect learning. The components of the input vector are weighted by a set of coefficients, the weight vector $\boldsymbol{W}_k = [w_{0_k}, w_{1_k}, w_{2_k}, \cdots, w_{n_k}]^T$. The sum of the weighted inputs is then computed, producing a linear output, the inner product $s_k = \boldsymbol{X}_k^T \boldsymbol{W}_k$. The components of $\boldsymbol{X}_k$ may be either

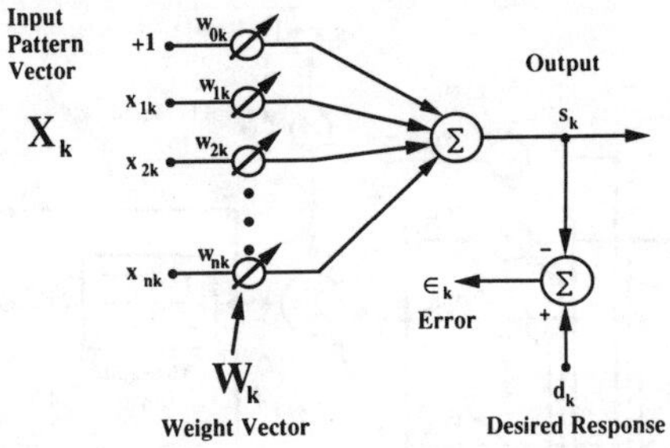

Fig. 1. Adaptive linear combiner.

continuous analog values or binary values. The weights are essentially continuously variable, and can take on negative as well as positive values.

During the training process, input patterns and corresponding desired responses are presented to the linear combiner. An adaptation algorithm automatically adjusts the weights so that the output responses to the input patterns will be as close as possible to their respective desired reponses. In signal processing applications, the most popular method for adapting the weights is the simple LMS (least mean square) algorithm [58], [59], often called the Widrow-Hoff delta rule [42]. This algorithm minimizes the sum of squares of the linear errors over the training set. The linear error ϵ_k is defined to be the difference between the desired response d_k and the linear output s_k, during presentation k. Having this error signal is necessary for adapting the weights. When the adaptive linear combiner is embedded in a multi-element neural network, however, an error signal is often not directly available for each individual linear combiner and more complicated procedures must be devised for adapting the weight vectors. These procedures are the main focus of this paper.

B. A Linear Classifier—The Single Threshold Element

The basic building block used in many neural networks is the "adaptive linear element," or Adaline[3] [58] (Fig. 2).

This is an adaptive threshold logic element. It consists of an adaptive linear combiner cascaded with a hard-limiting quantizer, which is used to produce a binary ± 1 output, $Y_k = \text{sgn}(s_k)$. The bias weight w_{0_k} which is connected to a constant input $x_0 = +1$, effectively controls the threshold level of the quantizer.

In single-element neural networks, an adaptive algorithm (such as the LMS algorithm, or the Perceptron rule) is often used to adjust the weights of the Adaline so that it responds correctly to as many patterns as possible in a training set that has binary desired responses. Once the weights are adjusted, the responses of the trained element can be tested by applying various input patterns. If the Adaline responds correctly with high probability to input patterns that were not included in the training set, it is said that generalization has taken place. Learning and generalization are among the most useful attributes of Adalines and neural networks.

Linear Separability: With n binary inputs and one binary

[3]In the neural network literature, such elements are often referred to as "adaptive neurons." However, in a conversation between David Hubel of Harvard Medical School and Bernard Widrow, Dr. Hubel pointed out that the Adaline differs from the biological neuron in that it contains not only the neural cell body, but also the input synapses and a mechanism for training them.

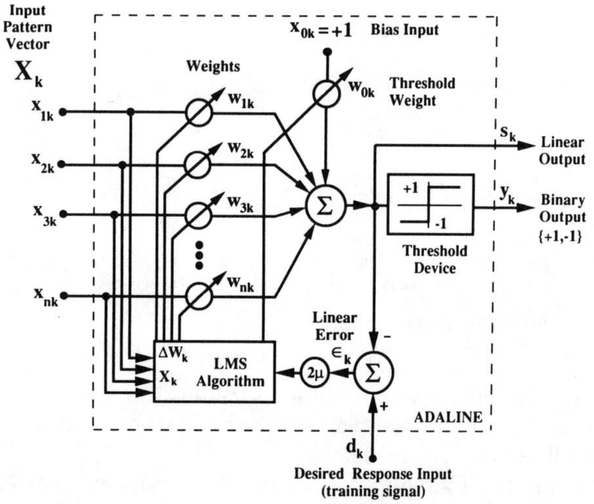

Fig. 2. Adaptive linear element (Adaline).

output, a single Adaline of the type shown in Fig. 2 is capable of implementing certain logic functions. There are 2^n possible input patterns. A general logic implementation would be capable of classifying each pattern as either $+1$ or -1, in accord with the desired response. Thus, there are 2^{2^n} possible logic functions connecting n inputs to a single binary output. A single Adaline is capable of realizing only a small subset of these functions, known as the linearly separable logic functions or threshold logic functions [60]. These are the set of logic functions that can be obtained with all possible weight variations.

Figure 3 shows a two-input Adaline element. Figure 4 represents all possible binary inputs to this element with four large dots in pattern vector space. In this space, the components of the input pattern vector lie along the coordinate axes. The Adaline separates input patterns into two categories, depending on the values of the weights. A critical

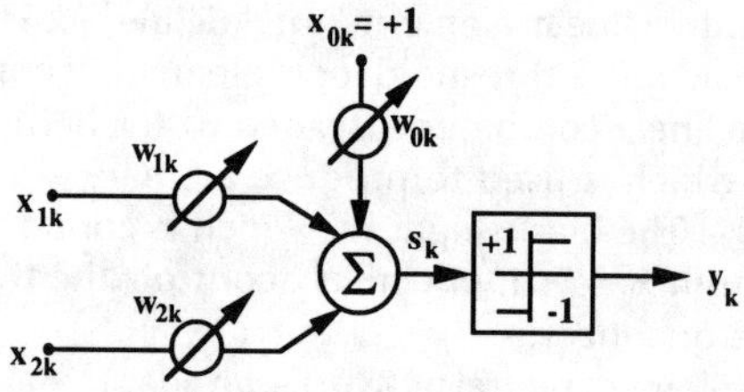

Fig. 3. Two-input Adaline.

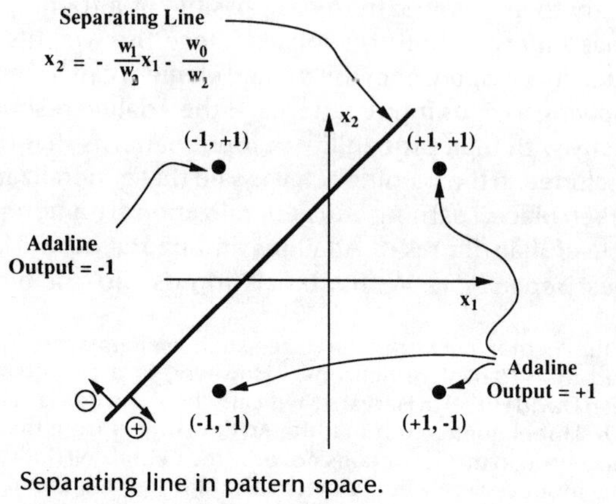

Fig. 4. Separating line in pattern space.

thresholding condition occurs when the linear output s equals zero:

$$s = x_1w_1 + x_2w_2 + w_0 = 0, \tag{1}$$

therefore

$$x_2 = -\frac{w_1}{w_2}x_1 - \frac{w_0}{w_2}. \tag{2}$$

Figure 4 graphs this linear relation, which comprises a separating line having slope and intercept given by

$$\text{slope} = -\frac{w_1}{w_2}$$

$$\text{intercept} = -\frac{w_0}{w_2}. \tag{3}$$

The three weights determine slope, intercept, and the side of the separating line that corresponds to a positive output. The opposite side of the separating line corresponds to a negative output. For Adalines with four weights, the separating boundary is a plane; with more than four weights, the boundary is a hyperplane. Note that if the bias weight is zero, the separating hyperplane will be homogeneous—it will pass through the origin in pattern space.

As sketched in Fig. 4, the binary input patterns are classified as follows:

$$\begin{aligned}(+1, +1) &\rightarrow +1\\ (+1, -1) &\rightarrow +1\\ (-1, -1) &\rightarrow +1\\ (-1, +1) &\rightarrow -1\end{aligned} \tag{4}$$

This is an example of a linearly separable function. An example of a function which is not linearly separable is the two-input exclusive NOR function:

$$\begin{aligned}(+1, +1) &\rightarrow +1\\ (+1, -1) &\rightarrow -1\\ (-1, -1) &\rightarrow +1\\ (-1, +1) &\rightarrow -1\end{aligned} \tag{5}$$

No single straight line exists that can achieve this separation of the input patterns; thus, without preprocessing, no single Adaline can implement the exclusive NOR function.

With two inputs, a single Adaline can realize 14 of the 16 possible logic functions. With many inputs, however, only a small fraction of all possible logic functions is realizable, that is, linearly separable. Combinations of elements or networks of elements can be used to realize functions that are not linearly separable.

Capacity of Linear Classifiers: The number of training patterns or stimuli that an Adaline can learn to correctly classify is an important issue. Each pattern and desired output combination represents an inequality constraint on the weights. It is possible to have inconsistencies in sets of simultaneous inequalities just as with simultaneous equalities. When the inequalities (that is, the patterns) are determined at random, the number that can be picked before an inconsistency arises is a matter of chance.

In their 1964 dissertations [61], [62], T. M. Cover and R. J. Brown both showed that the average number of random patterns with random binary desired responses that can be absorbed by an Adaline is approximately equal to twice the number of weights.[4] This is the *statistical pattern capacity* C_s of the Adaline. As reviewed by Nilsson [46], both theses included an analytic formula describing the probability that such a training set can be separated by an Adaline (i.e., it is linearly separable). The probability is a function of N_p, the number of input patterns in the training set, and N_w, the number of weights in the Adaline, including the threshold weight, if used:

$$P_{\text{Separable}} = \begin{cases} 2^{-(N_p-1)} \sum_{i=0}^{N_w-1} \binom{N_p-1}{i} & \text{for } N_p > N_w \\ 1 & \text{for } N_p \le N_w. \end{cases} \tag{6}$$

In Fig. 5 this formula was used to plot a set of analytical curves, which show the probability that a set of N_p random patterns can be trained into an Adaline as a function of the ratio N_p/N_w. Notice from these curves that as the number of weights increases, the statistical pattern capacity of the Adaline $C_s = 2N_w$ becomes an accurate estimate of the number of responses it can learn.

Another fact that can be observed from Fig. 5 is that a

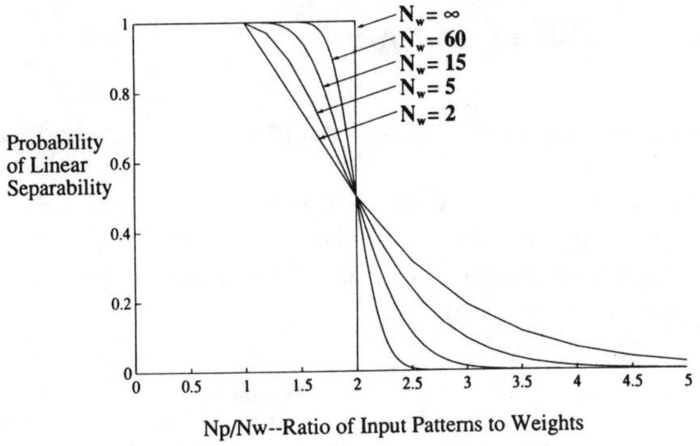

Fig. 5. Probability that an Adaline can separate a training pattern set as a function of the ratio N_p/N_w.

problem is guaranteed to have a solution if the number of patterns is equal to (or less than) half the statistical pattern capacity; that is, if the number of patterns is equal to the number of weights. We will refer to this as the *deterministic pattern capacity* C_d of the Adaline. An Adaline can learn *any* two-category pattern classification task involving no more patterns than that represented by its deterministic capacity, $C_d = N_w$.

Both the statistical and deterministic capacity results depend upon a mild condition on the positions of the input patterns: the patterns must be in general position with respect to the Adaline.[5] If the input patterns to an Adaline are continuous valued and smoothly distributed (that is, pattern positions are generated by a distribution function containing no impulses), general position is assured. The general position assumption is often invalid if the pattern vectors are binary. Nonetheless, even when the points are not in general position, the capacity results represent useful upper bounds.

The capacity results apply to randomly selected training patterns. In most problems of interest, the patterns in the training set are not random, but exhibit some statistical regularities. These regularities are what make generalization possible. The number of patterns that an Adaline can learn in a practical problem often far exceeds its statistical capacity because the Adaline is able to generalize within the training set, and learns many of the training patterns before they are even presented.

C. Nonlinear Classifiers

The linear classifier is limited in its capacity, and of course is limited to only linearly separable forms of pattern discrimination. More sophisticated classifiers with higher capacities are nonlinear. Two types of nonlinear classifiers are described here. The first is a fixed preprocessing network connected to a single adaptive element, and the other is the multi-element feedforward neural network.

Polynomial Discriminant Functions: Nonlinear functions of the inputs applied to the single Adaline can yield nonlinear decision boundaries. Useful nonlinearities include the polynomial functions. Consider the system illustrated in Fig. 6 which contains only linear and quadratic input

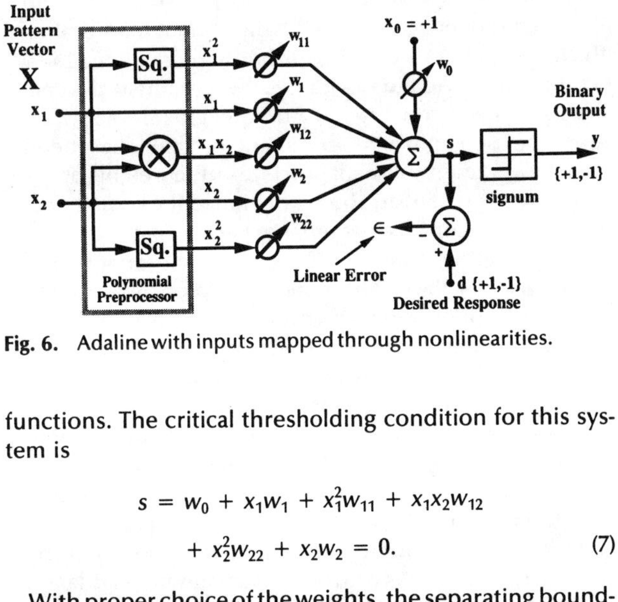

Fig. 6. Adaline with inputs mapped through nonlinearities.

functions. The critical thresholding condition for this system is

$$s = w_0 + x_1w_1 + x_1^2w_{11} + x_1x_2w_{12} + x_2^2w_{22} + x_2w_2 = 0. \tag{7}$$

With proper choice of the weights, the separating boundary in pattern space can be established as shown, for example, in Fig. 7. This represents a solution for the exclusive NOR function of (5). Of course, all of the linearly separable functions are also realizable. The use of such nonlinearities can be generalized for more than two inputs and for higher degree polynomial functions of the inputs. Some of the first work in this area was done by Specht [66]–[68] at Stanford in the 1960s when he successfully applied polynomial discriminants to the classification and analysis of electrocardiographic signals. Work on this topic has also been done

[4]Underlying theory for this result was discovered independently by a number of researchers including, among others, Winder [63], Cameron [64], and Joseph [65].

[5]Patterns are in general position with respect to an Adaline with no threshold weight if any subset of pattern vectors containing no more than N_w members forms a linearly independent set or, equivalently, if no set of N_w or more input points in the N_w-dimensional pattern space lie on a homogeneous hyperplane. For the more common case involving an Adaline with a threshold weight, general position means that no set of N_w or more patterns in the $(N_w - 1)$-dimension pattern space lie on a hyperplane not constrained to pass through the origin [61], [46].

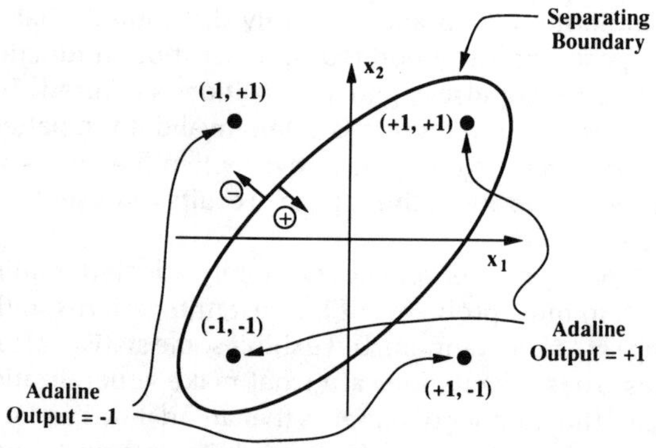

Fig. 7. Elliptical separating boundary for realizing a function which is not linearly separable.

by Barron and Barron [69]–[71] and by Ivankhnenko [72] in the Soviet Union.

The polynomial approach offers great simplicity and beauty. Through it one can realize a wide variety of adaptive nonlinear discriminant functions by adapting only a single Adaline element. Several methods have been developed for training the polynomial discriminant function. Specht developed a very efficient noniterative (that is, single pass through the training set) training procedure: the polynomial discriminant method (PDM), which allows the polynomial discriminant function to implement a nonparametric classifier based on the Bayes decision rule. Other methods for training the system include iterative error-correction rules such as the Perceptron and α-LMS rules, and iterative gradient-descent procedures such as the μ-LMS and SER (also called RLS) algorithms [30]. Gradient descent with a single adaptive element is typically much faster than with a layered neural network. Furthermore, as we shall see, when the single Adaline is trained by a gradient descent procedure, it will converge to a unique global solution.

After the polynomial discriminant function has been trained by a gradient-descent procedure, the weights of the Adaline will represent an approximation to the coefficients in a multidimensional Taylor series expansion of the desired response function. Likewise, if appropriate trigonometric terms are used in place of the polynomial preprocessor, the Adaline's weight solution will approximate the terms in the (truncated) multidimensional Fourier series decomposition of a periodic version of the desired response function. The choice of preprocessing functions determines how well a network will generalize for patterns outside the training set. Determining "good" functions remains a focus of current research [73], [74]. Experience seems to indicate that unless the nonlinearities are chosen with care to suit the problem at hand, often better generalization can be obtained from networks with more than one adaptive layer. In fact, one can view multilayer networks as single-layer networks with trainable preprocessors which are essentially self-optimizing.

Madaline I

One of the earliest trainable layered neural networks with multiple adaptive elements was the Madaline I structure of Widrow [2] and Hoff [75]. Mathematical analyses of Madaline I were developed in the Ph.D. theses of Ridgway [76], Hoff [75], and Glanz [77]. In the early 1960s, a 1000-weight Madaline I was built out of hardware [78] and used in pattern recognition research. The weights in this machine were memistors, electrically variable resistors developed by Widrow and Hoff which are adjusted by electroplating a resistive link [79].

Madaline I was configured in the following way. Retinal inputs were connected to a layer of adaptive Adaline elements, the outputs of which were connected to a fixed logic device that generated the system output. Methods for adapting such systems were developed at that time. An example of this kind of network is shown in Fig. 8. Two Adalines are connected to an AND logic device to provide an output.

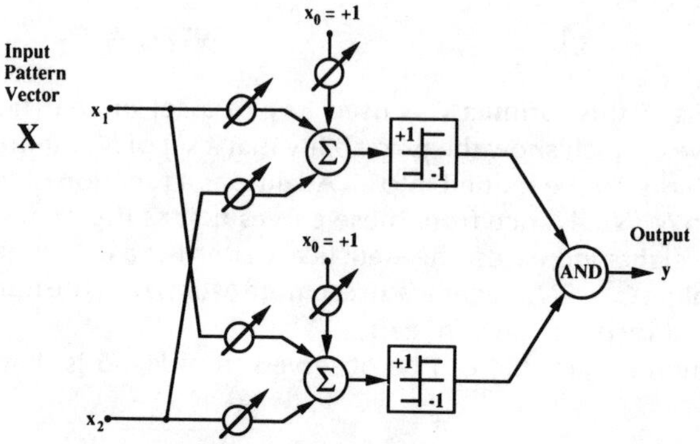

Fig. 8. Two-Adaline form of Madaline.

With weights suitably chosen, the separating boundary in pattern space for the system of Fig. 8 would be as shown in Fig. 9. This separating boundary implements the exclusive NOR function of (5).

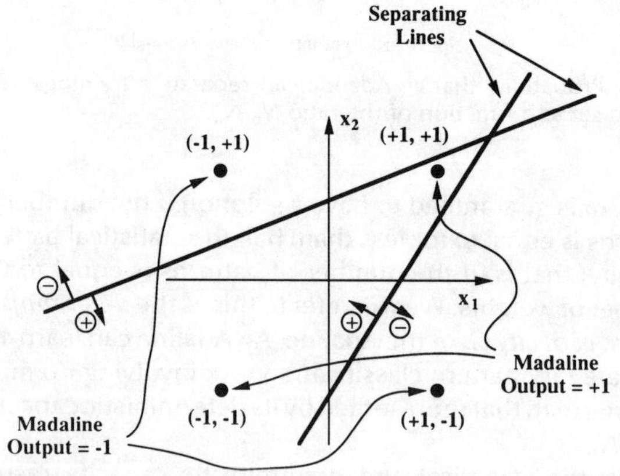

Fig. 9. Separating lines for Madaline of Fig. 8.

Madalines were constructed with many more inputs, with many more Adaline elements in the first layer, and with various fixed logic devices such as AND, OR, and majority-vote-taker elements in the second layer. Those three functions (Fig. 10) are all threshold logic functions. The given weight values will implement these three functions, but the weight choices are not unique.

Feedforward Networks

The Madalines of the 1960s had adaptive first layers and fixed threshold functions in the second (output) layers [76],

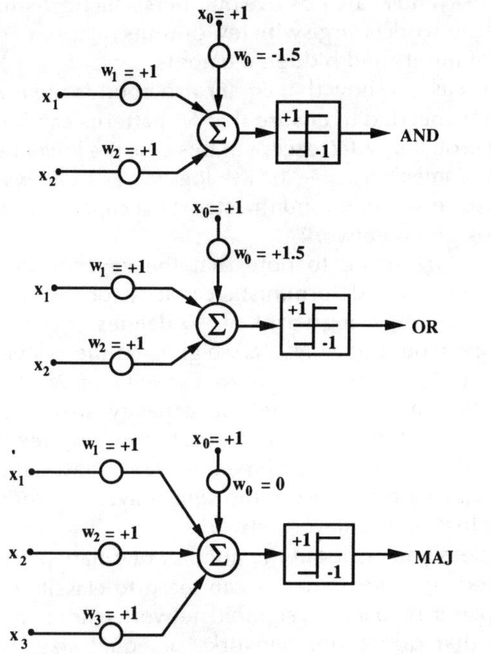

Fig. 10. Fixed-weight Adaline implementations of AND, OR, and MAJ logic functions.

[46]. The feedfoward neural networks of today often have many layers, and usually all layers are adaptive. The backpropagation networks of Rumelhart *et al.* [47] are perhaps the best-known examples of multilayer networks. A fully connected three-layer[6] feedforward adaptive network is illustrated in Fig. 11. In a fully connected layered network,

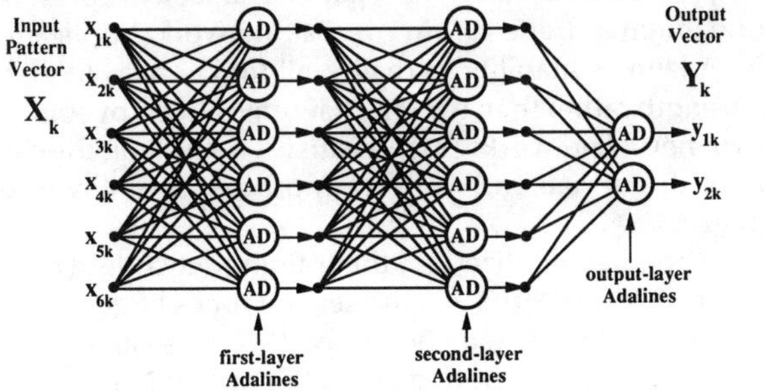

Fig. 11. Three-layer adaptive neural network.

each Adaline receives inputs from every output in the preceding layer.

During training, the response of each output element in the network is compared with a corresponding desired response. Error signals associated with the output elements are readily computed, so adaptation of the output layer is straightforward. The fundamental difficulty associated with adapting a layered network lies in obtaining "error signals" for hidden-layer Adalines, that is, for Adalines in layers other than the output layer. The backpropagation and Madaline III algorithms contain methods for establishing these error signals.

[6]In Rumelhart *et al.*'s terminology, this would be called a four-layer network, following Rosenblatt's convention of counting layers of signals, including the input layer. For our purposes, we find it more useful to count only layers of computing elements. We do not count as a layer the set of input terminal points.

There is no reason why a feedforward network must have the layered structure of Fig. 11. In Werbos's development of the backpropagation algorithm [37], in fact, the Adalines are ordered and each receives signals directly from each input component and from the output of each preceding Adaline. Many other variations of the feedforward network are possible. An interesting area of current research involves a generalized backpropagation method which can be used to train "high-order" or "σ–π" networks that incorporate a polynomial preprocessor for each Adaline [47], [80].

One characteristic that is often desired in pattern recognition problems is invariance of the network output to changes in the position and size of the input pattern or image. Various techniques have been used to achieve translation, rotation, scale, and time invariance. One method involves including in the training set several examples of each exemplar transformed in size, angle, and position, but with a desired response that depends only on the original exemplar [78]. Other research has dealt with various Fourier and Mellin transform preprocessors [81], [82], as well as neural preprocessors [83]. Giles and Maxwell have developed a clever averaging approach, which removes unwanted dependencies from the polynomial terms in high-order threshold logic units (polynomial discriminant functions) [74] and high-order neural networks [80]. Other approaches have considered Zernike moments [84], graph matching [85], spatially repeated feature detectors [9], and time-averaged outputs [86].

Capacity of Nonlinear Classifiers

An important consideration that should be addressed when comparing various network topologies concerns the amount of information they can store.[7] Of the nonlinear classifiers mentioned above, the pattern capacity of the Adaline driven by a fixed preprocessor composed of smooth nonlinearities is the simplest to determine. If the inputs to the system are smoothly distributed in position, the outputs of the preprocessing network will be in general position with respect to the Adaline. Thus, the inputs to the Adaline will satisfy the condition required in Cover's Adaline capacity theory. Accordingly, the deterministic and statistical pattern capacities of the system are essentially equal to those of the Adaline.

The capacities of Madaline I structures, which utilize both the majoritiy element and the OR element, were experimentally estimated by Koford in the early 1960s. Although the logic functions that can be realized with these output elements are quite different, both types of elements yield essentially the same statistical storage capacity. The average number of patterns that a Madaline I network can learn to classify was found to be equal to the capacity per Adaline multiplied by the number of Adalines in the structure. The statistical capacity C_s is therefore approximately equal to twice the number of adaptive weights. Although the Madaline and the Adaline have roughly the same capacity per adaptive weight, without preprocessing the Adaline can separate only linearly separable sets, while the Madaline has no such limitation.

[7]We should emphasize that the information referred to here corresponds to the maximum number of binary input/output mappings a network achieve with properly adjusted weights, not the number of bits of information that can be stored directly into the network's weights.

A great deal of theoretical and experimental work has been directed toward determining the capacity of both Adalines and Hopfield networks [87]–[90]. Somewhat less theoretical work has been focused on the pattern capacity of multilayer feedforward networks, though some knowledge exists about the capacity of two-layer networks. Such results are of particular interest because the two-layer network is surprisingly powerful. With a sufficient number of hidden elements, a signum network with two layers can implement any Boolean function.[8] Equally impressive is the power of the two-layer sigmoid network. Given a sufficient number of hidden Adaline elements, such networks can implement any continuous input–output mapping to arbitrary accuracy [92]–[94]. Although two-layer networks are quite powerful, it is likely that some problems can be solved more efficiently by networks with more than two layers. Nonfinite-order predicate mappings (such as the connectedness problem [95]) can often be computed by small networks using signal feedback [96].

In the mid-1960s, Cover studied the capacity of a feedforward signum network with an arbitrary number of layers[9] and a single output element [61], [97]. He determined a lower bound on the minimum number of weights N_w needed to enable such a network to realize any Boolean function defined over an arbitrary set of N_p patterns in general position. Recently, Baum extended Cover's result to multi-output networks, and also used a construction argument to find corresponding upper bounds for the special case of the two-layer signum network [98]. Consider a two-layer fully connected feedforward network of signum Adalines that has N_x input components (excluding the bias inputs) and N_y output components. If this network is required to learn to map any set containing N_p patterns that are in general position to any set of binary desired response vectors (with N_y components), it follows from Baum's results[10] that the minimum requisite number of weights N_w can be bounded by

$$\frac{N_y N_p}{1 + \log_2(N_p)} \le N_w < N_y \left(\frac{N_p}{N_x} + 1\right)(N_x + N_y + 1) + N_y. \quad (8)$$

From Eq. (8), it can be shown that for a two-layer feedforward network with several times as many inputs and hidden elements as outputs (say, at least 5 times as many), the deterministic pattern capacity is bounded below by something slightly smaller than N_w/N_y. It also follows from Eq. (8) that the pattern capacity of any feedforward network with a large ratio of weights to outputs (that is, N_w/N_y at least several thousand) can be bounded above by a number of somewhat larger than $(N_w/N_y) \log_2 (N_w/N_y)$. Thus, the deterministic pattern capacity C_d of a two-layer network can be bounded by

$$\frac{N_w}{N_y} - K_1 \le C_d \le \frac{N_w}{N_y} \log_2 \left(\frac{N_w}{N_y}\right) + K_2 \quad (9)$$

[8]This can be seen by noting that any Boolean function can be written in the sum-of-products form [91], and that such an expression can be realized with a two-layer network by using the first-layer Adalines to implement AND gates, while using the second-layer Adalines to implement OR gates.

[9]Actually, the network can be an arbitrary feedforward structure and need not be layered.

[10]The upper bound used here is Baum's loose bound: minimum number hidden nodes $\le N_y \lceil N_p/N_x \rceil < N_y(N_p/N_x + 1)$.

where K_1 and K_2 are positive numbers which are small terms if the network is large with few outputs relative to the number of inputs and hidden elements.

It is easy to show that Eq. (8) also bounds the number of weights needed to ensure that N_p patterns can be learned with probability 1/2, except in this case the lower bound on N_w becomes: $(N_y N_p - 1)/(1 + \log_2 (N_p))$. It follows that Eq. (9) also serves to bound the statistical capacity C_s of a two-layer signum network.

It is interesting to note that the capacity bounds (9) encompass the deterministic capacity for the single-layer network comprising a bank of N_y Adalines. In this case each Adaline would have N_w/N_y weights, so the system would have a deterministic pattern capacity of N_w/N_y. As N_y becomes large, the statistical capacity also approaches N_w/N_y (for N_x finite). Until further theory on feedforward network capacity is developed, it seems reasonable to use the capacity results from the single-layer network to estimate that of multilayer networks.

Little is known about the number of binary patterns that layered sigmoid networks can learn to classify correctly. The pattern capacity of sigmoid networks cannot be smaller than that of signum networks of equal size, however, because as the weights of a sigmoid network grow toward infinity, it becomes equivalent to a signum network with a weight vector in the same direction. Insight relating to the capabilities and operating principles of sigmoid networks can be winnowed from the literature [99]–[101].

A network's capacity is of little utility unless it is accompanied by useful generalizations to patterns not presented during training. In fact, if generalization is not needed, we can simply store the associations in a look-up table, and will have little need for a neural network. The relationship between generalization and pattern capacity represents a fundamental trade-off in neural network applications: the Adaline's inability to realize all functions is in a sense a strength rather than the fatal flaw envisioned by some critics of neural networks [95], because it helps limit the capacity of the device and thereby improves its ability to generalize.

For good generalization, the training set should contain a number of patterns at least several times larger than the network's capacity (i.e., $N_p \gg N_w/N_y$). This can be understood intuitively by noting that if the number of degrees of freedom in a network (i.e., N_w) is larger than the number of constraints associated with the desired response function (i.e., $N_y N_p$), the training procedure will be unable to completely constrain the weights in the network. Apparently, this allows effects of initial weight conditions to interfere with learned information and degrade the trained network's ability to generalize. A detailed analysis of generalization performance of signum networks as a function of training set size is described in [102].

A Nonlinear Classifier Application

Neural networks have been used successfully in a wide range of applications. To gain some insight about how neural networks are trained and what they can be used to compute, it is instructive to consider Sejnowski and Rosenberg's 1986 NETtalk demonstration [51], [52]. With the exception of work on the traveling salesman problem with Hopfield networks [103], this was the first neural network application since the 1960s to draw widespread attention. NETtalk is a two-layer feedforward sigmoid network with 80 Adalines in the first layer and 26 Adalines in the second layer. The network is trained to convert text into phonetically correct speech, a task well suited to neural implementation. The pronunciation of most words follows general rules based upon spelling and word context, but there are many exceptions and special cases. Rather than programming a system to respond properly to each case, the network can learn the general rules and special cases by example.

One of the more remarkable characteristics of NETtalk is that it learns to pronounce words in stages suggestive of the learning process in children. When the output of NETtalk is connected to a voice synthesizer, the system makes babbling noises during the early stages of the training process. As the network learns, it next conquers the general rules and, like a child, tends to make a lot of errors by using these rules even when not appropriate. As the training continues, however, the network eventually abstracts the exceptions and special cases and is able to produce intelligible speech with few errors.

The operation of NETtalk is surprisingly simple. Its input is a vector of seven characters (including spaces) from a transcript of text, and its output is phonetic information corresponding to the pronunciation of the center (fourth) character in the seven-character input field. The other six characters provide context, which helps to determine the desired phoneme. To read text, the seven-character window is scanned across a document in computer memory and the network generates a sequence of phonetic symbols that can be used to control a speech synthesizer. Each of the seven characters at the network's input is a 29-component binary vector, with each component representing a different alphabetic character or punctuation mark. A one is placed in the component associated with the represented character; all other components are set to zero.[11]

The system's 26 outputs correspond to 23 articulatory features and 3 additional features which encode stress and syllable boundaries. When training the network, the desired response vector has zeros in all components except those which correspond to the phonetic features associated with the center character in the input field. In one experiment, Sejnowski and Rosenberg had the system scan a 1024-word transcript of phonetically transcribed continuous speech. With the presentation of each seven-character window, the system's weights were trained by the backpropagation algorithm in response to the network's output error. After roughly 50 presentations of the entire training set, the network was able to produce accurate speech from data the network had not been exposed to during training.

Backpropagation is not the only technique that might be used to train NETtalk. In other experiments, the slower Boltzmann learning method was used, and, in fact, Madaline Rule III could be used as well. Likewise, if the sigmoid network was replaced by a similar signum network, Madaline Rule II would also work, although more first-layer Adalines would likely be needed for comparable performance.

The remainder of this paper develops and compares various adaptive algorithms for training Adalines and artificial neural networks to solve classification problems such as NETtalk. These same algorithms can be used to train networks for other problems such as those involving nonlinear control [50], system identification [50], [104], signal processing [30], or decision making [55].

III. Adaptation—The Minimal Disturbance Principle

The iterative algorithms described in this paper are all designed in accord with a single underlying principle. These techniques—the two LMS algorithms, Mays's rules, and the Perceptron procedure for training a single Adaline, the MRI rule for training the simple Madaline, as well as MRII, MRIII, and backpropagation techniques for training multilayer Madalines—all rely upon the principle of minimal disturbance: *Adapt to reduce the output error for the current training pattern, with minimal disturbance to responses already learned.* Unless this principle is practiced, it is difficult to simultaneously store the required pattern responses. The minimal disturbance principle is intuitive. It was the motivating idea that led to the discovery of the LMS algorithm and the Madaline rules. In fact, the LMS algorithm had existed for several months as an error-reduction rule before it was discovered that the algorithm uses an instantaneous gradient to follow the path of steepest descent and minimize the mean-square error of the training set. It was then given the name "LMS" (least mean square) algorithm.

IV. Error Correction Rules—Single Threshold Element

As adaptive algorithms evolved, principally two kinds of on-line rules have come to exist. *Error-correction rules* alter the weights of a network to correct error in the output response to the present input pattern. *Gradient rules* alter the weights of a network during each pattern presentation by gradient descent with the objective of reducing mean-square error, averaged over all training patterns. Both types of rules invoke similar training procedures. Because they are based upon different objectives, however, they can have significantly different learning characteristics.

Error-correction rules, of necessity, often tend to be *ad hoc*. They are most often used when training objectives are not easily quantified, or when a problem does not lend itself to tractable analysis. A common application, for instance, concerns training neural networks that contain discontinuous functions. An exception is the α-LMS algorithm, an error-correction rule that has proven to be an extremely useful technique for finding solutions to well-defined and tractable linear problems.

We begin with error-correction rules applied initially to single Adaline elements, and then to networks of Adalines.

A. Linear Rules

Linear error-correction rules alter the weights of the adaptive threshold element with each pattern presentation to make an error correction proportional to the error itself. The one linear rule, α-LMS, is described next.

[11]The input representation often has a considerable impact on the success of a network. In NETtalk, the inputs are sparsely coded in 29 components. One might consider instead choosing a 5-bit binary representation of the 7-bit ASCII code. It should be clear, however, that in this case the sparse representation helps simplify the network's job of interpreting input characters as 29 distinct symbols. Usually the appropriate input encoding is not difficult to decide. When intuition fails, however, one sometimes must experiment with different encodings to find one that works well.

The α-LMS Algorithm: The α-LMS algorithm or Widrow-Hoff delta rule applied to the adaptation of a single Adaline (Fig. 2) embodies the *minimal disturbance principle.* The weight update equation for the original form of the algorithm can be written as

$$W_{k+1} = W_k + \alpha \frac{\epsilon_k X_k}{|X_k|^2}. \tag{10}$$

The time index or adaptation cycle number is k. W_{k+1} is the next value of the weight vector, W_k is the present value of the weight vector, and X_k is the present input pattern vector. The present linear error ϵ_k is defined to be the difference between the desired response d_k and the linear output $s_k = W_k^T X_k$ before adaptation:

$$\epsilon_k \triangleq d_k - W_k^T X_k. \tag{11}$$

Changing the weights yields a corresponding change in the error:

$$\Delta\epsilon_k = \Delta(d_k - W_k^T X_k) = -X_k^T \Delta W_k. \tag{12}$$

In accordance with the α-LMS rule of Eq. (10), the weight change is as follows:

$$\Delta W_k = W_{k+1} - W_k = \alpha \frac{\epsilon_k X_k}{|X_k|^2}. \tag{13}$$

Combining Eqs. (12) and (13), we obtain

$$\Delta\epsilon_k = -\alpha \frac{\epsilon_k X_k^T X_k}{|X_k|^2} = -\alpha\epsilon_k. \tag{14}$$

Therefore, the error is reduced by a factor of α as the weights are changed while holding the input pattern fixed. Presenting a new input pattern starts the next adaptation cycle. The next error is then reduced by a factor of α, and the process continues. The initial weight vector is usually chosen to be zero and is adapted until convergence. In nonstationary environments, the weights are generally adapted continually.

The choice of α controls stability and speed of convergence [30]. For input pattern vectors independent over time, stability is ensured for most practical purposes if

$$0 < \alpha < 2. \tag{15}$$

Making α greater than 1 generally does not make sense, since the error would be overcorrected. Total error correction comes with $\alpha = 1$. A practical range for α is

$$0.1 < \alpha < 1.0. \tag{16}$$

This algorithm is self-normalizing in the sense that the choice of α does not depend on the magnitude of the input signals. The weight update is collinear with the input pattern and of a magnitude inversely proportional to $|X_k|^2$. With binary ±1 inputs, $|X_k|^2$ is equal to the number of weights and does not vary from pattern to pattern. If the binary inputs are the usual 1 and 0, no adaptation occurs for weights with 0 inputs, while with ±1 inputs, all weights are adapted each cycle and convergence tends to be faster. For this reason, the symmetric inputs +1 and −1 are generally preferred.

Figure 12 provides a geometrical picture of how the α-LMS rule works. In accord with Eq. (13), W_{k+1} equals W_k added to ΔW_k, and ΔW_k is parallel with the input pattern vector X_k. From Eq. (12), the change in error is equal to the negative dot product of X_k and ΔW_k. Since the α-LMS algorithm

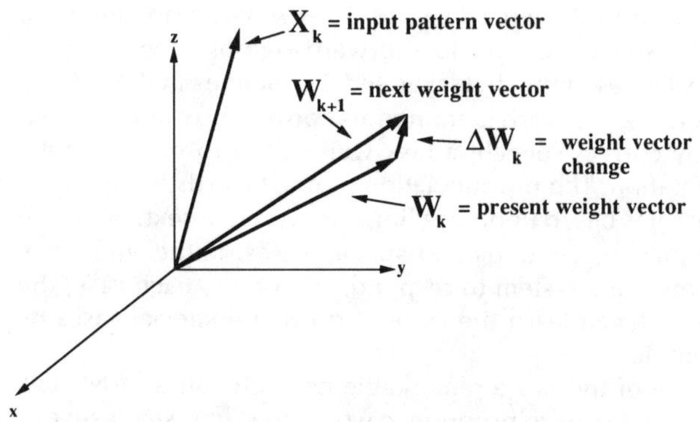

Fig. 12. Weight correction by the LMS rule.

selects ΔW_k to be collinear with X_k, the desired error correction is achieved with a weight change of the smallest possible magnitude. When adapting to respond properly to a new input pattern, the responses to previous training patterns are therefore minimally disturbed, on the average.

The α-LMS algorithm corrects error, and if all input patterns are all of equal length, it minimizes mean-square error [30]. The algorithm is best known for this property.

B. Nonlinear Rules

The α-LMS algorithm is a linear rule that makes error corrections that are proportional to the error. It is known [105] that in some cases this linear rule may fail to separate training patterns that are linearly separable. Where this creates difficulties, nonlinear rules may be used. In the next sections, we describe early nonlinear rules, which were devised by Rosenblatt [106], [5] and Mays [105]. These nonlinear rules also make weight vector changes collinear with the input pattern vector (the direction which causes minimal disturbance), changes that are based on the linear error but are not directly proportional to it.

The Perceptron Learning Rule: The Rosenblatt α-Perceptron [106], [5], diagrammed in Fig. 13, processed input pat-

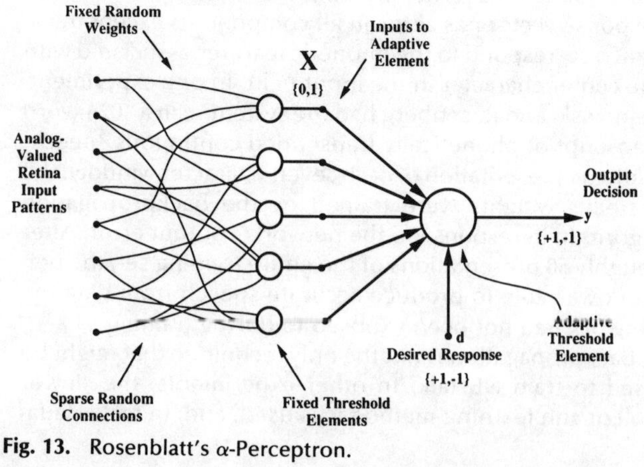

Fig. 13. Rosenblatt's α-Perceptron.

terns with a first layer of sparse randomly connected fixed logic devices. The outputs of the fixed first layer fed a second layer, which consisted of a single adaptive linear threshold element. Other than the convention that its input signals were {1, 0} binary, and that no bias weight was included, this element is equivalent to the Adaline element. The learning rule for the α-Perceptron is very similar to LMS, but its behavior is in fact quite different.

It is interesting to note that Rosenblatt's Perceptron learning rule was first presented in 1960 [106], and Widrow and Hoff's LMS rule was first presented the same year, a few months later [59]. These rules were developed independently in 1959.

The adaptive threshold element of the α-Perceptron is shown in Fig. 14. Adapting with the Perceptron rule makes

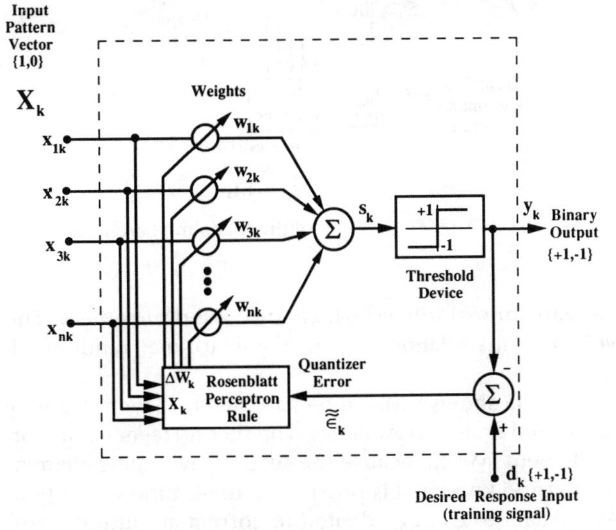

Fig. 14. The adaptive threshold element of the Perceptron.

use of the "quantizer error" $\tilde{\tilde{\epsilon}}_k$, defined to be the difference between the desired response and the output of the quantizer

$$\tilde{\tilde{\epsilon}}_k \triangleq d_k - y_k. \tag{17}$$

The Perceptron rule, sometimes called the Perceptron convergence procedure, does not adapt the weights if the output decision y_k is correct, that is, if $\tilde{\tilde{\epsilon}}_k = 0$. If the output decision disagrees with the binary desired response d_k, however, adaptation is effected by adding the input vector to the weight vector when the error $\tilde{\tilde{\epsilon}}_k$ is positive, or subtracting the input vector from the weight vector when the error $\tilde{\tilde{\epsilon}}_k$ is negative. Thus, half the product of the input vector and the quantizer error $\tilde{\tilde{\epsilon}}_k$ is added to the weight vector. The Perceptron rule is identical to the α-LMS algorithm, except that with the Perceptron rule, half of the quantizer error $\tilde{\tilde{\epsilon}}_k/2$ is used in place of the normalized linear error $\epsilon_k/|\mathbf{X}_k|^2$ of the α-LMS rule. The Perceptron rule is nonlinear, in contrast to the LMS rule, which is linear (compare Figs. 2 and 14). Nonetheless, the Perceptron rule can be written in a form very similar to the α-LMS rule of Eq. (10):

$$\mathbf{W}_{k+1} = \mathbf{W}_k + \alpha \frac{\tilde{\tilde{\epsilon}}_k}{2} \mathbf{X}_k. \tag{18}$$

Rosenblatt normally set α to one. In contrast to α-LMS, the choice of α does not affect the stability of the Perceptron algorithm, and it affects convergence time only if the initial weight vector is nonzero. Also, while α-LMS can be used with either analog or binary desired responses, Rosenblatt's rule can be used only with binary desired responses.

The Perceptron rule stops adapting when the training patterns are correctly separated. There is no restraining force controlling the magnitude of the weights, however. The direction of the weight vector, not its magnitude, determines the decision function. The Perceptron rule has been proven to be capable of separating any linearly separable set of training patterns [5], [107], [46], [105]. If the training patterns are not linearly separable, the Perceptron algorithm goes on forever, and often does not yield a low-error solution, even if one exists. In most cases, if the training set is not separable, the weight vector tends to gravitate toward zero[12] so that even if α is very small, each adaptation can dramatically affect the switching function implemented by the Perceptron.

This behavior is very different from that of the α-LMS algorithm. Continued use of α-LMS does not lead to an unreasonable weight solution if the pattern set is not linearly separable. Nor, however, is this algorithm guaranteed to separate any linearly separable pattern set. α-LMS typically comes close to achieving such separation, but its objective is different—error reduction at the linear output of the adaptive element.

Rosenblatt also introduced variants of the fixed-increment rule that we have discussed thus far. A popular one was the absolute-correction version of the Perceptron rule.[13] This rule is identical to that stated in Eq. (18) except the increment size α is chosen with each presentation to be the smallest integer which corrects the output error in one presentation. If the training set is separable, this variant has all the characteristics of the fixed-increment version with α set to 1, except that it usually reaches a solution in fewer presentations.

Mays's Algorithms: In his Ph.D. thesis [105], Mays described an "increment adaptation" rule[14] and a "modified relaxation adaptation" rule. The fixed-increment version of the Perceptron rule is a special case of the increment adaptation rule.

Increment adaptation in its general form involves the use of a "dead zone" for the linear output s_k, equal to $\pm\gamma$ about zero. All desired responses are ± 1 (refer to Fig. 14). If the linear output s_k falls outside the dead zone ($|s_k| \geq \gamma$), adaptation follows a normalized variant of the fixed-increment Perceptron rule (with $\alpha/|\mathbf{X}_k|^2$ used in place of α). If the linear output falls within the dead zone, whether or not the output response y_k is correct, the weights are adapted by the normalized variant of the Perceptron rule as though the output response y_k had been incorrect. The weight update rule for Mays's increment adaptation algorithm can be written mathematically as

$$\mathbf{W}_{k+1} = \begin{cases} \mathbf{W}_k + \alpha \tilde{\tilde{\epsilon}}_k \dfrac{\mathbf{X}_k}{2|\mathbf{X}_k|^2} & \text{if } |s_k| \geq \gamma \\[2ex] \mathbf{W}_k + \alpha d_k \dfrac{\mathbf{X}_k}{|\mathbf{X}_k|^2} & \text{if } |s_k| < \gamma \end{cases} \tag{19}$$

where $\tilde{\tilde{\epsilon}}_k$ is the quantizer error of Eq. (17).

With the dead zone $\gamma = 0$, Mays's increment adaptation algorithm reduces to a normalized version of the Percep-

[12]This results because the length of the weight vector decreases with each adaptation that does not cause the linear output s_k to change sign and assume a magnitude greater than that before adaptation. Although there are exceptions, for most problems this situation occurs only rarely if the weight vector is much longer than the weight increment vector.

[13]The terms "fixed-increment" and "absolute correction" are due to Nilsson [46]. Rosenblatt referred to methods of these types, respectively, as quantized and nonquantized learning rules.

[14]The increment adaptation rule was proposed by others before Mays, though from a different perspective [107].

tron rule (18). Mays proved that if the training patterns are linearly separable, increment adaptation will always converge and separate the patterns in a finite number of steps. He also showed that use of the dead zone reduces sensitivity to weight errors. If the training set is not linearly separable, Mays's increment adaptation rule typically performs much better than the Perceptron rule because a sufficiently large dead zone tends to cause the weight vector to adapt away from zero when any reasonably good solution exists. In such cases, the weight vector may sometimes appear to meander rather aimlessly, but it will typically remain in a region associated with relatively low average error.

The increment adaptation rule changes the weights with increments that generally are not proportional to the linear error ϵ_k. The other Mays rule, modified relaxation, is closer to α-LMS in its use of the linear error ϵ_k (refer to Fig. 2). The desired response and the quantizer output levels are binary ± 1. If the quantizer output y_k is wrong or if the linear output s_k falls within the dead zone $\pm\gamma$, adaptation follows α-LMS to reduce the linear error. If the quantizer output y_k is correct and the linear output s_k falls outside the dead zone, the weights are not adapted. The weight update rule for this algorithm can be written as

$$W_{k+1} = \begin{cases} W_k & \text{if } \tilde{\epsilon}_k = 0 \text{ and } |s_k| \geq \gamma \\ W_k + \alpha\epsilon_k \dfrac{X_k}{|X_k|^2} & \text{otherwise} \end{cases} \quad (20)$$

where $\tilde{\epsilon}_k$ is the quantizer error of Eq. (17).

If the dead zone γ is set to ∞, this algorithm reduces to the α-LMS algorithm (10). Mays showed that, for dead zone $0 < \gamma < 1$ and learning rate $0 < \alpha \leq 2$, this algorithm will converge and separate any linearly separable input set in a finite number of steps. If the training set is not linearly separable, this algorithm performs much like Mays's increment adaptation rule.

Mays's two algorithms achieve similar pattern separation results. The choice of α does not affect stability, although it does affect convergence time. The two rules differ in their convergence properties but there is no consensus on which is the better algorithm. Algorithms like these can be quite useful, and we believe that there are many more to be invented and analyzed.

The α-LMS algorithm, the Perceptron procedure, and Mays's algorithms can all be used for adapting the single Adaline element or they can be incorporated into procedures for adapting networks of such elements. Multilayer network adaptation procedures that use some of these algorithms are discussed in the following.

V. Error-Correction Rules—Multi-Element Networks

The algorithms discussed next are the Widrow-Hoff Madaline rule from the early 1960s, now called Madaline Rule I (MRI), and Madaline Rule II (MRII), developed by Widrow and Winter in 1987.

A. Madaline Rule I

The MRI rule allows the adaptation of a first layer of hard-limited (signum) Adaline elements whose outputs provide inputs to a second layer, consisting of a single fixed-threshold-logic element which may be, for example, the OR gate, AND gate, or majority-vote-taker discussed previously. The weights of the Adalines are initially set to small random values.

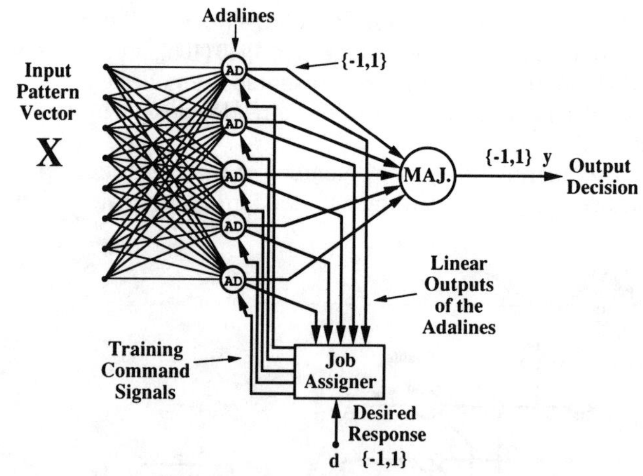

Fig. 15. A five-Adaline example of the Madaline I architecture.

Figure 15 shows a Madaline I architecture with five fully connected first-layer Adalines. The second layer is a majority element (MAJ). Because the second-layer logic element is fixed and known, it is possible to determine which first-layer Adalines can be adapted to correct an output error. The Adalines in the first layer assist each other in solving problems by automatic load-sharing.

One procedure for training the network in Fig. 15 follows. A pattern is presented, and if the output response of the majority element matches the desired response, no adaptation takes place. However, if, for instance, the desired response is $+1$ and three of the five Adalines read -1 for a given input pattern, one of the latter three must be adapted to the $+1$ state. The element that is adapted by MRI is the one whose linear output s_k is closest to zero—the one whose analog response is closest to the desired response. If more of the Adalines were originally in the -1 state, enough of them are adapted to the $+1$ state to make the majority decision equal $+1$. The elements adapted are those whose linear outputs are closest to zero. A similar procedure is followed when the desired response is -1. When adapting a given element, the weight vector can be moved in the LMS direction far enough to reverse the Adaline's output (absolute correction, or "fast" learning), or it can be adapted by the small increment determined by the α-LMS algorithm (statistical, or "slow" learning). The one desired response d_k is used for all Adalines that are adapted. The procedure can also be modified to allow one of Mays's rules to be used. In that event, for the case we have considered (majority output element), adaptations take place if at least half of the Adalines either have outputs differing from the desired response or have analog outputs which are in the dead zone. By setting the dead zone of Mays's increment adaptation rule to zero, the weights can also be adapted by Rosenblatt's Perceptron rule.

Differences in initial conditions and the results of subsequent adaptation cause the various elements to take "responsibility" for certain parts of the training problem. The basic principle of load sharing is summarized thus: *Assign responsibility to the Adaline or Adalines that can most easily assume it.*

In Fig. 15, the "job assigner," a purely mechanized process, assigns responsibility during training by transferring the appropriate adapt commands and desired response signals to the selected Adalines. The job assigner utilizes linear-output information. Load sharing is important, since it results in the various adaptive elements developing individual weight vectors. If all the weights vectors were the same, there would be no point in having more than one element in the first layer.

When training the Madaline, the pattern presentation sequence should be random. Experimenting with this, Ridgway [76] found that cyclic presentation of the patterns could lead to cycles of adaptation. These cycles would cause the weights of the entire Madaline to cycle, preventing convergence.

The adaptive system of Fig. 15 was suggested by common sense, and was found to work well in simulations. Ridgway found that the probability that a given Adaline will be adapted in response to an input pattern is greatest if that element had taken such responsibility during the previous adapt cycle when the pattern was most recently presented. The division of responsibility stabilizes at the same time that the responses of individual elements stabilize to their share of the load. When the training problem is not perfectly separable by this system, the adaptation process tends to minimize error probability, although it is possible for the algorithm to "hang up" on local optima.

The Madaline structure of Fig. 15 has 2 layers—the first layer consists of adaptive logic elements, the second of fixed logic. A variety of fixed-logic devices could be used for the second layer. A variety of MRI adaptation rules were devised by Hoff [75] that can be used with all possible fixed-logic output elements. An easily described training procedure results when the output element is an OR gate. During training, if the desired output for a given input pattern is +1, only the one Adaline whose linear output is closest to zero would be adapted if any adaptation is needed—in other words, if all Adalines give −1 outputs. If the desired output is −1, all elements must give −1 outputs, and any giving +1 outputs must be adapted.

The MRI rule obeys the "minimal disturbance principle" in the following sense. No more Adaline elements are adapted than necessary to correct the output decision and any dead-zone constraint. The elements whose linear outputs are nearest to zero are adapted because they require the smallest weight changes to reverse their output responses. Furthermore, whenever an Adaline is adapted, the weights are changed in the direction of its input vector, providing the requisite error correction with minimal weight change.

B. Madaline Rule II

The MRI rule was recently extended to allow the adaptation of multilayer binary networks by Winter and Widrow with the introduction of Madaline Rule II (MRII) [43], [83], [108]. A typical two-layer MRII network is shown in Fig. 16. The weights in both layers are adaptive.

Training with the MRII rule is similar to training with the MRI algorithm. The weights are initially set to small random values. Training patterns are presented in a random sequence. If the network produces an error during a training presentation, we begin by adapting first-layer Adalines.

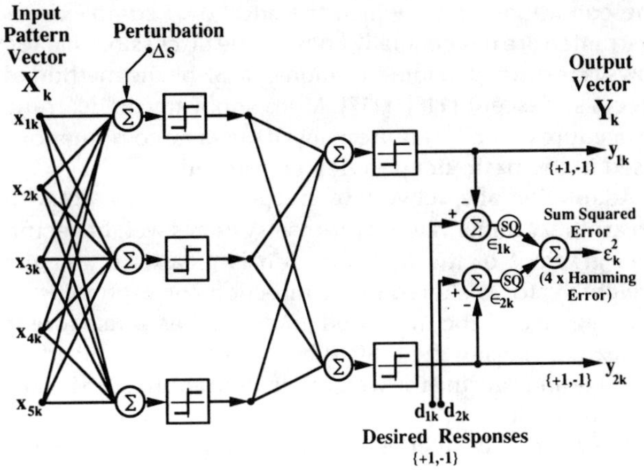

Fig. 16. Typical two-layer Madaline II architecture.

By the minimal disturbance principle, we select the first-layer Adaline with the smallest linear output magnitude and perform a "trial adaptation" by inverting its binary output. This can be done without adaptation by adding a perturbation Δs of suitable amplitude and polarity to the Adaline's sum (refer to Fig. 16). If the output Hamming error is reduced by this bit inversion, that is, if the number of output errors is reduced, the perturbation Δs is removed and the weights of the selected Adaline element are changed by α-LMS in a direction collinear with the corresponding input vector—the direction that reinforces the bit reversal with minimal disturbance to the weights. Conversely, if the trial adaptation does not improve the network response, no weight adaptation is performed.

After finishing with the first element, we perturb and update other Adalines in the first layer which have "sufficiently small" linear-output magnitudes. Further error reductions can be achieved, if desired, by reversing pairs, triples, and so on, up to some predetermined limit. After exhausting possibilities with the first layer, we move on to the next layer and proceed in a like manner. When the final layer is reached, each of the output elements is adapted by α-LMS. At this point, a new training pattern is selected at random and the procedure is repeated. The goal is to reduce Hamming error with each presentation, thereby hopefully minimizing the average Hamming error over the training set. Like MRI, the procedure can be modified so that adaptations follow an absolute correction rule or one of Mays's rules rather than α-LMS. Like MRI, MRII can "hang up" on local optima.

VI. Steepest-Descent Rules—Single Threshold Element

Thus far, we have described a variety of adaptation rules that act to reduce error with the presentation of each training pattern. Often, the objective of adaptation is to reduce error averaged in some way over the training set. The most common error function is mean-square error (MSE), although in some situations other error criteria may be more appropriate [109]–[111]. The most popular approaches to MSE reduction in both single-element and multi-element networks are based upon the method of steepest descent. More sophisticated gradient approaches such as quasi-Newton [30], [112]–[114] and conjugate gradient [114], [115] techniques often have better convergence properties, but the conditions under which the additional complexity is warranted are not generally known. The discussion that follows is restricted to minimization of MSE by the method of steepest descent [116], [117]. More sophisticated learning procedures usually require many of the same computations used in the basic steepest-descent procedure.

Adaptation of a network by steepest-descent starts with an arbitrary initial value $\boldsymbol{W}_0$ for the system's weight vector. The gradient of the MSE function is measured and the weight vector is altered in the direction corresponding to the negative of the measured gradient. This procedure is repeated, causing the MSE to be successively reduced on average and causing the weight vector to approach a locally optimal value.

The method of steepest descent can be described by the relation

$$\boldsymbol{W}_{k+1} = \boldsymbol{W}_k + \mu(-\nabla_k) \tag{21}$$

where μ is a parameter that controls stability and rate of convergence, and ∇_k is the value of the gradient at a point on the MSE surface corresponding to $\boldsymbol{W} = \boldsymbol{W}_k$.

To begin, we derive rules for steepest-descent minimization of the MSE associated with a single Adaline element. These rules are then generalized to apply to full-blown neural networks. Like error-correction rules, the most practical and efficient steepest-descent rules typically work with one pattern at a time. They minimize mean-square error, approximately, averaged over the entire set of training patterns.

A. Linear Rules

Steepest-descent rules for the single threshold element are said to be linear if weight changes are proportional to the linear error, the difference between the desired response d_k and the linear output of the element s_k.

Mean-Square Error Surface of the Linear Combiner: In this section we demonstrate that the MSE surface of the linear combiner of Fig. 1 is a quadratic function of the weights, and thus easily traversed by gradient descent.

Let the input pattern $\boldsymbol{X}_k$ and the associated desired response d_k be drawn from a statistically stationary population. During adaptation, the weight vector varies so that even with stationary inputs, the output s_k and error ϵ_k will generally be nonstationary. Care must be taken in defining the MSE since it is time-varying. The only possibility is an ensemble average, defined below.

At the kth iteration, let the weight vector be $\boldsymbol{W}_k$. Squaring and expanding Eq. (11) yields

$$\epsilon_k^2 = (d_k - \boldsymbol{X}_k^T\boldsymbol{W}_k)^2 \tag{22}$$

$$= d_k^2 - 2d_k\boldsymbol{X}_k^T\boldsymbol{W}_k + \boldsymbol{W}_k^T\boldsymbol{X}_k\boldsymbol{X}_k^T\boldsymbol{W}_k. \tag{23}$$

Now assume an ensemble of identical adaptive linear combiners, each having the same weight vector $\boldsymbol{W}_k$ at the kth iteration. Let each combiner have individual inputs $\boldsymbol{X}_k$ and d_k derived from stationary ergodic ensembles. Each combiner will produce an individual error ϵ_k represented by Eq. (23). Averaging Eq. (23) over the ensemble yields

$$E[\epsilon_k^2]_{W=W_k} = E[d_k^2] - 2E[d_k\boldsymbol{X}_k^T]\boldsymbol{W}_k + \boldsymbol{W}_k^T E[\boldsymbol{X}_k\boldsymbol{X}_k^T]\boldsymbol{W}_k. \tag{24}$$

Defining the vector $\boldsymbol{P}$ as the crosscorrelation between the desired response (a scalar) and the $\boldsymbol{X}$-vector[15] then yields

$$\boldsymbol{P}^T \triangleq E[d_k\boldsymbol{X}_k^T] = E[d_k, d_kx_{1k}, \cdots, d_kx_{nk}]^T. \tag{25}$$

The input correlation matrix $\boldsymbol{R}$ is defined in terms of the ensemble average

$$\boldsymbol{R} \triangleq E[\boldsymbol{X}_k\boldsymbol{X}_k^T]$$

$$= E\begin{bmatrix} 1 & x_{1k} & \cdots & x_{nk} \\ x_{1k} & x_{1k}x_{1k} & \cdots & x_{1k}x_{nk} \\ \vdots & \vdots & & \vdots \\ x_{nk} & x_{nk}x_{1k} & \cdots & x_{nk}x_{nk} \end{bmatrix}. \tag{26}$$

This matrix is real, symmetric, and positive definite, or in rare cases, positive semi-definite. The MSE ξ_k can thus be expressed as

$$\xi_k \triangleq E[\epsilon_k^2]_{W=W_k}$$

$$= E[d_k^2] - 2\boldsymbol{P}^T\boldsymbol{W}_k + \boldsymbol{W}_k^T\boldsymbol{R}\boldsymbol{W}_k. \tag{27}$$

Note that the MSE is a quadratic function of the weights. It is a convex hyperparaboloidal surface, a function that never goes negative. Figure 17 shows a typical MSE surface for a linear combiner with two weights. The position of a point on the grid in this figure represents the value of the Adaline's two weights. The height of the surface at each point represents MSE over the training set when the Adaline's weights are fixed at the values associated with the grid point. Adjusting the weights involves descending along this surface toward the unique minimum point ("the bottom of the bowl") by the method of steepest descent.

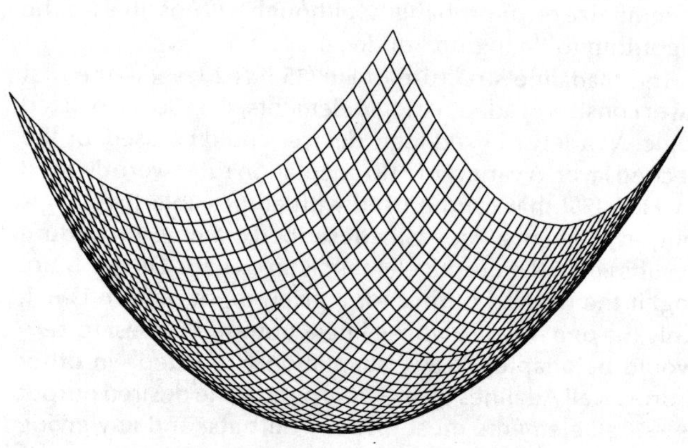

Fig. 17. Typical mean-square-error surface of a linear combiner.

The gradient ∇_k of the MSE function with $\boldsymbol{W} = \boldsymbol{W}_k$ is obtained by differentiating Eq. (27):

$$\nabla_k \triangleq \left\{\begin{matrix} \dfrac{\partial E[\epsilon_k^2]}{\partial w_{0k}} \\ \vdots \\ \dfrac{\partial E[\epsilon_k^2]}{\partial w_{nk}} \end{matrix}\right\}_{W=W_k} = -2\boldsymbol{P} + 2\boldsymbol{R}\boldsymbol{W}_k. \tag{28}$$

[15]We assume here that $\boldsymbol{X}$ includes a bias component $x_{0k} = +1$.

This is a linear function of the weights. The optimal weight vector W^*, generally called the Wiener weight vector, is obtained from Eq. (28) by setting the gradient to zero:

$$W^* = R^{-1}P. \tag{29}$$

This is a matrix form of the Wiener–Hopf equation [118]–[120]. In the next section we examine μ-LMS, an algorithm which enables us to obtain an accurate estimate of W^* without first computing R^{-1} and P.

The μ-LMS Algorithm: The μ-LMS algorithm works by performing approximate steepest descent on the MSE surface in weight space. Because it is a quadratic function of the weights, this surface is convex and has a unique (global) minimum.[16] An instantaneous gradient based upon the square of the instantaneous linear error is

$$\hat{\nabla}_k = \frac{\partial \epsilon_k^2}{\partial W_k} = \begin{Bmatrix} \dfrac{\partial \epsilon_k^2}{\partial w_{0k}} \\ \vdots \\ \dfrac{\epsilon_k^2}{\partial w_{nk}} \end{Bmatrix}. \tag{30}$$

LMS works by using this crude gradient estimate in place of the true gradient ∇_k of Eq. (28). Making this replacement into Eq. (21) yields

$$W_{k+1} = W_k + \mu(-\hat{\nabla}_k) = W_k - \mu \frac{\partial \epsilon_k^2}{\partial W_k}. \tag{31}$$

The instantaneous gradient is used because it is readily available from a single data sample. The true gradient is generally difficult to obtain. Computing it would involve averaging the instantaneous gradients associated with all patterns in the training set. This is usually impractical and almost always inefficient.

Performing the differentiation in Eq. (31) and replacing the linear error by definition (11) gives

$$\begin{aligned} W_{k+1} &= W_k - 2\mu\epsilon_k \frac{\partial \epsilon_k}{\partial W_k} \\ &= W_k - 2\mu\epsilon_k \frac{\partial(d_k - W_k^T X_k)}{\partial W_k}. \end{aligned} \tag{32}$$

Noting that d_k and X_k are independent of W_k yields

$$W_{k+1} = W_k + 2\mu\epsilon_k X_k. \tag{33}$$

This is the μ-LMS algorithm. The learning constant μ determines stability and convergence rate. For input patterns independent over time, convergence of the mean and variance of the weight vector is ensured [30] for most practical purposes if

$$0 < \mu < \frac{1}{\text{trace } [R]} \tag{34}$$

where trace $[R] = \Sigma$(diagonal elements of R) is the average signal power of the X-vectors, that is, $E(X^T X)$. With μ set within this range,[17] the μ-LMS algorithm converges in the mean to W^*, the optimal Wiener solution discussed above. A proof of this can be found in [30].

In the μ-LMS algorithm, and other iterative steepest-descent procedures, use of the instantaneous gradient is perfectly justified if the step size is small. For small μ, W will remain essentially constant over a relatively small number of training presentations K. The total weight change during this period will be proportional to

$$\begin{aligned} -\sum_{l=0}^{K-1} \frac{\partial \epsilon_{k+l}^2}{\partial W_{k+l}} &\simeq -K\left(\frac{1}{K}\sum_{l=0}^{K-1} \frac{\partial \epsilon_{k+l}^2}{\partial W_k}\right) \\ &= -K \frac{\partial}{\partial W_k}\left(\frac{1}{K}\sum_{l=0}^{K-1} \epsilon_{k+l}^2\right) \\ &\simeq -K \frac{\partial \xi}{\partial W_k} \end{aligned} \tag{35}$$

where ξ denotes the MSE function. Thus, on average the weights follow the true gradient. It is shown in [30] that the instantaneous gradient is an unbiased estimate of the true gradient.

Comparison of μ-LMS and α-LMS: We have now presented two forms of the LMS algorithm, α-LMS (10) in Section IV-A and μ-LMS (33) in the last section. They are very similar algorithms, both using the LMS instantaneous gradient. α-LMS is self-normalizing, with the parameter α determining the fraction of the instantaneous error to be corrected with each adaptation. μ-LMS is a constant-coefficient linear algorithm which is considerably easier to analyze than α-LMS. Comparing the two, the α-LMS algorithm is like the μ-LMS algorithm with a continually variable learning constant. Although α-LMS is somewhat more difficult to implement and analyze, it has been demonstrated experimentally to be a better algorithm than μ-LMS when the eigenvalues of the input autocorrelation matrix R are highly disparate, giving faster convergence for a given level of gradient noise[18] propagated into the weights. It will be shown next that μ-LMS has the advantage that it will always converge in the mean to the minimum MSE solution, while α-LMS may converge to a somewhat biased solution.

We begin with α-LMS of Eq. (10):

$$W_{k+1} = W_k + \alpha \frac{\epsilon_k X_k}{|X_k|^2} \tag{36}$$

Replacing the error with its definition (11) and rearranging terms yields

$$W_{k+1} = W_k + \alpha \frac{(d_k - W_k^T X_k) X_k}{|X_k|^2} \tag{37}$$

$$= W_k + \alpha\left(\frac{d_k}{|X_k|} - W_k^T \frac{X_k}{|X_k|}\right)\frac{X_k}{|X_k|}. \tag{38}$$

We define a new training set of pattern vectors and desired responses $\{\tilde{\tilde{X}}_k, \tilde{\tilde{d}}_k\}$ by normalizing elements of the original training set as follows,[19]

$$\begin{aligned} \tilde{\tilde{X}}_k &\triangleq \frac{X_k}{|X_k|} \\ \tilde{\tilde{d}}_k &\triangleq \frac{d_k}{|X_k|}. \end{aligned} \tag{39}$$

[16]If the autocorrelation matrix of the pattern vector set has m zero eigenvalues, the minimum MSE solution will be an m-dimensional subspace in weight space [30].

[17]Horowitz and Senne [121] have proven that (34) is not sufficient in general to guarantee convergence of the weight vector's variance. For input patterns generated by a zero-mean Gaussian process independent over time, instability can occur in the worst case if μ is greater than 1/(3 trace $[R]$).

[18]Gradient noise is the difference between the gradient estimate and the true gradient.

[19]The idea of a normalized training set was suggested by Derrick Nguyen.

Eq. (38) then becomes

$$W_{k+1} = W_k + \alpha(\tilde{\tilde{d}}_k - W_k^T \tilde{\tilde{X}}_k)\tilde{\tilde{X}}_k. \quad (40)$$

This is the μ-LMS rule of Eq. (33) with 2μ replaced by α. The weight adaptations chosen by the α-LMS rule are equivalent to those of the μ-LMS algorithm presented with a different training set—the normalized training set defined by (39). The solution that will be reached by the μ-LMS algorithm is the Wiener solution of this training set

$$\tilde{\tilde{W}}^* = (\tilde{\tilde{R}})^{-1}\tilde{\tilde{P}} \quad (41)$$

where

$$\tilde{\tilde{R}} = E[\tilde{\tilde{X}}_k \tilde{\tilde{X}}_k^T] \quad (42)$$

is the input correlation matrix of the normalized training set and the vector

$$\tilde{\tilde{P}} = E[\tilde{\tilde{d}}_k \tilde{\tilde{X}}_k] \quad (43)$$

is the crosscorrelation between the normalized input and the normalized desired response. Therefore α-LMS converges in the mean to the Wiener solution of the normalized training set. When the input vectors are binary with ± 1 components, all input vectors have the same magnitude and the two algorithms are equivalent. For nonbinary training patterns, however, the Wiener solution of the normalized training set generally is no longer equal to that of the original problem, so α-LMS converges in the mean to a somewhat biased version of the optimal least-squares solution.

The idea of a normalized training set can also be used to relate the stable ranges for the learning constants α and μ in the two algorithms. The stable range for α in the α-LMS algorithm given in Eq. (15) can be computed from the corresponding range for μ given in Eq. (34) by replacing R and μ in Eq. (34) by $\tilde{\tilde{R}}$ and $\alpha/2$, respectively, and then noting that trace$[\tilde{\tilde{R}}]$ is equal to one:

$$0 < \alpha < \frac{2}{\text{trace}[\tilde{\tilde{R}}]}, \text{ or}$$

$$0 < \alpha < 2. \quad (44)$$

B. Nonlinear Rules

The Adaline elements considered thus far use at their outputs either hard-limiting quantizers (signums), or no nonlinearity at all. The input-output mapping of the hard-limiting quantizer is $y_k = \text{sgn}(s_k)$. Other forms of nonlinearity have come into use in the past two decades, primarily of the sigmoid type. These nonlinearities provide saturation for decision making, yet they have differentiable input-output characteristics that facilitate adaptivity. We generalize the definition of the Adaline element to include the possible use of a sigmoid in place of the signum, and then determine suitable adaptation algorithms.

Fig. 18 shows a "sigmoid Adaline" element which incorporates a sigmoidal nonlinearity. The input-output relation of the sigmoid can be denoted by $y_k = \text{sgm}(s_k)$. A typical sigmoid function is the hyperbolic tangent:

$$y_k = \tanh(s_k) = \left(\frac{1 - e^{-2s_k}}{1 + e^{-2s_k}}\right). \quad (45)$$

We shall adapt this Adaline with the objective of minimizing the mean square of the sigmoid error $\tilde{\epsilon}_k$, defined as

$$\tilde{\epsilon}_k \triangleq d_k - y_k = d_k - \text{sgm}(s_k). \quad (46)$$

Backpropagation for the Sigmoid Adaline: Our objective is to minimize $E[(\tilde{\epsilon}_k)^2]$, averaged over the set of training patterns, by proper choice of the weight vector. To accomplish this, we shall derive a backpropagation algorithm for the sigmoid Adaline element. An instantaneous gradient is obtained with each input vector presentation, and the method of steepest descent is used to minimize error as was done with the μ-LMS algorithm of Eq. (33).

Referring to Fig. 18, the instantaneous gradient estimate

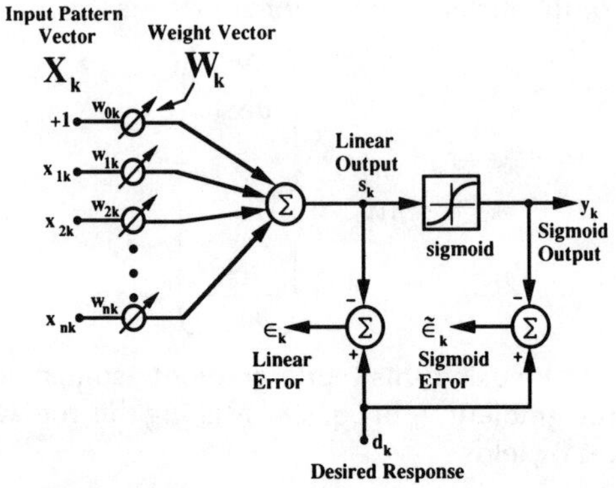

Fig. 18. Adaline with sigmoidal nonlinearity.

obtained during presentation of the kth input vector X_k is given by

$$\hat{\nabla}_k = \frac{\partial(\tilde{\epsilon}_k)^2}{\partial W_k} = 2\tilde{\epsilon}_k \frac{\partial \tilde{\epsilon}_k}{\partial W_k}. \quad (47)$$

Differentiating Eq. (46) yields

$$\frac{\partial \tilde{\epsilon}_k}{\partial W_k} = -\frac{\partial \, \text{sgm}(s_k)}{\partial W_k} = -\text{sgm}'(s_k)\frac{\partial s_k}{\partial W_k}. \quad (48)$$

We may note that

$$s_k = X_k^T W_k. \quad (49)$$

Therefore,

$$\frac{\partial s_k}{\partial W_k} = X_k. \quad (50)$$

Substituting into Eq. (48) gives

$$\frac{\partial \tilde{\epsilon}_k}{\partial W_k} = -\text{sgm}'(s_k) X_k. \quad (51)$$

Inserting this into Eq. (47) yields

$$\hat{\nabla}_k = -2\tilde{\epsilon}_k \, \text{sgm}'(s_k) X_k. \quad (52)$$

Using this gradient estimate with the method of steepest descent provides a means for minimizing the mean-square error even after the summed signal s_k goes through the nonlinear sigmoid. The algorithm is

$$W_{k+1} = W_k + \mu(-\hat{\nabla}_k) \quad (53)$$

$$= W_k + 2\mu\tilde{\epsilon}_k \, \text{sgm}'(s_k) X_k. \quad (54)$$

Algorithm (54) is the backpropagation algorithm for the sigmoid Adaline element. The backpropagation name makes more sense when the algorithm is utilized in a lay-

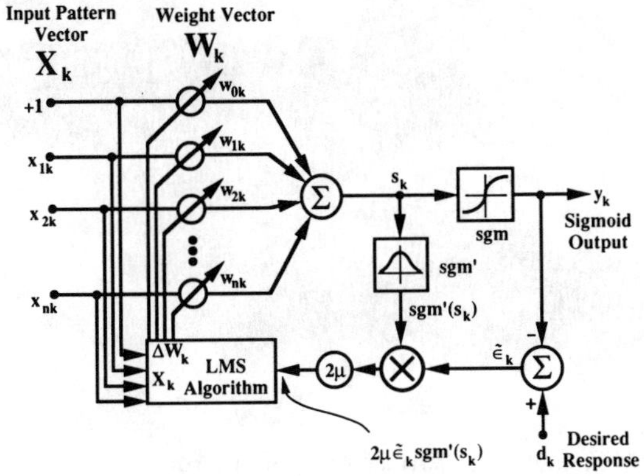

Fig. 19. Implementation of backpropagation for the sigmoid Adaline element.

ered network, which will be studied below. Implementation of algorithm (54) is illustrated in Fig. 19.

If the sigmoid is chosen to be the hyperbolic tangent function (45), then the derivative sgm′ (s_k) is given by

$$\begin{aligned}\text{sgm}'(s_k) &= \frac{\partial(\tanh(s_k))}{\partial s_k}\\ &= 1 - (\tanh(s_k))^2 = 1 - y_k^2. \end{aligned}\tag{55}$$

Accordingly, Eq. (54) becomes

$$W_{k+1} = W_k + 2\mu\tilde{\epsilon}_k(1 - y_k^2)X_k. \tag{56}$$

Madaline Rule III for the Sigmoid Adaline: The implementation of algorithm (54) (Fig. 19) requires accurate realization of the sigmoid function and its derivative function. These functions may not be realized accurately when implemented with analog hardware. Indeed, in an analog network, each Adaline will have its own individual nonlinearities. Difficulties in adaptation have been encountered in practice with the backpropagation algorithm because of imperfections in the nonlinear functions.

To circumvent these problems, a new algorithm has been devised by David Andes for adapting networks of sigmoid Adalines. This is the Madaline Rule III (MRIII) algorithm.

The idea of MRIII for a sigmoid Adaline is illustrated in Fig. 20. The derivative of the sigmoid function is not used here. Instead, a small perturbation signal Δs is added to the sum s_k, and the effect of this perturbation upon output y_k and error $\tilde{\epsilon}_k$ is noted.

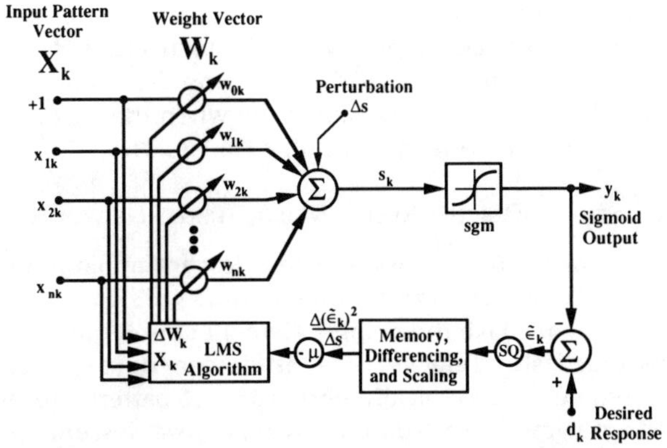

Fig. 20. Implementation of the MRIII algorithm for the sigmoid Adaline element.

An instantaneous estimated gradient can be obtained as follows:

$$\hat{\nabla}_k = \frac{\partial(\tilde{\epsilon}_k)^2}{\partial W_k} = \frac{\partial(\tilde{\epsilon}_k)^2}{\partial s_k}\frac{\partial s_k}{\partial W_k} = \frac{\partial(\tilde{\epsilon}_k)^2}{\partial s_k}X_k. \tag{57}$$

Since Δs is small,

$$\hat{\nabla}_k \simeq \left(\frac{\Delta(\tilde{\epsilon}_k)^2}{\Delta s}\right)X_k. \tag{58}$$

Another way to obtain an approximate instantaneous gradient by measuring the effects of the perturbation Δs can be obtained from Eq. (57).

$$\hat{\nabla}_k = \frac{\partial(\tilde{\epsilon}_k)^2}{\partial s_k}X_k = 2\tilde{\epsilon}_k\frac{\partial\tilde{\epsilon}_k}{\partial s_k}X_k \simeq 2\tilde{\epsilon}_k\left(\frac{\Delta\tilde{\epsilon}_k}{\Delta s}\right)X_k. \tag{59}$$

Accordingly, there are two forms of the MRIII algorithm for the sigmoid Adaline. They are based on the method of steepest descent, using the estimated instantaneous gradients:

$$W_{k+1} = W_k - \mu\left(\frac{\Delta(\tilde{\epsilon}_k)^2}{\Delta s}\right)X_k \tag{60}$$

or,

$$W_{k+1} = W_k - 2\mu\tilde{\epsilon}_k\left(\frac{\Delta\tilde{\epsilon}_k}{\Delta s}\right)X_k. \tag{61}$$

For small perturbations, these two forms are essentially identical. Neither one requires *a priori* knowledge of the sigmoid's derivative, and both are robust with respect to natural variations, biases, and drift in the analog hardware. Which form to use is a matter of implementational convenience. The algorithm of Eq. (60) is illustrated in Fig. 20.

Regarding algorithm (61), some changes can be made to establish a point of interest. Note that, in accord with Eq. (46),

$$\tilde{\epsilon}_k = d_k - y_k. \tag{62}$$

Adding the perturbation Δs causes a change in ϵ_k equal to

$$\Delta\tilde{\epsilon}_k = -\Delta y_k. \tag{63}$$

Now, Eq. (61) may be rewitten as

$$W_{k+1} = W_k + 2\mu\tilde{\epsilon}_k\left(\frac{\Delta y_k}{\Delta s}\right)X_k. \tag{64}$$

Since Δs is small, the ratio of increments may be replaced by a ratio of differentials, finally giving

$$W_{k+1} \simeq W_k + 2\mu\tilde{\epsilon}_k\frac{\partial y_k}{\partial s_k}X_k \tag{65}$$

$$= W_k + 2\mu\tilde{\epsilon}_k\,\text{sgm}'(s_k)X_k. \tag{66}$$

This is identical to the backpropagation algorithm (54) for the sigmoid Adaline. Thus, backpropagation and MRIII are mathematically equivalent if the perturbation Δs is small, but MRIII is robust, even with analog implementations.

MSE Surfaces of the Adaline: Fig. 21 shows a linear combiner connected to both sigmoid and signum devices. Three errors, ϵ, $\tilde{\epsilon}_k$, and $\tilde{\tilde{\epsilon}}$ are designated in this figure. They are:

$$\begin{aligned}\text{linear error} &= \epsilon = d - s\\ \text{sigmoid error} &= \tilde{\epsilon} = d - \text{sgm}(s)\\ \text{signum error} &= \tilde{\tilde{\epsilon}} = d - \text{sgn}(\text{sgm}(s))\\ &= d - \text{sgn}(s). \end{aligned}\tag{67}$$

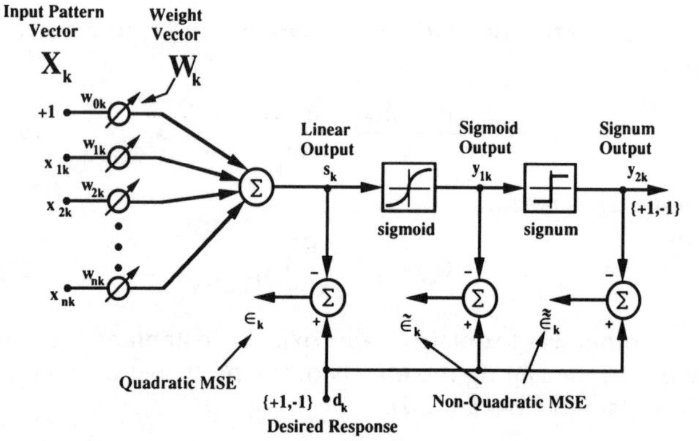

Fig. 21. The linear, sigmoid, and signum errors of the Adaline.

To demonstrate the nature of the square error surfaces associated with these three types of error, a simple experiment with a two-input Adaline was performed. The Adaline was driven by a typical set of input patterns and their associated binary $\{+1, -1\}$ desired responses. The sigmoid function used was the hyperbolic tangent. The weights could have been adapted to minimize the mean-square error of ϵ, $\tilde{\epsilon}$, or $\tilde{\tilde{\epsilon}}$. The MSE surfaces of $E[(\epsilon)^2]$, $E[(\tilde{\epsilon})^2]$, $E[(\tilde{\tilde{\epsilon}})^2]$ plotted as functions of the two weight values, are shown in Figs. 22, 23, and 24, respectively.

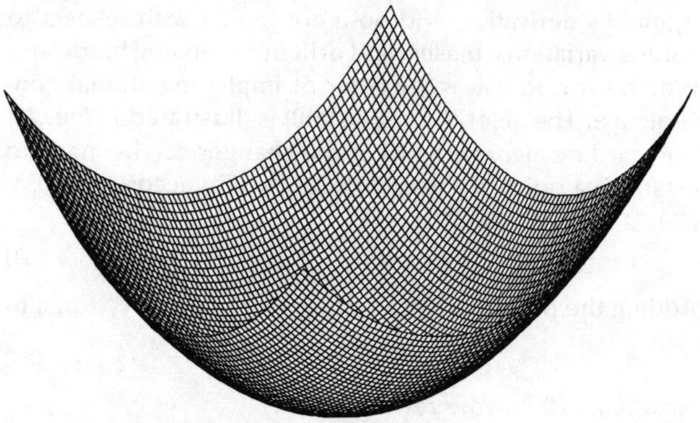

Fig. 22. Example MSE surface of linear error.

Fig. 23. Example MSE surface of sigmoid error.

Although the above experiment is not all encompassing, we can infer from it that minimizing the mean square of the linear error is easy and minimizing the mean square of the sigmoid error is more difficult, but typically much easier

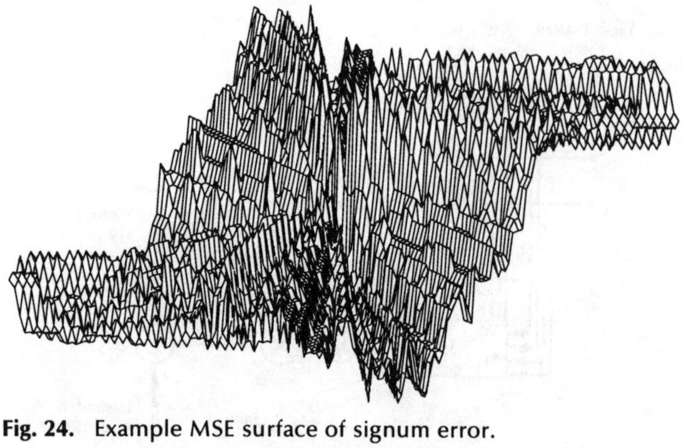

Fig. 24. Example MSE surface of signum error.

than minimizing the mean square of the signum error. Only the linear error is guaranteed to have an MSE surface with a unique global minimum (assuming invertible $\mathbf{R}$-matrix). The other MSE surfaces can have local optima [122], [123].

In nonlinear neural networks, gradient methods generally work better with sigmoid rather than signum nonlinearities. Smooth nonlinearities are required by the MRIII and backpropagation techniques. Moreover, sigmoid networks are capable of forming internal representations that are more complex than simple binary codes and, thus, these networks can often form decision regions that are more sophisticated than those associated with similar signum networks. In fact, if a noiseless infinite-precision sigmoid Adaline could be constructed, it would be able to convey an infinite amount of information at each time step. This is in contrast to the maximum Shannon information capacity of one bit associated with each binary element.

The signum does have some advantages over the sigmoid in that it is easier to implement in hardware and much simpler to compute on a digital computer. Furthermore, the outputs of signums are binary signals which can be efficiently manipulated by digital computers. In a signum network with binary inputs, for instance, the output of each linear combiner can be computed without performing weight multiplications. This involves simply adding together the values of weights with +1 inputs and subtracting from this the values of all weights that are connected to −1 inputs.

Sometimes a signum is used in an Adaline to produce decisive output decisions. The error probability is then proportional to the mean square of the output error $\tilde{\tilde{\epsilon}}$. To minimize this error probability approximately, one can easily minimize $E[(\epsilon)^2]$ instead of directly minimizing $E[(\tilde{\tilde{\epsilon}})^2]$ [58]. However, with only a little more computation one could minimize $E[(\tilde{\epsilon})^2]$ and typically come much closer to the objective of minimizing $E[(\tilde{\tilde{\epsilon}})^2]$. The sigmoid can therefore be used in training the weights even when the signum is used to form the Adaline output, as in Fig. 21.

VII. Steepest-Descent Rules—Multi-Element Networks

We now study rules for steepest-descent minimization of the MSE associated with entire networks of sigmoid Adaline elements. Like their single-element counterparts, the most practical and efficient steepest-descent rules for multi-element networks typically work with one pattern presentation at a time. We will describe two steepest-descent rules for multi-element sigmoid networks, backpropagation and Madaline Rule III.

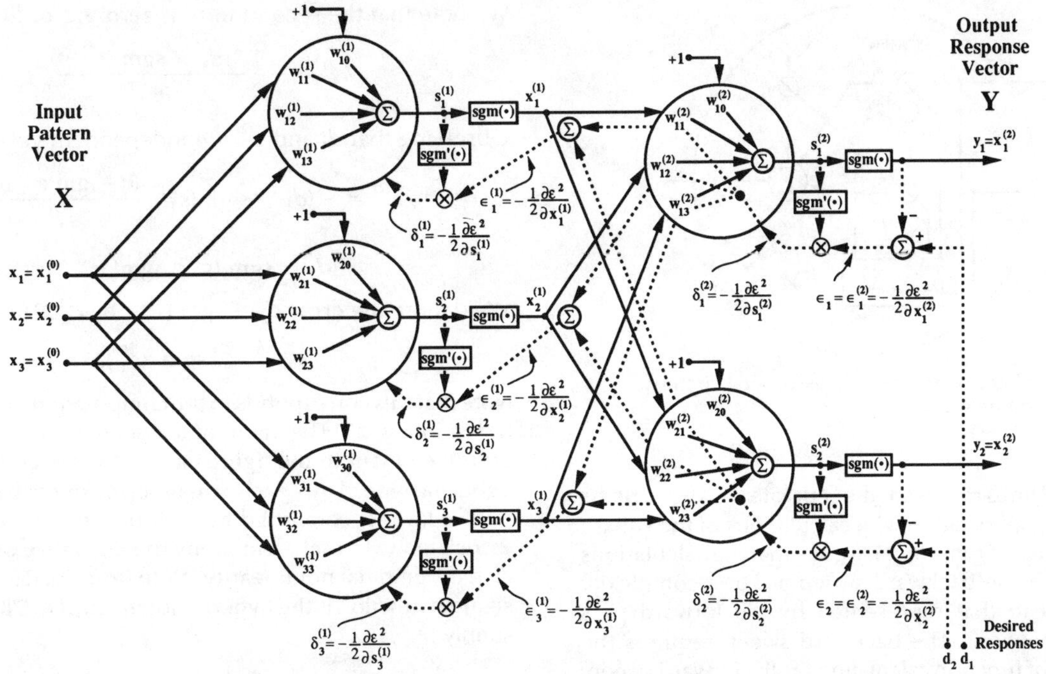

Fig. 25. Example two-layer backpropagation network architecture.

A. Backpropagation for Networks

The publication of the backpropagation technique by Rumelhart *et al.* [42] has unquestionably been the most influential development in the field of neural networks during the past decade. In retrospect, the technique seems simple. Nonetheless, largely because early neural network research dealt almost exclusively with hard-limiting nonlinearities, the idea never occurred to neural network researchers throughout the 1960s.

The basic concepts of backpropagation are easily grasped. Unfortunately, these simple ideas are often obscured by relatively intricate notation, so formal derivations of the backpropagation rule are often tedious. We present an informal derivation of the algorithm and illustrate how it works for the simple network shown in Fig. 25.

The backpropagation technique is a nontrivial generalization of the single sigmoid Adaline case of Section VI-B. When applied to multi-element networks, the backpropagation technique adjusts the weights in the direction opposite the instantaneous error gradient:

$$\hat{\nabla}_k = \frac{\partial \varepsilon_k^2}{\partial \mathbf{W}_k} = \left. \begin{matrix} \dfrac{\partial \varepsilon_k^2}{\partial w_{1k}} \\ \vdots \\ \dfrac{\varepsilon_k^2}{\partial w_{mk}} \end{matrix} \right\} . \tag{68}$$

Now, however, $\mathbf{W}_k$ is a long m-component vector of all weights in the entire network. The instantaneous sum squared error ε_k^2 is the sum of the squares of the errors at each of the N_y outputs of the network. Thus

$$\varepsilon_k^2 = \sum_{i=1}^{N_y} \epsilon_{ik}^2. \tag{69}$$

In the network example shown in Fig. 25, the sum square error is given by

$$\varepsilon^2 = (d_1 - y_1)^2 + (d_2 - y_2)^2 \tag{70}$$

where we now suppress the time index k for convenience.

In its simplest form, backpropagation training begins by presenting an input pattern vector $\mathbf{X}$ to the network, sweeping forward through the system to generate an output response vector $\mathbf{Y}$, and computing the errors at each output. The next step involves sweeping the effects of the errors backward through the network to associate a "square error derivative" δ with each Adaline, computing a gradient from each δ, and finally updating the weights of each Adaline based upon the corresponding gradient. A new pattern is then presented and the process is repeated. The initial weight values are normally set to small random numbers. The algorithm will not work properly with multilayer networks if the initial weights are either zero or poorly chosen nonzero values.[20]

We can get some idea about what is involved in the calculations associated with the backpropagation algorithm by examining the network of Fig. 25. Each of the five large circles represents a linear combiner, as well as some associated signal paths for error backpropagation, and the corresponding adaptive machinery for updating the weights. This detail is shown in Fig. 26. The solid lines in these diagrams represent forward signal paths through the network,

[20]Recently, Nguyen has discovered that a more sophisticated choice of initial weight values in hidden layers can lead to reduced problems with local optima and dramatic increases in network training speed [100]. Experimental evidence suggests that it is advisable to choose the initial weights of each hidden layer in a quasi-random manner, which ensures that at each position in a layer's input space the outputs of all but a few of its Adalines will be saturated, while ensuring that each Adaline in the layer is unsaturated in some region of its input space. When this method is used, the weights in the output layer are set to small random values.

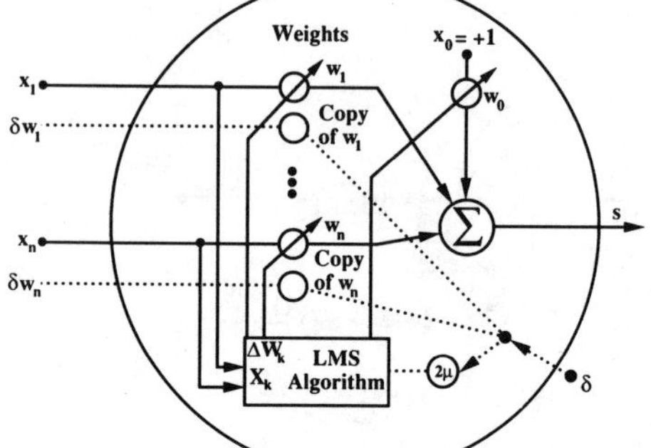

Fig. 26. Detail of linear combiner and associated circuitry in backpropagation network.

and the dotted lines represent the separate backward paths that are used in association with calculations of the square error derivatives δ. From Fig. 25, we see that the calculations associated with the backward sweep are of a complexity roughly equal to that represented by the forward pass through the network. The backward sweep requires the same number of function calculations as the forward sweep, but no weight multiplications in the first layer.

As stated earlier, after a pattern has been presented to the network, and the response error of each output has been calculated, the next step of the backpropagation algorithm involves finding the instantaneous square-error derivative δ associated with each summing junction in the network. The square error derivative associated with the jth Adaline in layer l is defined as[21]

$$\delta_j^{(l)} \triangleq -\frac{1}{2}\frac{\partial \varepsilon^2}{\partial s_j^{(l)}}. \tag{71}$$

Each of these derivatives in essence tells us how sensitive the sum square output error of the network is to changes in the linear output of the associated Adaline element.

The instantaneous square-error derivatives are first computed for each element in the output layer. The calculation is simple. As an example, below we derive the required expression for $\delta_1^{(2)}$, the derivative associated with the top Adaline element in the output layer of Fig. 25. We begin with the definition of $\delta_1^{(2)}$ from Eq. (71)

$$\delta_1^{(2)} \triangleq -\frac{1}{2}\frac{\partial \varepsilon^2}{\partial s_1^{(2)}}. \tag{72}$$

Expanding the squared-error term ε^2 by Eq. (70) yields

$$\delta_1^{(2)} = -\frac{1}{2}\frac{\partial((d_1 - y_1)^2 + (d_2 - y_2)^2)}{\partial s_1^{(2)}} \tag{73}$$

$$= -\frac{1}{2}\frac{\partial(d_1 - \text{sgm}\,(s_1^{(2)}))^2}{\partial s_1^{(2)}}$$

$$-\frac{1}{2}\frac{\partial(d_2 - \text{sgm}\,(s_1^{(2)}))^2}{\partial s_1^{(2)}}. \tag{74}$$

[21]In Fig. 25, all notation follows the convention that superscripts within parentheses indicate the layer number of the associated Adaline or input node, while subscripts identify the associated Adaline(s) within a layer.

We note that the second term is zero. Accordingly,

$$\delta_1^{(2)} = -\frac{1}{2}\frac{\partial(d_1 - \text{sgm}\,(s_1^{(2)}))^2}{\partial s_1^{(2)}}. \tag{75}$$

Observing that d_1 and $s_1^{(2)}$ are independent yields

$$\delta_1^{(2)} = -(d_1 - \text{sgm}\,(s_1^{(2)}))\frac{\partial(-\text{sgm}\,(s_1^{(2)}))}{\partial s_1^{(2)}} \tag{76}$$

$$= (d_1 - \text{sgm}\,(s_1^{(2)}))\,\text{sgm}'\,(s_1^{(2)}). \tag{77}$$

We denote the error $d_1 - \text{sgm}\,(s_1^{(2)})$, by $\epsilon_1^{(2)}$. Therefore,

$$\delta_1^{(2)} = \epsilon_1^{(2)}\,\text{sgm}'\,(s_1^{(2)}). \tag{78}$$

Note that this corresponds to the computation of $\delta_1^{(2)}$ as illustrated in Fig. 25. The value of δ associated with the other output element in the figure can be expressed in an analogous fashion. Thus each square-error derivative δ in the output layer is computed by multiplying the output error associated with that element by the derivative of the associated sigmoidal nonlinearity. Note from Eq. (55) that if the sigmoid function is the hyperbolic tangent, Eq. (78) becomes simply

$$\delta_1^{(2)} = \epsilon_1^{(2)}(1 - (y_1)^2). \tag{79}$$

Developing expressions for the square-error derivatives associated with hidden layers is not much more difficult (refer to Fig. 25). We need an expression for $\delta_1^{(1)}$, the square-error derivative associated with the top element in the first layer of Fig. 25. The derivative $\delta_1^{(1)}$ is defined by

$$\delta_1^{(1)} \triangleq -\frac{1}{2}\frac{\partial \varepsilon^2}{\partial s_1^{(1)}}. \tag{80}$$

Expanding this by the chain rule, noting that ε^2 is determined entirely by the values of $s_1^{(2)}$ and $s_2^{(2)}$, yields

$$\delta_1^{(1)} = -\frac{1}{2}\left(\frac{\partial \varepsilon^2}{\partial s_1^{(2)}}\frac{\partial s_1^{(2)}}{\partial s_1^{(1)}} + \frac{\partial \varepsilon^2}{\partial s_2^{(2)}}\frac{\partial s_2^{(2)}}{\partial s_1^{(1)}}\right). \tag{81}$$

Using the definitions of $\delta_1^{(2)}$ and $\delta_2^{(2)}$, and then substituting expanded versions of Adaline linear outputs $s_1^{(2)}$ and $s_2^{(2)}$ gives

$$\delta_1^{(1)} = \delta_1^{(2)}\frac{\partial s_1^{(2)}}{\partial s_1^{(1)}} + \delta_2^{(2)}\frac{\partial s_2^{(2)}}{\partial s_1^{(1)}} \tag{82}$$

$$= \delta_1^{(2)}\frac{\partial}{\partial s_1^{(1)}}\left(w_{10}^{(2)} + \sum_{i=1}^{3} w_{1i}^{(2)}\,\text{sgm}\,(s_i^{(1)})\right)$$

$$+ \delta_2^{(2)}\frac{\partial}{\partial s_1^{(1)}}\left(w_{20}^{(2)} + \sum_{i=1}^{3} w_{2i}^{(2)}\,\text{sgm}\,(s_i^{(1)})\right). \tag{83}$$

Noting that $\partial[\text{sgm}\,(s_i^{(l)})]/\partial s_j^{(l)} = 0,\ i \neq j$, leaves

$$\delta_1^{(1)} = \delta_1^{(2)}w_{11}^{(2)}\,\text{sgm}'\,(s_1^{(1)}) + \delta_2^{(2)}w_{21}^{(2)}\,\text{sgm}'\,(s_1^{(1)}) \tag{84}$$

$$= [\delta_1^{(2)}w_{11}^{(2)} + \delta_2^{(2)}w_{21}^{(2)}]\,\text{sgm}'\,(s_1^{(1)}). \tag{85}$$

Now, we make the following definition:

$$\epsilon_1^{(1)} \triangleq \delta_1^{(2)}w_{11}^{(2)} + \delta_2^{(2)}w_{21}^{(2)}. \tag{86}$$

Accordingly,

$$\delta_1^{(1)} = \epsilon_1^{(1)}\,\text{sgm}'\,(s_1^{(1)}). \tag{87}$$

Referring to Fig. 25, we can trace through the circuit to verify that $\delta_1^{(1)}$ is computed in accord with Eqs. (86) and (87).

The easiest way to find values of δ for all the Adaline elements in the network is to follow the schematic diagram of Fig. 25.

Thus, the procedure for finding $\delta^{(l)}$, the square-error derivative associated with a given Adaline in hidden layer l, involves respectively multiplying each derivative $\delta^{(l+1)}$ associated with each element in the layer immediately downstream from a given Adaline by the weight that connects it to the given Adaline. These weighted square-error derivatives are then added together, producing an error term $\epsilon^{(l)}$, which, in turn, is multiplied by sgm$'(s^{(l)})$, the derivative of the given Adaline's sigmoid function at its current operating point. If a network has more than two layers, this process of backpropagating the instantaneous square-error derivatives from one layer to the immediately preceding layer is successively repeated until a square-error derivative δ is computed for each Adaline in the network. This is easily shown at each layer by repeating the chain rule argument associated with Eq. (81).

We now have a general method for finding a derivative δ for each Adaline element in the network. The next step is to use these δ's to obtain the corresponding gradients. Consider an Adaline somewhere in the network which, during presentation k, has a weight vector $\boldsymbol{W}_k$, an input vector $\boldsymbol{X}_k$, and a linear output $s_k = \boldsymbol{W}_k^T\boldsymbol{X}_k$.

The instantaneous gradient for this Adaline element is

$$\hat{\nabla}_k = \frac{\partial \varepsilon_k^2}{\partial \boldsymbol{W}_k}. \tag{88}$$

This can be written as

$$\hat{\nabla}_k = \frac{\partial \varepsilon_k^2}{\partial \boldsymbol{W}_k} = \frac{\partial \varepsilon_k^2}{\partial s_k}\frac{\partial s_k}{\partial \boldsymbol{W}_k}. \tag{89}$$

Note that $\boldsymbol{W}_k$ and $\boldsymbol{X}_k$ are independent so

$$\frac{\partial s_k}{\partial \boldsymbol{W}_k} = \frac{\partial \boldsymbol{W}_k^T\boldsymbol{X}_k}{\partial \boldsymbol{W}_k} = \boldsymbol{X}_k. \tag{90}$$

Therefore,

$$\hat{\nabla}_k = \frac{\partial \varepsilon_k^2}{\partial s_k}\boldsymbol{X}_k. \tag{91}$$

For this element,

$$\delta_k = -\frac{1}{2}\frac{\partial \varepsilon_k^2}{\partial s_k}. \tag{92}$$

Accordingly,

$$\hat{\nabla}_k = -2\delta_k\boldsymbol{X}_k. \tag{93}$$

Updating the weights of the Adaline element using the method of steepest descent with the instantaneous gradient is a process represented by

$$\boldsymbol{W}_{k+1} = \boldsymbol{W}_k + \mu(-\hat{\nabla}_k) = \boldsymbol{W}_k + 2\mu\delta_k\boldsymbol{X}_k. \tag{94}$$

Thus, after backpropagating all square-error derivatives, we complete a backpropagation iteration by adding to each weight vector the corresponding input vector scaled by the associated square-error derivative. Eq. (94) and the means for finding δ_k comprise the general weight update rule of the backpropagation algorithm.

There is a great similarity between Eq. (94) and the μ-LMS algorithm (33), but one should view this similarity with caution. The quantity δ_k, defined as a squared-error derivative, might appear to play the same role in backpropagation as that played by the error in the μ-LMS algorithm. However, δ_k is not an error. Adaptation of the given Adaline is effected to reduce the squared output error ε_k^2, not δ_k of the given Adaline or of any other Adaline in the network. The objective is not to reduce the δ_k's of the network, but to reduce ε_k^2 at the network output.

It is interesting to examine the weight updates that backpropagation imposes on the Adaline elements in the output layer. Substituting Eq. (77) into Eq. (94) reveals the Adaline which provides output y_1 in Fig. 25 is updated by the rule

$$\boldsymbol{W}_{k+1} = \boldsymbol{W}_k + 2\mu\epsilon_1^{(2)}\,\text{sgm}'(s_1^{(2)})\boldsymbol{X}_k. \tag{95}$$

This rule turns out to be identical to the single Adaline version (54) of the backpropagation rule. This is not surprising since the output Adaline is provided with both input signals and desired responses, so its training circumstance is the same as that experienced by an Adaline trained in isolation.

There are many variants of the backpropagation algorithm. Sometimes, the size of μ is reduced during training to diminish the effects of gradient noise in the weights. Another extension is the momentum technique [42] which involves including in the weight change vector $\Delta\boldsymbol{W}_k$ of each Adaline a term proportional to the corresponding weight change from the previous iteration. That is, Eq. (94) is replaced by a pair of equations:

$$\Delta\boldsymbol{W}_k = 2\mu(1-\eta)\delta_k\boldsymbol{X}_k + \eta\Delta\boldsymbol{W}_{k-1} \tag{96}$$

$$\boldsymbol{W}_{k+1} = \boldsymbol{W}_k + \Delta\boldsymbol{W}_k. \tag{97}$$

where the momentum constant $0 \le \eta < 1$ is in practice usually set to something around 0.8 or 0.9.

The momentum technique low-pass filters the weight updates and thereby tends to resist erratic weight changes caused either by gradient noise or high spatial frequencies in the MSE surface. The factor $(1-\eta)$ in Eq. (96) is included to give the filter a DC gain of unity so that the learning rate μ does not need to be stepped down as the momentum constant η is increased. A momentum term can also be added to the update equations of other algorithms discussed in this paper. A detailed analysis of stability issues associated with momentum updating for the μ-LMS algorithm, for instance, has been described by Shynk and Roy [124].

In our experience, the momentum technique used alone is usually of little value. We have found, however, that it is often useful to apply the technique in situations that require relatively "clean"[22] gradient estimates. One case is a normalized weight update equation which makes the network's weight vector move the same Euclidean distance with each iteration. This can be accomplished by replacing Eq. (96) and (97) with

$$\Delta_k = \delta_k\boldsymbol{X}_k + \eta\Delta_{k+1} \tag{98}$$

$$\boldsymbol{W}_{k+1} = \boldsymbol{W}_k + \frac{\mu\Delta_k}{\sqrt{\sum_{\text{all Adalines}} |\Delta_k|^2}}. \tag{99}$$

where again $0 < \eta < 1$. The weight updates determined by Eqs. (98) and (99) can help a network find a solution when a relatively flat local region in the MSE surface is encoun-

[22] "Clean" gradient estimates are those with little gradient noise.

tered. The weights move by the same amount whether the surface is flat or inclined. It is reminiscent of α-LMS because the gradient term in the weight update equation is normalized by a time-varying factor. The weight update rule could be further modified by including terms from both techniques associated with Eqs. (96) through (99). Other methods for speeding up backpropagation training include Fahlman's popular quickprop method [125], as well as the delta-bar-delta approach reported in an excellent paper by Jacobs [126].[23]

One of the most promising new areas of neural network research involves backpropagation variants for training various recurrent (signal feedback) networks. Recently, backpropagation rules have been derived for training recurrent networks to learn static associations [127], [128]. More interesting is the on-line technique of Williams and Zipser [129] which allows a wide class of recurrent networks to learn dynamic associations and trajectories. A more general and computationally viable variant of this technique has been advanced by Narendra and Parthasarathy [104]. These on-line methods are generalizations of a well-known steepest-descent algorithm for training linear IIR filters [130], [30].

An equivalent technique that is usually far less computationally intensive but best suited for off-line computation [37], [42], [131], called "backpropagation through time," has been used by Nguyen and Widrow [50] to enable a neural network to learn without a teacher how to back up a computer-simulated trailer truck to a loading dock (Fig. 27). This is a highly nonlinear steering task and it is not yet known how to design a controller to perform it. Nevertheless, with just 6 inputs providing information about the current position of the truck, a two-layer neural network with only 26 Adalines was able to learn of its own accord to solve this problem. Once trained, the network could successfully back up the truck from any initial position and orientation in front of the loading dock.

B. Madaline Rule III for Networks

It is difficult to build neural networks with analog hardware that can be trained effectively by the popular backpropagation technique. Attempts to overcome this difficulty have led to the development of the MRIII algorithm. A commercial analog neurocomputing chip based primarily on this algorithm has already been devised [132]. The method described in this section is a generalization of the single Adaline MRIII technique (60). The multi-element generalization of the other single element MRIII rule (61) is described in [133].

The MRIII algorithm can be readily described by referring to Fig. 28. Although this figure shows a simple two-layer feedforward architecture, the procedure to be developed will work for neural networks with any number of Adaline

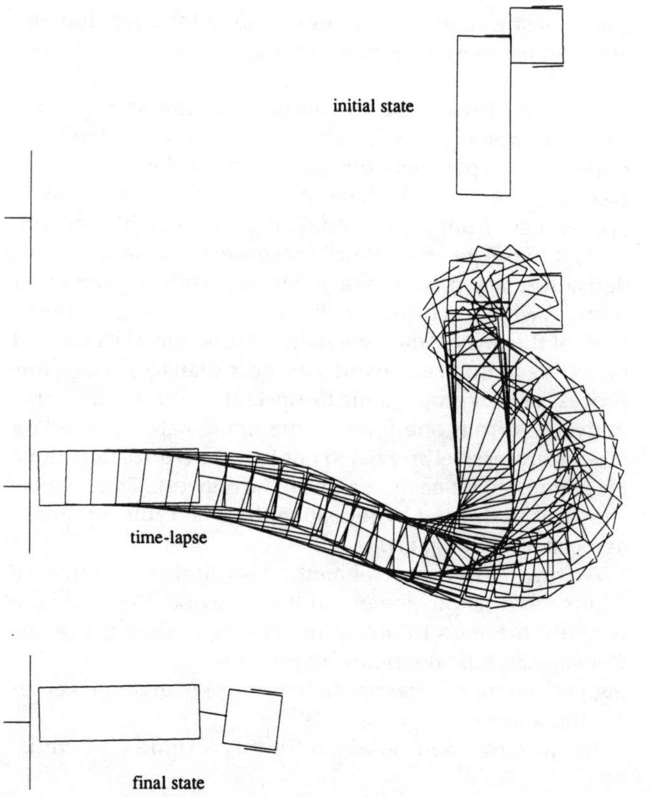

Fig. 27. Example truck backup sequence.

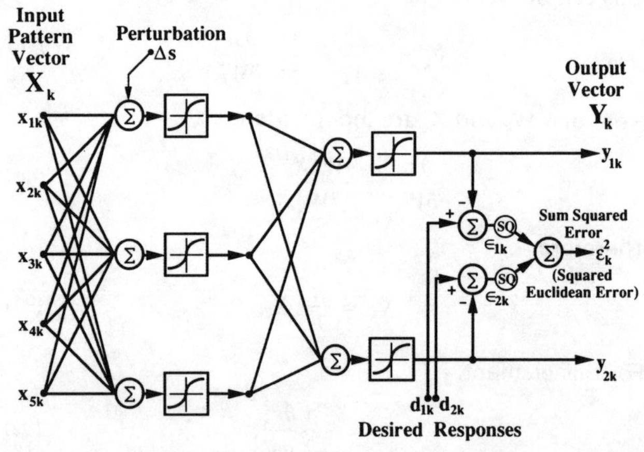

Fig. 28. Example two-layer Madaline III architecture.

elements in any feedforward structure. In [133], we discuss variants of the basic MRIII approach that allow steepest-descent training to be applied to more general network topologies, even those with signal feedback.

Assume that an input pattern X and its associated desired output responses d_1 and d_2 are presented to the network of Fig. 28. At this point, we measure the sum squared output response error $\varepsilon^2 = (d_1 - y_1)^2 + (d_2 - y_2)^2 = \epsilon_1^2 + \epsilon_2^2$. We then add a small quantity Δs to a selected Adaline in the network, providing a perturbation to the element's linear sum. This perturbation propagates through the network, and causes a change in the sum of the squares of the errors, $\Delta(\varepsilon^2) = \Delta(\epsilon_1^2 + \epsilon_2^2)$. An easily measured ratio is

$$\frac{\Delta(\varepsilon^2)}{\Delta s} = \frac{\Delta(\epsilon_1^2 + \epsilon_2^2)}{\Delta s} \simeq \frac{\partial(\varepsilon^2)}{\partial s}. \qquad (100)$$

[23] Jacob's paper, like many other papers in the literature, assumes for analysis that the true gradients rather than instantaneous gradients are used to update the weights, that is, that weights are changed periodically, only after all training patterns are presented. This eliminates gradient noise but can slow down training enormously if the training set is large. The delta-bar-delta procedure in Jacob's paper involves monitoring changes of the true gradients in response to weight changes. It should be possible to avoid the expense of computing the true gradients explicitly in this case by instead monitoring changes in the outputs of, say, two momentum filters with different time constants.

Below we use this to obtain the instantaneous gradient of ε_k^2 with respect to the weight vector of the selected Adaline. For the kth presentation, the instantaneous gradient is

$$\hat{\nabla}_k = \frac{\partial(\varepsilon_k^2)}{\partial \boldsymbol{W}_k} = \frac{\partial(\varepsilon_k^2)}{\partial s_k}\frac{\partial s_k}{\partial \boldsymbol{W}_k} = \frac{\partial(\varepsilon_k^2)}{\partial s_k}\boldsymbol{X}_k. \tag{101}$$

Replacing the derivative with a ratio of differences yields

$$\hat{\nabla}_k \simeq \frac{\Delta(\varepsilon_k^2)}{\Delta s}\boldsymbol{X}_k. \tag{102}$$

The idea of obtaining a derivative by perturbing the linear output of the selected Adaline element is the same as that expressed for the single element in Section VI-B, except that here the error is obtained from the output of a multi-element network rather than from the output of a single element.

The gradient (102) can be used to optimize the weight vector in accord with the method of steepest descent:

$$\boldsymbol{W}_{k+1} = \boldsymbol{W}_k - \mu\frac{\Delta(\varepsilon_k^2)}{\Delta s}\boldsymbol{X}_k. \tag{103}$$

Maintaining the same input pattern, one could either perturb all the elements in the network in sequence, adapting after each gradient calculation, or else the derivatives could be computed and stored to allow all Adalines to be adapted at once. These two MRIII approaches both involve the same weight update equation (103), and if μ is small, both lead to equivalent solutions. With large μ, experience indicates that adapting one element at a time results in convergence after fewer iterations, especially in large networks. Storing the gradients, however, has the advantage that after the initial unperturbed error is measured during a given training presentation, each gradient estimate requires only the perturbed error measurement. If adaptations take place after each error measurement, both perturbed and unperturbed errors must be measured for each gradient calculation. This is because each weight update changes the associated unperturbed error.

C. Comparison of MRIII with MRII

MRIII was derived from MRII by replacing the signum nonlinearities with sigmoids. The similarity of these algorithms becomes evident when comparing Fig. 28, representing MRIII, with Fig. 16, representing MRII.

The MRII network is highly discontinuous and nonlinear. Using an instantaneous gradient to adjust the weights is not possible. In fact, from the MSE surface for the signum Adaline presented in Section VI-B, it is clear that even gradient descent techniques that use the true gradient could run into severe problems with local minima. The idea of adding a perturbation to the linear sum of a selected Adaline element is workable, however. If the Hamming error has been reduced by the perturbation, the Adaline is adapted to reverse its output decision. This weight change is in the LMS direction, along its $\boldsymbol{X}$-vector. If adapting the Adaline would not reduce network output error, it is not adapted. This is in accord with the minimal disturbance principle. The Adalines selected for possible adaptation are those whose analog sums are closest to zero, that is, the Adalines that can be adapted to give opposite responses with the smallest weight changes. It is useful to note that with binary ± 1 desired responses, the Hamming error is equal to 1/4 the sum square error. Minimizing the output Hamming error is therefore equivalent to minimizing the output sum square error.

The MRIII algorithm works in a similar manner. All the Adalines in the MRIII network are adapted, but those whose analog sums are closest to zero will usually be adapted most strongly, because the sigmoid has its maximum slope at zero, contributing to high gradient values. As with MRII, the objective is to change the weights for the given input presentation to reduce the sum square error at the network output. In accord with the minimal disturbance principle, the weight vectors of the Adaline elements are adapted in the LMS direction, along their $\boldsymbol{X}$-vectors, and are adapted in proportion to their capabilities for reducing the sum square error (the square of the Euclidean error) at the output.

D. Comparison of MRIII with Backpropagation

In Section VI-B, we argued that for the sigmoid Adaline element, the MRIII algorithm (61) is essentially equivalent to the backpropagation algorithm (54). The same argument can be extended to the network of Adaline elements, demonstrating that if Δs is small and adaptation is applied to all elements in the network at once, then MRIII is essentially equivalent to backpropagation. That is, to the extent that the sample derivative $\Delta\varepsilon_k^2/\Delta s$ from Eq. (103) is equal to the analytical derivtive $\partial\varepsilon_k^2/\partial s_k$ from Eq. (91), the two rules follow identical instantaneous gradients, and thus perform identical weight updates.

The backpropagation algorithm requires fewer operations than MRIII to calculate gradients, since it is able to take advantage of *a priori* knowledge of the sigmoid nonlinearities and their derivative functions. Conversely, the MRIII algorithm uses no prior knowledge about the characteristics of the sigmoid functions. Rather, it acquires instantaneous gradients from perturbation measurements. Using MRIII, tolerances on the sigmoid implementations can be greatly relaxed compared to acceptable tolerances for successful backpropagation.

Steepest-descent training of multilayer networks implemented by computer simulation or by precise parallel digital hardware is usually best carried out by backpropagation. During each training presentation, the backpropagation method requires only one forward computation through the network followed by one backward computation in order to adapt all the weights of an entire network. To accomplish the same effect with the form of MRIII that updates all weights at once, one measures the unperturbed error followed by a number of perturbed error measurements equal to the number of elements in the network. This could require a lot of computation.

If a network is to be implemented in analog hardware, however, experience has shown that MRIII offers strong advantages over backpropagation. Comparison of Fig. 25 with Fig. 28 demonstrates the relative simplicity of MRIII. All the apparatus for backward propagation of error-related signals is eliminated, and the weights do not need to carry signals in both directions (see Fig. 26). MRIII is a much simpler algorithm to build and to understand, and in principle it produces the same instantaneous gradient as the backpropagation algorithm. The momentum technique and most other common variants of the backpropagation algorithm can be applied to MRIII training.

E. MSE Surfaces of Neural Networks

In Section VI-B, "typical" mean-square-error surfaces of sigmoid and signum Adalines were shown, indicating that sigmoid Adalines are much more conducive to gradient approaches than signum Adalines. The same phenomena result when Adalines are incorporated into multi-element networks. The MSE surfaces of MRII networks are reasonably chaotic and will not be explored here. In this section we examine only MSE surfaces from a typical backpropagation training problem with a sigmoidal neural network.

In a network with more than two weights, the MSE surface is high-dimensional and difficult to visualize. It is possible, however, to look at slices of this surface by plotting the MSE surface created by varying two of the weights while holding all others constant. The surfaces plotted in Figs. 29 and 30 show two such slices of the MSE surface from a typical learning problem involving, respectively, an untrained sigmoidal network and a trained one. The first surface resulted from varying two first-layer weights of an untrained network. The second surface resulted from varying the same two weights after the network was fully trained. The two surfaces are similar, but the second one has a deeper minimum which was carved out by the backpropagation learning process. Figs. 31 and 32 resulted from varying a different set of two weights in the same network. Fig. 31 is the result from varying a first-layer weight and third-layer weight in the untrained network, whereas Fig. 32 is the surface that resulted from varying the same two weights after the network was trained.

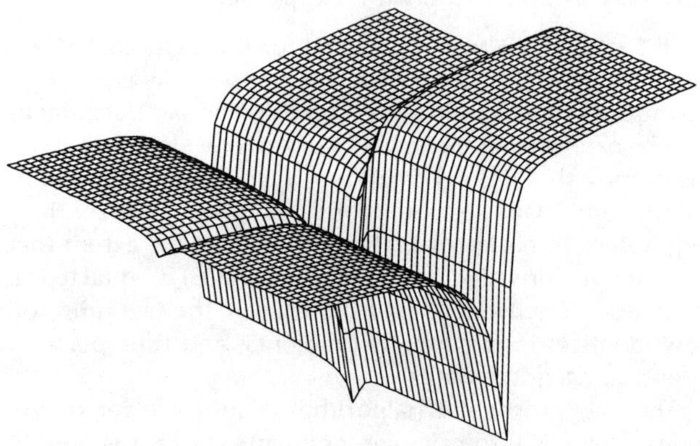

Fig. 29. Example MSE surface of untrained sigmoidal network as a function of two first-layer weights.

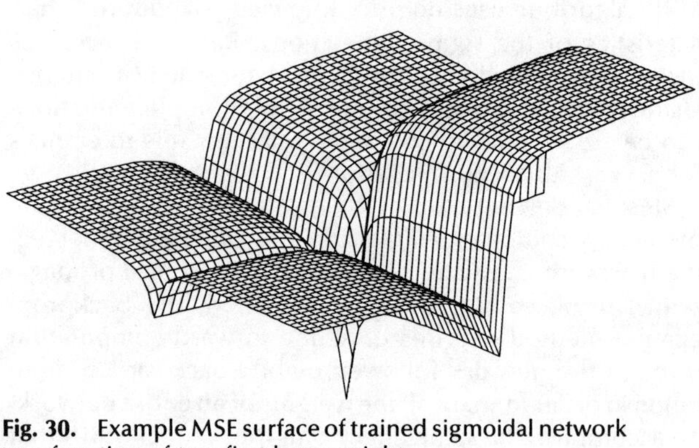

Fig. 30. Example MSE surface of trained sigmoidal network as a function of two first-layer weights.

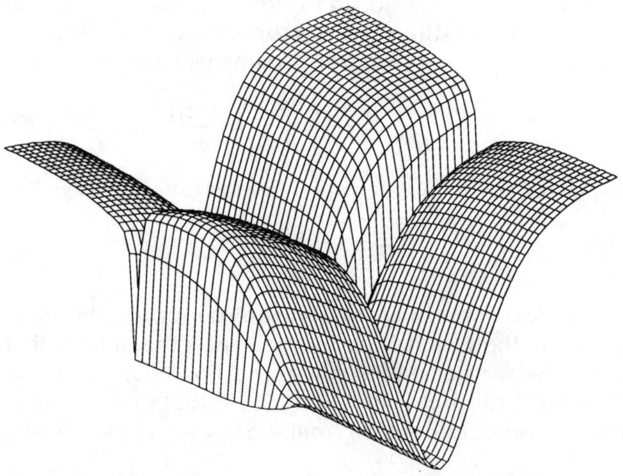

Fig. 31. Example MSE surface of untrained sigmoidal network as a function of a first-layer weight and a third-layer weight.

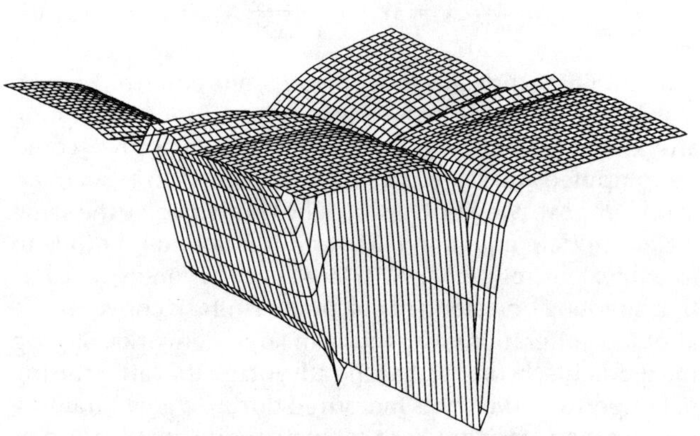

Fig. 32. Example MSE surface of trained sigmoidal network as a function of a first-layer weight and a third-layer weight.

By studying many plots, it becomes clear that backpropagation and MRIII will be subject to convergence on local optima. The same is true for MRII. The most common remedy for this is the sporadic addition of noise to the weights or gradients. Some of the "simulated annealing" methods [47] do this. Another method involves retraining the network several times using differnt random initial weight values until a satisfactory solution is found.

Solutions found by people in everyday life are usually not optimal, but many of them are useful. If a local optimum yields satisfactory performance, often there is simply no need to search for a better solution.

VIII. Summary

This year is the 30th anniversary of the publication of the Perceptron rule by Rosenblatt and the LMS algorithm by Widrow and Hoff. It has also been 16 years since Werbos first published the backpropagation algorithm. These learning rules and several others have been studied and compared. Although they differ significantly from each other, they all belong to the same "family."

A distinction was drawn between error-correction rules and steepest-descent rules. The former includes the Perceptron rule, Mays' rules, the α-LMS algorithm, the original Madaline I rule of 1962, and the Madaline II rule. The latter includes the μ-LMS algorithm, the Madaline III rule, and the

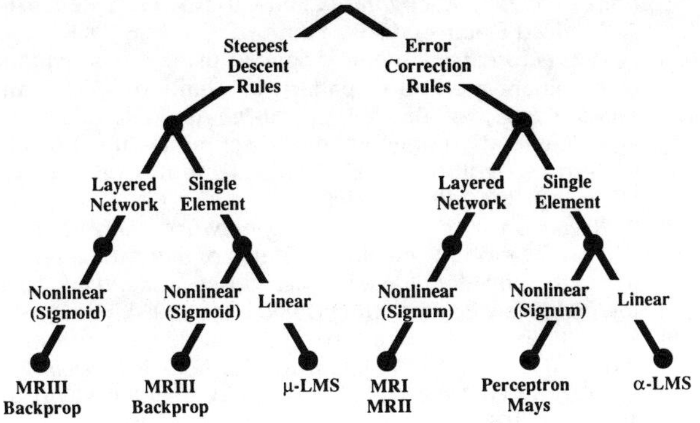

Fig. 33. Learning rules.

backpropagation algorithm. Fig. 33 categorizes the learning rules that have been studied.

Although these algorithms have been presented as established learning rules, one should not gain the impression that they are perfect and frozen for all time. Variations are possible for every one of them. They should be regarded as substrates upon which to build new and better rules. There is a tremendous amount of invention waiting "in the wings." We look forward to the next 30 years.

References

[1] K. Steinbuch and V. A. W. Piske, "Learning matrices and their applications," *IEEE Trans. Electron. Comput.*, vol. EC-12, pp. 846–862, Dec. 1963.

[2] B. Widrow, "Generalization and information storage in networks of adaline 'neurons,' in *Self-Organizing Systems 1962*, M. Yovitz, G. Jacobi, and G. Goldstein, Eds. Washington, DC: Spartan Books, 1962, pp. 435–461.

[3] L. Stark, M. Okajima, and G. H. Whipple, "Computer pattern recognition techniques: Electrocardiographic diagnosis," *Commun. Ass. Comput. Mach.*, vol. 5, pp. 527–532, Oct. 1962.

[4] F. Rosenblatt, "Two theorems of statistical separability in the perceptron," in *Mechanization of Thought Processes: Proceedings of a Symposium held at the National Physical Laboratory, Nov. 1958*, vol. 1 pp. 421–456. London: HM Stationery Office, 1959.

[5] F. Rosenblatt, *Principles of Neurodynamics: Perceptrons and the Theory of Brain Mechanisms*. Washington, DC: Spartan Books, 1962.

[6] C. von der Malsburg, "Self-organizing of orientation sensitive cells in the striate cortex," *Kybernetik*, vol. 14, pp. 85–100, 1973.

[7] S. Grossberg, "Adaptive pattern classification and universal recoding, I: Parallel development and coding of neural feature detectors," *Biolog. Cybernetics*, vol. 23, pp. 121–134, 1976.

[8] K. Fukushima, "Cognitron: A self-orgainizing multilayered neural network," *Biolog. Cybernetics*, vol. 20, pp. 121–136, 1975.

[9] —, "Neocognitron: A self-organizing neural network model for a mechanism of pattern recognition unaffected by shift in position," *Biolog. Cybernetics*, vol. 36, pp. 193–202, 1980.

[10] B. Widrow, "Bootstrap learning in threshold logic systems," presented at the American Automatic Control Council (Theory Committee), IFAC Meeting, London, England, June 1966.

[11] B. Widrow, N. K. Gupta, and S. Maitra, "Punish/reward: Learning with a critic in adaptive threshold systems," *IEEE Trans. Syst., Man, Cybernetics*, vol. SMC-3, pp. 455–465, Sept. 1973.

[12] A. G. Barto, R. S. Sutton, and C. W. Anderson, "Neuronlike adaptive elements that can solve difficult learning control problems," *IEEE Trans. Syst., Man, Cybernetics*, vol. SMC-13, pp. 834–846, 1983.

[13] J. S. Albus, "A new approach to manipulator control: the cerebellar model articulation controller (CMAC)," *J. Dyn. Sys., Meas., Contr.*, vol. 97, pp. 220–227, 1975.

[14] W. T. Miller, III, "Sensor-based control of robotic manipulators using a general learning algorithm." *IEEE J. Robotics Automat.*, vol. RA-3, pp. 157–165, Apr. 1987.

[15] S. Grossberg, "Adaptive pattern classification and universal recoding, II: Feedback, expectation, olfaction, and illusions," Biolog. Cybernetics, vol. 23, pp. 187–202, 1976.

[16] G. A. Carpenter and S. Grossberg, "A massively parallel architecture for a self-organizing neural pattern recognition machine," *Computer Vision, Graphics, and Image Processing*, vol. 37, pp. 54–115, 1983.

[17] —, "Art 2: Self-organization of stable category recognition codes for analog output patterns," *Applied Optics*, vol. 26, pp. 4919–4930, Dec. 1, 1987.

[18] —, "Art 3 hierarchical search: Chemical transmitters in self-organizing pattern recognition architectures," in *Proc. Int. Joint Conf. on Neural Networks*, vol. 2, pp. 30–33, Wash., DC, Jan. 1990.

[19] T. Kohonen, "Self-organized formation of topologically correct feature maps," *Biolog. Cybernetics*, vol. 43, pp. 59–69, 1982.

[20] —, Self-Organization and Associative Memory. New York: Springer-Verlag, 2d ed., 1988.

[21] D. O. Hebb, *The Organization of Behavior*. New York: Wiley, 1949.

[22] J. J. Hopfield, "Neural networks and physical systems with emergent collective computational abilities," *Proc. Natl. Acad. Sci.*, vol. 79, pp. 2554–2558, Apr. 1982.

[23] —, "Neurons with graded response have collective computational properties like those of two-state neurons," *Proc. Natl. Acad. Sci.*, vol. 81, pp. 3088–3092, May 1984.

[24] B. Kosko, "Adaptive bidirectional associative memories," *Appl. Optics*, vol. 26, pp. 4947–4960, Dec. 1, 1987.

[25] G. E. Hinton, R. J. Sejnowski, and D. H. Ackley, "Boltzmann machines: Constraint satisfaction networks that learn," Tech. Rep. CMU-CS-84-119, Carnegie-Mellon University, Dept. of Computer Science, 1984.

[26] G. E. Hinton and T. J. Sejnowski, "Learning and relearning in Boltzmann machines," in *Parallel Distributed Processing*, vol. 1, ch. 7, D. E. Rumelhart and J. L. McClelland, Eds. Cambridge, MA, M.I.T. Press, 1986.

[27] L. R. Talbert *et al.*, "A real-time adaptive speech-recognition system," Tech. rep., Stanford University, 1963.

[28] M. J. C. Hu, *Application of the Adaline System to Weather Forecasting*. Thesis, Tech. Rep. 6775-1, Stanford Electron. Labs., Stanford, CA, June 1964.

[29] B. Widrow, "The original adaptive neural net broom-balancer," *Proc. IEEE Intl. Symp. Circuits and Systems*, pp. 351–357, Phila., PA, May 4–7 1987.

[30] B. Widrow and S. D. Stearns, *Adaptive Signal Processing*. Englewood Cliffs, NJ: Prentice-Hall, 1985.

[31] B. Widrow, P. Mantey, L. Griffiths, and B. Goode, "Adaptive antenna systems," *Proc. IEEE*, vol. 55, pp. 2143–2159, Dec. 1967.

[32] B. Widrow, "Adaptive inverse control," *Proc. 2d Intl. Fed. of Automatic Control Workshop*, pp. 1–5, Lund, Sweden, July 1–3, 1986.

[33] B. Widrow, *et al.*, "Adaptive noise cancelling: Principles and applications," *Proc. IEEE*, vol. 63, pp. 1692–1716, Dec. 1975.

[34] R. W. Lucky, "Automatic equalization for digital communication," *Bell Syst. Tech. J.*, vol. 44, pp. 547–588, Apr. 1965.

[35] R. W. Lucky, *et al.*, *Principles of Data Communication*. New York: McGraw-Hill, 1968.

[36] M. M. Sondhi, "An adaptive echo canceller," *Bell Syst. Tech. J.*, vol. 46, pp. 497–511, Mar. 1967.

[37] P. Werbos, *Beyond Regression: New Tools for Prediction and Analysis in the Behavioral Sciences*. Ph.D. thesis, Harvard University, Cambridge, MA, Aug. 1974.

[38] Y. le Cun, "A theoretical framework for back-propagation," in *Proc. 1988 Connectionist Models Summer School*, D. Touretzky, G. Hinton, and T. Sejnowski, Eds. June 17–26, pp. 21–28. San Mateo, CA; Morgan Kaufmann.

[39] D. Parker, "Learning-logic," Invention Report S81-64, File 1, Office of Technology Licensing, Stanford University, Stanford, CA, Oct. 1982.

[40] —, "Learning-logic," Technical Report TR-47, Center for

Computational Research in Economics and Management Science, M.I.T., Apr. 1985.

[41] D. E. Rumelhart, G. E. Hinton, and R. J. Williams, "Learning internal representations by error propagation," ICS Report 8506, Institute for Cognitive Science, University of California at San Diego, La Jolla, CA, Sept. 1985.

[42] —, "Learning internal representations by error propagation," in *Parallel Distributed Processing*, vol. 1, ch. 8, D. E. Rumelhart and J. L. McClelland, Eds., Cambridge, MA: M.I.T. Press, 1986.

[43] B. Widrow, R. G. Winter, and R. Baxter, "Learning phenomena in layered neural networks," *Proc. 1st IEEE Intl. Conf. on Neural Networks*, vol. 2, pp. 411–429, San Diego, CA, June 1987.

[44] R. P. Lippmann, "An introduction to computing with neural nets," *IEEE ASSP Mag.*, Apr. 1987.

[45] J. A. Anderson and E. Rosenfeld, Eds., *Neurocomputing: Foundations of Research*. Cambridge, MA: M.I.T. Press, 1988.

[46] N. Nilsson, *Learning Machines*. New York: McGraw-Hill, 1965.

[47] D. E. Rumelhart and J. L. McClelland, Eds., *Parallel Distributed Processing*. Cambridge, MA: M.I.T. Press, 1986.

[48] B. Moore, "Art 1 and pattern clustering," in *Proc. 1988 Connectionist Models Summer School*, D. Touretzky, G. Hinton, and T. Sejnowski, Eds., June 17–26 1988, pp. 174–185, San Mateo, CA: Morgan Kaufmann.

[49] *DARPA Neural Network Study*. Fairfax, VA: AFCEA International Press, 1988.

[50] D. Nguyen and B. Widrow, "The truck backer-upper: An example of self-learning in neural networks," *Proc. Intl. Joint Conf. on Neural Networks, vol. 2, pp. 357–363, Wash., DC, June 1989.*

[51] T. J. Sejnowski and C. R. Rosenberg, "Nettalk: a parallel network that learns to read aloud," Tech. Rep. JHU/EECS-86/01, Johns Hopkins University, 1986.

[52] —, "Parallel networks that learn to pronounce English text," *Complex Systems*, vol. 1, pp. 145–168, 1987.

[53] P. M. Shea and V. Lin, "Detection of explosives in checked airline baggage using an artificial neural system," *Proc. Intl. Joint Conf. on Neural Networks*, vol. 2, pp. 31–34, Wash., DC, June 1989.

[54] D. G. Bounds, P. J. Lloyd, B. Mathew, and G. Waddell, "A multilayer perceptron network for the diagnosis of low back pain," *Proc. 2d IEEE Intl. Conf. on Neural Networks*, vol. 2, pp. 481–489, San Diego, CA, July 1988.

[55] G. Bradshaw, R. Fozzard, and L. Ceci, "A connectionist expert system that actually works," in *Advances in Neural Information Processing Systems I*, D. S. Touretzky, Ed. San Mateo, CA: Morgan Kaufmann, 1989, pp. 248–255.

[56] N. Mokhoff, "Neural nets making the leap out of lab," *Electronic Engineering Times*, p. 1, Jan. 22, 1990.

[57] C. A. Mead, *Analog VLSI and Neural Systems*. Reading, MA: Addison-Wesley, 1989.

[58] B. Widrow and M. E. Hoff, Jr., "Adaptive switching circuits." *1960 IRE Western Electric Show and Convention Record, Part 4*, pp. 96–104, Aug. 23, 1960.

[59] —, "Adaptive switching circuits," Tech. Rep. 1553-1, Stanford Electron. Labs., Stanford, CA June 30, 1960.

[60] P. M. Lewis II and C. Coates, *Threshold Logic*. New York: Wiley, 1967.

[61] T. M. Cover, *Geometrical and Statistical Properties of Linear Threshold Devices*. Ph.D. thesis, Tech. Rep. 6107-1, Stanford Electron. Labs., Stanford, CA, May 1964.

[62] R. J. Brown, *Adaptive Multiple-Output Threshold Systems and Their Storage Capacities*. Thesis, Tech. Rep. 6771-1, Stanford Electron. Labs., Stanford, CA, June 1964.

[63] R. O. Winder, *Threshold Logic*. Ph.D. thesis, Princeton University, Princeton, NJ, 1962.

[64] S. H. Cameron, "An estimate of the complexity requisite in a universal decision network," *Proc. 1960 Bionics Symposium*, Wright Air Development Division Tech. Rep. 60-600, pp. 197–211, Dayton, OH, Dec. 1960.

[65] R. D. Joseph, "The number of orthants in *n*-space intersected by an *s*-dimensional subspace," *Tech. Memorandum 8*, Project PARA, Cornell Aeronautical Laboratory, Buffalo, New York 1960.

[66] D. F. Specht, *Generation of Polynomial Discriminant Functions for Pattern Recognition*. Ph.D. thesis, Tech. Rep. 6764-5, Stanford Electron. Labs., Stanford, CA, May 1966.

[67] —, "Vectorcardiographic diagnosis using the polynomial discriminant method of pattern recognition," *IEEE Trans. Biomed. Eng.*, vol. BME-14, pp. 90–95, Apr. 1967.

[68] —, "Generation of polynomial discriminant functions for pattern recognition," IEEE Trans. Electron. Comput., vol. EC-16, pp. 308–319, June 1967.

[69] A. R. Barron, "Adaptive learning networks: Development and application in the United States of algorithms related to gmdh," in *Self-Organizing Methods in Modeling*, S. J. Farlow, Ed., New York: Marcel Dekker Inc., 1984, pp. 25–65.

[70] —, "Predicted squared error: A criterion for automatic model selection," *Self-Organizing Methods in Modeling*, in S. J. Farlow, Ed. New York: Marcel Dekker Inc., 1984, pp. 87–103.

[71] A. R. Barron and R. L. Barron, "Statistical learning networks: A unifying view," *1988 Symp. on the Interface: Statistics and Computing Science*, pp. 192–203, Reston, VA, Apr. 21–23, 1988.

[72] A. G. Ivakhnenko, "Polynomial theory of complex systems," *IEEE Trans. Syst., Man, Cybernetics*, SMC-1, pp. 364–378, Oct. 1971.

[73] Y. H. Pao, "Functional link nets: Removing hidden layers." *AI Expert*, pp. 60–68, Apr 1989.

[74] C. L. Giles and T. Maxwell, "Learning, invariance, and generalization in high-order neural networks," *Applied Optics*, vol. 26, pp. 4972–4978, Dec. 1, 1987.

[75] M. E. Hoff, Jr., *Learning Phenomena in Networks of Adaptive Switching Circuits*. Ph.D. thesis, Tech. Rep. 1554-1, Stanford Electron. Labs., Stanford, CA, July 1962.

[76] W. C. Ridgway III, *An Adaptive Logic System with Generalizing Properties*. Ph.D. thesis, Tech. Rep. 1556-1, Stanford Electron. Labs., Stanford, CA, April 1962.

[77] F. H. Glanz, *Statistical Extrapolation in Certain Adaptive Pattern-Recognition Systems*. Ph.D. thesis, Tech. Rep. 6767-1, Stanford Electron. Labs., Stanford, CA, May 1965.

[78] B. Widrow, "Adaline and Madaline—1963, plenary speech," *Proc. 1st IEEE Intl. Conf. on Neural Networks*, vol. 1, pp. 145–158, San Diego, CA, June 23, 1987.

[79] —, "An adaptive "adaline" neuron using chemical 'memistors.'" Tech. Rep. 1553-2, Stanford Electron. Labs., Stanford, CA, Oct. 17, 1960.

[80] C. L. Giles, R. D. Griffin, and T. Maxwell, "Encoding geometric invariances in higher order neural networks," *Neural Information Processing Systems*, in D. Z. Anderson, Ed. New York: American Institute of Physics, 1988, pp. 301–309.

[81] D. Casasent and D. Psaltis, "Position, rotation, and scale invariant optical correlation," *Appl. Optics*, vol. 15, pp. 1795–1799, July 1976.

[82] W. L. Reber and J. Lyman, "An artificial neural system design for rotation and scale invariant pattern recognition," *Proc. 1st IEEE Intl. Conf. on Neural Networks*, vol. 4, pp. 277–283, San Diego, CA, June 1987.

[83] B. Widrow and R. G. Winter, "Neural nets for adaptive filtering and adaptive pattern recognition," *IEEE Computer*, pp. 25–39, Mar. 1988.

[84] A. Khotanzad and Y. H. Hong, "Rotation invariant pattern recognition using zernike moments," *Proc. 9th Intl. Conf. on Pattern Recognition*, vol. 1, pp. 326–328, 1988.

[85] C. von der Malsburg, "Pattern recognition by labeled graph matching," *Neural Networks*, vol. 1, pp. 141–148, 1988.

[86] A. Waibel, T. Hanazawa, G. Hinton, K. Shikano, and K. J. Lang, "Phoneme recognition using time delay neural networks," *IEEE Trans. Acoust., Speech, and Signal Processing*, vol. ASSP-37, pp. 328–339, Mar. 1989.

[87] C. M. Newman, "Memory capacity in neural network models: Rigorous lower bounds," *Neural Networks*, vol. 1, pp. 223–238, 1988.

[88] Y. S. Abu-Mostafa and J. St. Jacques, "Information capacity of the hopfield model," *IEEE Trans. Inform. Theory*, vol. IT-31, pp. 461–464, 1985.

[89] Y. S. Abu-Mostafa, "Neural networks for computing?" in *Neural Networks for Computing, Amer. Inst. of Phys. Conf. Proc. No. 151*, J. S. Denker, Ed. New York: American Institute of Physics, 1986, pp. 1–6.

[90] S. S. Venkatesh, "Epsilon capacity of neural networks," in

Neural Networks for Computing, Amer. Inst. of Phys. Conf. Proc. No. 151, J. S. Denker, Ed. New York: American Institute of Physics, 1986, pp. 440–445.

[91] J. D. Greenfield, *Practical Digital Design Using IC's. 2d ed., New York: Wiley, 1983.*

[92] M. Stinchombe and H. White, "Universal approximation using feedforward networks with non-sigmoid hidden layer activation functions," *Proc. Intl. Joint Conf. on Neural Networks*, vol. 1, pp. 613–617, Wash., DC, June 1989.

[93] G. Cybenko, "Continuous valued neural networks with two hidden layers are sufficient," Tech. Rep., Dept. of Computer Science, Tufts University, Mar. 1988.

[94] B. Irie and S. Miyake, "Capabilities of three-layered perceptrons," *Proc. 2d IEEE Intl. Conf. on Neural Networks*, vol. 1, pp. 641–647, San Diego, CA, July 1988.

[95] M. L. Minsky and S. A. Papert, *Perceptrons: An Introduction to Computational Geometry*. Cambridge, MA: M.I.T. Press, expanded ed., 1988.

[96] M. W. Roth, "Survey of neural network technology for automatic target recognition," *IEEE Trans. Neural Networks*, vol. 1, pp. 28–43, Mar. 1990.

[97] T. M. Cover, "Capacity problems for linear machines,"*Pattern Recognition*, in L. N. Kanal, Ed. Wash., DC: Thompson Book Co., 1968, pp. 283–289, part 3.

[98] E. B. Baum, "On the capabilities of multilayer perceptrons," *J. Complexity*, vol. 4, pp. 193–215, Sept. 1988.

[99] A. Lapedes and R. Farber, "How neural networks work," Tech. Rep. LA-UR-88-418, Los Alamos Nat. Laboratory, Los Alamos, NM, 1987.

[100] D. Nguyen and B. Widrow, "Improving the learning speed of 2-layer neural networks by choosing initial values of the adaptive weights," *Proc. Intl. Joint Conf. on Neural Networks*, San Diego, CA, June 1990.

[101] G. Cybenko, "Approximation by superpositions of a sigmoidal function," *Mathematics of Control, Signals, and Systems*, vol. 2, 1989.

[102] E. B. Baum and D. Haussler, "What size net gives valid generalization?" *Neural Computation*, vol. 1, pp. 151–160, 1989.

[103] J. J. Hopfield and D. W. Tank, "Neural computations of decisions in optimization problems," *Biolog. Cybernetics*, vol. 52, pp. 141–152, 1985.

[104] K. S. Narendra and K. Parthasarathy, "Identification and control of dynamical systems using neural networks," *IEEE Trans. Neural Networks*, vol. 1, pp. 4–27, Mar. 1990.

[105] C. H. Mays, *Adaptive Threshold Logic*. Ph.D. thesis, Tech. Rep. 1557-1, Stanford Electron. Labs., Stanford, CA, Apr. 1963.

[106] F. Rosenblatt, "On the convergence of reinforcement procedures in simple perceptrons," *Cornell Aeronautical Laboratory Report VG-1196-G-4*, Buffalo, NY, Feb. 1960.

[107] H. Block, "The perceptron: A model for brain functioning, I," *Rev. Modern Phys.*, vol. 34, pp. 123–135, Jan. 1962.

[108] R. G. Winter, *Madaline Rule II: A New Method for Training Networks of Adalines*. Ph.D. thesis, Stanford University, Stanford, CA, Jan. 1989.

[109] E. Walach and B. Widrow, "The least mean fourth (lmf) adaptive algorithm and its family," *IEEE Trans. Inform. Theory*, vol. IT-30, pp. 275–283, Mar. 1984.

[110] E. B. Baum and F. Wilczek, "Supervised learning of probability distributions by neural networks," in *Neural Information Processing Systems*, D. Z. Anderson, Ed. New York: American Institute of Physics, 1988, pp. 52–61.

[111] S. A. Solla, E. Levin, and M. Fleisher, "Accelerated learning in layered neural networks," *Complex Systems*, vol. 2, pp. 625–640, 1988.

[112] D. B. Parker, "Optimal algorithms for adaptive neural networks: Second order back propagation, second order direct propagation, and second order Hebbian learning," *Proc. 1st IEEE Intl. Conf. on Neural Networks*, vol. 2, pp. 593–600, San Diego, CA, June 1987.

[113] A. J. Owens and D. L. Filkin, "Efficient training of the back propagation network by solving a system of stiff ordinary differential equations," *Proc. Intl. Joint Conf. on Neural Networks*, vol. 2, pp. 381–386, Wash., DC, June 1989.

[114] D. G. Luenberger, *Linear and Nonlinear Programming*. Reading, MA: Addison-Wesley, 2d ed., 1984.

[115] A. Kramer and A. Sangiovanni-Vincentelli, "Efficient parallel learning algorithms for neural networks," in *Advances in Neural Information Processing Systems I*, D. S. Touretzky, Ed., pp. 40–48, San Mateo, CA: Morgan Kaufmann, 1989.

[116] R. V. Southwell, *Relaxation Methods in Engineering Science*. New York: Oxford, 1940.

[117] D. J. Wilde; *Optimum Seeking Methods*. Englewood Cliffs, NJ: Prentice-Hall, 1964.

[118] N. Wiener, *Extrapolation, Interpolation, and Smoothing of Stationary Time Series, with Engineering Applications*. New York: Wiley, 1949.

[119] T. Kailath, "A view of three decades of linear filtering theory," *IEEE Trans. Inform. Theory*, vol. IT-20, pp. 145–181, Mar. 1974.

[120] H. Bode and C. Shannon, "A simplified derivation of linear least squares smoothing and prediction theory," *Proc. IRE*, vol. 38, pp. 417–425, Apr. 1950.

[121] L. L. Horowitz and K. D. Senne, "Performance advantage of complex LMS for controlling narrow-band adaptive arrays," *IEEE Trans. Circuits, Systems*, vol. CAS-28, pp. 562–576, June 1981.

[122] E. D. Sontag and H. J. Sussmann, "Backpropagation separates when perceptrons do," *Proc. Intl. Joint Conf. on Neural Networks*, vol. 1, pp. 639–642, Wash., DC, June 1989.

[123] —, "Backpropagation can give rise to spurious local minima even for networks without hidden layers," *Complex Systems*, vol. 3, pp. 91–106, 1989.

[124] J. J. Shynk and S. Roy, "The lms algorithm with momentum updating," *ISCAS 88*, Espoo, Finland, June 1988.

[125] S. E. Fahlman, "Faster learning variations on backpropagation: An empirical study," in *Proc. 1988 Connectionist Models Summer School*, D. Touretzky, G. Hinton, and T. Sejnowski, Eds. June 17–26, 1988, pp. 38–51, San Mateo, CA: Morgan Kaufmann.

[126] R. A. Jacobs, "Increased rates of convergence through learning rate adaptation, *Neural Networks*, vol. 1, pp. 295–307, 1988.

[127] F. J. Pineda, "Generalization of backpropagation to recurrent neural networks," *Phys. Rev. Lett.*, vol. 18, pp. 2229–2232, 1987.

[128] L. B. Almeida, "A learning rule for asynchronous perceptrons with feedback in a combinatorial environment," *Proc. 1st IEEE Intl. Conf. on Neural Networks*, vol. 2, pp. 609–618, San Diego, CA, June 1987.

[129] R. J. Williams and D. Zipser, "A learning algorithm for continually running fully recurrent neural networks," ICS Report 8805, Inst. for Cog. Sci., University of California at San Diego, La Jolla, CA, Oct. 1988.

[130] S. A. White, "An adaptive recursive digital filter," *Proc. 9th Asilomar Conf. Circuits Syst. Comput.*, p. 21, Nov. 1975.

[131] B. Pearlmutter, "Learning state space trajectories in recurrent neural networks," in *Proc. 1988 Connectionist Models Summer School*, D. Touretzky, G. Hinton, and T. Sejnowski, Eds. June 17–26, 1988, pp. 113–117. San Mateo, CA: Morgan Kaufmann.

[132] M. Holler, *et al.*, "An electrically trainable artificial neural network (etann) with 10240 'floating gate' synapses," *Proc. Intl. Joint Conf. on Neural Networks*, vol. 2, pp. 191–196, Wash., DC, June 1989.

[133] D. Andes, B. Widrow, M. Lehr, and E. Wan, "MRIII: A robust algorithm for training analog neural networks, *Proc. Intl. Joint Conf. on Neural Networks*, vol. 1, pp. 533–536, Wash., DC, Jan. 1990.

Mathematical Foundations of Neurocomputing

SHUN-ICHI AMARI

Neurocomputing makes use of parallel dynamical interactions of modifiable neuron-like elements. It is important to show, by mathematical treatments, the capabilities and limitations of information processing by various architectures of neural networks. This paper, part tutorial and part review, tries to give mathematical foundations to neurocomputing. It considers the capabilities of transformations by layered networks, statistical neurodynamics, the dynamical characteristics of associative memory, a general theory of neural learning, and self-organization of neural networks.

I. Introduction

The human brain makes use of two different methods of information processing. One is the sequential and logical inferential processing in terms of symbols. This method is also used in modern computers. The other is parallel processing, which is realized by the dynamics of mutually interacting neurons. This method uses a distributed information representation with learning ability. Modern technology has so developed that it is expected to realize this type of information processing in the near future.

It is necessary for this purpose to elucidate the fundamental principles of parallel information processing in the brain. One important method of approach is to study the architecture and functioning of the brain, and then to formulate and to analyze their models. This is a natural way of understanding the principles underlying the brain. On the other hand, we can first suppose *a priori*, from the purely theoretical point of view, that information processing may be possible by using the parallel dynamics of mutually interacting elements with learning ability. Its characteristics could be summarized mathematically in the fundamental principles of parallel information processing. From this point of view, the brain is one realization, a biological realization, of these principles. The principles have been discovered and realized in the brain through a random search in the process of evolution, so that they might not be a very sophisticated realization. This makes it difficult to study the principles from biology and by experimental methods only. On the other hand, we may invent a technological realization of these principles in a different and more sophisticated architecture.

Manuscript received April 11, 1990.
The author is with the Faculty of Engineering, University of Tokyo, Tokyo 113, Japan.
IEEE Log Number 9038825.

A theoretical or mathematical method, among others, can elucidate the principles. We build various architectures of simple neural network models, and analyze their dynamical and learning behaviors, mathematically, in order to understand the capabilities and limitations of these architectures. These analyses are accumulated to form a mathematical theory of general neural networks, which elucidates the basic principles of parallel information processing. This theory can then be applied to elucidate brain functioning, as well as to designing neurocomputing systems.

It is without doubt important to propose various powerful models of neural information processing based on brain functioning, but it is nonetheless important to construct mathematical theories to show its intrinsic mechanisms, capabilities, and limitations.

The present paper recapitulates the author's endeavor to construct such a theory ([1]–[22]). This paper contains some well established important results, which are not widely known, as well as some new results. Since the rise of connectionism, some topics such as the backpropagation method, the Hopfield network, and the Boltzmann machine, are prevailing in the world. However, much wider and deeper mathematical treatments of neural networks have been done. This paper will be a good tutorial review of such mathematical theories of neural networks from another point of view.

The paper consists of six sections. The first section is an introduction. The second section gives a method of statistical analysis of one-layer neural networks. The third section considers a fundamental problem of statistical neurodynamics, in a way which is different from the spin-glass approach. The fourth section is devoted to the dynamical analysis of associative memory models. The fifth section covers the general theory of neural learning, in which the learning potential function plays a role. The sixth section gives an advanced theory of learning and self-organization.

II. Statistical Analysis of Neural Transformation

A. One-Layer Neural Network

Let us consider one-layer network consisting of k neural elements, which receive the same input signals $\mathbf{x} = (x_1, x_2, \cdots, x_n)$ in common, and emit respective outputs $z_1, \cdots, z_k$ (Fig. 1). Let w_{ji} be the synaptic connection weight from

Reprinted from *Proc. IEEE*, vol. 78, no. 9, Sept. 1990, pp. 1443–1463.

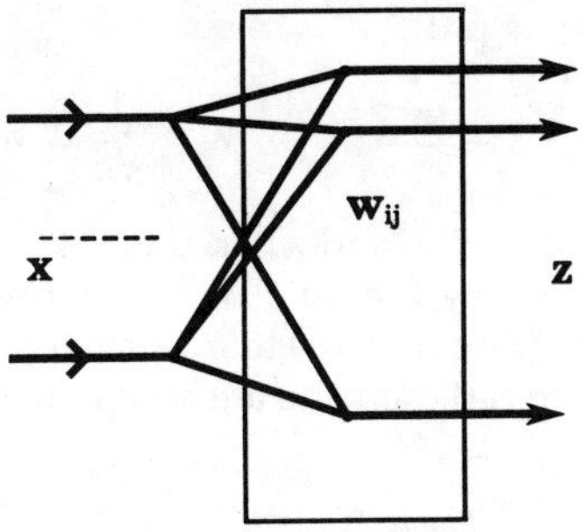

Fig. 1. One-layer network.

the ith input component x_i to the jth neuron. The output z_j of the jth neuron is then written as

$$z_j = f\left(\sum_{i=1}^{n} w_{ji}x_i - h_j\right), \qquad j = 1, \cdots, k \tag{1}$$

where f is a nonlinear output function and h_j is a threshold value. This is the behavior of a simple one-layer network without recurrent connections.

Let us denote a bundle of output signals by a vector $\mathbf{z} = (z_1, \cdots, z_k)$. The network transforms a vector input signal $\mathbf{x}$ to a vector output signal $\mathbf{z}$. We denote this transformation by

$$\mathbf{z} = T_W\mathbf{x} \tag{2}$$

where T_W is a nonlinear mapping defined by (1) and $W = (w_{ji})$ is called the connection matrix. A one-layer neural network thus defines a transformation or mapping from the input signal space $X = \{\mathbf{x}\}$ to the output signal space $Z = \{\mathbf{z}\}$,

$$T_W: X \rightarrow Z.$$

It is important to study typical characteristics of the mapping T_W realized by a neural network. This, however, is not an easy task, because of the nonlinearity of T_W. We use in this section a simple binary neuron model to demonstrate a mathematical method of approach, such that input and output signals x_i and z_i take on the binary values $+1$ and -1, so that the function f is the sign function,

$$\text{sgn}(u) = \begin{cases} 1, & u \geqq 0, \\ -1, & u < 0. \end{cases}$$

Moreover, we put $h_j = 0$ for the sake of simplicity so that

$$\mathbf{z} = T_W\mathbf{x} = \text{sgn}(W\mathbf{x})$$

where the sgn function operates on the vector $W\mathbf{x}$ componentwise.

There are a number of approaches to study characteristics of T_W. For example, one can define the capacity of the class of one-layer networks by the maximum number m of input-output pairs $(\mathbf{s}_i, \mathbf{q}_i)$, $i = 1, \cdots, m$, such that for almost all such pairs there exists a network which realizes the input-output relation

$$\mathbf{q}_i = T_W\mathbf{s}_i, \qquad i = 1, \cdots, m.$$

It is known that the capacity is $m = 2n$ by a number of interesting but different methods [23], [24], [25].

In the present paper, we focus on the statistical method of approach. When a network is complex, the connection weights may be regarded as if they are determined randomly. The statistical method is applicable to such networks. In the special case where the connection matrix $W = (w_{ij})$ is determined randomly subject to a probability distribution, we can apply the statistical method to elucidate the characteristics of the mapping T_W. When the network size is large, we find those properties which hold for almost all randomly generated networks under the same probability law (see [3], [4], [6]). Obviously, the typical characteristics depend on the probability distribution of w_{ij}. We treat the two typical cases as examples: 1) totally random networks in which all the components w_{ij} are independently and identically distributed, and 2) associative memory networks in which w_{ij} are not independent but are determined by a smaller number of random parameters.

Although we use here very simplified models for the ease of calculation, it is easy to apply our method to more general models.

B. Stability of Mapping by Totally Random Networks

We first show properties of the mapping by a totally random network where w_{ij} are the realization of independent random variables subject to a normal distribution $N(\overline{w}, \sigma_w^2)$ with mean $\overline{w}$ and variance σ_w^2. Such a network is said to be totally random. Let us put

$$u_i = \sum_{j=1}^{n} w_{ij}x_j$$

which is the weighted sum of input stimuli, and the output is written as

$$z_i = \text{sgn}\, u_i.$$

Since w_{ij} are randomly determined, then given $\mathbf{x}$ the u_i ($i = 1, \cdots, k$) are also randomly distributed. Moreover, they are independently and identically distributed. More precisely, u_i is a linear combination of w_{ij}, so that it is also normally distributed. Its mean is given by

$$\overline{u} = E\left[\sum w_{ij}x_j\right] = \sum \overline{w}x_j = n\overline{w}A_X$$

where $E[u]$ denotes the expectation of u and A_X is the mean activity of the input vector $\mathbf{x}$ defined by

$$A_X = \frac{1}{n}\sum x_i. \tag{3}$$

The variance σ^2 of u_i is given by

$$\sigma^2 = V\left[\sum_j w_{ij}x_j\right] = \sum_j x_j^2 V[w_{ij}] = n\sigma_w^2$$

where $V[u]$ denotes the variance of u.

The probability p of $z_i = 1$ is given by

$$p = \text{Prob}\,\{z_i = 1\} = \text{Prob}\,\{u_i > 0\} = \Phi\left(\frac{\overline{u}}{\sigma}\right)$$

where Φ is the error integral,

$$\Phi(u) = \int_{-\infty}^{u} (1/\sqrt{2\pi}) \exp\{-v^2/2\}\, dv. \tag{4}$$

Since all the z_i are independent subject to the same probability distribution, the output activity

$$A_Z = \frac{1}{k}\sum_{i=1}^{k} z_i$$

converges in probability to

$$A_Z = E[z_i] = \Psi(\alpha A_X) \tag{5}$$

when k is large, where we put

$$\alpha = \sqrt{n}\,\frac{\overline{w}}{\sigma_w} \tag{6}$$

and

$$\Psi(u) = 2\Phi(u) - 1$$

$$= \int_{-u}^{u} (1/\sqrt{2\pi}) \exp\{-v^2/2\}\, dv. \tag{7}$$

When we partition the input and output signal space X and Z, according to the activity, T_W maps input signals of activity A_X to output signals of activity A_Z given by (5). This is a macroscopic characteristic of T_W. When $\overline{w} = 0$, we have $\alpha = 0$ so that the activity A_Z is concentrated around 0.

We study more subtle microscopic properties of the mapping T_W. Let us assume that $\mathbf{x}$ is mapped to $\mathbf{z}$,

$$\mathbf{z} = T_W\mathbf{x}.$$

It is then expected that signals $\mathbf{x}'$ belonging to a neighborhood of $\mathbf{x}$ are mapped to a neighborhood of $\mathbf{z}$. To show this, we introduce the normalized distance between $\mathbf{x}$ and $\mathbf{x}'$ by

$$D_X(\mathbf{x}, \mathbf{x}') = \frac{1}{2n}\sum_{i=1}^{n} |x_i - x_i'|. \tag{8}$$

This is the normalized Hamming distance, satisfying $0 \leqq D_X \leqq 1$. The distance $D_Z(\mathbf{z}, \mathbf{z}')$ between $\mathbf{z}$ and $\mathbf{z}'$ is defined similarly.

Let $\mathbf{x}'$ be a signal whose distance from $\mathbf{x}$ is D_X. How far is the distance D_Z between $\mathbf{z} = T_W\mathbf{x}$ and $\mathbf{z}' = T_W\mathbf{x}'$? See Fig. 2. The relation between D_X and D_Z defines a stability or

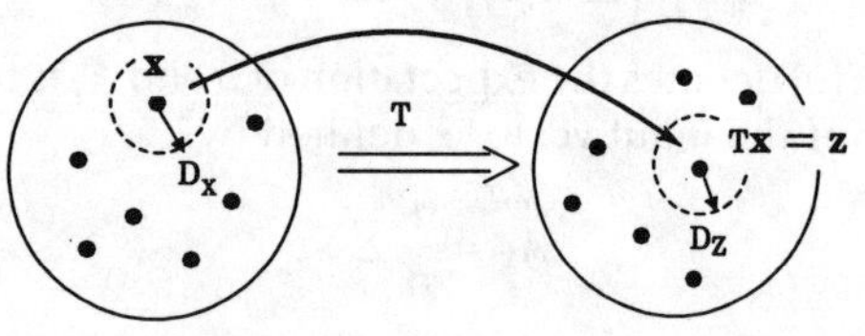

Fig. 2. Stability of transformation T_W.

robustness of the mapping T_W, because when $\mathbf{x}'$ is regarded as a noisy version of $\mathbf{x}$ with noise rate D_X, the noise rate of the output $\mathbf{z}'$ is given by D_Z. When $D_Z < D_X$, the noise is reduced by the transformation, and if $D_X < D_Z$, the noise is amplified. The next theorem shows that the noise is amplified by a totally random network [6]. This type of network enlarges small differences around $\mathbf{x}$ so that they are convenient for detecting differences among similar signals.

The following theorem holds for networks with $\overline{w} = 0$. Similar properties hold for any totally random networks.

Theorem 1: When the distance between $\mathbf{x}$ and $\mathbf{x}'$ is $D_X(\mathbf{x}, \mathbf{x}')$, the distance $D_Z(T_W\mathbf{x}, T_W\mathbf{x}')$ of their transforms is given by

$$D_Z = \frac{2}{\pi}\sin^{-1}\sqrt{D_X}. \tag{9}$$

Proof: Let us put

$$u_i = \frac{1}{\sqrt{n}}\sum w_{ij}x_j, \qquad v_i = \frac{1}{\sqrt{n}}\sum w_{ij}x_j'.$$

When $u_iv_i > 0$, $z_i = z_i'$ and when $u_iv_i < 0$, $z_i = -z_i'$. Therefore, D_Z is given by the ratio of the number of the components i satisfying $u_iv_i > 0$ to k. Since (u_i, v_i) are a pair of normal random variables and are independent for different i, we have

$$D_Z = \text{Prob}\,\{u_iv_i < 0\}$$

when k is large. The means of u_i and v_i are zero, and the variances of u_i and v_i are σ_w^2. Their covariance is given by

$$\sigma_{uv}^2 = E[u_iv_i] = \frac{1}{n}\sigma_w^2 \sum x_jx_j' = (1 - 2D_X)\sigma_w^2.$$

Therefore,

$$D_Z = \int_{uv<0} \frac{1}{2\pi}\exp\left\{-\frac{1}{2}\begin{pmatrix}u\\v\end{pmatrix}'\Sigma^{-1}\begin{pmatrix}u\\v\end{pmatrix}\right\} du\, dv,$$

where

$$\Sigma = \begin{bmatrix}\sigma_w^2 & \sigma_{uv}^2\\ \sigma_{uv}^2 & \sigma_w^2\end{bmatrix}.$$

This can easily be calculated, giving (9). □

Fig. 3 gives the graph of relation (9). When D_X is small, we

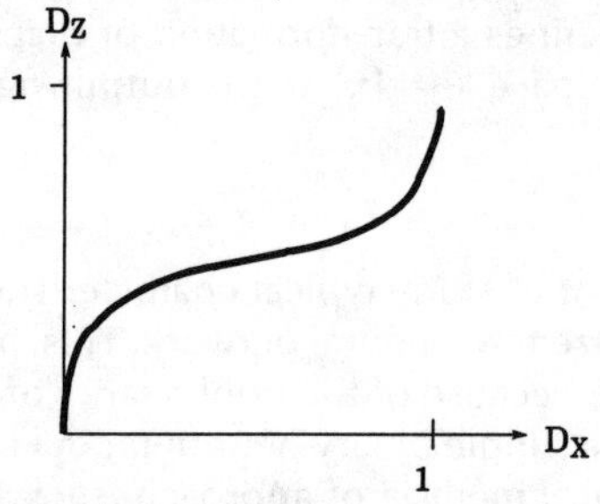

Fig. 3. Graph of 2.9.

have approximately

$$D_Z = \frac{2}{\pi}\sqrt{D_X}.$$

The approximate derivative

$$\frac{dD_Z}{dD_X} = \frac{1}{\pi}\frac{1}{\sqrt{D_X}}$$

becomes infinitely large at $D_X = 0$. This implies that a small neighborhood of $\mathbf{x}$ is expanded and mapped to a very large neighborhood of $\mathbf{z} = T_W\mathbf{x}$. Such a mapping is useful for recognizing differences among similar signals in a small neighborhood of $\mathbf{x}$, because the differences are enlarged in the corresponding output signals. This is contrary to the noise reduction property which reduces noise added to $\mathbf{x}$ in transforming it to $\mathbf{z}$.

C. Stability of Associative Mapping

Given m pairs of signals $(\mathbf{s}^1, \mathbf{q}^1), \cdots, (\mathbf{s}^m, \mathbf{q}^m)$, we next consider a network which transforms $\mathbf{s}^\mu$ to $\mathbf{q}^\mu$ $(\mu = 1, 2,$

$\cdots, m$). The network should satisfy the given m input-output relations

$$T_W \mathbf{s}^\mu = \mathbf{q}^\mu, \qquad \mu = 1, \cdots, m. \tag{10}$$

The network should have a strong noise reduction property such that, when a noisy version of $\mathbf{s}^\mu$ is input, the noise is eliminated in its output. There are many ways of constructing such a network.

The cross-correlation matrix memory proposed by Kohonen [26], Anderson [27], Nakano [28], Amari [5], and many others, provides one way of realizing the m specified pairs of input-output transformations. The correlation matrix W is defined by

$$W = \frac{1}{n} \sum_{\mu=1}^{m} \mathbf{q}^\mu (\mathbf{s}^\mu)' \tag{11}$$

where $(\mathbf{s}^\mu)'$ is the transposition of the column vector $\mathbf{s}^\mu$. This is given in the component form by

$$w_{ij} = \frac{1}{n} \sum_{\mu=1}^{m} q_i^\mu s_j^\mu$$

where s_i^μ is the ith component of $\mathbf{s}^\mu$. If $\mathbf{s}^\mu$s are mutually orthogonal,

$$W\mathbf{s}^\nu = \mathbf{q}^\nu$$

holds for any ν. Therefore, $T\mathbf{s}^\nu = \mathbf{q}^\nu$ holds in this case. However, when $\mathbf{s}^\mu$ are not mutually orthogonal, the correlation matrix memory does not work well. The capacity of such a network is specified by the maximum number of memorizable pairs. In order to show typical performances of a cross-correlation associative network, we treat the case where $\mathbf{s}^\mu$ and $\mathbf{q}^\mu$ are randomly generated vectors. More precisely, their components s_i^μ and q_i^μ are determined randomly and independently, to be equal to 1 or -1 with probability 1/2. The connection matrix $W = (w_{ij})$ is then randomly determined, but w_{ij} are not independent in this case. The statistical method is applicable in this case, too.

It has already been proved [29], [30] that, when

$$m < \frac{n}{2 \log n}$$

(10) almost surely holds. Let r be the ratio of the number m of the pattern pairs to the input dimension number n, $r = m/n$. When $r > 0$, (10) does not hold exactly but approximately.

Let $\mathbf{x}$ be a noisy version of one of memorized $\mathbf{s}^\mu$, say $\mathbf{s}^1$, whose distance from $\mathbf{s}^1$ is D_X. We then search for the distance D_Z between the output $T_W\mathbf{x}$ and the desired $\mathbf{q}^1$,

$$D_Z = D_Z(T_W\mathbf{x}, \mathbf{q}^1).$$

When a certain relation

$$D_Z = K(D_X)$$

holds for some function K, this function shows the stability of a correlation type associative memory net [31], [8]. In particular $K(0)$ denotes the accuracy of the mapping $\mathbf{s}^\mu \to \mathbf{q}^\mu$.

Theorem 2: The output error rate D_Z is given by

$$D_Z = \Phi\left(-\frac{1 - 2D_X}{\sqrt{r}}\right). \tag{12}$$

Proof: Let us put

$$u_i = \frac{1}{n} \sum w_{ij} x_j = \frac{1}{n} \sum_{\mu=1}^{m} q_i^\mu \mathbf{s}^\mu \cdot \mathbf{x} \tag{13}$$

where $\mathbf{s}^\mu \cdot \mathbf{x}$ is the inner product of $\mathbf{s}^\mu$ and $\mathbf{x}$. When the distance between $\mathbf{x}$ and $\mathbf{s}^1$ is D_X, we have

$$\mathbf{s}^1 \cdot \mathbf{x} = n(1 - 2D_X).$$

Therefore, (13) is rewritten as

$$u_i = (1 - 2D_X)q_i^1 + N_i,$$

where

$$N_i = \frac{1}{n} \sum_{\mu=2}^{m} \sum_{j=1}^{n} q_i^\mu s_j^\mu x_j$$

is a sum of $n(m - 1)$ independent random variables. By virtue of the central limit theorem, N_i is asymptotically normally distributed with mean 0 and variance

$$\sigma^2 = \frac{1}{n^2} n(m - 1) \doteq r.$$

The ith component $z_i = \operatorname{sgn} u_i$ is different from the desired output q_i^1, when N_i or $-N_i$ is larger than $1 - 2D_X$ depending on $q_i^1 = -1$ or 1. Therefore, the expected error rate of the distance D_Z is given by

$$D_Z = \text{Prob}\,\{N_i > 1 - 2D_X\} = \Phi\left(-\frac{1 - 2D_X}{\sqrt{r}}\right). \qquad \square$$

When r is not very large, D_Z is negligibly small compared with D_X (see Fig. 4). The derivative is given by

$$\frac{dD_Z}{dD_X} = \sqrt{\frac{2}{\pi r}} \exp\left\{-\frac{(1 - 2D_X)^2}{2r}\right\}$$

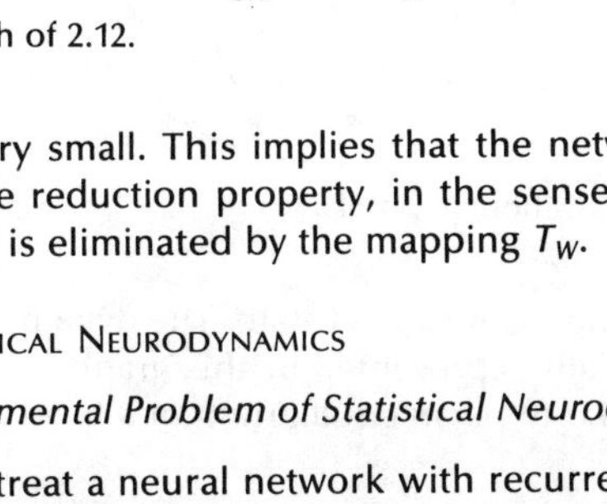

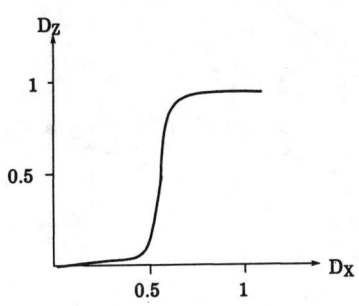

Fig. 4. Graph of 2.12.

which is very small. This implies that the network has a strong noise reduction property, in the sense that noise added to $\mathbf{s}^\mu$ is eliminated by the mapping T_W.

III. Statistical Neurodynamics

A. A Fundamental Problem of Statistical Neurodynamics

We now treat a neural network with recurrent connections (Fig. 5). Let w_{ij} be the connection weight from the jth neuron to the ith neuron, and let $x_i(t)$ be the state or the output of the ith neuron at time t, taking values $+1$ or -1. When each neuron works synchronously at discrete times $t = 0, 1, 2, \cdots$, the behavior of the nework is written as

$$x_i(t + 1) = \operatorname{sgn}\left(\sum_{j=1}^{n} w_{ij} x_j(t) - h_i + a_i\right) \tag{14}$$

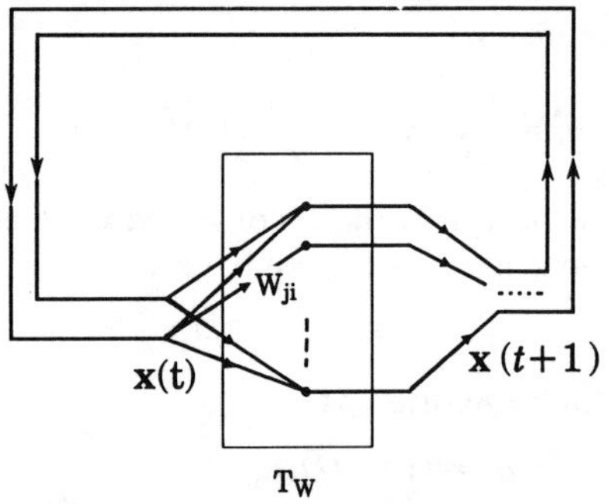

Fig. 5. Network with recurrent connections.

where h_i is the threshold and a_i is the weighted sum of stimuli coming to the ith neuron from the outside. For the sake of simplicity, we let this a_i be included in the term h_i, by putting $h_i - a_i$ as the new h_i and neglect the term a_i.

By using the nonlinear operator T_W,

$$T_W\mathbf{x} = \text{sgn}(W\mathbf{x} - h)$$

as before, Eq. (14) is written as

$$\mathbf{x}(t+1) = T_W\mathbf{x}(t). \tag{15}$$

The vector $\mathbf{x}(t)$ is regarded as the state of the network at time t, and (15) is the state transition equation describing the dynamical behavior of the network. The stae space X consists of 2^n vectors $\mathbf{x}$ whose components are ± 1 in the present case. The state transition T_W defines a mapping from X to itself, where $T_W\mathbf{x}$ is called the next state of $\mathbf{x}$. The state transition graph is constructed in X by adding directed edges connecting two nodes $\mathbf{x}$ and $T_W\mathbf{x}$ in this order (Fig. 6). Each node (state) has one, and only one, edge starting

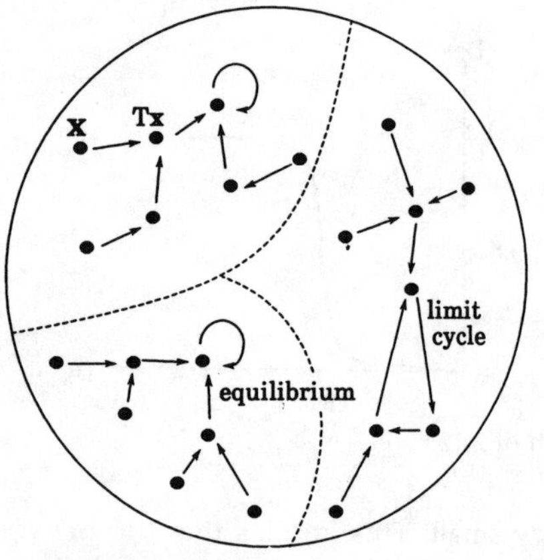

Fig. 6. State transition graph of T_W.

from it and ending at its next state. The dynamic property of the net is fully represented by this graph.

State $\mathbf{x}$ is said to be an equilibrium or a fixed point of X, when

$$\mathbf{x} = T_W\mathbf{x}$$

holds. When and only when $\mathbf{x}$ has a self-closed edge, i.e., an edge starting form $\mathbf{x}$ and entering in $\mathbf{x}$, it is a fixed point. A sequence $\{\mathbf{x}_1, \cdots, \mathbf{x}_k\}$ of nodes is said to be a cycle of period k, when

$$\mathbf{x}_{t+1} = T_W\mathbf{x}_t, \qquad t = 1, \cdots, k-1$$
$$\mathbf{x}_1 = T_W\mathbf{x}_k$$

hold and all $\mathbf{x}_t$s are different. This is represented by a primitive loop of length k in the graph.

It is not easy to analyze the behavior of the dynamics (15) of a nonlinear network. When the connection weights w_{ij} are randomly determined subject to some probability distribution, there exist common dynamical properties that are shared by almost all randomly generated networks by the same probability law. Obviously such properties depend on the probability distribution. Statistical neurodynamics studies such properties by using macroscopic state variables [3], [4], [6], [11].

A macroscopic state variable is a function of the (microscopic) state $\mathbf{x}$, summarizing some average features of the state. A simple example is the activity level,

$$A(\mathbf{x}) = \frac{1}{n}\sum_{i=1}^{n} x_i \tag{16}$$

of state $\mathbf{x}$ which shows the ratio of the excited neurons. The activity level A_t at time t is written as

$$A_t = A\{\mathbf{x}(t)\}$$

and it is expected that the dynamical equation of the type

$$A_{t+1} = F(A_t) \tag{17}$$

holds for almost all randomly generated networks with a desired accuracy as n tends to infinity. Such a quantity is called a macroscopic state variable [6], [11]. It is not necessarily a scalar but may be a vector quantity, as will be shown later. In order to elucidate common microscopic characteristics of the state transition graph, it is useful to define a macroscopic variable, which is a function of two or more microscopic states. For example, we may use the distance $D(\mathbf{x}, \mathbf{y})$ between two states as a macroscopic variable and put

$$D_t = D\{\mathbf{x}(t), \mathbf{y}(t)\} \tag{18}$$

where $\mathbf{x}(t) = T_W^t\mathbf{x}(0)$ and $\mathbf{y}(t) = T_W^t\mathbf{y}(0)$ are the state transition sequences starting at $\mathbf{x}(0)$ and $\mathbf{y}(0)$, respectively. If we have such a dynamical relation as

$$D_{t+1} = G(D_t) \tag{19}$$

we can study how an initial difference in the state develops in the course of the state transition dynamics.

How can we find a macroscopic state? Let $M = M(\mathbf{x})$ be a candidate of the macroscopic state. Given initial state $\mathbf{x}_0$ and $M_0 = M(\mathbf{x}_0)$, it is not difficult to check whether the next macrostate $M_1 = M(T\mathbf{x}_0)$ is determined only as a function of the present macrostate M_0,

$$M_1 = K(M_0) \tag{20}$$

for almost all random nets with sufficient accuracy. In the case of the activity, we obtain

$$A_1 = \Psi(\alpha A_0)$$

in the same manner as obtaining (5). By substituting $\mathbf{x}(t)$ for $\mathbf{x}(0)$ in (20), one may think that for the macrostate $M_t = M(\mathbf{x}(t))$ at time t,

$$M_{t+1} = K(M_t) \tag{21}$$

holds as well, which is the macroscopic state equation.

However, even when (20) holds, (21) does not necessarily hold. When we obtain (20), we use the stochastic properties of $T_W\mathbf{x}_0$, where $\mathbf{x}_0$ is a given constant and W are random variables. When we calculate the stochastic properties of $T_W \mathbf{x}(t)$, we cannot neglect the correlations between the operator T_W and the operand $\mathbf{x}(t) = T_W^t \mathbf{x}_0$, because $\mathbf{x}(t)$ is a random variable depending on W in a very complex manner [32]. When the correlations can be neglected, we have the macroscopic equation (21). The situation is the same as the one we encounter in deriving the famous H-theorem of Boltzmann in statistical dynamics of gasses [33]. Whether (21) holds or not is a fundamental problem of statistical neurodynamics.

We now state the precise meaning of (20).

Postulate. A macroscopic variable $M(\mathbf{x})$ should satisfy, for any $\mathbf{x}$,

$$\lim_{n \to \infty} E[|M(T_W \mathbf{x}) - K(M(\mathbf{x}))|^2] = 0 \tag{22}$$

for some function K. Equation (20) holds in this case.

Let

$$M_t = M(T_W^t \mathbf{x}_0)$$

be the actual macroscopic value of $\mathbf{x}(t)$, and let M_t^* be the solution of the equation (21) with the initial condition $M_0^* = M(\mathbf{x}_0)$. The above postulate does not necessarily guarantee that the actual M_t is close to M_t^*. In this regard, we state two propositions:

Weak Proposition. For any $t = 1, 2, \cdots$,

$$\lim_{n \to \infty} E[|M_t - M_t^*|^2] = 0. \tag{23}$$

Strong Proposition.

$$\lim_{n \to \infty} \sup_t E[|M_t - M_t^*|^2] = 0. \tag{24}$$

The implications of the two propositions are a little different. The weak proposition states that M_t is very close to M_t^* until some prescribed t^*, which depends on n. The t^* becomes infinitely large as $n \to \infty$. The strong proposition states that M_t becomes as close to M_t^* as desired for all $t = 1, 2, \cdots$, when n is sufficiently large. Amari, Yoshida, and Kanatani [11] proved the weak proposition for some classes of randomly generated nets. The strong proposition has not been proved except for very limited special cases, although it is believed to hold for many cases. However, we see in the case of associative memory, the weak proposition does not necessarily hold even when the macroscopic variable satisfies the postulate (22).

B. Macroscopic Dynamics of Activity

When w_{ij} are independent subject to the same distribution of the average w^* and variable σ_w^2, say the normal distribution $N(w^*, \sigma_w^2)$, and h_i are subject to another independent distribution $N(h^*, \sigma_h^2)$, the dynamical equation of the activity is given by

$$A_{t+1} = \Psi(W^* A_t + H^*) \tag{25}$$

where

$$W^* = \frac{w^*}{\sigma}, \quad H^* = \frac{h^*}{\sigma}, \quad \sigma^2 = \sigma_w^2 + \sigma_h^2.$$

Totally random networks are classified into the three categories depending on the behaviors of the macroscopic equation or the parameters W^* and H^* [3]: 1) monostable, converging to the unique equilibrium macrostate A^* from whatever initial state it starts, 2) bistable, converging to one of the two stable equilibrium macrostates depending on the initial state, and 3) oscillatory with period 2. Fig. 7 shows how the dynamic behavior depends on the macroparameters W^* and H^*. This is the catastrophe curve of the macroscopic dynamics. It should be noted that h_i or H^* can be controlled by stimulation from the outside.

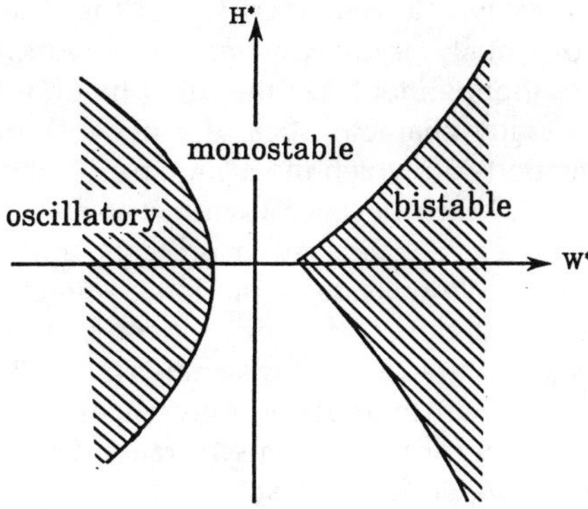

Fig. 7. Catastrophe of macrodynamics.

We next consider a random network consisting of several different types of neurons. Let $w_{ij}^{\alpha\beta}$ be the connection weight from the jth neuron of type β to the ith neuron of type α. It is a realization subject to the normal distribution with mean $w_{\alpha\beta}^*$ and variance $\sigma_{\alpha\beta}^2$. The threshold h_i^α of the ith neuron of type α is also assumed to be subject to the normal distribution with mean h_α^* and variance $\sigma_{h\alpha}^2$. Let A_t^α be the activity of the neurons of type α at time t,

$$A_t^\alpha = \frac{1}{n_\alpha} \sum_i x_i^\alpha(t)$$

where n_α is the number of the neurons of type α and $x_i^\alpha(t)$ is the state at time t of the ith neuron of type α. It is easy to show that the vector

$$\mathbf{A} = (A^\alpha)$$

is a macroscopic state satisfying the postulate (22). The macroscopic dynamics is given by

$$A_{t+1}^\alpha = \Psi\left(\sum_\beta W_{\alpha\beta}^* A_t^\beta + H_\alpha^*\right) \tag{26}$$

where the macroparameters $W_{\alpha\beta}^*$ and H_α^* are given by

$$W_{\alpha\beta}^* = \frac{1}{\sigma_\alpha} w_{\alpha\beta}^*, \quad H_\alpha^* = \frac{1}{\sigma_\alpha} h_\alpha^*$$

$$\sigma_\alpha^2 = \sum_\beta \sigma_{\alpha\beta}^2 + \sigma_{h\alpha}^2.$$

Amari [3] studied the dynamical behavior of (26), especially in the case consisting of two different types of neurons. There exist at most 9 equilibrium macrostates in such a network (see also Harth *et al.* [34]). When type 1 neurons are excitatory and type 2 neurons are inhibitory, it was shown that there exists a stable oscillatory solution with a long period. Similar results were found also by Wilson and Cowan [35]. Not only the oscillatory behavior but also its period can be controlled by stimuli from the outside, so that such a network is convenient for modeling temporal behaviors. Amari [4] also studied similar behaviors in random nets of continuous-time analog neurons described by a set of differential equations.

C. Characteristics of Microstate Transition in Totally Random Networks

We now study typical characteristics of the state transition graph of a totally random asymmetric network, where w_{ij} and w_{ji} are independent. On the other hand, it is also important to study characteristics of a network of symmetric connections, in which the symmetry condition $w_{ij} = w_{ji}$ is imposed. This is because a symmetric network can be used to solve the optimization problem under constraints [36], [37]. We consider a random symmetric network, too, where all the w_{ij} are independently, identically, and normally distributed under the symmetric condition $w_{ij} = w_{ji}$. As will be shown, there are big differences in the characteristics of symmetric and asymmetric random networks.

1) Number of Stable States: A state **x** is said to be equilibrium or stable, when its next state $T_W\mathbf{x}$ is equal to **x** itself. The expected number of stable states can be calculated by the statistical neurodynamical method.

Theorem 3. The expected number of stable states is equal to 1 for an asymmetric random net, and is equal to $e^{0.199n}$ for a symmetric random net.

Proof: The proof for the asymmetric net is easy [6]. The proof for the symmetric case was given by Tanaka and Edwards [38] in connection with the SK-model of spin glass. Here, we give a simple proof. We first calculate the probability that $\mathbf{x} = (1, 1, \cdots, 1)$ is a stable state. For the above **x**, we put

$$u_i = \sum w_{ij}x_j = \sum_{j=1}^{n} w_{ij}.$$

The state **x** is stable, if and only if $u_i > 0$ for all i. Therefore, the probability p that $T_W\mathbf{x} = \mathbf{x}$ is written as

$$p = \text{Prob}\,\{u_1 > 0, \cdots, u_n > 0\}.$$

In the asymmetric case, all the u_i are independently and normally distributed with mean 0. Therefore, because of $\text{Prob}\,\{u_1 > 0\} = 0.5$,

$$P\,\text{asym} = \prod_{i=1}^{n} \text{Prob}\,\{u_i > 0\} = 2^{-n}.$$

In the symmetric case, u_i are normally distributed with mean 0 and variance

$$\sigma^2 = V[\sum w_{ij}] = n\sigma_w^2.$$

However, u_i and u_j are not independent because of $w_{ij} = w_{ji}$, and their covariance is given by

$$\text{Cov}\,[u_i, u_j] = \text{Cov}\,[w_{ij}, w_{ji}] = \sigma_w^2.$$

These correlated u_i can be represented by using mutually independent normal random variables s_i and r subject to $N(0, 1)$, as

$$u_i = \sigma_w(\sqrt{n-1}\,s_i - r).$$

The probability then becomes

$$P\,\text{sym} = \text{Prob}\,\{u_1 > 0, \cdots, u_n > 0\}$$
$$= \text{Prob}\left\{s_1 > \frac{r}{\sqrt{n-1}}, \cdots, s_n > \frac{r}{\sqrt{n-1}}\right\}$$

In order to calculate this, we first fix r, and calculate the probability. We then take the expectation with respect to r. When r is fixed, the events $s_i > r/\sqrt{n-1}$ are independent in the sense of the conditional probability. Therefore, because of $\text{Prob}\,\{s > c\} = 1 - \Phi(c)$,

$$P\,\text{sym} = E_r\left[\prod_{i=1}^{n} (1 - \Phi(r/\sqrt{n-1}))\right]$$
$$= \frac{1}{\sqrt{2\pi}} \int \exp\left\{-\frac{r^2}{2} + n \log\left\{1 - \Phi\left(\frac{r}{\sqrt{n-1}}\right)\right\}\right\} dr$$
$$= \sqrt{\frac{n-1}{2\pi}} \int \exp\left[-n\left\{\left(\frac{1}{2} + \frac{1}{2n}\right) y^2 - \log\{1 - \Phi(y)\}\right\}\right] dy$$

By using the saddle-point approximation, we have

$$P_{\text{sym}} = \exp\{-n[\tfrac{1}{2}y_0^2 - \log\{1 - \Phi(y_0)\}]\},$$

where y_0 is the value of y minimizing $(1/2)y^2 - \log\{1 - \Phi(y)\}$. Numerical calculations give

$$P\,\text{sym} \doteq e^{-0.494n}$$

It is easy to show that P asym and P sym do not depend on specific **x** but are the same for any **x**. Since there are 2^n states, the expected number of stable points are 2^n times the probability.

2) Stability of State Transition: For two states $\mathbf{x}_1$ and $\mathbf{x}_2$ whose distance is D, we search for the distance D' between their next states $T_W\mathbf{x}_1$ and $T_W\mathbf{x}_2$ [6].

Theorem 4: When the distance between $\mathbf{x}_1$ and $\mathbf{x}_2$ is D, the distance D' between $T_W\mathbf{x}_1$ and $T_W\mathbf{x}_2$ is given by

$$D' = \frac{2}{\pi} \sin^{-1} \sqrt{D} \tag{27}$$

in both cases of the asymmetric and symmetric random connections.

Proof: Since D' is written as

$$D' = \frac{1}{2n} \sum_{i=1}^{n} |z_i - z_i'|$$

when n is large, it converges to

$$D' = \text{Prob}\,\{u_iv_i < 0\}$$

where

$$u_i = \frac{1}{\sqrt{n}} \sum w_{ij}x_{1j}, \qquad v_i = \frac{1}{\sqrt{n}} \sum w_{ij}x_{2j}.$$

The joint probability distribution of (u_i, v_i) is normal with mean 0 and their variance and covariance are

$$\sigma^2 = \sigma_w^2, \qquad \sigma_{\text{cov}}^2 = \sigma_w^2(1 - 2D).$$

In the symmetric case, (u_i, v_i) and (u_j, v_j) are not independent. But their marginal distributions are the same as the asymmetric case. Therefore, we have (27) by the same reasoning that obtained Theorem 1.

The theorem shows the diverging characteristic of the state transitions in a randomly connected network. This implies that a stable equilibrium state does not have a large basin of attraction. This is also shown by the following argument. Let **x** be a stable point. Let **x**′ be a state location at a distance D from $\mathbf{x}$. What is then the distance D' between $\mathbf{x} = T_W\mathbf{x}$ and $T_W\mathbf{x}'$? If $D' > D$, $\mathbf{x}'$ is leaving $\mathbf{x}$. The relation (27) holds between D and D', so that $\mathbf{x}'$ is leaving the fixed point by the state transition.

3) Concentricity of Parent States: Every state $\mathbf{x}$ has a unique next state $T_W\mathbf{x}$. When $\mathbf{x} = T_W\mathbf{y}$ holds, $\mathbf{y}$ is called a predecessor or a parent state of $\mathbf{x}$. The distribution of the number of the parent states is not uniform, because some states have no parent and some have a large number of parents. We denote by $T_W^{-1}\mathbf{x}$ the set of parent states of $\mathbf{x}$, and by $|T_W^{-1}\mathbf{x}|$ its size.

Let p_k ($k = 0, 1, \cdots, 2^n$) be the probability that a state $\mathbf{x}$ has k parents,

$$p_k = \text{Prob}\,\{|T_W^{-1}\mathbf{x}| = k\}. \tag{28}$$

This probability distribution is the same for all $\mathbf{x}$, and satisfies

$$\sum p_k = 1, \qquad \sum kp_k = 1,$$

showing that the expected number of the parent states is one for any $\mathbf{x}$. If the next state of $\mathbf{x}$ is chosen randomly and independently out of 2^n states for all $\mathbf{x}$, the distribution of the number of parent states is subject to the Poisson distribution of average 1, when n is large. In this case, the variance of the number of the parent states is one. However, in our case of randomly connected networks, the connections w_{ij} are randomly determined, and the next state is calculated therefrom. We will show that the variance V of the parent number is quite large in a randomly connected network. This implies that a very small number of special states keep a very large number of parent states. This monopoly is a characteristic feature of the state transition graph of a random neural net [6]. This is related to the fact that the transient period is very short in the state transition dynamics of a neural net.

To show this, we introduce the following probability

$$r_k = \text{Prob}\,\{|T_W^{-1}\mathbf{x}| = k \mid T_W\mathbf{y} = \mathbf{x}\} \tag{29}$$

i.e., the probability that $\mathbf{x}$ has k parents under the condition that $\mathbf{y}$ is a parent of $\mathbf{x}$. The probability does not depend on a given specific pair $(\mathbf{y}, \mathbf{x})$.

Theorem 5: The expected number of the parent states of $\mathbf{x}$ which satisfies the condition $T_W\mathbf{y} = \mathbf{x}$ is equal to the unconditional variance of the number of parent states, and is given asymptotically by

$$V = 2^{0.226n} \tag{30}$$

when n is large.

Proof: Given any two states $\mathbf{x}$ and $\mathbf{y}$, we have

$$\text{Prob}\,\{T_W\mathbf{y} = \mathbf{x}\} = 2^{-n}.$$

Moreover, the conditional probability of $T_W\mathbf{y} = \mathbf{x}$ under the condition that $\mathbf{x}$ has k parent states is given by

$$\text{Prob}\,\{T_W\mathbf{y} = \mathbf{x} \mid |T_W^{-1}\mathbf{x}| = k\} = k2^{-n}.$$

We now rewrite the probability r_k as

$$\begin{aligned} r_k &= \text{Prob}\,\{|T_W^{-1}\mathbf{x}| = k \mid T_W\mathbf{y} = \mathbf{x}\} \\ &= \frac{\text{Prob}\,\{|T_W^{-1}\mathbf{x}| = k,\ T_W\mathbf{y} = \mathbf{x}\}}{\text{Prob}\,\{T_W\mathbf{y} = \mathbf{x}\}} \\ &= \frac{\text{Prob}\,\{|T_W^{-1}\mathbf{x}| = k\}\ \text{Prob}\,\{T_W\mathbf{y} = \mathbf{x} \mid |T_W^{-1}\mathbf{x}| = k\}}{\text{Prob}\,\{T_W\mathbf{y} = \mathbf{x}\}} \\ &= kp_k. \end{aligned}$$

Therefore, we have

$$\begin{aligned} V' &= E[|T_W^{-1}\mathbf{x}| \mid T_W\mathbf{y} = \mathbf{x}] \\ &= \sum kr_k = \sum k^2p_k = V + 1. \end{aligned}$$

We now calculate the conditional expectation V'. Let $\mathbf{z}$ be a state whose distance from $\mathbf{y}$ is D. By putting

$$u_i = \sum w_{ij}y_j, \qquad v_i = \sum w_{ij}z_j$$

the probability that u_i and v_i have different signs is given from (30) by

$$\text{Prob}\,\{u_iv_i < 0\} = \tau(D) = \frac{2}{\pi}\sin^{-1}\sqrt{D}$$

For an asymmetric net, (u_i, v_i) are independent. Therefore, the probability that $\mathbf{z}$ is a parent of $\mathbf{x}$, i.e., $T_W\mathbf{y} = T_W\mathbf{z}$, is given by

$$\text{Prob}\,\{u_iv_i > 0 \ \text{ for all } i\} = \{1 - \tau(D)\}^n.$$

The number of states whose distances are D from $\mathbf{y}$ is given by the binomial coefficient

$${}_nC_{nD} = \exp\{nH(D)\}.$$

where $H(D)$ is the entropy $H(D) = -D\log D - (1 - D)\log(1 - D)$. The expected number is, hence, given by

$$\begin{aligned} V' &= \sum {}_nC_{nD}\{1 - \tau(D)\}^n \\ &= \int \exp\{n[\log(1 - \tau(D)) + H(D)]\}\,dD \end{aligned}$$

When n is large, by using the saddlepoint approximation, this integral is given asymptotically by

$$\begin{aligned} V' &= \exp\{n[\log(1 - \tau(D_0)) + H(D_0)]\} \\ &\doteq 2^{0.226n} \end{aligned}$$

where D_0 is the point which maximizes the function in the bracket.

4) Potential Function: In the case of symmetric connections, a potential function monotonically decreases as the state evolves by the networks dynamics. This is a characteristic feature of a symmetric connection network. Let

$$E(\mathbf{x}) = -\tfrac{1}{2}\sum w_{ij}x_ix_j - \sum h_ix_i \tag{31}$$

where we assume $w_{ii} = 0$ for all i. When each neuron changes its state (output) one by one in a nonsynchronized manner depending on the sign of the weighted sum of input stimuli, it is easy to show that $E(\mathbf{x}_t)$ is monotonically nonincreasing as the state transition takes place, [39], [40]. This implies that the state of a network converges to one of the local minima of the potential function $E(\mathbf{x})$. This also proves that there is no oscillatory behavior in such a network. See also [41], [36] for the Lyapunov or potential function in the continuous-time case.

When all the neurons change the state synchronously, the situation is slightly different. The potential function $E(\mathbf{x})$ does not necessarily decrease as time goes on. We can instead define the following function of two states $\mathbf{x}$ and $\mathbf{y}$,

$$E^*(\mathbf{x}, \mathbf{y}) = -\sum w_{ij}x_iy_j - \tfrac{1}{2}\sum h_i(x_i + y_i). \tag{32}$$

It is easy to show that $E^*(\mathbf{x}_t, \mathbf{x}_{t+1})$ monotonically decreases under the synchronous state transition, [42]. Obviously $E^*(\mathbf{x}, \mathbf{x}) = E(\mathbf{x})$. Therefore, this implies that the state converges to one of the local minima of $E(\mathbf{x})$, or otherwise the state falls into an oscillation of period 2.

In a symmetric random network, for any two states $\mathbf{x}$ and $\mathbf{y}$, we can show that

$$\text{Prob}\,\{T_W\mathbf{x} = \mathbf{y},\ T_W\mathbf{y} = \mathbf{x}\} = \text{Prob}\,\{T_W\mathbf{x} = \mathbf{x},\ T_W\mathbf{y} = \mathbf{y}\}.$$

This probability depends on the distance D between $\mathbf{x}$ and $\mathbf{y}$.

IV. Dynamical Behaviors of Autocorrelation Associative Memory

A. Autocorrelation Associative Memory

We have so far studied the dynamical properties of totally randomly connected networks, where w_{ij} are independently distributed. We now consider a neural network with recurrent connections whose connection matrix is determined by

$$w_{ij} = \frac{1}{n}\sum_{\mu=1}^{m} s_i^\mu s_j^\mu, \qquad W = \frac{1}{n}\sum_{\mu=1}^{m} \mathbf{s}^\mu(\mathbf{s}^\mu)'.$$

This is an autocorrelation associative memory model, where m given vectors $\mathbf{s}^\mu$ are expected to be equilibrium states of the network. One may say that m vectors $\mathbf{s}^\mu$ are memorized in the network in the form of its equilibrium states. They are stored in a distributed and superimposed manner, and they can be recalled by the dynamical recalling process. Indeed, if $\mathbf{s}^\mu$ are mutually orthogonal, we have

$$W\mathbf{s}^\mu = n\mathbf{s}^\mu$$

or $T_W\mathbf{s}^\mu = \mathbf{s}^\mu$. Therefore, the m specified vectors $\mathbf{s}^1, \cdots, \mathbf{s}^m$ are equilibrium states of the network. In order to evaluate the behaviors of such networks, it is convenient to analyze the case where $\mathbf{s}^\mu = (s_i^\mu)$, $\mu = 1, 2, \cdots, m$, is a set of m randomly and independently determined vectors, each component s_i^μ being determined to be equal to 1 or -1 with probability 1/2 each. In the case that $\mathbf{s}^\mu$ are randomly generated, they are not necessarily equilibrium states unless the number m of the superimposed pattern vectors is extremely small. In the present case, $W = (w_{ij})$ becomes a random matrix depending on $\mathbf{s}^\mu$, but w_{ij} are not mutually independent but strongly correlated. Therefore, the dynamical behaviors are quite different from the previous independent case.

When $\mathbf{s}^\mu$ are stable equilibrium states of the network, starting at an initial state $\mathbf{x}$ close to $\mathbf{s}^\mu$, it is expected that the state converges to $\mathbf{s}^\mu$ by state transition. Even when $\mathbf{s}^\mu$ itself is not an equilibrium state, if equilibrium states exist in a small neighborhood of $\mathbf{s}^\mu$, starting at $\mathbf{x}$, the state approaches $\mathbf{s}^\mu$ and is trapped at one of them, remaining close to $\mathbf{s}^\mu$. This network is regarded as a model of associative memory, in which a number of patterns $\mathbf{s}^\mu$ are stored in a distributed and superimposed manner. This type of model was proposed by Nakano [28], Kohonen [26], and Anderson [27], and its behavior was analyzed by Amari [5], [8]. Since Hopfield [39] introduced the concept of the energy function by using the spin glass analogy, many deeper theoretical works have been published by physicists (e.g., Amit *et al.* [43], [44], Gardner [45], Sompolinsky [46]). However, its dynamical behavior is difficult to analyze.

We show a simple and comprehensive analysis of the dynamical behavior of the associative memory model. Without loss of generality, we put

$$\mathbf{s}^1 = (1, \cdots, 1)$$

and study the dynamical behavior of the state transition

$$\mathbf{x}(t+1) = T_W\mathbf{x}(t)$$

in a neighborhood of $\mathbf{s}^1$. All the components of the other $\mathbf{s}^\mu$ $(\mu \neq 1)$ are randomly and independently determined. Let $\mathbf{x}$ be a state whose distance is D from $\mathbf{s}^1$. We search for the next state $\mathbf{x}' = T_W\mathbf{x}$. We put

$$a^\mu = \frac{1}{n}\mathbf{s}^\mu \cdot \mathbf{x} \tag{33}$$

where

$$a^1 = \frac{1}{n}\mathbf{s}^1 \cdot \mathbf{x} = 1 - 2D. \tag{34}$$

By introducing a vector $\mathbf{u} = W\mathbf{x}$, we have $\mathbf{x}' = \text{sgn}\,(\mathbf{u})$. Its components are written as

$$u_i = \frac{1}{n}\sum_{\mu,j} s_i^\mu s_j^\mu x_j = (1 - 2D) + N_i, \tag{35}$$

$$N_i = \frac{1}{n}\sum_{\mu=2}^{m} s_i^\mu \mathbf{s}^\mu \cdot \mathbf{x} = \sum_{\mu=2}^{m} s_i^\mu a^\mu. \tag{36}$$

The vector $\mathbf{N} = (N_i)$ is regarded as a crosstalk noise which intervenes the correct recalling of $\mathbf{s}^1$ by virtue of the other superimposed patterns $\mathbf{s}^\mu$.

The random variable N_i is the sum of a large number of independent random variables, so that it is asymptotically normally distributed as the central limit theorem guarantees. The expectation of N_i is equal to 0, and the variance $\sigma^2 = V[N_i]$ is

$$\sigma^2 = mV[a^\mu] = \frac{m-1}{n} \doteq r, \tag{37}$$

where $r = m/n$ is the ratio of memorized patterns to the number of neurons. Two components N_i and N_j are jointly normal with the covariance

$$\text{Cov}\,[N_i, N_j] = (m/n^2)\,\text{Cov}\,[s_i^\mu s_j^\mu x_j, s_j^\mu s_i^\mu x_i] = \frac{r}{n} x_i x_j. \tag{38}$$

It is not clear whether $\mathbf{N}$ itself is subject to the multidimensional normal distribution, because the dimension number n increases as the number m of independent terms to be added increases, provided r is fixed. We tentatively assume that $\mathbf{N}$ are jointly normal. We then have the following expression,

$$N_i = \sqrt{r}\left(q_i + \frac{1}{\sqrt{n}} a x_i\right) \tag{39}$$

by using mutually independent normal random variables q_i $(i = 1, \cdots, n)$ and a subject to $N(0, 1)$.

B. Dynamical Behavior of Recalling Process

Starting at $\mathbf{x}$ in a neighborhood of $\mathbf{s}^1$, it is expected that the next state $T_W\mathbf{x}$ is closer to $\mathbf{s}^1$ than $\mathbf{x}$ itself is. To see this, we calculate the distance D' between $\mathbf{s}^1$ and $T_W\mathbf{x}$. The probability that the ith component of $T_W\mathbf{x}$ is the same as $\mathbf{s}^1$ is given by

$$P = \text{Prob}\,\{u_i > 0\} = \text{Prob}\,\{(1 - 2D) + N_i > 0\}$$
$$= \Phi\left(\frac{1 - 2D}{\sqrt{r}}\right),$$

because N_i is subject to the normal distribution with mean 0 and variance r. The distance D' is given by $1 - P$, so that we have

$$D' = \Phi\left(\frac{1 - 2D}{\sqrt{r}}\right). \tag{40}$$

The curve of (40) is shown in Fig. 8, where we see that, when r is not so large, $D' < D$. This implies that $\mathbf{x}$ approaches $\mathbf{s}^1$ by the state transition.

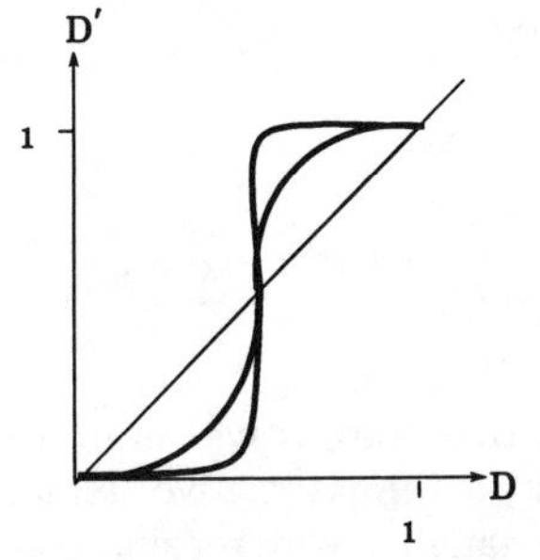

Fig. 8. Curve of 4.8.

Let D_t be the distance between $\mathbf{x}(t) = T_W^t\mathbf{x}(0)$ and $\mathbf{s}^1$. It is natural to expect that

$$D_{t+1} = \Phi\left(-\frac{1 - 2D_t}{\sqrt{r}}\right)$$

is the dynamical process of recalling $\mathbf{s}^1$, showing how $\mathbf{x}(t)$ approaches $\mathbf{s}^1$ by the state transition. This indea was first discussed by Amari [8] and then by Kinzel [47]. However, this is not the case. This implies that even the weak proposition of statistical neurodynamics does not hold in this case. Let us define

$$N_i(t) = \frac{1}{n}\sum_{\mu,j} s_i^\mu s_j^\mu x_j(t). \tag{41}$$

The variance of $N_i(t)$ is not equal to r, because $\mathbf{x}(t) = T_W^t\mathbf{x}(0)$ already depends on W or $\mathbf{s}^\mu$ and the correlation between W and $\mathbf{x}(t)$ cannot be neglected. Amari and Maginu [18] gave the dynamical equation of recalling by taking this correlation into account, as

$$D_{t+1} = \Phi\left(-\frac{1 - 2D_t}{\sigma_t}\right) \tag{42}$$

$$\sigma_{t+1}^2 = r + 4\{p(\bar{a}_t)\}^2 + 4r\bar{a}_t\bar{a}_{t+1}\sigma_{t+1}p(\bar{a}_t)$$

$$\bar{a}_t = \frac{1 - 2D_t}{\sigma_t} \qquad p(u) = \frac{1}{\sqrt{2\pi}}\exp\left\{-\frac{u^2}{2}\right\}. \tag{43}$$

There are no other theories treating dynamical or transient aspects of recalling processes of the associative memory model. Although the equations are not exact but approximate, the equations explain the actual recalling behavior very well [18].

One interesting feature of the recalling process is that a threshold value $r_c \doteq 0.15$ exists such that, when $r < r_c$, D_t approaches nearly equal to 0 when the initial value D_0 is within a limit $D^*(r)$ determined by r. This was shown by Hopfield [39] by computer simulation and by Amit *et al.* [43] by the spin glass replica method. Moreover, when the network fails to recall $\mathbf{s}^1$ in the case of $D_0 > D^*(r)$, the next state $\mathbf{x}(1)$ approaches $\mathbf{s}^1$ in general and D_1 may become smaller than $D^*(r)$. This implies that $\mathbf{x}(t)$ becomes once very close to $\mathbf{s}^1$ but then it fails to approach it beccause of the past history. This suggests that the basin of attraction of $\mathbf{s}^\mu$ has a very complicated fractal shape [18].

C. Equilibrium States of Associative Memory

The original pattern $\mathbf{s}^\mu$ does not become a stable equilibrium state unless r is negligibly small. But when $r < r_c$, a number of equilibrium states exist very close to $\mathbf{s}^\mu$, and the network keeps very good approximate memory patterns. We now study where the equilibrium states exist. An excellent analysis was given by Gardner [45], which will be introduced in the following by a different approach.

Let $\mathbf{x}$ be a state whose distance from $\mathbf{s}^1$ is D. The number of such states is given by

$${}_nC_{nD} \doteq \exp\{nH(D)\}$$

where ${}_nC_{nD}$ is the binomial coefficient and $H(D)$ is the entropy function

$$H(D) = -D\log D - (1 - D)\log(1 - D).$$

Let us calculate the probability that $\mathbf{x}$ is an equilibrium state, that is $\mathbf{x} = \text{sgn}(W\mathbf{x})$ or $u_i x_i > 0$ for all i. This is written as

$$P(D) = \text{Prob}\{\mathbf{x} = T_W\mathbf{x}\} = \text{Prob}\{u_i x_i > 0 \text{ for all } i\}.$$

The expected number of equilibrium states which are at the distance D from $\mathbf{s}^1$ is then given by $P(D)e^{nH(D)}$. In order to calculate $P(D)$, we need to evaluate the joint probability distribution of $\mathbf{N}$. If we take a finite number of its components, say N_1, N_2, N_3, they are asymptotically normally distributed. However, $\mathbf{N}$ itself is not necessarily so, because its dimensionality increases as n does.

Let $\Psi(\boldsymbol{\omega})$, $\boldsymbol{\omega} = (\omega_1, \omega_2, \cdots, \omega_n)$, be the characteristic function of $\mathbf{N}$ defined by

$$\Psi(\boldsymbol{\omega}) = E[\exp\{i\mathbf{N}\cdot\boldsymbol{\omega}\}]. \tag{44}$$

After some calculations, we then have an asymptotic expression

$$\Psi(\boldsymbol{\omega}) = e^{-im\Omega_1}(1 - 2i\Omega_1 + \Omega_2 - \Omega_1^2)^{-(m/2)}. \tag{45}$$

where

$$\Omega_1 = \frac{1}{n}\sum_{i=1}^{n}\omega_i$$

$$\Omega_2 = \frac{1}{n}\sum_{i=1}^{n}\omega_i^2.$$

It is, however, not easy to obtain the distribution function of $\mathbf{N}$ by taking the inverse Fourier transform. We use another expression of $\mathbf{N}$ in terms of independent random variables.

Let v_μ be m independent normal random variables subject to $N(0, 1)$, and let

$$v^2 = \frac{1}{m}\sum v_\mu^2. \tag{46}$$

Let z_j be also n normal variables subject to $N(0, 1)$, satisfying

$$\sum_{j=1}^{n} z_j = 0.$$

The random variable $\mathbf{N}$ is then represented by

$$N_j = \sqrt{r}vz_j + r(v^2 - 1).$$

Moreover, by using $n+1$ independent normal random variables t_j and a, we may put

$$z_j = t_j + \frac{i}{\sqrt{n}} a$$

where the imaginary number i is introduced to realize the negative correlation among z_j, which makes it possible to calculate the probability related to **N**. This procedure leads to the following theorem.

Theorem 6: The probability $P(D)$ is asymptotically given by

$$P(D) = \exp\left[-n\left\{\tfrac{1}{2}y_0^2 + \tau(y_0; D, r)\right\}\right] \tag{47}$$

where

$$\tau(y_0; D, r) = (1-D)\,\Phi\left(y + \frac{1-2D}{\sqrt{r}}\right) + D\Phi\left(y - \frac{1-2D}{\sqrt{r}}\right)$$

and y_0 is the point which minimizes $(1/2)y^2 + \tau(y; D, r)$.

Proof: The event $u_i x_i > 0$ is rewritten as

$$x_i(1 - 2D + \sqrt{r}q_i + \sqrt{r/n}\,a x_i) > 0$$

which is further rewritten as

$$q_i > -\frac{1-2D}{\sqrt{r}} - \frac{a}{\sqrt{n}}$$

when $x_i = 1$ and

$$q_i < -\frac{1-2D}{\sqrt{r}} + \frac{a}{\sqrt{n}}$$

when $x_i = -1$. When the random variable a is fixed, the above inequalities are stochastically independent and their probabilities are, respectively, equal to

$$\Phi\left(\frac{1-2D}{\sqrt{r}} + \frac{a}{\sqrt{n}}\right), \quad \Phi\left(-\frac{1-2D}{\sqrt{r}} + \frac{a}{\sqrt{n}}\right).$$

Since the number of i for which $x_i = 1$ is $n(1-D)$ and that for $x_i = -1$ is nD, the conditional probability conditioned on a is given by

$$\Phi\left(\frac{1-2D}{\sqrt{r}} + \frac{a}{\sqrt{n}}\right)^{n(1-D)} \Phi\left(-\frac{1-2D}{\sqrt{r}} + \frac{a}{\sqrt{n}}\right)^{nD}$$

and its expectation with respect to a gives $P(D)$,

$$P(D) = \int \frac{1}{\sqrt{2\pi}} \exp\left\{-\frac{a^2}{2} + n\tau\left(\frac{a}{\sqrt{n}}; D, r\right)\right\} da$$

$$= \frac{\sqrt{n}}{\sqrt{2\pi}} \int \exp\left\{-n\left[\frac{1}{2}y^2 + \tau(y; D, r)\right]\right\} dy.$$

By virtue of the saddle point approximation, the probability is finally given asymptotically by (47). □

We now search for the condition which guarantees that $\mathbf{s}^\mu$ itself is an equilibrium state. This condition was given by Weisbuch [29] and by McEliece *et al.* [30].

Theorem 7: When the number m of stored patterns are of order

$$m = \frac{n}{2\log n} \tag{48}$$

$\mathbf{s}^\mu$ is an equilibrium state with probability as close to 1 as desired.

Proof: The probability that $\mathbf{s}^1$ is an equilibrium is given $P(0)$. For $D = 0$, the point y_0 is given by $y_0 = 0$, so that

$$\log P(0) = -n\tau(0; 0, r)$$

where $r = m/n$. In order that $P(0) \to 1$,

$$-n\tau(0; 0, r) = -n \log \phi\left(\sqrt{\frac{n}{m}}\right) \to 0$$

holds. By using the asymptotic relation

$$\Phi(x) \sim 1 - \frac{1}{x}\exp\left\{-\frac{1}{2}x^2\right\}$$

when x is large, we have

$$\exp\left\{-\frac{1}{2}\frac{n}{m} + \log n - \frac{1}{2}\log\frac{n}{m}\right\} \to 0$$

from which (48) is obtained. □

The theorem shows that, if we require recalling of $\mathbf{s}^\mu$ exactly, the capacity of the associative memory is very small. However, if we are satisfied with recalling one which is very close to $\mathbf{s}^\mu$, the capacity m of the network is about $0.15n$. (If we use the sparse encoding, the capacity is of the order $n^2/(\log n)$, as will be shown later.)

Theorem 8: The expected number of equilibrium states which lies at distance D from $\mathbf{s}^\mu$ is given by

$$\exp\left\{n(H(D) - \tfrac{1}{2}y_0^2 - \tau(y_0; D, r)\right\}. \tag{49}$$

Proof: Since there are $e^{nH(D)}$ states whose distance from $\mathbf{s}^\mu$ is D, the expected number of equilibrium states is given by (49). By calculating

$$k(D, r) = H(D) - \tfrac{1}{2}y_0^2 - \tau(y_0; D, r)$$

we see that, for $r < 0.113$, a gap exists between a set of equilibrium states close to the memorized pattern and another set of equilibrium states at around $D = 1/2$ [45]. There is always a positive region at around $D = 1/2$, which includes a large number of spurious memories.

D. Associative Memory of Spatio-Temporal Pattern

The associative memory model is used not only for storing m spatial patterns in the form of equilibria, but also for storing sequences of patterns in the form of dynamic state transitions. Let $S = \{\mathbf{s}_1, \cdots, \mathbf{s}_m\}$ be a sequence of patterns of length m. When

$$T_W \mathbf{s}_i = \mathbf{s}_{i+1}$$

holds, the network recalls the sequence S one by one by the state transition. This is the dynamical recalling of the sequence.

More generally, let S^μ $(\mu = 1, 2, \cdots, k)$ be a number of sequences, where $S^\mu = \{\mathbf{s}_1^\mu, \cdots, \mathbf{s}_{m(\mu)}^\mu\}$ is a sequence of patterns of length $m(\mu)$. It is a cycle of length $m(\mu) - 1$, when $\mathbf{s}_1^\mu = \mathbf{s}_{m(\mu)+1}^\mu$ holds. Let us consider k such sequences or cycles $\mathbf{s}^\mu$ $(\mu = 1, 2, \cdots, k)$. They altogether include

$$m = \sum_{\mu=1}^{k} m(\mu)$$

patterns. The neural network is capable of memorizing such sequences or cycles in its dynamical state transition such that

$$T_W s_i^\mu = s_{i+1}^\mu$$

holds. Starting at initial state $\mathbf{x}(0)$ in a neighborhood of $\mathbf{s}_i^\mu$, it recalls the sequence or cycle following $\mathbf{s}_i^\mu$ by the state transition. Such a model was proposed by Amari [5] and its dynamical behavior was mathematically analyzed. He used the correlation type memory,

$$W = \frac{1}{n} \sum_\mu \sum_i \mathbf{s}_i^\mu \mathbf{s}_{i+1}^\mu$$

where W is not symmetric. A similar idea was followed and generalized by many researchers [48], [49]. This is still an interesting problem waiting for further study.

Amari [17] also showed that the memory capacity of the above dynamic network is larger than the network memorizing m patterns as equilibrium states. The capacity is approximatley

$$m = 0.27n$$

which is equal to the capacity of a cascaded associative network analyzed by Meir and Domany [50].

E. Sparse Encoding

We have so far treated a model in which the components of each signal $\mathbf{s}^\mu$ takes values ± 1 with probability 1/2. However, the number of excited neurons is much smaller than that of the nonexcited neurons in the actual neural network. Moreover, x_i is not ± 1 but 0 or 1. It has been known that, when the number of excited components is very small compared to the entire n components in $\mathbf{s}^\mu$, the memory capacity becomes drastically large [51], [52].

It is possible to give a mathematical analysis [19] for a sparsely encoded associative memory model. We assume that, among n components of $\mathbf{s}^\mu$, only $c \log n$ components are active, i.e., taking value 1. Such a sparse vector is realized by choosing $c \log n$ components s_i^μ among n components, independently for each $\mathbf{s}^\mu$ ($\mu = 1, \cdots, m$), which are put equal to 1 and all the other components are put equal to 0. The connection matrix W is defined in the same manner as before. In the state transition dynamics, it is assumed that the number Σx_i of the excited elements of a state $\mathbf{x}(t)$ is always controlled to be equal to a fixed value $c \log n$. This can easily be done by controlling the threshold value h of each neuron adequately. The state transition dynamics is given by

$$\mathbf{x}(t+1) - 1(W\mathbf{x} - h)$$

where the function $1(u)$ is the unit step function,

$$1(u) = \begin{cases} 1, & u > 0 \\ 0, & \text{otherwise} \end{cases}$$

and 1 is operated componentwise.

We now define the notion of the D-noisy version of $\mathbf{s}^\mu$ instead of the distance, because the state transition takes place only at a fixed activity level. When $Dc \log n$ components of the active components (those $s_i^\mu = 1$) of $\mathbf{s}^\mu$ are changed into 0, and $Dc \log n$ components of the inactive components (those $s_i^\mu = 0$) are changed into 1 for compensation, the resultant $\mathbf{x}$ is said to be a D-noisy version of $\mathbf{s}^\mu$. When we regard $\mathbf{s}^\mu$ as a vector composed of $c \log n$ active features, a D-noisy version $\mathbf{x}$ loses $100D$% of active features and instead captures $100D$% of false features. The following theorem shows the behavior of sparsely encoded associative memory.

Theorem 9: When

$$m < \frac{(1-2D)^2}{24c(\log n)^2} n^2 \tag{50}$$

the probability that $\mathbf{s}^\mu$ is correctly recalled from its D-noisy version by one-step state transition approaches 1 as n tends to infinity.

The proof is omitted (see [19]). The theorem shows that the capacity of the network is of order

$$m \approx \left(\frac{n}{\log n}\right)^2$$

if the one-step correct recalling is required. In the case of approximate recalling, the capacity is of order

$$m \approx \frac{n}{\log n}.$$

This is much larger than the non-sparsely encoded associative memory. It should be noted that the amount of information contained in a pattern $\mathbf{s}^\mu$ is smaller in the sparsely encoded case, and is given by

$$I = c(\log n)^2.$$

However, the total informtion mI is

$$mI = \frac{1}{24} n^2 \tag{51}$$

which is still far larger than the non-sparsely encoded case where

$$mI = \frac{1}{32 \log n} n^2. \tag{52}$$

The sparse encoding scheme is very promising not only for its large capacity but also from the point of view of hardware implementation. The connection weight

$$w_{ij} = \frac{1}{n} \sum_\mu s_i^\mu s_j^\mu$$

is subject to the normal distribution in the nonsparse case, so that we need an analog memory for w_{ij}. In the sparse case, nw_{ij} is subject to the Poisson distribution, taking values on the integers 0, 1, 2, $\cdots$, with mean

$$\lambda = \frac{c^2}{b}$$

when the number of patterns is

$$m = b\left(\frac{n}{\log n}\right)^2.$$

When λ is small, nw_{ij} is equal to 0 or 1 with a large probability. This implies that a digital memory is sufficient for w_{ij} (see also [51]).

V. Mathematical Theory of Neural Learning

A. General Learning Equation

A neuron has the ability to modify its connection weights $\mathbf{w} = (w_1, \cdots, w_n)$ depending on the input signals $\mathbf{x} = (x_1, \cdots, x_n)$ which it receives and the associated teacher signals or error signals. The teacher or error signal is not provided in some cases, where a neuron modifies its weights depending only on its state and input signal. This is the case of nonsupervised learning, and such a learning scheme is sometimes called self-organization. In order to build a geneal theory of neural learning, we consider the following situation [8]: A neuron receives input signals $\mathbf{x}$ from an information source I, to which it is to adapt. A set of training signals $\mathbf{x}_\alpha$, $\alpha = 1, \cdots, k$, may be regarded as a set of examples from the information source (Fig. 9). The probability

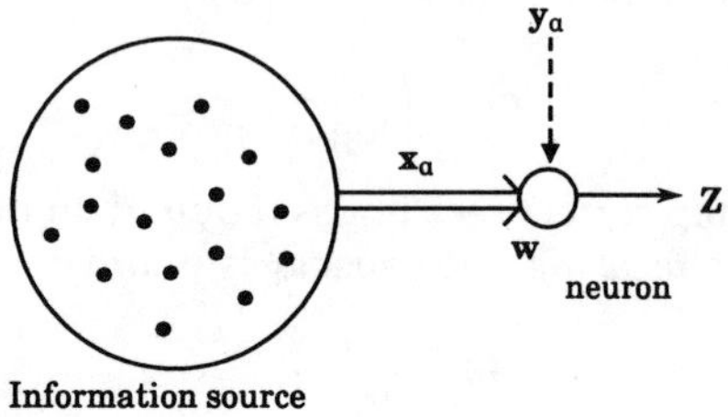

Fig. 9. Learning scheme.

or relative frequency of $\mathbf{x}_\alpha$ is denoted by p_α, $\Sigma\, p_\alpha = 1$. Let y_α be the teacher signal associated with input $\mathbf{x}_\alpha$. One may use the error signal e_α instead of y_α.

The environmental information source I is, henceforth, specified by a probability structure of signal pairs

$$I = \{(\mathbf{x}_\alpha, y_\alpha, p_\alpha),\ \alpha = 1, \cdots, k\},$$

or more generally by

$$I = \{(\mathbf{x}, y, p(\mathbf{x}, y))\},$$

where $p(\mathbf{x}, y)$ represents the probability distribution of a pair $(\mathbf{x}, y)$ of an input $\mathbf{x}$ and the associated y. In some cases, y is missing, so that

$$I = \{(\mathbf{x}, p(\mathbf{x}))\}.$$

We assume the following general learning rule: The synaptic weight vecotr $\mathbf{w}$ increases in proportion to the product of the input $\mathbf{x}$ and a *learning signal* r, and slightly decays at the same time. Here, the learning signal r is determined as a function of $\mathbf{x}$, $\mathbf{w}$, as well as y or e when such a teacher or error signal is provided. By choosing an adequate function r, most learning rules proposed so far are formulated in the following scheme.

The learning rule is expressed mathematically as

$$\mathbf{w}(t+1) = (1-\epsilon)\,\mathbf{w}(t) + cr\mathbf{x}(t) \tag{53}$$

in the discrete time case, and

$$\dot{\mathbf{w}}(t) - -c\mathbf{w}(t) + cr\mathbf{x}(t) \tag{54}$$

in the continuous time case, where $\dot{\mathbf{w}}$ denotes the time derivative $d\mathbf{w}/dt$. One may replace the decay term $(1-\epsilon)\mathbf{w}$ or $-\epsilon\mathbf{w}$ by $(1-\epsilon r)\mathbf{w}$ or $-\epsilon r\mathbf{w}$, respectively, so that the decay term vanishes when $r = 0$. The analysis is almost the same in this latter case. The above equation is called the *learning equation*.

We show some typical examples of the learning signal. When r is equal to the output z, as is given by

$$r = z = f(\mathbf{w} \cdot \mathbf{x} - h)$$

the learning rule is Hebbian. When f is approximated by the unit step function, the weight $\mathbf{w}$ increases in proportion to the input $\mathbf{x}$, when and only when the input excites the neuron. When r is given by the error signal $r = y - z$ we have the Perceptron learning rule. When the learning signal r is the teacher signal y itself, $r = y$, we have the correlation learning rule which is used in the associative memory model. When $r = \mathbf{w} \cdot \mathbf{x} - y$, we have the orthogonal or the least-square learning rule of Widrow type.

It is noted that the learning signal r is a function of the membrane potential (the weighted sum of input stimuli) $u = \mathbf{w} \cdot \mathbf{x}$ and the teacher signal y in most cases, including all of the above examples, so that we may put

$$r = r(u, y). \tag{55}$$

In this case, we have a potential function [8]

$$R(\mathbf{x}, \mathbf{w}, y) = \tfrac{1}{2}\epsilon\,|\mathbf{w}|^2 - \int_0^{\mathbf{w}\cdot\mathbf{x}} r(u, y)\, du \tag{56}$$

with which the learning equation (54) is written as

$$\tau\dot{\mathbf{w}} = -\frac{\partial}{\partial \mathbf{w}} R\{\mathbf{x}(t), \mathbf{w}(t), y(t)\}. \tag{57}$$

The function R is called the *instantaneous learning potential*, and the synaptic weight vector $\mathbf{w}$ changes in the direction of decreasing R.

B. Statistical Analysis of Learning Equation

The learning behavior of $\mathbf{w}(t)$ depends on all the past history of the input signal sequence $\mathbf{x}(t)$, which represents the environmental information structure I. More definitely, we assume that I is an ergodic information source. It chooses one signal $\mathbf{x}$ randomly with probability $p(\mathbf{x})$, applies it to the neuron for a fixed time interval Δt, and then chooses another signal $\mathbf{x}'$ with probability $p(\mathbf{x}')$ independently, repeating this procedure. Mathematically speaking, an input time series $\mathbf{x}(t)$ is, therefore, an independent stochastic process in which a signal $\mathbf{x}_\alpha$ appears approximately with frequency $p(\mathbf{x}_\alpha)$. This is the ergodic property which shows that the temporal average over a typical sequence $\mathbf{x}(t)$ is the same as the average over the probability distribution $p(\mathbf{x})$ of I.

The learning equation (57) is a stochastic differential equation, because $\mathbf{x}(t)$ is a stochastic process. Let us define

$$L(\mathbf{w}) = \langle R(\mathbf{x}, \mathbf{w}, y)\rangle = \int R(\mathbf{x}, \mathbf{w}, y)\, p(\mathbf{x}, y)\, d\mathbf{x}\, dy \tag{58}$$

where $\langle\ \rangle$ implies averaging over possible pairs $(\mathbf{x}, y)$ with respect to the probability structure I. We then have

$$\left\langle \frac{\partial}{\partial \mathbf{w}} R(\mathbf{x}, \mathbf{w}, y) \right\rangle = \frac{\partial}{\partial \mathbf{w}} L(\mathbf{w}).$$

In Eq. (57), $\mathbf{w}$ is changed in random directions depending on the random variable $\mathbf{x}(t)$. Its average direction is given by $-(\partial/\partial\, \mathbf{w})\, L(\mathbf{w})$. This process is repeated again and again, so that we can expect that the averaged equation

$$\tau\dot{\mathbf{w}} = -\frac{\partial}{\partial \mathbf{w}} L(\mathbf{w}) \tag{59}$$

holds approximately. We call this the *average learning equation*. Mathematically speaking, the average learning equation is obtained by substituting the ensemble average of $\mathbf{w}$ in r and then taking the ensemble average of the equation (57).

The solution of the average learning equation converges to one of the local minima of the potential function $L(\mathbf{w})$. The actual $\mathbf{w}(t)$, subject to the stochastic equation (57), also approaches one of the local minima of L, and randomly fluctuates around it. More precisely, the actual $\mathbf{w}(t)$ is a Markov process having a stationary distribution with peaks at the local minima of L. Therefore, the solution of the *average equation*

$$\tau\dot{\mathbf{w}} = -\epsilon\mathbf{w}(t) + c\langle r(\mathbf{x}, \mathbf{w}, y)\mathbf{x}\rangle \tag{60}$$

explains the learning behavior of a neuron, even when the right hand of (60) does not possess a potential function. See [8]. Some mathematical aspects of this type of learning equation were studied by Geman [53].

The local minima of L, or the equilibria of the average learning equation, are given by the equation

$$\mathbf{w}^* = \frac{c}{\epsilon}\langle r(\mathbf{x}, \mathbf{w}^*, y)\mathbf{x}\rangle. \tag{61}$$

C. Characteristics of Various Learning Schema

1) Hebbian Learning: When the learning signal is given by $r = z = 1(\mathbf{w}\cdot\mathbf{x} - h)$, the learning rule is said to be Hebbian. The instantaneous potential is given by

$$R(\mathbf{x}, \mathbf{w}) = \frac{\epsilon}{2}|\mathbf{w}|^2 - cg(\mathbf{w}\cdot\mathbf{x} - h)$$

where $1(u)$ is the unit step function and

$$g(u) = \begin{cases} u, & u > 0,\\ 0, & u \leqq 0.\end{cases}$$

The potential is given by

$$L(\mathbf{w}) = \frac{\epsilon}{2}|\mathbf{w}|^2 - c\langle g(\mathbf{w}\cdot\mathbf{x} - h)\rangle.$$

The local minima $\mathbf{w}^*$ are given by the solutions of

$$\mathbf{w}^* = \frac{c}{\epsilon}\langle 1(\mathbf{w}^*\cdot\mathbf{x} - h)\mathbf{x}\rangle. \tag{62}$$

This shows that an equilibrium $\mathbf{w}^*$ is given by the average of those $\mathbf{x}$ that excite this neuron. The equation may have many solutions, and a number of local minima exist depending on the information structure I.

Self-organization is a fundamental ability for a neural system to adapt to its environmental information structure. The Hebbian learning rule underlies most of the self-organizing neural network models. To study its characteristics, we show the following simple model, in which a neuron receives not only excitatory signal $\mathbf{x}$ through connection weight $\mathbf{w}$ but also an inhibitory input x_0 through inhibitory connection w_0. The input-output relation of this neuron is given by

$$z = 1(\mathbf{w}\cdot\mathbf{x} - w_0 z_0), \tag{63}$$

where we put $h = 0$. We also assume that x_0 is a constant for the sake of simplicity. The learning equations are

$$\tau\dot{\mathbf{w}} = -\epsilon\mathbf{w} + cz\mathbf{x} \tag{64}$$

$$\tau\dot{w}_0 = \epsilon w_0 + c'zx_0. \tag{65}$$

The inhibitory connection w_0 is also modifiable, but its learning efficacy may be different from that of $\mathbf{w}$. Hence, c and c' are different constants, so that the learning equations do not have a potential. However, it doesn't matter, and the equilibrium solution of the average learning equations are obtained by solving

$$\mathbf{w}^* = \frac{c}{\epsilon}\langle 1(\mathbf{w}^*\cdot\mathbf{x} - w_0^*x_0)\mathbf{x}\rangle \tag{66}$$

$$w_0^* = \frac{c'}{\epsilon}\langle 1(\mathbf{w}^*\cdot\mathbf{x} - w_0^*x_0)x_0\rangle. \tag{67}$$

We now study a characteristic of self-organization. A neuron is said to be a *categorizer* or a *detector* of a set C of signals when it is excited by any signals belonging to C, but is not excited by any signals outside C. When a neuron is a categorizer of C, its connection weight satisfies

$$\begin{aligned}\mathbf{w}^*\cdot\mathbf{x} - w_0^*x_0 > 0, &\quad \text{for } \mathbf{x}\in C,\\ \mathbf{w}^*\cdot\mathbf{x} - w_0^*x_0 < 0, &\quad \text{for } \mathbf{x}\notin C.\end{aligned} \tag{68}$$

We study what kinds of categorizers are formed automatically by self-organization under a given environmental information source I. To show this, we define the following quantities. Let $\mathbf{x}_C$ be the average of signals in a set C. This is defined by

$$\mathbf{x}_C = \frac{1}{p(C)}\int_{\mathbf{x}\in C} p(\mathbf{x})\mathbf{x}\,d\mathbf{x}$$

where

$$p(C) = \int_{\mathbf{x}\in C} p(\mathbf{x})\,d\mathbf{x}$$

is the probability of signals in C. We also define

$$\lambda = \frac{c'}{c}x_0^2. \tag{69}$$

The next theorem shows the ability of Hebbian learning [12].

Theorem 10: A necessary and sufficient condition that a set C becomes to have its categorizer by the Hebbian self-organization is that the set C satisfies $\mathbf{x}\cdot\mathbf{x}_C > \lambda$ for any signals $\mathbf{x}\in C$ and $\mathbf{x}\cdot\mathbf{x}_C < \lambda$ for any signals $\mathbf{x}\notin C$.

Proof: When a categorizer of C has synaptic weights $\mathbf{w}^*$, w_0^*, they satisfy (68). Moreover, they should be an equilibrium point of the average learning equations, so that they satisfy (66), (67). By using (68), the averages of (66), (67) are calculated as

$$\mathbf{w}^* = \frac{c}{\epsilon}P(C)\mathbf{x}_C$$

$$w_0^* = \frac{c'}{\epsilon}P(C)x_0. \tag{70}$$

If they really satisfy (68), a neuron with synaptic weights $\mathbf{w}^*$, w_0^* is a categorizer of C formed by self-organization. By substituting (70) in (68), we have the theorem. □

Intuitively speaking, a categorizer is formed for such a cluster C of signals that are concentrated around its center $\mathbf{x}_C$. The concentration is measured by the inner product. In particular, when all the signals are normalized, i.e., $|\mathbf{x}| = 1$, $\mathbf{x}\cdot\mathbf{x}_C > \lambda$ implies that the direction cosine or the similarity of $\mathbf{x}$ and $\mathbf{x}_C$ is larger than λ. Therefore, the theorem states that, for a cluster C of signals in which any two $\mathbf{x}\in$

C have a similarity larger than λ, its categorizer is automatically formed by self-organization. Therefore, λ is an important quantity called the *resolution factor*.

This can be shown more clearly in the case when I consists of a finite number of signals $\mathbf{x}_1, \cdots, \mathbf{x}_k$, where $|\mathbf{x}_i| = 1$ is assumed. We assume that any two signals $\mathbf{x}_i$ and $\mathbf{x}_j$ have a similarity less than b, $\mathbf{x}_i \cdot \mathbf{x}_j < b$. An interesting problem is to find when a categorizer C_i is formed for each $\mathbf{x}_i$ separately, C_i containing $\mathbf{x}_i$ but no other $\mathbf{x}_j$ ($j \neq i$). This C_i is a detector of $\mathbf{x}_i$.

Corollary: When $1 > \lambda > b$, the categorizer C_i can be formed for any single $\mathbf{x}_i$ by self-organization. When $\lambda > (1 + b)/2$, no other categorizers are formed.

When the similarity of some $\mathbf{x}_i$ and $\mathbf{x}_j$ are larger than λ, a common categorizer of $\mathbf{x}_i$ and $\mathbf{x}_j$, which is excited by any of $\mathbf{x}_i$ and $\mathbf{x}_j$, is formed instead of separate categorizers of $\mathbf{x}_i$ and $\mathbf{x}_j$. The resolution factor λ is controlled by changing the intensity x_0 of the inhibitory signal.

2) Potential Learning and Principal Component Analyzer: We next consider another unsupervised learning rule, where the learning signal r is given by the weighted sum, or the membrane potential, of the input signal $r = w \cdot \mathbf{x}$. It is easy to show that the instantaneous potential is given by $R = (1/2)\,[\epsilon|\mathbf{w}|^2 - c(\mathbf{w} \cdot \mathbf{x})^2]$ so that the learning potential is

$$L = \tfrac{1}{2}[\epsilon|\mathbf{w}|^2 - c\mathbf{w}'X\mathbf{w}] \tag{71}$$

where $X = \langle \mathbf{x}\mathbf{x}' \rangle = \int p(\mathbf{x})\mathbf{x}\mathbf{x}'\,d\mathbf{x}$ is the correlation or moment matrix of input signals.

Theorem 11: When the absolute value of the synaptic weight vector is kept constant, a neuron becomes the principal component analyzer of the input signals.

The function L has rather trivial minima, because it is a homogeneous quadratic function in $\mathbf{w}$. Therefore, we consider the case where the absolute value $|\mathbf{w}|$ of the synaptic vector is kept constant. This can be done by modifying the decay constant ϵ depending on $|\mathbf{w}|$. In this case, $L(\mathbf{w})$ is minimized when $\mathbf{w}$ is the eigenvector of the matrix X that has the largest eigenvalue. This eigenvector is called the principal direction of the set I of signals, and $\mathbf{w} \cdot \mathbf{x}$ is called the principal component of $\mathbf{x}$. A neuron, whose $\mathbf{w}$ is given by the principal direction, is called a principal component analyzer. When the output function f is linear, it emits the principal component of an input signal. This fact was first discovered by Amari [8] and was analyzed in detail by Oja [54]. An interesting model was proposed recently which learns not the largest but all the principal components [55].

Theorem 12: When the learning signal is given by $r = \mathbf{w} \cdot \mathbf{x}$, the principal component analyzer is formed by self-organization.

We next show some typical examples of supervised learning.

3) Perceptron Error Correction Learning: When the learning signal r is given by $r(\mathbf{w}, \mathbf{x}, y) = y - z$, where y is the desired output and z is the actual output, both taking the value 0 or 1, learning takes place only when $y \neq z$. This is called the error correction learning rule, which is used in the perceptron model by putting $\epsilon = 0$. This rule has the following potentials

$$R(\mathbf{w}, \mathbf{x}, y) = \tfrac{1}{2}\epsilon|\mathbf{w}|^2 - c(y - z)\,(\mathbf{w} \cdot \mathbf{x} - h)$$

$$L(\mathbf{w}) = \tfrac{1}{2}\epsilon|\mathbf{w}|^2 - c\langle\{y - 1 \cdot (\mathbf{w} \cdot \mathbf{x} - h)\} \cdot (\mathbf{w} \cdot \mathbf{x} - h)\rangle. \tag{72}$$

The signals in I are said to be linearly separable, when the set C_0 of the signals whose desired output is $y = 0$ can be separated by a hyperplane from the set C_1 of the signals with the output $y = 1$. It was proved that $L(\mathbf{w})$ is unimodal, having one connected bottom area with $L(\mathbf{w}) = 0$, when the signals in I are linearly separable and $\epsilon = 0$. This is the reason why the perceptron learning rule works well in the linearly separable case.

4) Correlation Learning: When the learning signal is given directly by the teacher signal y,

$$r(\mathbf{w} \cdot \mathbf{x}, y) = y,$$

this is called the correlation learning rule. We have

$$R = \frac{\epsilon}{2}|\mathbf{w}|^2 - cy\mathbf{w} \cdot \mathbf{x}$$

$$L = \tfrac{1}{2}|\mathbf{w}|^2 - c\mathbf{w} \cdot \langle y\mathbf{x}\rangle \tag{73}$$

so that L is unimodal. Its minimum is given by $\mathbf{w} = c\langle y\mathbf{x}\rangle$, which is the correlation of the input $\mathbf{x}$ and the associated output y. This is used in the model of associative memory.

We have another interpretation of this learning rule, when x_i and y are 0 or 1. When a pair $(\mathbf{x}, y)$ of signals is subject to a joint probability distribution, we put the conditional probability $p_i = \text{Prob}\,\{x_i = 1 \mid y = 1\}$ and $q = \text{Prob}\,\{y = 1\}$. We then have $\langle y\mathbf{x}\rangle = q\mathbf{p}$. Hence, a neuron studies the conditional probability of signals under the condition $y = 1$ given by the teacher signal.

5) Least Square or Orthogonal Learning Rule: Let $(\mathbf{x}_\alpha, y_\alpha)$, $\alpha = 1, \cdots, m$ be m pairs of desired input-output relations, where $\mathbf{x}_\alpha$ are assumed to be linearly independent. When the learning signal is given by $r = \mathbf{w} \cdot \mathbf{x} - y$, we have

$$R = \frac{\epsilon}{2}|\mathbf{w}|^2 + \frac{c}{2}(y - \mathbf{w} \cdot \mathbf{x})^2$$

$$L = \frac{\epsilon}{2}|\mathbf{w}|^2 + \frac{c}{2}\langle(y - \mathbf{w} \cdot \mathbf{x})^2\rangle. \tag{74}$$

When $\epsilon = 0$, L is the expected value of the square of the error signal $e = y - \mathbf{w} \cdot \mathbf{x}$, provided the output function is linear. This gives the least square learning rule, when $\epsilon = 0$. This rule is used in the Widrow adaline model.

The potential L is unimodal, and the weight vector of a neuron converges to the unique minimum. Here, a decay constant ϵ plays an important role. To show this, we define the dual set of vectors $\{\mathbf{x}^*_\alpha\}$ for a given set $\{\mathbf{x}_\alpha\}$ of linearly independent vectors, by

i) $\mathbf{x}^*_\alpha \cdot \mathbf{x}_\beta = \delta_{\alpha\beta}$

ii) $\mathbf{x}^*_\alpha$ is a linear combination of $\mathbf{x}_\beta$, (75)

where $\delta_{\alpha\beta} = 1$ when $\alpha = \beta$, and 0 otherwise. The dual vectors are explicitly given by

$$\mathbf{x}^*_\alpha = \sum_\beta (g^{-1})^{\alpha\beta}\mathbf{x}_\beta \tag{76}$$

where $G^{-1} = ((g^{-1})^{\alpha\beta})$ is the inverse matrix of $G = (g_{\alpha\beta})$, $g_{\alpha\beta} = \mathbf{x}_\alpha \cdot \mathbf{x}_\beta$. The least square solution when $\epsilon = 0$ is given by $\mathbf{w} = \Sigma\, y_\alpha \mathbf{x}^*_\alpha$, so that $\mathbf{w} \cdot \mathbf{x}_\beta = y_\beta$ holds for any β.

When two signals $\mathbf{x}_\alpha$ anmd $\mathbf{x}_\beta$ are similar, the magnitudes of $\mathbf{x}^*_\alpha$ and $\mathbf{x}^*_\beta$ cannot but be very large. When they are very close, it may be better to regard them versions of one and the same signal. More generally, given an information source I, it is desirable to treat a cluster of signals as noisy versions of one and the same prototype signal. It was proved that the constant ϵ determines the resolution of such clustering [8].

Theorem 13: When ϵ is small, the equilibrium $\mathbf{w}$ is given by

$$\mathbf{w} = \sum_{\alpha} y_\alpha \mathbf{x}_\alpha^* - \frac{\epsilon}{n} \sum_{\alpha,\beta} \frac{1}{p_\beta} y_\alpha (g^{-1})^{\alpha\beta} \mathbf{x}_\beta^* + O(\epsilon^2) \quad (77)$$

where p_β is the probability of $\mathbf{x}_\beta$. When the direction cosine of two signals is smaller than a, the two signals are treated automatically as versions of the same signal if $\epsilon > 2a^2$.

VI. Learning Neural Networks

Learning behaviors of a single neuron are treated in the previous section, where we fix the environmental information source I. When a neural network modifies its behavior cooperatively, each neuron changes its connection weights according to the learning equation. The environmental information source I of each neuron, however, is not fixed but changes as the other neurons modify their connection weights, because the information source I of one neuron is given by the behaviors of other neurons in the network. Hence, we need to solve a set of the mutually coupled learning equations.

We give two examples of learning networks.

A. Backpropagation and Its Generalization

1) General Learning Scheme: Let us consider a neural network N, which receives a vector input signal $\mathbf{x}$, processes it, and emits a vector output $\mathbf{z}$. Let S be the set of modifiable parameters (connection weights and thresholds), which specify the network. The output is determined as a function of input $\mathbf{x}$ and the parameter values S as

$$\mathbf{z} = \mathbf{f}(\mathbf{x}; S)$$

depending on the network architecture.

Let I be the information source of the network, which emits signal $\mathbf{x}$ with probability $p(\mathbf{x})$. For each signal $\mathbf{x}$ there is associated the desired output $\mathbf{y} = \mathbf{d}(\mathbf{x})$. Amari [1] formulated a general learning scheme of neural networks in the following manner. Let $l(\mathbf{x}; S)$ be a loss when input $\mathbf{x}$ is processed by a network whose parameter values are S. A simple example of the loss is the squared error

$$l(\mathbf{x}; S) = \tfrac{1}{2} |\mathbf{f}(\mathbf{x}; S) - \mathbf{d}(\mathbf{x})|^2 \quad (78)$$

which is used in the back propagation learning rule. However, there are many other types of reasonable loss. The expected loss is given by

$$L(S) = \langle l(\mathbf{x}; S) \rangle = \int p(\mathbf{x})\, l(\mathbf{x}; S)\, d\mathbf{x}. \quad (79)$$

The parameters which minimize $L(S)$ give the best network, which satisfies

$$\frac{\partial L(S)}{\partial S} = 0. \quad (80)$$

The best parameters may be obtained by the gradient method.

The learning rule is given by the gradient method as

$$S_{t+1} = S_t - c_t \frac{\partial l(\mathbf{x}_t; S_t)}{\partial S} \quad (81)$$

where S_t are the values of S at time t and $\mathbf{x}_t$ is the input at t. The parameter S_t approaches one of the local minima of $L(S)$. Amari [1] proposed, more than 20 years ago, this type of general learning and studied the trade-off between the speed and the accuracy of convergence. He also applied the method to layered neural networks (Fig. 10), and gave a general learning rule including that of the so-called hidden units. We show in Fig. 11 an example of computer simulation [2] as a historical remark for learning of hidden units, where input signals $\mathbf{x} = (x_1, x_2)$ is two-dimensional, and the network has four hidden units and one output unit. The set C_1 is the set of signals whose desired output is 1, and C_0 is the set of signals whose desired output is 0. They are not linearly separable. After a number of steps of learning, three hidden units came to work together such that they separate C_1 and C_0. Here, the output unit was fixed to be an OR element

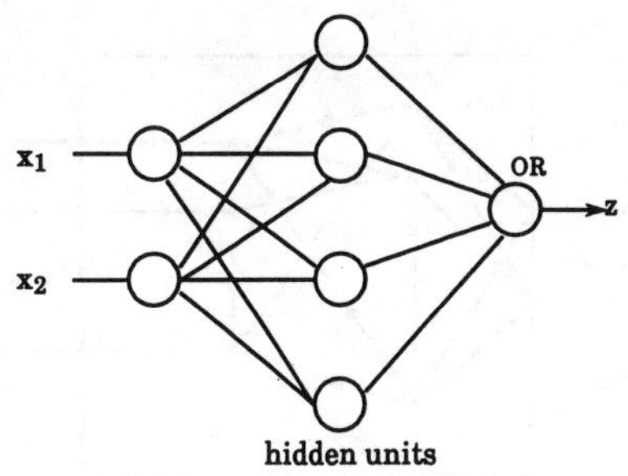

Fig. 10. Layered neural net.

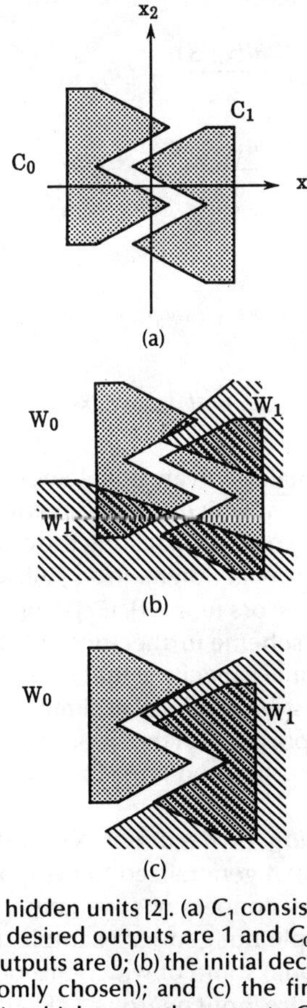

Fig. 11. Learning hidden units [2]. (a) C_1 consists of signals $\mathbf{x} = (x_1, x_2)$ whose desired outputs are 1 and C_0 consists of $\mathbf{x}$ whose desired outputs are 0; (b) the initial decision region W_1 and W_0 (randomly chosen); and (c) the final decision regions W_1 and W_0, which correctly separate C_1 and C_0

ment. He used an analog sigmoid output function for hidden units. It was impossible to perform a larger scale computer simulation by a Japanese computer at that time.

2) Backpropagation of Layered Networks: We show the famous backpropagation learning rule as an example of the general scheme. Here we use three layer networks (one hidden layer, see Fig. 12), but the same rule holds for more general layered networks. For input $\mathbf{x}$, the ith element of the hidden unit emits $q_i = f(\Sigma\, w_{ik}x_k)$ and the jth element of the output unit emits

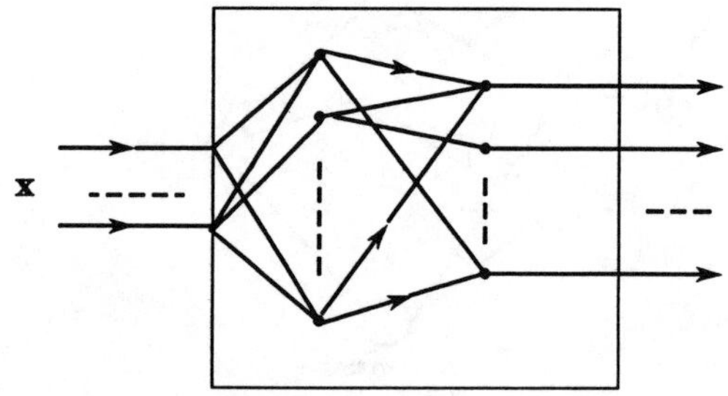

Fig. 12. Backpropagation learning.

$$z_j = f\left(\Sigma\, v_{ji}q_i\right) = f\left(\sum_i v_{ji} f\left(\sum_k w_{ik}x_k\right)\right)$$

where w_{ik} and v_{ji} are the connection weights from the input layer to the hidden layer, and from the hidden layer to the output layer. Threshold values may be included in the above by adding a unit which emits a constant value.

The modifiable parameters are $S = (v_{ji}, w_{ik})$. For the squared error loss $l = 0.5e^2$, $e = |\mathbf{z} - \mathbf{d}|$,

$$\frac{\partial l(\mathbf{x}_t; S)}{\partial v_{ji}} = r_j q_i \tag{82}$$

$$\frac{\partial l(\mathbf{x}_t; S)}{\partial w_{ik}} = r_i^* x_k \tag{83}$$

where

$$r_j = ef'\left(\Sigma\, v_{ji}q_i\right) \tag{84}$$

$$r_i^* = \sum_j w_{ji} f'\left(\sum_k w_{ik}x_k\right) r_j \tag{85}$$

are the learning signals of jth and ith elements of the output and hidden units, respectively. Since the learning signals r_i^* are determined by backpropagating the error signals, this is called the backpropagation method [56], although there were many predecessors (e.g., [1], [57]–[59]). Amari did not study this learning scheme further, not only because of the limited computational capacity at that time, but because he did not like the existence of local minima of L and failed to understand the importance of this approach. It is, however, proved later that this method is useful in many interesting cases (e.g., [60]).

3) Backpropagation of Recurrent Networks: The backpropagation has been generalized to be applicable to networks with recurrent connections by many researchers [61], [62]. We give a simple but general example. let N be a network with n neurons, some of which are output neurons and some of which are input neurons. Let $z_i(t)$ be the output of the ith neuron at time t, which is determined by

$$z_i(t) = f[u_i(t)] \tag{86}$$

$$u_i(t) = \Sigma\, w_{ij}z_j(t-1) + \Sigma\, s_{ik}x_k(t-1). \tag{87}$$

Here, w_{ij} is the weight of the recurrent connection from the jth unit to the ith unit, and s_{ik} is the connection weight from the kth input x_k to the ith unit. When the ith unit is not an input neuron, $s_{ik} = 0$. The input is a time sequence $\{\mathbf{x}(t)\}$, $t = 1, 2, \cdots$, and the network is in the quiescent state at time 0. For each input time sequence $\mathbf{x}(t)$, a sequence $\mathbf{y}(t)$ of the desired outputs is given at $t = 2, 3, \cdots$, to the output neurons.

The parameters are (w_{ij}, s_{ik}), some of which may be fixed to 0 or to prescribed values. We denote by S only modifiable parameters. The squared error loss at time t is given by

$$l(\mathbf{x}, t; S) = \frac{1}{2}\sum_{k\in O} |z_k(t) - y_k(t)|^2$$

where the summation is taken over the set O of the output neurons.

The connection weights are changed in the learning phase by $w_{ij}(t+1) = w_{ij}(t) - c\partial l/\partial w_{ij}$, $s_{ij}(t+1) = s_{ij}(t) - c\partial l/\partial s_{ij}$. However, $\partial l/\partial w_{ij}$ and $\partial l/\partial s_{ij}$ are not simple, because of the recurrent connections. We have the following theorem.

Theorem 14: The learning rule of a recurrent network is given by

$$w_{ij}(t+1) = w_{ij}(t) - c\sum_{k\in O} e_k r_{kij}(t) \tag{88}$$

$$s_{ij}(t+1) = s_{ij}(t) - c\sum_{k\in O} e_k q_{kij}(t) \tag{89}$$

where

$$e_k = \Sigma\, |z_k(t) - y_k(t)|^2 \tag{90}$$

and r_{kij}, q_{kij} are calculated recurrently by

$$r_{kij}(t) = f'(u_k(t))\, z_j(t-1)\delta_{ki} + \sum_m w_{km} r_{mij}(t-1) \tag{91}$$

$$q_{kij}(t) = f'(u_k(t))\, x_j(t-1)\delta_{ki} + \sum_m w_{km} q_{mij}(t-1) \tag{92}$$

δ_{ki} being the Kronecker delta.

Proof: From

$$\frac{\partial l(\mathbf{x}, t; S)}{\partial w_{ij}} = \sum_{k\in O} e_k \partial z_k(t)/\partial w_{ij}$$

we need to calculate

$$r_{kij}(t) = \partial z_k(t)/\partial w_{ij}.$$

From (86), (87), we have $\partial z_k(t)/\partial w_{ij} = f'[(u_k(t)]\, \partial u_k(t)/\partial w_{ij} = f'[(u_k(t)]\, \{\delta_{ki}z_j(t-1) + \Sigma_m w_{km}\partial z_m(t-1)/\partial w_{ij}\}$, which gives (91). The recurrent equation (92) is obtained similarly.

When the dynamics of the neural network converges to $\mathbf{z} = \mathbf{f}(\mathbf{z}; S)$, and if we want the final output $\mathbf{z}$ to be equal to the desired $\mathbf{y}(\mathbf{x})$, we may use the equilibrium solution of (86) and (87) by solving the simultaneous equations. This method is proposed by Pineda [63]. He also gave the dynamical approach to solve it. See also Almeida [64]. Recently, Sato [65] and Pearlmutter [66] gave an interesting learning scheme, related to the Pontrjagin theory of control.

B. Formation of Topological Maps and Neural Representations of Information

Given a set I of information signals, a neural network is capable of automatically forming an inner representation of signals. In particular, when each signal in I is represented by a local excitation at a specific position of a neural field, we have a map of the signals on the neural field. Here, a neural field implies a network in which neurons are arranged on a two-dimensional space like a cortex. This is called a cortical map or a neural map of information. It is interesting to know the basic properties of a map; the topological relation between the map and the original signal space I, the resolution and stability of a map, the amplification factor of each signal in the map, etc.

A self-organizing mechanism of this type of a cortical map was proposed by Willshaw and von der Malsburg [67]. It was studied by many researchers (e.g., [13], [22], [68], [69]) in various versions. Kohonen [70], [71] also proposed a simplified but powerful model, and studied its properties by computer simulation. He also utilized this map to form a vector quantizer, emphasizing its discrete characteristics.

A series of mathematical analysis has been performed [13], [14], [22]. It seems to be one of the deepest mathematical theories on neural networks, although it is not widely known. The theory predicts that a frequently applied signal is mapped to a wider area of the neural field to have a finer resolution. This fact is observed by Merzenich [72] in the somatosensory cortex. The theory also predicts that a micro-columnar structure is automatically formed even when the signal space I is continuous. This explains the topological properties of the cortical map. We summarize the theory briefly.

Let us consider a nerural field F with recurrent connections, which is a two-dimensional continuum of neurons like a cortex. Let $\xi = (\xi_1, \xi_2)$ be the position coordinates of the neural field F, specifying the spatial positions of neurons in F (Fig. 13). Let $u(\xi, t)$ be the average potential of neurons at position ξ at time t. The average output firing rate of these neurons is

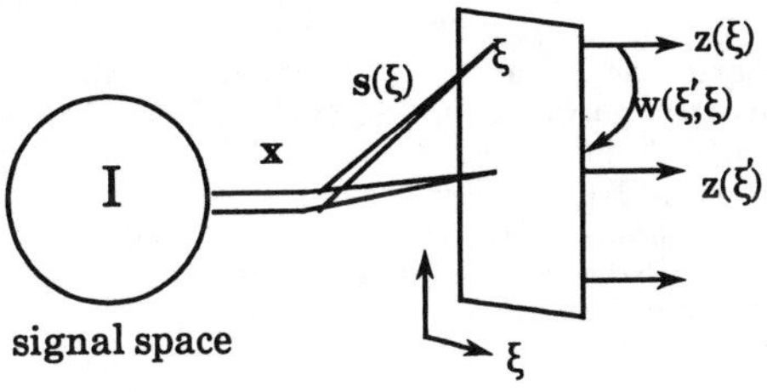

Fig. 13. Self-organizing neural field.

$$z(\xi, t) = f[u(\xi, t)]. \tag{93}$$

Let $w(\xi - \xi')$ be the connection weight from the neurons at ξ' to the neurons at ξ. The dynamics of neural excitation patterns in F is then written as

$$\tau \frac{\partial u(\xi, t)}{\partial t} = -u(\xi, t) + w \circ f[u] + S(\xi), \tag{94}$$

where

$$w \circ f[u] = \int w(\xi - \xi') \, f[u\text{–}(\xi', t)] \, d\xi' \tag{95}$$

is the total weighted sum of recurrent stimuli from the neurons of the other positions, and $S(\xi)$ is the total weighted sum of direct stimuli from the information source I to the neurons at ξ.

The dynamics of such a neural field were studied in detail [9], [20], in the case where $w(\xi - \xi')$ is of the on-center off-surround type. The equilibrium solution satisfies the equation

$$U(\xi) = w \circ f[U] + S(\xi). \tag{96}$$

This $U(\xi)$ shows the equilibrium activity pattern aroused in the field F by the distributed stimuli $S(\xi)$.

We consider the case where a common excitatory signal $\mathbf{x}$ and an inhibitory signal x_0 are applied to the neural field from the environmental information source I, and that the neurons at ξ receive them with connection weights $\mathbf{s}(\xi)$ and $s_0(\xi)$, respectively. Hence, when $\mathbf{x}$ is applied, the direct stimuli at position ξ are summarized in

$$S(\xi; \mathbf{x}) = \mathbf{s}(\xi) \cdot \mathbf{x} - s_0(\xi) x_0 \tag{97}$$

where x_0 is a constant as before. The equilibrium solution of (96) is denoted by $U(\xi; \mathbf{x})$, when the input signal is $\mathbf{x}$.

When the recurrent connections are strongly off-surround inhibitory, given any $\mathbf{x}$, only a local excitation pattern is aroused as the equilibrium $U(\xi; \mathbf{x})$. A local excitation is a pattern where the excitation is concentrated on neurons in a small local region alone. Let

$$\xi = m(\mathbf{x}) \tag{98}$$

be the position of the center of the local excitation aroused by input $\mathbf{x}$. This implies that $U(\xi; \mathbf{x})$ is positive only at a small neighborhood of $\xi = m(\mathbf{x})$. This $m(\mathbf{x})$ is a mapping from the signal space I to the neural field showing that signal $\mathbf{x}$ is represented by the position $\xi = m(\mathbf{x})$ of the neural field (Fig. 14). It thus represents the cortical map of I in field F.

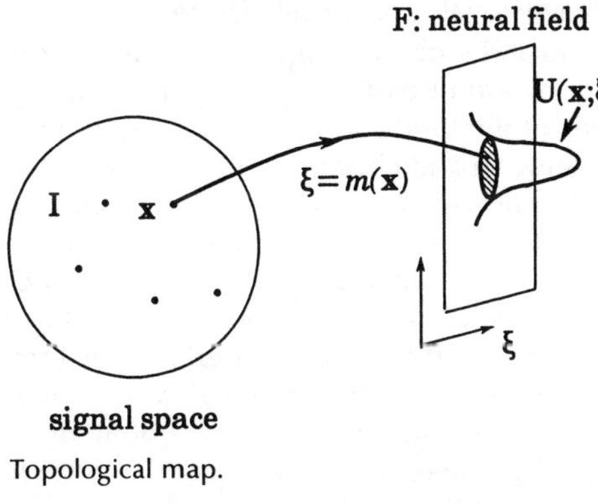

Fig. 14. Topological map.

When the connections $\mathbf{s}(\xi)$ and $s_0(\xi)$ are modifiable but $w(\xi - \xi')$ is fixed, the cortical map is formed by learning or self-organization. It is important to study what kind of map is formed by Hebbian self-organization. The average learning equation is written as

$$\tau' \frac{\partial \mathbf{s}(\xi, t)}{\partial t} = -\epsilon \mathbf{s} + c \langle f[U(\xi; \mathbf{x})] \mathbf{x} \rangle \tag{99}$$

$$\tau' \frac{\partial s_0(\xi, t)}{\partial t} = -\epsilon s_0 + c' \langle f[U(\xi; \mathbf{x})] x_0 \rangle. \tag{100}$$

Since the stimulus distribution $S(\xi; \mathbf{x})$ aroused by $\mathbf{x}$ changes as $\mathbf{s}$ and s_0 do, we have the following equation

$$\tau' \frac{\partial S(\xi, \mathbf{x})}{\partial t} = -S(\xi, \mathbf{x}) + k * f[U] \quad (101)$$

where

$$k(\mathbf{x}, \mathbf{x}') = c\mathbf{x} \cdot \mathbf{x}' - c_0 x_0^2 \quad (102)$$

$$k * f[u] = \int p(\mathbf{x}')\, k(\mathbf{x}, \mathbf{x}')\, f[U(\xi, \mathbf{x}')]\, d\mathbf{x}'. \quad (103)$$

The function $k(\mathbf{x}, \mathbf{x}')$ represents the similarity of two signals $\mathbf{x}$ and $\mathbf{x}'$ in I and hence the topology of the signal space [22].

We have thus derived a set of the fundamental equations (96) and (101) governing the dynamics of self-organization of a neural field. They include two operators $w \circ$ and $k *$. The two-dimensional topology of the neural field is represented by the recurrent connections w of the field. The topology of the signal space I is represented by the correlation or similarity k of signals in I. Therefore, the fundamental equations relate the topology of I with that of F.

It is in general difficult to solve the fundamental equations. However, some properties of the formation of the self-organizing map are revealed from the equations in some special but important cases, as has been studied mathematically [13]–[16], [22]. It was proved that, when $\mathbf{x}$ is more frequently applied, i.e., when $p(\mathbf{x})$ is larger, $\mathbf{x}$ occupies a larger area and has a finer resolution in the cortical map. The topological properties are much more interesting. When the applied signals $\mathbf{x}$ occupy two-dimensional submanifold M in I, it is very natural that the cortical map m: $M \rightarrow F$ is a homeomorphism, i.e., a topology preserving mapping. However, what will happen when M is 3-dimensional or higher dimensional? In the visual cortex, the neural field is divided into a hypercolumnar patch structure such that the patches are retinotopically arranged, preserving the 2-dimensional topology. A microstructure exists in each patch such that the orientation-detecting cells are arranged in a 1-dimensional topological manner.

Takeuchi and Amari [22] analyzed the dynamical stability of the formation of cortical maps by using the variational equations of the fundamental equations around the equilibrium solution and checking the real parts of the eigenvalues. They proved that, even if M is continuous, a discrete patch structure automatically emerges in the cortical map. This enables a cortical map to form a microstructure preserving a higher-dimensional topology. This also predicted and explained the mechanism underlying the formation of patches, studied later by physiological experiments [72]. Recently, a mathematical analysis was done by Ritter and Schulten [73], where Kohonen's simplified model of the topological mapping is used. This is also a very interesting mathematical analysis, treating the dynamical stability of a topological map. However, this type of block structure does not emerge in the simple Kohonen type map.

VII. Concluding Remarks

Neurocomputing is one of the very important methods of information processing. However, it has been neglected for long years, and it is only recently that researchers are studying it enthusiastically. In order for neurocomputing to get a fixed position in the field of information processing, we need to construct its mathematical foundations by studying its capacities and limitations in a systematic way.

The present paper showed such directions, summarizing the author's endeavor for these 20 years, although some topics were only touched upon and some were neglected. They are, for example, neural dynamics in continuous time [4], [21], neural field theory [9], [20], and self-organization [13]–[16], [22]. See also [74].

It should be noted that there are many other promising methods of approach. One is an algorithmic approach, e.g., [4]. Another is the physicists' approach [46]. A large number of computer scientists, information theorists, applied mathematicians, and physicists are joining in this field. Although the mathematics of neurocomputing is still in its infancy, I believe that it grows gradually and steadily to become a giant.

References

[1] S. Amari, "Theory of adapative pattern classifiers," *IEEE Trans. Electron. Computers*, vol. EC-16, pp. 299–307, June 1967.

[2] —, *Geometrical Theory of Information* (in Japanese). Tokyo: Kyoritsu-Shuppan, 1968.

[3] —, "Characteristics of randomly connected threshold-element networks and network systems," *Proc. IEEE.*, vol. 59, pp. 35–47, Jan. 1971.

[4] —, "Characteristics of random nets of analog neuron-like elements," *IEEE Trans. Syst., Man, Cybernetics*, vol. SMC-2, pp. 643–657, Nov. 1972.

[5] —, "Learning patterns and pattern sequences by self-organizing nets of threshold elements," *IEEE Trans. Comput.*, vol. C-21, pp. 1197–1206, Nov. 1972.

[6] —, "A method of statistical neurodynamics," *Kybernetik*, vol. 14, pp. 201–215, Apr. 1974.

[7] —, "Homogeneous nets of neuron-like elements," *Biol. Cybernetics*, vol. 17, pp. 221–235, 1975.

[8] —, "Neural theory of association and concept-formation," *Biol. Cybernetics*, vol. 26, pp. 175–185, 1977.

[9] —, "Dynamics of pattern formation in lateral-inhibition type neural fields," *Biol. Cybernetics*, vol. 27, pp. 77–87, 1977.

[10] S. Amari and M. A. Arbib, "Competition and cooperation in neural nets," in *Systems Neuroscience*, J. Metzler, ed. New York: Academic Press, pp. 119–165, 1977.

[11] S. Amari, K. Yoshida and K. Kanatani, "A mathematical foundation for statistical neurodynamics," *SIAM J. Appl. Math.*, vol. 33, pp. 95–126, 1977.

[12] S. Amari and A. Takeuchi, "Mathematical theory on formation of category detecting nerve cells," *Biol. Cybernetics*, vol. 29, pp. 127–136, 1978.

[13] S. Amari, "Topographic organization of nerve fields," *Bull. of Math. Biology*, vol. 42, pp. 339–364, 1980.

[14] —, "Field theory of self-organizing neural nets," *IEEE Trans. Syst., Man, Cybernetics*, vol. SMC-13, pp. 741–748, Sep./Oct. 1983.

[15] S. Amari and M. Maruyama, "On the topological representation of signals in self-organizing nerve fields," in *Mathematical Topics in Population Biology, Morphogenesis and Neurosciences*, E. Teramoto and M. Yamaguti, eds. New York: Springer Lecture Notes in Biomathematics, vol. 71, pp. 282–291, 1986.

[16] S. Amari, "Dynamical stability of formation of cortical maps," in *Dynamic Interactions in Neural Networks: Models and Data*, M. A. Arbib and S. Amari, eds. Springer Research Notes in Neural Computation, vol. 1, pp. 15–34, 1988.

[17] —, "Associative memory and its statistical-neurodynamical analysis," in *Neural and Synergetic Computers*, H. Haken, ed. New York: Springer Series in Synergetics, vol. 42, pp. 85–99, 1988.

[18] S. Amari and K. Maginu, "Statistical neurodynamics of associative memory," *Neural Networks*, vol. 1, pp. 63–73, 1988.

[19] S. Amari, "Characteristics of sparsely encoded associative memory," *Nerural Networks*, vol. pp. 451–457, 1989.

[20] K. Kishimoto and S. Amari, "Existence and stability of local

excitations in homogeneous neural fields," *J. Math. Biology*, vol. 7, pp. 303-318, 1979.
[21] I. Lieblich and S. Amari, "An extended first approximation model for the amygdaloid kindling phenomenon," *Biol. Cybernetics*, vol. 28, pp. 129-135, 1978.
[22] A. Takeuchi and S. Amari, "Formation of topographic maps and columnar microstructures," *Biol. Cybernetics*, vol. 35, pp. 63-72, 1979.
[23] T. Cover, "Geometrical and statistical properties of systems of linear inequalities with applications to pattern recognition," *IEEE Trans. Electron. Computers*, vol. 14, pp. 326-334, 1965.
[24] E. B. Baum and D. Haussler, "What size net gives valid generalization?," *Neural Computation*, vol. 1, pp. 151-160, 1989.
[25] E. Gardner, "The space of interactions in neural network models," *J. Phys. A*, vol. 21, pp. 257-270, 1988.
[26] T. Kohonen, "Correlation matrix memories," *IEEE Trans. Comput.*, vol. C-21, pp. 353-359, 1972.
[27] J. A. Anderson, "A simple neural network generating interactive memory," *Math. Biosciences*, vol. 14, pp. 197-220, 1972.
[28] K. Nakano, "Association—A model of associative memory," *IEEE Trans. Syst., Man, Cybernetics*, vol. SMC-2, pp. 381-388, 1972.
[29] G. Weisbuch, "Scaling laws for the attractors of Hopfield networks," *J. Phys. Lett.*, vol. 46, pp. 623-630, 1972.
[30] R. J. McEliece *et al.*, "The capacity of the Hopfield associative memory," *IEEE Trans. Inform. Theory*, vol. IT-33, pp. 461-482, 1987.
[31] Y. Uesaka and K. Ozeki, "Some properties of associative type memories," *J. Inst. Electron. Commun. Eng. Jap.*, vol. 55-D, pp. 323-330, 1972.
[32] L. I. Rozonoer, "Random logical nets: I," *Automat. Telemek.*, vol. 5, pp. 137-147, 1969.
[33] M. Kac, *Probability and Related Topics in Physical Sciences* New York: Wiley Interscience, 1959.
[34] E. M. Harth, T. J. Csermely, B. Beek, and R. D. Lindsay, "Brain functions and neural dynamics," *J. Theoret. Biol.*, vol. 26, pp. 93-120, 1970.
[35] H. R. Wilson and J. D. Cowan, "Excitatory and inhibitory interactions in localized populations of model neurons," *Biophys. J.*, vol. 12, pp. 1-24, 1972.
[36] J. J. Hopfield and D. W. Tank, "Neural computation of decisions in optimization problems," *Biol. Cybernetics*, vol. 52, pp. 141-152, 1985.
[37] D. E.f Rumelhart and J. L. McClelland, *Parallel Distributed Processing*, vols. I, II. Cambridge: M.I.T. Press, 1986.
[38] F. Tanaka and S. F. Edwards, "Analytic theory of the ground state properties of a spin glass: I, Ising spin glass," *J. Phys. F.*, vol. 10, pp. 2769-2778, 1980.
[39] J. J. Hopfield, "Neural networks and physical systems with emergent collective computational abilities," *Proc. Nat. Acad. Sci. U.S.*, vol. 79, pp. 2445-2458, 1982.
[40] J. J. Hopfield, "Neurons with graded response have collective computational properties like those of two-state neurons," *Proc. Nat. Acad. Sci. U.S.*, vol. 81, pp. 3088-3092, 1984.
[41] M. Cohen and S. Grossberg, "Absolute stability of global pattern formation and parallel memory stage by competitive neural networks," *IEEE Trans. Syst., Man, Cybernetics*, vol. SMC-13, pp. 815-826, 1983.
[42] E. Goles-Chacc, F. Fogelman-Soulie and D. Pellegrin, "Decreasing energy functions as a tool for studying threshold networks," *Discrete Mathematics*, vol. 12, pp. 261-277, 1985.
[43] D. J. Amit, H. Gutfreund, and H. Sompolinsky, "Spin-glass models of neural networks," *Phys. Rev.*, vol. A2, pp. 1007-1018, 1985.
[44] ——, "Storing infinite numbers of patterns in a spin glass model of neural networks," *Phys. Rev. Lett.*, vol. 55, pp. 1530-1533, 1985.
[45] E. Gardner, "Structure of metastable states in the Hopfield model," *J. Phys. A*, vol. 19, pp. 1047-1052, 1986.
[46] H. Sompolinsky, "Statistical mechanics of neural networks," *Phys. Today*, vol. 41, pp. 70-80, December 1988.
[47] W. Kinzel, "Learning and pattern recognition in spin glass models," *Z. Angew. Physik*, vol. B60, pp. 205-213, 1985.
[48] K. Fukushima, "A model of associative memory in the brain," *Kybernetik*, vol. 12, pp. 58-63, 1988.
[49] D. Kleinfeld and H. Sompolinsky, "Associative neural network model for the generation of temporal patterns," *Biophys. J.*, vol. 54, pp. 1039-1051, 1988.
[50] R. Meir and E. Domany, "Exact solution of a layered neural network memory," *Phys. Rev. Lett.*, vol. 59, pp. 359-362, 1987.
[51] D. J. Willshaw, O. P. Buneman and H. C. Longuett-Higins, "Nonholographic associative memory," *Nature*, vol. 222, pp. 960-962, 1969.
[52] G. Palm, "On associative memory," *Biol. Cybernetics*, vol. 36, pp. 646-658, 1980.
[53] S. Geman, "Some averaging and stability results for random differential equations," *SIAM J. Appl. Math.*, vol. 36, pp. 86-105, 1979.
[54] E. Oja, "A simplified neuron model as a principal component analyzer," *J. Math. Biol.*, vol. 15, pp. 267-273, 1982.
[55] P. Baldi and K. Hornik, "Neural networks and principal component analysis: learning from examples without local minima," *Neural Networks*, vol. 2, pp. 53-58, 1989.
[56] D. E. Rumelhart, G. E. Hinton, and R. J. Williams, "Learning internal representations by error propagation," in *Parallel Distributed Processing*, vol. 1, D. E. Rumelhart, and J. L. McCelland, eds. Cambridge: M.I.T. Press, 1986, pp. 318-362.
[57] P. Werbos, *Beyond Regression: New Tool for Prediction and Analysis in the Behavioral Sciences*, Ph.D. thesis, Harvard Univ., 1974.
[58] Y. le Cun, "A learning scheme for asymmetric threshold networks," *Proc. Cognitiva*, vol. 85, Paris, pp. 599-604, 1985.
[59] D. B. Parker, "Learning logic," Tech. Rep. TGR-47, M.I.T. Sloan School of Management, Cambridge, MA, 1982.
[60] T. J. Sejnowski and C. R. Rosenberg, "NET talk: A parallel network that learns to read aloud," *Complex Systems*, vol. 1, pp. 145-168, 1987.
[61] R. J. Williams and D. Zipser, "A learning algorithm for continuously running fully recurrent neural networks," *Neural Computation*, vol. 1, pp. 270-280, 1989.
[62] K. Doya and S. Yoshizawa, "Adaptive neural oscillator using continuous-time backpropagation learning," *Neural Networks*, vol. 2, pp. 375-385, 1989.
[63] F. J. Pineda, "Generalization of back-propagation to recurrent neural networks," *Phys. Rev. Lett.*, vol. 59, pp. 2229-2232, 1987.
[64] L. B. Almeida, "A learning rule for asynchronous perceptions with feedback in a combinatorial environment," *Proc. 1st ICNN, II*, pp. 609-618, 1987.
[65] M. Sato, "A learning algorithm to teach spatiotemporal patterns to recurrent neural networks," *Biol. Cybernetics*, vol. 62, pp. 259-263, 1990.
[66] B. A. Pearlmutter, "Learning state space trajectories in recurrent neural networks," *Neural Computation*, vol. 1, pp. 263-269, 1989.
[67] D. J. Willshaw and C. von der Malsburg, "How patterned neural connections can be set up by self-organization," *Proc. Roy. Soc.*, vol. B-194, pp. 431-445, 1976.
[68] E. Bienenstock, L. N. Cooper, and P. W. Munro, "A theory for the development of neuron selectivity: orientation specificity and binocular interaction in the visual cortex," *J. Neuroscience*, vol. 2, pp. 32-48, 1982.
[69] R. Linsker, "From basic network principles to neural architecture," *Proc. Nat. Acad. Sci. U.S.*, vol. 83, pp. 7508 7512; 8390-8394; 8779-8783, 1986.
[70] T. Kohonen, "Self-organized formation of topologically correct feature maps,"*Biol. Cybernetics*, vol. 43, pp. 59-69, 1982.
[71] ——, *Associative Memory and Self-Organization.* New York: Springer-Verlag, 1984.
[72] M. M. Merzenich, "Dynamic neocortical processes and the origins of higher brain functions," in *The Neural and Molecular Bases of Learning*, J.-P. Changeux and M. Konishi, eds., Dahlem Conference, 38. New York: Wiley, 1987.
[73] H. Ritter and K. Schulten, "Convergency properties of Kohonen's topology conserving maps: Fluctuations, stability and dimension selection," *Biol. Cybernetics*, vol. 60, pp. 59-71, 1988.
[74] M. A. Arbib and S. Amari, "Sensori-motor transformations in the brain (with a critique of the tensor theory of cerebellum)," *J. Theoret. Biol.*, vol. 112, pp. 123-155, Jan. 1985.

The Self-Organizing Map

TEUVO KOHONEN, SENIOR MEMBER, IEEE

Invited Paper

Among the architectures and algorithms suggested for artificial neural networks, the Self-Organizing Map has the special property of effectively creating spatially organized "internal representations" of various features of input signals and their abstractions. One novel result is that the self-organization process can also discover semantic relationships in sentences. In this respect the resulting maps very closely resemble the topographically organized maps found in the cortices of the more developed animal brains. After supervised fine tuning of its weight vectors, the Self-Organizing Map has been particularly successful in various pattern recognition tasks involving very noisy signals. In particular, these maps have been used in practical speech recognition, and work is in progress on their application to robotics, process control, telecommunications, etc. This paper contains a survey of several basic facts and results.

I. Introduction

A. On the Role of the Self-Organizing Map Among Neural Network Models

The network architectures and signal processes used to model nervous systems can roughly be divided into three categories, each based on a different philosophy. *Feedforward networks* [94] transform sets of input signals into sets of output signals. The desired input-output transformation is usually determined by external, supervised adjustment of the system parameters. In *feedback networks* [27], the input information defines the initial activity state of a feedback system, and after state transitions the asymptotic final state is identified as the outcome of the computation. In the third category, neighboring cells in a neural network compete in their activities by means of mutual lateral interactions, and develop adaptively into specific detectors of different signal patterns. In this category learning is called *competitive*, *unsupervised*, or *self-organizing*.

The Self-Organizing Map discussed in this paper belongs to the last category. It is a sheet-like artificial neural network, the cells of which become specifically tuned to various input signal patterns or classes of patterns through an unsupervised learning process. In the basic version, only one cell or local group of cells at a time gives the active response to the current input. The locations of the responses tend to become ordered as if some meaningful coordinate system for different input features were being created over the network. The spatial location or coordinates of a cell in the network then correspond to a particular domain of input signal patterns. Each cell or local cell group acts like a separate *decoder* for the same input. It is thus the presence or absence of an active response at that location, and not so much the exact input–output signal transformation or magnitude of the response, that provides an interpretation of the input information.

The Self-Organizing Map was intended as a viable alternative to more traditional neural network architectures. It is possible to ask just how "neural" the map is. Its analytical description has already been developed further in the technical than in the biological direction. But the learning results achieved seem very natural, at least indicating that the adaptive processes themselves at work in the map may be similar to those encountered in the brain. There may therefore be sufficient justification for calling these maps "neural networks" in the same sense as their traditional rivals.

Self-Organizing Maps, or systems consisting of several map modules, have been used for tasks similar to those to which other more traditional neural networks have been applied: pattern recognition, robotics, process control, and even processing of semantic information. The spatial segregation of different responses and their organization into topologically related subsets results in a high degree of efficiency in typical neural network operations.

Although the largest map we have used in practical applications has only contained about 1000 cells, its learning speed, especially when using computational shortcuts, can be increased to orders of magnitude greater than that of many other neural networks. Thus much larger maps than those used so far are quite feasible, although it also seems that practical applications favor hierarchical systems made up of many smaller maps.

It may be appropriate to observe here that if the maps are used for pattern recognition, their classification accuracy can be multiplied if the cells are fine-tuned using supervised learning principles (cf. Sec. III).

Although the Self-Organizing Map principle was introduced in early 1981, no complete review has appeared in compact form, except perhaps in [44], which does not contain the latest results. I have therefore tried to collect a variety of basic material in the present paper.

Manuscript received August 18, 1989; revised March 15, 1990.
The author is with the Department of Computer Science, Helsinki University of Technology, 02150 Espoo, and the Academy of Finland, 00550 Helsinki, Finland.
IEEE Log Number 9038826.

Reprinted from *Proc. IEEE*, vol. 78, no. 9, Sept. 1990, pp. 1464–1480.

B. Brain Maps

As much as a hundred years ago, a quite detailed topographical organization of the brain, and especially of the cerebral cortex, could be deduced from functional deficits and behavioral impairments induced by various kinds of lesion, or by hemorrhages, tumors, or malformations. Different regions in the brain thereby seemed to be dedicated to specific tasks. One modern systematic technique for causing controllable, reversible simulated lesions is to stimulate a particular site with small electric currents, thereby eventually inducing both excitatory and inhibitory effects and disturbing the assumed local function [75]. If such a spatially confined stimulus then disrupts a specific cognitive ability such as naming of objects, it gives at least some indication that this site is essential to that task.

One straightforward method for locating a response is to record the electric potential or train of neural impulses associated with it. Many detailed mappings, especially from the primary sensory and associative areas of the brain, have been made using various electrophysiological recording techniques.

Direct evidence for any localization of brain functions can also be obtained using modern imaging techniques that display the strength and spatial distribution of neural responses simultaneously over a large area, with a spatial resolution of a few millimeters. The two principal methods which use radioactive tracers are positron emission tomography (PET) [80] and autoradiography of the brain through very narrow collimators (gamma camera). PET reveals changes in oxygen uptake and phosphate metabolism. The gamma camera method directly detects changes in cerebral blood flow. Both phenomena correlate with local neural activity, but they are unable to monitor rapid phenomena. In magnetoencephalography (MEG), the low magnetic field caused by electrical neural responses is detected, and by computing its sources, quite rapid neural responses can be directly analyzed, with a spatial resolution of a few millimeters. The main drawback of MEG is that only current dipoles parallel to the surface of the skull are detectable; and since the dipoles are oriented perpendicular to the cortex, only the sulci can be studied with this method. A review of experimental techniques and results relating to these studies can be found in [32].

After a large number of such observations, a fairly detailed organizational view of the brain has evolved [32]. Especially in higher animals, the various cortices in the cell mass seem to contain many kinds of "map" [33], such that a particular location of the neural response in the map often directly corresponds to a specific modality and quality of sensory signal. The field of vision is mapped "quasiconformally" onto the primary visual cortex. Some of the maps, especially those in the primary sensory areas, are ordered according to some feature dimensions of the sensory signals; for instance, in the visual areas, there are line orientation and color maps [11], [116], and in the auditory cortex there are the so-called tonotopic maps [91], [103], [104], which represent pitches of tones in terms of the cortical distance, or other auditory maps [98]. One of the sensory maps is the somatotopic map [29], [30] which contains a representation of the body, i.e., the skin surface. Adjacent to it is a motor map [70] that is topographically almost identically organized. Its cells mediate voluntary control actions on muscles. Similar maps exist in other parts of the brain [97]. On the higher levels the maps are usually unordered, or at most the order is a kind of ultrametric topological order that is not easily interpretable. There are also singular cells that respond to rather complex patterns, such as the human face [9], [93].

Some maps represent quite abstract qualities of sensory and other experiences. For instance, in the word-processing areas, neural responses seem to be organized according to categories and semantic values of words ([6], [15], [65], [67], [106–109], and [114]; cf. also Sec. V).

It thus seems as if the *internal representations* of information in the brain are generally organized *spatially*. Although there is only partial biological evidence for this, enough data are already available to justify further theoretical studies of this principle. Artificial self-organizing maps and brain maps thus have many features in common, and what is even more intriguing, we now fully understand the processes by which such artificial maps can be formed adaptively and completely automatically.

C. Early Work on Competitive Learning

The basic idea underlying what is called competitive learning is roughly as follows: Assume a sequence of statistical samples of a vectorial observable $\boldsymbol{x} = \boldsymbol{x}(t) \in \mathbb{R}^n$, where t is the time coordinate, and a set of variable reference vectors $\{\boldsymbol{m}_i(t): \boldsymbol{m}_i \in \mathbb{R}^n, i = 1, 2, \cdots, k\}$. Assume that the $\boldsymbol{m}_i(0)$ have been initialized in some proper way; random selection will often suffice. If $\boldsymbol{x}(t)$ can somehow be simultaneously compared with each $\boldsymbol{m}_i(t)$ at each successive instant of time, taken here to be an integer $t = 1, 2, 3, \cdots$, then the best-matching $\boldsymbol{m}_i(t)$ is to be updated to match even more closely the current $\boldsymbol{x}(t)$. If the comparison is based on some distance measure $d(\boldsymbol{x}, \boldsymbol{m}_i)$, altering $\boldsymbol{m}_i$ must be such that, if $i = c$ is the index of the best-matching reference vector, then $d(\boldsymbol{x}, \boldsymbol{m}_c)$ is decreased, and all the other reference vectors $\boldsymbol{m}_i$, with $i \neq c$, are left intact. In this way the different reference vectors tend to become specifically "tuned" to different domains of the input variable $\boldsymbol{x}$. It will be shown below that if p is the probability density function of the samples $\boldsymbol{x}$, then the $\boldsymbol{m}_i$ tend to be located in the input space $\mathbb{R}^n$ in such a way that they approximate to p in the sense of some minimal residual error.

Vector Quantization (*VQ*) (cf., e.g., [19], [54], [58]) is a classical method, that produces an approximation to a continuous probability density function $p(\boldsymbol{x})$ of the vectorial input variable $\boldsymbol{x}$ using a finite number of codebook vectors $\boldsymbol{m}_i$, $i = 1, 2, \cdots, k$. Once the "codebook" is chosen, the approximation of $\boldsymbol{x}$ involves finding the reference vector $\boldsymbol{m}_c$ closest to $\boldsymbol{x}$. One kind of optimal placement of the $\boldsymbol{m}_i$ minimizes E, the expected rth power of the reconstruction error:

$$E = \int \|\boldsymbol{x} - \boldsymbol{m}_c\|^r p(\boldsymbol{x})\, d\boldsymbol{x} \tag{1}$$

where $d\boldsymbol{x}$ is the volume differential in the $\boldsymbol{x}$ space, and the index $c = c(\boldsymbol{x})$ of the best-matching codebook vector ("winner") is a function of the input vector $\boldsymbol{x}$:

$$\|\boldsymbol{x} - \boldsymbol{m}_c\| = \min_i \{\|\boldsymbol{x} - \boldsymbol{m}_i\|\}. \tag{2}$$

In general, no closed-form solution for the optimal placement of the $\boldsymbol{m}_i$ is possible, and iterative approximation schemes must be used.

It has been pointed out in [14], [64], and [115] that (1)

defines a placement of the codebook vectors into the signal space such that their point density function is an approximation to $[p(\mathbf{x})]^{n/(n+r)}$, where n is the dimensionality of $\mathbf{x}$ and $\mathbf{m}_i$. We usually consider the case $r = 2$. In most practical applications $n \gg r$, and then the optimal VQ can be shown to approximate $p(\mathbf{x})$.

Using the square-error criterion ($r = 2$), it can also be shown that the following stepwise "delta rule," in the discrete-time formalism ($t = 0, 1, 2, \cdots$), defines the optimal values asymptotically. Let $\mathbf{m}_c = \mathbf{m}_c(t)$ be the closest codebook vector to $\mathbf{x} = \mathbf{x}(t)$ in the Euclidean metric. The steepest-descent gradient-step optimization of E in the $\mathbf{m}_c$ space yields the sequence

$$\mathbf{m}_c(t+1) = \mathbf{m}_c(t) + \alpha(t)\,[\mathbf{x}(t) - \mathbf{m}_c(t)],$$

$$\mathbf{m}_i(t+1) = \mathbf{m}_i(t) \qquad \text{for } i \neq c \tag{3}$$

with $\alpha(t)$ being a suitable, monotonically decreasing sequence of scalar-valued gain coefficients, $0 < \alpha(t) < 1$. This is then the simplest analytical description of competitive learning.

In general, if we express the dissimilarity of $\mathbf{x}$ and $\mathbf{m}_i$ in terms of a general distance function $d(\mathbf{x}, \mathbf{m}_i)$, we have first to identify the "winner" $\mathbf{m}_c$ such that

$$d(\mathbf{x}, \mathbf{m}_c) = \min_i \{d(\mathbf{x}, \mathbf{m}_i)\}. \tag{4}$$

After that an updating rule should be used such that d decreases monotonically: the correction $\delta\mathbf{m}_i$ of $\mathbf{m}_i$ must be such that

$$[\text{grad}_{\mathbf{m}_i}\, d(\mathbf{x}, \mathbf{m}_i)]^T \cdot \delta\mathbf{m}_i < 0. \tag{5}$$

If (1) is used for signal approximation, it often turns out to be more economical to first observe a number of training samples $\mathbf{x}(t)$, which are "classified" (labeled) on the basis of (2) according to the closest codebook vectors $\mathbf{m}_i$, and then to perform the updating operation in a single step. For the new codebook vector $\mathbf{m}_i$, the average is taken of those $\mathbf{x}(t)$ that were identified with codebook vector i. This algorithm, termed the *k-means algorithm* is widely used in digital telecommunications engineering [58].

The $\mathbf{m}_i(t)$, in the above processes, actually develop into a set of *feature-sensitive detectors*. Feature-sensitive cells are also known to be common in the brain. Neural modelers like Nass and Cooper [72], Pérez *et al.* [79], and Grossberg [21] have been able to suggest how such feature-sensitive cells can emerge from simplified membrane equations of model neurons.

In the above process and its biophysical counterparts, all the cells act independently. Therefore the *order* in which they are assigned to the different domains of input signals is more or less haphazard, most strongly depending on the initial values of the $\mathbf{m}_i(0)$. In fact, in 1973, v.d. Malsburg [59] had already published a computer simulation in which he demonstrated *local* ordering of feature-sensitive cells, such that in small subsets of cells roughly corresponding to the so-called columns of the cortex, the cells were tuned more closely than were more remote cells. Later, Amari [1] formulated and analyzed the corresponding system of differential equations, relating them to spatially continuous two-dimensional media. Such continuous layers interacted in the lateral direction; the arrangement was called a *nerve field*. The above studies are of great theoretical importance because they involve a self-organizing tendency. The ordering power they demonstrated was, however, still weak as nerve-field type equations only describe this tendency as a marginal effect. In spite of numerous attempts, no "maps" of practical importance could be produced; ordering was either restricted to a one-dimensional case, or confined to small parcelled areas of the network [60], [77], [78], [99], [100], [110], [111].

Indeed it later transpired that system equations have to involve much stronger, idealized self-organizing effects, and that the organizing effect has to be maximized in every possible way before useful global maps can be created. The present author, in early 1981, was experimenting with various architectures and system equations, and found a process description [34]–[36] that seemed generally to produce globally well-organized maps. Because all the other system models known at that time only yielded results that were significantly more "brittle" with respect to the selection of parameters and to success in achieving the desired results, we may skip them here and concentrate on the computationally optimized algorithm known as the *Self-Organizing Map* algorithm.

II. An Algorithm that Orders Responses Spatially

Readers who are not yet familiar with the Self-Organizing Maps may benefit from a quick look at Figs. 5 and 6 or Fig. 9 to find out what spatial ordering of output responses means.

The Self-Organizing Map algorithm that I shall now describe has evolved during a long series of computer experiments. The background to this research has been expounded in [44]. While the purpose of each detail of the final equations may be clear in concrete simulations, it has proved extremely difficult, in spite of numerous attempts, to express the dynamic properties of this process in mathematical theorems. Strict mathematical analysis only exists for simplified cases. And even they are too lengthy to be reviewed here: cf. [7], [8], [24], [57], [83], [86], [89], [90]. It is therefore hoped that the simulation experiments and practical applications reported below in Secs. II-C, II-E, IV, V, and VI will suffice to convince the reader about the utility of this algorithm.

It may also be necessary to emphasize again that for practical purposes we are trying to extract or explain the self-organizing function in its purest, most effective form, whereas in genuine biological networks this tendency may be more or less disguised by other functions. It may thus be conceivable, as has been verified by numerous simulation experiments, that the two essential effects leading to spatially organized maps are: 1) *spatial concentration* of the network activity on the cell (or its neighborhood) that is *best tuned* to the present input, and 2) further *sensitization or tuning* of the best-matching cell *and its topological neighbors* to the present input.

A. Selection of the Best-Matching Cell

Consider the two-dimensional network of cells depicted in Fig. 1. Their arrangement can be hexagonal, rectangular, etc. Let (in matrix notation) $\mathbf{x} = [x_1, x_2, \cdots, x_n]^T \in \mathbb{R}^n$ be the *input vector* that, for simplicity and computational efficiency, is assumed to be connected in parallel to all the neurons i in this network. (We have also shown that subsets of the same input signals can be connected at random to the

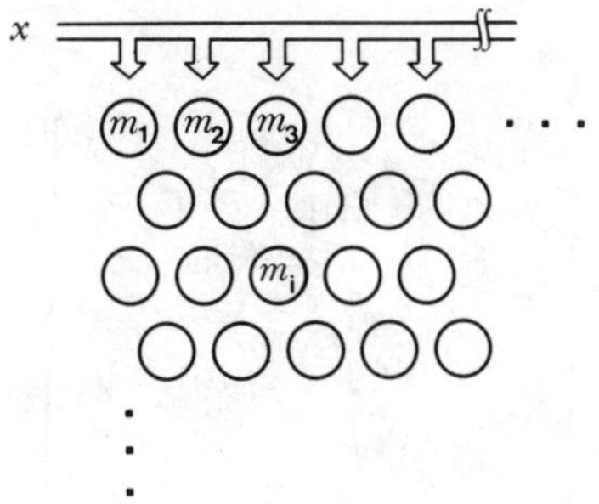

Fig. 1. Cell arrangement for the map and definition of variables.

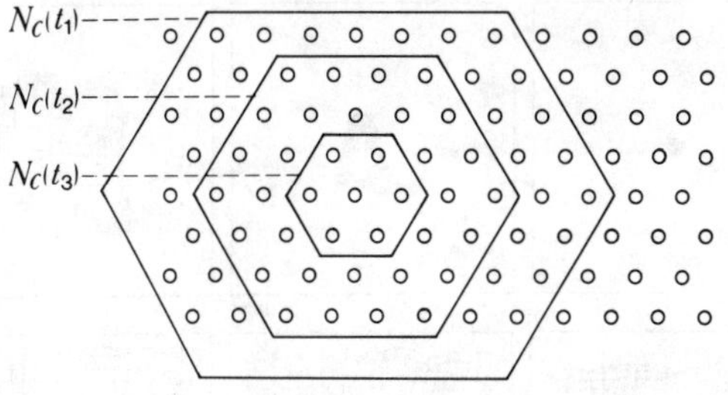

Fig. 2. Examples of topological neighborhood $N_c(t)$, where $t_1 < t_2 < t_3$.

cells; cf. the "tonotopic map" discussed in [35] and [44]. Experiments are in progress in which the input connections to the cells can be made in a cascade.) The *weight vector* of cell i shall henceforth be denoted by $\boldsymbol{m}_i = [\boldsymbol{m}_{i1}, \boldsymbol{m}_{i2}, \cdots, \boldsymbol{m}_{in}]^T \in \mathbb{R}^n$.

The simplest analytical measure for the match of $\boldsymbol{x}$ with the $\boldsymbol{m}_i$ may be the inner product $\boldsymbol{x}^T\boldsymbol{m}_i$. If, however, the self-organizing algorithm is to be used for, say, natural signal patterns relating to metric vector spaces, a better and more convenient (cf. the adaptation law below) matching criterion may be used, based on the *Euclidean distances* between $\boldsymbol{x}$ and $\boldsymbol{m}_i$. The minimum distance defines the "winner" $\boldsymbol{m}_c$ (cf. (2)). A shortcut algorithm to find $\boldsymbol{m}_c$ has been presented in [49].

Comment. Definition of the input vector, $\boldsymbol{x}$, as an ordered set of signal values is only possible if the interrelation between the signals is simple. In many practical problems, such as image analysis (cf. Discussion, Sec. VII) it will generally be necessary to use some kind of preprocessing to extract a set of invariant features for the components of $\boldsymbol{x}$.

B. Adaptation (Updating) of the Weight Vectors

It is crucial to the formation of ordered maps that the cells doing the learning are not affected independently of each other (cf. competitive learning in Sec. I-C), but as *topologically related subsets*, on each of which a similar kind of correction is imposed. During the process, such selected subsets will then encompass different cells. The net corrections at each cell will thus tend to be smoothed out in the long run. An even more intriguing result from this sort of spatially correlated learning is that *the weight vectors tend to attain values that are ordered along the axes of the network.*

In biophysically inspired neural network models, correlated learning by spatially neighboring cells can be implemented using various kinds of lateral feedback connection and other lateral interactions. In the present process we want to enforce lateral interaction directly in a general form, for arbitrary underlying network structures, by defining a *neighborhood set* N_c around cell c. At each learning step, all the cells within N_c are updated, whereas cells outside N_c are left intact. This neighborhood is centered around that cell for which the best match with input $\boldsymbol{x}$ is found:

$$\|\boldsymbol{x} - \boldsymbol{m}_c\| = \min_i \{\|\boldsymbol{x} - \boldsymbol{m}_i\|\}. \qquad (2')$$

The width or radius of N_c can be time-variable; in fact, for good global ordering, it has experimentally turned out to be advantageous to let N_c be very wide in the beginning and shrink monotonically with time (Fig. 2). The explanation for this may be that a wide initial N_c, corresponding to a coarse spatial resolution in the learning process, first induces a rough global order in the $\boldsymbol{m}_i$ values, after which narrowing the N_c improves the spatial resolution of the map; the acquired global order, however, is not destroyed later on. It is even possible to end the process with $N_c = \{c\}$, that is, finally updating the best-matching unit ("winner") only, in which case the process is reduced to simple competitive learning. Before this, however, the "topological order" of the map would have to be formed.

The updating process (in discrete-time notation) may read

$$\boldsymbol{m}_i(t+1) = \begin{cases} \boldsymbol{m}_i(t) + \alpha(t)[\boldsymbol{x}(t) - \boldsymbol{m}_i(t)] & \text{if } i \in N_c(t), \\ \boldsymbol{m}_i(t) & \text{if } i \notin N_c(t), \end{cases} \qquad (6)$$

where $\alpha(t)$ is a scalar-valued "adaptation gain" $0 < \alpha(t) < 1$. It is related to a similar gain used in the stochastic approximation processes [49], [92], and as in these methods, $\alpha(t)$ should decrease with time.

An alternative notation is to introduce a scalar "kernel" function $h_{ci} = h_{ci}(t)$,

$$\boldsymbol{m}_i(t+1) = \boldsymbol{m}_i(t) + h_{ci}(t)[\boldsymbol{x}(t) - \boldsymbol{m}_i(t)] \qquad (7)$$

whereby, above, $h_{ci}(t) = \alpha(t)$ within N_c, and $h_{ci}(t) = 0$ outside N_c. On the other hand, the definition of h_{ci} can also be more general; a biological lateral interaction often has the shape of a "bell curve". Denoting the coordinates of cells c and i by the vectors $\boldsymbol{r}_c$ and $\boldsymbol{r}_i$, respectively, a proper form for h_{ci} might be

$$h_{ci} = h_0 \exp(-\|\boldsymbol{r}_i - \boldsymbol{r}_c\|^2/\sigma^2), \qquad (8)$$

with $h_0 = h_0(t)$ and $\sigma = \sigma(t)$ as suitable decreasing functions of time.

C. Demonstrations of the Ordering Process

The first computer simulations presented here are intended to illustrate the effect that the weight vectors tend to approximate to the density function of the input vectors in an orderly fashion. In these examples, the input vectors were chosen to be two-dimensional for visual display purposes, and their probability density function was arbitrarily selected to be uniform over the area demarcated by the borderlines (square or triangle). Outside the frame the density was zero. The vectors $\boldsymbol{x}(t)$ were drawn from this density function independently and at random, after which they caused adaptive changes in the weight vectors $\boldsymbol{m}_i$.

The $\boldsymbol{m}_i$ vectors appear as points in the same coordinate system as that in which the $\boldsymbol{x}(t)$ are represented; in order to indicate to which unit each $\boldsymbol{m}_i$ value belongs, the points

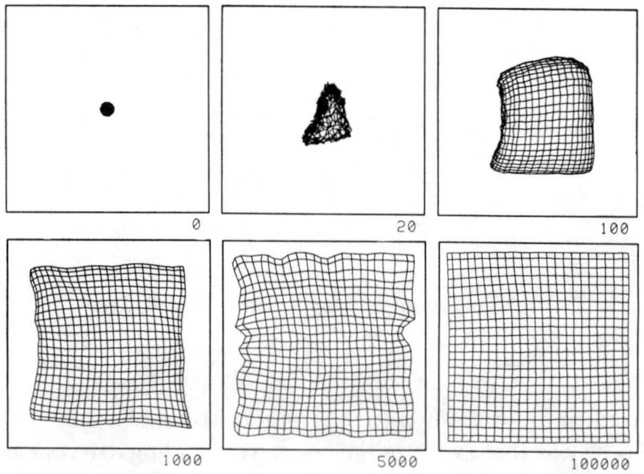

Fig. 3. Weight vectors during the ordering process, two-dimensional array.

corresponding to the $\boldsymbol{m}_i$ vectors have been connected by a lattice of lines conforming to the topology of the processing unit array. In other words, a line connecting two weight vectors $\boldsymbol{m}_i$ and $\boldsymbol{m}_j$ is only used to indicate that the corresponding units *i* and *j* are adjacent in the array. In Fig. 3 the arrangement of the cells is rectangular (square), whereas in Fig. 4 the cells are interconnected in a linear chain.

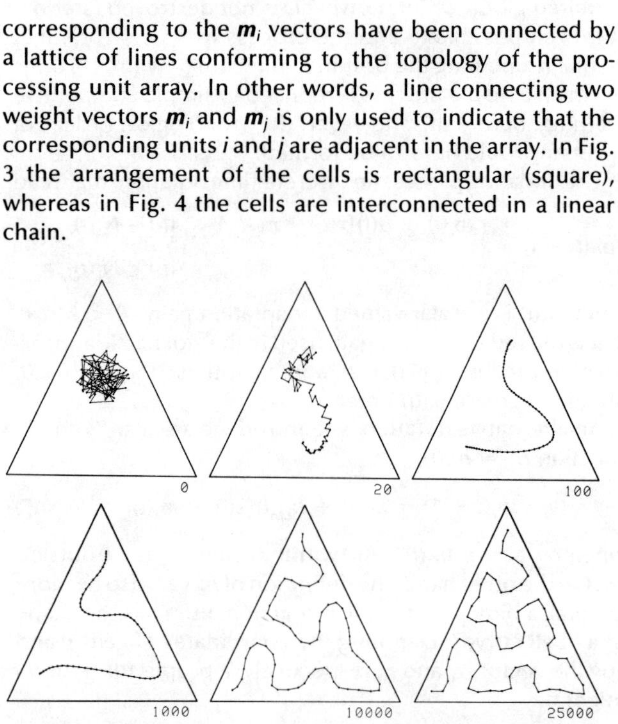

Fig. 4. Weight vectors during the ordering process, one-dimensional array.

Examples of intermediate phases during the self-organizing process are given in Figs. 3 and 4. The initial values $\boldsymbol{m}_i(0)$ were selected at random from a certain domain of values.

As stated above, in Fig. 3 the array was two-dimensional. The results, however, are particularly interesting if the distribution and the array have different dimensionalities: Fig. 4 illustrates a case in which the distribution of $\boldsymbol{x}$ is two-dimensional, but the array is one-dimensional (linear row of cells). The weight vectors of linear arrays tend to approximate to higher-dimensional distributions by Peano curves. A two-dimensional network representing three-dimensional "bodies" (uniform-density function) is shown in Fig. 5.

In practical applications, the input and output weight vectors are usually high-dimensional; e.g., in speech recognition, the dimensionality *n* may be 15 to 100.

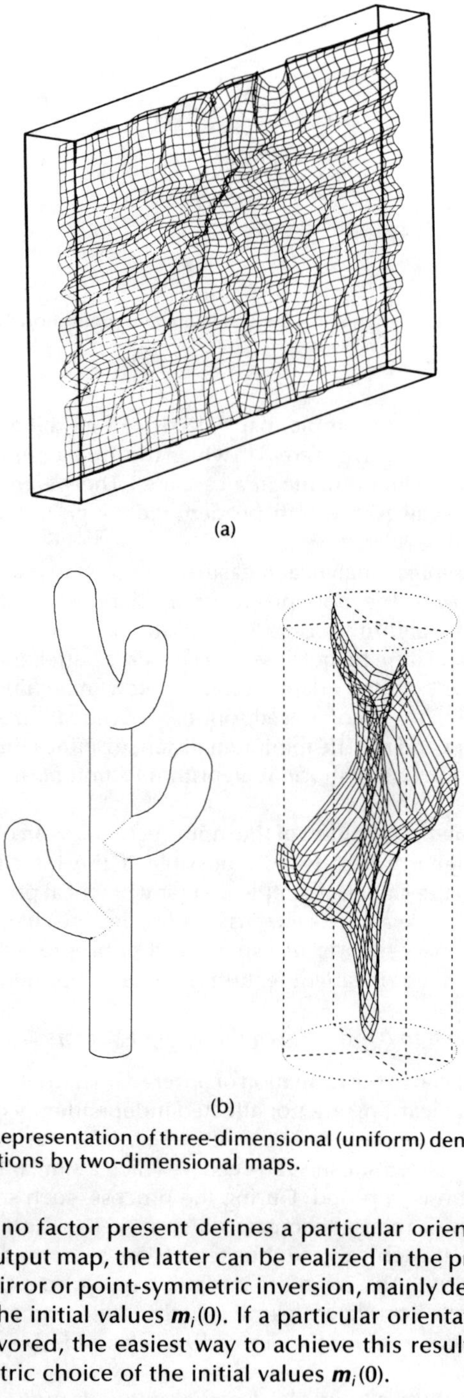

Fig. 5. Representation of three-dimensional (uniform) density functions by two-dimensional maps.

Since no factor present defines a particular orientation in the output map, the latter can be realized in the process in any mirror or point-symmetric inversion, mainly depending on the initial values $\boldsymbol{m}_i(0)$. If a particular orientation is to be favored, the easiest way to achieve this result is by asymmetric choice of the initial values $\boldsymbol{m}_i(0)$.

D. Some Practical Hints for the Application of the Algorithm

When applying the map algorithm, (2) or (2′) and (6) alternate. Input $\boldsymbol{x}$ is usually a random variable with a density function $p(\boldsymbol{x})$, from which the successive values $\boldsymbol{x}(t)$ are drawn. In real-world observations, such as speech recognition, the $\boldsymbol{x}(t)$ can simply be successive samples of the input observables in their natural order of occurrence.

The process may be started by choosing arbitrary, even random, initial values for the $\boldsymbol{m}_i(0)$, the only restriction being that they should be different.

We shall give numerical examples of efficient process parameters with the simulation examples. It may also be helpful to emphasize the following general conditions.

1) Since learning is a stochastic process, the final statistical accuracy of the mapping depends on the number of steps, which must be reasonably large; there is no way to circumvent this requirement. A "rule of thumb" is that, for good statistical accuracy, the number of steps must be at least 500 times the number of network units. On the other hand, the number of components in $\boldsymbol{x}$ has no effect on the number of iteration steps, and if hardware neural computers are used, a very high dimensionality of input is allowed. Typically we have used up to 100 000 steps in our simulations, but for "fast learning," e.g., in speech recognition, 10 000 steps and even less may sometimes be enough. Note that the algorithm is computationally extremely light. If only a small number of samples are available, they must be recycled for the desired number of steps.

2) For approximately the first 1000 steps, $\alpha(t)$ should start with a value that is close to unity, thereafter decreasing monotonically. An accurate rule is not important: $\alpha = \alpha(t)$ can be linear, exponential, or inversely proportional to t. For instance, $\alpha(t) = 0.9(1 - t/1000)$ may be a reasonable choice. The *ordering* of the $\boldsymbol{m}_i$ occurs during this initial period, while the remaining steps are only needed for the fine adjustment of the map. After the ordering phase, $\alpha = \alpha(t)$ should attain small values (e.g., of the order of or less than .01) over a long period. Neither is it crucial whether the law for $\alpha(t)$ decreases linearly or exponentially during the final phase.

3) Special caution is required in the choice of $N_c = N_c(t)$. If the neighborhood is too small to start with, the map will not be ordered globally. Instead various kinds of mosaic-like parcellations of the map are seen, between which the ordering direction changes discontinuously. This phenomenon can be avoided by starting with a fairly wide $N_c = N_c(0)$ and letting it shrink with time. The initial radius of N_c can even be more than half the diameter of the network! During the first 1000 steps or so, when the proper ordering takes place, and $\alpha = \alpha(t)$ is fairly large, the radius of N_c can shrink linearly to, say, one unit; during the fine-adjustment phase, N_c can still contain the nearest neighbors of cell c.

Parallel implementations of the algorithm have been discussed in [25] and [61].

E. Example: Taxonomy (Hierarchical Clustering) of Abstract Data

Although the more practical applications of the Self-Organizing Maps are available, for example, in pattern recognition and robotics, it may be interesting to apply this principle first to abstract data vectors consisting of hypothetical *attributes* or *characteristics*. We will look at an example with implicitly defined (*hierarchical*) structures in the primary data, which the map algorithm is then able to reveal. Although this system is a single-level network, it can produce a hierarchical representation of the relations between the primary data.

The central result in self-organization is that if the input signals have a well-defined probability density function, then the weight vectors of the cells try to imitate it, however complex its form. It is even possible to perform a kind of numerical taxonomy on this model. Because there are no restrictions on the semantic content of the input signals, they can be regarded as arbitrary attributes, with discrete or continuous values. In Table 1, 32 items, each with five hypothetical attributes, are recorded in a data matrix. (This example is completely artificial.) Each of the columns represents one item, and for later inspection the items are labeled "A" through "6", although these labels were not referred to during the learning.

The attribute values $(a_1, a_2, \cdots, a_5)$ constitute the pattern vector $\boldsymbol{x}$ which acts as a set of signal values at the inputs to the network of the type shown in Fig. 1. During training, the vectors $\boldsymbol{x}$ were selected from Table 1 at random. Sampling and adaptation were continued iteratively until the asymptotic state could be considered stationary. Such a "learned" network was then calibrated using the items from Table 1 and labeling the best-matching map cells according to the different calibration items. Such a labeled map is shown in Fig. 6. It can be seen that the "images" of different items are related according to a taxonomic graph where the different branches are visible. For comparison, Fig. 7 illustrates

B	C	D	E	*	Q	R	*	Y	Z
A	*	*	*	*	P	*	*	X	*
*	F	*	N	O	*	W	*	*	1
*	G	*	M	*	*	*	*	2	*
H	K	L	*	T	U	*	3	*	*
*	I	*	*	*	*	*	*	4	*
*	J	*	S	*	*	V	*	5	6

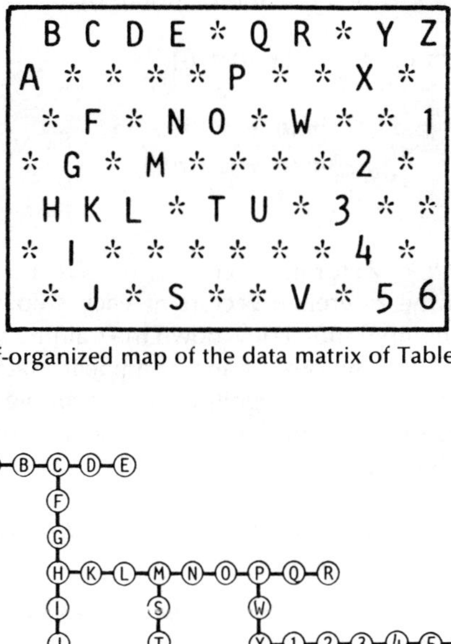

Fig. 6. Self-organized map of the data matrix of Table 1.

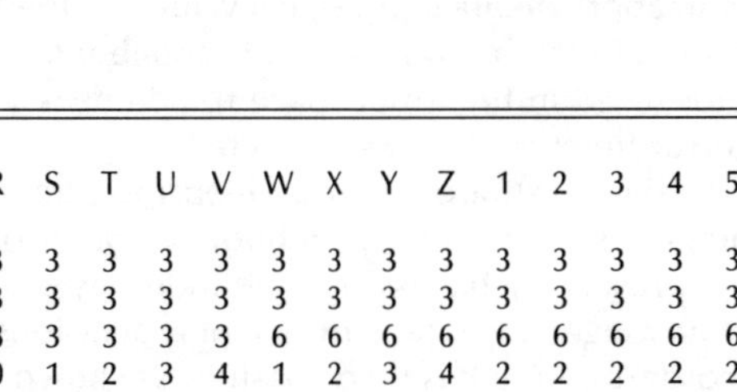

Fig. 7. Minimal spanning tree corresponding to Table 1.

Table 1 Input Data Matrix

Attribute \ Item	A	B	C	D	E	F	G	H	I	J	K	L	M	N	O	P
a_1	1	2	3	4	5	3	3	3	3	3	3	3	3	3	3	3
a_2	0	0	0	0	0	1	2	3	4	5	3	3	3	3	3	3
a_3	0	0	0	0	0	0	0	0	0	0	1	2	3	4	5	6
a_4	0	0	0	0	0	0	0	0	0	0	0	0	0	0	0	0
a_5	0	0	0	0	0	0	0	0	0	0	0	0	0	0	0	0

Attribute \ Item	Q	R	S	T	U	V	W	X	Y	Z	1	2	3	4	5	6
a_1	3	3	3	3	3	3	3	3	3	3	3	3	3	3	3	3
a_2	3	3	3	3	3	3	3	3	3	3	3	3	3	3	3	3
a_3	7	8	3	3	3	3	6	6	6	6	6	6	6	6	6	6
a_4	0	0	1	2	3	4	1	2	3	4	2	2	2	2	2	2
a_5	0	0	0	0	0	0	0	0	0	0	1	2	3	4	5	6

trates the minimal spanning tree (where the most closely similar pairs of items are linked) describing the similarity relations of the items in Table 1. The system parameters in this process were:

$\alpha = \alpha(t)$: During the first 1000 steps, α decreased linearly with time from .5 to .04 (the initial value could have been closer to unity, say, .9). During the subsequent 10 000 steps, α decreased from .04 to zero linearly with time.

$N_c = N_c(t)$: The lattice was hexagonal, 7 by 10 units, and during the first 1000 steps, the *radius* of N_c decreased from the value six (encompassing the majority of cells in the network) to one (encompassing neuron c and its six neighbors) linearly with time, thereafter keeping the value one.

F. Another Variant of the Algorithm

One further remark may be necessary. It has sometimes been suggested that $\mathbf{x}$ be normalized before it is used in the algorithm. Normalization is not necessary in principle, but it may improve numerical accuracy because the resulting reference vectors then tend to have the same dynamic range.

Another aspect, as mentioned above, is that it is also possible to apply a general distance measure in the matching; then, however, the matching and updating laws should be mutually compatible with respect to the same metric. For instance, if the inner-product measure of similarity were applied, the learning equations should read:

$$\mathbf{x}^T(t)\mathbf{m}_c(t) = \max_i \{\mathbf{x}^T(t)\mathbf{m}_i(t)\}, \tag{9}$$

$$\mathbf{m}_i(t+1) = \begin{cases} \dfrac{\mathbf{m}_i(t) + \alpha'(t)\mathbf{x}(t)}{\|\mathbf{m}_i(t) + \alpha'(t)\mathbf{x}(t)\|} & \text{if } i \in N_c(t), \\ \mathbf{m}_i(t) & \text{if } i \notin N_c(t), \end{cases} \tag{10}$$

and $0 < \alpha'(t) < \infty$; for instance, $\alpha'(t) = 100/t$. This process normalizes the reference vectors at each step. The normalization computations slow down the training algorithm significantly. On the other hand, the linear matching criterion applied during recognition is very simple and fast, and amenable to many kinds of simple analog computation, both electronic and optical.

III. Fine Tuning of the Map by Learning Vector Quantization (LVQ) Methods

If the Self-Organizing Map is to be used as a *pattern classifier* in which the cells or their responses are grouped into subsets, each of which corresponds to a discrete class of patterns, then the problem becomes a decision process and must be handled differently. The original Map, like any classical Vector Quantization (VQ) method (cf. Sec. I-D) is mainly intended to approximate input signal values, or their probability density function, by quantized "codebook" vectors that are localized in the input space to minimize a quantization error functional (cf. Sec. III-A below). On the other hand, if the signal sets are to be *classified* into a finite number of categories, then several codebook vectors are usually made to represent each class, and their identity *within* the classes is no longer important. In fact, only decisions made at class borders count. It is then possible, as shown below, to define *effective* values for the codebook vectors such that they directly define *near-optimal decision borders* between the classes, even in the sense of classical Bayesian decision theory. These strategies and learning algorithms were introduced by the present author [38], [43], [45] and called *Learning Vector Quantization (LVQ)*.

A. Type One Learning Vector Quantization (LVQ1)

If several codebook vectors $\mathbf{m}_i$ are assigned to each class, and each of them is labeled with the corresponding class symbol, the class regions in the $\mathbf{x}$ space are defined by simple nearest-neighbor comparison of $\mathbf{x}$ with the $\mathbf{m}_i$; the label of the closest $\mathbf{m}_i$ defines the classification of $\mathbf{x}$.

To define the optimal placement of $\mathbf{m}_i$ in an iterative learning process, initial values for them must first be set using any classical VQ method or by the Self-Organizing Map algorithm. The initial values in both cases roughly correspond to the overall statistical density function $p(\mathbf{x})$ of the input. The next phase is to determine the labels of the codebook vectors, by presenting a number of input vectors with known classification, and assigning the cells to different classes by majority voting, according to the frequency with which each $\mathbf{m}_i$ is closest to the calibration vectors of a particular class.

The classification accuracy is improved if the $\mathbf{m}_i$ are updated according to the following algorithm [41], [43]–[45]. The idea is to pull codebook vectors away from the decision surfaces to demarcate the class borders more accurately. Let $\mathbf{m}_c$ be the codebook vector closest to $\mathbf{x}$ in the Euclidean metric (cf. (2), (2')); this then also defines the classification of $\mathbf{x}$. Apply training vectors $\mathbf{x}$ the classification of which is known. Update the $\mathbf{m}_i = \mathbf{m}_i(t)$ as follows:

$$\begin{aligned} \mathbf{m}_c(t+1) &= \mathbf{m}_c(t) + \alpha(t)[\mathbf{x}(t) - \mathbf{m}_c(t)] \\ &\qquad \text{if } x \text{ is classified correctly,} \\ \mathbf{m}_c(t+1) &= \mathbf{m}_c(t) - \alpha(t)[\mathbf{x}(t) - \mathbf{m}_c(t)] \\ &\qquad \text{if the classification of } x \text{ is incorrect,} \\ \mathbf{m}_i(t+1) &= \mathbf{m}_i(t) \text{ for } i \neq c. \end{aligned} \tag{11}$$

Here $\alpha(t)$ is a scalar gain ($0 < \alpha(t) < 1$), which is decreasing monotonically in time, as in earlier formulas. Since this is a fine-tuning method, one should start with a fairly small value, say $\alpha(0) = 0.01$ or 0.02 and let it decrease to zero, say, in 100 000 steps.

This algorithm tends to reduce the point density of the $\mathbf{m}_i$ around the Bayesian decision surfaces. This can be deduced as follows. The minus sign in the second equation may be interpreted as *defining corrections in the same direction as if (10) were used for the class to which $\mathbf{m}_c$ belongs, but with the probability density function of the neighboring (overlapping) class subtracted from that of $\mathbf{m}_c$.* In other words, we would perform a classical Vector Quantization of the function $|p(\mathbf{x}|C_i)P(C_i) - p(\mathbf{x}|C_j)P(C_j)|$ where C_i and C_j are the neighboring classes, $p(\mathbf{x}|C_i)$ is the conditional probability density function of samples $\mathbf{x}$ belonging to class C_i, and $P(C_i)$ is the *a priori* probability of occurrences of the class C_i samples. The difference between the density functions of the neighboring classes, by definition, drops to zero at the Bayes border, inducing the above "depletion layer" of the codebook vectors.

After training, the $\mathbf{m}_i$ will have acquired values such that classification using the "nearest neighbor" principle, by

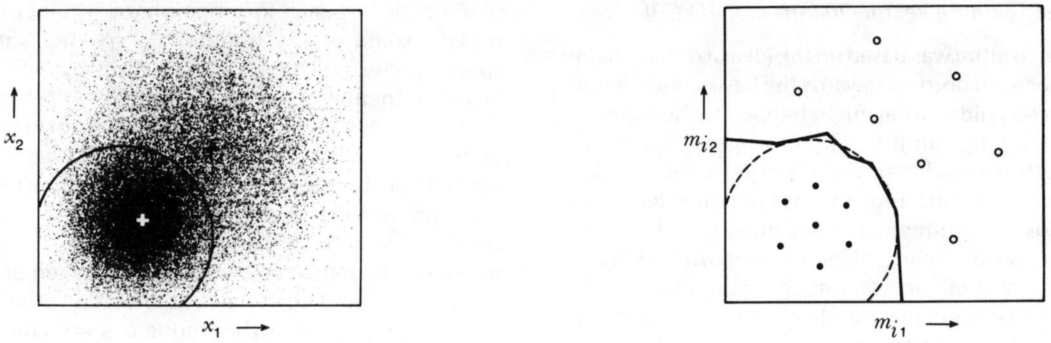

(a) (b)

Fig. 8. (a) An illustrative example in which x is two-dimensional and the probability density functions of the classes substantially overlap. (a) The probability density function of $x = [x_1, x_2]^T$ is represented here by its samples, the small dots. The superposition of two symmetric Gaussian density functions corresponding to two different classes C_1 and C_2, with their centroids shown by the white and the dark cross, respectively, is shown. Solid curve: the theoretically optimal Bayes decision surface. (b) Large black dots: reference vectors of class C_1. Open circles: reference vectors of class C_2. Solid curve: decision surface in the Learning Vector Quantization. Broken curve: Bayes decision surface.

comparing of $\boldsymbol{x}$ with the $\boldsymbol{m}_i$, already rather closely coincides with that of the Bayes classifier. Figure 8 represents an illustrative example in which x is two-dimensional, and the probability density functions of the classes substantially overlap. The decision surface defined by this classifier seems to be near-optimal, although piecewise linear, and the classification accuracy in this rather difficult example is within a fraction of a percent of that achieved with the Bayes classifier. For practical applications of the LVQ1, cf. [12], [76]. A rigorous mathematical discussion of the LVQ1, and suggestions to improve its stability, have been represented in [51].

B. Type Two Learning Vector Quantization (LVQ2)

The previous algorithm can easily be modified to comply even better with Bayes' decisionmaking philosophy [43]–[45]. Assume that two codebook vectors $\boldsymbol{m}_i$ and $\boldsymbol{m}_j$ that belong to different classes and are closest neighbors in the vector space are initially in a wrong position. The (incorrect) discrimination surface, however, is always defined as the midplane of $\boldsymbol{m}_i$ and $\boldsymbol{m}_j$. Let us define a symmetric *window* of nonzero width around the midplane, and stipulate that *corrections to* $\boldsymbol{m}_i$ *and* $\boldsymbol{m}_j$ *shall only be made if* $\boldsymbol{x}$ *falls into the window on the wrong side of the midplane* (cf. Fig. 9).

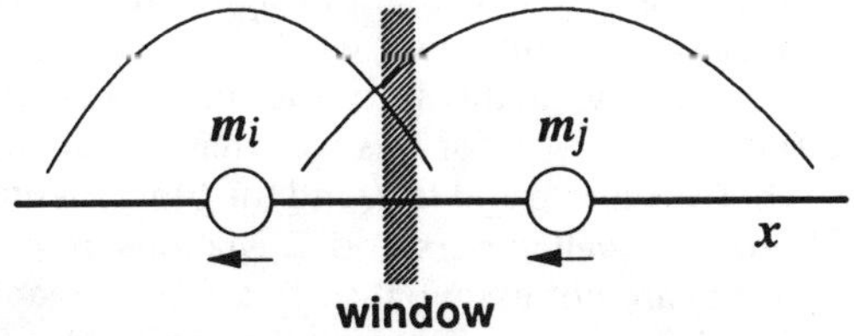

Fig. 9. Illustration of the "window" used in the LVQ2 and LVQ3 algorithms. The curves represent class distributions of x samples.

If the corrections are made according to (12), it is easy to see that for vectors falling into the window, the corrections of both $\boldsymbol{m}_i$ and $\boldsymbol{m}_j$, on average, have such a direction that the midplane moves towards the crossing surface of the class distributions, and thus asymptotically coincides with the Bayes decision border.

$$\boldsymbol{m}_i(t+1) = \boldsymbol{m}_i(t) - \alpha(t)[\boldsymbol{x}(t) - \boldsymbol{m}_i(t)],$$

$$\boldsymbol{m}_j(t+1) = \boldsymbol{m}_j(t) + \alpha(t)[\boldsymbol{x}(t) - \boldsymbol{m}_j(t)],$$

if C_i is the nearest class, but $\boldsymbol{x}$ belongs to $C_j \neq C_i$ where C_j is the next-to-nearest class ("runner-up"); furthermore $\boldsymbol{x}$ must fall into the "window". In all the other cases,

$$\boldsymbol{m}_k(t+1) = \boldsymbol{m}_k(t). \tag{12}$$

The optimal width of the window must be determined experimentally, and it depends on the number of available samples. With a relatively small number of training samples, a width 10 to 20% of the difference between $\boldsymbol{m}_i$ and $\boldsymbol{m}_j$ seems to be proper.

One question concerns the practical definition of the "window". If we are working in a high-dimensional signal space, it seems reasonable to define the "window" in terms of relative distances d_i and d_j from $\boldsymbol{m}_i$ and $\boldsymbol{m}_j$, respectively, having constant ratio s. In this way the borders of the "window" are Apollonian hyperspheres. The vector $\boldsymbol{x}$ is defined to lie in the "window" if

$$\min(d_i/d_j, d_j/d_i) > s. \tag{13}$$

If w is the relative width of the window in its narrowest point, then $s = (1 - w)/(1 + w)$. The optimal size of the window depends on the number of available training samples. If we had a large number of samples, a narrow window would guarantee the most accurate location of the border; but for good statistical accuracy the number of samples falling into the window must be sufficient, too, so a 20% window seems a good compromise, at least in the experiments reported below.

For reasons explained in the next section, the classification accuracy of the LVQ2 is first improved when the decision surface is shifted towards the Bayes limit; after that, however, the $\boldsymbol{m}_i$ continue "drifting away". Therefore this algorithm ought to be applied for a relatively short time only, say, starting with $\alpha = 0.02$ and letting it to decrease to zero in at most 10 000 steps.

C. Type Three Learning Vector Quantization (LVQ3)

The LVQ2 algorithm was based on the idea of *differentially* shifting the decision borders towards the Bayes limits, while no attention was paid to what might happen to the location of the $\mathbf{m}_i$ in the long run if this process were continued. Thus, although researchers have reported good results, some have had problems, too. It turns out that at least two different kinds of detrimental effect must be taken into account. First, because corrections are proportional to the difference of $\mathbf{x}$ and $\mathbf{m}_i$, or $\mathbf{x}$ and $\mathbf{m}_j$, the correction on $\mathbf{m}_j$ (correct class) is of larger magnitude than that on $\mathbf{m}_i$ (wrong class); this results in monotonically decreasing distances $\|\mathbf{m}_i - \mathbf{m}_j\|$. One remedy is to compensate for this effect, approximately at least, by accepting *all the training vectors from the "window,"* and the only condition is that *one* of $\mathbf{m}_i$ and $\mathbf{m}_j$ must belong to the *correct* class, and *the other* to the *incorrect class*. The second problem arises from the fact that if the process in (12) is continued, it may lead to another asymptotic equilibrium of $\mathbf{m}_i$ that is no longer optimal. Therefore it seems necessary to include corrections that ensure that the $\mathbf{m}_i$ continue approximating the class distributions, at least roughly. Combining these ideas, we now obtain an improved algorithm that may be called LVQ3:

$$\mathbf{m}_i(t+1) = \mathbf{m}_i(t) - \alpha(t)[\mathbf{x}(t) - \mathbf{m}_i(t)],$$

$$\mathbf{m}_j(t+1) = \mathbf{m}_j(t) + \alpha(t)[\mathbf{x}(t) - \mathbf{m}_j(t)],$$

where $\mathbf{m}_i$ and $\mathbf{m}_j$ are the two closest codebook vectors to $\mathbf{x}$, and $\mathbf{x}$ and $\mathbf{m}_j$ belong to the same class, while $\mathbf{x}$ and $\mathbf{m}_i$ belong to different classes; furthermore $\mathbf{x}$ must fall into the "window";

$$\mathbf{m}_k(t+1) = \mathbf{m}_k(t) + \epsilon\alpha(t)[\mathbf{x}(t) - \mathbf{m}_k(t)]$$

for $k \in \{i, j\}$, if $\mathbf{x}$, $\mathbf{m}_i$, and $\mathbf{m}_j$ belong to the same class. (14)

In a series of experiments, applicable values for ϵ between 0.1 and 0.5 were found. The optimal value of ϵ seems to depend on the size of the window, being smaller for narrower windows. This algorithm seems to be self-stabilizing, i.e., the optimal placement of the $\mathbf{m}_i$ does not change in continued learning.

Notice that whereas in LVQ1 only one of the $\mathbf{m}_i$ values was changed at each step, LVQ2 and LVQ3 change two codebook vectors simultaneously.

IV. Application of the Map to Speech Recognition

When artificial neural networks are to be used for a practical pattern recognition application such as speech recognition, the first task is to make clear whether it is desirable to perform the complete chain of processing operations starting, e.g., from the pre-analysis of the microphone signal and leading on to some form of linguistic encoding of speech using "all-neural" operations, or whether "neural networks" should only be applied at the most critical stage, whereby the rest of the processing operations can be implemented on standard computing equipment. This choice mainly depends on whether the objective is commercial or academic.

Another issue is whether the aim is to demonstrate the ultimate capabilities of "neural networks" in the analysis of dynamical speech information, or whether it is only to replace some of the traditional "spectral" and "vector space" pattern recognition algorithms by highly adaptive, learning "neural network" principles.

In a speech recognizer, a proper place for artificial neural networks is in the *phonemic recognition stage* where exacting statistical analysis is needed. It should be remembered that if phonemes, i.e., classes of different phonological realizations of vowels and consonants, are selected for the basic phonetic units, then account has to be taken of their transformations due to *coarticulation effects*. In other words, the spectral properties of the phonemes are changed in the context or frame of other phonemes. In an "all-neural" speech recognizer it may not be necessary to distinguish or consider phonemes at all, because interpretation of speech is then regarded as an integral, implicit process. Introduction of the phoneme concept already implies that the system must be able to automatically identify them in one form or another and to label the corresponding time interval. Correction of coarticulation effects may then already be implemented in the acoustic analysis itself, by regarding the speech states as Markov processes, and analyzing the state transitions statistically [53]. A different approach altogether is first to apply some vector quantization classification, whereby the speech waveform is only labeled by class symbols of stationary phonemes, as if no coarticulation effects were being taken into account. Corrections can then be made afterwards in a separate postprocessing stage, in symbolic form. We have used the latter approach.

We have implemented a practical "phonetic typewriter" for unlimited speech input using the Self-Organizing Map to spot and recognize phonemes in continuous speech (Finnish and Japanese) [42], [46], [48]. The "network" was fine-tuned for optimal decision accuracy by the Learning Vector Quantization. After that, in the postprocessing stage we applied a self-learning grammar that corrects the majority of coarticulation errors and derives its numerous transformation rules automatically from given examples. This principle, termed *"Dynamically Expanding Context"* [37], [40], actually belongs to the category of learning Artificial Intelligence methods, and thus falls outside the scope of this article (cf. Sec. IV-D below).

A. Acoustic Preprocessing of the Speech Signal

It is known that biological sensory organs such as the inner ear are usually able to adapt to signal transients in a fast, nonlinear way. Nonetheless, we decided to apply conventional frequency analysis to the preprocessing of speech. The main reason for this was that digital Fourier analysis is both accurate and fast, and the fundamentals of digital filtering are well understood. Deviations from physiological reality are not essential since the self-organizing neural network can accept many alternative kinds of preprocessing and can compensate for minor imperfections.

The technical details of the acoustic preprocessing stage are briefly as follows: 1) 5.3-kHz low-pass switched-capacitor filter, 2) 12-bit A/D-converter with 13.02-kHz sampling rate, 3) 256-point FFT formed every 9.83 ms using a Hamming window, 4) logarithmization and smoothing of the power spectrum, 5) combination of spectral channels from the frequency range 200 Hz–5 kHz into a 15-component pattern vector, 6) subtraction of the average from the components, 7) normalization of the pattern vectors. Except for steps 1) and 2), an integrated-circuit signal processor, TMS32010, is used for the computation.

B. Phoneme Map

The simplest type of speech maps formed by self-organization is the static *phoneme map*. There are 21 phonemes in Finnish: /u, o, a, œ, ø, y, e, i, s, m, n, η, l, r, j, v, h, d, k, p, t/. For their representation we used *short-time spectra* as the input patterns $x(t)$. The spectra were evaluated every 9.83 ms. They were computed by the 256-point FFT, from which a 15-component spectral vector was formed by grouping of the channels. In the present study all the spectral samples, even those from the transitory regions, were employed and presented to the algorithm in the natural order of their utterance. During learning, the spectra were not segmented or labeled in any way: any features present in the speech waveform contributed to the self-organized map. After adaptation, the map was calibrated using known stationary phonemes (Fig. 10). The map resembles the well-known *formant maps* used in phonetics; the main difference is that in our maps *complete spectra*, not just two of their resonant frequencies as in formant maps, are used to define the mapping.

Recognition of discrete phonemes is a decision-making process in which the final accuracy only depends on the rate of misclassification errors. It is therefore necessary to try to minimize them using a decision-controlled (supervised) learning scheme, using a training set of speech spectra with known classification.

In practice, for a new speaker, it will be sufficient to dictate 200 to 300 words which are then analyzed by an automatic segmentation method. The latter picks up the training spectra that are applied in the supervised learning algorithm. The finite set of training spectra (of the order of 2000) must be repeated in the algorithm either cyclically or in a random permutation. LVQ1, LVQ2, or LVQ3 can be used as the fine tuning algorithm. A map created for a typical (standard) speaker can then be modified for a new speaker very quickly, using 100 more dictated words, and LVQ fine tuning only.

C. Specific Problems with Transient Phonemes

Generally, the spectral properties of consonants behave more dynamically than those of vowels. Especially in the case of stop consonants, it seems to be better to pay attention to the plosive burst and transient region between the consonant and the subsequent vowel in order to identify the consonant. In our system transient information is coded in additional "satellite" maps (called *transient maps*) and they are trained, using transient spectral samples alone, to describe the dynamic features with higher resolution [48]. Our system was in fact developed in two versions: one for Finnish and one for Japanese. In the Japanese version, four transient maps have been constructed to distinguish the following cases:

1) voiceless stops /k, p, t/ and glottal stop (vowel at the beginning of utterance),
2) voiceless stops /k, p, t/ without comparison with the glottal stop,
3) voiced stops /b, d, g/,
4) nasals /m, n, η/.

Only one transient map has been adopted for the Finnish version, making the distinction between /k, p, t/ and the glottal stop. (/b/ and /g/ do not exist in original Finnish.)

D. Compensation for Coarticulation Effects using the "Dynamically Expanding Context"

Because of coarticulation effects, i.e., transformation of the speech spectra due to neighboring phonemes, systematic errors appear in phonemic transcriptions. For instance, the Finnish word "hauki" (meaning pike) is almost invariably recognized as the phoneme string /haouki/ by our acoustic processor. It may then be suggested that if a transformation rule /aou/ → /au/ is introduced, this error will be corrected. It might also be imagined that it is possible to list and take into account all such variations. However, there may be hundreds of different frames or contexts of neighboring phonemes in which a particular phoneme may occur, and in many cases such empirical rules are contradictory; they are only statistically correct. The frames may

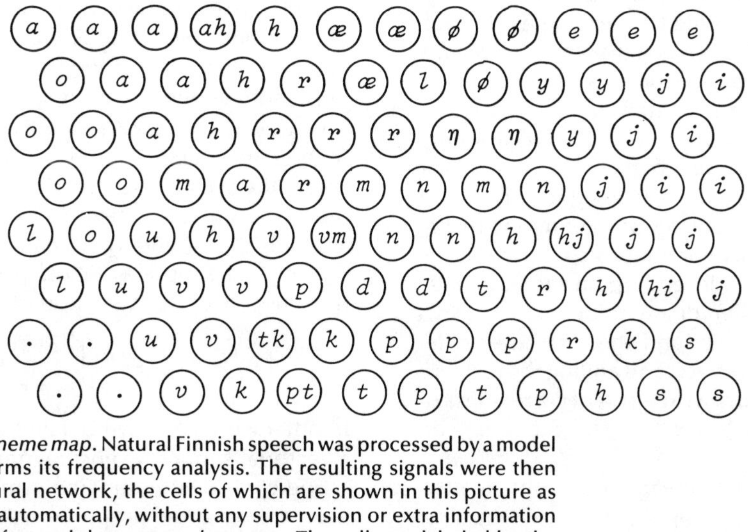

Fig. 10. An example of a *phoneme map*. Natural Finnish speech was processed by a model of the inner ear which performs its frequency analysis. The resulting signals were then connected to an artificial neural network, the cells of which are shown in this picture as circles. The cells were tuned automatically, without any supervision or extra information given, to the acoustic units of speech known as *phonemes*. The cells are labeled by the symbols of those phonemes to which they "learned" to give responses; most cells give a unique answer, whereas the double labels show which cells respond to two phonemes.

also be erroneous. In order to find an optimal and very large system of rules, the *Dynamically Expanding Context* grammar mentioned above was applied [37], [40]. Its rules or productions can be used to transform erroneous symbol strings into correct ones, and even into orthographic text.

Because the correction rules are made accessible in memory using a software content-addressing method (hash coding), they can be applied very quickly, such that the overall operation of the grammar, even with 15 000 rules, is almost in real time. This algorithm is able to correct up to 70% of the errors left by the phoneme map recognizer.

E. Performance of the "Phonetic Typewriter"

In order to get some idea of the accuracy of the map algorithm, we first show a comparative benchmarking of five different methods, namely, classification of manually selected phonemic spectra by the classical parametric Bayes classification, the well-known k-Nearest-Neighbor method (kNN), and LVQ1, LVQ2 and LVQ3.

In this partial experiment, the spectral samples were of Finnish phonemes (divided into 19 classes and using 15 frequency channels for the spectral decomposition). There were 1550 training vectors, and 1550 statistically independent vectors that were only used for testing. The error percentages are given in Table 2.

Table 2 Speech Recognition Experiments with Error Percentages for Independent Test Data

	Parametric Bayes	kNN	LVQ1	LVQ2	LVQ3
Test 1	12.1	12.0	10.2	9.8	9.6
Test 2	13.8	12.1	13.2	12.0	11.5

Note that the parametric Bayes classifier is not even theoretically the best because it assumes that the class samples are normally distributed. We have not been able to find any method, theoretical or heuristic, that classifies speech spectra better than LVQ1, LVQ2 or LVQ3.

In its complete form, the "Phonetic Typewriter" has been tested on several Finnish and Japanese speakers over a long period. To someone familiar with practical speech recognizers it will be clear that it would be meaningless to evaluate and compare different test runs statistically; the results obtained in each isolated test depend so much on the experimental situation and the content of text, the status and tuning of the equipment, as well as on the physical condition of the speaker. The number of tests performed over many years is also too large to be discussed fully here. Let it suffice to mention that the accuracy of spotting and recognizing phonemes in arbitrary continuous speech typically varies between 80 and 90% (depending on the automatic segmentation and recognition of any phoneme), and this figure depends on the speaker and the text. After compensation for coarticulation effects and editing the text into orthographic form, the accuracy, in terms of correctness of any letter, is of the order of 92 to 97%, again depending on the speaker and the text.

The Phonetic Typewriter has already been implemented in several hardware versions using signal processor chips. The latest versions operate in genuine real time with continuous dictation.

It may be of interest here to mention other results, independent of ours. McDermott and Katagiri [28], [66] have carried out experiments on all the Japanese phonemes, and report that LVQ2 gave consistently higher accuracies than Backpropagation Time Delay Neural Networks [105] and was faster in learning.

V. Semantic Map

Demonstrations such as those reported above have indicated that the Self-Organizing Map is indeed able to extract abstract information from multidimensional primary signals, and to represent it as a location, say, in a two-dimensional network. Although this is already a step towards generalization and symbolism, it must be admitted that the extraction of features from geometrically or physically relatable data elements is still a very concrete task, in principle at least.

The operation of the brain at the higher levels relies heavily on abstract concepts, symbolism, and language. It is an old notion that the deepest semantic elements of any language should also be physiologically represented in the neural realms. There is now new physiological evidence for linguistic units being locatable in the human brain [6], [15].

In attempting to devise Neural Network models for linguistic representations, the first difficulty is encountered when trying to find metric distance relations between symbolic items. Unlike with primary sensory signal patterns for which similarity is easily derivable from their mutual distances in the vector spaces in which they are represented, it can not be assumed that encodings of symbols in general have any relationship with the observable characteristics of the corresponding items. How could it then be possible to represent the "logical similarity" of pairs of items, and to map such items topographically? The answer lies in the fact that *the symbol, during the learning process, is presented in context*, i.e., in conjunction with the encodings of a set of other concurrent items. In linguistic representations context might mean a few adjacent words. Similarity between items would then be reflected through the *similarity of the contexts*. Note that for ordered sets of arbitrary encodings, invariant similarity can be expressed, e.g., in terms of the number of items they have in common. On the other hand, it may be evident that the meaning (semantics) of a symbolic encoding is only derivable from the conditional probabilities of its occurrences with other encodings, independent of the type of encoding [68].

However, in the learning process, the literal encodings of the symbols must be memorized, too. Let vector $\mathbf{x}_s$ represent the symbolic expression of an item, and $\mathbf{x}_c$ the representation of its context. The simplest neural model then assumes that $\mathbf{x}_s$ and $\mathbf{x}_c$ are connected to the same neural units, i.e., the representation (pattern) vector $\mathbf{x}$ of the item is formed as a concatenation of $\mathbf{x}_s$ and $\mathbf{x}_c$:

$$\mathbf{x} = \begin{bmatrix} \mathbf{x}_s \\ \mathbf{x}_c \end{bmatrix} = \begin{bmatrix} \mathbf{x}_s \\ 0 \end{bmatrix} + \begin{bmatrix} 0 \\ \mathbf{x}_c \end{bmatrix}. \tag{15}$$

In other words, the symbol part and the context part form a vectorial sum of two orthogonal components.

The core idea underlying symbol maps is that the two parts are weighted properly such that *the norm of the context part predominates over that of the symbol part during the self-organizing process;* the topographical mapping then mainly reflects the metric relationships of the sets of associated encodings. But since the inputs for symbolic signals are also active all the time, memory traces of them are formed in the corresponding inputs of those cells in the map that have been selected (or actually enforced) by the context part. *If then, during recognition of input information, the context signals are missing or are weaker, the (same) map units are selected solely on the basis of the symbol part. In this way the symbols become encoded into a spatial order reflecting their logical (or semantic) similarities.*

In the following, I shall demonstrate this idea, which was originated by H. Ritter, using a simple language [84]. The simplest definition of the context of a word is to take all those words (together with their serial order) that occur in a certain "window" around the selected word. For simplicity, we shall imagine that the content of each "window" can somehow be presented to the x_c input ports of the neural system. We are not interested here in any particular means for the conversion of, say, temporal signal patterns into parallel ones (this task could be done using paths with different delays, eigenstates that depend on sequences, or any other mechanisms implementable in short-term memory).

The vocabulary used in this experiment is listed in Fig. 11(a) and comprises nouns, verbs, and adverbs. Each word

Bob/Jim/Mary	1
horse/dog/cat	2
beer/water	3
meat/bread	4
runs/walks	5
works/speaks	6
visits/phones	7
buys/sells	8
likes/hates	9
drinks/eats	10/11
much/little	12
fast/slowly	13
often/seldom	14
well/poorly	15

(a)

Sentence Patterns:		
1-5-12	1-9-2	2-5-14
1-5-13	1-9-3	2-9-1
1-5-14	1-9-4	2-9-2
1-6-12	1-10-3	2-9-3
1-6-13	1-11-4	2-9-4
1-6-14	1-10-12	2-10-3
1-6-15	1-10-13	2-10-12
1-7-14	1-10-14	2-10-13
1-8-12	1-11-12	2-10-14
1-8-2	1-11-13	2-11-4
1-8-3	1-11-14	2-11-12
1-8-4	2-5-12	2-11-13
1-9-1	2-5-13	2-11-14

(b)

Mary likes meat
Jim speaks well
Mary likes Jim
Jim eats often
Mary buys meat
dog drinks fast
horse hates meat
Jim eats seldom
Bob buys meat
cat walks slowly
Jim eats bread
cat hates Jim
Bob sells beer
(etc.)

(c)

Fig. 11. Outline of vocabulary used in this experiment. (a) List of used words (nouns, verbs, and adverbs), (b) sentence patterns, and (c) some examples of generated three-word-sentences.

class has further categorial subdivisions, such as names of persons, animals, and inanimate objects. To study semantic relationships in their purest form, it must be stipulated that the semantic meaning be not inferable from any patterns used for the encoding of the individual words, but only from the context in which the words occur (i.e., combinations of words). To this end each word was encoded by a random vector of unit length (here, seven-dimensional).

A sequence of randomly generated meaningful three-word sentences was used as the input data to the self-organizing process. Meaningful sentence patterns had therefore first to be constructed on the basis of word categories (Fig. 11(b)). Each explicit sentence was then constructed by randomly substituting the numbers in a randomly selected sentence pattern from Fig. 11(b) by words with compatible numbering in Fig. 11(a). A total of 498 different three-word sentences are possible, a few of which are exemplified in Fig. 11(c). These sentences were concatenated into a single continuous string, *S*.

The context of a word in this string was restricted to the pair of words formed by its immediate predecessor and successor in *S* (ignoring any sentence borders; i.e., words from adjacent sentences in *S* are uncorrelated, and act like random noise in that field). The code vectors of the predecessor/successor-pair forming the context to a word were concatenated into a single 14-dimensional code vector $\mathbf{x}_c$. In this simple demonstration we thus only took into account the context provided by the immediately adjacent textual environment of each word occurrence. Even this restricted context already contains interesting semantic relationships.

In our computer experiments it turned out that instead of presenting each phrase separately to the algorithm, a much more efficient learning strategy is first to consider each word *in its average context* over a set of possible "windows". The (mean) context of a word was thus first defined as *the average over 10 000 sentences of all code vectors of predecessor/successor-pairs surrounding that particular word.* The resulting thirty 14-dimensional "average word contexts", normalized to unit length, assumed the role of the "context fields" $\mathbf{x}_c$ in (14). Each "context field" was combined with a 7-dimensional "symbol field" $\mathbf{x}_s$, consisting of the code vector for the word itself, but scaled to length *a*. The parameter *a* determines the relative influence of the symbol part $\mathbf{x}_s$ in comparison to the context part $\mathbf{x}_c$ and was set to 0.2.

For the simulation, a planar, rectangular lattice of 10 by 15 cells was used. The initial weight vectors of the cells were chosen randomly, so that no initial order was present. Updating was based on (7) and (8). The learning step size was $h_0 = 0.8$ and the radius $\sigma(t)$ of the adjustment zone (cf. (8)) was gradually decreased from an initial value $\sigma_i = 4$ to a final value $\sigma_f = 0.5$ according to the law $\sigma(t) = \sigma_i(\sigma_f/\sigma_i)^{t/t_{max}}$. Here *t* counts the number of adaptation steps.

After $t_{max} = 2000$ input presentations the responses of the neurons to presentation of the symbol parts alone were tested. In Fig. 12, the symbolic label is written to that site at which the symbol signal $\mathbf{x} = [\mathbf{x}_s, 0]^T$ gave the maximum response. We clearly see that *the contexts "channel" the word items to memory positions whose arrangements reflects both grammatical and semantic relationships.* Words of same type, i.e., nouns, verbs, and adverbs, are segregated into separate, large domains. Each of these domains is further organized according to similarities on the semantic level. Adverbs with opposite meaning tend to be close to each other, because sentences differing in one word only are regarded as semantically correlated, and the words that are different then usually have the opposite meaning. The groupings of the verbs correspond to differences in the ways they can co-occur with adverbs, persons, animals, and nonanimate objects such as, e.g., food.

It could be argued that the structures resulting in the map were artificially created by a preplanned choice of the sentence patterns allowed as input. This is not the case, however, since it is easy to check that the categorial sentence patterns in Fig. 11(b) almost completely exhaust the possibilities for forming semantically meaningful three-word sentences.

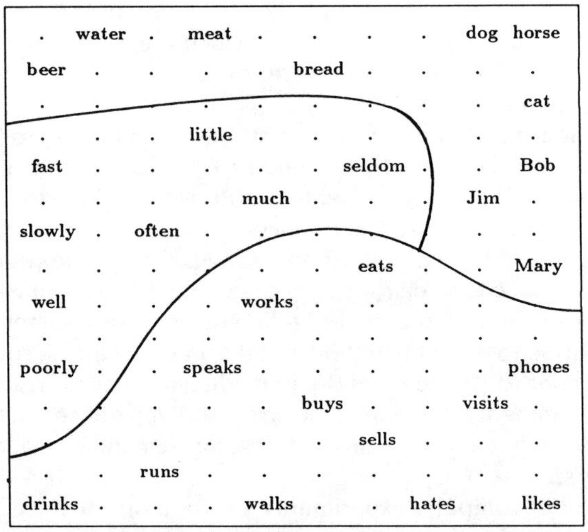

Fig. 12. "Semantic map" obtained on a network of 10 × 15 cells after 2000 presentations of word-context-pairs derived from 10 000 random sentences of the kind shown in Fig. 10(c). Nouns, verbs, and adverbs are segregated into different domains. Within each domain a further grouping according to aspects of meaning is discernible.

VI. Survey of Practical Applications of the Map

In addition to numerous more abstract simulations, theoretical developments, and "toy examples," the following practical problem areas have been suggested for the Self-Organizing Map or the LVQ algorithms. In some of them concrete work is already in progress.

- Statistical pattern recognition, especially recognition of speech [42], [48];
- control of robot arms, and other problems in robotics [17], [18], [63], [85], [87], [88];
- control of industrial processes, especially diffusion processes in the production of semiconductor substrates [62], [102];
- automatic synthesis of digital systems [23];
- adaptive devices for various telecommunications tasks [2], [4], [47];
- image compression [71];
- radar classification of sea-ice [76];
- optimization problems [2];
- sentence understanding [95];
- application of expertise in conceptual domains [96]; and even
- classification of insect courtship songs [73].

Of these, the application to speech recognition has the longest tradition in demonstrating the power of the map method when dealing with difficult stochastic signals. My personal expectations are, however, that the greatest industrial potential of this method may lie in process control and telecommunications.

On the other hand, it is a little surprising that so few applications of the maps to computer vision are being studied. This does not mean that the problems of vision are not important. It is rather that automatic analysis and extraction of visual features, without heuristic or analytical approach, has turned out to be an extremely difficult problem. Biological and artificial vision probably require very complicated hierarchical systems using many stages (e.g., several different maps) [55], [56]. One unclarified problem is how the maps should be interconnected, e.g., whether special nonlinear interfaces are needed [82]; and in hierarchical systems, adaptive normalization of input (cf. [31]) also seems necessary. Only a few isolated problems, such as texture analysis that is under study in our laboratory, might be amenable to the basic method as such.

VII. Discussion

It was stated in Secs. I and III that it is not advisable to use the Self-Organizing Map for classification problems because decision accuracy can be significantly increased if fine tuning such as LVQ is used. Another important notion, that not only concerns the maps but most of the other neural network models as well, is that it would often be absurd to use primary signal elements, such as temporal samples of speech waveform or pixels of an image, for the components of $\boldsymbol{x}$ directly. This is especially true if the input patterns are fine-structured, like line drawings. It is not possible to achieve any *invariances* in perception unless the primary information is first *transformed*, using, e.g., various convolutions with, say, Gabor functions [13], or other, possibly nonlinear functionals of the image field [81], as components of $\boldsymbol{x}$. Which particular choice of functionals should be used for preprocessing in a particular task is a very difficult and delicate question, and cannot be discussed here.

One question concerns the maximum capacity achievable in the maps. Is it possible to increase their size, to eventually use them for data storage in large knowledge data bases? It can at least be stated that the brain's maps are not particularly extensive; they mainly seem to provide for efficient encoding of a particular subset of signals to enhance the operation and capacity of associative memory [44]. If more extensive systems are required, it might be more efficient to develop hierarchical structures of abstract representations.

The hardware used for the maps has so far only consisted of co-processor boards (cf., e.g., [42], [48]). If the simple algorithm is to be directly built into special hardware, one of its essential operations will be the global extremum selector, for which conventional parallel computing hardware is available [39]. Analog "winner-take-all" circuits can also be used [20], [21], [52]. Another question is whether the learning operations ought to be performed on the board, or whether fixed values for weights could be loaded into the cells. Note that in the latter case the function of the cells can be very simple, like that of the conventional formal neurons. One beneficial property of the maps is that their parameters usually stabilize out into a narrow dynamic range, and the accuracy requirements are then modest. In this case even integer arithmetic operations can provide for sufficient accuracy.

What is the most significant difference between the Self-Organizing Map and other contemporary neural-model approaches? Most of the latter strongly emphasize the aspect of distributed processing, and only consider spatial organization of the processing units as a secondary aspect. The map principle, on the other hand, is in some ways complementary to this idea. The intrinsic potential of this particular self-organizing process for creating a localized, structured arrangement of representations in the basic network module is emphasized.

Actually, we should not talk of the localization of a "function": it is only the response that is localized. I am thus not opposed to the view that neural networks are distributed systems. The massive interconnects that underlie all neural processing are certainly spread over the network; their *effects*, on the other hand, may be "focused" on local sites.

It seems inevitable, however, that any complex processing task requires *organization of information into separate parts*. Distributed processing models in general underrate this issue. Consequently, many models that process features of input data without structuring exhibit slow convergence and poor generalization ability, usually ensuing from ignorance of the localization of the adaptive processes.

On the lower perceptual levels, localization of responses in topographically organized maps has already been demonstrated long time ago, and it is known that such maps need not be prespecified in detail, but can instead organize themselves on the basis of the statistics of the incoming signals. Such maps have already been applied with success in many complex pattern recognition and robot control tasks.

On the higher levels of representation, relationships between items seem to be based on more subtle roles in their occurrence, and are less apparent from their immediate intrinsic properties. Nonetheless it has also been shown recently that even with a simple modeling assumption of semantic roles, topological self-organization of semantic data will take place. To describe the role of an item, it is sufficient that the input data are presented together with a sufficient amount of context. This then controls the adaptation process.

In the practical application that we have studied most carefully, viz. speech recognition, a statistical accuracy of phonemic recognition has been achieved that is clearly equal to or better than the results produced by more conventional methods, even when the latter are based on analysis of signal dynamics [28], [66].

It should be emphasized that the map method is not restricted to using of any particular form of preprocessing, such as amplitude spectra in speech recognition, or even to phonemes as basic phonological units. For instance, analogous maps may be formed for diphones, syllables, or demisyllables, and other spectral representations such as linear prediction coding (LPC) coefficients or cepstra may be used as the input information to the maps.

Although the basic one-level map, as demonstrated in Sec. II-E, has already been shown to be capable of creating hierarchical (ultrametric) representations of structured data distributions, it might be expected that the real potential of the map lies in a genuine hierarchical or otherwise structured system that consists of several interconnected map modules. In a more natural system, such modules might also correspond to contiguous areas in a single large sheet, where each area receives a different kind of external input, as in the different areas in the cortex. In that case, the borders between the modules might be diffuse. The problem of hierarchical maps, however, has turned out to be very difficult. One of the particular difficulties arises if the inputs to a cell come from very different sources; it then seems inevitable that for the comparison of input patterns, an asymmetrical distance function, in which the signal components are provided with adaptive tensorial weights, must be applied [31]. Another aspect concerns the interfaces of modules in a hierarchical map system: the signals merging from different modules may have to be combined nonlinearly [82]. On the other hand, it has already been demonstrated that the map, or the LVQ algorithms, can be used as a preprocessing stage for other models [26], [69], [101]. In the Counterpropagation Network of Hecht-Nielsen [22], competitive learning is neatly integrated into a hierarchical system as a special layer. Combinations of maps have also been studied in [74], [112], and [113].

It should be noted that slightly different self-organization ideas have recently been suggested [5], [10], [16]. They, however, fall outside the scope of this article.

One of the strongest original motives for starting the development of (artificial) neural networks was their use as learning systems that might effectively be able to utilize the vast capacities of active circuits that can be manufactured using semiconductor or optical technologies. It is therefore a little surprising that most of the theoretical research on and simulations of neural networks have been restricted to relatively small networks containing only a few tens to a few thousands of nodes (let alone parallel networks for preprocessing images). The main problem with most circuits seems to be slow convergence of learning, which again indicates that the best learning mechanisms are yet to be found.

References

[1] S.-I. Amari, "Topographic organization of nerve fields," *Bull. Math. Biology*, vol. 42, pp. 339–364, 1980.

[2] B. Angéniol, G. de la Croix Vaubois, and J.-Y. Le Texier, "Self-organizing feature maps and the travelling salesman problem," *Neural Networks*, vol. 1, pp. 289–293, 1988.

[3] N. Ansari and Y. Chen, "Dynamic digital satellite communication network management by self-organization," *Proc. Int. Joint Conf. on Neural Networks, IJCNN-90-WASH-DC* (Washington, DC, 1990) pp. II-567–II-570.

[4] D. S. Bradburn, "Reducing transmission error effects using a self-organizing network," *Proc. Int. Joint Conf. on Neural Networks, IJCNN 89* (Washington, D.C., 1989) pp. II-531–537.

[5] D. J. Burr, "An improved elastic net method for the traveling salesman problem," *Proc. IEEE Int. Conf. on Neural Networks, ICNN-88* (San Diego, Cal., 1988) pp. I-69–I-76.

[6] A. Caramazza, "Some aspects of language processing revealed through the analysis of acquired aphasia: The lexical system," *Ann. Rev. Neurosci.*, vol. 11, pp. 395–421, 1988.

[7] M. Cottrell and J.-C. Fort, "A stochastic model of retinotopy: A self-organizing process," *Biol. Cybern.*, vol. 53, pp. 405–411, 1986.

[8] ——, "Étude d'un processus d'auto-organisation," *Ann. Inst. Henri Poincaré*, vol. 23, pp. 1–20, 1987.

[9] A. R. Damasio, H. Damasio, and G. W. Van Hoesen, "Prosopagnosia: Anatomic basis and behavioral mechanisms," *Neurology*, vol. 24, pp. 89–93, 1975.

[10] R. Durbin and D. Willshaw, "An analogue approach to the travelling salesman problem using an elastic net method," *Nature*, vol. 326, pp. 689–691, 1987.

[11] D. Essen, "Functional organization of primate visual cortex," in *Cerebral Cortex*, vol. 3, A. Peters, E. G. Jones (Eds.). New York: Plenum Press, 1985, pp. 259–329.

[12] J. Fuller and A. Farsaie, "Invariant target recognition using feature extraction," *Proc. Int. Joint. Conf. on Neural Networks, IJCNN-90-WASH-DC* (Washington, DC, 1990) pp. II-595–II-598.

[13] D. Gabor, "Theory of communication," *J.I.E.E.*, vol. 93, pp. 429–459, 1946.

[14] A. Gersho, "On the structure of vector quantizers," *IEEE Trans. Inform. Theory*, vol. IT-25, no. 4, pp. 373–380, July 1979.

[15] H. Goodglass, A. Wingfield, M. R. Hyde, and J. C. Theurkauf, "Category specific dissociations in naming and recognition by aphasic patients," *Cortex*, vol. 22, pp. 87–102, 1986.

[16] I. Grabec, "Self-organization based on the second maximum entropy principle," *First IEE Int. Conf. on Artificial Neural Networks*, Conference Publication No. 313. (London, 1989) pp. 12–16.

[17] D. H. Graf and W. R. LaLonde, "A neural controller for collision-free movement of general robot manipulators," *Proc. IEEE Int. Conf. on Neural Networks, ICNN-88* (San Diego, Cal., 1988) pp. I-77–I-84.

[18] D. H. Graf and W. R. LaLonde, "Neuroplanners for hand/eye coordination," *Proc. Int. Joint Conf. on Neural Networks, IJCNN 89* (Washington, DC, 1989) pp. II-543–II-548.

[19] R. M. Gray, "Vector quantization," *IEEE ASSP Mag.*, vol. 1, pp. 4–29, 1984.

[20] S. Grossberg, "On the development of feature detectors in the visual cortex with applications to learning and reaction-diffusion systems," *Biol. Cybern.*, vol. 21, pp. 145–159, 1976.

[21] —, "Adaptive pattern classification and universal recoding: I. Parallel development and coding of neural feature detectors; II. Feedback, expectation, olfaction, illusions," *Biol. Cybern.*, vol. 23, pp. 121–134 and 187–202, 1976.

[22] R. Hecht-Nielsen, "Applications of counterpropagation network," *Neural Networks*, vol. 1, pp. 131–139, 1988.

[23] A. Hemani and A. Postula, "Scheduling by self organisation," *Proc. Int. Joint. Conf. on Neural Networks, IJCNN-90-WASH-DC* (Washington, DC, 1990) pp. II-543–II-546.

[24] R. E. Hodges and C.-H. Wu, "A method to establish an autonomous self-organizing feature map," *Proc. Int. Joint. Conf. on Neural Networks, IJCNN-90-WASH-DC* (Washington, DC, 1990) pp. I-517–I-520.

[25] R. E. Hodges, C.-H. Wu, and C.-J. Wang, "Parallelizing the self-organizing feature map on multi-processor systems," *Proc. Int. Joint. Conf. on Neural Networks, IJCNN-90-WASH-DC* (Washington, DC, 1990) pp. II-141–II-144.

[26] R. M. Holdaway, "Enhancing supervised learning algorithms via self-organization," *Proc. Int. Joint Conf. on Neural Networks, IJCNN 89* (Washington, D.C., 1989) pp. II-523–II-529.

[27] J. J. Hopfield, "Neural networks and physical systems with emergent collective computational abilities," *Proc. Natl. Acad. Sci. USA*, vol. 79, pp. 2554–2558, 1982.

[28] H. Iwamida, S. Katagiri, E. McDermott, and Y. Tohkura, "A hybrid speech recognition system using HMMs with an LVQ-trained codebook," ATR Technical Report TR-A-0061, ATR Auditory and Visual Perception Research Laboratories, 1989.

[29] J. H. Kaas, R. J. Nelson, M. Sur, C. S. Lin, and M. M. Merzenich, "Multiple representations of the body within the primary somatosensory cortex of primates," *Science*, vol. 204, pp. 521–523, 1979.

[30] J. H. Kaas, M. M. Merzenich, and H. P. Killackey, "The reorganization of somatosensory cortex following peripheral nerve damage in adult and developing mammals," *Annual Rev. Neurosci.*, vol. 6, pp. 325–356, 1983.

[31] J. Kangas, T. Kohonen, and J. Laaksonen, "Variants of self-organizing maps," *IEEE Trans. Neural Networks*, vol. 1, pp. 93–99, 1990.

[32] A. Kertesz, Ed., *Localization in Neuropsychology.* New York, N.Y.: Academic Press, 1983.

[33] E. I. Knudsen, S. du Lac, and S. D. Esterly, "Computational maps in the brain," *Ann. Rev. Neurosci.*, vol. 10, pp. 41–65, 1987.

[34] T. Kohonen, "Automatic formation of topological maps of patterns in a self-organizing system," *Proc. 2nd Scandinavian Conf. on Image Analysis* (Espoo, Finland, 1981) pp. 214–220.

[35] —, "Self-organized formation of topologically correct feature maps," *Biol. Cybern.*, vol. 43, pp. 59–69, 1982.

[36] —, "Clustering, taxonomy, and topological maps of patterns," *Proc. Sixth Int. Conf. on Pattern Recognition* (Munich, Germany, 1982) pp. 114–128.

[37] —, "Dynamically expanding context, with application to the correction of symbol strings in the recognition of continuous speech," *Proc. Eighth Int. Conf. on Pattern Recognition* (Paris, France, 1986) pp. 1148–1151.

[38] —, "Learning Vector Quantization," Helsinki University of Technology, Laboratory of Computer and Information Science, Report TKK-F-A-601, 1986.

[39] —, *Content-Addressable Memories*, 2nd ed. Berlin, Heidelberg, Germany: Springer-Verlag, 1987.

[40] —, "Self-learning inference rules by dynamically expanding context," *Proc. IEEE First Ann. Int. Conf. on Neural Networks* (San Diego, CA, 1987) pp. II-3–II-9.

[41] —, "An introduction to neural networks," *Neural Networks*, vol. 1, pp. 3–16, 1988.

[42] —, "The 'neural' phonetic typewriter," *Computer*, vol. 21, pp. 11–22, March 1988.

[43] —, "Learning vector quantization," *Neural Networks*, vol. 1, suppl. 1, p. 303, 1988.

[44] —, *Self-Organization and Associative Memory*, 3rd ed. Berlin, Heidelberg, Germany: Springer-Verlag, 1989.

[45] T. Kohonen, G. Barna, and R. Chrisley, "Statistical pattern recognition with neural networks: Benchmarking studies," *Proc. IEEE Int. Conf. on Neural Networks, ICNN-88* (San Diego, Cal., 1988) pp. I-61–I-68.

[46] T. Kohonen, K. Mäkisara, and T. Saramäki, "Phonotopic maps—insightful representation of phonological features for speech recognition," *Proc. Seventh Int. Conf. on Pattern Recognition* (Montreal, Canada, 1984) pp. 182–185.

[47] T. Kohonen, K. Raivio, O. Simula, O. Ventä, and J. Henriksson, "An adaptive discrete-signal detector based on self-organizing maps," *Proc. Int. Joint. Conf. on Neural Networks, IJCNN-90-WASH-DC* (Washington, DC, 1990) pp. II-249–II-252.

[48] T. Kohonen, K. Torkkola, M. Shozakai, J. Kangas, and O. Ventä, "Microprocessor implementation of a large vocabulary speech recognizer and phonetic typewriter for Finnish and Japanese," *Proc. European Conference on Speech Technology* (Edinburgh, 1987) pp. 377–380.

[49] H. J. Kushner and D. S. Clark, *Stochastic Approximation Methods for Constrained and Unconstrained Systems.* New York, Berlin: Springer-Verlag, 1978.

[50] J. Lampinen and E. Oja, "Fast self-organization by the probing algorithm," *Proc. Int. Joint Conf. on Neural Networks, IJCNN 89* (Washington, DC, 1989) pp. II-503–II-507.

[51] A. LaVigna, "Nonparametric classification using learning vector quantization," Ph.D. Thesis, University of Maryland, 1989.

[52] J. Lazarro, S. Ryckebusch, M. A. Mahowald, and C. A. Mead, "Winner-take-all network of O(N) complexity," in *Advances in Neural Information Processing Systems I*, D. S. Touretzky, Ed. San Mateo, CA: Morgan Kaufmann Publishers, 1989.

[53] S. E. Levinson, L. R. Rabiner, and M. M. Sondhi, "An introduction to the application of the theory of probabilistic functions of a Markov process to automatic speech recognition," *Bell Syst. Tech. J.*, pp. 1035–1073, Apr. 1983.

[54] Y. Linde, A. Buzo, and R. M. Gray, "An algorithm for vector quantization," *IEEE Trans. Communication*, vol. COM-28, pp. 84–95, 1980.

[55] S. P. Luttrell, "Self-organizing multilayer topographic mappings," *Proc. IEEE Int. Conf. on Neural Networks, ICNN-88* (San Diego, CA, 1988) pp. I-93–I-100.

[56] —, "Hierarchical self-organizing networks," *First IEE Int. Conf. on Artificial Neural Networks*, Conference Publication No. 313. (London, 1989) pp. 2–6.

[57] —, "Self-organization: A derivation from first principles of a class of learning algorithms," *Proc. Int. Joint Conf. on Neural Networks, IJCNN 89* (Washington, DC, 1989) pp. II-495–II-498.

[58] J. Makhoul, S. Roucos, and H. Gish, "Vector quantization in speech coding," *Proc. IEEE*, vol. 73, pp. 1551–1588, 1985.

[59] Ch. v.d Malsburg, "Self-organization of orientation sensitive cells in the striate cortex," *Kybernetik*, vol. 14, pp. 85–100, 1973.

[60] Ch. v.d. Malsburg and D. J. Willshaw, "How to label nerve cells so that they can interconnect in an ordered fashion," *Proc. Natl. Acad. Sci. USA*, vol. 74, pp. 5176–5178, 1977.

[61] R. Mann and S. Haykin, "A parallel implementation of Kohonen feature maps on the Warp systolic computer," *Proc. Int. Joint. Conf. on Neural Networks, IJCNN-90-WASH-DC* (Washington, DC, 1990) pp. II-84–II-87.

[62] K. M. Marks and K. F. Goser, "Analysis of VLSI process data based on self-organizing feature maps," *Proc. Neuro-Nîmes'88* (Nîmes, France, 1988) pp. 337–347.

[63] J. Martinetz, H. J. Ritter, and K. J. Schulten, "Three-dimensional neural net for learning visuomotor coordination of a robot arm," *IEEE Trans. Neural Networks*, vol. 1, pp. 131-136, 1990.
[64] J. Max, "Quantizing for minimum distortion," *IRE Trans. Inform. Theory*, vol. IT-6, no. 2, pp. 7-12, Mar. 1960.
[65] R. A. McCarthy and E. K. Warrington, "Evidence for modality specific meaning systems in the brain," *Nature*, vol. 334, pp. 428-430, 1988.
[66] E. McDermott and S. Katagiri, "Shift-invariant, multi-category phoneme recognition using Kohonen's LVQ2," *Proc. Int. Conf. on Acoustics, Signals, and Speech, ICASSP 89* (Glasgow, Scotland) pp. 81-84.
[67] P. McKenna and E. K. Warrington, "Category-specific naming preservation: A single case study," *J. Neurol. Neurosurg. Psychiatry*, vol. 41, pp. 571-574, 1978.
[68] R. Miikkulainen and M.-G. Dyer, "Forming global representations with extended backpropagation," *Proc. IEEE Int. Conf. on Neural Networks, ICNN 88* (San Diego, CA, 1988) pp. 285-292.
[69] P. Morasso, "Neural models of cursive script handwriting," *Proc. Int. Joint Conf. on Neural Networks, IJCNN 89* (Washington, DC, 1989) pp. II-539-II-542.
[70] J. T. Murphy, H. C. Kwan, W. A. MacKay, and Y. C. Wong, "Spatial organization of precentral cortex in awake primates, III, Input-output coupling," *J. Neurophysiol.*, vol. 41, pp. 1132-1139, 1977.
[71] N. M. Nasrabadi and Y. Feng, "Vector quantization of images based upon the Kohonen Self-Organizing Feature Maps," *Proc. IEEE Int. Conf. on Neural Networks, ICNN-88* (San Diego, CA, 1988) pp. I-101-I-108.
[72] M. M. Nass and L. N. Cooper, "A theory for the development of feature detecting cells in visual cortex," *Biol. Cybern.*, vol. 19, pp. 1-18, 1975.
[73] E. K. Neumann, D. A. Wheeler, J. W. Burnside, A. S. Bernstein, and J. C. Hall, "A technique for the classification and analysis of insect courtship song," *Proc. Int. Joint. Conf. on Neural Networks, IJCNN-90-WASH-DC*, (Washington, DC, 1990) pp. II-257-262.
[74] Y. Nishikawa, H. Kita, and A. Kawamura, "NN/I: a neural network which divides and learns environments," *Proc. Int. Joint. Conf. on Neural Networks, IJCNN-90-WASH-DC*, (Washington, DC, 1990) pp. I-684-I-687.
[75] G. A. Ojemann, "Brain organization for language from the perspective of electrical stimulation mapping," *Behav. Brain Sci.*, vol. 2, pp. 189-230, 1983.
[76] J. Orlando, R. Mann, and S. Haykin, "Radar classification of sea-ice using traditional and neural classifiers," *Proc. Int. Joint. Conf. on Neural Networks, IJCNN-90-WASH-DC*, (Washington, DC, 1990) pp. II-263-II-266.
[77] K. J. Overton and M. A. Arbib, "The branch arrow model of the formation of retinotectal connections," *Biol. Cybern.*, vol. 45, pp. 157-175, 1982.
[78] K. J. Pearson, L. H. Finkel, and G. M. Edelman, "Plasticity in the organization of adult cerebral maps: a computer simulation based on neuronal group selection," *J. Neurosci.*, vol. 12, pp. 4209-4223, 1987.
[79] R. Pérez, L. Glass, and R. J. Shlaer, "Development of specificity in cat visual cortex," *J. Math. Biol.*, vol. 1, pp. 275-288, 1975.
[80] S. E. Petersen, P. T. Fox, M. I. Ponsner, M. Mintun, and M. E. Raichle, "Positron emission tomographic studies of the cortical anatomy of single-word processing," *Nature*, vol. 331, pp. 585-589, 1988.
[81] M. Porat and Y. Y. Zeevi, "The generalized Gabor scheme of image representation in biological and machine vision," *IEEE Trans. Pattern Anal. Machine Intell.*, vol. PAMI-10, pp. 452-468, 1988.
[82] H. Ritter, "Combining self-organizing maps," *Proc. Int. Joint Conf. on Neural Networks, IJCNN 89* (Washington, DC, 1989) pp. II-499-II-502.
[83] —, "Asymptotic level density for a class of vector quantization processes," Helsinki University of Technology, Lab. of Computer and Information Science, Report A9, 1989.
[84] H. Ritter and T. Kohonen, "Self-organizing semantic maps," *Biol. Cybern.*, vol. 61, pp. 241-254, 1989.
[85] H. J. Ritter, T. M. Martinetz, and K. J. Schulten, "Topology conserving maps for learning visuo-motor-coordination," *Neural Networks*, vol. 2, pp. 159-168, 1989.
[86] H. Ritter and K. Schulten, "On the stationary state of Kohonen's self-organizing sensory mapping," *Biol. Cybern.*, vol. 54, pp. 99-106, 1986.
[87] —, "Topology conserving mappings for learning motor tasks," *Proc. Neural Networks for Computing*, AIP Conference (Snowbird, Utah, 1986) pp. 376-380.
[88] —, "Extending Kohonen's self-organizing mapping algorithm to learn ballistic movements," *NATO ASI Series*, vol. F41, pp. 393-406, 1988.
[89] —, "Kohonen's self-organizing maps: exploring their computational capabilities," *Proc. IEEE Int. Conf. on Neural Networks, ICNNN 88* (San Diego, CA, 1988) pp. I-109-I-116.
[90] —, "Convergency properties of Kohonen's topology conserving maps: Fluctuations, stability and dimension selection," *Biol. Cybern.*, vol. 60, pp. 59-71, 1989.
[91] R. A. Reale and T. J. Imig, "Tonotopic organization in auditory cortex of the cat," *J. Comp. Neurol.*, vol. 192, pp. 265-291, 1980.
[92] H. Robbins and S. Monro, "A stochastic approximation method," *Ann. Math. Statist.*, vol. 22, pp. 400-407, 1951.
[93] E. T. Rolls, "Neurons in the cortex of the temporal lobe and in the amygdala of the monkey with responses selective for faces," *Hum. Neurobiol.*, vol. 3, pp. 209-222, 1984.
[94] D. E. Rumelhart, G. E. Hinton, and R. J. Williams, "Learning internal representations by error propagation," in *Parallel Distributed Processing: Explorations in the Microstructure of Cognition. Vol. 1.: Foundations*, D. E. Rumelhart, J. L. McClelland and the PDP research group, Eds. Cambridge, Mass.: MIT Press, 1986, pp. 318-362.
[95] J. K. Samarabandu and O. E. Jakubowicz, "Principles of sequential feature maps in multi-level problems," *Proc. Int. Joint. Conf. on Neural Networks, IJCNN-90-WASH-DC* (Washington, DC, 1990) pp. II-683-II-686.
[96] P. G. Schyns, "Expertise acquisition through concepts refinement in a self-organizing architecture," *Proc. Int. Joint. Conf. on Neural Networks, IJCNN-90-WASH-DC* (Washington, DC, 1990) pp. I-236-I-239.
[97] D. L. Sparks and J. S. Nelson, "Sensory and motor maps in the mammalian superior colliculus," *TINS*, vol. 10, pp. 312-317, 1987.
[98] N. Suga and W. E. O'Neill, "Neural axis representing target range in the auditory cortex of the mustache bat," *Science*, vol. 206, pp. 351-353, 1979.
[99] N. V. Swindale, "A model for the formation of ocular dominance stripes," *Proc. R. Soc.*, vol. B.208, pp. 243-264, 1980.
[100] A. Takeuchi and S. Amari, "Formation of topographic maps and columnar microstructures," *Biol. Cybern.*, vol. 35, pp. 63-72, 1979.
[101] T. Tanaka, M. Naka, and K. Yoshida, "Improved back-propagation combined with LVQ," *Proc. Int. Joint. Conf. on Neural Networks, IJCNN-90-WASH-DC* (Washington, DC, 1990) pp. I-731-734.
[102] V. Tryba, K. M. Marks, U. Rückert, and K. Goser, "Selbstorganisierende Karten als lernende klassifizierende Speicher," *ITG Fachbericht*, vol. 102, pp. 407-419, 1988.
[103] A. R. Tunturi, "Physiological determination of the arrangement of the afferent connections to the middle ectosylvian auditory area in the dog," *Am. J. Physiol.*, vol. 162, pp. 489-502, 1950.
[104] —, "The auditory cortex of the dog," *Am. J. Physiol.*, vol. 168, pp. 712-717, 1952.
[105] A. Waibel, T. Hanazawa, G. Hinton, K. Shikano, and K. J. Lang, "Phoneme recognition using time-delay neural networks," *IEEE Trans. Acoust. Speech and Signal Processing*, vol. ASSP-37, pp. 382-339, 1989.
[106] E. K. Warrington, "The selective impairment of semantic memory," *Q. J. Exp. Psychol.*, vol. 27, pp. 635-657, 1975.
[107] E. K. Warrington and R. A. McGarthy, "Category specific access dysphasia," *Brain*, vol. 106, pp. 859-878, 1983.
[108] —, "Categories of knowledge," *Brain*, vol. 110, pp. 1273-1296, 1987.
[109] E. K. Warrington and T. Shallice, "Category-specific impairments," *Brain*, vol. 107, pp. 829-854, 1984.

[110] D. J. Willshaw and Ch. v.d. Malsburg, "How patterned neural connections can be set up by self-organization," *Proc. R. Soc. London*, vol. B 194, pp. 431–445, 1976.
[111] ——, "A marker induction mechanism for the establishment of ordered neural mappings: its application to the retinotectal problem," *Proc. R. Soc. London*, vol. B 287, pp. 203–243, 1979.
[112] L. Xu and E. Oja, "Vector pair correspondence by a simplified counter-propagation model: a twin topographic map," *Proc. Int. Joint. Conf. on Neural Networks, IJCNN-90-WASH-DC* (Washington, DC, 1990) pp. II-531–534.
[113] ——, "Adding top-down expectation into the learning procedure of self-organizing maps," *Proc. Int. Joint. Conf. on Neural Networks, IJCNN-90-WASH-DC* (Washington, DC, 1990) pp. I-735–738.
[114] A. Yamadori and M. L. Albert, "Word category aphasia," *Cortex*, vol. 9, pp. 112–125, 1973.
[115] P. L. Zador, "Asymptotic quantization error of continuous signals and the quantization dimension," *IEEE Trans. Inform. Theory*, vol. IT-28, pp. 139–149, March 1982.
[116] S. Zeki, "The representation of colours in the cerebral cortex," *Nature*, vol. 284, pp. 412–418, 1980.

Networks for Approximation and Learning

TOMASO POGGIO, ASSOCIATE MEMBER, IEEE, AND FEDERICO GIROSI

Learning an input-output mapping from a set of examples, of the type that many neural networks have been constructed to perform, can be regarded as synthesizing an approximation of a multi-dimensional function, that is solving the problem of hypersurface reconstruction. From this point of view, this form of learning is closely related to classical approximation techniques, such as generalized splines and regularization theory. This paper considers the problem of the approximation of nonlinear mappings—especially continuous mappings. We develop a theoretical framework for approximation based on regularization techniques that leads to a class of three-layer networks that we call regularization networks and include as a special case the well-known Radial Basis Functions method. Regularization networks are not only equivalent to generalized splines, but are also closely related to pattern recognition methods such as Parzen windows and potential functions and to several neural network algorithms, such as Kanerva's associative memory, backpropagation, and Kohonen's topology preserving map. They also have an interesting interpretation in terms of prototypes that are synthesized and optimally combined during the learning stage. This paper generalizes the theory of regularization networks to a formulation that turns out to include task-dependent clustering and dimensionality reduction. We also discuss briefly some intriguing analogies with neurobiological data.

I. Learning as Approximation

The problem of learning a mapping between an input and an output space is equivalent to the problem of synthesizing an associative memory that retrieves the appropriate output when presented with the input and *generalizes* when presented with new inputs. It is also equivalent to the problem of estimating the system that transforms inputs into outputs given a set of examples of input-output pairs. A classical framework for this problem is *approximation theory*. Related fields are *system identification techniques* (when it is possible to choose the input set) and *system estimation techniques* (when the input-output pairs are given).

Manuscript received August 15, 1989; revised March 20, 1990. This work was supported in part by a grant from the Office of Naval Research (ONR), Cognitive and Neural Sciences Division, by the Artificial Intelligence Center of Hughes Aircraft Corporation, and by the NATO Scientific Affairs Division (0403/87). Support for the Artificial Intelligence Laboratory's artificial intelligence research is provided by the Advanced Research Projects Agency of the Department of Defense, under Army contract DACA76-85-C-0010, and in part under Office of Naval Research contract N00014-85-K-0124. The work of T. Poggio is supported by the Uncas and Ellen Whitaker chair.

The authors are with the Artificial Intelligence Laboratory and Center for Biological Information Processing, Massachusetts Institute of Technology, Cambridge, MA 02139, USA.

IEEE Log Number 9038827.

A suggestive point of view on networks and classical approximation methods is provided by Omohundro [1] and an interesting review of networks, statistical inference, and estimation techniques has been given by Barron and Barron [2]. Learning from the point of view of approximation has been also considered among others by Schwartz [3], Poggio *et al.* [4], [5], Aloimonos [6], Moody and Darken [7], and Poggio [8]. A related area of research, concerned with learning of Boolean functions, has been developing rapidly since the seminal work of Valiant [9].

Approximation theory deals with the problem of *approximating* or *interpolating* a continuous, multivariate function $f(X)$ by an approximating function $F(W, X)$ having a fixed number of parameters W belonging to some set P (X and W are real vectors $X = (x_1, x_2, \cdots, x_n)$ and $W = (w_1, w_2, \cdots, w_m)$). For a choice of a specific F, the problem is then to find the set of parameters W that provides the best possible approximation of f on the set of "examples." This is the *learning* step. Needless to say, it is very important to choose an approximating function F that can represent f as well as possible. There would be little point in trying to learn, if the chosen approximation function $F(W, X)$ could only give a very poor representation of $f(X)$, even with optimal parameter values. Therefore, it is useful to distinguish three main problems:

1) the problem of which approximation to use, i.e., which classes of functions $f(X)$ can be effectively approximated by which approximating functions $F(W, X)$. This is a *representation* problem.
2) the problem of *which* algorithm to use for finding the optimal values of the parameters W for a given choice of F.
3) the problem of an efficient implementation of the algorithm in parallel, possibly analog, hardware.

This paper deals with the first two of these problems. It is especially focused on the question of a good representation for learning continuous functions.

A. Networks and Approximation Schemes

Almost all approximation schemes can be mapped into some kind of network that can be dubbed as a "neural network." Networks, after all, can be regarded as a graphic notation for a large class of algorithms. In the context of our discussion, a network is a function represented by the composition of many basic functions. To see how the approx-

Reprinted from *Proc. IEEE*, vol. 78, no. 9, Sept. 1990, pp. 1481–1497.

imation problem maps into such a network formulation, let us introduce some definitions.

To measure the quality of the approximation, one introduces a *distance function* ρ to determine the distance $\rho[f(X), F(W, X)]$ of an approximation $F(W, X)$ from $f(X)$. The distance is usually induced by a norm, for instance the standard L_2 norm. The approximation problem can then be stated formally as:

Approximation problem: *If f(X) is a continuous function defined on set* **X**, *and F(W, X) is an approximating function that depends continuously on $W \in P$ and X, the approximation problem is to determine the parameters W^* such that*

$$\rho[F(W^*, X), f(X)] \leq \rho[F(W, X), f(X)]$$

for all W in the set P.

A solution to this problem, if it exists, is said to be a *best approximation*. The existence of a best approximation depends ultimately on the class of functions to whom $F(W, X)$ belongs [10].

With these definitions we can consider a few examples of approximating functions $F(W, X)$: $R^n \rightarrow R$, that correspond to multilayer networks (see [11]):

- the classical linear case is

$$F(W, X) = W \cdot X$$

where W and X are n-dimensional vectors. It corresponds to a network without hidden units;

- the classical approximation scheme is linear in a suitable basis $\{\Phi_i\}_{i=1}^m$ of functions of the original inputs X, that is

$$F(W, X) = \sum_{i=1}^{m} W_i \Phi_i(X)$$

and corresponds to a network with one layer of hidden units. Spline interpolation and many approximation schemes, such as expansions in series of orthogonal polynomials, are included in this representation. When the Φ_i are products and powers of the input components, F is a polynomial.

- the nested sigmoids scheme (of the type used with the backpropagation learning scheme, see [12]) can be written as

$$F(W, X) = \sigma\left(\sum_n w_n \sigma\left(\sum_i v_i \sigma\left(\cdots \sigma\left(\sum_j u_j X_j\right)\cdots\right)\right)\right)$$

where σ is a sigmoid function. It corresponds to a multilayer network of units that sum their inputs with "weights" $W = \{w_n, v_i, u_j, \cdots\}$ and then perform a sigmoidal transformation of this sum. This scheme (of nested nonlinear functions) is unusual in the classical theory of the approximation of continuous functions. Its motivation is that

$$F(W, X) = \sigma\left(\sum_n w_n \sigma\left(\sum_j u_j X_j\right)\right)$$

with σ being a linear threshold function, can represent all Boolean functions (any mapping $S: \{0, 1\}^N \rightarrow \{0, 1\}$ can be written as a disjunction of conjunctions, which in terms of threshold elements becomes the above expression, where biases or dummy inputs are allowed). Networks of this type, with one layer of hidden units, can approximate arbitrarily well any continuous multivariate functions [13], [14] (Cybenko [15] and Moore and Poggio [16], among others, proved the same result for the case of two layers of hidden units).

In general, each approximation scheme has some specific algorithm for finding the optimal set of parameters W. An approach that works in general, though it may not be the most efficient in any specific case, is some relaxation method, such as gradient descent or conjugate gradient or simulated annealing in parameter space, attempting to minimize the error ρ over the set of examples. In any case, our discussion suggests that networks of the type used recently for simple learning tasks can be considered as specific methods of function approximation. This observation suggests that the network version of the problem of learning can be approached from the point of view of classical approximation theory.

In this paper, we will be mainly concerned with the first of the problems listed earlier, that is the problem of developing a well-founded and sufficiently general approximation scheme, which maps into multilayer networks.

Before discussing more extensively the approximation problem, it is obviously important to answer the question of whether an *exact* representation exists for continuous functions in terms of simpler functions. For instance, if all multivariate functions could be represented exactly and *nicely* as sums or products of univariate ones, we could use networks consisting of units with just one input and one output. Recently, it has been claimed that a theorem of this type, due to Kolmogorov [17], could be used to justify the use of multilayer networks [2] (see also [18]). Unfortunately, the claim is not warranted, as revealed by an analysis of Kolmogorov's result [19] to which we refer the reader.

Thus, exact representations with the required properties do not exist. Good and general approximating representations, however, may exist. The next section discusses the formulation of the problem of learning from examples as the problem of approximation of mappings. From this point of view, regularization techniques used for surface reconstruction are a natural framework for the problem of learning. This leads to the following problem: is there a connection between regularization techniques and feedforward, multilayer networks? Sections III and IV provide a solution to this problem by showing that regularization leads to an approximation scheme which is general, powerful, and maps into a class of networks with one layer of hidden units that we call *regularization networks.* We show that regularization networks are strictly related to the well-known interpolation method of Radial Basis Functions (RBF). A subset of regularization networks consists of Radial Basis Functions (though not all of them). The Appendix reviews some of the existing results about RBF. Section IV also provides powerful extensions of the basic regularization networks. In this paper we refer to the most powerful and general of the regularization networks as Hyper Basis Functions (HyperBF). The possible relevance of the work to neurophysiology is then briefly outlined in section V, together with a number of properties of Gaussian radial basis functions. Section VI sketches some of the applications of the technique, while the last section mentions several classical algorithms that can be regarded as special cases of HyperBF. We conclude with some comments on the crucial problem of dimensionality faced by this and almost any other learning or approximation technique.

II. Learning as Hypersurface Reconstruction

If we consider learning from the perspective of approximation, we can draw an equivalence between learning smooth mappings and a standard approximation problem, surface reconstruction from sparse data points. In this analogy, learning simply means collecting the *examples*, i.e., the input coordinates x_i, y_i and the corresponding output values at those locations, the height of the surface d_i. This builds a look-up table. *Generalization* means estimating d in locations x, y where there are no examples, i.e., no data. This requires interpolating or, more generally, approximating the surface between the data points. Interpolation is the limit of approximation when there is no noise in the data. This example, given for a surface, i.e., the graph in $R^2 \times R$, corresponding to the mapping from R^2 to R, can be immediately extended to mappings from R^n to R^m (and graphs in $R^n \times R^m$). In this sense learning is a problem of *hypersurface reconstruction*. Notice that tasks of classification and of learning Boolean functions may be regarded in a similar way. They correspond to the problems of approximating a mapping $R^n \to \{0, 1\}$ and a mapping $\{0, 1\}^n \to \{0, 1\}$, respectively.

B. Approximation, Regularization, and Generalized Splines

From the point of view of learning as approximation, the problem of learning a smooth mapping from examples is ill-posed [20], [21] in the sense that the information in the data is not sufficient to reconstruct uniquely the mapping in regions where data are not available. In addition, the data are usually noisy. *A priori* assumptions about the mapping are needed to make the problem well-posed. Generalization is not possible if the mapping is completely random. For instance, any number of examples for the mapping represented by a telephone directory (people's names into telephone numbers) do not help in estimating the telephone number corresponding to a new name. Generalization is based on the fact that the world in which we live is usually—at the appropriate level of description—redundant. In particular, it may be *smooth:* small changes in some input parameters determine a correspondingly small change in the output (it may be necessary in some cases to accept *piecewise smoothness*). This is one of the most general and weakest constraints that makes approximation possible. Other, stronger *a priori* constraints may be known before approximating a mapping, for instance that the mapping is linear, or has a positive range, or a limited domain or is invariant to some group of transformations. Smoothness of a function corresponds to the function being not fully local: the value at one point depends on other values nearby. Smoothness can be measured in a number of different ways. As we will explain later, our measure of deviation from smoothness is some functional containing derivatives of the function considered. The results of Stone [22] (see section VII-C) suggest that, if nothing else is known about a high dimensional function to be approximated, the only option may be to assume a high degree of smoothness. Otherwise, the number of examples required would be totally unpractical.

B. Regularization Techniques for Learning

Techniques that exploit smoothness constraints in approximation problems are well known under the term of standard regularization. Consider the inverse problem of finding the hypersurface values z, given sparse data d. Standard regularization replaces the problem with the variational problem of finding the surface that minimizes a cost functional consisting of two terms [21], [23] (the first to introduce this technique in computer vision was Grimson, in 1981 [24]). The first term measures the distance between the data and the desired solution z; the second term measures the cost associated with a functional of the solution $\|Pz\|^2$ that embeds the *a priori* information on z. P is usually a differential operator. Thus, the problem is to find the hypersurface z that minimizes

$$\sum_i (z_i - d_i)^2 + \lambda\|Pz\|^2 \qquad (1)$$

where i is a collective index representing the points in feature space where data are available and λ, the regularization parameter, controls the compromise between the degree of smoothness of the solution and its closeness to the data. Therefore λ is directly related to the degree of generalization that is enforced. It is well known that standard regularization provides solutions that are equivalent to generalized splines [25]. A large body of results in fitting and approximating with splines may be therefore exploited.

C. Learning, Bayes Theorem and Minimum Length Principle

The formulation of the learning problem in terms of regularization is satisfying from a theoretical point of view. A variational principle such as equation (1) can be solidly grounded on Bayesian estimation (see [11]). Using Bayes theorem one expresses the conditional probability distribution $P_{z/d}(z; d)$ of the hypersurface z given the examples d in terms of a prior probability $P_z(z)$ that embeds the constraint of smoothness and the conditional probability $P_{d/z}(d; z)$ of d given z, equivalent to a model of the nosie:

$$P_{z/d}(z; d) \propto P_z(z)\, P_{d/z}(d; z).$$

This can be rewritten in terms of *complexities* of hypothesis, defined as $C(\cdot) = -\log P(\cdot)$

$$C(z|d) = C(z) + C(d|z) + c \qquad (2)$$

where c, which is related to $P_d(d)$, depends only on d. The MAP estimate corresponds to considering the z with minimum complexity $C(z|d)$. Maximum likelihood is the special case of MAP for uniform $C(z)$ (perfect *a priori* ignorance).

The maximum of this posterior probability (the MAP estimate) coincides with standard regularization, that is equation (1), provided that the noise is additive and Gaussian and the prior is a Gaussian distribution of a linear functional of z (see [11]). Under these conditions, the first term $-\Sigma_i (z_i - d_i)^2$—in the regularization principle of equation (1) corresponds to $C(d|z)$, whereas the second term—$\|Pz\|^2$—corresponds to the prior $C(z)$ [26].

Outside the domain of standard regularization, the prior probability distribution may represent other *a priori* knowledge than just smoothness. Piecewise constancy, for instance, could be used for classification tasks. Notice that in practice as much a priori information as possible must be supplied in order to make the learning problem manageable. *Space invariance* or other invariances to appropriate groups of transformations can play a very important role in effectively countering the curse of dimensionality (see [18]).

As pointed out by Rivest (in preparation), one can reverse the relationship between prior probabilities and complexity (see (2)). Instead of determining the complexity $C(z)$ in (2) from the prior, one may measure the *complexity* of the *a priori* hypotheses to determine the prior probabilities. Rissanen [27] for instance, proposes to measure the complexity of a hypothesis in terms of the bit length needed to encode it. In this sense, the MAP estimate is equivalent to the Minimum Description Length Principle: the hypothesis z which for given d can be described in the most compact way is chosen as the "best" hypothesis. Similar ideas have been explored by others (for instance [28]). They connect data compression and coding with Bayesian inference, regularization, hypersurface reconstruction, and learning.

D. From Hypersurface Reconstruction to Networks

In the section above we have sketched the strict relations between learning, Bayes estimation, regularization, and splines; splines are equivalent to standard regularization, itself a special case of MRF models, which are a subset of Bayesian estimators. All these methods can be implemented in terms of parallel networks: in particular, we and others have proposed that MRFs can be implemented in terms of hybrid networks of coupled analog and digital elements [26]. Standard regularization can be implemented by resistive grids, and has been implemented on an analog VLSI chip [29]. It is then natural to ask whether splines, and more generally standard regularization, can be implemented by feedforward multilayer networks. The answer is positive, and will be given in the next few sections in terms of what we call Regularization Networks. Regularization Networks are closely related to an interpolation technique called Radial Basis Functions (RBF), which has recent theoretical foundations (see the review of Powell [30]) and has been used with very promising results [31]–[36].

III. Regularization Theory and Regularization Networks

In this section we apply regularization theory to the approximation/interpolation problem and we show the equivalence between regularization and a class of three-layer networks that we call regularization networks. These networks are not only equivalent to generalized splines, but are also closely related to the classical Radial Basis Functions used for interpolation tasks, which are discussed in some detail in Appendix A.

A. Regularization Theory

Let $S = \{(\mathbf{x}_i, y_i) \in R^n \times R \mid i = 1, \cdots N\}$ be a set of data that we want to approximate by means of a function f. The regularization approach [37], [21], [38], [23] determines the function f that minimizes the functional

$$H[f] = \sum_{i=1}^{N} (y_i - f(\mathbf{x}_i))^2 + \lambda \|Pf\|^2 \qquad (3)$$

where P is a constraint operator (usually a differential operator), $\|\cdot\|$ is a norm on the function space to which Pf belongs (usually the L^2 norm) and λ is a positive real number, the so called *regularization parameter.* The structure of the operator P embodies the *a priori* knowledge about the solution, and therefore depends on the nature of the particular problem that has to be solved. Minimization of the functional H leads to the associated Euler–Lagrange equations [39], that in this case can always be written as

$$\hat{P}Pf(\mathbf{x}) = \frac{1}{\lambda} \sum_{i=1}^{N} (y_i - f(\mathbf{x}))\delta(\mathbf{x} - \mathbf{x}_i) \qquad (4)$$

where $\hat{P}$ is the adjoint of the differential operator P and the right side comes from the functional derivative with respect to f of the data term of H.

Equation (4) is a partial differential equation, and it is well known that its solution can be written as the integral transformation of its right side with a kernel given by the Green's function of the differential operator $\hat{P}P$, that is the function G satisfying the following distributional differential equation:

$$\hat{P}PG(\mathbf{x}; \mathbf{y}) = \delta(\mathbf{x} - \mathbf{y}).$$

Because of the delta functions appearing in (4) the integral transformation becomes a discrete sum and f can then be written as

$$f(\mathbf{x}) = \frac{1}{\lambda} \sum_{i=1}^{N} (y_i - f(\mathbf{x}_i))G(\mathbf{x}; \mathbf{x}_i). \qquad (5)$$

Equation (5) says that the solution of the regularization problem lies in an N-dimensional subspace of the space of smooth functions. A basis for this subspace is given by the N functions $G(\mathbf{x}; \mathbf{x}_i)$. In the following we will refer to $G(\mathbf{x}; \mathbf{x}_i)$ as to the Green's function "centered" at the point $\mathbf{x}_i$, and to the points $\mathbf{x}_i$ as to the "centers" of the expansion. The reason for this lies in the fact that usually the Green's function is translationally invariant, that is $G = G(\mathbf{x} - \mathbf{x}_i)$, and in this case $G(\mathbf{x})$ and $G(\mathbf{x} - \mathbf{x}_i)$ are equivalent modulo a coordinates translation that maps $\mathbf{x}_i$ in the origin.

A set of equations for the unknown coefficients $c_i = y_i - f(\mathbf{x}_i)/\lambda$ is easily obtained by evaluating equation (5) at the N data points $\mathbf{x}_i$. A straightforward calculation yields the following linear system:

$$(G + \lambda I)\mathbf{c} = \mathbf{y} \qquad (6)$$

where I is the identity matrix, and we have defined

$$(\mathbf{y})_i = y_i, \quad (\mathbf{c})_i = c_i, \quad (G)_{ij} = G(\mathbf{x}_i; \mathbf{x}_j).$$

We then conclude that *the solution to the regularization problem is given by*

$$f(\mathbf{x}) = \sum_{i=1}^{N} c_i G(\mathbf{x}; \mathbf{x}_i) \qquad (7)$$

where the coefficients satisfy the linear system (6).

We notice however that this expression is not the complete solution of the minimization problem. In fact all the functions that lie in the null space of the operator P are "invisible" to the smoothing term in the functional (3), so that the previous expansion is the solution *modulo* a term that lies in the null space of P. The form of this term depends on the stabilizer that has been chosen and on the boundary conditions, and therefore on the particular problem that has to be solved. For this reason, and since its inclusion does not modify the main conclusions, we will disregard it in the following. We just mention that for a stabilizer that is a homogeneous, rotationally invariant operator of degree n, the null space is the space of polynomials of degree $2n - 1$. This and other aspects of the minimization problem (3) can be found in the book of Wahba [40], where a result similar to the one of (7) is derived in a rigorous way by means of the technique of reproducing kernels.

Since the operator $\hat{P}P$ in equation (4) is self-adjoint, its Green's function is symmetric: $G(\mathbf{x}; \mathbf{y}) = G(\mathbf{y}; \mathbf{x})$. As a consequence the matrix G of equation (6) is symmetric and its eigenvalues are real numbers. The matrix $G + \lambda I$ is then of full rank (unless $-\lambda$ is equal to one of its eigenvalues) and the linear system (6) always has a solution. The existence of a solution in the case of $\lambda = 0$, that corresponds to pure interpolation, depends on the properties of the Green's function G. If the Green's function is positive definite this limit always exists, and an expansion of the type (7) interpolates the data without any null space term. If the Green's function is conditionally positive definite of some order (see Appendix A), well known results of approximation theory [41] guarantee that the addition to the expansion (7) of a polynomial of appropriate degree, that is the polynomial that lies in the null space of P, makes it always possible to interpolate the data points. Conditionally positive definiteness of the Green's function, as well as other properties, derives from the structure of the stabilizer P (see the next section for some examples). If the operator P is translationally invariant, G will depend on the difference of its arguments ($G = G(\mathbf{x} - \mathbf{y})$) and if it is rotationally and translationally invariant G will be a radial function: $G = G(\|\mathbf{x} - \mathbf{y}\|)$. In the last case the regularized solution is given by the following expansion:

$$f(\mathbf{x}) = \sum_{i=1}^{N} c_i G(\|\mathbf{x} - \mathbf{x}_i\|) \tag{8}$$

and the method of Radial Basis Functions may be recovered (see Appendix A). There are strict connections between the Radial Basis Function method and variational principles, some of which are sketched in the following subsection. Interesting results can be found in the paper of Dyn [42], where the work of Madych and Nelson [43] on semi-reproducing kernels and variational principles is discussed.

Notice that the requirement of rotational and translational invariance on P is very common in practical applications. Clearly, regularization with a non-radial stabilizer P justifies the use of appropriate non-radial basis functions, retaining all the approximation properties associated with the Tikhonov technique. An example involving non-radial stabilizers is the case of tensor product splines. Tensor product splines correspond to non-radial stabilizing operators that are the product of "one-dimensional" operators. In two dimensions, for example, they correspond to stabilizers of the form $P = P_x P_y$, where P_x (P_y) is a differential operator involving only derivatives with respect to x (y). The Green's function associated to $P_x P_y$ is the product of the Green's functions associated to P_x and P_y. The two dimensional problem is then regarded as the "tensor product" of two one-dimensional problems.

We now give some examples of stabilizers P and of their properties.

1) Examples

Multidimensional Splines: A widely used class of stabilizers is given by the functionals considered by Duchon [44] and Meinguet [45] in their variational approach to multivariate interpolation. In particular they considered functionals of the form

$$\|O^m f\|^2 = \sum_{i_1 \cdots i_m}^{n} \int_{R^n} d\mathbf{x} (\partial_{i_1 \cdots i_m} f(\mathbf{x}))^2$$

where $\partial_{i_1 \cdots i_m} = \partial^m / \partial x_{i_1} \cdots \partial x_{i_m}$ and $m \geq 1$. Stabilizers of this type are invariant under rotations and translations. Moreover, since the differential operator involved is homogeneous, a scale transformation of the variables affects this functional multiplying it by a constant, implying that the operations of finding the solution and scaling the data commute.

The Green's function associated to this stabilizer is radial, translation invariant and satisfies the following differential equation (in the sense of the distributions):

$$(-1)^m \nabla 2^m G(\mathbf{x}) = \delta(\mathbf{x})$$

where ∇^{2m} is the m-iterated Laplacian in n dimensions. The solution of this differential equation can be found using the method of generalized Fourier transforms, and it is shown to be (see Gelfand and Vilenkin, pp. 202, 1964)

$$G(\mathbf{x}) = \begin{cases} \|\mathbf{x}\|^{2m-n} \ln \|\mathbf{x}\| & \text{if } 2m > n \text{ and } n \text{ is even} \\ \|\mathbf{x}\|^{2m-n} & \text{otherwise.} \end{cases} \tag{9}$$

It is clear from equation (9) that the constraint $2m > n$ has to be imposed on the degree of smoothness m in order to obtain a Green's function that is not singular in the origin. Suppose now that the condition $2m > n$ is fulfilled: it is well known from spline theory that if the stabilizer is of order m then the Green's function is conditionally positive definite of the same order. This means that, given m, in order to interpolate the set $\mathcal{S}$ of data, $\mathcal{S} = \{(\mathbf{x}_i, y_i) \in R^n \times R | i = 1, \cdots N\}$, the following function can be used:

$$f(\mathbf{x}) = \sum_{k=1}^{N} c_i G(\mathbf{x} - \mathbf{x}_i) + p_{m-1}(\mathbf{x})$$

where $p_{m-1}(\mathbf{x})$ is a polynomial of degree $m - 1$.

In the case $n = m = 2$ the functional to be minimized is

$$\|O^2 f\|^2 = \int_{R^2} dx\, dy \left[\left(\frac{\partial^2 f}{\partial x^2} \right)^2 + 2 \left(\frac{\partial^2 f}{\partial x \partial y} \right)^2 + \left(\frac{\partial^2 f}{\partial y^2} \right)^2 \right]$$

and the Green's function h is the well known "thin plate spline" $h(r) = r^2 \ln r$. In this case a linear term appears as the second term of the right hand side of equation (9). Thin plate splines have been introduced by engineers for aeroelastic calculations [46], their name coming from the fact that $\| O^2 f\|^2$ is the bending energy of a thin plate of infinite extent.

A Generalization of Multidimensional Splines: We now consider the following generalization of the class of stabilizers previously shown:

$$\|P^M f\|^2 = \sum_{n=0}^{M} a_n \|O^n f\|^2 \tag{10}$$

The stabilizer is rotationally and translationally invariant and the Green's function satisfies the distributional differential equation:

$$\sum_{m=0}^{M} (-1)^m a_m \nabla^{2m} G(\mathbf{x} - \mathbf{y}) = \delta(\mathbf{x} - \mathbf{y}). \quad (11)$$

By Fourier transforming both sides of equation (11) we obtain:

$$\sum_{m=0}^{M} a_m(\mathbf{s} \cdot \mathbf{s})^m \, G(\mathbf{s}) = 1$$

and by Fourier anti-transforming $G(\mathbf{s})$ we have for the Green's function $G(\mathbf{x})$:

$$G(\mathbf{x}) = \int_{R^n} d\mathbf{s} \frac{e^{i\mathbf{s}\cdot\mathbf{x}}}{\sum_{m=0}^{M} a_m(\mathbf{s} \cdot \mathbf{s})^m} = \int_{R^n} d\mathbf{s} e^{i\mathbf{s}\cdot\mathbf{x}} \, dV(\mathbf{s}) \quad (12)$$

where $V(\mathbf{s})$ is a bounded non-decreasing function if $a_0 \neq 0$. Now we can apply Bochner's theorem [47], which states that a function is positive definite if and only if it can be written in the form (12), to conclude that $G(\mathbf{x})$ is positive definite. Notice that the condition $a_0 > 0$ is crucial in this particular derivation, and, as it has been pointed out by Yuille and Grzywacz [48], *it is a necessary and sufficient condition for the Green's function to fall asymptotically to zero.* If a_0 is zero a similar result holds, the Green's function being *conditionally* positive definite of some order, as in the case of the spline functions previously shown.

One simple one-dimensional example is provided by the following choice of the coefficients:

$$a_n = \begin{cases} q^2 & q > 0, \text{ if } n = 0 \\ 1 & \text{if } n = 1 \\ 0 & \text{otherwise.} \end{cases}$$

The Green's function for $q \neq 0$ is shown to be [49]:

$$G_q(x - y) = \frac{1}{2q} e^{-q|x-y|}.$$

Clearly this function is not very smooth, reflecting the fact that the stabilizer consists of derivatives of order 0 and 1 only. Smoother functions can be obtained allowing a larger number of coefficients to be different from zero. Here we give an example of a stabilizer of the type (10) in which the degree, and then the number M of terms, is let go to infinity. In this case the differential operator defining the Green's function ceases to be a differential operator in the standard sense, and it is called a pseudo-differential operator. As an example we consider the choice $a_m = \sigma^{2m}/m!2^m$, that leads to the pseudodifferential equation:

$$\sum_{n=0}^{\infty} (-1)^n \frac{\sigma^{2m}}{m!2^m} \nabla^{2n} G(\mathbf{x}) = \delta(\mathbf{x}).$$

Standard Fourier techniques yield the Green's function

$$G(\mathbf{x}) = Ae^{-(\mathbf{x}^2/2\sigma^2)}$$

where A is a normalization constant. The regularized solution is then a linear superposition of Gaussians centered on the data points $\mathbf{x}_i$, and has interesting properties that will be shown in section (7).

B. Regularization Networks

An obvious property of this technique is that it can be implemented by a simple network with just one layer of hidden units, as shown in Fig. 1. The first layer of this network, that we call *regularization network* consists of "input" units whose number is equivalent to the number of independent variables of the problem. The second layer is composed of nonlinear "hidden" units fully connected to the first layer. There is one hidden unit for each data point $\mathbf{x}_i \equiv (x_i, y_i, z_i, \cdots)$, and the connections between the ith hidden unit and the input units are given by the coordinates $(x_i, y_i, z_i, \cdots)$ of the ith data point. The "activation function" of the hidden units is the Green's function G, so that the output of the ith hidden unit is $G(\mathbf{x}; \mathbf{x}_i)$. The output layer, fully connected to the hidden layer, consists of one (or more) linear unit(s), whose "weights" are the unknown coefficients of the expansion (7). It is straightforward to see that gradient descent, that minimizes the interpolation error on the data points, can be used to solve the system (6) with λ set to zero. If the Green's function is positive definite this solution will be the "optimal" interpolant, that is the interpolant that minimizes the functional $\|Pf\|^2$, even without the polynomial terms. If the Green's function is conditionally positive definite some appropriate polynomial units should be added to the network in order to obtain the optimal interpolant (Fig. 1 shows the case of a polynomial of order 1, i.e., linear).

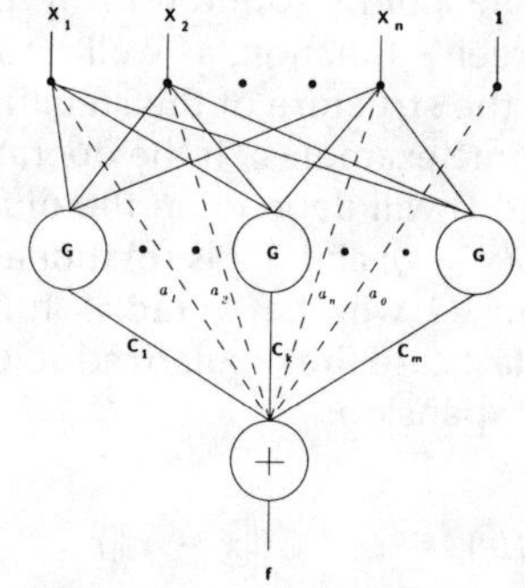

Fig. 1. The regularization network used to approximate a mapping between $x_1, x_2, \cdots, x_n$ and y, given a set of sparse, noisy data. In addition to the linear combination of Green's functions constant and linear terms are shown here as direct connections from the input to the output with weights a_0, $a_1, a_2, \cdots, a_n$. Constant, linear and higher order polynomials may be needed, depending on the stabilizer P.

Notice that the architecture of the regularization network is completely determined by the learning problem, and that, unlike most of the current "neural" networks, all weights between the input and the hidden layer are known. From the point of view of approximation theory the regularization network has three desirable properties:

1. It has been shown [50] that a regularization network can approximate arbitrarily well any multivariate continuous function on a compact domain, given a sufficiently high number of units. This property is shared by algebraic and trigonometric polynomials, as is shown by the classical Weierstrass Theorem, and by a large class of networks with one layer of hidden units [13], [15], [14], [16], [51].
2. Since the approximation scheme derived from regularization theory is linear in the unknown coefficients, it is easy to prove that it has the so called *best-approximation property* [50]. This means that

given a function f, there always exists a choice of coefficients that approximates f better than all other possible choices. This property, which is important mainly from the theoretical point of view, is shared by all the classical approximating schemes, such as approximation by polynomial and splines with fixed knots, in which the approximating solution depends *linearly* on the unknown parameters. It can be shown [50], that multilayer feedforward networks, of the type usually considered for back-propagation schemes, do not have this property.

3. The solution computed by the regularization network is "optimal" in the sense that it minimizes a functional that measures how much it oscillates. This eliminates solutions that perfectly interpolate the data points but badly oscillate where there are no data. This property is typical of the spline interpolation method, but it is not shared, for example, by the polynomial interpolation scheme.

Notice that in the regularization networks output units may also compute a fixed, nonlinear, invertible function σ ([11]), as already observed by Broomhead and Lowe [34]. This is useful for instance in the case of classification tasks, the function σ being naturally chosen to be a sigmoid function. Clearly a similar nonlinear function could be applied to each of the inputs. It seems possible that in some cases suitable input and output processing of this type may be advantageous. Poggio (see [18]) following Resnikoff [52], has argued that the input and the output of the mapping to be approximated should be processed by a nonlinear function in order to match the domain and the range of the approximating function. Resnikoff had proposed as nonlinear functions for this processing the birational functions, the exponential function, the logarithmic function, and the composition of these functions, since they achieve the necessary conversion of domain and range with minimal disruption of the algebraic structure of the input and output spaces. Input and output coding of this type tries to linearize the approximation as much as possible by exploiting *a priori* information about the range and the domain of the mapping to be approximated. Interestingly, the sigmoid function used at the output of many neural networks can be derived from the composition of a rational function and an exponential and matches the range of functions used for binary classification.

IV. Extensions of the Regularization Approach

In this section we extend the theory by defining a more general form of regularization networks, that can perform task-dependent clustering and dimensionality reduction and that we call Hyper Basis Functions. The extensions we propose are two:

1. The network associated with equation (7) has a complexity (number of units) that is independent of the dimensionality of the input space but is on the order of the dimensionality of the training set (number of examples), which is usually high. We show how to justify an approximation of equation (7) in which the number of units is much smaller than the number of examples and the positions of the "centers" of the expansion are modified during learning [11]. This scheme can be further extended by considering in equation (7) the superposition of different types of functions G, such as Gaussians of different scales.
2. The norm $\|x - x_i\|$ may be considered as a *weighted norm*

$$\|x - x_i\|_W^2 = (x - x_i)^T W^T W (x - x_i)$$

where W is a square matrix and the superscript T indicates the transpose. In the simple case of diagonal W the diagonal elements w_{ii} assign a specific weight to each input coordinate, and the standard Euclidean norm is obtained when W is set to the identity matrix. They play a critical role whenever different types of inputs are present. We will show how the weighted norm idea can be derived rigorously from a slightly more general regularization principle than equation (3).

In the following we will introduce these two extensions and show that the *moving centers* are related to clustering techniques and that the *norm-weights* correspond to dimensionality reduction. We also mentioned two further extensions: learning in the presence of unreliable examples and learning from positive *and* negative examples.

A. Moving Centers: An Approximation to the Regularization Solution

The solution given by standard regularization theory to the approximation problem can be very expensive in computational terms when the number of examples is very high. The computation of the coefficients of the expansion can become then a very time consuming operation: its complexity grows polynomially with N, (roughly as N^3) since an $N \times N$ matrix has to be inverted. In addition, the probability of ill-conditioning is higher for larger and larger matrices (it grows like N^3 for a $N \times N$ uniformly distributed random matrix) [53]. In this section, we show how to reduce the complexity of the problem, introducing an approximation to the regularized solution.

A standard technique that has been used to find approximate solutions of variational problems is to expand the solution on a finite basis. The approximated solution $f^*(x)$ has then the following form:

$$f^*(x) = \sum_{i=1}^{n} c_i \phi_i(x) \tag{13}$$

where $\{\phi_i\}_{i=1}^n$ is a set of linearly independent functions [54]. The coefficients c_i are usually found according to some rule that guarantees a minimum deviation from the true solution. In the case of standard regularization, when the functional to minimize is given by equation (3), this method gives the *exact* solution if n is equal to the number of data points N, and $\{\phi_i\}_{i=1}^n = \{G(x; x_i)\}_{i=1}^N$, where G is the Green's function of the operator $\hat{P}P$. In this case the unknown coefficients of the expansion (13) can be obtained in a simple way by substituting expansion (13) in the regularization functional (3), that becomes a *function* $H[f^*] = H^*(c_1, \cdots, c_N)$, and then by minimizing $H[f^*]$ with respect to the coefficients, that is by setting:

$$\frac{\partial H[f^*]}{\partial c_i} = 0 \qquad i = 1, \cdots, N. \tag{14}$$

It can be easily shown [11] that if the Green's function vanishes on the boundary of the region that is considered the set of equations (14) is equivalent to the linear system (6). In more general cases the basis $\{\phi_i\}_{i=1}^n$ should be enlarged, to include terms that generate the null space of P, in order to obtain the correct solution. For simplicity, we disregard these terms in the following, since they do not change the main conclusions. A natural approximation to the exact solution will then be of the form:

$$f^*(x) = \sum_{\alpha=1}^{n} c_\alpha G(x; t_\alpha) \tag{15}$$

where the parameters t_α, that we call "centers", and the coefficients c_α are unknown, and are in general fewer than the data points ($n \leq N$). This form of solution has the desirable property to be a universal approximator for continuous functions [50] and to be the only choice that guarantees that in the case of $n = N$ and $\{t_\alpha\}_{\alpha=1}^n = \{x_i\}_{i=1}^n$ the correct solution (of equation (3)) is consistently recovered. We will see later how to find the unknown parameters of this expansion.

B. Different Types of Basis Functions and Multiple Scales

This scheme can be further extended by considering in equation (15) the superposition of different types of functions G, such as Gaussians at different scales. The function f to be approximated is regarded as the sum of p components f^m, $m = 1, \cdots, p$, each component having a different prior probability. Therefore the functional $H[f]$ to minimize will contain p stabilizers P^m and will be written as

$$H[f] = \sum_{i=1}^{N} \left(\sum_{m=1}^{p} f^m(x_i) - y_i \right)^2 + \sum_{m=1}^{p} \lambda_m \|P^m f^m\|^2. \tag{16}$$

Analyzing the structure of the Euler-Lagrange equations associated to equation (16) it can be shown that the function $F(x)$ that minimizes the functional (16) is a *linear superposition of linear superpositions* of the Green's functions G^m corresponding to the stabilizers P^m. Exactly as in the previous section, an approximated solution f^* to the variational problem is sought of the following form:

$$f^*(x) = \sum_{m=1}^{p} \sum_{\alpha=1}^{K_m} c_\alpha^m G^m(x; t_\alpha^m) \tag{17}$$

where $K_m < N$ and the coefficients c_α^m and the *centers* t_α^m are to be found.

This method leads in particular to radial basis functions of multiple scales for the reconstruction of the function f. Suppose we know *a priori* that the function to be approximated has components on a number p of scales $\sigma_1, \cdots, \sigma_p$: we can use this information to choose a set of p stabilizers whose Green's functions are, for example, Gaussians of variance $\sigma_1, \cdots, \sigma_p$. As a result, the solution will be a *superposition of superpositions* of Gaussians of different variance. Of course, the Gaussians with large σ should be preset, depending on the nature of the problem, to be fewer and therefore on a sparser grid, than the Gaussians with a small σ.

This method yields also non-radial Green's functions—by using appropriate stabilizers—and also Green's functions with a lower dimensionality—by using the associated f^m and P^m in a suitable lower-dimensional subspace. Again this reflects *a priori* information that may be available about the nature of the mapping to be learned. In the latter case the information is that the mapping is of lower dimensionality or has lower dimensional components.

C. Weighted Norm and Regularization

The norm in equation (15) is usually intended as an Euclidean norm. If the components of x are of different types, it is natural to consider a *weighted norm* defined as $\|x\|_W^2 = x^T W^T W x$, since the relative scale of the components is otherwise arbitrary. The case in which the matrix W is known (from prior information) does not present any difficulty. It is interesting, however, to see what it means in terms of the underlying regularization principle.

The regularization principle consists of finding the f that minimizes the functional:

$$H_W[f] = \sum_{i=1}^{N} (y_i - f(x_i))^2 + \lambda \|Pf\|_y^2 \tag{18}$$

where we assume that P is radially symmetric in the variable y and that $y = Wx$ (i.e. y is a known linear transformation of x that depends on the parameters W). This means that the smoothness constraint is given in a space that is an affine transformation of the original x space. The Green's function associated with equation (18) is $G(\|y\|^2) = G(\|x\|_W^2)$. If this formulation is used together with the moving center scheme, the approximated solution of the regularization problem has the form:

$$f^*(x) = \sum_{\alpha=1}^{n} c_\alpha G(\|x - t_\alpha\|_W^2) \tag{19}$$

Suppose now that the parameters W are unknown. We can formulate the problem of finding f and W that minimize the functional $H_W(f)$. Thus finding the optimal W corresponds to finding the best stabilizer among those that are expressed in a coordinate system which is a linear transformation of the original one.

The simplest case is the case of W diagonal and $G(x) = e^{-x^2}$. In this case

$$G(\|x\|_W^2) = e^{-x_1^2 w_1^2} e^{-x_2^2 w_2^2} \cdots e^{-x_n^2 w_n^2}$$

and thus the diagonal elements w_i of W are equivalent to the inverse of the variance σ of each component of the multidimensional Gaussian.

D. Learning with Unreliable and Negative Examples

In the standard regularization approach, as well as in the extensions shown above, the set of data g is fixed, and all the data points are used in order to obtain a solution. It is possible to modify the functional (3) to take in account the possibility of excluding unreliable data, that are "spurious" or "too noisy". An analysis, similar to the one performed by Geiger and Girosi [55] on the problem of reconstructing piecewise smooth surfaces, shows that in the presence of unreliable data the functional (3) has to be replaced with the functional [56]

$$H'[f] = \sum_{i=1}^{N} V(\Delta_i) + \lambda \|Pf\|^2. \tag{20}$$

Here we have defined the "effective potential" V as the function

$$V(x) = x^2 - \frac{1}{\beta} \ln (1 + e^{-\beta(\epsilon - x^2)})$$

where ϵ is a positive number and β is a positive parameter, that is usually let go to infinity. In the case of β going to infinity the meaning of the effective potential is the following: closeness to the ith data point is enforced only if the interpolation error Δ_i is smaller that $\sqrt{\epsilon}$ (in this region $V(x) = x^2$ as in the standard regularization case). If the interpolation error is larger than $\sqrt{\epsilon}$ it is very likely that the datum is spurious, so that there is no need to enforce the function to go through that datum ($V(x)$ = constant = ϵ, while in the standard regularization case it is still quadratic).

The effective potential can be used also to deal with the problem of *negative examples*. Suppose we know that the function at the points $\{\mathbf{t}_\alpha\}_{\alpha=1}^K$ has to assume values that are *far* from the values $\{y_\alpha\}_{\alpha=1}^K$. This *a priori* knowledge can be introduced in the standard regularization functional by adding an appropriate term, that is, by minimizing

$$H''[f] = \sum_{i=1}^{N} \Delta_i^2 - \sum_{\alpha=1}^{N} V(\Delta_\alpha) + \lambda\|Pf\|^2. \quad (21)$$

where γ is a positive parameter. Due to the minus sign in equation (21) the interpolation error Δ_α at the points $\{\mathbf{t}_\alpha\}_{\alpha=1}^K$ is enforced to be larger than $\sqrt{\gamma}$. Notice that the solutions of the minimization problems (20) and (21) still have the form of linear superposition of Green's functions, and then can be implemented by a regularization network whose "weights" are found using a gradient-descent procedure.

E. How to Learn Centers' Positions and Norm Weights

Suppose that we look for an approximated solution of the regularization problem of the form (19). We now have the problem of finding the n coefficients c_α, the $d \times n$ coordinates of the centers $\mathbf{t}_\alpha$ and the d^2 elements of the matrix $\mathbf{W}$ so that the expansion (19) is optimal. In this case we can make use of a natural definition of optimality, given by the functional H. We then impose the condition that the set $\{c_\alpha, \mathbf{t}_\alpha | \alpha = 1, \cdots, n\}$ and the matrix $\mathbf{W}$ must be such that they minimizes $H[f^*]$, and the following equations must be satisfied:

$$\frac{\partial H[f^*]}{\partial c_\alpha} = 0, \quad \frac{\partial H[f^*]}{\partial \mathbf{t}_\alpha} = 0, \quad \frac{\partial H[f^*]}{\partial \mathbf{W}} = 0,$$

$$\alpha = 1, \cdots, n.$$

Gradient-descent is probably the simplest approach for attempting to find the solution to this problem, though, of course, it is not guaranteed to converge. Several other iterative methods, such as versions of conjugate gradient and simulated annealing [57] or variations of the Metropolis algorithm (Caprile and Girosi, in preparation) may be better than gradient descent and should be used in practice. Since the function $H[f^*]$ to minimize is in general non-convex, a stochastic term in the gradient descent equations may be advisable to avoid local minima. In the gradient descent method the values of c_α, $\mathbf{t}_\alpha$, and $\mathbf{W}$ that minimize $H[f^*]$ are regarded as the coordinates of the stable fixed point of the following dynamical system:

$$\dot{c}_\alpha = -\omega \frac{\partial H[f^*]}{\partial c_\alpha}, \quad \dot{\mathbf{t}}_\alpha = -\omega \frac{\partial H[f^*]}{\partial \mathbf{t}_\alpha}, \quad \dot{\mathbf{W}} = -\omega \frac{\partial H[f^*]}{\partial \mathbf{W}},$$

$$\alpha = 1, \cdots, n$$

where ω is a parameter determining the microscopic timescale of the problem and is related to the rate of convergence to the fixed point. Defining

$$\Delta_i \equiv y_i - f^*(\mathbf{x}) = y_i - \sum_{\alpha=1}^{n} c_\alpha G(\|\mathbf{x}_i - \mathbf{t}_\alpha\|_{\mathbf{W}}^2)$$

and setting $\lambda = 0$ for simplicity (the more general case can be approached in a similar way) in equation (3) we obtain

$$H[f^*] = H_{c,\mathbf{w},\mathbf{t}} = \sum_{i=1}^{N} (\Delta_i)^2.$$

The important quantities—that can be used in more efficient schemes than gradient descent—are:

- for the c_α

$$\frac{\partial H[f^*]}{\partial c_\alpha} = -2 \sum_{i=1}^{N} \Delta_i G(\|\mathbf{x}_i - \mathbf{t}_\alpha\|_{\mathbf{W}}^2); \quad (22)$$

- for the centers $\mathbf{t}_\alpha$

$$\frac{\partial H[f^*]}{\partial \mathbf{t}_\alpha} = 4c_\alpha \sum_{i=1}^{N} \Delta_i G'(\|\mathbf{x}_i - \mathbf{t}_\alpha\|_{\mathbf{W}}^2)\, \mathbf{W}^T\mathbf{W}(\mathbf{x}_i - \mathbf{t}_\alpha) \quad (23)$$

- and for $\mathbf{W}$

$$\frac{\partial H[f^*]}{\partial \mathbf{W}} = -4\mathbf{W} \sum_{\alpha=1}^{N} c_\alpha \sum_{i=1}^{N} \Delta_i G'(\|\mathbf{x}_i - \mathbf{t}_\alpha\|_{\mathbf{W}}^2) Q_{i,\alpha} \quad (24)$$

  where $Q_{i,\alpha} = (\mathbf{x}_i - \mathbf{t}_\alpha)(\mathbf{x}_i - \mathbf{t}_\alpha)^T$ is a dyadic product and G' is the first derivative of G. Instead of $\mathbf{W}$ we have also used $\mathbf{M} = \mathbf{W}^T\mathbf{W}$ with the appropriate equivalent of equation (24).

Remarks

1. Equation (22) has a simple interpretation: the correction is equal to the sum over the examples of the products between the error on that example and the "activity" of the "unit" that represents with its center that example. Notice that $H[f^*]$ is quadratic in the coefficients c_α, and if the centers and the matrix $\mathbf{W}$ are kept fixed, it can be shown [11] that the optimal coefficients are given by

$$\mathbf{c} = (G^TG + \lambda g)^{-1}G^T\mathbf{y} \quad (25)$$

   where we have defined $(\mathbf{y})_i = y_i$, $(\mathbf{c})_\alpha = c_\alpha$, $(G)_{i\alpha} = G(\mathbf{x}_i; \mathbf{t}_\alpha)$ and $(g)_{\alpha\beta} = G(\mathbf{t}_\alpha; \mathbf{t}_\beta)$. If λ is let go to zero the matrix on the right side of equation (25) converges to the pseudoinverse of G [58], and if the Green's function is radial the approximation method of Broomhead and Lowe [34] is recovered.
2. Equation (23) is similar to task-dependent clustering [11]. This can be best seen by assuming that Δ_i are constant: then the gradient descent updating rule makes the centers move towards the majority of the data, to find the position of the cluster. Equating $\partial H[f^*]/\partial \mathbf{t}_\alpha$ to zero we notice that, when the matrix $\mathbf{W}$ is set to the identity matrix, the optimal centers $\mathbf{t}_\alpha$ satisfy the following set of nonlinear equations:

$$\mathbf{t}_\alpha = \frac{\sum_i P_i^\alpha \mathbf{x}_i}{\sum_i P_i^\alpha} \qquad \alpha = 1, \cdots, n$$

   where $P_i^\alpha = \Delta_i G'(\|\mathbf{x}_i - \mathbf{t}_\alpha\|^2)$. The optimal centers are then a weighted sum of the data points. The weight P_i^α of the data point i for a given center $\mathbf{t}_\alpha$ is high if the interpolation error Δ_i is high there *and* the radial basis function centered on that knot changes quickly in a neighborhood of the data point. This observation could suggest faster methods for finding a quasi-optimal set of knots [7].

3. Equation (24) contains the quantity $\Sigma_{i=1}^{N} Q_{i,\alpha}$ which is an estimate of the correlation matrix of all the examples relative to $\boldsymbol{t}_\alpha$ (modulus a normalization factor). Notice that $\Sigma_{i=1}^{N} Q_{i,\alpha}$ can be written as the product of a matrix containing N columns, each being one example (minus the quantity $\boldsymbol{t}_\alpha$) times the transpose of the same matrix: it is therefore a $d \times d$ matrix (d being the number of components of $\boldsymbol{x}$). It can be shown [59] that equation (24), under strong simplifying conditions, converges to a $\boldsymbol{W}$ with rows that are close to the eigenvectors of Q with the smallest eigenvalues. In other words, the equation would then converge to rows of $\boldsymbol{W}$ that span the space orthogonal to the space spanned by the principal components of the input examples (i.e. the eigenvectors of Q with the largest eigenvalues).
4. Equation (24) is similar to an operation of (task-dependent) dimensionality reduction [60] whereas equation (23) is similar to a clustering process. It is conceivable that learning the weights of the norm is even more important than learning the centers and that in many cases it may be preferable to set the centers to a representative subset of the data and to keep them fixed thereafter.
5. A specific matrix $\boldsymbol{W}$ corresponds to a specific metric in the multidimensional input space: $\boldsymbol{W}$ projects the input vector into the subspace spanned by its rows. In the case of the rows of $\boldsymbol{W}$ spanning the space orthogonal to the principal components of the inputs, $\boldsymbol{W}$ assigns a metric ellipsoid with the larges axes (corresponding to a large σ, if the Green's function is a Gaussian) along the principal components and the small axis (corresponding to a small σ in the Gaussian) orthogonal to it: thus even vectors that are far away (in the ordinary Euclidean metric) are close in this metric if they lie in the hyperplane of the principal components and even close vectors (in the ordinary metric) are far away in the metric induced by $\boldsymbol{W}$ if they are orthogonal to the principal components.
6. In the case of N examples, $n = N$ fixed centers and $\boldsymbol{W} = I$, there are enough data to constrain the N c_α to be found. Moving centers add another $n \times d$ parameters (d is the number of input components) and the matrix $\boldsymbol{W}^T\boldsymbol{W}$ another d^2 parameters. Thus the number of examples N must be sufficiently large to constrain adequately the free parameters—n d-dimensional centers, n coefficients c_α and d^2 entries of the matrix $\boldsymbol{W}$ (notice that only $(d^2 + d)/2$ entries will be independent). Thus the condition $N > K + Kd + d^2$ should be satisfied.
7. In the case of Gaussian basis functions, learning the entries of a diagonal $\boldsymbol{W}$ is equivalent to learn the σ of each two-dimensional (or one-dimensional) Gaussian receptive field for each center.
8. In the gradient descent equations nothing forbids that two or more centers may move towards each other until they coincide. Clearly, this should be avoided, for example adding to the functional (3) a term of the form $\Sigma_{\alpha \neq \beta} \Psi(\|\boldsymbol{t}_\alpha - \boldsymbol{t}_\beta\|)$, where Ψ is an appropriate repulsive potential. The gradient descent equation can be easily modified to reflect this additional term.

F. A Practical Algorithm

It seems natural to try to find a reasonable initial value for the parameters c_α, $\boldsymbol{t}_\alpha$, and $\boldsymbol{W}$ to start the minimization process. In absence of more specific prior information the following heuristics seems reasonable.

- Set the number of centers n and set the centers positions to a subset of the examples;
- Set the rows of $\boldsymbol{W}$ to be vectors orthogonal to the eigenvectors of $\Sigma_\alpha \Sigma_i Q_{i,\alpha}$ with largest eigenvalues;
- Use matrix pseudo-inversion to find the c_α;
- Use the $\boldsymbol{t}_\alpha$, $\boldsymbol{W}$ and c_α found so far as initial values for gradient descent equations.

As discussed in [59] even more general strategies may make sense.

V. Gaussian Basis Functions and Science-Fiction Neurobiology

In this section we point out some remarkable properties of Gaussian Basis Functions, that may have significant implications for neurobiology and, to a lesser extent, for VLSI circuit implementations.

A. Factorizable Radial Basis Functions

The synthesis of radial basis functions in many dimensions may be easier if they are factorizable. It can be easily proven that *the only radial basis function which is factorizable is the Gaussian* (tensor product splines correspond to factorizable Green functions which are not radial). A multidimensional Gaussian function can be represented as the product of lower dimensional Gaussians. For instance a 2D Gaussian radial function centered in $\boldsymbol{t}$ can be written as:

$$G(\|\boldsymbol{x} - \boldsymbol{t}\|^2) \equiv e^{-\|\boldsymbol{x}-\boldsymbol{t}\|^2} = e^{-(x-t_x)^2} e^{-(y-t_y)^2}. \qquad (26)$$

This dimensionality factorization is especially attractive from the physiological point of view, since it is difficult to imagine how neurons could compute $G(\|\boldsymbol{x} - \boldsymbol{t}_\alpha\|^2)$ in a simple way for dimensions higher than two. The scheme of Fig. 2, on the other hand, is physiologically plausible. Gaussian radial functions in one and two dimensions can be readily implemented as *receptive fields* by weighted connections from the sensor arrays (or some retinotopic array of units representing with their activity the position of features).

Physiological speculations aside, this scheme has three interesting features from the point of view of a hardware implementation and also in purely conceptual terms. Consider the example of a Gaussian Radial Basis Function network operating on images:

1. The multidimensional radial functions are synthesized directly by appropriately weighted connections from the sensor arrays, without any need of an explicit computation of the norm and the exponential.

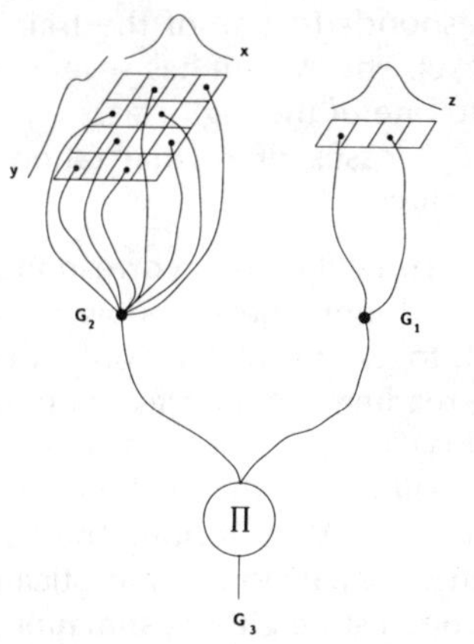

Fig. 2. A three-dimensional radial Gaussian implemented by multiplying two-dimensional Gaussian and one-dimensional Gaussian receptive fields. The latter two functions are synthesized directly by appropriately weighted connections from the sensor arrays, as neural receptive fields are usually thought to arise. Notice that they transduce the implicit position of stimuli in the sensor array into a number (the activity of the unit). They serve the dual purpose of providing the required "number" representation from the activity of the sensor array and of computing a Gaussian function. 2D Gaussians acting on a retinotopic map can be regarded as representing 2D "features," while the radial basis function represents the "template" resulting from the conjunction of those lower-dimensional features.

2. 2D Gaussians operating on the sensor array or on a retinotopic array of features extracted by some preprocessing transduce the implicit position of features in the array into a number (the activity of the unit). They thus serve the purpose of providing the required "number" representation from the "array" representation.
3. 2D Gaussians acting on a retinotopic map can be regarded as representing 2D "features", while each radial basis function represents the "template" resulting from the conjunction of those lower-dimensional features. Notice that in this analogy the radial basis function is the AND of several features and could also include the negation of certain features, that is the AND NOT of them. The scheme is also hierarchical, in the sense that a multidimensional Gaussian "template" unit may be a "feature" input for another radial function (again because of the factorization property of the Gaussian). Of course a whole network may be one of the inputs to another network.

B. *Style of Computation and Physiological Predictions*

The multiplication operation required by the previous interpretation of Gaussian networks to perform the "conjunction" of Gaussian receptive fields is not too implausible from a biophysical point of view. It could be performed by several biophysical mechanisms, as discussed in more detail by [11], directly on the dendritic tree of the neuron representing the corresponding radial function.

The scheme also requires a certain amount of memory per basis unit, in order to store the center vector. In the Gaussian case the center vector is effectively stored in the position of the 2D (or 1D) receptive fields and in their connections to the product unit(s). This is plausible physiologically. The update equations are probably not. Equation (22) or a somewhat similar, quasi-hebbian scheme is not too unlikely and may require only a small amount of plausible neural circuitry. Equations (23) seem more difficult to implement for a network of real neurons. It should be stressed, however, that the centers may be moved in other ways—or not at all! In the Gaussian case, with basis functions synthesized through the product of Gaussian receptive fields, moving the centers means establishing or erasing connections to the product unit. This can be done on the basis of rules that are different from the full equation (23), such as, for instance, competitive learning, and that are biologically more plausible. The same can be said about the process that determines the weights in the norm.

Regularization networks with a Gaussian Green's function suggest an intriguing metaphor for a computational strategy that the brain may use. Computation, in the sense of generalization from examples, would be done by superposition of receptive fields in a multidimensional input space. In the case of Gaussian radial basis functions, the multidimensional receptive fields could be synthesized by combining lower dimensional receptive fields, possibly in multiple stages. From this point of view, some cells would correspond to radial functions with centers in a high dimensional input space, somewhat similar to prototypes or coarse "grandmother cells," a picture that seems superficially consistent with physiological evidence. They could be synthesized as the conjunction of Gaussian weighted positive and negative features in 2D retinotopic arrays.

Notice that from this perspective the computation is performed by *Gaussian receptive fields* and their combination (through some approximation to multiplication), rather than by threshold functions. The basis units may not even need to be all radial, as obvious from the regularization formulation. The view is in the spirit of the key role that the concept of receptive field has always played in neurophysiology. It predicts the existence of low-dimensional feature-like cells and multidimensional Gaussian-like receptive fields, somewhat similar to template-like cells, a fact that could be tested experimentally on cortical cells.

VI. Some Applications

Many problems in several different fields such as system estimation, computer vision, speech understanding, statistical estimation, analysis of time series, signal processing can be formulated as problems of approximating multivariate functions from sparse data or, equivalently, as problems of learning from examples. In all these cases, especially when the problem involves continuous output values rather than binary (as in classification tasks), regularization networks can be used. This section sketches just three applications.

A. *Recognizing a 3D Object from its Perspective Views*

Consider the problem of recognizing a wire-frame 3D object from any of its perspective views. A view of the object is represented, for instance, as a $2N$ vector $x_1, y_1, x_2, y_2, \cdots, x_N, y_N$ of the coordinates on the image plane of N labeled and visible points on the object. Additional different types of features can also be used, such as angles between vertices. The network learns to map any view of the object into a classification function. The results with images generated with computer graphics tools are encouraging, using a small number of training views [61]. Other encoding schemes are roughly equivalent, such as angles between the edges or segments lengths. A similar network with the same centers but different c can be used to provide the attitude of the object in space for any of its views [62].

B. Learning Dynamical Systems

HyperBF can be used to "learn" a dynamical system from the time course of its output. In fact, RBF have been often suggested as a good technique for this problem and have been successfully tested in some cases [34, 36]. The technique involves the approximation of the "iterated map" underlying the dynamical system (the crucial problem is, of course, the estimation of the dimension of the attractor and the choice of the input variables). We have every reason to believe that HyperBF will perform on this problem at least as well as the linear techniques of Farmer and Sidorowich [63] and the backpropagation algorithm of Lapedes and Farber [64]. The task of learning filters, especially recursive filters, for signal processing applications, is a closely related problem.

C. Learning Perceptual and Motor Tasks

Regularization networks have a good chance of being capable of synthesizing several vision algorithms from examples, since several problems in vision have satisfactory solutions in terms of regularization. The use of regularization networks is not restricted to sensory processes and they may also be used to learn motor tasks and even to model biological motor control. In support of this latter point, notice that simple biological trajectory control seems to be well explained by variational formulations of the regularization type [65]. Regularization networks are equivalent to regularization *and* may have attractive neural interpretations: basis functions, possibly radial, may correspond to motor units with a multidimensional motor field, whereas their sum may be implicitly performed by the whole mechanical system, say a multijoint arm.

VII. Conclusions

In this final section we discuss the structure of HyperBF, their relation to classical techniques, some general points about the most crucial problem of learning, the "curse of dimensionality", and its relation with the key assumption underlying regularization and regularization networks—the assumption of smoothness.

A. How Regularization Networks Really Work

Regularization networks have a rather simple structure that seems to capture some of the main lessons that are becoming evident in the fields of statistics and neural networks.

To have a feeling of how regularization networks work let us consider a specific, extreme case, in which we consider a regularization network as a classifier, something the formal theory does not actually allow. Imagine using a regularization scheme to classify patterns, such as handwritten digits, in different classes. Assume that the input is a binary 8-bit vector of length N and each of the basis functions is initially centered on the point in the N-dimensional input space that corresponds to one of the training examples (fixed centers case). The system has several outputs, each corresponding to one of the digit classes. Let us consider a series of special cases of regularization networks of increasing generality:

1. Each of the unit (its center corresponds to an example) is an hypersphere and is connected, with weight 1, to its output class only. Classification is done by reading out the class with maximum output. In this case, the system is performing a Parzen window estimate of the posterior probability and then using a MAP criterion. The Parzen-window approach is similar (and asymptotically equivalent) to the k_n nearest-neighbor estimation, of which the nearest-neighbor rule is a special case. The network is equivalent here to a hypersphere classifier.
2. We now replace the hypersphere by a multidimensional Gaussian that is an allowed radial basis function (the hypersphere does not satisfy Micchelli's condition and cannot be derived from regularization). At least for the task of approximating smooth functions the network should perform better than in the non-Gaussian case. The centers of the radial basis functions may be regarded as representing "templates" against which the input vectors are matched (think, for instance of a radial Gaussian with small σ, centered on its center, which is a point in the n-dimensional space of inputs).
3. We may do even better by allowing arbitrary c values between the radial units (as many as examples) and the output. The c can then be found by the pseudoinverse techniques (or gradient descent) and are guaranteed to be optimal in the L_2 sense.
4. We now allow a number of (movable) centers, which is less than the number of examples. Moving a center is equivalent to modifying the corresponding template. Thus equation (23) attempts to develop better templates by modifying during training the existing ones. In our case, this means changing the pixel values in the arrays representing the digits.
5. We allow an arbitrary weighted norm, with the weights to be found during the learning stage. This corresponds to finding which new features, synthesized as linear combinations of the inputs components, optimally capture the information in the input set, necessary for the task. Irrelevant features, in our example irrelevant pixels, will be assigned negligible weights.
6. Finally the most general network, in addition to the above features, also contains radial units, for instance of the Gaussian type, of different scale (i.e. σ), together with non-radial units associated to appropriate stabilizers and units that may receive only subsets of the inputs. This is the HyperBF scheme.

This list shows that the HyperBF scheme is an extension of some of the simplest and most efficient approximation and learning algorithms which can be regarded as special cases of it. In addition, it illuminates a few interesting aspects of the HyperBF algorithm, such as its massive parallelism and its use of prototypes. The network is massively parallel in the sense that it may in general require a large number of basis units. While this property could have been regarded quite negatively a few years ago, this is not so anymore. The advent of parallel machines such as the Connection Machine with about 65 000 processors and of special purpose parallel hardware has changed the perspective towards massive parallelism. The use of prototypes by HyperBF suggest that, in a sense, HyperBF networks are an extension of massive template matchers or look-up tables. We believe that this property makes them intriguingly attractive: after all, if memory is cheap, look-up tables are a good starting point. The HyperBF scheme says how to extend look-up tables into a powerful approximation scheme equivalent to generalized splines, which are probably the most powerful approximation method known. From another perspective, Gaussian HyperBF can be regarded as *disjunction of conjunctions* and seem therefore a natural and satisfying way to connect the representation of Boolean functions with the approximation of continuous, smooth multivariate functions.

B. Relations with Other Methods

Many existing schemes for networks that learn are encompassed by the framework of regularization networks. In this section, we will mention briefly some of the most obvious connections with existing methods. Because of space limitations, we refer the reader to the appropriate references and to [11] for a detailed discussion of the methods we consider.

Regularization networks are the feedforward network versions of regularization, and are therefore equivalent to generalized splines. They are similar to the architecture used for backpropagation, being multilayer networks with one hidden layer and two or even three sets of adjustable parameters. Their Boolean limit version carves the input space into hyperspheres, each corresponding to a center: a radial unit is active if the input vector is within a certain radius of its center and is otherwise silent. The Boolean limit of backpropagation carves the space with hyperplanes. With an arbitrary number of units each network can approximate the other, since each network can approximate arbitrarily well continuous functions on a limited interval [13, 50]. Multilayer networks with sigmoid units do not have, however, the best approximation property that regularization networks have [50]. The Boolean limit of regularization networks is almost identical to Kanerva's associative memory algorithm [66], which is itself closely related to vector quantization. Parzen windows, potential techniques in pattern recognition and, more in general, kernel estimation methods can be regarded as special cases of our method. Close analogies between Kanerva's model and Marr's [67] and Albus' [68] models of the cerebellum also exist [69, 11]. The update equation that controls the evolution of the centers $\mathbf{t}_\alpha$ is also similar to Kohonen's topology preserving algorithm [70, 11] (which is also similar to the k-means algorithm [71]) and can be interpreted as a learning scheme in which the centers of the radial functions move to find centers of clusters of input vectors. Coarse coding techniques can be interpreted within the HyperBF framework (for the special case of Gaussian Radial Basis functions) [11]. Regularization networks have also similarities with the class of Memory-Based Reasoning methods, recently used by D. Waltz and coworkers [72] on massively parallel machines, since in their simplest version (as many centers as examples) they are essentially look-up tables that find those past instances that are sufficiently close to the new input. In fact, regularization networks can be regarded as a powerful and simple extension of Memory-Based Reasoning that makes it equivalent to generalized splines.

C. Networks and Learning: The Pervasive Problem of Dimensionality

Our main result shows that for the learning problem regularization theory yields naturally a class of feedforward multilayer networks. This is highly satisfactory from a theoretical point of view, but in practice another fundamental question must also be addressed: *how many samples are needed to achieve a given degree of accuracy* [22], [2]? It is well known that the answer depends on the dimensionality d and on the degree of smoothness p of the class of functions that has to be approximated [73], [22], [74]. This problem has been extensively studied and some fundamental results have been obtained by Stone [22]. He considered a class of nonparametric estimation problems, like surface approximation, and computed the optimal rate of convergence ϵ_n, that is a measure of how accurately a function can be approximated knowing n samples of its graph. He showed that using a local polynomial regression the optimal rate of convergence $\epsilon_n = n^{-(p/2p+d)}$ can be achieved, generalizing previous results based on local averages. This means that the number of examples needed to approximate a function reasonably well grows *exponentially with the ratio between the dimensionality d and its degree of smoothness p*.

Other interesting results have been obtained by Baum and Haussler on the statistical reliability of networks for binary classification [75], [76], whereas another approach to dimensionality reduction has been pursued by J. Schwartz [3] (similar to [77]). He solves the learning problem for many data sets, obtained from the original one dropping some dimensions, and then selects the one that gives the best result. This method is more similar to Generalized Cross Validation [78], [79] and even without a priori information on the dimensionality of the problem, turned out to be effective in computer simulations [3].

D. Summary

Approaching the problem of learning in networks from the point of view of approximation theory provides several useful insights. It illuminates what network architectures are doing; it suggests more principled ways of obtaining the same results and ways of extending further the approach; and finally, it suggests fundamental limitations of all approximation methods, including neural networks.

In this paper, we developed a theoretical framework based on regularization techniques that leads to a class of three-layer networks, useful for approximation, that we call regularization networks. The most general form of them is called Hyper Basis Functions, since they are related to the well-known Radial Basis Functions, mainly used for strict interpolation tasks. We have introduced several new extensions of the method and its connections with splines, regularization, Bayes formulation and clustering. Regularization networks have a feedforward, multilayer network architecture with good theoretical foundations. They may provide the best framework within which we can study general issues for learning techniques of the neural network type.

A Radial Basis Functions: A Review

The Radial Basis Function (RBF) method is one of the possible solutions to the real multivariate *interpolation problem*, that can be stated as follows:

Interpolation problem: *Given N different points $\{x_i \in R^n | i = 1, \cdots N\}$ and N real numbers $\{y_i \in R | i = 1, \cdots N\}$ find a function F from R^n to R satisfying the interpolation conditions:*

$$F(\mathbf{x}_i) = y_i \qquad i = 1, \cdots, N.$$

The RBF approach consists in choosing a function F of the following form:

$$F(\mathbf{x}) = \sum_{i=1}^{N} c_i h(\|\mathbf{x} - \mathbf{x}_i\|) + \sum_{i=1}^{m} d_i p_i(\mathbf{x}) \qquad m \le n \qquad (27)$$

where h is a continuous function from R^+ to R, usually called the *radial basis function*, $\|\cdot\|$ is the Euclidean norm on R^n, $\{p_i | i = 1, \cdots, m\}$ is a basis of the linear space $\pi_{k-1}(R^n)$ of algebraic polynomials of degree at most $k-1$ from R^n to R, and k is given. The interpolation conditions give N linear equations for the $(N + m)$ coefficients c_i and d_i in equation (27), so that the remaining degrees of freedom are fixed by imposing the following constraints:

$$\sum_{i=1}^{N} c_i p_j(\mathbf{x}_i) = 0, \qquad j = 1, \cdots, m.$$

In order to discuss the solvability of the interpolation problem by means of this representation we need the following definition [80, 41]:

Definition A.1 *A continuous function $f(t)$, defined on $[0, \infty)$, is said to be conditionally (strictly) positive definite of order k on R^n if for any distinct points $\mathbf{x}_1, \cdots, \mathbf{x}_N \in R^n$ and scalars $c_1, \cdots, c_N$ such that $\Sigma_{i=1}^N c_i p(\mathbf{x}_i) = 0$ for all $p \in \pi_{k-1}(R^n)$, the quadratic form $\Sigma_{i=1}^N \Sigma_{j=1}^N c_i c_j f(\|\mathbf{x}_i - \mathbf{x}_j\|)$ is (positive) nonnegative.*

Notice that for $k = 0$ this class of functions, that we denote by $\mathcal{P}_k(R^n)$, reduces to the class of the (strictly) positive definite functions, that is the class of functions such that the quadratic form $\Sigma_{i=1}^N \Sigma_{j=1}^N c_i c_j f(\|\mathbf{x}_i - \mathbf{x}_j\|)$ is (positive) nonnegative [81].

Well known results of approximation theory assert that a sufficient condition for the existence of a solution of the form (27) to the interpolation problem is that $h \in \mathcal{P}_k(R^n)$, where we have defined $\mathcal{P}_k(R^n)$ as the set of conditionally positive definite functions of order k. It is then an important problem to give a full characterization of this class. In particular it is important to characterize the set of functions that are conditionally positive definite of order k over any R^n, that we define as simply $\mathcal{P}_k$.

An interesting characterization of $\mathcal{P}_k$ has been recently obtained by C. A. Micchelli [41]. Before stating his result we first give the following:

Definition A.2 *A function f is said to be completely monotonic on $(0, \infty)$ provided that it is $C^\infty(0, \infty)$ and $(-1)^l(\partial^l f/\partial x^l)(x) \ge 0$, $\forall x \in (0, \infty)$, $\forall l \in \mathfrak{N}$, where $\mathfrak{N}$ is the set of natural numbers.*

We define $\mathfrak{M}_k$ the set of all the functions whose kth derivative is completely monotonic on $(0, \infty)$. Micchelli showed that there is a deep connection between $\mathfrak{M}_k$ and $\mathcal{P}_k$. In fact he proved the following theorem:

Theorem A.1 (Micchelli, 1986) *For every natural number k, $h(r^2) \in \mathcal{P}_k$ whenever $h(r)$ is continuous on $[0, \infty)$ and $(-1)^k(\partial^k h(r)/\partial r^k$ is completely monotonic on $(0, \infty)$.*

To our extents the practical implication of this theorem is the following: if the kth derivative of $h(r)$ is completely monotonic the expansion (27) can be used to solve the interpolation problem. It has been noticed [41, 30] that this theorem encompasses the results obtained by Duchon [44] and Meinguet [45] in their variational approach to splines. For instance the functions $h(r) = r^{3/2}$ and $g(r) = \frac{1}{2} r \log \sqrt{r}$ belong to $\mathfrak{M}_2$, and by theorem A.1 the functions $h(r^2) = r^3$ and $g(r^2) = r^2 \log r$ ("thin plate splines") belong to $\mathcal{P}_2$: therefore it is possible to interpolate any set of data points using $h(r^2)$ and $g(r^2)$ as radial basis functions in the expansion (27), where the polynomial is of degree one. This corresponds exactly to the result derived by Duchon and Meinguet, but without some of their limitations (see Example 2 in section V-A-2). Since this method has been shown to embody natural spline interpolation in one dimension [30], can then be considered as an extension of natural splines to multivariable interpolation.

We notice that when $k = 0$ the theorem of Micchelli gives, as a particular case, a well known theorem of Schoenberg on the positive definite functions [81, 82]. In this case the radial basis functions expansion (27) becomes

$$F(\mathbf{x}) = \sum_{i=1}^{N} c_i h(\|\mathbf{x} - \mathbf{x}_i\|). \qquad (28)$$

The unknown coefficients c_i can be recovered by imposing the interpolation conditions $F(\mathbf{x}_j) = y_j (j = 1, \cdots N)$, that substituted in equation (28) yields the linear system

$$Hc = y. \qquad (29)$$

where we have defined $(y)_j = y_j$, $(c)_i = c_i$, $(H)_{ij} = h(\|\mathbf{x}_i - \mathbf{x}_j\|)$. The theorem of Micchelli ensures that the solution of system (29) always exists, since the matrix H can be inverted, being strictly positive definite.

From equation (29) it turns out that a necessary and sufficient condition to solve the interpolation problem is the invertibility of the matrix H. Theorem (A.1), however, gives only a sufficient condition, so that many other functions could be used as radial basis functions without being strictly positive definite. Another sufficient condition has been given by Micchelli, who proved the following theorem [41]:

Theorem A.2 (Micchelli, 1986) *Let h be a continuous function on $[0, \infty)$ and positive on $(0, \infty)$. Suppose its first derivative is completely monotonic but not constant on $(0, \infty)$. Then for any distinct vectors $\mathbf{x}_1, \cdots, \mathbf{x}_N \in R^n$*

$$(-1)^{N-1} \det h(\|\mathbf{x}_i - \mathbf{x}_j\|^2) > 0.$$

The essence of this theorem is that if the first derivative of a function is completely monotonic this function can be used as radial basis function, since the matrix H associated to it can be inverted. A new class of functions is then allowed to be used as radial basis functions. For instance the function $(c^2 + r)^\alpha$, with $0 < \alpha < 1$ and c possibly zero, is not completely monotonic, but satisfies the conditions of theorem (A.2), so that the choice $(c^2 + r^2)^\alpha$ is possible for the function h in (28).

A list of functions that can be used in practice for data interpolation by means of the RBF expansion (28) is given below, and their use is justified by the results of Micchelli:

$$h(r) = e^{-(r/c)^2} \quad \text{(Gaussian)}$$

$$h(r) = \frac{1}{(c^2 + r^2)^\alpha} \quad \alpha > 0$$

$$h(r) = (c^2 + r^2)^\beta \quad 0 < \beta < 1$$

$$h(r) = r \quad \text{(linear)}$$

Notice that the linear case corresponds, in one dimension, to piecewise linear interpolation, that is the simplest case of spline interpolation. In the case $\beta = \frac{1}{2}$ the radial basis function corresponds to the "Hardy's multiquadric" [31], that has been extensively used in surface interpolation with very good results [32], [33]. Some of the functions listed above have been used in practice.

Almost all of these functions share the unpleasant property of depending on a parameter, that will generally depend on the distribution of the data points. However it has been noticed [32] that the results obtained with Hardy's multiquadrics (in 2 dimensions) seem not to depend strongly on this parameter, and that the surfaces obtained are usually very smooth. It is interesting to notice that, in spite of the excellent results, no theoretical basis existed for Hardy's multiquadrics before Micchelli's theorem [41]. On the contrary, in the case of several functions, including the Gaussian, a mathematical justification can be given in the context of regularization theory, as we have seen in section III.

Acknowledgment

We are grateful to C. Atkeson, S. Edelman, E. Hildreth, D. Hillis, A. Hurlbert, C. Furlanello, E. Grimson, B. Kahle, A. Singer, L. Tucker, S. Ullman, and D. Weinshall for useful discussions and suggestions.

References

[1] S. Omohundro, "Efficient algorithms with neural network behavior," *Complex Systems*, vol. 1, p. 273, 1987.

[2] A. R. Barron and R. L. Barron, "Statistical learning networks: A unifying view," in *Symposium on the Interface: Statistics and Computing Science*, Reston, Virginia, April 1988.

[3] J. Schwartz, "On the effectiveness of backpropagation learning in trainable N^2 nets, and of other related form of discrimination learning, preprint, 1988.

[4] T. Poggio and the staff, "MIT progress in understanding images," in *Proceedings Image Understanding Workshop*, Cambridge, MA, April 1988. Morgan Kaufmann, San Mateo, CA.

[5] T. Poggio and the staff, "MIT progress in understanding images," in *Proceedings Image Understanding Workshop*, pages 56–74, Palo Alto, CA, May 1989. Morgan Kaufmann, San Mateo, CA.

[6] J. Y. Aloimonos, "Unification and integration of visual modules: An extension of the Marr paradigm," in *Proceedings Image Understanding Workshop*, pages 507–551, Palo Alto, CA, May 1989. Morgan Kaufmann, San Mateo, CA.

[7] J. Moody and C. Darken, "Fast learning in networks of locally-tuned processing units," *Neural Computation*, vol. 1, no. 2, pp. 281–294, 1989.

[8] T. Poggio, "On optimal nonlinear associative recall," *Biological Cybernetics*, vol. 19, pp. 201–209, 1975.

[9] L. G. Valiant, "A theory of learnable," *Proc. of the 1984 STOC*, pp. 436–445, 1984.

[10] J. R. Rice, *The Approximation of Functions*, Vol. 1. Addison-Wesley, Reading, MA, 1964.

[11] T. Poggio and F. Girosi, "A theory of networks for approximation and learning," A.I. Memo No. 1140, Artificial Intelligence Laboratory, Massachusetts Institute of Technology, 1989.

[12] D. E. Rumelhart, G. E. Hinton, and R. J. Williams, "Learning internal representations by error propagation," in *Parallel Distributed Processing*, ch. 8, pp. 318–362. MIT Press, Cambridge, MA, 1986.

[13] G. Cybenko, "Approximation by superposition of a sigmoidal function," *Math. Control Systems Signals*, in press, 1989.

[14] K. Funahashi, "On the approximate realization of continuous mappings by neural networks," *Neural Networks*, vol. 2, pp. 183–192, 1989.

[15] G. Cybenko, "Continuous valued neural networks with two hidden layers are sufficient," Technical report, Dept. of Computer Sciences, Tufts Univ., Medford, MA, 1988.

[16] B. Moore and T. Poggio, "Representations properties of multilayer feedforward networks," in *Abstracts of the First Annual INNS Meeting*, p. 502, New York, 1988, Pergamon Press.

[17] A. N. Kolmogorov, "On the representation of continuous functions of several variables by superposition of continuous functions of one variable and addition," *Dokl. Akad. Nauk SSSR*, vol. 114, pp. 953–956, 1957.

[18] T. Poggio, "Visual algorithms," in O. J. Braddick and A. C. Sleigh, editors, *Physical and Biological Processing of Images*, pp. 128–153, Springer-Verlag, Berlin, 1982.

[19] F. Girosi and T. Poggio, "Representation properties of networks: Kolmogorov's theorem is irrelevant," *Neural Computation*, vol. 1, no. 4, pp. 465–469, 1989.

[20] J. Hadamard, *La theorie des equations aux derivees partielles*. Editions Scientifiques, Pekin, 1964.

[21] A. N. Tikhonov and V. Y. Arsenin, *Solutions of Ill-posed Problems*. W. H. Winston, Washington, D.C., 1977.

[22] C. J. Stone, "Optimal global rates of convergence for nonparametric regression," *Ann. Stat.*, vol. 10, pp. 1040–1053, 1982.

[23] M. Bertero, "Regularizations methods for linear inverse problems," in C. G. Talenti, editor, *Inverse Problems*. Springer-Verlag, Berlin, 1986.

[24] W. E. L. Grimson, *From Images to Surfaces*. MIT Press, Cambridge, Mass., 1981.

[25] M. Bertero, T. Poggio, and V. Torre, "Ill-posed problems in early vision," *Proceedings of the IEEE*, vol. 76, pp. 869–889, 1988.

[26] J. L. Marroquin, S. Mitter, and T. Poggio, "Probabilistic solution of ill-posed problems in computational vision," *J. Amer. Stat. Assoc.*, vol. 82, pp. 76–89, 1987.

[27] J. Rissanen, "Modeling by shortest data description," *Automatica*, vol. 14, pp. 465–471, 1978.

[28] R. J. Solomonoff, "Complexity-based induction systems: Comparison and convergence theorems," *IEEE Transactions on Information Theory*, p. 24, 1978.

[29] J. G. Harris, "An analog VLSI chip for thin-plate surface interpolation," in D. S. Touretzky, editor, *Advances in Neural Information Processing Systems I*. Morgan Kaufmann Publishers, Carnegie Mellon University, 1989.

[30] M. J. D. Powell, "Radial basis functions for multivariable interpolation: A review," in J. C. Mason and M. G. Cox, editors, *Algorithms for Approximation*. Clarendon Press, Oxford, 1987.

[31] R. L. Hardy, "Multiquadric equations of topography and other irregular surfaces," *J. Geophys. Res.*, vol. 76, pp. 1905–1915, 1971.

[32] R. Franke, "Scattered data interpolation: Tests of some method," *Math. Comp.*, vol. 38(5), pp. 181–200, 1982.

[33] E. J. Kansa, "Multiquadrics—a scattered data approximation scheme with applications to computational fluid dynamics—I," *Computers Math. Appl.*, vol. 19, no. 8/9, pp. 127–145, 1990.

[34] D. S. Broomhead and D. Lowe, "Multivariable functional interpolation and adaptive networks," *Complex Systems*, vol. 2, pp. 321–355, 1988.

[35] S. Renals and R. Rohwer, "Phoneme classification experiments using radial basis functions," in *Proceedings of the International Joint Conference on Neural Networks*, pp. I-461–

I-467, Washington, D.C., June 1989, IEEE TAB Neural Network Committee.

[36] M. Casdagli, "Nonlinear prediction of chaotic time-series," *Physica D*, vol. 35, pp. 335–356, 1989.

[37] A. N. Tikhonov, "Solution of incorrectly formulated problems and the regularization method," *Soviet Math. Dokl.*, vol. 4, pp. 1035–1038, 1963.

[38] V. A. Morozov, *Methods for Solving Incorrectly Posed Problems*. Springer-Verlag, Berlin, 1984.

[39] R. Courant and D. Hilbert, *Methods of Mathematical Physics*, Vol. 2. Interscience, London, England, 1962.

[40] G. Wahba, *Splines Models for Observational Data*, Series in Applied Mathematics, Vol. 59, SIAM, Philadelphia, 1990.

[41] C. A. Micchelli, "Interpolation of scattered data: Distance matrices and conditionally positive definite functions," *Constr. Approx.*, vol. 2, pp. 11–22, 1986.

[42] N. Dyn, "Interpolation of scattered data by radial functions," in C. K. Chui, L. L. Schumaker, and F. I. Utreras, editors, *Topics in Multivariate Approximation*. Academic Press, New York, 1987.

[43] W. R. Madych and S. A. Nelson, "Multivariate interpolation and conditionally positive definite functions, II," *Mathematics of Computation*, vol. 54, no. 189, pp. 211–230, Jan. 1990.

[44] J. Duchon, "Spline minimizing rotation-invariant semi-norms in Sobolev spaces," in W. Schempp and K. Zeller, editors, *Constructive Theory of Functions of Several Variables*, Lecture Notes in Mathematics, 571. Springer-Verlag, Berlin, 1977.

[45] J. Meinguet, "Multivariate interpolation at arbitrary points made simple," *J. Appl. Math. Phys.*, vol. 30, pp. 292–304, 1979.

[46] R. L. Harder and R. M. Desmarais, "Interpolation using surface splines," *J. Aircraft*, vol. 9, pp. 189–191, 1972.

[47] S. Bochner, "Vorlesungen ueber Fouriersche Integrale," in *Akademische Verlagsgesellschaft*, Leipzig, 1932.

[48] A. Yuille and N. Grzywacz, "The motion coherence theory," in *Proceedings of the International Conference on Computer Vision*, pp. 344–354, Washington, D.C., December 1988, IEEE Computer Society Press.

[49] I. Stakgold, *Green's Functions and Boundary Problems*. John Wiley and Sons, New York, 1979.

[50] F. Girosi and T. Poggio, "Networks and the best approximation property," *Biological Cybernetics*, vol. 63, pp. 169–176, 1990.

[51] M. Stinchcombe and H. White, "Universal approximation using feedforward networks with non-sigmoid hidden layer activation functions," in *Proceedings of the International Joint Conference on Neural Networks*, pp. I-607–I-611, Washington, D.C., June 1989, IEEE TAB Neural Network Committee.

[52] H. L. Resnikoff, "On the psychophysical function," *J. Math. Biol.*, vol. 2, pp. 265–276, 1975.

[53] J. Demmel, "The geometry of ill-conditioning," *J. Complexity*, vol. 3, pp. 201–229, 1987.

[54] S. G. Mikhlin, *The Problem of the Minimum of a Quadratic Functional*. Holden-Day, San Francisco, CA, 1965.

[55] D. Geiger and F. Girosi, "Parallel and deterministic algorithms for MRFs: surface reconstruction and integration," in *Lecture Notes in Computer Science*, Vol. 427: Computer Vision—ECCV 90, O. Faugeras, Ed. Berlin: Springer-Verlag, 1990.

[56] F. Girosi, T. Poggio, and B. Caprile, "Extensions of a theory of networks for approximation and learning: Outliers and negative examples," A.I. Memo 1220, Artificial Intelligence Laboratory, Massachusetts Institute of Technology, 1990.

[57] S. Kirkpatrick, C. D. Gelatt, and M. P. Vecchi, "Optimization by simulated annealing," *Science*, vol. 220, pp. 219–227, 1983.

[58] A. Albert, *Regression and the Moore-Penrose Pseudoinverse*. Academic Press, New York, 1972.

[59] T. Poggio and F. Girosi, "Extension of a theory of networks for approximation and learning: Dimensionality reduction and clustering," A.I. Memo 1167, Artificial Intelligence Laboratory, Massachusetts Institute of Technology, 1990.

[60] R. O. Duda and P. E. Hart, *Pattern Classification and Scene Analysis*. Wiley, New York, 1973.

[61] T. Poggio and S. Edelman, "A network that learns to recognize 3D objects," *Nature*, vol. 343, pp. 263–266, 1990.

[62] S. Edelman and T. Poggio, "Bringing the grandmother back into the picture: A memory-based view of object recognition," A.I. Memo 1181, Artificial Intelligence Laboratory, Massachusetts Institute of Technology, 1990.

[63] J. D. Farmer and J. J. Sidorowich, "Exploiting chaos to predict the future and reduce noise," Technical report, Los Alamos National Laboratory, New Mexico, 1988.

[64] A. Lapedes and R. Farber, "Nonlinear signal processing using neural networks: Prediction and system modelling," Los Alamos National Laboratory LA-UR-87-2662, 1987, submitted to Proc. IEEE.

[65] T. Flash and N. Hogan, "The coordination of arm movements: An experiment confirmed mathematical model," *The Journal of Neuroscience*, vol. 5(7), pp. 1688–1703, 1985.

[66] P. Kanerva, *Sparse Distributed Memory*, MIT Press, Cambridge, MA, 1988.

[67] D. Marr, "A theory of cerebellar cortex," *J. Physiology*, vol. 202, pp. 437–470, 1969.

[68] J. S. Albus, "A theory of cerebellar functions," *Math. Bio.*, vol. 10, pp. 25–61, 1971.

[69] J. D. Keeler, "Comparison between Kanerva's SDM and Hopfield-type neural networks," *Cognitive Science*, vol. 12, pp. 299–329, 1988.

[70] T. Kohonen, "Self organized formation of topologically correct feature maps in the brain," *Biological Cybernetics*, vol. 43, pp. 59–69, 1982.

[71] J. MacQueen, "Some methods of classification and analysis of multivariate observations," in L. M. LeCam and J. Neyman, editors, *Proc. 5th Berkeley Symposium on Math., Stat., and Prob.*, p. 281. U. California Press, Berkeley, CA, 1967.

[72] C. Stanfill and D. Waltz, "Towards memory-based reasoning," *Comm. of the ACM*, vol. 29, pp. 1213–1228, 1986.

[73] G. G. Lorentz, *Approximation of Functions*. Chelsea Publishing Co., New York, 1986.

[74] C. J. Stone, "Additive regression and other nonparametric models," *Ann. Stat.*, vol. 13, pp. 689–705, 1985.

[75] E. B. Baum, "On the capabilities of multilayer perceptrons," *J. Complexity*, vol. 4, pp. 193–215, 1988.

[76] E. B. Baum and D. Haussler, "What size net gives valid generalization?" in D. S. Touretzky, editor, *Advances in Neural Information Processing Systems I*, pp. 81–90. Morgan Kaufmann Publishers, Carnegie Mellon University, 1989.

[77] F. Girosi and T. Poggio, "Networks for learning: A view from the theory of approximation of functions," in *Proc. of the Genoa Summer School on Neural Networks and Their Applications*, Genoa, Italy, June 1989, Prentice-Hall (in press).

[78] G. Wahba, "Practical approximate solutions to linear operator equations when the data are noisy," *SIAM J. Numer. Anal.*, p. 14, 1977.

[79] P. Craven and G. Wahba, "Smoothing noisy data with spline functions: Estimating the correct degree of smoothing by the method of generalized cross validation," *Numer. Math*, vol. 31, pp. 377–403, 1979.

[80] I. M. Gelfand and N. Ya. Vilenkin, *Generalized Functions. Vol. 4: Applications of Harmonic Analysis*, Academic Press, New York, 1964.

[81] I. J. Schoenberg, "Metric spaces and positive definite functions," *Ann. of Math.*, vol. 44, pp. 522–536, 1938.

[82] J. Stewart, "Positive definite functions and generalizations, an historical survey," *Rocky Mountain J. Math.*, vol. 6, pp. 409–434, 1976.

Part 3
Neural Modeling

Synthetic Neural Modeling: The "Darwin" Series of Recognition Automata

GEORGE N. REEKE, JR., OLAF SPORNS, AND GERALD M. EDELMAN

Synthetic neural modeling is a multilevel theoretical approach to the problem of understanding the neuronal bases of adaptive behavior. It uses simultaneous large-scale computer simulations of the nervous system, the phenotype, and the environment of a particular organism to study events and their interactions at these three levels. The simulations are based on physiological and anatomical data. They incorporate detailed models for synaptic modification, for the organization of cells into neuronal groups and larger assemblies, and for the integrated action of multiple cortical layers and brain regions to generate behavior in the context of a particular environment and the unique history of an organism. Synthetic neural modeling takes into account possible evolutionary origins and modes of development of the nervous system, permitting a wide range of psychophysical and behavioral phenomena to be studied within a common framework.

The automata discussed here deal first with certain abstract properties of pattern recognition (Darwin I) and then with categorization and association (Darwin II). The discussion culminates in a description of an automaton with sensory and motor systems and autonomous behavior (Darwin III). The behavior of this automaton is not programmed but results from its encounter with events in its world under constraints of neuronal and synaptic selection.

Darwin III exists in an environment of simple two-dimensional shapes moving on a background; its phenotype comprises a sessile "creature" with an eye and a multijointed arm provided with senses of touch and kinesthesia; its nervous system consists of some 50 interconnected networks containing over 50 000 cells and 620 000 synaptic junctions. By interaction with its environment, Darwin III develops sensorimotor coordination, permitting it to track moving objects with its eye, to reach out and touch objects with its arm, to categorize certain objects according to combinations of visual, tactile, and kinesthetic cues, and to respond to objects based on previous categorizations. These elementary behaviors provide a microcosm in which it is possible to analyze critical problems involving the acquisition and maturation of integrated sensory and motor behavior in animals.

Manuscript received September 1, 1989; revised March 22, 1990.

This research has been supported by the Neurosciences Research Foundation through grants from the Office of Naval Research, the John D. and Catherine T. MacArthur Foundation, the Lucille P. Markey Charitable Trust, the Pew Charitable Trusts, the van Ameringen Foundation, and the Charles and Mildred Schnurmacher Foundation. O. Sporns is a Fellow of the Charles and Mildred Schumacher Foundation. Some of this research was carried out using facilities of the Cornell National Supercomputer Facility, a resource of the Center for Theory and Simulation in Science and Engineering at Cornell University, which is funded in part by the National Science Foundation, New York State, the IBM Corporation, and members of the Corporate Research Institute. An expanded version of this paper appears in [69].

The authors are with The Neurosciences Institute and the Rockefeller University, New York, NY 10021, USA.

IEEE Log Number 9038828.

Introduction

The extent to which the particular structure and mode of operation of the nervous system play critical roles in the determination of animal and human behavior has been widely debated. Some believe that intelligent behavior can only arise from living tissue of a particular kind, while others believe that only certain computational properties of the nervous system are significant, not the details of its physiology. Many neurobiologists take the position that the answers to such questions will emerge in time from the empirical data. However, we do not see how the massive amounts of available and forthcoming data can be interpreted without a theory. The understanding of brain function is widely viewed as requiring an abstract approach based on theories of information, logic, computation, and cybernetic control [1]–[4]. We present here an analysis which suggests that the application of many of these abstract principles to animal behavior is inconsistent with what is known about the nervous system. We also present a series of closely related neural models that are based on a different set of principles. As biologists, we emphasize that a computational formalism applied in isolation to behavior can give only a very incomplete and potentially misleading picture of the nature of the mind.

Information-processing models incorporate two fundamental assumptions that in our view do not give an adequate description of reality [5]. The first of these is that the world can be described in terms of *a priori* categories that are defined by lists of features and that may be represented symbolically, for example, by appropriate coded impulses in the nervous system. The second is that, given such a representation, percepts and behaviors can be computed by formal symbol manipulation without reference to meaning, as occurs in a digital computer. These assumptions neglect the role of the unique history of each individual (as an organism and as a member of a species) in shaping its unique perceptions and responses.

The computational approach based on classical *a priori* categories thus leads to a number of problems. To avoid an infinite regress of definitions, one must assume that at least some undefined primitive categories exist. How can the developing nervous system associate these primitive categories with appropriate sensory signals on the one hand, and with the arbitrary neuronal impulses by which they

Reprinted from *Proc. IEEE*, vol. 78, no. 9, Sept. 1990, pp. 1498–1530.

must be represented on the other? How can either primitive or composite categories be associated in different contexts with constantly varying or novel referents in the world outside the nervous system? How can information-processing algorithms be built up by trial and error and transmitted between generations when, as far as we know, DNA sequences encode only chemical structures and not symbol definitions or instruction sequences? If algorithms were encoded genetically, mutations affecting single steps in even minor ways would be likely to render them entirely useless. In computer programming, algorithms are arrived at *by design*, but in biological systems origin by design is excluded because it is contrary to the most basic and well-established principles of the theory of evolution.

Rather than discard or disregard the theory of evolution, we look to it to provide the solution to these dilemmas. One way to avoid the simultaneous need for instructed or preexisting categories, codes, and algorithms that is implicit in information-processing models is to assume that these elements do not exist *a priori*, but that *selection upon variance* plays a major role in the establishment of working neuronal circuitry during the lifetime of each individual. A theory describing how this might happen, the theory of neuronal group selection (TNGS), has been proposed and described in some detail [6]–[8]. This theory is selective rather than instructive in the sense that variability occurs *prior* to encounter with the environment rather than *after* it; it is a population theory because it deals with selection and differential amplification of connections in collectives of neurons rather than in single units. Similar principles in relation to differential reproduction in populations of organisms constitute the heart of Darwin's theory of natural selection; accordingly, the term "Neural Darwinism" has been applied to the extension of population thinking to the nervous system.

In this paper, we show how the TNGS can form the basis for an approach to computer modeling of the nervous system that deals with the foregoing issues. This approach has been called *synthetic neural modeling* because it involves the synthesis in the computer of an entire model nervous system along with the phenotype of a representative creature in a particular environment. The individual components of a synthetic neural model are chosen for their heuristic value in helping us to understand the organization of the nervous system as a whole. Present computer capabilities do not usually permit the use of explicit models of particular brain regions; instead, one attempts to incorporate the critical features of each region that are most important for its function in the system as a whole. The choice of these features is strongly constrained by the biological facts and itself constitutes a result of synthetic neural modeling that can be checked against experimental data. These principles are illustrated by a series of models with which we have investigated some basic principles of recognition in selective matching systems, some purely perceptual aspects of pattern recognition and category association, and, finally, how extensive interactions among multiple sensory and neural systems can lead to adaptive interactions with the environment in a behaving automaton.

The Theory of Neuronal Group Selection

The TNGS proposes that the fundamental unit of organization of the nervous system is the *neuronal group*, a collection of hundreds to thousands of strongly interconnected neurons that act in collaboration. Three basic mechanisms govern the formation, adaptation, and interactions of neuronal groups: *developmental selection*, *experiential selection*, and *reentrant mapping*. During embryogenesis, the macroscopic anatomical order of the nervous system that is characteristic for each animal species is generated. Within this overall order, the precise arborization patterns of neurons show enormous variation both within and between individuals. This structural diversity must be the result of epigenetic regulatory processes acting during development. The local interactions of cells are thought to be regulated by dynamic place-dependent control loops involving the expression of cell adhesion molecules (CAMs) and substrate adhesion molecules (SAMs) [9]–[11]. The generation of diversity in growing neuronal structures is a necessary outcome of these morphoregulatory control processes, which lead to the formation of *primary repertoires* comprising circuits of variant localized neuronal groups in a given anatomical region.

Postnatally, after most of the neural connections have been laid down, the anatomical structure tends to become more or less fixed while synaptic mechanisms become the main agents of plasticity and adaptation. The functional specificity of neuronal groups in primary repertoires is subject to additional, experiential selectional mechanisms to form *secondary repertoires* within which competition occurs for access to incoming and outgoing signaling pathways. The resulting populations of variant groups in a brain region are called repertoires in reference to their collective potential to respond to any of a wide class of inputs. Experiential selection among synaptic populations effectively provides a basis for defining the significance of neuronal signals in terms of perceptual categories and behavior; as in evolution itself, the ultimate criterion of success is the enhanced fitness of the organism. Indeed, evolutionary selection for fitness must itself depend in part upon the varying success of these somatic neuronal group selection processes. It is beyond the scope of this paper to discuss in detail the implications of these ideas for theories of animal nervous systems and behavior; a recent book is devoted to this subject [8].

In order for somatic selection to operate in the nervous system, each neuronal group must be exposed (either directly or through intermediate units) to a sufficient sample of the afferent sensory signals to permit it to respond differentially to various objects and events in the environment. Each neuronal group must be able to contribute, through the output signals it emits, to some aspect of the behavior of the organism. Finally, neuronal groups must have the capacity to change their responses according to the relative success of the behaviors to which they contribute. According to the TNGS, such groups are formed dynamically and correspond loosely, but not obligatorily, to regions of heavy anatomical connectivity. The interactions of neurons both within and between groups change continually as a result of selection occurring in response to changes in input patterns. Thus the set of neurons that constitutes a particular group can vary over time, but at any one time neighboring groups are nonoverlapping.

Group organization has several advantages for the nervous system: it provides spatially extended targets for neurite growth during map formation; it provides a way for units with fixed anatomy to undergo functional reorganization as required by the changing needs and growth of the organism; it permits essential mappings to be maintained during such reorganization; it provides a mechanism for the coordination of interdependent synaptic changes by bringing together collections of neurons with related function; and it fosters the long-term stability of connections receiving common patterns of correlated input, reducing the danger that useful outputs will be disrupted by uncoordinated synaptic changes induced by any unusual, strong inputs. The general importance of groups in the nervous system is attested to by the widespread occurrence of group-like local structures such as ocular dominance columns, blobs, slabs, barrels, fractured somatotopies, and so on. In any event, the dense interconnections throughout the nervous system make it most unlikely that cells could ever function as individuals.

Recent experimental evidence has revealed the occurrence of synchronous oscillations at 40 Hz in local populations of orientation-selective neurons in the primary visual cortex during presentation of a light bar at optimal or near-optimal orientation [12]. These oscillations presumably involve many or all cells in an orientation column, occur in awake or lightly anesthetized animals, and appear to be generated by an intracortical mechanism. Moreover, oscillations in distant columns within area 17 or in areas 17 and 18 having similar orientational selectivity are highly correlated in frequency and in phase if these columns are presented with spatially and temporally correlated stimuli [13], [14]. These experiments confirm some of the theoretical predictions of the TNGS [6], which have been worked out in detail in a recent model [15]. The results provide clear evidence for the existence of neuronal groups in the primary visual cortex.

Connections between cells in the same or different neuronal groups are strengthened or weakened according to locally acting synaptic rules. We formulate and apply several such rules in the models that we shall discuss. These rules differ in the degree to which they are abstractions of the known biochemistry and biophysics of synaptic function. All the rules deviate from simple Hebb rules [16], most significantly by the explicit incorporation of temporal and heterosynaptic effects [17], [18]. Heterosynaptic modification at a given site depends in direction or extent on events occurring at nearby synapses on the same cell, mediated through second messengers.

We assume that, in order for a system to display adaptive behavior, the modification of synapses of certain classes must be biased by heterosynaptic inputs from specialized neuronal repertoires that reflect the global evaluation of recent behavior. These repertoires have connectivities that predispose them to respond to the sequelae of adaptive behaviors, but their constituent groups are normal in all other respects. Such repertoires are called "value repertoires" and they instantiate what we have called "value schemes." Value schemes are the basic evolutionary adaptations that define broad behavioral goals for an organism.

Characteristic features of value repertoires include the presence of sensory afferents, a relative lack of internal order and topography, and diffuse and widespread efferents that heterosynaptically influence large populations of synapses. Value repertoires influence other areas in a diffuse and modulatory fashion. Thus they do not predefine the *exact* way a behavioral response is executed or determine *particular* perceptual categories; rather, they impose biases on synaptic modifications depending on the outcome of previous interactions with the environment. (Several specific examples will be discussed in the course of our presentation of Darwin III.) The emergence of value repertoires, as well as the general, but not the detailed, layout of all the groups and repertoires in a nervous system, may be assumed to be under evolutionary control, which assures that the neuronal structures existing in any particular organism are appropriate in a general way to generate the behavioral diversity necessary for its survival.

A selective system does not need *a priori* information about the particular stimuli that it might encounter, other than evolutionarily established boundary conditions implicit in the construction of its recognizing elements according to anatomic rules. In order to be assured of *some* response to *any* stimulus, the system must contain units having specificities responsive to the entire range of possible stimuli. The number of units required increases with the number of potential stimuli as well as with the degree of specificity required in each act of recognition. Given the indefinite nature of the boundaries in the world between possible categories, the only reasonable strategy is to construct units with arbitrary but overlapping functional specificities. The overlap provides assurance of coverage of the range of possible stimuli and permits the system to continue operating when some of its units fail. We call this important property *degeneracy*, to suggest the presence of multiple, *nonisomorphic* but functionally interreplaceable units, and to distinguish it from simple *redundancy* which denotes duplication of *isomorphic* structural units to achieve fault tolerance.

Besides being able to recognize relevant stimuli and categories in the environment, the nervous system must be able to associate stimuli according to their temporal and spatial correlations, as well as, in higher animals, various abstract properties. Association requires comparison, and hence memory. In order for comparison and association to take place, recognition events relating to different times and places must be correlated with each other. The TNGS proposes that this conjunction is brought about by *reentry*, the ongoing and often recursive exchange of signals between different repertoires along parallel anatomical connections (Fig. 1). Reentry can take many forms, including connections backwards from a repertoire to earlier repertoires in the same pathway, as well as horizontally, between repertoires in different pathways. Reentry is typically reciprocal, involving the exchange of signals in both directions between two repertoires. Often these repertoires are mappings located in different sensory pathways, and reentry provides a mechanism for the correlation of responses to different aspects of the same objects or events in the environment. These different forms of reentry are of course associated with different functional roles; several of them occur in the various models to be presented in this paper and each is discussed in its place.

Reentry gives meaning to the dominant feature of the mammalian neocortex—the vast system of interareal connections—extending well beyond the feedback functions often ascribed to them. As Ashby [19] has pointed out, "such complex systems cannot be treated as an interlaced set of more or less independent feedback circuits, but only as a whole." It is therefore important at the outset to distinguish

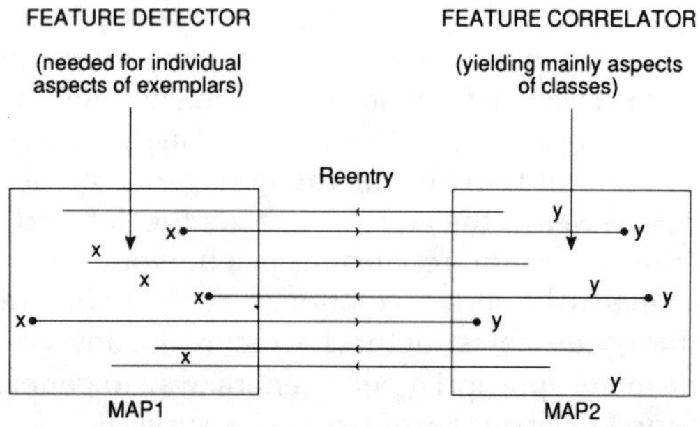

Fig. 1. One kind of classification couple using reentry. Neurons—in the visual system, for example—can act as feature detectors. These features detectors map onto some higher-order lamina in the brain (Map 1, left). Other neurons—related, for example, to light touch on a moving finger—can act as feature correlators by moving across an object. These neurons map onto another lamina (Map 2, right). Maps project onto each other by locally distributed reentrant connections so that groups in one map may excite groups in the other. *x*s and *y*s represent synaptic domains undergoing changes in synaptic strengths as a result of such reentrant signals. Black dots represent synapses that have been strengthened, leading to parallel coupling of the two domains. (From [67], reproduced with permission.)

the properties of reentry from those typically associated with the notion of feedback. Reentry is inherently parallel and involves populations of interconnected units, whereas feedback involves the recursion of a single scalar variable. Reentry is distributed, that is, each area simultaneously reenters to many other areas (note that reentry can occur between areas at the same heterarchical level as well as between higher and lower levels in a system). Reentry has a statistical nature, inasmuch as not all connections are used at all times. Finally, as we will show, reentry can give rise to the construction of novel operations, and is used more for correlation than for error correction or gain control.

In the Darwin automata, reentry provides a structural and functional basis for associative memory, in that the responses of reentrantly activated groups often reflect the existence of stimulus correlations having potential significance to the automaton. The modification of synapses involved in these responses, biased according to the strength of the reentrant response, provides the physical substrate for association. Functionally, memory appears as the facilitation of categorical responses that have previously been selected in response to similar stimuli in the past. These responses are modified, of course, according to the current context. In this view, memory is a process of *recategorization* rather than a replicative storage of discrete data. Associations are developed across appropriate reentrant signaling pathways through the same mechanisms of synaptic modification that are used elsewhere to stabilize initial categorical responses. Frequently these associations are formed between neuronal maps and reflect different aspects of a stimulus complex.

Synthetic Neural Modeling and the "Darwin" Series of Models

Computer modeling has been used extensively in the past to examine hypotheses relating to very specific parts of the nervous system, for example, to explore the electrical properties of membranes and single cells or small circuits (reviewed in MacGregor [20]). Recently, a few models of entire brain areas, such as the olfactory cortex [21] and the hippocampus [22] have appeared. We have applied the principles of synthetic neural modeling to study the formation of neuronal groups in sensory cortex and the plasticity of cortical maps in response to changing inputs during adult life [23]. A "reentrant cortical integration" (RCI) model illustrates the role of reentry in the integration of distributed cortical systems. The RCI model shows how responses to occluding stimuli, illusory contours, and structure-from-motion may be mediated by a single, reentrant architecture in the visual cortex. It successfully predicts a new visual illusion that combines illusory contours with structure-from-motion [24]. A related model of the visual cortex incorporating more detailed aspects of neuronal group interactions shows how responses to related stimulus features may be correlated in the brain by means of phase-locked oscillations occurring in multiple, spatially separated groups with similar receptive field properties [15]. This model is in full accord with the experimental data already mentioned [12]–[14].

Heretofore, however, very little has been done to incorporate detailed models of cellular and synaptic properties into large scale simulations of interconnected networks in multilevel systems. A new, more complete approach is needed to analyze the properties of entire nervous systems in relation to a phenotype and an environment. Such an approach permits one to check the consistency of theoretical ideas that may not be currently accessible to experiment. In this section, we show how synthetic neural modeling can be used to approach these goals. The models used for this purpose take the form of a series of related automata, which, in their currently most advanced form, constitute a one-eyed, one-armed "creature" we call Darwin III.

The aim of these studies is to demonstrate that automata constructed according to the principles of the TNGS can have, in a crude form, some of the sensorimotor capabilities of animals, without the use of *a priori* definitions of categories, codes, or information-processing algorithms. In a single system of interconnected neuronal repertoires, we examine sensory acts involving recognition and classification, as well as motor acts such as visual saccades, reaching, and touch exploration. Sensory and motor systems are combined in Darwin III to produce a behaving automaton that constructs global mappings involving perception, categorization, and response. In this system, behavior can influence subsequent perceptual categorizations through the rearrangement of objects in the environment. Darwin III thus presents a unique opportunity to study the effects of such global loops in a controlled fashion that is not yet feasible with real, behaving animals.

Darwin I

We began with a system, Darwin I, which was designed only to examine the process of pattern recognition and some general factors relating to degeneracy and amplification in selective systems [7]. As such, this model was highly abstract and was most definitely not intended to reflect the workings of the nervous system. In Darwin I, recognition is based upon the number of matches between individual binary digits in random 32-bit strings designated as stimuli and other strings acting as recognizing elements in a repertoire. The model consists of a repertoire generator that produces a collection of random bit strings, a stimulus generator that produces the "stimuli" to be matched, a matching rule that scores the similarity between a given stimulus and individual elements of the repertoire, and an amplifier that increases the probability of response by those repertoire elements that match a stimulus above a specified threshold level. No information on the nature of the stimuli is available to the repertoire before matching begins.

In a typical experiment, the repertoire consists of 10^4 32-bit patterns randomly chosen from the total of $2^{32} \approx 4.3 \times 10^9$ possible patterns. Stimuli consist of 32-bit patterns chosen from the same set. To give some structure to the stimuli, they are not chosen randomly but are constrained by arbitrarily fixing 16 of the 32 bits to constant values. The matching function simply counts the number of bits that are identical in corresponding positions in the two strings. A threshold score is then set for accepting a match as a "recognition," and for any chosen threshold score and stimulus, the entire repertoire is scanned for matches.

The amplification scheme is at the heart of the adaptive behavior of the system. A list of matches is made for each stimulus, and the repertoire elements giving the highest match scores are amplified by making some predetermined number of copies of them and depositing these copies in random locations in the repertoire array. The number of copies may be made to depend on the match score or may be fixed. For convenient implementation on a computer, the size of the repertoire is kept constant, and amplified elements simply replace other elements at random. (For a sufficiently large repertoire, this procedure gives almost the same behavior as expansion of the repertoire during amplification.)

As shown in Fig. 2, statistics of actual matches for various threshold scores M and numbers of repertoire elements N

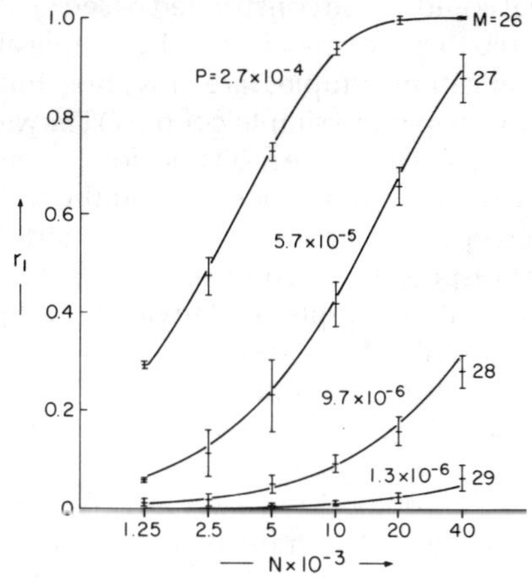

Fig. 2. Comparison of theoretical and experimental recognition functions r_1 as a function of match threshold and repertoire size in Darwin I. r_1 = fraction of stimuli presented that are expected to be recognized. Solid curves were calculated acccording to $r_1 = 1 - (1 - p)^N$, where p = probability of recognizing any one stimulus, N = number of elements in repertoire. Experimental data are presented as dashes with vertical error bars, representing standard deviations of r_1 for four series of 100 trials each. Each curve is labeled with the match threshold M (number of bits out of 32 that must be identical in stimulus and repertoire element for a "recognition" to occur) and the corresponding recognition probability p. As expected, the statistical distribution of matches obtained from the model closely approaches theoretical values. (From [7], reproduced with permission.)

are entirely consistent with theoretical predictions. Moreover, recognition in Darwin I is degenerate—many recognition elements can respond above threshold to any one stimulus and be amplified accordingly. The response to unrelated control stimuli (stimuli in which the above-mentioned constraint on half the bits is omitted) undergoes only a slight reduction during the amplification procedure, showing that significant capacity remains for recognizing new stimuli of novel classes that might be presented later.

A most interesting form of cross-recognition between stimuli occurs if the threshold for amplification is set lower than that for recognition under conditions where there is a sufficient degree of degeneracy (overlapping specificity) in the repertoire. In this case, some of the poorer matches to a given stimulus that are amplified turn out to give matches above threshold to related stimuli that happen to be presented later; this process may be described as stimulus generalization in the sense that stimuli related to the original test stimulus (by having a certain number of bits in common) are more likely to be recognized above threshold after copying than are unrelated stimuli. A similar effect can be produced by introducing errors in the copying process.

Darwin I served to demonstrate the fundamental role of thresholding in recognition and generalization and showed how selective mechanisms for these processes can lead to dramatic improvements in performance toward novel stimuli. Although the mechanism of amplification in the nervous system is entirely different, the results with Darwin I were suggestive of the power of selective mechanisms in biological recognition processes and encouraged us to proceed with more complex models embodying the network architecture of the nervous system.

Darwin II

A more advanced selective recognition model, Darwin II, introduced recognition units with some of the properties of neuronal groups, connected in reentrant networks to permit exploration of aspects of the recognition process leading to categorization, generalization, and associative memory [25], [26]. Its main purpose was to show the role of reentry in categorization. Accordingly, Darwin II has two sets of repertoires operating in parallel and linked by reentrant connections. These arrangements are shown schematically in Fig. 3. One set of repertoires (Darwin, left) is constructed to respond uniquely to combinations of local features that define *individual* stimuli, while the other set (Wallace, right) responds to correlations of features that define *class properties* of stimuli. Each set has an initial layer, which responds to primary sensory signals, and a second layer, which responds to combinations of active units in the primary layer. The responses in each subsystem correspond in their own ways to different categorizations of objects in the world, but it is through their reentrant connection to form what we have called a "classification couple" that the full potential of the automaton for categorization is realized. We will describe these arrangements in some detail because they provide a basis for understanding the architecture of Darwin III; we begin with the individual repertoires and then proceed to consider the reentrant interactions.

The primary layer of the first set of repertoires (R, Fig. 3, upper left) contains local feature-detecting units mod-

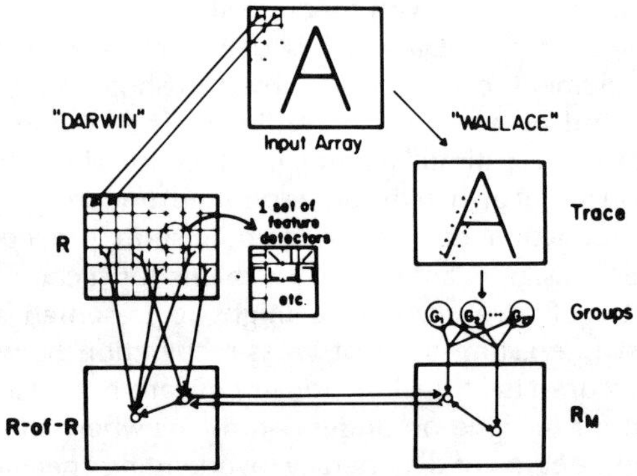

Fig. 3. Simplified plan of construction for Darwin II. (From [68], reproduced with permission.)

eled loosely after some of the cell types found in visual cortex [27], [28]. These units respond to oriented line segments, line terminations, or angles, as suggested in the inset. The selective properties of these units arise from their initial connection strengths, which, unlike other units in Darwin II, are assigned systematically, not randomly. Groups having all of the available selectivities are replicated across the *R* layer, so that the response of one of these units signals both the nature and the location of a particular local feature in the stimulus object. The responses of these units thus correspond to only parts of stimuli, and in no way embody a predetermined solution to the categorization problem in the manner of the "grandmother" or "cardinal" neurons proposed by others [29].

The second layer of the Darwin set of networks is called *R*-of-*R*, for "recognizer of recognizers" (Fig. 3, lower left). The purpose of this layer is to respond to nonlocal combinations of the purely local features detected by the *R* layer, thus giving patterns of response corresponding to the individual properties of entire stimulus objects. (Such patterns may be indicative of categories in relatively trivial cases, but in general the participation of both members of the classification couple is needed for the formation of interesting categories.) To make nonlocal responses possible, each *R*-of-*R* group has numerous input connections from randomly selected units in *R*. Because these connections can be inhibitory as well as excitatory (with thresholds), responses in *R*-of-*R* can be *vetoed* as well as *activated* by activity in certain *R* groups. This design gives *R*-of-*R* the ability to respond nonlinearly to combinations of features in *R* and thus to make categorical responses to compound stimuli that are not simple linear superpositions of the responses to the individual parts of the stimulus.

The Wallace system has the same two-layered structure as Darwin, but in this case the primary layer responds not to static local features, but rather to larger-scale correlations of features of a kind that are relatively invariant to translations and rotations of the stimulus. These include, for example, various types of line intersections, such as "L" or "T" junctions. Detection of these feature correlations is accomplished in Darwin II by a separate computer program, Trace (upper right), which is designed to produce responses of a kind that might be obtained from motion-sensitive units in the visual cortex during object movement or during active tracing around the contours of an object by eye or arm movements, without the costs of actual simulation of such units. (We will discuss later the replacement of this somewhat artificial mechanism in Darwin II by actual neuronal repertoires carrying out tracing functions in Darwin III.) The output of Trace is expressed in the activation of a special class of neuronal groups ($G_1 \cdots G_{27}$, Fig. 3). These groups play the same role in Wallace as the *R* groups do in Darwin; both types of groups provide a primary repertoire of visual feature-related responses that form the basis for categorical responses at a higher level. In no way do they correspond *in themselves* to categories, nor do they contain hidden descriptions of the categories with which the automaton will be tested; they merely provide a different submodality of visual information suitable for input to the categorization process, which takes place at higher levels.

The higher layer of Wallace that provides this categorization function is called R_M, for "recognizer of motion." The construction of R_M is parallel to that of *R*-of-*R*, that is, its groups respond to random combinations of the more elementary responses in the primary layer. It is here in R_M that correlations of features are formed in Wallace; as a consequence of the particular properties of the primary inputs to R_M, these correlations are relatively insensitive to motions and distortions of the stimulus. The categories formed in Wallace thus tend to correspond more than those in Darwin to the normal human concept of the class characteristics of an object.

It is important to note that categorization in Darwin II is expressed as partially overlapping patterns of response to related stimuli in each of two reentrantly interconnected subsystems. The Darwin and Wallace pathways of Darwin II are joined by reentrant connections between *R*-of-*R* and R_M to form a classification couple, a structure in which responses representative of two different sensory modalities or submodalities are integrated to generate perceptual categories that could not be constructed based on the information available to either member of the couple alone. (In general, classification *n*-tuples are possible, but all the examples in this paper are simple couples.) Darwin II thus shows how reentry, which is responsible for the integration of *patterned* responses to visual stimuli in the RCI model, can lead to perceptual categorization when repertoires with more *abstract* responses are coupled.

In the classification couple in Darwin II, one pathway (Darwin) is responsible for responding in a unique way to aspects of each individual stimulus object, while the other pathway (Wallace) is responsible for responding to correlations of features that can contribute to definitions of categories based on nonlocal (or even topological; cf. [63]) properties of an object. Reentrant interactions between the pathways permit the two types of responses to be integrated, tying the overall categorical response to the appropriate object features in a possibly complex environment. During this process, each pathway retains its own ability to respond independently, and neither member of the couple acts as a "teacher" for the other.

Reentry between the two systems also provides a mechanism for increased generalization and for associative memory. Although each subsystem has some generalizing capacity on its own as a consequence of its degeneracy, generalization is enhanced by reentry because a new stimulus belonging to a previously encountered class is more likely to excite some groups in common with other members of the class in one or the other pathway of the classification couple than in any single pathway. These common groups then act to tie together the responses in the other pathway through reentry. Similarly, the two subsystems are able by reentry to associate individual stimuli (characterized predominantly by responses in Darwin) that are members of the same class (characterized predominantly by responses in Wallace). Association operates by exchange of signals in both directions across reentrant connections that have been strengthened as a result of selection during past exposure to stimuli similar to those in question. For example, when one of a set of associated stimuli gives rise to a response in Darwin, that activity excites units in Wallace that are members of the response pattern common to the entire set of related stimuli; that activity in turn excites other units in Darwin which, in the absence of reentry, would have responded only to other members of the set. These indirect responses constitute a form of associative recall. Examples of both generalization and reentry in Darwin II have been presented [26], [30].

Group responses in Darwin II are subject to amplification, which is carried out by a local synaptic rule [25] that increases the strength of connections between active cells in a manner similar to the rule proposed by Hebb [16]. However, the rule has been modified to remove the instability inherent in Hebb's rule by providing, among other possibilities, for the weakening of connections between pairs of units of which one, but not both, is active. Amplification leads to tuning of responses that occur initially by chance and hence leads to improved recognition and categorization of familiar stimuli with increased experience. It does this by selectively *strengthening* the responses that are most characteristic of a particular stimulus, while *weakening* marginal responses that might lead to confusion with other stimuli.

In Darwin II, these crucial aspects of the recognition process are demonstrated in a system that does not have an output function capable of interacting with its environment. An observer assesses its responses by a statistical analysis of patterns of activity in its neuronal groups rather than by evaluating its behavior. This lack of interaction with the environment precludes any measure of adaptive value in Darwin II, and all responses are equally valid *a priori*. The automaton is capable of tuning its responses and enhancing its recognition abilities, but not of adaptively changing them or discriminating among them according to internal criteria of value. For this reason, true learning is not possible, and a Hebb-like synaptic change rule is sufficient. This limitation was recognized from the outset in designing Darwin II, which nonetheless provides a reasonably good model for perceptual categorization processes. In the next section, we apply the synthetic neural modeling method more fully to deal with phenotype and behavior. We discuss an automaton that has output and that is able to interact with its environment, to categorize, and to learn. As we shall see, a more elaborate, heterosynaptic amplification rule is required for this kind of learning system.

Darwin III

In contrast to Darwin II, Darwin III is a behaving automaton, the responses of which can be evaluated by direct observation of its motor acts. The nervous system of Darwin III consists of a set of interconnected repertoires of neuronal groups. Groups may be simulated at the level of their constituent cells, but in most cases are simulated for convenience by abstract units of the kind used in Darwin II. The connections, initial connection strengths, and rules for cell responses and synaptic modifications are specified parametrically for each repertoire, but no prior information about particular stimuli and no explicit algorithms for "neural computations" are specified. Training of behavioral responses proceeds in the absence of any internal or external representation of desired responses or feedback of detailed error signals into the system. The adaptive value of responses is determined solely by their consequences; criteria for the selection of responses are given neural expression by value repertoires of the kind discussed earlier.

Darwin III adds a new element to the categories of nervous system function considered in the previous models, namely, motor control. The TNGS proposes that motor control, like perception, is a selective process. The primary entities subject to selection in this case are taken to be elementary motor acts ("gestures") that result from spontaneous neural activity in the motor cortex. Gestures that form a part of behavioral sequences having adaptive value for the organism are selected (via synaptic modification), increasing the probability that they will occur again under similar circumstances in the future. The mechanism of synaptic change is the same as that used for purely perceptual systems, sometimes with and sometimes without biasing by value. Several examples of motor control achieved by this mechanism are presented in the following detailed description of Darwin III and its performance.

Overall Description of Darwin III

The simulation program ("CNS") that implements Darwin III permits the construction of very general neural network systems. A particular model may have any number of repertoires of neuronal groups. Cells of one or more kinds may be arranged in layers within each repertoire. Each cell may have as many connections as desired, selected from three generic types: specific (constructed according to some specified rule, for example to form a topographic mapping), geometric (constructed with a specified density-distance relationship, often to provide lateral inhibition), or modulatory (receiving input corresponding to the average activity of all cells in some source layer).

In the experiments presented here, four sets of interconnected repertoires were constructed (Fig. 4): a foveation and fine-tracking oculomotor system, a reaching system using a multijointed arm, a touch-exploration system using a different set of "muscles" in the same arm, and a reentrant categorizing system. The numbers and types of units in each functional system are summarized in Table 1. The four systems together form an automaton capable of autonomous behavior, involving sensorimotor coordination and categorization of stimulus objects.

Darwin III currently implements three sensory modalities: vision, touch, and kinesthesia. In each case, signals from the simulated senses are generated in the form of neuronal activity in specialized cells that can be connected as desired to any of the neural repertoires in the model. On the motor side, there may be one or more eyes with lateral and vertical orbital motions and one or more arms with multiple joints, each controlled by neurons in specified repertoires that are designated as "motor repertoires." (In the

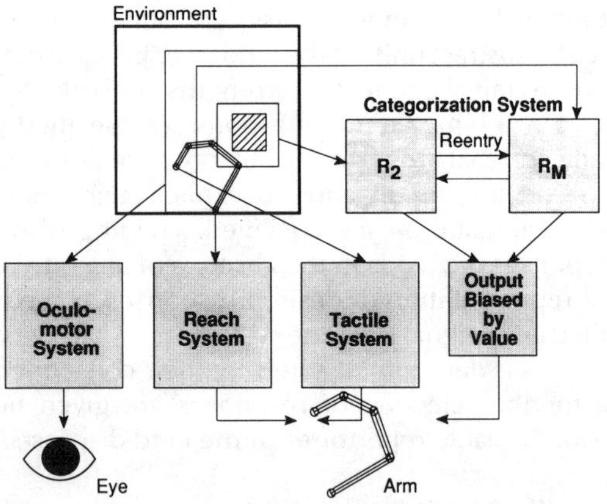

Fig. 4. Schematic diagram of Darwin III and its subsystems. The "environment" (heavy square at upper left) contains moving objects (one of which is indicated by the shaded square). A portion of the environment is viewed by the eye (large square only partially visible within border of environment, limits of peripheral vision; small square surrounding hatched object, central vision). Movements of the eye and the four-jointed arm (bottom) are controlled by oculomotor and reach systems, respectively. The distal digit of the arm contains touch sensors used by the tactile system to trace the edges of objects. The categorization system receives sensory inputs from the central part of the visual field and from joint receptors signaling arm movements as tracing of object edges occurs. These inputs connect, via intermediate layers not shown, to higher-order visual center R_2 and to area correlating motion signals over time R_M. R_2 and R_M are reciprocally connected to form a classification couple according to the scheme in Fig. 1. Correlation of firing patterns in R_2 and R_M via reentry leads to classification of objects and eventually yields output biased by value that can activate reflex movements of the arm. (This figure and Figs. 5-8, 10-15, and 17 are from [69], reproduced with permission.)

instantiations described here, a single eye and a single arm are used.)

Every cell in a Darwin III model has a scalar activity variable determined by a "response function." This function has terms corresponding to synaptic inputs, noise, decay of previous activity, depression and refractory periods, and long-term potentiation (LTP), which is here treated as a property of a *class* of synapses. (Rules for synaptic changes at individual synapses, which, in contrast to LTP, may be permanent, are discussed in the next section.) The relative magnitudes of all the terms in the response function can be varied parametrically. Symbolically (omitting unnecessary details):

$$s_i(t) = [(A + G + M)\phi(I_s)]\phi(D) + N + W \quad (1)$$

where (Greek letters are used for adjustable parameters, Roman letters for dynamic variables):

- $s_i(t)$ state of cell i at time t
- A total input from specific connections $= \Sigma_k w_k \Sigma_j c_{ij}(s_{l_{ij}} - \theta_{Ek})$, w_k = scale factor that determines overall strength of connections of type k, c_{ij} = strength of connection from input j to cell i ($c_{ij} > 0$, excitatory; $c_{ij} < 0$, inhibitory), l_{ij} = index number of cell connected to input j of cell i, θ_{Ek} = excitation threshold ($s_{l_{ij}} < \theta_{Ek}$ ignored), k = index over connection types, j = index over individual connections
- G total geometrically defined input $= \Sigma_k \beta_k \Sigma_j (s_{g_{ij}} - \theta_G)$, β_k = strength of connections from ring k around cell i, g_{ij} = index number of cell connected to geometrically defined input j of cell i, θ_G = activity threshold for geometric inputs ($s_{g_{ij}} < \theta_G$ ignored)
- M total modulatory input, defined similarly to G except that all cells in the source layer are included with equal weight
- I_s total shunting inhibition, sum of all specific and geometric inputs designated as shunting inputs [shunting inhibition multiplies the excitatory terms $(A + G + M)$ and is thus able to overcome any amount of excitatory input to a group. Accordingly, it is of critical importance in assuring the stability of repertoires]
- D depression $= \upsilon_D s_i(t-1) + \omega_D D(t-1)$, υ_D = growth coefficient for depression, ω_D = decay coefficient for depression. When $D > \theta_D$, where θ_D is a refractory threshold, then $\phi(D)$ is set to 0 for a specified number of cycles, after which D is set to 0 and $\phi(D)$ returns to 1.0
- N noise, which may be shot noise or Gaussian noise
- W decay term $= \omega s_i(t-1)$
- $\phi(x)$ sigmoidal function, approximated as $\phi(x) = 1 - 2x^2 + x^4$.

The entire collection of terms $[(A + G + M)\phi(I_s)]\phi(D)$, as well as the input from each individual connection type (which may be thought of as the input to a local region of a dendritic tree), must exceed a given firing threshold or it is ignored. These connection type thresholds θ_K are modulated by LTP according to

$$\theta'_K = \theta_K - \sigma_L L \quad (2)$$

$$L = \omega_L L(t-1) + \upsilon_L(s_i(t-1) - \theta_L) + \sum_k \upsilon_{L_k}(\pm A_k - \theta_{L_k}) \quad (3)$$

where

- θ'_K modified value of connection type threshold θ_K
- σ_L LTP scaling factor, L = LTP value, ω_L = decay coefficient for LTP, υ_L, υ_{L_k} = homo- and heterosynaptic growth factors for LTP, θ_L, θ_{L_k} = homo- and heterosynaptic LTP action thresholds, A_k = total input from connection type k. σ_L may be negative to implement long-term depression; unlike the D (normal depression) term, the LTP term may have different effects on different afferent connection types. These rules for LTP currently do not incorporate the recently discovered short-term component of this phenomenon [31].

Training in Darwin III takes place by permanent alterations in synaptic weights according to principles of the TNGS, and not by LTP, which is subject to eventual decay. The rules for long-lasting synaptic modification are patterned after those used in Darwin II [25], which essentially involve making positive or negative changes in c_{ij} according to the degree of correlation of pre- and postsynaptic activities. There are two major changes in Darwin III, however, both of which are aimed at implementing the principle of *value-dependent modification* and both of which mark significant departures from Hebb-like rules: (1) the changes in c_{ij} values of a given type may be made to depend hetero-

Table 1 Properties of Darwin III Repertoires

Repertoire	Afferents	Efferents	Details of Unit Dynamics and Connectivity
OCULOMOTOR SYSTEM			
VR	Input Array	SC	Layers 1 & 2: 841 excitatory and 841 inhibitory units (29×29 grid). Every excitatory unit receives one topographical connection from the portion of the environment currently viewed through the eye. Local excitatory and lateral inhibitory connectivity provides sharpening of responses and attentional bias. Excitatory units have depression (see Equation 1), with four refractory cycles after eight consecutive cycles of maximal firing.
SC	VR	OM	Layers 1 & 2: 256 excitatory and 256 inhibitory units (16×16 grid). Every excitatory unit receives four topographical connections. Local connectivity as in VR.
FO	Input Array	Value Scheme 1	121 excitatory units (11×11 grid). Each unit receives one excitatory topographically mapped connection from the entire visual field, as well as one additional connection from the central 15% and 3% of the visual field, respectively. Global average of activity in the repertoire is used for heterosynaptic value input into connections from SC to OM.
OM	SC (VALUE 1)	Move eye muscles	36 motor units (four groups of nine units). Each unit receives 256 excitatory connections from the entire array of SC units. Two inhibitory connections from opposing units provide lateral inhibition (sharpening response).
REACHING SYSTEM (4 JOINTS)			
HV	Input Array	VALUE	256 units for hand vision (16×16 grid). One excitatory connection from the visual field.
WD	Input Array WD	Value, WD	Layer 1: 1024 units (32×32 grid). One excitatory topographic connection from input array. Layer 2: Inhibitory units provided to sharpen responses in layer 1.

Table 1 (*Continued*)

Repertoire	Afferents	Efferents	Details of Unit Dynamics and Connectivity
VALUE	HV, WD	**Value Scheme 2**	256 units (16×16 grid). 30 excitatory topographical connections from an 11×11 region in HV, 40 excitatory topographical connections from a 17×17 region in WD. Both inputs are required to elicit a response. Global average of activity in the repertoire is used for heterosynaptic value input into connections from WD and KE to MC.
KE	From arm joints	MC, GR	12 units per arm joint (12×4 grid). Units are tuned using a Gaussian function to respond preferably to a particular joint position (angle).
MC	**WD (VALUE 2), KE (VALUE 2)**	IO, IN	Layer 1: 192 units (1×4 grid), predominantly moving extensor muscles. 16 connections (e/i ratio, 2.33) from 13×13 regions of WD, 16 connections (e/i ratio, 1.5) from the entire array WD (these connections only to the first joint), 16 connections, mapped and unmapped, (e/i ratio, 1.0) from all joint levels in KE, six excitatory connections from MC joint level n-1 to n, and 18 inhibitory connections from MC joint level n to n-1. If value is positive, connections from WD and KE to MC are strengthened if pre- and postsynaptic unit are coactive; if value is negative, these connections are weakened. Layer 2: 192 flexor units (1×4 grid). Same connectivity as layer 1.
IO	MC, VALUE 2	PK	Layer 1: 96 flexor units (1×4 grid). Five connections (e/i ratio, 4.0) from MC. Unit activity is modulated by value 2--cells fire only if positive value is present. Layer 2: 96 extensor units (1×4 grid). Connectivity as in layer 1.
GR	WD, KE	PK	288 units (12×24 grid). Six connections (e/i ratio, 1.22) from KE, and nine connections (e/i ratio, 4.0) from 8×8 regions in WD. Both inputs required to fire unit.
PK	GR, IO	IN	Layer 1: 96 flexor units (1×4 grid). Four strong excitatory topographical connections from IO flexor units, 216 initially weak connections (e/i ratio, 1.5) from GR units. These connections are strengthened if pre- and postsynaptic units are coactive and weakened if presynaptic unit is active but postsynaptic is not. PK units remain active for several cycles after excitation, before entering a refractory period of several cycles. Layer 2: 96 extensor units (1×4 grid). Connectivity as in layer 1.

Table 1 *(Continued)*

Repertoire	Afferents	Efferents	Details of Unit Dynamics and Connectivity
IN	PK, MC	SG	Layer 1: 192 flexor units (1×4 grid). Six excitatory connections from MC flexors, from topographically corresponding and neighboring joint levels, 24 inhibitory connections from the corresponding joint level in PK, both extensors and flexors. These connections become less inhibitory if pre- and postsynaptic units are coactive and more inhibitory if presynaptic unit is active but postsynaptic is not. Layer 2: 192 extensor units. Connectivity as in layer 1.
SG	IN, TH	Move arm joints	Layer 1: 128 flexor units (1×4 grid). 16 connections from IN flexors or extensors (e/i ratio, 1.86), all-or-none inhibitory connections from TH to joints 1 and 2. These connections inhibit gross arm movement when touch is established. Layer 2: 128 extensor units (1×4 grid). Connectivity as in layer 1.
REACHING SYSTEM (2 JOINTS)			
EKX, EKY	From eye muscles	MX, MY	21 units each (21×1 or 1×21 grid). One excitatory afferent from eye muscles signaling eye position. Units form one-dimensional map of x- and y-coordinates.
MX, MY	EKX, EKY, VR	WD	609 units (21×29 grid). 29 excitatory connections from topographically corresponding units distributed along a line in VR and one excitatory mapped connection from KEX or KEY (signaling eye position). Both inputs are required to fire the unit.
WD	MX, MY	K1, K2	Layers 1&2: 1024 excitatory and 1024 inhibitory units (32×32 grid). Local interactions are similar to those in VR and SC. Topographically mapped afferents terminate on excitatory units arriving from regions in MX or MY, distributed along diagonal lines in those repertoires. Inputs from both sources are required to fire a WD unit. Layer 3: An additional 1024 units receive excitatory connections from local regions (3×3) in layer 1. They have addititional intrinsic connectivity that further sharpens the response. This layer connects to repertoires K1 and K2.
HV			See four-jointed arm.
VALUE			See four-jointed arm.

Table 1 (*Continued*)

Repertoire	Afferents	Efferents	Details of Unit Dynamics and Connectivity
KE	from arm joints	K1, K2, JM1, JM2	24 units per arm joint (24×2 grid) and an additional 24 units for report of shoulder joint motion in tracing. Units are tuned using a Gaussian function to respond preferably to a particular joint position (angle).
K1, K2	WD, KE	JM1, JM2	24 units each (1×24 grid). One excitatory connection comes from a corresponding position in KE, and 512 initially weak excitatory connections spread out homogeneously over layer 3 in WD. These connections are strengthened if pre- and postsynaptic units fire and weakened if presynaptic unit fires but postsynaptic does not.
JM1, JM2	KE, K1, K2	SG	576 units each (24×24 grid). There is one JM repertoire for each arm joint. One excitatory topographical connection from KE and one topographical connection from K1 or K2 converge onto each unit. Two inputs are required for firing.
SG	JM1, JM2 (VALUE 2), RX	Move arm joints	32 units, 16 for each arm joint (eight flexors, eight extensors), with 576 initially weak excitatory inputs from all positions in either JM1 or JM2. If value is positive connections are strengthened if pre-and postsynaptic units are coactive, and weakened if postsynaptic unit is active, but presynaptic is not. If value is negative, connections are weakened if pre- and postsynaptic units are coactive. Moderate noise level to generate initially random arm motions.
TACTILE SYSTEM			
TH	From touch receptors, RX	TC, E1, E2, E3, E4	64 units (8×8 grid). One excitatory connection from grid of touch receptors on last arm joint.
TC	TH	TM	36 units (6×6 grid). Nine connections arranged in an on-center, off-surround matrix.
E1, E2, E3, E4	TH	TM	36 units each (6×6 grid). Nine connections arranged in a matrix allowing edge detection.

Table 1 *(Continued)*

Repertoire	Afferents	Efferents	Details of Unit Dynamics and Connectivity
TM	TC, E1, E2, E3, E4	Move shoulder joint	16 units, four each for up, down, left, and right motion. 36 excitatory connections from all positions in TC. Connections to each of the four motor neuron groups have one-dimensional gradients in their connection strength. Additional connections from E1, E2, E3, and E4 terminate on their respective groups of motor neurons to further bias joint motion.
CATEGORIZATION SYSTEM			
LGN	Input Array	R	Layers 1 & 2: 7056 on-center units and 7056 off-center units (84×84 grid). 16 inputs in a topographic map from the central 15% of the visual field arranged in a matrix of connections.
R	LGN	R_2	6561 units each of four types (81×81 grid). Nine topographically mapped connections arranged in a matrix to produce orientation-selective units. Each position in R contains four units responding optimally to horizontal, vertical, and diagonal lines.
R_2	R, R_M, TR	R_M, RF	Layer 1: 484 units (11×11 grid). 10 excitatory connections spread out over the entire R array. Layer 2: 484 units. One topographically mapped connection from layer 1. Units will not fire if only these connections are active. They also receive connections from the trigger unit TR and 48 **reentrant** connections from R_M. Activity in these connections can lower the excitation threshold ("LTP", see Equations 2 and 3) of the unit.
M_T	KE, TR	R_M	Layer 1: 12 units (12×1 grid). One temporally delayed connection from layer 2. Layer 2: 12 units (12×1 grid). One excitatory connection from a group of units in KE. Responsible for detecting motion of the shoulder joint in tracing. Layer 3: 48 units (12×1 grid). One topographically mapped excitatory connection each from layer 1 and layer 2, nine inhibitory connections from noncorresponding positions in layer 1 and layer 2. One inhibitory connection from trigger repertoire. Units detect correlation of motion in one direction ("smooth edges"). Layer 4: 48 units (12×1 grid). One excitatory topographical connection from layer 2, one inhibitory topographical connection from layer 1, nine excitatory nonmapped connections from layer 1, nine inhibitory nonmapped connections from layer 2, one inhibitory connection from trigger repertoire. Units detect absence of correlation in motion ("bumpy edges").

Table 1 (*Continued*)

Repertoire	Afferents	Efferents	Details of Unit Dynamics and Connectivity
R_M	M_T, R_2, TR	R_2, RF	Layer 1: 192 units (12×1 grid). Four excitatory topographical connections from M_T, layer 4. Units also receive input from TR to reexcite units that have been recently active ("LTP"). Layer 2: 192 units (12×1 grid). One excitatory mapped input from layer 1. This input alone will not fire the unit, which also receive 24 **reentrant** connections from R_2. An additional input from TR can influence firing threshold of unit by "LTP".
TR	M_T, TR	R_2, R_M	Layer 1: 48 units (12×1 grid). One topographical excitatory connection from M_T, layer 3. Units are active for several cycles after activation and then enter a refractory period. They detect novel smooth contours--the absence of firing in this layer indicates the absence of such features. Layer 2: 48 units (12×1 grid). One topographical excitatory connection from M_T, layer 4. Responses like layer 2, but for "bumpy" contours. Layer 3: One unit, 48 excitatory connections each from layers 1 and 2. Novelty detector. Layer 4: One unit, 48 inhibitory connections each from layers 1 and 2, one excitatory connection from layer 3. Fires if no novel stimuli features are detected.
RF	R_2, R_M	OP	16 units (1×1 grid). 32 connections each from widespread regions in R_2 and R_M. Inputs from both R_2 and R_M are required to fire a unit.
OP	RF, R_M	RX	16 units (1×1 grid). 32 excitatory connections from RF, eight excitatory connections from R_M, layer 2. Two inputs are required to fire a unit.
RX	OP	SG	12 units arranged in three layers. Form oscillatory circuit.

Note: The connection strengths of afferents in **bold** type are modifiable, under the heterosynaptic influence of a value scheme if one is listed. The e/i ratios for certain connection types give the ratio of the number of excitatory to the number of inhibitory connections. An excitatory connection cannot become inhibitory by amplification or vice-versa. Connections within a repertoire are not listed in the affferents or efferents columns.

synaptically on the activity of cells in some repertoire reflecting the organism's evaluation of its recent behavior according to a specified value scheme; and (2) the dependence on pre- and postsynaptic activity may be based on moving-window time averages of these quantities rather than instantaneous values. Further flexibility is provided by the inclusion of a "rule selector" factor (R), which can be manipulated to generate value-dependent synaptic modification or to reproduce the original Darwin II rules or even the classical Hebb rule. The complete modification equation is

$$c_{ij}(t+1) = c_{ij}(t) + \delta \cdot \phi(c_{ij}) \cdot (\bar{s}_i - \theta_I) \cdot (m_{ij} - \theta_J) \cdot (v - \theta_V) \cdot R \tag{4}$$

where

- δ amplification factor, a parameter that adjusts the overall rate of synaptic change
- $\bar{s}_i$ time-averaged activity of cell i, calculated according to $\bar{s}_i(t) = \lambda s_i(t) + (1 - \lambda)\bar{s}_i(t-1)$, where λ = damping constant for averaged activity
- θ_I amplification threshold relating to postsynaptic activity
- m_{ij} average concentration of hypothetical postsynaptic "modifying substance" produced at a synapse made on cell i by cell j according to

$$m_{ij}(t) = m_{ij}(t-1) + \upsilon_M s_j - \text{Min}\,(\tau_M m_{ij}(t-1), \tau_M^0) \tag{5}$$

  where υ_M = production rate for m_{ij}, τ_M = decay constant for m_{ij}, τ_M^0 = maximum decay rate for m_{ij} (m_{ij} may be replaced simply by s_j if desired)
- θ_J amplification threshold relating to presynaptic activity
- v magnitude of heterosynaptic input from relevant value scheme neurons
- θ_V amplification threshold relating to value
- R rule selector. R may be independently set to +1, 0, or −1 for each of the eight combinations of signs of the three thresholded terms in the amplification function, giving a total of $3^8 = 6561$ possible amplification rules. Positive values of R lead to enhancement of synapses with correlated pre- and postsynaptic activity (selection); negative values of R lead to suppression of such synapses (homeostasis). By choice of a particular rule, it is possible to simulate any of a wide variety of different kinds of synapses, with properties corresponding, for example, to those of synapses using different neurotransmitters. Selective setting of a subset of the R values to zero makes it possible to suppress synaptic modification under certain conditions, as might be the case with certain pharmacological agents. Typically, we choose a rule in which R is +1 when $(v - \theta_V) > 0$ and either of $(\bar{s}_i - \theta_I)$ or $(m_{ij} - \theta_J) > 0$, that is, when a value signal is present, a synapse is strengthened when both presynaptic and postsynaptic cells are active but weakened when one is active and the other is not. If the value factor and time averaging are omitted, the rule reduces to the rule used in Darwin II and then resembles a Hebb rule [16].

There are significant differences between the neuronal dynamics of Darwin III and those of other recent models incorporating neuron-like elements (see, for example, [32], [33]). Unlike the case with these other models, the repertoires in Darwin III are *not* operated under conditions designed to seek a minimum in some potential function that reflects the degree of disparity in the responses of interconnected units, and recognition events are not associated with energy minima. Instead, network activity is always driven strongly by current input and is "far from equilibrium" in the statistical physical sense. In this view, patterns of activity in networks involved in recognizing patterns have no static symbolic meaning, and one can usually not interpret them at any given time point. Instead, they represent categorizations of input signals that acquire meaning only in terms of the motor outputs they engender; their internal consistency or lack of it is of no consequence to the system as a whole. Another important point is that since no learning or minimization algorithms are applied, there are no formal restrictions on the way cellular or modular units are connected and operate dynamically. This allows us to choose more or less realistic arrangements of networks that are free of the unnatural simplifying assumptions such as the complete n^2 connectivity or the use of bidirectional synapses that are characteristic of models such as multilayer PDP networks [34], [35] or Hopfield networks [32].

Functional Subsystems of Darwin III

Darwin III offers a unique opportunity to relate events at different levels—synapse, cell, group, network, system, and behavior. As we discuss the functional subsystems of Darwin III, we will frequently cross the borders between these levels to gain some insight into their interdependence. However, it is necessary to be cautious concerning the difficult issue of animal learning and how it relates to the simulations described here. Although Darwin III has made a few steps in the direction of conditioned learning, it is not yet able to learn in a fashion that would enable it to change its behavioral responses toward environmental stimuli as a consequence of its own experience. Learning in this sense would require more elaboration of internal value-related states and the ability to couple these into connections between category and motor output (studies of this kind are currently under way). Darwin III is, however, able to link its responses to perceptual categorizations and is capable of self-organization leading to sensorimotor coordination. The selectional processes involved in these behaviors are of a different, simpler nature, and we consistently refer to them as "training" rather than "learning" in order to make this distinction stand out clearly.

Caution is also in order concerning the relationship between neuronal repertoires in Darwin III and cytoarchitectonic areas in real brains. In the following descriptions of the component subsystems of Darwin III, neuronal repertoires are designated by two-letter names. In some cases, these names are abbreviations of names of cytoarchitectonic areas in real brains; the coincidence of names is intended only to be suggestive of the general function of these repertoires as well as their relative position in an overall scheme and is not meant to imply that they are accurate models of the corresponding real brain regions.

The Oculomotor System of Darwin III

The oculomotor system of Darwin III exemplifies how selective mechanisms enable a simple motor control system to adapt to the requirements of an environment. Our main interest is to understand how such a system may develop over time and how various conditions involving the mechanics of effector organs, neuronal architecture, and sensory stimulation interact to shape its structure. We start with circuitry that is not programmed or precisely prespecified, in that the strengths of the connections linking sensory maps to motor output are assigned without prior knowledge of the task the system should perform. As in other parts of Darwin III, we have omitted much of the detail of real anatomy and physiology. We have not, for example, included a detailed model of the superior colliculus, which is heavily involved in oculomotor control (for a review, see [36]), nor have we distinguished between control mechanisms for the generation and scaling of visual saccades versus fine tracking movements as are found in real visual systems.

A schematic diagram of the repertoires and connections used in the current version of the oculomotor system is shown in Fig. 5. Visual signals impinge on VR, a retina-like

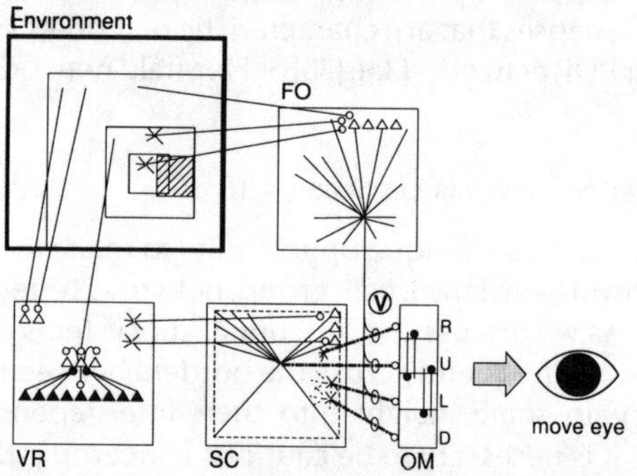

Fig. 5. Schematic connectivity of neural repertoires in oculomotor system of Darwin III. Visual signals coming from the portion of the environment viewed by the eye lead to responses in a simulated neuronal layer VR, a map of visual space. VR contains excitatory and inhibitory units; excitatory units make connections to neighboring excitatory units, thus enhancing activity locally. Inhibitory units influence excitatory units further away, thus providing lateral inhibition to limit extent of centers of activation and sharpen responses. VR is connected directly and in a topographic manner to another sensory area SC, which contains a similar arrangement of local excitatory and inhibitory connections to that of VR (not shown). Eye-motor area OM contains four groups of nine units each connected to four simulated "muscles" that move the eye right (*R*), up (*U*), left (*L*), or down (*D*), respectively. Each of these four areas receives 256 (128 in some experiments) excitatory connections from the entire SC array. These connections initially have random synaptic strength and are subject to modification biased by the state of a "value" repertoire FO, which responds more strongly when the central visual field is more strongly stimulated. FO receives denser and more numerous connections from the center of the visual field; the appearance of a stimulus in the center thus leads to an increase in activity in the FO network. (In schematic diagrams of Darwin III network connectivities: open and filled triangles denote excitatory and inhibitory units, respectively; open and filled circles denote excitatory and inhibitory synapses, respectively; modifiable connections are indicated by dashed bold lines (-·-·-); heterosynaptic influence of value is indicated by V.

visual repertoire containing two layers of cells, excitatory and inhibitory. The responses of the excitatory cells are mapped in a topographical and partially overlapping fashion to a second, smaller repertoire SC, that may be thought of as carrying out some of the functions of the superior colliculus in controlling eye movements. Excitatory cells in SC are connected directly to four separate collections of "ocular motor neurons" OM, which stimulate simulated muscles to move the eye up, down, left, or right in its orbit. These connections are excitatory, and initially their strengths are assigned by drawing them randomly from a normal distribution. Connection strengths are modifiable, following Eq. (4). In a typical simulation each motor neuron receives 256 connections from the entire array of units in SC. (Architectures in which the density of connections and their topographical arrangement were varied are discussed in the following.) Between opposing groups of motor neurons (up versus down, left versus right) local lateral inhibitory connections provide a sharpening of the responses evoked by activity in SC.

In order that motions of the eye with positive adaptive value for the organism may be selected, a value scheme is required. We have chosen to use one that effectively defines the goal "bring the eye toward bright spots and fixate on them." One way for the nervous system to accomplish this goal is to enhance motions that happen to bring visual stimuli into the foveal part of the retina. In the model, this is done by providing a specialized value repertoire that constantly monitors the responses of the visual repertoire VR. The value network contains units that receive excitatory connections with a probability (density) that is low at the periphery and increases toward the center of the visual field. These units thus respond more strongly as stimulus objects approach the fovea. The magnitude of these responses provides the heterosynaptic input that modulates the modification of connections from SC to OM (v factor in Eq. (4)). Activity in these connections causes the formation of a slowly decaying modifying substance (m_{ij} in Eq. (5)). Connections that have been active during any kind of motion are, as a result, "chemically" labeled and amenable to undergoing long-lasting changes. Connections that are so labeled because of activity occurring shortly before foveation of an object and consequent activation of the value repertoire are selected and strengthened. Selection in this model is continual, but strictly *a posteriori*: It acts on neuronal populations after their activity has produced an effect.

Because Darwin III's oculomotor system starts with connections and connection strengths equally distributed throughout the visual field, initial eye motions are mainly the result of spontaneous activity ("noise") in motor neurons and these motions are random. The initial repertoire of motions is constrained only by the mechanics of the eye itself and usually comprises motions in all directions with equal probability. After selection for foveation has occurred, the variability between individual eye trajectories is greatly decreased and the eye tends to move directly toward each newly presented object. In a standard training protocol, an object covering 3.5% of the input array is presented and then jumps randomly at intervals of 16 time steps. Occasionally an object jumps to a position outside the visual field. Figure 6 illustrates how the eye–object distance changes over time, before and after training of the oculomotor system. The improvement of the system can be

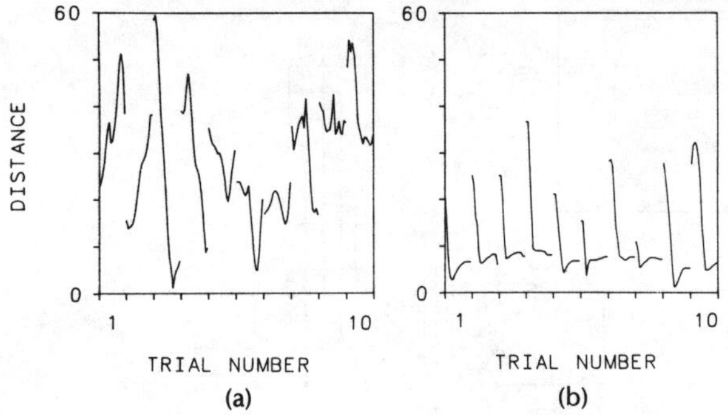

Fig. 6. Example showing how movements of Darwin III's output organs can be assessed. Distance of center of fovea from center of stimulus (in pixels) over time, (a) before and (b) after training of the oculomotor system for 5008 cycles. Sharp discontinuities arise because object randomly jumps to a new position every 16 cycles. Before training, eye movements are uncoordinated with respect to the object and most of the time there is no decrease of eye–object distance following a jump. After training is completed, a characteristic "comb" pattern emerges. Following a random jump, the eye quickly moves toward the new position, the object is kept foveated (radius of the foveal region is 10 pixels) and, if it moves, it is tracked.

assessed by noting the change in the slope of this curve in the time following the presentation of each new stimulus (jumps in eye–object distance at 16-cycle intervals). Figure 7 shows these data in another form. Motion of the eye with

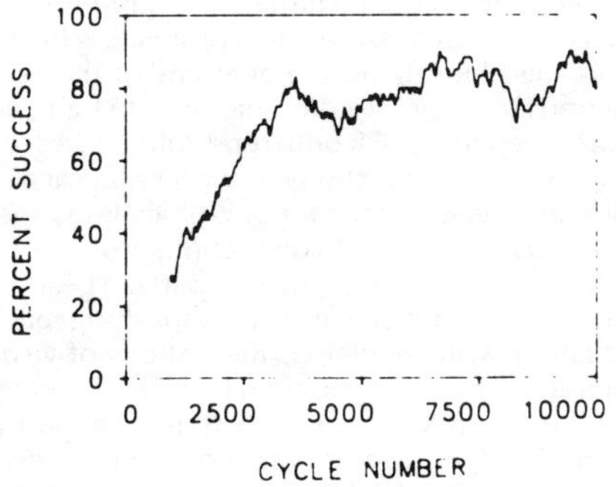

Fig. 7. Improvement of Darwin III's oculomotor system with training. Every trial (consisting of 16 cycles) in which the eye foveates on an object for at least six consecutive cycles is counted as a "success." Every graph point represents the average success rate for 60 trials (60 × 16 cycles) ending at cycle number plotted on the abscissa. After about 150 object presentations, foveation occurs in nearly every trial. Some trials are unsuccessful because the object jumps to a location outside the visual field and random search does not succeed in locating it within the time limit. Performance is stable at the end of training and remains at a constant high level for as long as testing is continued (up to 90 000 cycles).

respect to the object is scored by counting trials in which foveation successfully occurs in a series of overlapping time windows. A running average that serves as a performance index is calculated from these data. Even though synaptic modifications continue to take place, the adaptive nature of the value scheme keeps the system from deteriorating and a high level of performance is maintained over a long time (tested up to 90 000 cycles). Almost all simulations needed no more than 300, and often only 150 (Fig. 7) presentations of objects at different positions to reach optimal performance.

The development of satisfactory performance is insensitive to changes in the initial network parameters. For example, similar results are obtained when the efficiency of the ocular muscles (angular displacement of the eye per unit of afferent neuronal activity) is varied over a range of 5 to 1 (data not shown). When the muscles are relatively ineffective, the distribution of weights in OM between groups feeding opposing muscles tends to be asymmetrical. The variation in the strength of connections at a given position in the array is low. More effective muscles lead to a very shallow gradient of connection strengths across the SC network and the variation at any position is very high. In both cases conjoint activation of opposing groups of motor neurons is infrequent. The system adapts successfully regardless of which type of motor neuron is present, with no change in synaptic modification parameters.

The results discussed so far were obtained with every unit in SC connected systematically to every unit in OM. This configuration makes it possible to display the connection strengths in an easily interpreted format, but it clearly ignores an important aspect of variation in the nervous system. In fact, other configurations lead to equally satisfactory performance. In control runs, connections of the same density or half the density (256 or 128 connections per motor unit, respectively) were distributed at random over SC, so that many units in SC had more than one connection with a motor unit or none at all. Performance improved significantly during the course of simulation without additional adjustments in critical parameters, although at a somewhat slower pace than before. Sensitivity of the system to damage was tested by first running the system with 256 connections per cell and then, after training, eliminating half of these connections, chosen at random. The automaton continued to perform almost unperturbed, and subsequent synaptic changes in the remaining connections compensated for an initial decrease in the average firing rate of units in OM.

These simulations and others (data not shown) demonstrate the robustness of selective systems. Changes in the effectiveness of connections, in the density and distribution of connections, or in dynamic parameters such as time constants, thresholds, and so on do not, in general, prevent the system from converging to an effective mode of behavior. Each of the members of a family of such systems finds a different set of synaptic weights to bring about such behavior. Identical twin automata differing only in microscopic detail (by different choice of random number generating seeds) will differ as well when trained, reflecting the existence of degeneracy in the responses of their neural networks, but in general they cannot be distinguished from one another if only overall behavior is scored. This characteristic of selective systems also extends to varying conditions in the environment. For example, individual automata that frequently encounter large objects will come to differ from those that encounter small ones. Although otherwise identical, these automata will be optimally adapted to their respective worlds of stimuli. Moreover, they are able to readapt if external conditions change, a property of obvious value to the survival of an organism.

The value scheme is of crucial importance to the improvement of performance under training and, as expected, no improvement under any testing criterion is observed if it is disconnected. A different value scheme, however, will guide the system in a different direction. If, for example, the connectivity to the value repertoire is inverted so that the density of connections from the periphery of the retina is greater than from the fovea, then the value scheme of that automaton effectively favors the selection of motions that result in decreased light intensity on the retina, and after training the eye always moves away from visual stimuli. The final pattern of synaptic weights for connections originating close to the center of SC shows strong connections asymmetrically distributed between opposing pairs of motor units. Once more, the final outcome is consistent with the constraints imposed by the value scheme.

The simulations discussed so far show how, in a model system, changes in sensory inputs can be correlated with self-produced movements of a phenotypic organ. Selection based on value can shape the development of a simple sensorimotor system in which successful action requires little more than guidance in a particular direction through a topographic mapping. No such simple relationship between sensory and motor signals exists, however, for the problem of reaching using a multijointed arm.

The Reaching System

The versatility of the CNS simulation program makes it possible to construct a variety of models for any given problem. These models can differ significantly from each other, providing an excellent opportunity to compare different versions of a model with each other in isolation as well as during interactions with other components of the entire Darwin III automaton. This capability was exploited in connection with reaching movements, for which two quite different models were constructed.

The first model is more closely based on real anatomical structures. It contains a four-jointed arm moved by four sets of independent agonist-antagonist muscle pairs. The basic idea behind this model is the selection of gestures or gestural components from a set of initially unorganized motions. The model has two main components: a module corresponding to cerebal cortex where motor signals eventually leading to gestural motions are generated in a context-dependent manner, and a module corresponding to the cerebellum which correlates these motor signals with current sensory inputs and smooths the responses by eliminating inappropriate components. Hand and object vision as well as a simple form of kinesthesia (the sense of joint positions) provide the sensory signals utilized by the system. These signals are transformed through mapped and unmapped interactions of neuronal repertoires in the two component regions into motor signals that move the arm to new positions.

The circuitry is summarized schematically in Fig. 8. The first region contains repertoire MC (representing "motor cortex") that generates patterns of activity corresponding to primary gestural motions through a combination of spontaneous activity (noise) and responses to sensory inputs from target vision and arm kinesthesia. Activity in MC is transmitted to an intermediary network IN, which may be considered analogous in function to brain-stem nuclei (as, for example, the red nucleus) or to another motor cortical layer. Here the activity pattern is remodeled under

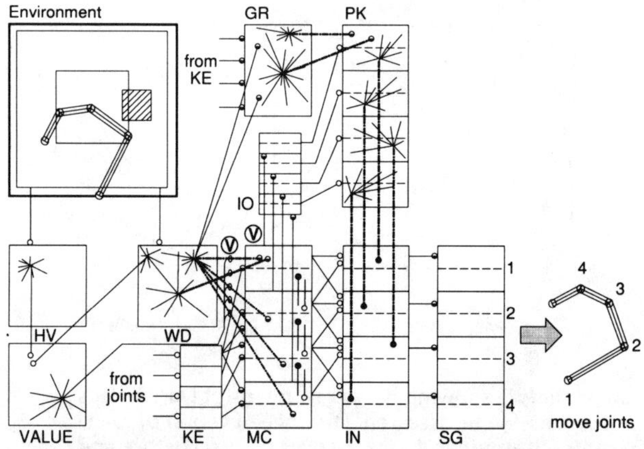

Fig. 8. Schematic of reaching system with four-jointed arm. The motor system proper contains a sequence of three repertoires, MC, IN, and SG, in which gestures are respectively generated, filtered, and converted to the activation of efferent motor neurons. MC corresponds to a primitive "motor cortex" and in the model is the area where actions are initiated in response to sensory inputs, in this case kinesthetic (from KE) and visual (from WD). In the model, unlike in real animals, the motor cortex is entirely autonomous, that is, unregulated by other brain regions. Each motor cortical unit receives a number of inputs from KE, some coming from the topographically corresponding joint, others from other joints. Reflecting the primacy of visual input for Darwin III and the absence of higher-level control, firing in MC cannot be stimulated by kinesthetic inputs alone, but requires visual inputs (mixed excitatory and inhibitory) as well. Some of these come from local regions on the WD map, others spread out over practically the entire array. Local connectivity in MC leading to a wave of activity from proximal to distal joint levels is indicated. The model includes the region responsible for the selective shaping of gestures originating in MC. This area is modeled loosely on the anatomy of the cerebellum. It functions by mapping combinations of KE and target visual inputs in repertoire GR onto repertoire PK. A great number of initially weak connections converges on each PK unit. A PK unit also receives strong topographically mapped input from repetoire IO. Efferent connections from PK act in motor repertoire IN to inhibit getures or parts of gestures found by selection to be ineffective in accomplishing reaching in past situations with similar configurations of visual stimulus and joint locations. Each unit in IN receives a number of connections from MC; connectivity is divergent to allow units in IN to respond to a combination of unit activity on different joint levels in MC. Efferent connections to SG are precisely topographic and activate appropriate motor units (extensors and flexors) to give arm motion. Connections from WD to MC are modifiable according to value (Eq. 4). Repertoire HV contains topographically mapped units that are selectively responsive to vision of Darwin III's "hand." VALUE receives a number of overlapping topographical connections from both WD and HV. Firing of units in VALUE thus reflects the relative proximity of Darwin III's hand to the target object. Global activity levels in VALUE are used to provide heterosynaptic influence on the modification of connections from WD to MC and to modulate the firing level in repertoire IO. The exact mechanisms by which connection strengths are modified to bring about mature functioning of this complex system are described in text. Half-filled circles indicate mixed excitatory and inhibitory connectivity, which eliminates the need for separate layers of inhibitory units and introduces greater stability. The relative numbers of the two types of connections are given in Table 1.

the influence of inhibitory connections descending onto IN from a set of networks forming the second module of the system. This component and its connectivity may be considered analogous in function to the cerebellum (explicit areas corresponding to deep cerebellar nuclei have been omitted in the model). IN sends out connections to four sets of motor neurons (one for each joint) organized in extensor/flexor pairs. The cerebellar networks receive sensory inputs as well as activity representing the current primary gesture emanating from MC. Target vision and kinesthetic inputs give rise to diffuse and fast-changing firing patterns in GR units, which are analogous to granule cells. Each GR pattern correlates an actual configuration of the arm in space with a target position. GR units connect densely to PK units, which are analogous to Purkinje cells. These connections are mixed excitatory and inhibitory to eliminate the need for a separate set of inhibitory interneurons analogous to stellate and basket cells. The connections from GR to PK provide a basis for associating actual positions of the arm and target with patterns corresponding to primary gestures that arise from MC and reach PK via repertoire IO (representing the inferior olive). The role of IO during exposure to environmental stimuli ("training") will be discussed below. Activity in PK inhibits a changing subset of units in IN and as a result selects or "filters out" appropriate gestures from the primary patterns transmitted to IN from MC. The topology of all these connections (Fig. 8) includes a reentrant signaling loop involving the MC, GR, IO, PK, and IN networks.

It must be understood that, while its components resemble those in real brains, this is not an explicit model of the cerebellum. The reaching system is designed as a gestural module representing parts of the cerebral and cerebellar cortices and their associated tracts. In its present version, it depends on saccadic eye motions for target location and selection. Coordinated hand motion should, however, be possible independent of position or relative motion of the eyes. Under these more general conditions, collections of similar modules acting in parallel and forming a cortical map of external space would be needed to guide gestural motions of the arm.

Motor cortical and cerebellar networks are topographically ordered in that they contain groups of units that primarily connect, in an ordered sequence, to single joint extensors or flexors. This arrangement is consistent with anatomical and physiological evidence for such motor maps. Intrinsic connections in the motor cortical network are biased to favor the spread of activity from units representing proximal to more distal joints. Gestural motions therefore tend to unfold proximodistally, a useful adaptation for the large-amplitude reaching movements under study here. A direct "point-to-point" topographical order of connections from MC to joint motor neurons was avoided in order to allow coordination between the MC level and the motor level to develop through the activity of the reentrant inhibitory loop. Although a certain degree of topography is present in the system from the beginning, there is no explicit representation of either "movements" or "muscles" over the area in MC. What is represented in the actual motor cortex is still an open and much debated question [37], [38].

As with the oculomotor system, the connectivity of the reaching system is initially uninstructed with respect to appropriate directions and amplitudes of movement. Coordinated motions of sets of joints occur only after gestural components have been selected from spontaneous movements by amplification of synaptic populations that give rise to such gestures. As with the oculomotor system, neuronal circuitry instantiating an intrinsic value scheme is required to detect and signal the *consequences* of successful motor activity. In the reaching system, this circuitry consists of a set of neurons designed to respond more actively as the moving hand approaches the vicinity of the foveated target object. These neurons receive topographically mapped visual inputs from two separate areas responsive to objects in the environment and to the hand of the automaton, respectively. Each of these inputs arborizes in an overlapping fashion over the surface of the value network, and thresholds are arranged so that correlated activity in both inputs is required for a vigorous response. The responses of the value units thus increase, independent of the absolute position of the target, as the hand approaches the target and the degree of overlap in the topographically mapped inputs increases.

The activity in the value repertoire is carried to the IO network by nonspecific modulatory connections. Bursts of activity in the value repertoire, which are associated with gestural motions that have brought the hand closer to the target, activate IO units, but only those that have already received subthreshold excitation from MC via the connections described earlier. The cellular distribution of the activity in IO is thus not determined by value but depends on the precise pattern of recent activity in MC. IO activity is in turn carried to the PK cells by connections analogous to those made by climbing fibers in the cerebellum. Climbing-fiber activity thus excites different subsets of PK cells according to the gestural pattern present at any given moment in MC, but this excitation is favored when the value network is also active. This scheme allows connections from active "parallel fibers" converging on PK units to be amplified preferentially when the target PK cell has been excited by a climbing fiber consequent to the initiation of a gesture that is in the process of being selected. The sensory conditions signaled by those active "parallel fibers" thus become associated at PK cells with gestures that are being selected as appropriate under those same conditions. The inhibitory consequences in IN of the firing of those PK units, whatever they may be, are perforce appropriate under the conditions in question, because the gesture that is being selected occurred in their presence. After repeated amplification, the "parallel fibers" become capable of exciting PK units on their own and thus acquire the ability to "preset" the pattern of PK cell activity to a configuration that is appropriated in a given context, even before a gesture is initiated in MC. These inhibitions thus come to be available for "filtering" gestures in IN just before they happen.

Activity in the value repertoire is also carried to MC, where active connections relating the position of the visual target to particular gestures are amplified according to value. Synaptic populations whose activity is associated with motions closer to the object are selectively favored in these modifications.

A precalculation of the relevant pathways for a given "desired" movement is neither necessary nor possible given the intricate anatomy and dynamics of the system. Unlike the case with the oculomotor system, there are multiple degenerate solutions for trajectories reaching a given end point, because the number of degrees of freedom of the arm exceeds the dimension of the task space. An online computational solution to the degrees-of-freedom problem by inverse dynamics is difficult and computationally expensive [39], [40], and in general it is not feasible at all. One way to reduce the number of degrees of freedom in a multilink kinematic chain composed of rotating joints is functionally to group muscles or joints together to form *synergies* [41], [42]. We will see shortly how selection constrains the envelope of possible motions by forming functional synergies; selection thus guarantees execution of one or another of the numerous solutions that lead to a successful outcome.

How these mechanisms work in practice to limit the range of gestures that are generated may be seen by considering a typical "training" run. An object (a 12 × 12 pixel square) is presented and spontaneous arm motion is allowed to occur for 6 cycles. After these 6 cycles, the arm is replaced in its initial position and a new trial begins. Initially, the connections from GR units to PK units are weak and only a few PK units fire weakly. As successful motions occur, patterns of MC activity are transmitted to the IO repertoire and IO units strongly excite a subset of PK units as already described. Consequent to this firing, excitatory connections between GR and active PK units and inhibitory connections from active PK units to IN are selectively modified. After training has proceeded for a time, units in PK tend to have weakened inhibitory connections to units in IN whose activity is correlated with positive value. Inhibitory connections to units that are only weakly active are strengthened. At the same time, GR units that correspond to certain sensory situations at the periphery (arm positions) strengthen their connections to simultaneously active PK units. After the training process has converged, sensory signals from the arm joints together with those coming from target vision establish patterns of activity in GR units, and thence in PK units, that in turn limit the possible patterns in IN and thus constrain the shapes of the resulting gestures. Only the gestural patterns most appropriate to the particular configuration of the arm and target position at any moment are able to pass through IN without inhibition. The actual primary gestures, however, can be initiated only by the MC network itself, presumably under the motivational and attentional control of other centers not considered here. Amplification has the effect of creating units in IN with a certain degree of directional selectivity. At least in the cases studied so far, activity in these units correlates with the onset of certain gestural motions, independent of the exact location of the starting or ending point. Interestingly, neurons with directional properties are readily found in real motor cortex and basal ganglia and are thought to play an important role in the directional specification of reaching movements [43]–[45].

Plots of bundles of trajectories illustrate the selectional process. The large initial variance among individual motions is progressively reduced to a narrow envelope of motions, most of which point toward the object (Fig. 9). This result corresponds well to experiments of Georgopoulos *et al.* ([44]; see especially their Fig. 3), who studied the acquisition of aiming arm movements in rhesus monkeys. They reported an exponential reduction in the variability of the movement trajectories. More detailed observation of single joints (such as "elbow" and "shoulder") in our own studies reveals that, after training, changes in joint angles are no longer independent of each other. Instead, joints act together in more or less stable ratios, and, as a result of this

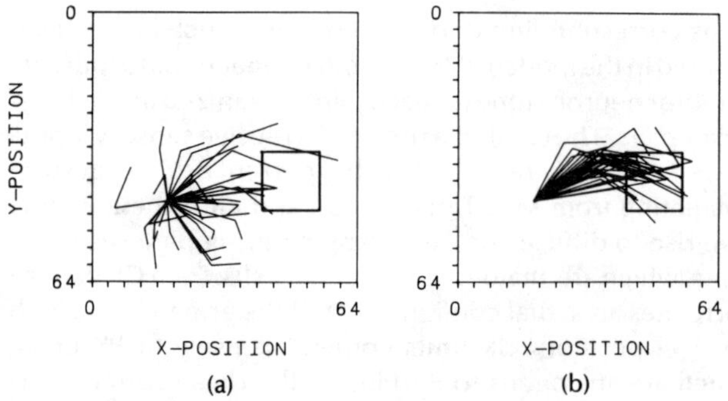

Fig. 9. Traces of paths taken by the distal tip of the four-jointed arm (a) before and (b) after 300 training cycles. Training proceeded as follows: For each of 50 trials, the arm was placed in a standard position with the tip at the point where the trajectories diverge (lower left). It was then allowed to move for 6 cycles, and synaptic changes occurred depending upon the success of the movements relative to a target object whose position is shown by square at right. After training, movements that reached the object on a direct path have been selected. Note that there is still variability in the exact paths taken. (From [66], reproduced with permission.)

synergic interaction, the effective number of degrees of freedom is smaller. Selection of synergic gestures allows the transformation of a redundant system into a controllable one, providing a solution to the "Bernstein problem" [41], [46].

In this model, the main function of the IO → PK connections is to activate patterns of PK units during training to allow modification of synaptic populations linking activity patterns in GR, PK, and IN at a given time; these connections are not required for practiced performance. This is different from the role of IO → PK connections in the Marr-Albus model of the cerebellum [47], [48], in which individual climbing fibers carry instructions for elemental movements. These fibers directly affect the modification of Purkinje cell input connections according to a Hebb rule. The Marr-Albus model requires that individual IO cells somehow "know" whether the output of the particular Purkinje cell to which they are connected is correct or not; our model has no such requirement because *value is transmitted indifferently to all variable synapses depending only on whether the output of the system as a whole, not of any individual unit, is of adaptive value to the organism as determined by the value repertoire.*

Evidently, in a system with many parallel gestural modules, the presentation of an object in different places relative to the arm must result in the selection of different gestures emanating from different modules. The system just described, however, has insufficient gestural richness to yield spatially differentiated solutions under these conditions. In the competition of gestures against each other only a small number prevail and other, less frequently produced gestures are eliminated. This is due to the absence of a defined mapping of external (target) space onto multiple gestural modules. If such a mapping were present, several gestural motions could coexist in the different gestural modules, each selected for one class of movement and each entering in parallel into a single output motor channel.

We have explored the implementation of such a scheme in a preliminary way by designing a second reaching system (Fig. 10). With this model, our main concern has been to achieve reliable and predictable performance over a wide

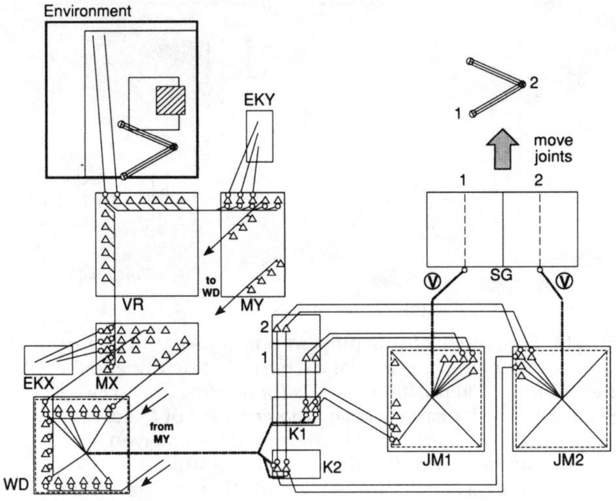

Fig. 10. Schematic of two-jointed reaching system. Repertoire VR (identical to the one used in the oculomotor system) receives topographically mapped excitatory connections from the portion of the visual field viewed through the eye. Strip-like portions of the array connect to networks MX and MY; units there receive additional connections from repertoires that report the eye position within the orbit (EKX, EKY). Units in MX and MY thus respond to particular conjunctions of eye position and target position. Units distributed in diagonal strips on maps MX and MY connect to horizontal and vertical strips in WD. Units there respond to combinations of input patterns from MX and MY, and the location of a center of activity in WD will, as a result of the topography of the mappings involved, more or less correspond to the location of an external target. The topographic mappings from VR to WD are not plastic. Repertoires K1 and K2 represent maps of target joint angles that specify the endpoint of an arm trajectory in response to signals relating the actual arm position (from KE) to the position of the target object (from WD). Initially weak connections from WD come from esentially all positions and are modifiable. Units in K1 and K2 are activated through afferents from KE, and connections between these active units and WD are amplified; inactive connections from WD to these units are deamplified. As a result, a target object presented to Darwin III will eventually activate units in K1 and K2 whose position in the topographic map defines a set of joint coordinates that corresponds to a configuration of the arm with the hand in that position. Maps of actual and target joint coordinates are recombined in JM1 and JM2 to generate an appropriate motor signal moving the arm closer to the target object. Arm motor units in SG receive connections with initially weak random strengths from all positions in JM1 and JM2, respectively. These connections are modified according to value following Eq. 4, using the same value scheme earlier described (Fig. 8) for the four-jointed arm.

range of input space. Neural maps serve as the basic adaptive units to achieve this goal. As before, a selective paradigm is used to train arm movements and generate an appropriate mapping of joint and target coordinates onto groups of motor neurons. In this version, however, the arm is simplified to two joints, thus limiting the number of possible gestural motions; the geometry of the system and its movement task are thus quite similar to planar point-to-point arm movements as studied in human or animal subjects (see, for example, [49], [50]).

The representation of the visual target that enters into the repertoires involved in generating suitable motor responses must ultimately be independent of self-generated eye movements. Neurons with gaze-dependent activity levels in the parietal cortex of primates [51], [52] are thought to be involved in the generation of an invariant representation of relevant objects in body coordinates. In Darwin III, the motor system receives input from a repertoire that responds to the location of the target independent of eye or arm motion in an absolute coordinate frame. This repertoire depends on a combination of visual and kinesthetic signals to compensate for the position of the eye at a given moment and involves no special nonneural mechanisms. Because our goal is only to show how this mapping can be carried out, and not how it might actually arise, the sensory networks that perform these coordinate transformations lack the plasticity that would almost certainly be a crucial property of real neuronal structures of this kind. A network of this kind that did involve plasticity, but of a biologically unrealistic kind, has been studied using a PDP learning algorithm [53]. Cells with receptive field properties analogous to those of the primate parietal cortex were indeed found in this study.

In our model, the two-jointed arm is trained in two stages that follow one another but could also occur in parallel. In the first, adaptive stage, a map is generated between visually detected hand positions and sets of kinesthetically sensed joint angles. This map, comprising networks K1 and K2 in Fig. 10, correlates joint configurations with the corresponding positions of the hand in space. The cells in this map receive kinesthetic inputs from both joints, as well as a great number of very weak connections from visual cells responding to essentially all positions of space. (In real animals, the mapping of limb positions to visual positions in space can presumably be carried out using cues other than kinesthesia, and with larger numbers of units having more restricted visual receptive fields.) In the map, only connections to units that receive both kinesthetic and visual inputs at the same time are strengthened, while connections to units that receive only one kind of input are weakened. The arm moves spontaneously and continuously in the environment as synaptic changes accumulate. The time needed to cover the entire visual space depends on the average movement velocity of the arm and the size of the field the hand covers. At the end of the first training stage, the map represents target arm positions, independent of current arm location. A visual point coming from a particular target location will now result in activity corresponding to the joint angles needed to reach the target. It is important to note that this strategy of defining the endpoint of a trajectory in joint coordinates can in general work only in a nonredundant system, for example, a two-jointed arm in two-dimensional space. A more realistic system would have multiple valid configurations of joints for any given position of the hand. Such a system could be constructed by combining the mapping principle used here with the gestural selection principle used with the four-jointed arm, but this combination has not yet been attempted.

In the second stage of training, input signals from the target joint map are used to guide motions of the arm joints that will bring the hand closer to the object. Two maps of actual versus target angles (one for each joint) make connections with four sets of arm motor neurons in a fashion similar to the connections used in the oculomotor system. The value scheme used is identical to the one used with the four-jointed arm, but here it enters directly into the modification of connections to motor neurons (via Eq. (4)). There are no connections between the networks involved in moving the two joints and thus no possibility of coordinated joint motion.

Training runs show rapid improvements of reaching movements to arbitrary positions in space for two versions with arms of different sizes (data not shown). There is a basic similarity in design to that of the oculomotor system, and consequently many of the adaptive and self-adjusting properties of that system can be found in this version of the reaching system as well. Gross changes of parameters are easily compensated for, and training is stable over time and robust against external disturbances. An interesting point is that after the first stage of training has ended, hand vision is no longer necessary to guide arm movements. Vision of the target is sufficient to define a trajectory end point in joint coordinates; afferent signals from kinesthetic joint receptors are then combined with these signals to produce an appropriate motor signal. If the hand happens to be outside the visual field of Darwin III when a target comes into sight, it will nevertheless approach it and make contact. Cutting the joint afferents at any time during training prevents further progress.

In order to collect data on spatial and temporal aspects of reaching movements, the performance of the reaching system was evaluated in more detail. Systematic presentation of test stimuli over the entire range of space reveals that a near-optimal mapping of external space into the joint system has been achieved, and all positions are reached from every initial position of the arm (an example is shown in Fig. 11(b), (c)). Fig. 12 shows that reaching movements are fast and target oriented; most successful trials terminate within the first four or five cycles.

The simulations of the reaching system so far described were carried out in isolation from movement and training of the eye, which was kept frozen in the center of the visual field. An important step toward a more integrated automaton is to connect the two sensorimotor components and let them interact simultaneously with environmental stimuli. The oculmotor system is not influenced by motions of the arm, but training of the arm is inevitably affected by the changing visual signals of hand and target object resulting from constant eye motion. As it turns out (Fig. 13), Darwin III is quite capable of creating adaptive sensorimotor mappings simultaneously in both components. However, an increase in training time for the arm is seen when the visual field is accidentally turned away from the object and when

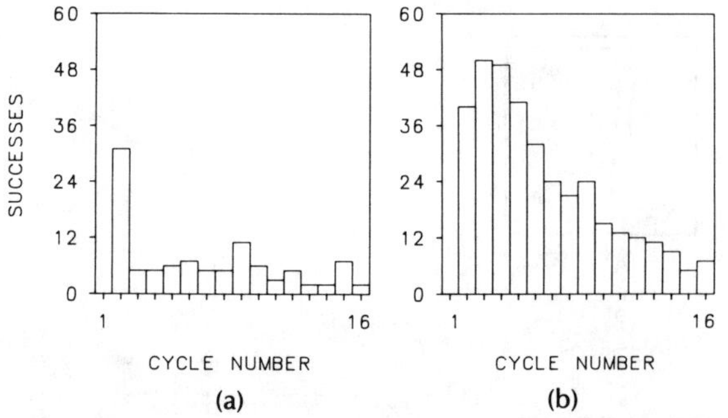

Fig. 12. Frequency of touching an object as a function of cycle number after the start of each trial, (a) before and (b) after training. 130 positions on the input array are covered systematically, four times each. The criterion of "success" is touching the object for at least one cycle in a given trial. Before training, only 102 trials are successful; after 5600 training cycles, 353 trials are successful (396 trials are within reach).

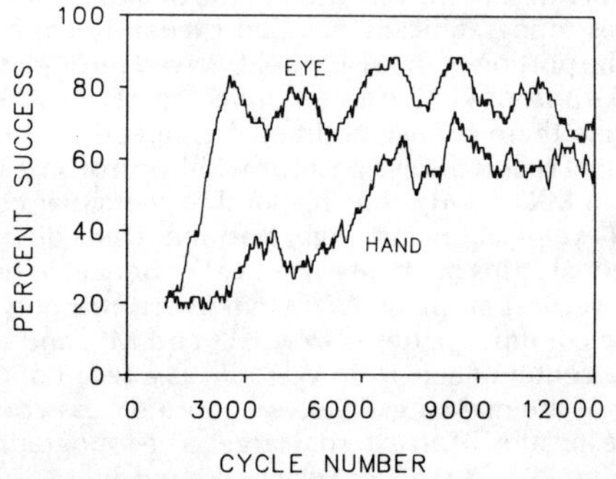

Fig. 13. Training curves of oculomotor and reaching systems for simultaneous simulation of eye and arm. Training of eye movements is independent of arm movements, but visual signals used in the reaching system change as eye moves. Progress in training the arm is somewhat delayed, but eventually a performance level comparable to that in an isolated system is reached and maintained. Absolute performance limits are 100% for the oculomotor system and about 80% for the reaching system.

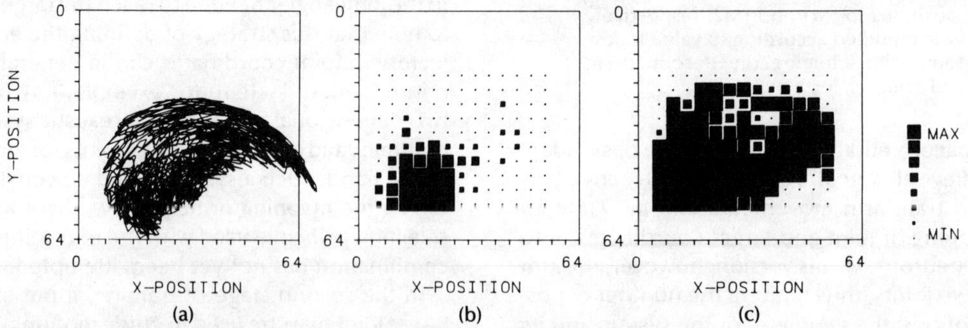

Fig. 11. Spatial range of reaching for two-jointed arm. Control panel (a) shows area of space hand is able to cover when moving freely on the input array (64 × 64 pixels). Tested positions [denoted by squares in panels (b) and (c)] encompass this area. An object is put in sequence at each of 13 × 10 locations, four times at each position. In each the test arm is reset to a standard position with the tip located at the lower left corner. Sizes of squares encode how often the arm touches an object at each position with maximum of 16 cycles allowed before the arm is reset. No synaptic modification is allowed during the evaluation runs. Initially (b), only positions very close to the starting point are covered, until after 5600 cycles of training (c) almost all positions within reach are covered with equal probability.

there are delays in the adjustment of current target positions in mappings as movement occurs. This simulation result is meaningful in the context of experimental findings that eye movements are important for the subsequent acquisition of other visual–motor skills, such as reaching for a target [54]. Even after training, arm movements of Darwin III in a combined fixation–reaching task are on the average somewhat delayed and follow after foveation. If Darwin III's eye is kept frozen, no such delay is observed and arm movements terminate on average two or three time steps earlier. Positioning the eye on the target favors a more precise approach of the hand in both training and final performance.

This second reaching system, like the first, acquires its ability to perform by means of selection, illustrating the broad power and applicability of selective mechanisms for a wide range of network architectures and tasks. Emergence of a narrow class of gestural motions as functional synergies was the key feature of the four-jointed, mechanically redundant system. Balanced performance over a large field of space using neural mappings with a limited number of degrees of freedom was the main characteristic of the second system. A combination of the two, in the form of emergent gestural components ordered in reentrant neural maps, would be a logical next step toward a biological solution to the problem of coordinated movements.

Touch

The third of Darwin III's senses that is used, along with vision and kinesthesia, to guide motor action and to explore objects in the environment is light touch at the end of its arm. The arm traces edges of arbitrarily shaped objects guided by touch and under control of a set of mechanisms, different from and complementary to the reaching system, which generate fine, nonballistic motions. The pattern of these motions is sensed by kinesthetic receptors, which provide signals that are used in Darwin III as one input to a categorization couple (described in the next section). These signals provide by simulated neuronal means the nonlocal features that in Darwin II were provided to Wallace by the Trace program, and make it possible to construct a recognition and categorization automaton (Darwin III) entirely by principles of synthetic neural modeling.

The arm has a built-in reflex-like response that causes it to assume a "canonical" exploratory position when it touches an object. In this position, all joints except the shoulder are immobilized. This arrangement makes it unnecessary to consider explicitly the impact of changes in the position of the intermediate joints on the orientation of the distal touch receptors. Exploratory motions are generated initially in random directions by spontaneous neural activity in the relevant motor repertoires (see schematic in Fig. 14). These random motions are biased by touch signals in two ways to produce coordinated tracing: 1) Touch receptors are responsive to varying pressure across the receptive sheet on the digit at the end of the arm. A pressure gradient sensed in a particular direction acts to enhance motor activity in *perpendicular* directions, thus biasing the arm motions to trace *along the edges* of objects. 2) When pressure decreases, it is normally a signal that the end of an object contour has been reached and tracing is proceeding off into empty space. Touch acts to inhibit the current direction of motion in such cases, with the frequent result that the digit moves back to the object and resumes tracing in another direction. As a result of these two mechanisms, once the hand finds the surface of an object and goes into its rigid exploratory position, tracing proceeds along the edges until interrupted by a burst of activity in the reentrant categorization system. This system which is the key one in the automaton, is described in the next section.

Categorization

The correlation of sensory signals of different modalities by reentry is fundamental to categorization in Darwin III (Fig. 15). The design of the system is based on the principles used in the construction of Darwin II [25], which we have described above. As exemplars of modalities that might be involved in categorization in real animals, we have used vision (for local feature detection) and kinesthesia (for feature correlation using the tracing mechanism just described in place of the programmed trace in Darwin II). The important point in this example, as with Darwin II, is the way the two modalities interact through reentry to form a classification couple, not the exact identity of the two sensory systems involved. Indeed, in recent work not described here, we have constructed versions of Darwin III containing classification couples based on two separate visual submodalities rather than on vision and kinesthesia.

Visual feature detection is carried out in Darwin III by a more realistic set of networks than those used in Darwin II. A simple "LGN" repertoire contains on- and off-center units somewhat analogous to those in the lateral geniculate nucleus, but with quite different dynamics (they respond to local nonmoving stimuli). The model LGN is connected at the next level to an R network, which, like that in Darwin II, is modeled loosely on cortical area $V1$. At each visual position, R has a number of units responsive to vertically, horizontally, or obliquely oriented line segments. The LGN and R networks form topographic images of the perceived object. This topography is lost at the next step, which is a repertoire called R_2 (similar to R-of-R in Darwin II). Units in R_2 receive connections from large, overlapping regions in R and respond to less localized combinations of the features to which R responds. The patterns of activity in R_2 thus bear no resemblance to the appearance of the object, but a unique pattern arises for every object that is presented.

The component of the categorization system dealing with motor patterns consists of a repertoire R_M, which comprises units responsive to two broad classes of stimulus shapes—smooth and rough. The inputs to these units come from kinesthetic receptors in the touch-exploration motor system. Smooth sensitive cells combine kinesthetic inputs corresponding to some angle of tracing with other excitatory inputs corresponding to the same angle but with some time delay. These units also have inhibitory inputs from other trace directions. They thus respond most strongly when tracing continues in a single direction and are inhibited when the direction of trace changes. Conversely, rough-sensitive units receive rapid excitatory inputs corresponding to some angle of tracing, and these are combined with time-delayed excitatory inputs from kinesthetic units with different orientation from the prompt (primary) input and inhibitory inputs from units with the same orientation. Rough-sensitive units thus respond most strongly when the

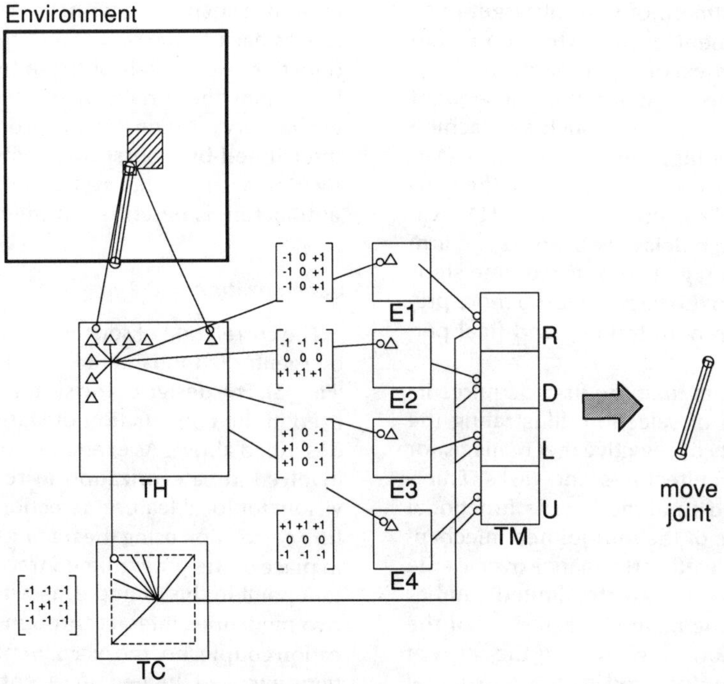

Fig. 14. Schematic of system used in Darwin III for touch-guided tracing of objects. Motor neurons in repertoire TM activate the muscles used for tracing when the arm is in the stiffened position (R, D, L, U indicate subrepertoires activating right, down, left, and up motions, respectively). Spontaneous activity in TM leads to "exploratory jitter" in the arm, which is modulated in two ways by tactile input. The first form of bias is mediated by pressure-sensitive touch receptors acting through repertoire TC, which contains cells with on-center responses (suggested by connection strength matrix to left of TC; +1 = excitatory connection; −1 = inhibitory connection) to enhance responses to regions of localized pressure. TC units act on TM in such a way as to favor motions that increase pressure on the distal digit. Each motor unit in TM receives input from the entire array of units in TC in a fashion analogous to connections in the oculomotor system. These connections have *a priori* gradients in connection strength; they could equally well have been trained using selective mechanisms similar to those used for reaching or for saccades. Inasmuch as pressure is maximal when the finger touches the edge of an object, TC-to-TM connections lead to edge-seeking behavior. The second form of bias is provided by repertoires E1, E2, E3, and E4, which contain units that respond preferentially to edges in orientations up, right, down, and left, respectively, by virtue of mapped inputs from primary touch repertoire TH (connection strengths for typical units shown as matrices to left of E1, · · · , E4). These units bias motion in the directions, right, down, left, and up, respectively, leading to counterclockwise tracing around edges.

direction of tracing changes and are inhibited when it remains the same. Both smooth- and rough-sensitive units integrate over short sequences of motor actions, giving rise to patterns of activity that are highly variable (dependent on direction, exact course, and initial position) and that capture class characteristics (for example, more smooth units will fire, on average, for smooth objects).

Since tracing an object requires a sequence of actions that is not in general completed in a fixed period of time, a triggering network is used to detect and signal the completion of tracing. This network depends on the idea that tracing a given object is profitable as long as new responses occur in the kinesthetic repertoires, but may be terminated when it does not produce any new information, that is, when no new responses have occurred for some time. The trigger network is constructed in a way that permits it to detect novelty in the R_M responses and integrate the appearance of novelty over time to recognize the completion of a trace. The network has two layers. Units in the first layer are stimulated by rough or smooth R_M units, but have long-lasting refractory periods that prevent them from resuming activity until some time after stimulation. These units inhibit a second, excitatory layer that has a high level of spontaneous activity. This second layer remains quiescent as long as new directions of trace are being discovered in the stimulus because of the inhibitory effect of the first layer, but it fires strongly once new inhibitory units cease to be recruited and the ones that have responded are all depressed. Firing in the second layer thus correlates with the completion of the examination of a stimulus but is indifferent to the category of that stimulus.

The trigger response is coupled back to R_2 and R_M, where it acts nonspecifically to reexcite units that were previously stimulated during the examination of the stimulus. Activity in most of these units will have decayed away by the time the trigger response occurs, but a mechanism analogous to LTP (see Eqs. (2) and (3), but shorter lasting, is used to sensitize these cells by lowering their activation threshold so that the relatively weak trigger input is sufficient to reactivate them. (Thresholds in these repertoires are such that the trigger signal alone is insufficient to activate units that were not sensitized by other inputs in the examination period prior to triggering.) Reciprocal reentrant connections between units in R_2 and R_M are also sensitized by LTP.

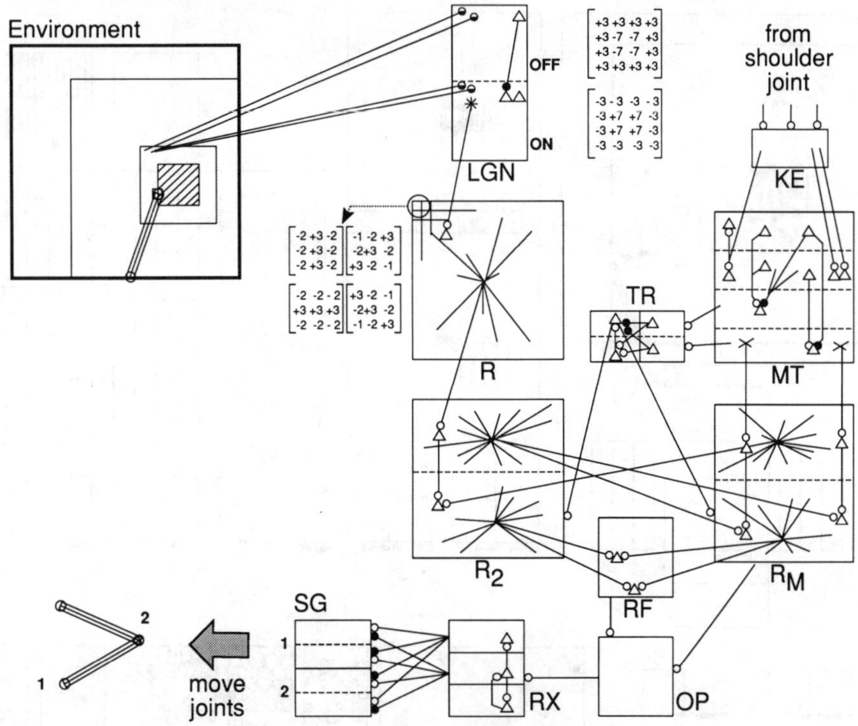

Fig. 15. Schematic of categorization system used in Darwin III. A classification couple is constructed, using for the left channel a series of repertoires responding to visual features and for the right channel a series of repertoires responding to correlations of features, detected in this case by kinesthetic responses to tracing motions of arm. The two-level systems in Figs. 1 and 3 are here augmented by addition of an early sensory area in each channel to form a three-level system. The visual system consists of repertoires LGN (containing on-center and off-center units similar to those found in the lateral geniculate nucleus), R (a low-level recognizing repertoire of feature-detecting units), and R_2 (a higher-level repertoire responding to patterns of activity in R representing arbitrary combinations of visual features). The feature-correlating system consists of KE (a primary kinesthetic area), M_T (an area corresponding to R that detects smooth and bumpy tracing motions), and R_M (a higher-level repertoire responding to patterns of activity in M_T representing arbitrary combinations of trace features). R_2 and R_M are joined by reciprocal reentrant connections that provide coordination between responses in the two distinct sensory channels. A triggering repertoire TR, described in detail in text, stimulates recapitulation of patterns of response in R_2 and R_M that have been sensitized over a trace sequence by an LTP-like mechanism. These patterns in turn stimulate a reflex-activating repertoire RF, in which categorical responses in the classification couple may become associated with motor responses under selectional bias provided by a value scheme (in the simulations described here, these associations were provided *a priori*). RF provides stimulation, via an output repertoire OP to a reflex pattern generator RX, which is responsible for the "swatting reflex" of the arm. Excitation is passed from RX to SG, the same "spinal ganglia" that provide innervation to the "arm muscles" for reaching.

Activation of these connections as a consequence of neural events occurring *independently* in the two repertoires constitutes reentry and is the decisive step in categorization. Only upon *coactivation* of appropriate visual groups in R_2 and correlated kinesthetic groups in R_M after a trace of the object has been completed is a categorical response elicited. To complete the behavioral loop, category-specific output centers are activated following such responses and those centers are linked to motor units. In the version of Darwin III described here, an output center specific to the formation of the category "rough-striped" is linked to motor units that generate a violent reflex oscillation of the arm. If it is in the path of the arm, the stimulus object is swatted away from the vicinity of the automaton by this reflex; otherwise, it is simply replaced by a new object at the beginning of the next trial.

Figure 16 shows selected frames from a movie we have made that displays Darwin III as it senses and explores an object. The environment is shown, along with the changing eye and arm positions of the automaton as it scans an object, categorizes it, and responds to it with a rejection reflex. The display of the environment is surrounded by a set of displays depicting the internal activity of the neuronal networks of Darwin III. An observer could score the behavior of the automaton as it responds to a variety of stimuli at various positions on the input array with no knowledge of its neural states, thus pursuing a kind of "machine behaviorism." At the same time, another observer could relate these events to the state of the automaton's networks and trace the activity of its neuronal units in fine detail.

An example of a classification experiment with Darwin III that followed the paradigm of "machine behaviorism" is shown in Fig. 17. In this experiment, 55 similar-sized objects of various shapes and textures were presented to

(a)

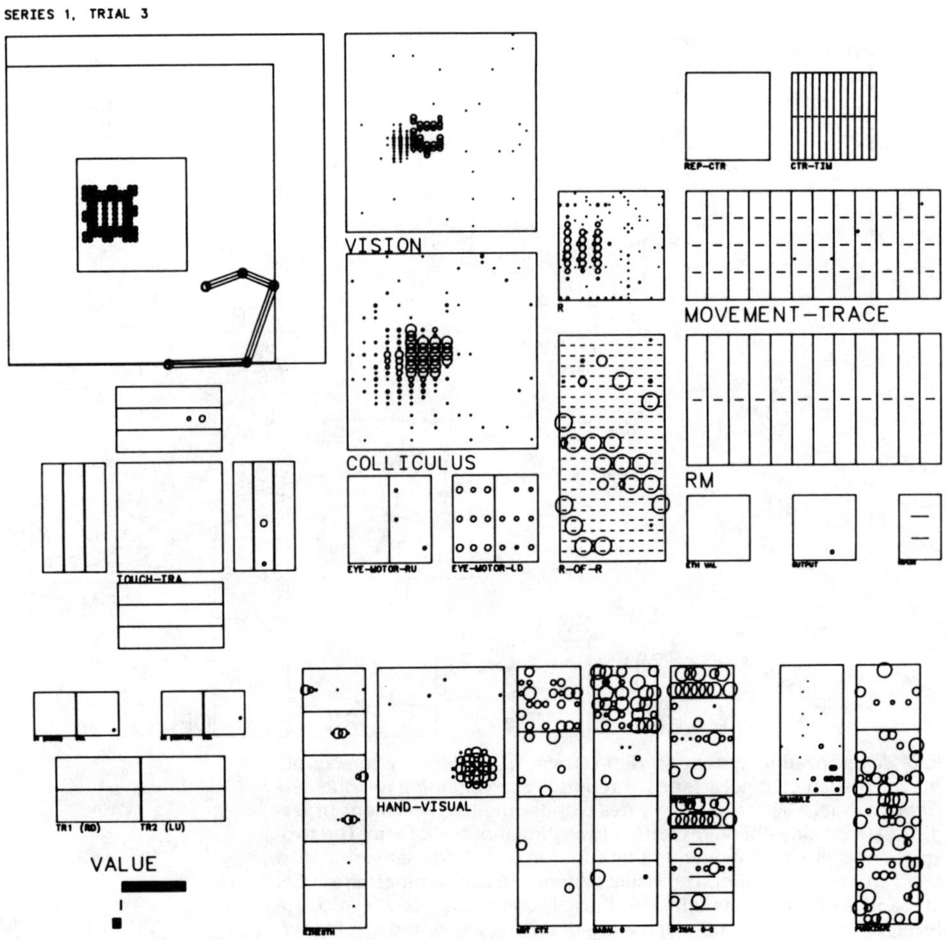

Fig. 16. Computer simulations showing Darwin III and its neuronal states during presentation of a striped bumpy object. Large square at upper left is the "environment," with the object located slightly left of center. The large square within the environment and the smaller square represent the field of peripheral vision and the foveal part of the visual field of the automaton, respectively.

At the beginning of the sequence, Darwin III has already had experience with seeing and reaching various objects; both arm and eye have developed a sufficient degree of sensorimotor coordination. (a) Both eye and arm are starting to move toward the object. Topographic representations of the object in various visual networks (labeled VISION, COLLICULUS, and R in this version) are clearly visible. There is activity in oculomotor neurons (EYE-MOTOR-LD) that move the eye to the left and down and in spinal extensors moving shoulder and wrist joints. Higher visual centers (R-of-R) show nontopographic signals in response to the stimulus. (b) The arm has nearly reached the object. (c) After the arm's distal digit touches the object, a reflex straightens arm. It then "feels" around the object, sending kinesthetic signals to a central neural map. There is very little activity in the motor neurons for eye or arm, since both organs have reached their targets. Activity of touch-sensitive neurons in the tip of the arm (TOUCH-TRA) is now clearly visible and activity of the specialized set of motor neurons moving arm along the edges of the object has begun. (d) A number of cycles has gone by and the automaton has finished visual and tactile inspection of the object. No new tactile features are discovered and the trigger (REP-CTR) repertoire has become active. All those synaptic populations that were facilitated (through "LTP") during the exploratory phase are now triggered and there is an explosion of reentrant activity between repertoires R-of-R and RM. As a result of this reentrant activity, a reflex repertoire is activated which now activates a swatting motion of the arm. (e) Slightly later stage. Reflex output is still active and the arm continues its wavelike motion. (f) This "rejection response" leads to the object's being struck. It is swept off to the left and down. The oculomotor system tracks the object as it moves away. (a)–(f) correspond to cycles 3, 9, 10, 62, 65, 66 of a Darwin III simulation. (From [70], reproduced with permission.)

the automaton eight times each and the behavioral responses were scored. A maximum exploration time of 50 time cycles was allowed; if no rejection response occurred within this time limit, a new object was presented. In Fig. 17 the objects have been grouped together according to the frequency with which a rejection response followed. Clearly, objects with a certain combination of visual and tactile features were rejected more frequently than others. Most objects that were striped and had a rough surface were classified as of "negative" adaptive vaule, or "bad" objects.

(b)

(c)

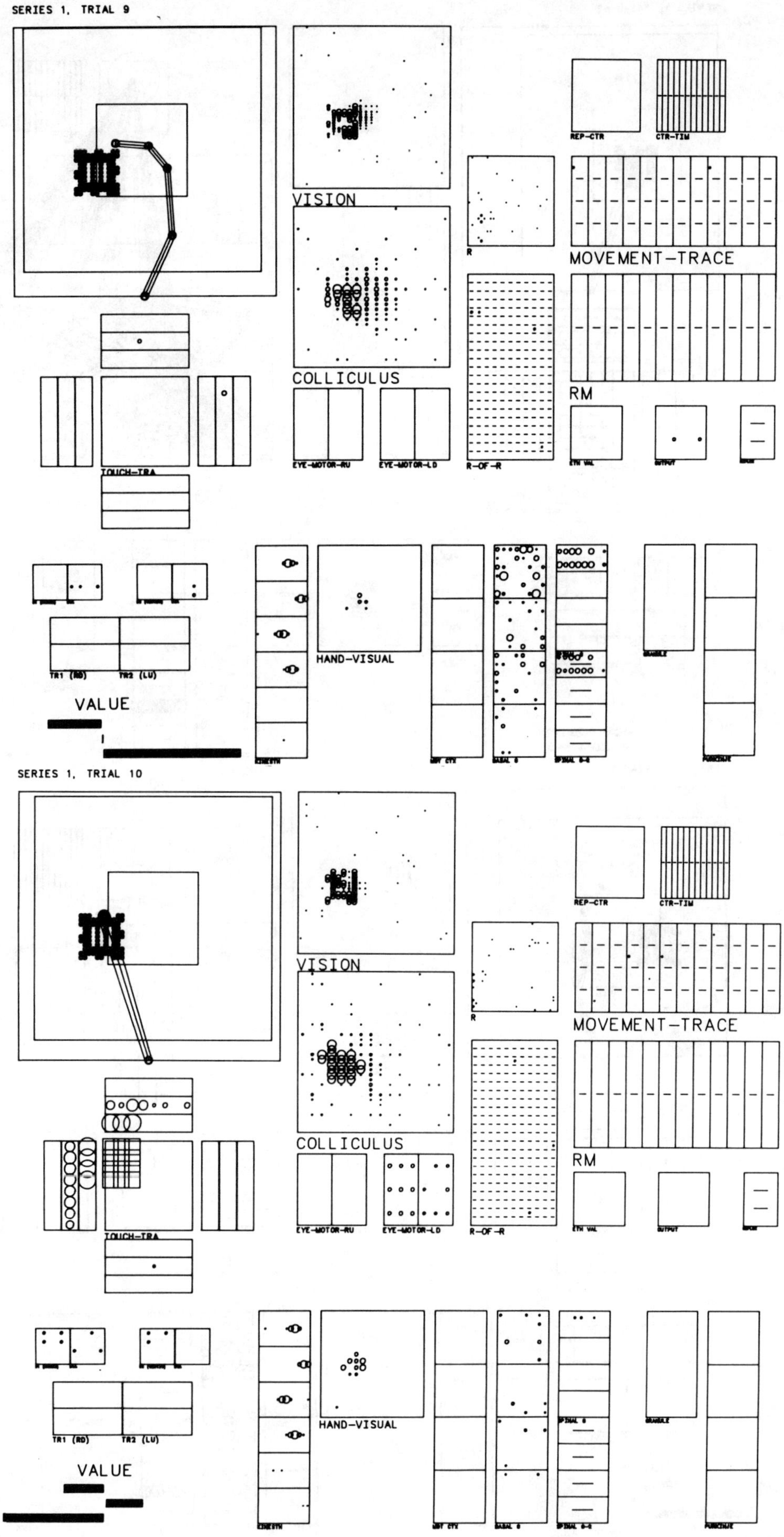

Fig. 16. *(Continued)*

(d)

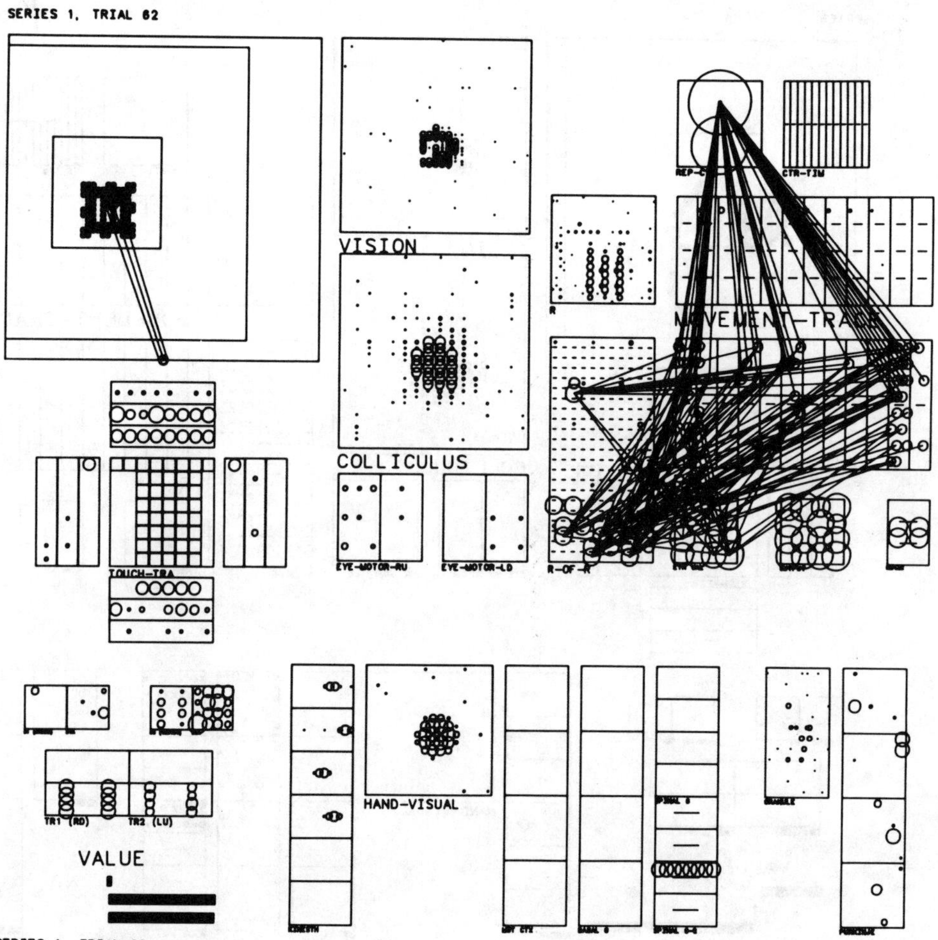

(e)

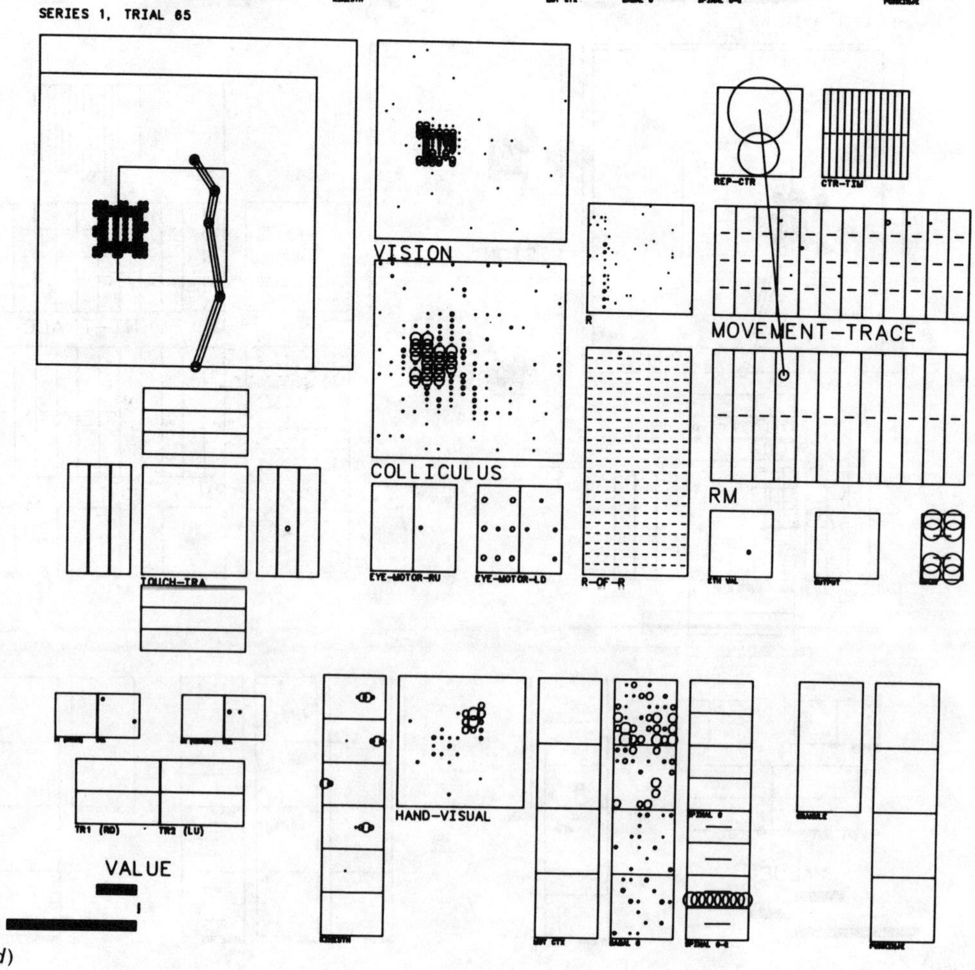

Fig. 16. (*Continued*)

(f)

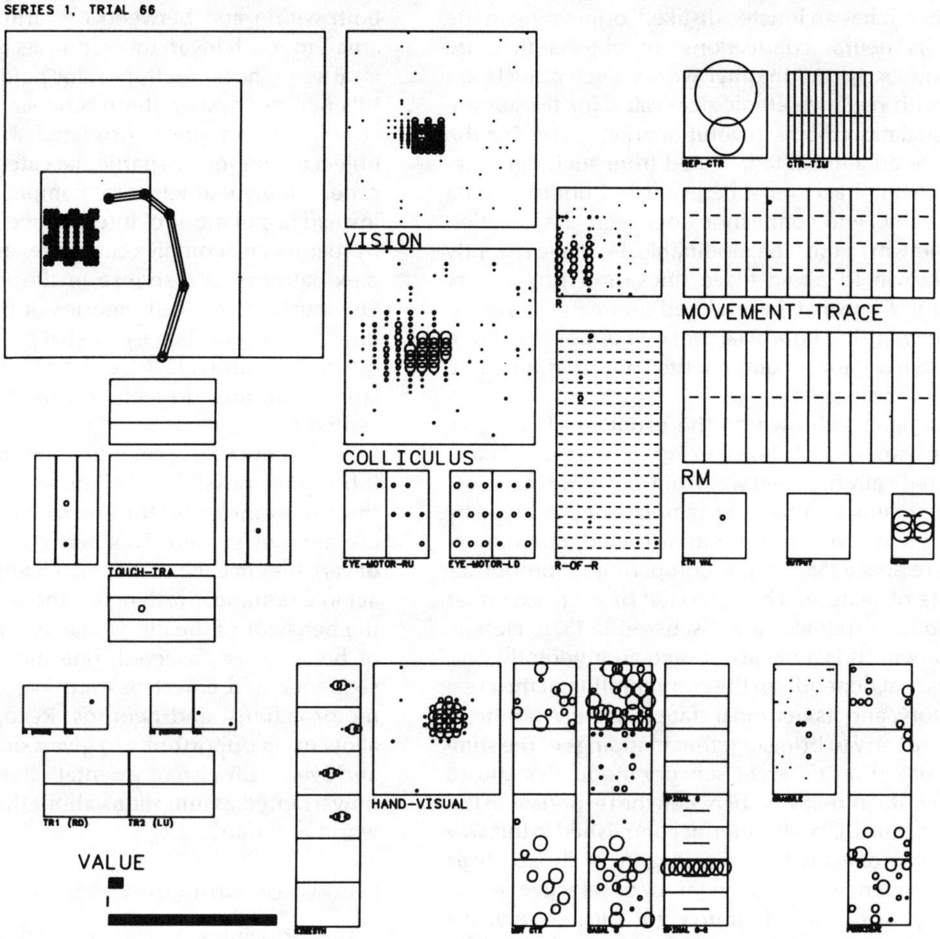

Fig. 16. *(Continued)*

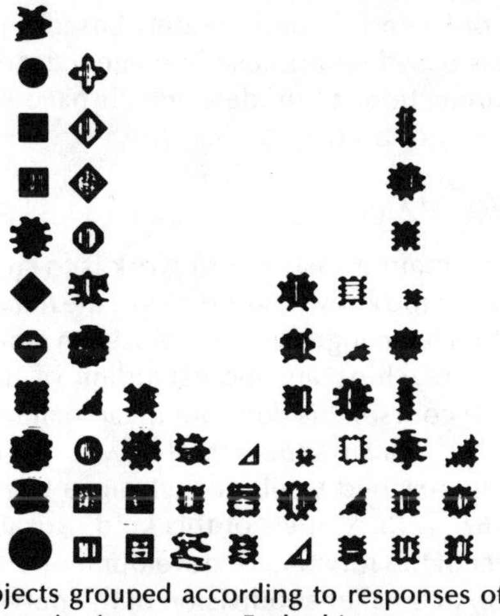

Fig. 17. Objects grouped according to responses of Darwin III's categorization system. Each object was presented eight times and a maximal tracing time of 50 cycles per object was allowed. Tracing started at different positions on the object (usually close to the center) and the activity of the reflex output was constantly recorded. In the case of a rejection response, the automaton's arm hit the object and removed it from the environment. Activation of the rejection response at any time within the 50-cycle time interval was counted as a "rejection" response. If no response occurred within the 50-cycle time limit, the trial was ended and a new object was entered. Objects are arranged in nine columns depending on the frequency with which they met with a response. In this version of Darwin III, an intrinsic negative ethological value is attached to "bumpy and striped" objects.

All others led to no response by the automaton. The rough and striped objects thus form a behaviorally defined probabilistic category. The responses and categories are unique to each individual version of the automaton, and somewhat different categories might well be defined if the starting conditions or precise sequence of stimulus presentations were different.

Autonomous Behavior of Darwin III

The current version of Darwin III embodies one of the largest and most complex simulations of a nervous system ever attempted. The simulations we have discussed force us to reexamine a series of questions ranging from synaptic function to behavioral psychology, some of which have been outlined already. At this point we will take up some problems of behavior and theoretical psychology.

First we return to the issue of value. It seems evident that the behavior of animals depends to a degree on which actions lead to the satisfaction of inner needs or avoid confronting pain or threat. This may be an oversimplification, especially when one looks at higher animals that have the ability to modify or postpone these simple goals as a result of higher-level considerations; nonetheless, it emphasizes the point of view that behavioral acts are not neutral but are coupled to the internal state of the organism. Darwin III in its present form has neither varied internal states nor a rich repertoire of behavioral responses allowing free choice. Rather, it has an innate "dislike," originating in the pattern of its neural connections, of objects that are "bumpy" and "striped." In other words, such objects are associated with negative ethological value for ths automaton, an association that is "evolutionarily" fixed. For the automaton (or an animal) to be freed from such rigid limitations, behavioral acts must be evaluated under criteria of adaptive value, and connections between classification and motor networks must be modifiable. We have recently modified Darwin III along these lines, and preliminary experiments indicate that the modified automaton is indeed capable of *learning* in a nontrivial sense (as opposed to mere *training* of sensorimotor components), and that it can be behaviorally conditioned.

Additional light is thrown on the problem of categorization by the experiment shown in Fig. 17. Darwin III categorizes in a radically different way from any other machine. Instead of matching a pattern to a template or prototype by representing it as a vector in some dissected multidimensional feature space [55], [56] or comparing its properties to static lists of features characteristic of each exemplar (these and other strategies are discussed in [57]), classification in Darwin III is a *behavioral act*, an inherently variable process that depends on the configuration of the creature, its history, and its neuronal state at any given time. It depends on reentry to bring together mappings of the stimulus world based on different sensory modalities and to resolve any conflicts that arise between the responses in the different modalities. Classification accomplished in this way is a stochastic process with a large degree of variability as a direct consequence of the degeneracy of selective neural networks It provides a rich source for further selective events to shape the overall behavioral characteristics of the automaton through experience and permit it to adapt.

In a real-world animal habitat such as a forest or a coral reef, objects cannot be categorized simply by placing fixed decision boundaries somewhere in an abstract feature space. Such boundaries are likely to be neither simple nor fixed. They are in general highly nonlinear, resembling the boundary "between a sponge and water when water penetrates the sponge. It is absolutely impossible to draw a completely smooth surface in such a way that on one side of it lies only water, and on another, only the sponge" [58, p. 13]. Moreover, the structure of the boundary will certainly vary with time, context, and the state of the animal. Such complexity may manifest itself statistically as a probabilistic gradient of a given behavioral response across a space of objects (a stimulus continuum). Such response statistics can be used to define "a class of behaviorally significant objects that share a set of invariant features" [59]. The particular shape of the probabilistic curve for an individual automaton will depend on its individual history. An innate criterion will only result in a general tendency, allowing responses to individual stimuli based on historical events and shaped by context and familiarity. The results obtained with Darwin III demonstrate "typicality" effects and the inadequacy of classical models of categorization based on the analysis of separable features [57], [60], [61].

Even neglecting these complexities of the real world, the simple version of Darwin III with one innate category is able to respond correctly to a great number of stimuli of various sizes and orientations at different positions in space. Its selective apparatus focuses its neuronal connectivities, both within and between its various sensory and motor areas, to reach invariant responses by very different behavioral sequences. An important point is that inside Darwin III's nervous system there is no single unit whose firing is strictly and uniquely correlated with the presence of an object belonging to a particular category. There are no high-order feature extractors for complex predicates or objects; instead populations of interconnected units are correlated by reentry and complex categories are represented by complex patterns of response in these populations of units. Obviously, single-cell theories of perception proposing a direct correspondence of visual perceptions to the activity of single neurons [29] are not proven wrong by our simulations, but they do seem less likely than the solution presented here.

With simulated recognition automata such as Darwin III it becomes possible to examine simultaneously events at three relevant levels: the environment, the phenotype, and the nervous system. This permits the relative importance of variables in each of these domains to be assessed as they act in a nonlinear fashion on the accumulated history and the behavior of the individual. After a particular sequence of behavior is observed, one may trace back the causal sequence and correlate events at the level of the world, motor actions, and neurons. Recognition automata thus allow us an opportunity to give a description of behavioral and eventually also of "mental" states, uncontaminated by unwarranted assumptions about the relationship between world and mind.

Comparison with Other Models

The principles of construction of Darwin III and the results obtained in our simulations may be compared with those of three different classes of models that also address questions of brain function: models based on neurobiology, models based on artificial intelligence, and the more recent "connectionist" models, which have some of the characteristics of both.

Neurobiological Models

One of the main thrusts of our work is to suggest that a close fidelity to the known properties of the nervous system is likely to be a main ingredient of success in modeling studies aimed at reaching an understanding of higher brain function. (Of course, this does not mean that models must be identical in detail to some actual nervous system.) Other authors have reached similar conclusions (see, for examples, [22], [62], [21]). Models of this kind ususally focus on some aspect of the function or development of a particular brain region or smaller subdivision of the nervous system. The value of such models lies primarily in helping us to understand which of the properties of neurons found in the laboratory are likely to be important for higher-level function, and what are the best ways to abstract these properties for inclusion in more comprehensive models. In developing synthetic neural modeling, we have attempted to go beyond these conventional neurobiological models to learn something about the function of the complete nervous system by considering the multiple levels of nervous system, phenotype, and environment in the context of an overall theoretical position, the theory of neuronal group selection.

Artificial Intelligence

The field of artificial intelligence (AI) encompasses a wide range of studies aimed at understanding the nature of human intelligence by trying to reproduce it in computers. These studies can perhaps best be characterized by their common acceptance of the view that intelligent behavior is essentially a manifestation of symbolic information-processing activity in the brain. In a recent analysis [5], we show how the basic assumptions of the AI approach to understanding intelligence are at odds with the properties of real environments faced by real animals. In particular, AI presumes the prior existence of categories, as distinct from observers, and a language for describing them. It deals with symbolic representations that permit *formal*, algorithmic analysis of perceptual and behavioral problems, reducing their solution to a matter of carrying out a prespecified sequence of steps. Because of these assumptions, AI intrinsically cannot address the question of how intelligent systems and their internal representations of the world come to exist. It does not describe how the steps of its algorithms can be assembled and then transmitted across generations, nor does it describe the nature of the entity that is required to interpret the results of its symbolic computations. This undescribed entity in fact amounts to a homunculus, a "little man" who bears the major part of the explanatory burden in an AI system, leading to an unacceptable infinite regress of explanation. We believe that the only way this "homunculus paradox" can be exorcised from computational models of behavior is to eliminate the symbolic interface with the experimenter and deal only with sensory signals and motor acts that are themselves embedded in the animal's world, standing in no need of interpretation as symbols do. A forthright confrontation of these questions of origins and interpretations severely constrains the range of acceptable theories capable of explaining intelligent behavior.

"Connectionist" Models

"Connectionist" or "parallel distributed processing" models [34], [35] stand in the tradition of perceptrons and other adaptive pattern recognition machines [55], [63] as well as the tradition of cognitive science. In accord with their origins, these models begin with assumptions about the nature of intelligent systems that are very similar to those made by AI, viewing the mind as governed by rules and representations. However, in a deviation from established AI methods they make use of distributed processors arranged in networks to carry out the necessary computations. Parallel algorithms that can be run on such systems have been derived for a number of interesting problems in information retrieval and optimization [64]. Some connectionist models share with synthetic neural modeling the idea that a properly constructed system can acquire useful responses through experience, but such systems still involve the concepts of formal representations and preestablished categories. The mechanism of learning is always instructional rather than selective in the sense that the "correct" *responses* (not *values*) are specified in advance and are imposed upon the system by a "teacher" from without under appropriate conditions and with appropriate error feedback to accomplish training. The network architectures used by many of these models are quite different from biological reality; symmetric and very dense matrix-like connectivities are usually required to implement the obligatory learning algorithms. We do not share the recently expressed view [65] that a valuable relationship exists between "realistic" and "abstract" neural models. Many of the features used in a variety of such "abstract" models to data seem to us simplistic and unbiological [66].

Implications for Further Work

Selective neural models can increase in complexity to incorporate additional systems in much the same way as additional parts are added to the nervous system in the course of evolution with retention of existing parts and their functions. This extensibility provides a strong indication that this style of modeling is robust and that it can help to provide us with an increasingly detailed picture of possible mechanisms of brain function.

Besides using synthetic neural models to study the brain, one can generate a whole new class of automata without explicit representations and programs, yet with powerful recognition and categorization capabilities, and one can potentially couple these devices to standard digital computers to give those computers the ability to interface more naturally with the "real world."

Further progress needs to be made on the adaptive control of behavior through internal value-related states. Initial simulations using modifiable connections between repertoires involved in perceptual categorization and others involved in the generation of motor output have been carried out successfully. Such plasticity will provide us with a mechanism to incorporate higher-order learning and memory.

The philosophical question of whether real brains are or are not Turing machines carrying out "computations" on "information" is much more than just a matter of vocabulary. The information-processing view demands mechanisms for the genetic specification of codes, for the definition of categories, and for the generation and replication of sequences of instructions for computation that are essentially incompatible with what we currently know about the nature of development in biological systems. Unlike the information-processing analogy, neuronal group selection with reentry takes into account those aspects of individual history that enter into each and every neuronal response. It is such a selectional history that endows us with the unpredictability and individuality that make us human.

Synthetic neural modeling is obviously still at an early embryonic stage. Nonetheless, it has allowed us to approach certain important psychological questions in terms of the basic biological components of which nervous systems are constructed. It allows us a glimpse at how we might eventually come to understand the means by which behavior and even consciousness itself [67] appear as consequences of the workings of selective mechanisms in the brain.

References

[1] W. S. McCulloch and W. Pitts, "A logical calculus of the ideas immanent in nervous activity," *Bull. Math. Biophys.*, vol. 5, pp. 115–133, 1943.

[2] N. Wiener, *Cybernetics*. Cambridge, Mass.: M.I.T. Press, 1948.

[3] A. M. Turing, "Computing machinery and intelligence," *Mind*, vol. 59, pp. 433–460, 1950.

[4] J. Von Neumann, *The Computer and the Brain*. New Haven, CT: Yale University, 1958.

[5] G. N. Reeke, Jr. and G. M. Edelman, "Real brains and artificial intelligence," *Daedalus, Proc. Am. Acad. Arts and Sciences*, vol. 117, pp. 143–173, 1988.

[6] G. M. Edelman, "Group selection and phasic reentrant signaling: A theory of higher brain function," in *The Mindful Brain: Cortical Organization and the Group-Selective Theory of Higher Brain Function*, G. M. Edelman and V. B. Mountcastle, Eds. Cambridge, Mass.: M.I.T. Press, pp. 51–100, 1978.

[7] G. M. Edelman, "Group selection as the basis for higher brain function," in *The Organization of the Cerebral Cortex*, F. O. Schmitt, F. G. Worden, G. Adelman and S. G. Dennis, Eds. Cambridge, Mass.: M.I.T. Press, pp. 535–563, 1981.

[8] G. M. Edelman, *Neural Darwinism: The Theory of Neuronal Group Selection*. New York: Basic Books, 1987.

[9] G. M. Edelman and J. -P. Thiery, *The Cell in Contact: Adhesions and Junctions as Morphogenetic Determinants*. New York: Wiley, 1985.

[10] G. M. Edelman, "Cell adhesion molecules in the regulation of animal form and tissue pattern," *Ann. Rev. Cell Biol.*, vol. 2, pp. 81–116, 1986.

[11] —, *Topobiology: An Introduction to Molecular Embryology*. New York: Basic Books, 1988.

[12] C. M. Gray and W. Singer, "Stimulus-specific neuronal oscillations in orientation columns of cat visual cortex," *Proc. Natl. Acad. Sci. USA*, vol. 86, pp. 1698–1702, 1989.

[13] R. Eckhorn, *et al.*, "Coherent oscillations: A mechanism of feature linking in the visual cortex? Multiple electrode and correlation analyses in the cat," *Biol. Cybern.*, vol. 60, pp. 121–130, 1988.

[14] C. M. Gray, P. König, A. K. Engel, and W. Singer, "Oscillatory reponses in cat visual cortex exhibit intercolumnar synchronization which reflects global stimulus properties," *Nature*, vol. 338, pp. 334–337, 1989.

[15] O. Sporns, J. A. Gally, G. N. Reeke, Jr., and G. M. Edelman, "Reentrant signaling among simulated neuronal groups leads to coherency in their oscillatory activity," *Proc. Natl. Acad. Sci. USA*, vol. 86, pp. 7265–7269, 1989.

[16] D. O. Hebb, *The Organization of Behavior: A Neuropsychological Theory*. New York: Wiley, 1949.

[17] L. H. Finkel and G. M. Edelman, "Interaction of synaptic modification rules within populations of neurons," *Proc. Natl. Acad. Sci. USA*, vol. 82, pp. 1291–1295, 1985.

[18] L. H. Finkel and G. M. Edelman, "Population rules for synapses in networks," in *Synaptic Function*, G. M. Edelman, W. E. Gall and W. M. Cowan, Eds. New York: Wiley, pp. 711–757, 1987.

[19] W. R. Ashby, *An Introduction to Cybernetics*. New York: Wiley, 1956.

[20] R. J. MacGregor, *Neural and Brain Modeling*. San Diego: Academic, 1987.

[21] R. Granger, J. Ambros-Ingerson, and G. Lynch," Derivation of encoding characteristics of layer II cerebral cortex," *J. Cogn. Neurosci.*, vol. 1, pp. 61–87, 1989.

[22] R. D. Traub, "Simulation of intrinsic bursting in CA3 hippocampal neurons," *Neuroscience*, vol. 7, pp. 1233–1242, 1982.

[23] J. C. Pearson, L. H. Finkel, and G. M. Edelman, "Plasticity in the organization of adult cortical maps: A computer model, based on neuronal group selection," *J. Neurosci.*, vol. 7, pp. 4209–4223, 1987.

[24] L. H. Finkel and G. M. Edelman, "The integration of distributed cortical systems by reentry: A computer simulation of interactive functionally segregated visual areas," *J. Neurosci.*, vol. 9, pp. 3188–3208, 1989.

[25] G. M. Edelman and G. N. Reeke, Jr., "Selective networks capable of representative transformations, limited generalizations, and associative memory," *Proc. Natl. Acad. Sci. USA*, vol. 79, pp. 2091–2095, 1982.

[26] G. N. Reeke and G. M. Edelman, "Selective networks and recognition automata," *Ann. N. Y. Acad. Sci.*, vol. 426, pp. 181–201, 1984.

[27] D. H. Hubel and T. N. Wiesel, "Receptive fields, binocular interaction and functional architecture in the cat's visual cortex," *J. Physiol (Lond.)*, vol. 160, pp. 106–154, 1962.

[28] —, "Receptive fields and functional architecture in two nonstriate visual areas (18 and 19) of the cat," *J. Neurophysiol.*, vol. 28, pp. 229–289, 1965.

[29] H. B. Barlow, "Single units and sensation: A neuron doctrine for perceptual psychology?," *Perception*, vol. 1, pp. 371–394, 1972.

[30] G. N. Reeke and G. M. Edelman, "Selective neural networks and their implications for recognition automata," *Int. J. Supercomputer. Appl.*, vol. 1, pp. 44–69, 1987.

[31] J. A. Kauer, R. C. Malenka, and R. A. Nicoll, "NMDA application potentiates synaptic transmission in the hippocampus," *Nature*, vol. 334, pp. 250–252, 1988.

[32] J. J. Hopfield, "Neural networks and physical systems with emergent collective computational abilities," *Proc. Natl. Acad. Sci. USA*, vol. 79, pp. 2554–2558, 1982.

[33] D. H. Ackley, G. E. Hinton, and T. J. Sejnowski, "A learning algorithm for Boltzmann machines," *Cognitive Sci.*, vol. 9, pp. 147–169, 1985.

[34] D. E. Rumelhart and J. L. McClelland, *Parallel Distributed Processing: Explorations in the Microstructure of Cognition*. Vol. 1: Foundations. Cambridge, Mass.: M.I.T. Press, 1986.

[35] J. L. McClelland and D. E. Rumelhart, *Parallel Distributed Processing: Explorations in the Microstructure of Cognition*. Vol. 2: Psychological and Biological Models. Cambridge, Mass.: M.I.T. Press, 1986.

[36] D. L. Sparks, "Translation of sensory signals into commands for control of saccadic eye movements: Role of primate superior colliculus," *Physiol. Rev.*, vol. 66, pp. 118–171, 1986.

[37] D. R. Humphrey, "Representation of movements and muscles within the primate precentral motor cortex: Historical and current perspectives," *Fed. Proc.*, vol. 45, pp. 2687–2699, 1986.

[38] R. Lemon, "The output map of the primate motor cortex," *Trends Neurosci.*, vol. 11, pp. 501–506, 1988.

[39] E. Saltzman, "Levels of sensorimotor representation," *J. Math. Biol.*, vol. 20, pp. 91–163, 1979.

[40] J. M. Hollerbach, "Computers, brains and the control of movement," *Trends Neurosci.*, vol. 5, pp. 189–192, 1982.

[41] N. A. Bernstein, *The Coordination and Regulation of Movements*. Oxford: Pergamon, 1967.

[42] I. M. Gelfand, V. S. Gurfinkel, M. L. Tsetlin, and M. L. Shik, "Some problems in the analysis of movements," in *Models of the Structural-Functional Organization of Certain Biological Systems*, I. M. Gelfand, V. S. Gurfinkel, S. V. Fomin, and M. L. Tsetlin, Eds. Cambridge, Mass.: M.I.T. Press, pp. 329–345, 1971.

[43] M. R. DeLong, G. E. Alexander, A. P. Georgopoulos, and M. D. Crutcher, "Role of basal ganglia in limb movements," *Hum. Neurobiol.*, vol. 2, pp. 235–244, 1984.

[44] A. P. Georgopoulos, A. B. K. Schwartz, and R. E. Kettner, "Neuronal population coding of movement direction," *Science*, vol. 233, pp. 1416–1419, 1986.

[45] A. P. Georgopoulos, "Neural integration of movement: Role of motor cortex in reaching," *FASEB J.*, vol. 2, pp. 2849–2857, 1988.

[46] H. T. A. Whiting, Ed., *Human Motor Actions. Bernstein Reassessed*. Amsterdam: North-Holland, 1984.

[47] D. Marr, "A theory of cerebellar cortex," *J. Physiol.* (Lond.), vol. 202, pp. 437–470, 1969.

[48] J. S. Albus, "A theory of cerebellar function," *Math. Biosci.*, vol. 10, pp. 25–61, 1971.

[49] A. P. Georgopoulos, J. F. Kalaska, and J. T. Massey, "Spatial trajectories and reaction time of aimed movements: Effects of practice, uncertainty, and change in target location," *J. Neurophysiol.*, vol. 46, pp. 725–743, 1981.

[50] P. Morasso, "Spatial control of arm movements," *Exp. Brain Res.*, vol. 42, pp. 223–227, 1981.

[51] R. A. Andersen, G. K. Essick, and R. M. Siegel, "Encoding of spatial location by posterior parietal neurons," *Science*, vol. 230, pp. 456–458, 1985.

[52] —, "Neurons of area 7 activated by both visual stimuli and oculomotor behavior," *Exp. Brain Res.*, vol. 67, pp. 316–322, 1987.

[53] D. Zipser and R. A. Andersen, "A back-propagation programmed network that simulates response properties of a subset of posterior parietal neurons," *Nature*, vol. 331, pp. 679–694, 1988.

[54] A. Hein, F. Vital-Durand, W. Salinger, and R. Diamond, "Eye movements initiate visual-motor development in the cat," *Science*, vol. 204, pp. 1321–1322, 1979.

[55] F. Rosenblatt, *Principles of Neurodynamics: Perceptrons and the Theory of Brain Mechanisms.* Washington, D. C.: Spartan, 1962.

[56] A. G. Knapp and J. A. Anderson, "Theory of categorization based on distributed memory storage," *J. Exp. Psychol. (Learn. Mem. Cogn.)*, vol. 10, pp. 616–637, 1984.

[57] E. E. Smith and D. L. Medin, *Categories and Concepts.* Cambridge, Mass.: Harvard University, 1981.

[58] M. Bongard, *Pattern Recognition*. Washington: Spartan, 1970.

[59] J.-P. Ewert, "Neuroethology of releasing mechanisms: Prey-catching in toads," *Behav. Brain Sci.*, vol. 10, pp. 337–368, 1987.

[60] C. B. Mervis and E. Rosch, "Categorization of natural objects," *Ann. Rev. Psychol.*, vol. 32, pp. 89–115, 1981.

[61] D. L. Medin and E. E. Smith, "Concepts and concept formation," *Ann. Rev. Psychol.*, vol. 35, pp. 113–138, 1984.

[62] J. Amros-Ingerson, R. Granger, and G. Lynch, "Simulation of paleocortex performs hierarchical clustering," *Science*, vol. 247, pp. 1344–1348, 1990.

[63] M. L. Minsky and S. A. Papert, *Perceptrons.* Cambridge, Mass.: M.I.T. Press, 1988.

[64] J. J. Hopfield and D. W. Tank, "Computing with neural circuits: A model," *Science*, vol. 223, pp. 625–633, 1986.

[65] T. J. Sejnowski, C. Koch, and P. S. Churchland, "Computational neuroscience," *Science*, vol. 241, pp. 1299–1306, 1988.

[66] G. N. Reeke, Jr., O. Sporns, and G. M. Edelman, "Synthetic neural modeling: Comparisons of population and connectionist approaches," in *Connectionism in Perspective*. R. Pfeifer, Z. Schreter, F. Fogelman-Soulié and L. Steels, Eds. Amsterdam: Elsevier, pp. 113–139. 1989.

[67] G. M. Edelman, *The Remembered Present: A Biological Theory of Consciousness. New York: Basic Books, 1989.*

[68] G. N. Reeke, Jr. and G. M . Edelman, "Selective networks and recognition automata," *Ann. N. Y. Acad. Sci.*, vol. 426, pp. 181–201, 1984.

[69] G. N. Reeke, Jr., L. H. Finkel, O. Sporns, and G. M. Edelman, "Synthetic neural modeling: A new approach to the analysis of brain complexity," in *Signal and Sense: Local and Global Order in Perceptual Maps*, G. M. Edelman, W. E. Gall and W. M. Cowan, Eds. New York: Wiley, 1990.

[70] G. M. Edelman and G. N. Reeke, Jr., "Neural Darwinism," in *Parallel Computers, Neural Networks, and Intelligent Systems*, J. A. Robinson and M. Arbib, Eds. Cambridge, Mass.: M.I.T. Press (in press).

Neural networks and physical systems with emergent collective computational abilities

(associative memory/parallel processing/categorization/content-addressable memory/fail-soft devices)

J. J. HOPFIELD

Division of Chemistry and Biology, California Institute of Technology, Pasadena, California 91125; and Bell Laboratories, Murray Hill, New Jersey 07974

Contributed by John J. Hopfield, January 15, 1982

ABSTRACT Computational properties of use to biological organisms or to the construction of computers can emerge as collective properties of systems having a large number of simple equivalent components (or neurons). The physical meaning of content-addressable memory is described by an appropriate phase space flow of the state of a system. A model of such a system is given, based on aspects of neurobiology but readily adapted to integrated circuits. The collective properties of this model produce a content-addressable memory which correctly yields an entire memory from any subpart of sufficient size. The algorithm for the time evolution of the state of the system is based on asynchronous parallel processing. Additional emergent collective properties include some capacity for generalization, familiarity recognition, categorization, error correction, and time sequence retention. The collective properties are only weakly sensitive to details of the modeling or the failure of individual devices.

Given the dynamical electrochemical properties of neurons and their interconnections (synapses), we readily understand schemes that use a few neurons to obtain elementary useful biological behavior (1–3). Our understanding of such simple circuits in electronics allows us to plan larger and more complex circuits which are essential to large computers. Because evolution has no such plan, it becomes relevant to ask whether the ability of large collections of neurons to perform "computational" tasks may in part be a spontaneous collective consequence of having a large number of interacting simple neurons.

In physical systems made from a large number of simple elements, interactions among large numbers of elementary components yield collective phenomena such as the stable magnetic orientations and domains in a magnetic system or the vortex patterns in fluid flow. Do analogous collective phenomena in a system of simple interacting neurons have useful "computational" correlates? For example, are the stability of memories, the construction of categories of generalization, or time-sequential memory also emergent properties and collective in origin? This paper examines a new modeling of this old and fundamental question (4–8) and shows that important computational properties spontaneously arise.

All modeling is based on details, and the details of neuroanatomy and neural function are both myriad and incompletely known (9). In many physical systems, the nature of the emergent collective properties is insensitive to the details inserted in the model (e.g., collisions are essential to generate sound waves, but any reasonable interatomic force law will yield appropriate collisions). In the same spirit, I will seek collective properties that are robust against change in the model details.

The model could be readily implemented by integrated circuit hardware. The conclusions suggest the design of a delocalized content-addressable memory or categorizer using extensive asynchronous parallel processing.

The publication costs of this article were defrayed in part by page charge payment. This article must therefore be hereby marked "*advertisement*" in accordance with 18 U. S. C. §1734 solely to indicate this fact.

The general content-addressable memory of a physical system

Suppose that an item stored in memory is "H. A. Kramers & G. H. Wannier *Phys. Rev.* **60,** 252 (1941)." A general content-addressable memory would be capable of retrieving this entire memory item on the basis of sufficient partial information. The input "& Wannier, (1941)" might suffice. An ideal memory could deal with errors and retrieve this reference even from the input "Vannier, (1941)". In computers, only relatively simple forms of content-addressable memory have been made in hardware (10, 11). Sophisticated ideas like error correction in accessing information are usually introduced as software (10).

There are classes of physical systems whose spontaneous behavior can be used as a form of general (and error-correcting) content-addressable memory. Consider the time evolution of a physical system that can be described by a set of general coordinates. A point in state space then represents the instantaneous condition of the system. This state space may be either continuous or discrete (as in the case of N Ising spins).

The equations of motion of the system describe a flow in state space. Various classes of flow patterns are possible, but the systems of use for memory particularly include those that flow toward locally stable points from anywhere within regions around those points. A particle with frictional damping moving in a potential well with two minima exemplifies such a dynamics.

If the flow is not completely deterministic, the description is more complicated. In the two-well problems above, if the frictional force is characterized by a temperature, it must also produce a random driving force. The limit points become small limiting regions, and the stability becomes not absolute. But as long as the stochastic effects are small, the essence of local stable points remains.

Consider a physical system described by many coordinates $X_1 \cdots X_N$, the components of a state vector X. Let the system have locally stable limit points $X_a, X_b, \cdots$. Then, if the system is started sufficiently near any X_a, as at $X = X_a + \Delta$, it will proceed in time until $X \approx X_a$. We can regard the information stored in the system as the vectors $X_a, X_b, \cdots$. The starting point $X = X_a + \Delta$ represents a partial knowledge of the item X_a, and the system then generates the total information X_a.

Any physical system whose dynamics in phase space is dominated by a substantial number of locally stable states to which it is attracted can therefore be regarded as a general content-addressable memory. The physical system will be a potentially useful memory if, in addition, any prescribed set of states can readily be made the stable states of the system.

The model system

The processing devices will be called neurons. Each neuron i has two states like those of McCullough and Pitts (12): $V_i = 0$

("not firing") and $V_i = 1$ ("firing at maximum rate"). When neuron i has a connection made to it from neuron j, the strength of connection is defined as T_{ij}. (Nonconnected neurons have $T_{ij} \equiv 0$.) The instantaneous state of the system is specified by listing the N values of V_i, so it is represented by a binary word of N bits.

The state changes in time according to the following algorithm. For each neuron i there is a fixed threshold U_i. Each neuron i readjusts its state randomly in time but with a mean attempt rate W, setting

$$\begin{matrix} V_i \to 1 \\ V_i \to 0 \end{matrix} \quad \text{if} \quad \sum_{j \neq i} T_{ij} V_j \quad \begin{matrix} > U_i \\ < U_i \end{matrix} \qquad [1]$$

Thus, each neuron randomly and asynchronously evaluates whether it is above or below threshold and readjusts accordingly. (Unless otherwise stated, we choose $U_i = 0$.)

Although this model has superficial similarities to the Perceptron (13, 14) the essential differences are responsible for the new results. First, Perceptrons were modeled chiefly with neural connections in a "forward" direction $A \to B \to C \to D$. The analysis of networks with strong backward coupling $A \rightleftarrows B \rightleftarrows C$ proved intractable. All our interesting results arise as consequences of the strong back-coupling. Second, Perceptron studies usually made a random net of neurons deal directly with a real physical world and did not ask the questions essential to finding the more abstract emergent computational properties. Finally, Perceptron modeling required synchronous neurons like a conventional digital computer. There is no evidence for such global synchrony and, given the delays of nerve signal propagation, there would be no way to use global synchrony effectively. Chiefly computational properties which can exist in spite of asynchrony have interesting implications in biology.

The information storage algorithm

Suppose we wish to store the set of states V^s, $s = 1 \cdots n$. We use the storage prescription (15, 16)

$$T_{ij} = \sum_s (2V_i^s - 1)(2V_j^s - 1) \qquad [2]$$

but with $T_{ii} = 0$. From this definition

$$\sum_j T_{ij} V_j^{s'} = \sum_s (2V_i^s - 1) \left[\sum_j V_j^{s'} (2V_j^s - 1) \right] \equiv H_j^{s'} . \qquad [3]$$

The mean value of the bracketed term in Eq. 3 is 0 unless $s = s'$, for which the mean is $N/2$. This pseudoorthogonality yields

$$\sum_j T_{ij} V_j^{s'} \equiv \langle H_i^{s'} \rangle \approx (2V_i^{s'} - 1)\, N/2 \qquad [4]$$

and is positive if $V_i^{s'} = 1$ and negative if $V_i^{s'} = 0$. Except for the noise coming from the $s \neq s'$ terms, the stored state would always be stable under our processing algorithm.

Such matrices T_{ij} have been used in theories of linear associative nets (15–19) to produce an output pattern from a paired input stimulus, $S_1 \to O_1$. A second association $S_2 \to O_2$ can be simultaneously stored in the same network. But the confusing simulus $0.6\, S_1 + 0.4\, S_2$ will produce a generally meaningless mixed output $0.6\, O_1 + 0.4\, O_2$. Our model, in contrast, will use its strong nonlinearity to make choices, produce categories, and regenerate information and, with high probability, will generate the output O_1 from such a confusing mixed stimulus.

A linear associative net must be connected in a complex way with an external nonlinear logic processor in order to yield true computation (20, 21). Complex circuitry is easy to plan but more difficult to discuss in evolutionary terms. In contrast, our model obtains its emergent computational properties from simple properties of many cells rather than circuitry.

The biological interpretation of the model

Most neurons are capable of generating a train of action potentials—propagating pulses of electrochemical activity—when the average potential across their membrane is held well above its normal resting value. The mean rate at which action potentials are generated is a smooth function of the mean membrane potential, having the general form shown in Fig. 1.

The biological information sent to other neurons often lies in a short-time average of the firing rate (22). When this is so, one can neglect the details of individual action potentials and regard Fig. 1 as a smooth input–output relationship. [Parallel pathways carrying the same information would enhance the ability of the system to extract a short-term average firing rate (23, 24).]

A study of emergent collective effects and spontaneous computation must necessarily focus on the nonlinearity of the input–output relationship. The essence of computation is nonlinear logical operations. The particle interactions that produce true collective effects in particle dynamics come from a nonlinear dependence of forces on positions of the particles. Whereas linear associative networks have emphasized the linear central region (14–19) of Fig. 1, we will replace the input–output relationship by the dot-dash step. Those neurons whose operation is dominantly linear merely provide a pathway of communication between nonlinear neurons. Thus, we consider a network of "on or off" neurons, granting that some of the interconnections may be by way of neurons operating in the linear regime.

Delays in synaptic transmission (of partially stochastic character) and in the transmission of impulses along axons and dendrites produce a delay between the input of a neuron and the generation of an effective output. All such delays have been modeled by a single parameter, the stochastic mean processing time $1/W$.

The input to a particular neuron arises from the current leaks of the synapses to that neuron, which influence the cell mean potential. The synapses are activated by arriving action potentials. The input signal to a cell i can be taken to be

$$\sum_j T_{ij} V_j \qquad [5]$$

where T_{ij} represents the effectiveness of a synapse. Fig. 1 thus

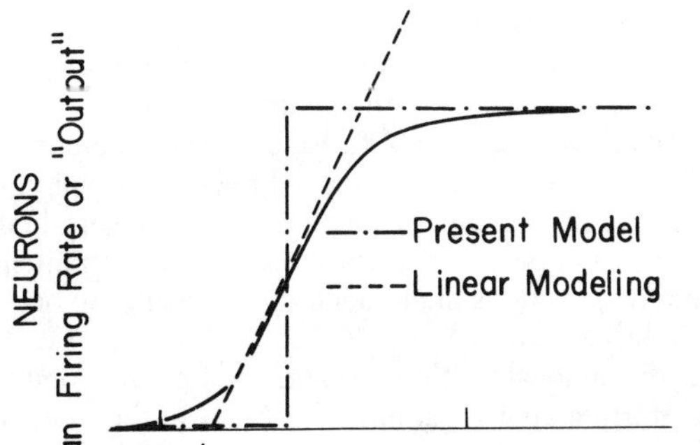

FIG. 1. Firing rate versus membrane voltage for a typical neuron (solid line), dropping to 0 for large negative potentials and saturating for positive potentials. The broken lines show approximations used in modeling.

becomes an input–output relationship for a neuron.

Little, Shaw, and Roney (8, 25, 26) have developed ideas on the collective functioning of neural nets based on "on/off" neurons and synchronous processing. However, in their model the relative timing of action potential spikes was central and resulted in reverberating action potential trains. Our model and theirs have limited formal similarity, although there may be connections at a deeper level.

Most modeling of neural learning networks has been based on synapses of a general type described by Hebb (27) and Eccles (28). The essential ingredient is the modification of T_{ij} by correlations like

$$\Delta T_{ij} = [V_i(t)V_j(t)]_{\text{average}} \qquad [6]$$

where the average is some appropriate calculation over past history. Decay in time and effects of $[V_i(t)]_{\text{avg}}$ or $[V_j(t)]_{\text{avg}}$ are also allowed. Model networks with such synapses (16, 20, 21) can construct the associative T_{ij} of Eq. 2. We will therefore initially assume that such a T_{ij} has been produced by previous experience (or inheritance). The Hebbian property need not reside in single synapses; small groups of cells which produce such a net effect would suffice.

The network of cells we describe performs an abstract calculation and, for applications, the inputs should be appropriately coded. In visual processing, for example, feature extraction should previously have been done. The present modeling might then be related to how an entity or *Gestalt* is remembered or categorized on the basis of inputs representing a collection of its features.

Studies of the collective behaviors of the model

The model has stable limit points. Consider the special case $T_{ij} = T_{ji}$, and define

$$E = -\frac{1}{2}\sum_{i \neq j}\sum T_{ij}V_iV_j \; . \qquad [7]$$

ΔE due to ΔV_i is given by

$$\Delta E = -\Delta V_i \sum_{j \neq i'} T_{ij}V_j \; . \qquad [8]$$

Thus, the algorithm for altering V_i causes E to be a monotonically decreasing function. State changes will continue until a least (local) E is reached. This case is isomorphic with an Ising model. T_{ij} provides the role of the exchange coupling, and there is also an external local field at each site. When T_{ij} is symmetric but has a random character (the spin glass) there are known to be many (locally) stable states (29).

Monte Carlo calculations were made on systems of $N = 30$ and $N = 100$, to examine the effect of removing the $T_{ij} = T_{ji}$ restriction. Each element of T_{ij} was chosen as a random number between -1 and 1. The neural architecture of typical cortical regions (30, 31) and also of simple ganglia of invertebrates (32) suggests the importance of 100–10,000 cells with intense mutual interconnections in elementary processing, so our scale of N is slightly small.

The dynamics algorithm was initiated from randomly chosen initial starting configurations. For $N = 30$ the system never displayed an ergodic wandering through state space. Within a time of about $4/W$ it settled into limiting behaviors, the commonest being a stable state. When 50 trials were examined for a particular such random matrix, all would result in one of two or three end states. A few stable states thus collect the flow from most of the initial state space. A simple cycle also occurred occasionally—for example, $\cdots A \rightarrow B \rightarrow A \rightarrow B \cdots$.

The third behavior seen was chaotic wandering in a small region of state space. The Hamming distance between two binary states A and B is defined as the number of places in which the digits are different. The chaotic wandering occurred within a short Hamming distance of one particular state. Statistics were done on the probability p_i of the occurrence of a state in a time of wandering around this minimum, and an entropic measure of the available states M was taken

$$\ln M = -\sum p_i \ln p_i \; . \qquad [9]$$

A value of $M = 25$ was found for $N = 30$. *The flow in phase space produced by this model algorithm has the properties necessary for a physical content-addressable memory* whether or not T_{ij} is symmetric.

Simulations with $N = 100$ were much slower and not quantitatively pursued. They showed qualitative similarity to $N = 30$.

Why should stable limit points or regions persist when $T_{ij} \neq T_{ji}$? If the algorithm at some time changes V_i from 0 to 1 or vice versa, the change of the energy defined in Eq. 7 can be split into two terms, one of which is always negative. The second is identical if T_{ij} is symmetric and is "stochastic" with mean 0 if T_{ij} and T_{ji} are randomly chosen. The algorithm for $T_{ij} \neq T_{ji}$ therefore changes E in a fashion similar to the way E would change in time for a symmetric T_{ij} but with an algorithm corresponding to a finite temperature.

About 0.15 N states can be simultaneously remembered before error in recall is severe. Computer modeling of memory storage according to Eq. 2 was carried out for $N = 30$ and $N = 100$. n random memory states were chosen and the corresponding T_{ij} was generated. If a nervous system preprocessed signals for efficient storage, the preprocessed information would appear random (e.g., the coding sequences of DNA have a random character). The random memory vectors thus simulate efficiently encoded real information, as well as representing our ignorance. The system was started at each assigned nominal memory state, and the state was allowed to evolve until stationary.

Typical results are shown in Fig. 2. The statistics are averages over both the states in a given matrix and different matrices. With $n = 5$, the assigned memory states are almost always stable (and exactly recallable). For $n = 15$, about half of the nominally remembered states evolved to stable states with less than 5 errors, but the rest evolved to states quite different from the starting points.

These results can be understood from an analysis of the effect of the noise terms. In Eq. 3, $H_i^{s'}$ is the "effective field" on neuron i when the state of the system is s', one of the nominal memory states. The expectation value of this sum, Eq. 4, is $\pm N/2$ as appropriate. The $s \neq s'$ summation in Eq. 2 contributes no mean, but has a rms noise of $[(n-1)N/2]^{1/2} \equiv \sigma$. For nN large, this noise is approximately Gaussian and the probability of an error in a single particular bit of a particular memory will be

$$P = \frac{1}{\sqrt{2\pi\sigma^2}} \int_{N/2}^{\infty} e^{-x^2/2\sigma^2}\, dx \; . \qquad [10]$$

For the case $n = 10$, $N = 100$, $P = 0.0091$, the probability that a state had no errors in its 100 bits should be about $e^{-0.91} \approx 0.40$. In the simulation of Fig. 2, the experimental number was 0.6.

The theoretical scaling of n with N at fixed P was demonstrated in the simulations going between $N = 30$ and $N = 100$. The experimental results of half the memories being well retained at $n = 0.15\,N$ and the rest badly retained is expected to

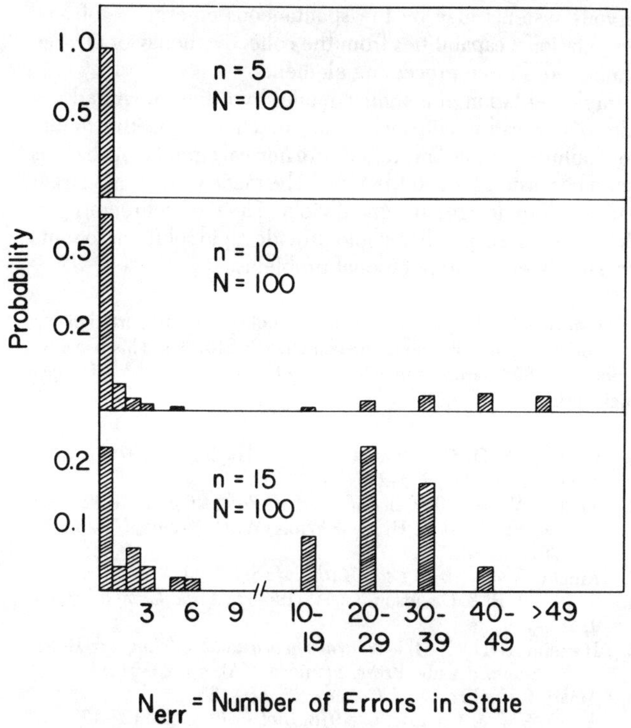

FIG. 2. The probability distribution of the occurrence of errors in the location of the stable states obtained from nominally assigned memories.

be true for all large N. The information storage at a given level of accuracy can be increased by a factor of 2 by a judicious choice of individual neuron thresholds. This choice is equivalent to using variables $\mu_i = \pm 1$, $T_{ij} = \Sigma_s \mu_i^s \mu_j^s$, and a threshold level of 0.

Given some arbitrary starting state, what is the resulting final state (or statistically, states)? To study this, evolutions from randomly chosen initial states were tabulated for $N = 30$ and $n = 5$. From the (inessential) symmetry of the algorithm, if $(101110\cdots)$ is an assigned stable state, $(010001\cdots)$ is also stable. Therefore, the matrices had 10 nominal stable states. Approximately 85% of the trials ended in assigned memories, and 10% ended in stable states of no obvious meaning. An ambiguous 5% landed in stable states very near assigned memories. There was a range of a factor of 20 of the likelihood of finding these 10 states.

The algorithm leads to memories near the starting state. For $N = 30$, $n = 5$, partially random starting states were generated by random modification of known memories. The probability that the final state was that closest to the initial state was studied as a function of the distance between the initial state and the nearest memory state. For distance ≤ 5, the nearest state was reached more than 90% of the time. Beyond that distance, the probability fell off smoothly, dropping to a level of 0.2 (2 times random chance) for a distance of 12.

The phase space flow is apparently dominated by attractors which are the nominally assigned memories, each of which dominates a substantial region around it. The flow is not entirely deterministic, and *the system responds to an ambiguous starting state by a statistical choice* between the memory states it most resembles.

Were it desired to use such a system in an Si-based content-addressable memory, the algorithm should be used and modified to hold the known bits of information while letting the others adjust.

The model was studied by using a "clipped" T_{ij}, replacing T_{ij} in Eq. 3 by ± 1, the algebraic sign of T_{ij}. The purposes were to examine the necessity of a linear synapse supposition (by making a highly nonlinear one) and to examine the efficiency of storage. Only $N(N/2)$ bits of information can possibly be stored in this symmetric matrix. Experimentally, for $N = 100$, $n = 9$, the level of errors was similar to that for the ordinary algorithm at $n = 12$. The signal-to-noise ratio can be evaluated analytically for this clipped algorithm and is reduced by a factor of $(2/\pi)^{1/2}$ compared with the unclipped case. For a fixed error probability, the number of memories must be reduced by $2/\pi$.

With the μ algorithm and the clipped T_{ij}, both analysis and modeling showed that the maximal information stored for $N = 100$ occurred at about $n = 13$. Some errors were present, and the Shannon information stored corresponded to about $N(N/8)$ bits.

New memories can be continually added to T_{ij}. The addition of new memories beyond the capacity overloads the system and makes all memory states irretrievable unless there is a provision for forgetting old memories (16, 27, 28).

The saturation of the possible size of T_{ij} will itself cause forgetting. Let the possible values of T_{ij} be 0, ± 1, ± 2, ± 3, and T_{ij} be freely incremented within this range. If $T_{ij} = 3$, a next increment of $+1$ would be ignored and a next increment of -1 would reduce T_{ij} to 2. When T_{ij} is so constructed, only the recent memory states are retained, with a slightly increased noise level. Memories from the distant past are no longer stable. How far into the past are states remembered depends on the digitizing depth of T_{ij}, and $0, \cdots, \pm 3$ is an appropriate level for $N = 100$. Other schemes can be used to keep too many memories from being simultaneously written, but this particular one is attractive because it requires no delicate balances and is a consequence of natural hardware.

Real neurons need not make synapses both of $i \rightarrow j$ and $j \rightarrow i$. Particular synapses are restricted to one sign of output. We therefore asked whether $T_{ij} = T_{ji}$ is important. Simulations were carried out with only one ij connection: if $T_{ij} \neq 0$, $T_{ji} = 0$. The probability of making errors increased, but the algorithm continued to generate stable minima. A Gaussian noise description of the error rate shows that the signal-to-noise ratio for given n and N should be decreased by the factor $1/\sqrt{2}$, and the simulations were consistent with such a factor. This same analysis shows that the system generally fails in a "soft" fashion, with signal-to-noise ratio and error rate increasing slowly as more synapses fail.

Memories too close to each other are confused and tend to merge. For $N = 100$, a pair of random memories should be separated by 50 ± 5 Hamming units. The case $N = 100$, $n = 8$, was studied with seven random memories and the eighth made up a Hamming distance of only 30, 20, or 10 from one of the other seven memories. At a distance of 30, both similar memories were usually stable. At a distance of 20, the minima were usually distinct but displaced. At a distance of 10, the minima were often fused.

The algorithm categorizes initial states according to the similarity to memory states. With a threshold of 0, the system behaves as a forced categorizer.

The state $00000\cdots$ is always stable. For a threshold of 0, this stable state is much higher in energy than the stored memory states and very seldom occurs. Adding a uniform threshold in the algorithm is equivalent to raising the effective energy of the stored memories compared to the 0000 state, and 0000 also becomes a likely stable state. The 0000 state is then generated by any initial state that does not resemble adequately closely one of the assigned memories and represents positive recognition that the starting state is not familiar.

Familiarity can be recognized by other means when the memory is drastically overloaded. We examined the case $N = 100$, $n = 500$, in which there is a memory overload of a factor of 25. None of the memory states assigned were stable. The initial rate of processing of a starting state is defined as the number of neuron state readjustments that occur in a time $1/2W$. Familiar and unfamiliar states were distinguishable most of the time at this level of overload on the basis of the initial processing rate, which was faster for unfamiliar states. This kind of familiarity can only be read out of the system by a class of neurons or devices abstracting average properties of the processing group.

For the cases so far considered, the expectation value of T_{ij} was 0 for $i \neq j$. A set of memories can be stored with average correlations, and $\overline{T}_{ij} = C_{ij} \neq 0$ because there is a consistent internal correlation in the memories. If now a partial new state X is stored

$$\Delta T_{ij} = (2X_i - 1)(2X_j - 1) \quad i,j \leq k < N \qquad [11]$$

using only k of the neurons rather than N, an attempt to reconstruct it will generate a stable point for all N neurons. The values of $X_{k+1} \cdots X_N$ that result will be determined primarily from the sign of

$$\sum_{j=1}^{k} c_{ij}\, x_j \qquad [12]$$

and X is completed according to the mean correlations of the other memories. The most effective implementation of this capacity stores a large number of correlated matrices weakly followed by a normal storage of X.

A nonsymmetric T_{ij} can lead to the possibility that a minimum will be only metastable and will be replaced in time by another minimum. Additional nonsymmetric terms which could be easily generated by a minor modification of Hebb synapses

$$\Delta T_{ij} = A \sum_s (2V_i^{s+1} - 1)(2V_j^s - 1) \qquad [13]$$

were added to T_{ij}. When A was judiciously adjusted, the system would spend a while near V_s and then leave and go to a point near V_{s+1}. But sequences longer than four states proved impossible to generate, and even these were not faithfully followed.

Discussion

In the model network each "neuron" has elementary properties, and the network has little structure. Nonetheless, collective computational properties spontaneously arose. Memories are retained as stable entities or *Gestalts* and can be correctly recalled from any reasonably sized subpart. Ambiguities are resolved on a statistical basis. Some capacity for generalization is present, and time ordering of memories can also be encoded. These properties follow from the nature of the flow in phase space produced by the processing algorithm, which does not appear to be strongly dependent on precise details of the modeling. This robustness suggests that similar effects will obtain even when more neurobiological details are added.

Much of the architecture of regions of the brains of higher animals must be made from a proliferation of simple local circuits with well-defined functions. The bridge between simple circuits and the complex computational properties of higher nervous systems may be the spontaneous emergence of new computational capabilities from the collective behavior of large numbers of simple processing elements.

Implementation of a similar model by using integrated circuits would lead to chips which are much less sensitive to element failure and soft-failure than are normal circuits. Such chips would be wasteful of gates but could be made many times larger than standard designs at a given yield. Their asynchronous parallel processing capability would provide rapid solutions to some special classes of computational problems.

The work at California Institute of Technology was supported in part by National Science Foundation Grant DMR-8107494. This is contribution no. 6580 from the Division of Chemistry and Chemical Engineering.

1. Willows, A. O. D., Dorsett, D. A. & Hoyle, G. (1973) *J. Neurobiol.* **4**, 207–237, 255–285.
2. Kristan, W. B. (1980) in *Information Processing in the Nervous System*, eds. Pinsker, H. M. & Willis, W. D. (Raven, New York), 241–261.
3. Knight, B. W. (1975) *Lect. Math. Life Sci.* **5**, 111–144.
4. Smith, D. R. & Davidson, C. H. (1962) *J. Assoc. Comput. Mach.* **9**, 268–279.
5. Harmon, L. D. (1964) in *Neural Theory and Modeling*, ed. Reiss, R. F. (Stanford Univ. Press, Stanford, CA), pp. 23–24.
6. Amari, S.-I. (1977) *Biol. Cybern.* **26**, 175–185.
7. Amari, S.-I. & Akikazu, T. (1978) *Biol. Cybern.* **29**, 127–136.
8. Little, W. A. (1974) *Math. Biosci.* **19**, 101–120.
9. Marr, J. (1969) *J. Physiol.* **202**, 437–470.
10. Kohonen, T. (1980) *Content Addressable Memories* (Springer, New York).
11. Palm, G. (1980) *Biol. Cybern.* **36**, 19–31.
12. McCulloch, W. S. & Pitts, W. (1943) *Bull. Math Biophys.* **5**, 115–133.
13. Minsky, M. & Papert, S. (1969) *Perceptrons: An Introduction to Computational Geometry* (MIT Press, Cambridge, MA).
14. Rosenblatt, F. (1962) *Principles of Perceptrons* (Spartan, Washington, DC).
15. Cooper, L. N. (1973) in *Proceedings of the Nobel Symposium on Collective Properties of Physical Systems*, eds. Lundqvist, B. & Lundqvist, S. (Academic, New York), 252–264.
16. Cooper, L. N., Liberman, F. & Oja, E. (1979) *Biol. Cybern.* **33**, 9–28.
17. Longuet-Higgins, J. C. (1968) *Proc. Roy. Soc. London Ser. B* **171**, 327–334.
18. Longuet-Higgins, J. C. (1968) *Nature (London)* **217**, 104–105.
19. Kohonen, T. (1977) *Associative Memory—A System-Theoretic Approach* (Springer, New York).
20. Willwacher, G. (1976) *Biol. Cybern.* **24**, 181–198.
21. Anderson, J. A. (1977) *Psych. Rev.* **84**, 413–451.
22. Perkel, D. H. & Bullock, T. H. (1969) *Neurosci. Res. Symp. Summ.* **3**, 405–527.
23. John, E. R. (1972) *Science* **177**, 850–864.
24. Roney, K. J., Scheibel, A. B. & Shaw, G. L. (1979) *Brain Res. Rev.* **1**, 225–271.
25. Little, W. A. & Shaw, G. L. (1978) *Math. Biosci.* **39**, 281–289.
26. Shaw, G. L. & Roney, K. J. (1979) *Phys. Rev. Lett.* **74**, 146–150.
27. Hebb, D. O. (1949) *The Organization of Behavior* (Wiley, New York).
28. Eccles, J. G. (1953) *The Neurophysiological Basis of Mind* (Clarendon, Oxford).
29. Kirkpatrick, S. & Sherrington, D. (1978) *Phys. Rev.* **17**, 4384–4403.
30. Mountcastle, V. B. (1978) in *The Mindful Brain*, eds. Edelman, G. M. & Mountcastle, V. B. (MIT Press, Cambridge, MA), pp. 36–41.
31. Goldman, P. S. & Nauta, W. J. H. (1977) *Brain Res.* **122**, 393–413.
32. Kandel, E. R. (1979) *Sci. Am.* **241**, 61–70.

A Massively Parallel Architecture for a Self-Organizing Neural Pattern Recognition Machine

GAIL A. CARPENTER*

Department of Mathematics, Northeastern University, Boston, Massachusetts 02215 and Center for Adaptive Systems, Department of Mathematics, Boston University, Boston, Massachusetts 02215

AND

STEPHEN GROSSBERG†

Center for Adaptive Systems, Department of Mathematics, Boston University, Boston, Massachusetts 02215

Received March 3, 1986

A neural network architecture for the learning of recognition categories is derived. Real-time network dynamics are completely characterized through mathematical analysis and computer simulations. The architecture self-organizes and self-stabilizes its recognition codes in response to arbitrary orderings of arbitrarily many and arbitrarily complex binary input patterns. Top-down attentional and matching mechanisms are critical in self-stabilizing the code learning process. The architecture embodies a parallel search scheme which updates itself adaptively as the learning process unfolds. After learning self-stabilizes, the search process is automatically disengaged. Thereafter input patterns directly access their recognition codes without any search. Thus recognition time does not grow as a function of code complexity. A novel input pattern can directly access a category if it shares invariant properties with the set of familiar exemplars of that category. These invariant properties emerge in the form of learned critical feature patterns, or prototypes. The architecture possesses a context-sensitive self-scaling property which enables its emergent critical feature patterns to form. They detect and remember statistically predictive configurations of featural elements which are derived from the set of all input patterns that are ever experienced. Four types of attentional process—priming, gain control, vigilance, and intermodal competition—are mechanistically characterized. Top—down priming and gain control are needed for code matching and self-stabilization. Attentional vigilance determines how fine the learned categories will be. If vigilance increases due to an environmental disconfirmation, then the system automatically searches for and learns finer recognition categories. A new nonlinear matching law (the $\frac{2}{3}$ Rule) and new nonlinear associative laws (the Weber Law Rule, the Associative Decay Rule, and the Template Learning Rule) are needed to achieve these properties. All the rules describe emergent properties of parallel network interactions. The architecture circumvents the noise, saturation, capacity, orthogonality, and linear predictability constraints that limit the codes which can be stably learned by alternative recognition models. © 1987 Academic Press, Inc.

1. INTRODUCTION: SELF-ORGANIZATION OF NEURAL RECOGNITION CODES

A fundamental problem of perception and cognition concerns the characterization of how humans discover, learn, and recognize invariant properties of the environments to which they are exposed. When such recognition codes sponta-

*Supported in part by the Air Force Office of Scientific Research Grants AFOSR 85-0149 and AFOSR 86-F49620-86-C-0037, the Army Research Office Grant ARO DAAG-29-85-K-0095, and the National Science Foundation Grant NSF DMS-84-13119.

†Supported in part by the Air Force Office of Scientific Research Grants AFOSR 85-0149 and AFOSR 86-F49620-86-C-0037 and the Army Research Office Grant ARO DAAG-29-85-K0095.

Reprinted with permission from *Computer, Vision, Graphics, and Image Processing* 37, pp. 54–115. Copyright © 1987 by Academic Press, Inc.

neously emerge through an individual's interaction with an environment, the processes are said to undergo *self-organization* [1]. This article develops a theory of how recognition codes are self-organized by a class of neural networks whose qualitative features have been used to analyse data about speech perception, word recognition and recall, visual perception, olfactory coding, evoked potentials, thalamocortical interactions, attentional modulation of critical period termination, and amnesias [2–13]. These networks comprise the *adaptive resonance theory* (ART) which was introduced in Grossberg [8].

This article describes a system of differential equations which completely characterizes one class of ART networks. The network model is capable of self-organizing, self-stabilizing, and self-scaling its recognition codes in response to arbitrary temporal sequences of arbitrarily many input patterns of variable complexity. These formal properties, which are mathematically proven herein, provide a secure foundation for designing a real-time hardware implementation of this class of massively parallel ART circuits.

Before proceeding to a description of this class of ART systems, we summarize some of their major properties and some scientific problems for which they provide a solution.

A. *Plasticity*

Each system generates recognition codes adaptively in response to a series of environmental inputs. As learning proceeds, interactions between the inputs and the system generate new steady states and basins of attraction. These steady states are formed as the system discovers and learns *critical feature patterns*, or prototypes, that represent invariants of the set of all experienced input patterns.

B. *Stability*

The learned codes are dynamically buffered against relentless recoding by irrelevant inputs. The formation of steady states is internally controlled using mechanisms that suppress possible sources of system instability.

C. *Stability–Plasticity Dilemma: Multiple Interacting Memory Systems*

The properties of plasticity and stability are intimately related. An adequate system must be able to adaptively switch between its stable and plastic modes. It must be capable of plasticity in order to learn about significant new events, yet it must also remain stable in response to irrelevant or often repeated events. In order to prevent the relentless degradation of its learned codes by the "blooming, buzzing confusion" of irrelevant experience, an ART system is sensitive to *novelty*. It is capable of distinguishing between familiar and unfamiliar events, as well as between expected and unexpected events.

Multiple interacting memory systems are needed to monitor and adaptively react to the novelty of events. Within ART, interactions between two functionally complementary subsystems are needed to process familiar and unfamiliar events. Familiar events are processed within an attentional subsystem. This subsystem establishes ever more precise internal representations of and responses to familiar events. It also builds up the learned top–down expectations that help to stabilize the learned bottom–up codes of familiar events. By itself, however, the attentional subsystem is unable simultaneously to maintain stable representations of familiar categories and to create new categories for unfamiliar patterns. An isolated attentional subsystem is either rigid and incapable of creating new categories for

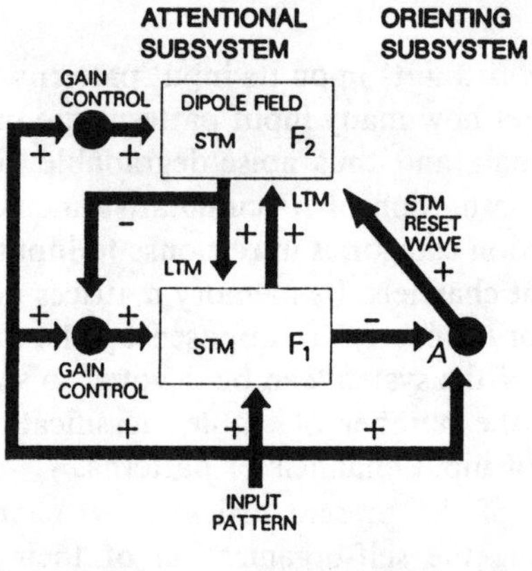

FIG. 1. Anatomy of the attentional-orienting system: Two successive stages, F_1 and F_2, of the attentional subsystem encode patterns of activation in short term memory (STM). Bottom-up and top-down pathways between F_1 and F_2 contain adaptive long term memory (LTM) traces which multiply the signals in these pathways. The remainder of the circuit modulates these STM and LTM processes. Modulation by gain control enables F_1 to distinguish between bottom-up input patterns and top-down priming, or template, patterns, as well as to match these bottom-up and top-down patterns. Gain control signals also enable F_2 to react supraliminally to signals from F_1 while an input pattern is on. The orienting subsystem generates a reset wave to F_2 when mismatches between bottom-up and top-down patterns occur at F_1. This reset wave selectively and enduringly inhibits active F_2 cells until the input is shut off. Variations of this architecture are depicted in Fig. 14.

unfamiliar patterns, or unstable and capable of ceaselessly recoding the categories of familiar patterns in response to certain input environments.

The second subsystem is an orienting subsystem that resets the attentional subsystem when an unfamiliar event occurs. The orienting subsystem is essential for expressing whether a novel pattern is familiar and well represented by an existing recognition code, or unfamiliar and in need of a new recognition code. Figure 1 schematizes the architecture that is analysed herein.

D. *Role of Attention in Learning*

Within an ART system, attentional mechanisms play a major role in self-stabilizing the learning of an emergent recognition code. Our mechanistic analysis of the role of attention in learning leads us to distinguish between four types of attentional mechanism: attentional priming, attentional gain control, attentional vigilance, and intermodality competition. These mechanisms are characterized below.

E. *Complexity*

An ART system dynamically reorganizes its recognition codes to preserve its stability-plasticity balance as its internal representations become increasingly complex and differentiated through learning. By contrast, many classical adaptive pattern recognition systems become unstable when they are confronted by complex input environments. The instabilities of a number of these models are identified in Grossberg [7, 11, 14]. Models which become unstable in response to nontrivial input environments are not viable either as brain models or as designs for adaptive machines.

Unlike many alternative models [15–19], the present model can deal with arbitrary combinations of binary input patterns. In particular, it places no orthogonality or linear predictability constraints upon its input patterns. The model computations remain sensitive no matter how many input patterns are processed. The model does not require that very small, and thus noise-degradable, increments in memory be made in order to avoid saturation of its cumulative memory. The model can store arbitrarily many recognition categories in response to input patterns that are defined on arbitrarily many input channels. Its memory matrices need not be square, so that no restrictions on memory capacity are imposed by the number of input channels. Finally, all the memory of the system can be devoted to stable recognition learning. It is not the case that the number of stable classifications is bounded by some fraction of the number of input channels or patterns.

Thus a primary goal of the present article is to characterize neural networks capable of self-stabilizing the self-organization of their recognition codes in response to an arbitrarily complex environment of input patterns in a way that parsimoniously reconciles the requirements of plasticity, stability, and complexity.

2. SELF-SCALING COMPUTATIONAL UNITS, SELF-ADJUSTING MEMORY SEARCH, DIRECT ACCESS, AND ATTENTIONAL VIGILANCE

Four properties are basic to the workings of the networks that we characterize herein.

A. *Self-Scaling Computational Units: Critical Feature Patterns*

Properly defining signal and noise in a self-organizing system raises a number of subtle issues. Pattern context must enter the definition so that input features which are treated as irrelevant noise when they are embedded in a given input pattern may be treated as informative signals when they are embedded in a different input pattern. The system's unique learning history must also enter the definition so that portions of an input pattern which are treated as noise when they perturb a system at one stage of its self-organization may be treated as signals when they perturb the same system at a different stage of its self-organization. The present systems automatically self-scale their computational units to embody context- and learning-dependent definitions of signal and noise.

One property of these self-scaling computational units is schematized in Fig. 2. In Fig. 2a, each of the two input patterns is composed of three features. The patterns agree at two of the three features, but disagree at the third feature. A mismatch of one out of three features may be designated as informative by the system. When this occurs, these mismatched features are treated as signals which can elicit learning of distinct recognition codes for the two patterns. Moreover, the mismatched features, being informative, are incorporated into these distinct recognition codes.

In Fig. 2b, each of the two input patterns is composed of 31 features. The patterns are constructed by adding identical subpatterns to the two patterns in Fig. 2a. Thus the input patterns in Fig. 2b disagree at the same features as the input patterns in Fig. 2a. In the patterns of Fig. 2b, however, this mismatch is less important, other things being equal, than in the patterns of Fig. 2a. Consequently, the system may treat the mismatched features as noise. A single recognition code may be learned to represent both of the input patterns in Fig. 2b. The mismatched features would not be learned as part of this recognition code because they are treated as noise.

The assertion that *critical feature patterns* are the computational units of the code learning process summarizes this self-scaling property. The term *critical feature*

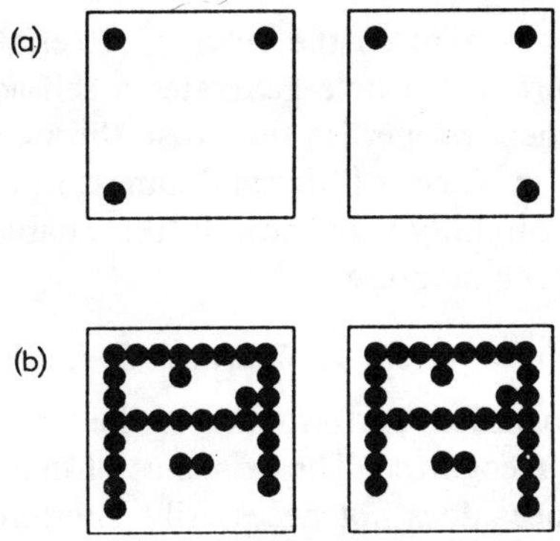

FIG. 2. Self-scaling property discovers critical features in a context-sensitive way: (a) Two input patterns of 3 features mismatch at 1 feature. When this mismatch is sufficient to generate distinct recognition codes for the two patterns, the mismatched features are encoded in LTM as part of the critical feature patterns of these recognition codes. (b) Identical subpatterns are added to the two input patterns in (a). Although the new input patterns mismatch at the same one feature, this mismatch may be treated as noise due to the additional complexity of the two new patterns. Both patterns may thus learn to activate the same recognition code. When this occurs, the mismatched feature is deleted from LTM in the critical feature pattern of the code.

indicates that not all features are treated as signals by the system. The learned units are *patterns* of critical features because the perceptual context in which the features are embedded influences which features will be processed as signals and which features will be processed as noise. Thus a feature may be a critical feature in one pattern (Fig. 2a) and an irrelevant noise element in a different pattern (Fig. 2b).

The need to overcome the limitations of featural processing with some of type of contextually sensitive pattern processing has long been a central concern in the human pattern recognition literature. Experimental studies have led to the general conclusions that "the trace system which underlies the recognition of patterns can be characterized by a central tendency and a boundary" [20, p. 54], and that "just listing features does not go far enough in specifying the knowledge represented in a concept. People also know something about the relations between the features of a concept, and about the variability that is permissible on any feature" [21, p. 83]. We illustrate herein how these properties may be achieved using self-scaling computational units such as critical feature patterns.

B. *Self-Adjusting Memory Search*

No pre-wired search algorithm, such as a search tree, can maintain its efficiency as a knowledge structure evolves due to learning in a unique input environment. A search order that may be optimal in one knowledge domain may become extremely inefficient as that knowledge domain becomes more complex due to learning.

The ART system considered herein is capable of a parallel memory search that adaptively updates its search order to maintain efficiency as its recognition code becomes arbitrarily complex due to learning. This self-adjusting search mechanism is part of the network design whereby the learning process self-stabilizes by engaging the orienting subsystem (Sect. 1C).

None of these mechanisms is akin to the rules of a serial computer program. Instead, the circuit architecture as a whole generates a self-adjusting search order and self-stabilization as emergent properties that arise through system interactions. Once the ART architecture is in place, a little randomness in the initial values of its memory traces, rather than a carefully wired search tree, enables the search to carry on until the recognition code self-stabilizes.

C. *Direct Access to Learned Codes*

A hallmark of human recognition performance is the remarkable rapidity with which familiar objects can be recognized. The existence of many learned recognition codes for alternative experiences does not necessarily interfere with rapid recognition of an unambiguous familiar event. This type of rapid recognition is very difficult to understand using models wherein trees or other serial algorithms need to be searched for longer and longer periods as a learned recognition code becomes larger and larger.

In an ART model, as the learned code becomes globally self-consistent and predictively accurate, the search mechanism is automatically disengaged. Subsequently, no matter how large and complex the learned code may become, familiar input patterns *directly access*, or activate, their learned code, or category. Unfamiliar patterns can also directly access a learned category if they share invariant properties with the critical feature pattern of the category. In this sense, the critical feature pattern acts as a prototype for the entire category. As in human pattern recognition experiments, an input pattern that matches a learned critical feature pattern may be better recognized than any of the input patterns that gave rise to the critical feature pattern [20, 22, 23].

Unfamiliar input patterns which cannot stably access a learned category engage the self-adjusting search process in order to discover a network substrate for a new recognition category. After this new code is learned, the search process is automatically disengaged and direct access ensues.

D. *Environment as a Teacher: Modulation of Attentional Vigilance*

Although an ART system self-organizes its recognition code, the environment can also modulate the learning process and thereby carry out a teaching role. This teaching role allows a system with a fixed set of feature detectors to function successfully in an environment which imposes variable performance demands. Different environments may demand either coarse discriminations or fine discriminations to be made among the same set of objects. As Posner [20, pp. 53–54] has noted:

> If subjects are taught a tight concept, they tend to be very careful about classifying any particular pattern as an instance of that concept. They tend to reject a relatively small distortion of the prototype as an instance, and they rarely classify a pattern as a member of the concept when it is not. On the other hand, subjects learning high-variability concepts often falsely classify patterns as members of the concept, but rarely reject a member of the concept incorrectly... The situation largely determines which type of learning will be superior.

In an ART system, if an erroneous recognition is followed by negative reinforcement, then the system becomes more *vigilant*. This change in vigilance may be interpreted as a change in the system's attentional state which increases its sensitivity to mismatches between bottom–up input patterns and active top–down critical feature patterns. A vigilance change alters the size of a single parameter in the network. The *interactions* within the network respond to this parameter change by learning recognition codes that make finer distinctions. In other words, if the network erroneously groups together some input patterns, then negative reinforcement can help the network to learn the desired distinction by making the system more vigilant. The system then behaves *as if* has a better set of feature detectors.

The ability of a vigilance change to alter the course of pattern recognition illustrates a theme that is common to a variety of neural processes: a one-dimensional parameter change that modulates a simple nonspecific neural process can have complex specific effects upon high-dimensional neural information processing.

Sections 3–7 outline qualitatively the main operations of the model. Sections 8–11 describe computer simulations which illustrate the model's ability to learn categories. Section 12 defines the model mathematically. The remaining sections characterize the model's properties using mathematical analysis and more computer simulations, with the model hypotheses summarized in Section 18.

3. BOTTOM–UP ADAPTIVE FILTERING AND CONTRAST-ENHANCEMENT IN SHORT TERM MEMORY

We begin by considering the typical network reactions to a single input pattern I within a temporal stream of input patterns. Each input pattern may be the output pattern of a preprocessing stage. Different preprocessing is given, for example, to speech signals and to visual signals before the outcome of such modality-specific preprocessing ever reaches the attentional subsystem. The preprocessed input pattern I is received at the stage F_1 of an attentional subsystem. Pattern I is transformed into a pattern X of activation across the nodes, or abstract "feature detectors," of F_1 (Fig. 3). The transformed pattern X represents a pattern in short term memory (STM). In F_1 each node whose activity is sufficiently large generates

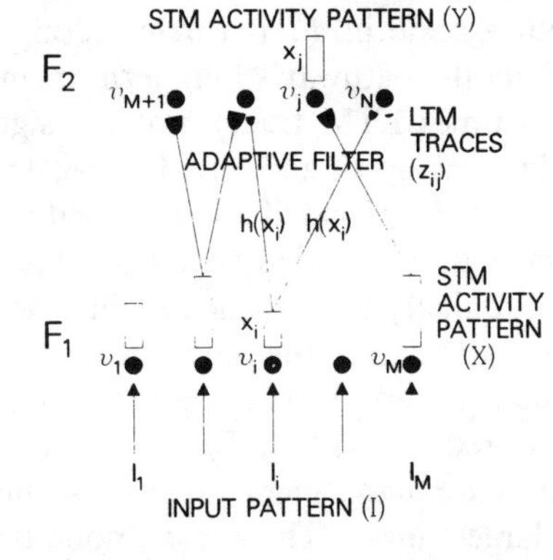

FIG. 3. Stages of bottom–up activation: The input pattern I generates a pattern of STM activation X across F_1. Sufficiently active F_1 nodes emit bottom–up signals to F_2. This signal pattern S is gated by long term memory (LTM) traces within the $F_1 \to F_2$ pathways. The LTM-gated signals are summed before activating their target nodes in F_2. This LTM-gated and summed signal pattern T generates a pattern of activation Y across F_2. The nodes in F_1 are denoted by $v_1, v_2, \ldots, v_M$. The nodes in F_2 are denoted by $v_{M+1}, v_{M+2}, \ldots, v_N$. The input to node v_i is denoted by I_i. The STM activity of node v_i is denoted by x_i. The LTM trace of the pathway from v_i to v_j is denoted by z_{ij}.

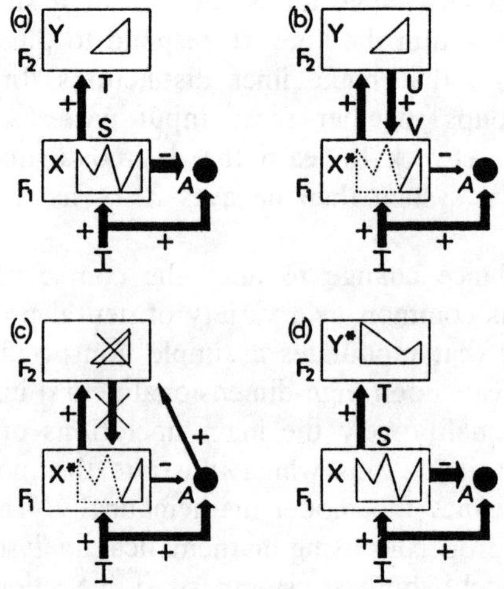

FIG. 4. Search for a correct F_2 code: (a) The input pattern I generates the specific STM activity pattern X at F_1 as it nonspecifically activates A. Pattern X both inhibits A and generates the output signal pattern S. Signal pattern S is transformed into the input pattern T, which activates the STM pattern Y across F_2. (b) Pattern Y generates the top–down signal pattern U which is transformed into the template pattern V. If V mismatches I at F_1, then a new STM activity pattern X^* is generated at F_1. The reduction in total STM activity which occurs when X is transformed into X^* causes a decrease in the total inhibition from F_1 to A. (c) Then the input-driven activation of A can release a nonspecific arousal wave to F_2, which resets the STM pattern Y at F_2. (d) After Y is inhibited, its top–down template is eliminated, and X can be reinstated at F_1. Now X once again generates input pattern T to F_2, but since Y remains inhibited T can activate a different STM pattern Y^* at F_2. If the top–down template due to Y^* also mismatches I at F_1, then the rapid search for an appropriate F_2 code continues.

excitatory signals along pathways to target nodes at the next processing stage F_2. A pattern X of STM activities across F_1 hereby elicits a pattern S of output signals from F_1. When a signal from a node in F_1 is carried along a pathway to F_2, the signal is multiplied, or *gated*, by the pathway's long term memory (LTM) trace. The LTM-gated signal (i.e., signal times LTM trace), not the signal alone, reaches the target node. Each target node sums up of all of its LTM-gated signals. In this way, pattern S generates a pattern T of LTM-gated and summed input signals to F_2 (Fig. 4a). The transformation from S to T is called an *adaptive filter*.

The input pattern T to F_2 is quickly transformed by interactions among the nodes of F_2. These interactions contrast-enhance the input pattern T. The resulting pattern of activation across F_2 is a new pattern Y. The contrast-enhanced pattern Y, rather than the input pattern T, is stored in STM by F_2.

A special case of this contrast-enhancement process is one in which F_2 chooses the node which receives the largest input. The chosen node is the only one that can store activity in STM. In general, the contrast enhancing transformation from T to Y enables more than one node at a time to be active in STM. Such transformations are designed to simultaneously represent in STM several groupings, or chunks, of an input pattern [9, 11, 24–26]. When F_2 is designed to make a choice in STM, it selects that global grouping of the input pattern which is preferred by the adaptive filter. This process automatically enables the network to partition all the input patterns which are received by F_1 into disjoint sets of recognition categories, each corresponding to a particular node (or "pointer," or "index") in F_2. Such a categorical mechanism is both interesting in itself and a necessary prelude to the analysis of recognition codes in which multiple groupings of X are simultaneously represented by Y. In the example that is characterized in this article, level F_2 is designed to make a choice.

All the LTM traces in the adaptive filter, and thus all learned past experiences of the network, are used to determine the recognition code Y via the transformation $I \to X \to S \to T \to Y$. However, only those nodes of F_2 which maintain stored activity in the STM pattern Y can elicit new learning at contiguous LTM traces. Because the recognition code Y is a more contrast-enhanced pattern than T, many F_2 nodes which receive positive inputs ($I \to X \to S \to T$) may not store any STM activity ($T \to Y$). The LTM traces in pathways leading to these nodes thus influence the recognition event but are not altered by the recognition event. Some memories which influence the focus of attention are not themselves attended.

4. TOP-DOWN TEMPLATE MATCHING AND STABILIZATION OF CODE LEARNING

As soon as the bottom-up STM transformation $X \to Y$ takes place, the STM activities Y in F_2 elicit a top-down excitatory signal pattern U back to F_1 (Fig. 4b). Only sufficiently large STM activities in Y elicit signals in U along the feedback pathways $F_2 \to F_1$. As in the bottom-up adaptive filter, the top-down signals U are also gated by LTM traces and the LTM-gated signals are summed at F_1 nodes. The pattern U of output signals from F_2 hereby generates a pattern V of LTM-gated and summed input signals to F_1. The transformation from U to V is thus also an adaptive filter. The pattern V is called a *top-down template*, or *learned expectation*.

Two sources of input now perturb F_1: the bottom-up input pattern I which gave rise to the original activity pattern X, and the top-down template pattern V that resulted from activating X. The activity pattern X^* across F_1 that is induced by I and V taken together is typically different from the activity pattern X that was previously induced by I alone. In particular, F_1 acts to match V against I. The result of this matching process determines the future course of learning and recognition by the network.

The entire activation sequence

$$I \to X \to S \to T \to Y \to U \to V \to X^* \tag{1}$$

takes place very quickly relative to the rate with which the LTM traces in either the bottom-up adaptive filter $S \to T$ or the top-down adaptive filter $U \to V$ can change. Even though none of the LTM traces changes during such a short time, their prior learning strongly influences the STM patterns Y and X^* that evolve within the network by determining the transformations $S \to T$ and $U \to V$. We now discuss how a match or mismatch of I and V at F_1 regulates the course of learning in response to the pattern I, and in particular solves the stability-plasticity dilemma (Sect. 1C).

5. INTERACTIONS BETWEEN ATTENTIONAL AND ORIENTING SUBSYSTEMS: STM RESET AND SEARCH

In Fig. 4a, an input pattern I generates an STM activity pattern X across F_1. The input pattern I also excites the orienting subsystem A, but pattern X at F_1 inhibits A before it can generate an output signal. Activity pattern X also elicits an output pattern S which, via the bottom–up adaptive filter, instates an STM activity pattern Y across F_2. In Fig. 4b, pattern Y reads a top–down template pattern V into F_1. Template V mismatches input I, thereby significantly inhibiting STM activity across F_1. The amount by which activity in X is attenuated to generate X^* depends upon how much of the input pattern I is encoded within the template pattern V.

When a mismatch attenuates STM activity across F_1, the total size of the inhibitory signal from F_1 to A is also attenuated. If the attenuation is sufficiently great, inhibition from F_1 to A can no longer prevent the arousal source A from firing. Fig. 4c depicts how disinhibition of A releases an arousal burst to F_2 which equally, or nonspecifically, excites all the F_2 cells. The cell populations of F_2 react to such an arousal signal in a state-dependent fashion. In the special case that F_2 chooses a single population for STM storage, the arousal burst selectively inhibits, or resets, the active population in F_2. This inhibition is long-lasting. One physiological design for F_2 processing which has these properties is a *gated dipole field* [10, 27]. A gated dipole field consists of opponent processing channels which are gated by habituating chemical transmitters. A nonspecific arousal burst induces selective and enduring inhibition of active populations within a gated dipole field.

In Fig. 4c, inhibition of Y leads to removal of the top–down template V, and thereby terminates the mismatch between I and V. Input pattern I can thus reinstate the original activity pattern X across F_1, which again generates the output pattern S from F_1 and the input pattern T to F_2. Due to the enduring inhibition at F_2, the input pattern T can no longer activate the original pattern Y at F_2. A new pattern Y^* is thus generated at F_2 by I (Fig. 4d). Despite the fact that some F_2 nodes may remain inhibited by the STM reset property, the new pattern Y^* may encode large STM activities. This is because level F_2 is designed so that its total suprathreshold activity remains approximately constant, or normalized, despite the fact that some of its nodes may remain inhibited by the STM reset mechanism. This property is related to the limited capacity of STM. A physiological process capable of achieving the STM normalization property is based upon on-center off-surround feedback interactions among cells obeying membrane equations [10, 28].

The new activity pattern Y^* reads out a new top–down template pattern V^*. If a mismatch again occurs at F_1, the orienting subsystem is again engaged, thereby leading to another arousal-mediated reset of STM at F_2. In this way, a rapid series of STM matching and reset events may occur. Such an STM matching and reset series controls the system's search of LTM by sequentially engaging the novelty-sensitive orienting subsystem. Although STM is reset sequentially in time via this mismatch-mediated, self-terminating LTM search process, the mechanisms which control the LTM search are all parallel network interactions, rather than serial algorithms. Such a parallel search scheme continuously adjusts itself to the system's evolving LTM codes. In general, the spatial configuration of LTM codes depends upon both the system's initial configuration and its unique learning history, and hence cannot be predicted a priori by a pre-wired search algorithm. Instead, the mismatch-mediated engagement of the orienting subsystem realizes the type of self-adjusting search that was described in Section 2B.

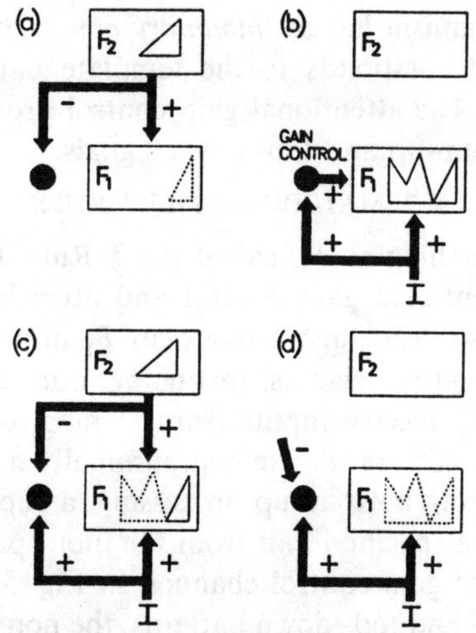

FIG. 5. **Matching by the $\frac{2}{3}$ Rule: (a) A top–down template from F_2 inhibits the attentional gain control source as it subliminally primes target F_1 cells. (b) Only F_1 cells that receive bottom–up inputs and gain control signals can become supraliminally active. (c) When a bottom–up input pattern and a top–down template are simultaneously active, only those F_1 cells that receive inputs from both sources can become supraliminally active. (d) Intermodality inhibition can shut off the F_1 gain control source and thereby prevent a bottom–up input from supraliminally activating F_1. Similarly, disinhibition of the F_1 gain control source may cause a top–down prime to become supraliminal.**

The mismatched-mediated search of LTM ends when an STM pattern across F_2 reads out a top–down template which matches I, to the degree of accuracy required by the level of attentional vigilance (Sect. 2D), or which has not yet undergone any prior learning. In the latter case, a new recognition category is then established as a bottom–up code and top–down template are learned.

6. ATTENTIONAL GAIN CONTROL AND ATTENTIONAL PRIMING

Further properties of the top–down template matching process can be derived by considering its role in the regulation of attentional priming. Consider, for example, a situation in which F_2 is activated by a level other than F_1 before F_1 can be activated by a bottom–up input (Fig. 5a). In such a situation, F_2 can generate a top–down template V to F_1. The level F_1 is then primed, or sensitized, to receive a bottom–up input that may or may not match the active expectancy. As depicted in Fig. 5a, level F_1 can be primed to receive a bottom–up input without necessarily eliciting suprathreshold output signals in response to the priming expectancy.

On the other hand, an input pattern I must be able to generate a suprathreshold activity pattern X even if no top–down expectancy is active across F_1 (Figs. 4a and 5b). How does F_1 know that it should generate a suprathreshold reaction to a bottom–up input pattern but not to a top–down input pattern? In both cases, excitatory input signals stimulate F_1 cells. Some auxiliary mechanism must exist to distinguish between bottom–up and top–down inputs. This auxiliary mechanism is called *attentional gain control* to distinguish it from *attentional priming* by the top–down template itself (Fig. 5a). While F_2 is active, the attentional priming mechanism delivers *excitatory specific learned* template patterns to F_1. The attentional gain control mechanism has an *inhibitory nonspecific unlearned* effect on the sensitivity with which F_1 responds to the template pattern, as well as to other patterns received by F_1. The attentional gain control process enables F_1 to tell the difference between bottom–up and top–down signals.

7. MATCHING: THE $\frac{2}{3}$ RULE

A rule for pattern matching at F_1, called the $\frac{2}{3}$ Rule, follows naturally from the distinction between attentional gain control and attentional priming. It says that two out of three signal sources must activate an F_1 node in order for that node to generate suprathreshold output signals. In Fig. 5a, during top–down processing, or priming, the nodes of F_1 receive inputs from at most one of their three possible input sources. Hence no cells in F_1 are supraliminally activated by the top–down template. In Fig. 5b, during bottom–up processing, a suprathreshold node in F_1 is one which receives both a specific input from the input pattern I and a nonspecific excitatory signal from the gain control channel. In Fig. 5c, during the matching of simultaneous bottom–up and top–down patterns, the nonspecific gain control signal to F_1 is inhibited by the top–down channel. Nodes of F_1 which receive sufficiently large inputs from both the bottom–up and the top–down signal patterns generate suprathreshold activities. Nodes which receive a bottom–up input or a top–down input, but not both, cannot become suprathreshold: mismatched inputs cannot generate suprathreshold activities. Attentional gain control thus leads to a matching process whereby the addition of top–down excitatory inputs to F_1 can lead to an overall decrease in F_1's STM activity (Figs. 4a and b). Figure 5d shows how competitive interactions across modalities can prevent F_1 from generating a supraliminal reaction to bottom–up signals when attention shifts from one modality to another.

8. CODE INSTABILITY AND CODE STABILITY

The importance of using the $\frac{2}{3}$ Rule for matching is now illustrated by describing how its absence can lead to a temporally unstable code (Fig. 6a). The system becomes unstable when the inhibitory top–down attentional gain control signals (Fig. 5c) are too small for the $\frac{2}{3}$ Rule to hold at F_1. Larger attentional gain control signals restore code stability by reinstating the $\frac{2}{3}$ Rule (Fig. 6b). Figure 6b also illustrates how a novel exemplar can directly access a previously established category; how the category in which a given exemplar is coded can be influenced by the categories which form to encode very different exemplars; and how the network responds to exemplars as coherent groupings of features, rather than to isolated feature matches or mismatches.

Code Instability Example

In Fig. 6, four input patterns, A, B, C, and D, are periodically presented in the order $ABCAD$. Patterns B, C, and D are all subsets of A. The relationships among the inputs that make the simulation work are as follows: $D \subset C \subset A$; $B \subset A$; $B \cap C = \phi$; and $|D| < |B| < |C|$, where $|I|$ denotes the number of features in input pattern I. The choice of input patterns in Fig. 6 is thus one of infinitely many examples in which, without the $\frac{2}{3}$ Rule, an alphabet of four input patterns cannot be stably coded.

The numbers $1, 2, 3, \ldots$, listed at the left in Fig. 6 itemize the presentation order. The next column, labeled BU for Bottom–Up, describes the input pattern that was

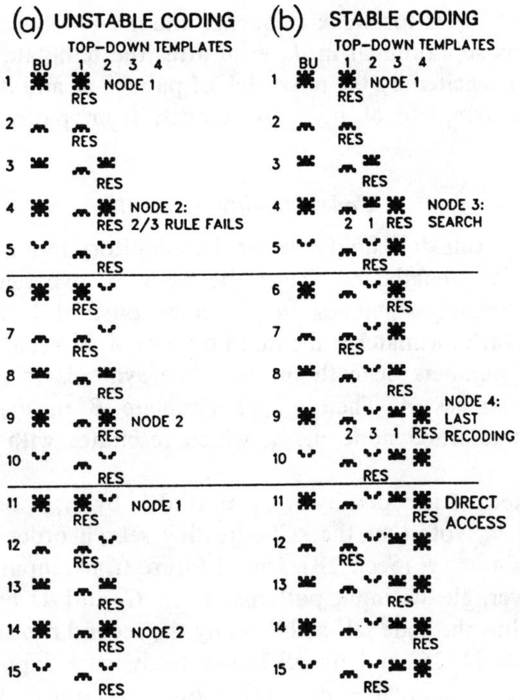

FIG. 6. Stabilization of categorical learning by the $\frac{2}{3}$ Rule: In both (a) and (b), four input patterns A, B, C, and D are presented repeatedly in the list order $ABCAD$. In (a), the $\frac{2}{3}$ Rule is violated because the top–down inhibitory gain control mechanism is weak (Fig. 5c). Pattern A is periodically coded by v_{M+1} and v_{M+2}. It is never coded by a single stable category. In (b), the $\frac{2}{3}$ Rule is restored by strengthening the top–down inhibitory gain control mechanism. After some initial recoding during the first two presentations of $ABCAD$, all patterns directly access distinct stable categories. A black square in a template pattern designates that the corresponding top–down LTM trace is large. A blank square designates that the LTM trace is small.

presented on each trial. Each Top–Down Template column corresponds to a different node in F_2. If M nodes $v_1, v_2, \ldots, v_M$ exist in F_1, then the F_2 nodes are denoted by $v_{M+1}, v_{M+2}, \ldots, v_N$. Column 1 corresponds to node v_{M+1}, column 2 corresponds to node v_{M+2}, and so on. Each row summarizes the network response to its input pattern. The symbol RES, which stands for *resonance*, designates the node in F_2 which codes the input pattern on that trial. For example, v_{M+2} codes pattern C on trial 3, and v_{M+1} codes pattern B on trial 7. The patterns in a given row describe the templates after learning has equilibrated on that trial.

In Fig. 6a, input pattern A is periodically recoded. On trial 1, it is coded by v_{M+1}; on trial 4, it is coded by v_{M+2}; on trial 6, it is coded by v_{M+1}; on trial 9, it is coded by v_{M+2}. This alternation in the nodes v_{M+1} and v_{M+2} which code pattern A repeats indefinitely.

Violation of the $\frac{2}{3}$ Rule occurs on trials 4, 6, 8, 9, and so on. This violation is illustrated by comparing the template of v_{M+2} on trials 3 and 4. On trial 3, the template of v_{M+2} is coded by pattern C, which is a subset of pattern A. On trial 4, pattern A is presented and directly activates node v_{M+2}. Since the inhibitory top–down gain control is too weak to quench the mismatched portion of the input, pattern A remains supraliminal in F_1 even after the template C is read out from v_{M+2}. No search is elicited by the mismatch of pattern A and its subset template C. Consequently the template of v_{M+2} is recoded from pattern C to its superset pattern A.

Code Stability Example

In Fig. 6b, the $\frac{2}{3}$ Rule does hold because the inhibitory top–down attentional gain control channel is strengthened. Thus the network experiences a sequence of recodings that ultimately stabilizes. In particular, on trial 4, node v_{M+2} reads-out the template C, which mismatches the input pattern A. Here, a search is initiated, as indicated by the numbers beneath the template symbols in row 4. First, v_{M+2}'s template C mismatches A. Then v_{M+1}'s template B mismatches A. Finally A activates the uncommitted node v_{M+3}, which resonates with F_1 as it learns the template A.

In Fig. 6b, pattern A is coded by v_{M+1} on trial 1; by v_{M+3} on trials 4 and 6; and by v_{M+4} on trial 9. Note that the self-adjusting search order in response to A is different on trials 4 and 9 (Sect. 2B). On all future trials, input pattern A is coded by v_{M+4}. Moreover, all the input patterns A, B, C, and D have learned a stable code by trial 9. Thus the code self-stabilizes by the second run through the input list $ABCAD$. On trials 11–15, and on all future trials, each input pattern chooses a different code ($A \rightarrow v_{M+4}$; $B \rightarrow v_{M+1}$; $C \rightarrow v_{M+3}$; $D \rightarrow v_{M+2}$). Each pattern belongs to a separate category because the vigilance parameter (Sect. 2D) was chosen to be large in this example. Moreover, after code learning stabilizes, each input pattern directly activates its node in F_2 without undergoing any additional search (Sect. 2C). Thus after trial 9, only the "RES" symbol appears under the top–down templates. The patterns shown in any row between 9 and 15 provide a complete description of the learned code.

Examples of how a novel exemplar can activate a previously learned category are found on trials 2 and 5 in Figs. 6a and b. On trial 2 pattern B is presented for the first time and directly accesses the category coded by v_{M+1}, which was previously learned by pattern A on trial 1. In other words, B activates the same categorical "pointer," or "marker," or "index" as A. In so doing, B may change the categorical template, which determines which input patterns will also be coded by this index on future trials. The category does not change, but its invariants may change.

9. USING CONTEXT TO DISTINGUISH SIGNAL FROM NOISE IN PATTERNS OF VARIABLE COMPLEXITY

The simulation in Fig. 7 illustrates how, at a fixed vigilance level, the network automatically rescales its matching criterion in response to inputs of variable complexity (Sect. 2A). On the first four trials, the patterns are presented in the order $ABAB$. By trial 2, coding is complete. Pattern A directly accesses node v_{M+1} on trial 3, and pattern B directly accesses node v_{M+2} on trial 4. Thus patterns A and B are coded by different categories. On trials 5–8, patterns C and D are presented in the order $CDCD$. Patterns C and D are constructed from patterns A and B, respectively, by adding identical upper halves to A and B. Thus, pattern C differs from pattern D at the same locations where pattern A differs from pattern B. Due to the addition of these upper halves, the network does not code C in the category v_{M+1} of

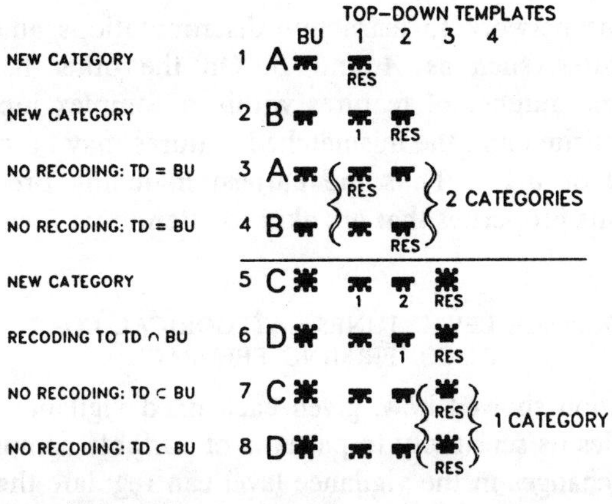

FIG. 7. Distinguishing noise from patterns for inputs of variable complexity: Input patterns A and B are coded by the distinct category nodes v_{M+1} and v_{M+2}, respectively. Input patterns C and D include A and B as subsets, but also possess identical subpatterns of additional features. Due to this additional pattern complexity, C and D are coded by the same category node v_{M+3}. At this vigilance level ($\rho = 0.8$), the network treats the difference between C and D as noise, and suppresses the discordant elements in the v_{M+3} template. By contrast, it treats the difference between A and B as informative, and codes the difference in the v_{M+1} and v_{M+2} templates, respectively.

A and does not code D in the category v_{M+2} of B. Moreover, because patterns C and D represent many more features than patterns A and B, the difference between C and D is treated as noise, whereas the identical difference between A and B is considered significant. In particular, both patterns C and D are coded within the same category v_{M+3} on trials 7 and 8, and the critical feature pattern which forms the template of v_{M+3} does not contain the subpatterns at which C and D are mismatched. In contrast, these subpatterns are contained within the templates of v_{M+1} and v_{M+2} to enable these nodes to differentially classify A and B.

Figure 7 illustrates that the matching process compares whole activity patterns across a field of feature-selective cells, rather than activations of individual feature detectors, and that the properties of this matching process which enable it to stabilize network learning also automatically rescale the matching criterion. Thus the network can both differentiate finer details of simple input patterns and tolerate larger mismatches of complex input patterns. This rescaling property also defines the difference between irrelevant features and significant pattern mismatches.

If a mismatch within the attentional subsystem does not activate the orienting subsystem, then no further search for a different code occurs. Thus on trial 6 in Fig. 7, mismatched features between the template of v_{M+3} and input pattern D are treated as noise in the sense that they are rapidly suppressed in short term memory (STM) at F_1, and are eliminated from the critical feature pattern learned by the v_{M+3} template. If the mismatch does generate a search, then the mismatched features may be included in the critical feature pattern of the category to which the search leads. Thus on trial 2 of Fig. 6, the input pattern B mismatches the template of node v_{M+1}, which causes the search to select node v_{M+2}. As a result, A and B are coded by the distinct categories v_{M+1} and v_{M+2}, respectively. If a template mismatches a simple input pattern at just a few features, a search may be elicited, thereby enabling the network to learn fine discriminations among patterns composed of few features, such as A and B. On the other hand, if a template mismatches the same number of features within a complex input pattern, then a search may not be elicited and the mismatched features may be suppressed as noise, as in the template of v_{M+3}. Thus the pattern matching process of the model automatically exhibits properties that are akin to attentional focussing, or "zooming in."

10. VIGILANCE LEVEL TUNES CATEGORICAL COARSENESS: DISCONFIRMING FEEDBACK

The previous section showed how, given each fixed vigilance level, the network automatically rescales its sensitivity to patterns of variable complexity. The present section shows that changes in the vigilance level can regulate the coarseness of the categories that are learned in response to a fixed sequence of input patterns. First we need to define the vigilance parameter ρ.

Let $|I|$ denote the number of input pathways which receive positive inputs when I is presented. Assume that each such input pathway sends an excitatory signal of fixed size P to A whenever I is presented, so that the total excitatory input to A is $P|I|$. Assume also that each F_1 node whose activity becomes positive due to I generates an inhibitory signal of fixed size Q to A, and denote by $|X|$ the number of active pathways from F_1 to A that are activated by the F_1 activity pattern X. Then the total inhibitory input from F_1 to A is $Q|X|$. When

$$P|I| > Q|X|, \tag{2}$$

the orienting subsystem A receives a net excitatory signal and generates a nonspecific reset signal to F_2 (Fig. 4c). The quantity

$$\rho \equiv \frac{P}{Q} \tag{3}$$

is called the *vigilance parameter* of A. By (2) and (3), STM reset is initiated when

$$\rho > \frac{|X|}{|I|}. \tag{4}$$

STM reset is prevented when

$$\rho \leq \frac{|X|}{|I|}. \tag{5}$$

In other words, the proportion $|X|/|I|$ of the input pattern I which is matched by the top–down template to generate X must exceed ρ in order to prevent STM reset at F_2.

While F_2 is inactive (Fig. 5b), $|X| = |I|$. Activation of A is always forbidden in this case to prevent an input I from resetting its correct F_2 code. By (5), this constraint is achieved if

$$\rho \leq 1; \tag{6}$$

that is, if $P \leq Q$.

In summary, due to the $\frac{2}{3}$ Rule, a bad mismatch at F_1 causes a large collapse of total F_1 activity, which leads to activation of A. In order for this to happen, the system maintains a measure of the original level of total F_1 activity and compares this criterion level with the collapsed level of total F_1 activity. The criterion level is computed by summing bottom–up inputs from I to A. This sum provides a stable criterion because it is proportional to the initial activation of F_1 by the bottom–up input, and it remains unchanged as the matching process unfolds in real-time.

We now illustrate how a low vigilance level leads to learning of coarse categories, whereas a high vigilance level leads to learning of fine categories. Suppose, for example, that a low vigilance level has led to a learned grouping of inputs which need to be distinguished for successful adaptation to a prescribed input environment, but that a punishing event occurs as a consequence of this erroneous grouping (Sect. 2D). Suppose that, in addition to its negative reinforcing effects, the punishing event also has the cognitive effect of increasing sensitivity to pattern mismatches. Such an increase in sensitivity is modelled within the network by an increase in the vigilance parameter, ρ, defined by (3). Increasing this single parameter enables the network to discriminate patterns which previously were lumped together. Once these patterns are coded by different categories in F_2, the different categories can be associated with different behavioral responses. In this way, environmental feedback can enable the network to parse more finely whatever input patterns happen to occur without altering the feature detection process per se. The vigilance parameter is increased if a punishing event amplifies all the signals from the input pattern to A so that parameter P increases. Alternatively, ρ may be increased either by a nonspecific decrease in the size Q of signals from F_1 to A, or by direct input signals to A.

Figure 8 describes a series of simulations in which four input patterns—A, B, C, D—are coded. In these simulations, $A \subset B \subset C \subset D$. The different parts of the figure show how categorical learning changes with changes of ρ. When $\rho = 0.8$ (Fig. 8a), 4 categories are learned: $(A)(B)(C)(D)$. When $\rho = 0.7$ (Fig. 8b), 3 categories are learned: $(A)(B)(C, D)$. When $\rho = 0.6$ (Fig. 8c), 3 different categories are learned: $(A)(B, C)(D)$. When $\rho = 0.5$ (Fig. 8d), 2 categories are learned: $(A, B)(C, D)$. When $\rho = 0.3$ (Fig. 8e), 2 different categories are learned: $(A, B, C)(D)$. When $\rho = 0.2$ (Fig. 8f), all the patterns are lumped together into a single category.

11. RAPID CLASSIFICATION OF AN ARBITRARY TYPE FONT

In order to illustrate how an ART network codifies a more complex series of patterns, we show in Fig. 9 the first 20 trials of a simulation using alphabet letters as input patterns. In Fig. 9a, the vigilance parameter $\rho = 0.5$. In Fig. 9b, $\rho = 0.8$. Three properties are notable in these simulations. First, choosing a different vigilance parameter can determine different coding histories, such that higher vigilance induces coding into finer categories. Second, the network modifies its search order on each trial to reflect the cumulative effects of prior learning, and

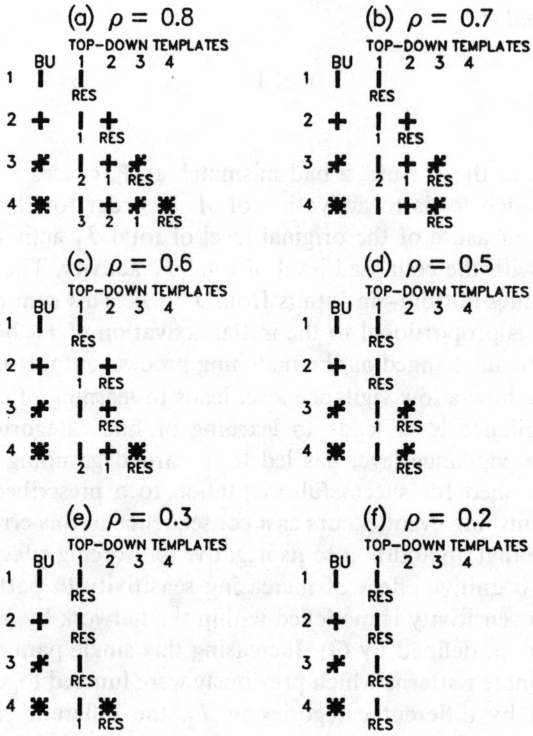

FIG. 8. **Influence of vigilance level on categorical groupings: As the vigilance parameter ρ decreases, the number of categories progressively decreases.**

bypasses the orienting subsystem to directly access categories after learning has taken place. Third, the templates of coarser categories tend to be more abstract because they must approximately match a larger number of input pattern exemplars.

Given $\rho = 0.5$, the network groups the 26 letter patterns into 8 stable categories within 3 presentations. In this simulation, F_2 contains 15 nodes. Thus 7 nodes remain uncoded because the network self-stabilizes its learning after satisfying criteria of vigilance and global self-consistency. Given $\rho = 0.8$ and 15 F_2 nodes, the network groups 25 of the 26 letters into 15 stable categories within 3 presentations. The 26th letter is rejected by the network in order to self-stabilize its learning while satisfying its criteria of vigilance and global self-consistency. Given a choice of ρ closer to 1, the network classifies 15 letters into 15 distinct categories within 2 presentations. In general, if an ART network is endowed with sufficiently many nodes in F_1 and F_2, it is capable of self-organizing an arbitrary ordering of arbitrarily many and arbitrarily complex input patterns into self-stabilizing recognition categories subject to the constraints of vigilance and global code self-consistency.

We now turn to a mathematical analysis of the properties which control learning and recognition by an ART network.

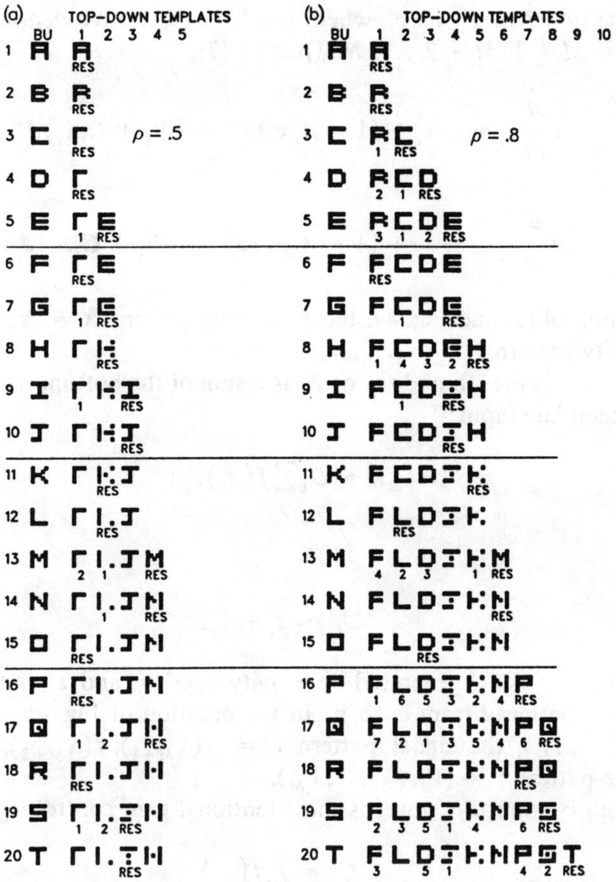

FIG. 9. Alphabet learning: different vigilance levels cause different numbers of letter categories and different critical feature patterns, or templates, to form.

12. NETWORK EQUATIONS: INTERACTIONS BETWEEN SHORT TERM MEMORY AND LONG TERM MEMORY PATTERNS

The STM and LTM equations are described below in dimensionless form [29], where the number of parameters is reduced to a minimum.

A. STM *Equations*

The STM activity x_k of any node v_k in F_1 or F_2 obeys a membrane equation of the form

$$\varepsilon \frac{d}{dt} x_k = -x_k + (1 - Ax_k) J_k^+ - (B + Cx_k) J_k^-, \tag{7}$$

where J_k^+ is the total excitatory input to v_k, J_k^- is the total inhibitory input to v_k, and all the parameters are nonnegative. If $A > 0$ and $C > 0$, then the STM activity $x_k(t)$ remains within the finite interval $[-BC^{-1}, A^{-1}]$ no matter how large the nonnegative inputs J_k^+ and J_k^- become.

We denote nodes in F_1 by v_i, where $i = 1, 2, \ldots, M$. We denote nodes in F_2 by v_j, where $j = M+1, M+2, \ldots, N$. Thus by (7),

$$\varepsilon \frac{d}{dt} x_i = -x_i + (1 - A_1 x_i) J_i^+ - (B_1 + C_1 x_i) J_i^- \tag{8}$$

and

$$\varepsilon \frac{d}{dt} x_j = -x_j + (1 - A_2 x_j) J_j^+ - (B_2 + C_2 x_j) J_j^-. \tag{9}$$

In the notation of (1) and Fig. 4a, the F_1 activity pattern $X = (x_1, x_2, \ldots, x_M)$ and the F_2 activity pattern $Y = (x_{M+1}, x_{M+2}, \ldots, x_N)$.

The input J_i^+ to the ith node v_i of F_1 is a sum of the bottom–up input I_i and the top–down template input V_i

$$V_i = D_1 \sum_j f(x_j) z_{ji}; \tag{10}$$

that is,

$$J_i^+ = I_i + V_i, \tag{11}$$

where $f(x_j)$ is the signal generated by activity x_j of v_j, and z_{ji} is the LTM trace in the top–down pathway from v_j to v_i. In the notation of Fig. 4b, the input pattern $I = (I_1, I_2, \ldots, I_M)$, the signal pattern $U = (f(x_{M+1}), f(x_{M+2}), \ldots, f(x_N))$, and the template pattern $V = (V_1, V_2, \ldots, V_M)$.

The inhibitory input J_i^- governs the attentional gain control signal

$$J_i^- = \sum_j f(x_j). \tag{12}$$

Thus $J_i^- = 0$ if and only if F_2 is inactive. When F_2 is active, $J_i^- > 0$ and hence term J_i^- in (8) has a nonspecific inhibitory effect on all the STM activities x_i of F_1. In Fig. 5c, this nonspecific inhibitory effect is mediated by inhibition of an active excitatory gain control channel. Such a mechanism is formally described by (12). The attentional gain control signal can be implemented in any of several formally equivalent ways. See the Appendix for some alternative systems.

The inputs and parameters of STM activities in F_2 are chosen so that the F_2 node which receives the largest input from F_1 wins the competition for STM activity. Theorems provide a basis for choosing these parameters [30–32]. The inputs J_j^+ and J_j^- to the F_2 node v_j have the following form.

Input J_j^+ adds a positive feedback signal $g(x_j)$ from v_j to itself to the bottom–up adaptive filter input T_j, where

$$T_j = D_2 \sum_i h(x_i) z_{ij}. \tag{13}$$

That is,

$$J_j^+ = g(x_j) + T_j, \tag{14}$$

where $h(x_i)$ is the signal emitted by the F_1 node v_i and z_{ij} is the LTM trace in the pathway from v_i to v_j. Input J_j^- adds up negative feedback signals $g(x_k)$ from all the other nodes in F_2,

$$J_j^- = \sum_{k \neq j} g(x_k). \tag{15}$$

In the notation of (1) and Fig. 4a, the output pattern $S = (h(x_1), h(x_2), \ldots, h(x_M))$ and the input pattern $T = (T_{M+1}, T_{M+2}, \ldots, T_N)$.

Taken together, the positive feedback signal $g(x_j)$ in (14) and the negative feedback signal J_j^- in (15) define an on-center off-surround feedback interaction which contrast-enhances the STM activity pattern Y of F_2 in response to the input pattern T. When F_2's parameters are chosen properly, this contrast-enhancement process enables F_2 to choose for STM activation only the node v_j which receives the largest input T_j. In particular, when parameter ε is small in Eq. (9), F_2 behaves approximately like a binary switching, or choice, circuit:

$$f(x_j) = \begin{cases} 1 & \text{if } T_j = \max\{T_k\} \\ 0 & \text{otherwise.} \end{cases} \tag{16}$$

In the choice case, the top–down template in (10) obeys

$$V_i = \begin{cases} D_1 z_{ji} & \text{if the } F_2 \text{ node } v_j \text{ is active} \\ 0 & \text{if } F_2 \text{ is inactive.} \end{cases} \tag{17}$$

Since V_i is proportional to the LTM trace z_{ji} of the active F_2 node v_j, we can define the template pattern that is read-out by each active F_2 node v_j to be $V^{(j)} \equiv D_1(z_{j1}, z_{j2}, \ldots, z_{jM})$.

B. LTM *Equations*

The equations for the bottom–up LTM traces z_{ij} and the top–down LTM traces z_{ji} between pairs of nodes v_i in F_1 and v_j in F_2 are formally summarized in this section to facilitate the description of how these equations help to generate useful learning and recognition properties.

The LTM trace of the bottom–up pathway from v_i to v_j obeys a learning equation of the form

$$\frac{d}{dt} z_{ij} = K_1 f(x_j)[-E_{ij} z_{ij} + h(x_i)]. \tag{18}$$

In (18), term $f(x_j)$ is a postsynaptic sampling, or learning, signal because $f(x_j) = 0$ implies $(d/dt)z_{ij} = 0$. Term $f(x_j)$ is also the output signal of v_j to pathways from v_j to F_1, as in (10).

The LTM trace of the top–down pathway from v_j to v_i also obeys a learning equation of the form

$$\frac{d}{dt} z_{ji} = K_2 f(x_j)[-E_{ji} z_{ji} + h(x_i)]. \tag{19}$$

In the present model, the simplest choice of K_2 and E_{ji} was made for the top–down LTM traces

$$K_2 = E_{ji} = 1. \tag{20}$$

A more complex choice of E_{ij} was made for the bottom–up LTM traces in order to generate the Weber Law Rule of Section 14. The Weber Law Rule requires that the positive bottom–up LTM traces learned during the encoding of an F_1 pattern X with a smaller number $|X|$ of active nodes be larger than the LTM traces learned during the encoding of an F_1 pattern with a larger number of active nodes, other things being equal. This inverse relationship between pattern complexity and bottom–up LTM trace strength can be realized by allowing the bottom–up LTM traces at each node v_j to compete among themselves for synaptic sites. The Weber Law Rule can also be generated by the STM dynamics of F_1 when competitive interactions are assumed to occur among the nodes of F_1. Generating the Weber Law Rule at F_1 rather than at the bottom–up LTM traces enjoys several advantages, and this model will be developed elsewhere [33]. In particular, implementing the Weber Law Rule at F_1 enables us to choose $E_{ij} = 1$.

Competition among the LTM traces which abut the node v_j is modelled herein by defining

$$E_{ij} = h(x_i) + L^{-1} \sum_{k \neq i} h(x_k) \tag{21}$$

and letting $K_1 =$ constant. It is convenient to write K_1 in the form $K_1 = KL$. A physical interpretation of this choice can be seen by rewriting (18) in the form

$$\frac{d}{dt} z_{ij} = Kf(x_j)\left[(1 - z_{ij})Lh(x_i) - z_{ij} \sum_{k \neq i} h(x_k)\right]. \tag{22}$$

By (22), when a postsynaptic signal $f(x_j)$ is positive, a positive presynaptic signal from the F_1 node v_i can commit receptor sites to the LTM process z_{ij} at a rate $(1 - z_{ij})Lh(x_i)Kf(x_j)$. In other words, uncommited sites—which number $(1 - z_{ij})$ out of the total population size 1—are committed by the joint action of signals $Lh(x_i)$ and $Kf(x_j)$. Simultaneously signals $h(x_k)$, $k \neq i$, which reach v_j at different patches of the v_j membrane, compete for the sites which are already committed to z_{ij} via the mass action competitive terms $-z_{ij}h(x_k)Kf(x_j)$. In other words, sites which are committed to z_{ij} lose their commitment at a rate $-z_{ij}\Sigma_{k \neq i}h(x_k)Kf(x_j)$ which is proportional to the number of committed sites z_{ij}, the total competitive input $-\Sigma_{k \neq i}h(x_k)$, and the postsynaptic gating signal $Kf(x_j)$.

Malsburg and Willshaw [34] have used a different type of competition among LTM traces in their model of retinotectal development. Translated to the present notation, Malsburg and Willshaw postulate that for each fixed F_1 node v_i, competition occurs among all the bottom–up LTM traces z_{ij} in pathways emanating from v_i in such a way as to keep the total synaptic strength $\Sigma_j z_{ij}$ constant through time. This model does not generate the Weber Law Rule. We show in Section 14 that the Weber Law Rule is essential for achieving direct access to learned categories of arbitrary input patterns in the present model.

C. STM *Reset System*

A simple type of mismatch-mediated activation of A and STM reset of F_2 by A were implemented in the simulations. As outlined in Section 10, each active input pathway sends an excitatory signal of size P to the orienting subsystem A. Potentials x_i of F_1 which exceed zero generate an inhibitory signal of size Q to A. These constraints lead to the following Reset Rule.

Reset Rule

Population A generates a nonspecific reset wave to F_2 whenever

$$\frac{|X|}{|I|} < \rho = \frac{P}{Q}, \tag{23}$$

where I is the current input pattern and $|X|$ is the number of nodes across F_1 such that $x_i > 0$. The nonspecific reset wave successively shuts off active F_2 nodes until the search ends or the input pattern I shuts off. Thus (16) must be modified as follows to maintain inhibition of all F_2 nodes which have been reset by A during the presentation of I:

F_2 Choice and Search

$$f(x_j) = \begin{cases} 1 & \text{if } T_j = \max\{T_k\colon k \in \mathbf{J}\} \\ 0 & \text{otherwise} \end{cases} \tag{24}$$

where $\mathbf{J}$ is the set of indices of F_2 nodes which have not yet been reset on the present learning trial. At the beginning of each new learning trial, $\mathbf{J}$ is reset at $\{M+1,\ldots,N\}$. (See Fig. 1.) As a learning trial proceeds, $\mathbf{J}$ loses one index at a time until the mismatch-mediated search for F_2 nodes terminates.

13. DIRECT ACCESS TO SUBSET AND SUPERSET PATTERNS

The need for a Weber Law Rule can be motivated as follows. Suppose that a bottom–up input pattern $I^{(1)}$ activates a network in which pattern $I^{(1)}$ is perfectly coded by the adaptive filter from F_1 to F_2. Suppose that another pattern $I^{(2)}$ is also perfectly coded and that $I^{(2)}$ contains $I^{(1)}$ as a subset; that is, $I^{(2)}$ equals $I^{(1)}$ at all the nodes where $I^{(1)}$ is positive. If $I^{(1)}$ and $I^{(2)}$ are sufficiently different, they should have access to distinct categories at F_2. However, since $I^{(2)}$ equals $I^{(1)}$ at their intersection, and since all the F_1 nodes where $I^{(2)}$ does not equal $I^{(1)}$ are inactive when $I^{(1)}$ is presented, how does the network decide between the two categories when $I^{(1)}$ is presented?

To accomplish this, the node $v^{(1)}$ in F_2 which codes $I^{(1)}$ should receive a bigger signal from the adaptive filter than the node $v^{(2)}$ in F_2 which codes a superset $I^{(2)}$ of $I^{(1)}$. In order to realize this constraint, the LTM traces at $v^{(2)}$ which filter $I^{(1)}$ should be smaller than the LTM traces at $v^{(1)}$ which filter $I^{(1)}$. Since the LTM traces at $v^{(2)}$ were coded by the superset pattern $I^{(2)}$, this constraint suggests that larger patterns are encoded by smaller LTM traces. Thus the absolute sizes of the LTM traces projecting to the different nodes $v^{(1)}$ and $v^{(2)}$ reflect the overall scale of the patterns $I^{(1)}$ and $I^{(2)}$ coded by the nodes. The quantitative realization of this inverse relationship between LTM size and input pattern scale is called the Weber Law Rule.

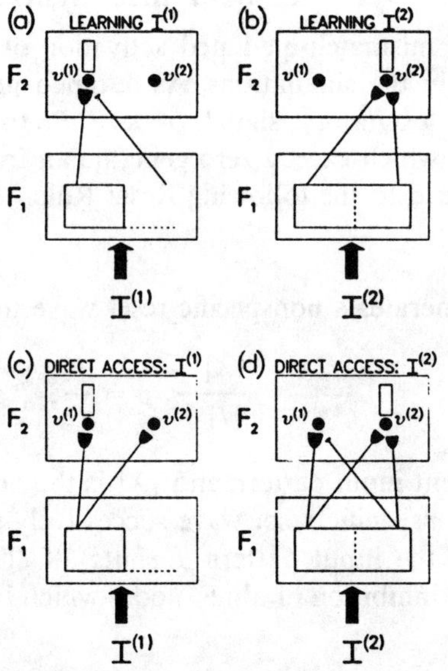

FIG. 10. The Weber Law Rule and the Associative Decay Rule enable both subset and superset input patterns to directly access distinct F_2 nodes: (a) and (b) schematize the learning induced by presentation of $I^{(1)}$ (a subset pattern) and $I^{(2)}$ (a superset pattern). Larger path endings designate larger learned LTM traces. (c) and (d) schematize how $I^{(1)}$ and $I^{(2)}$ directly access the F_2 nodes $v^{(1)}$ and $v^{(2)}$, respectively. This property illustrates how distinct, but otherwise arbitrary, input patterns can directly access different categories. No restrictions on input orthogonality or linear predictability are needed.

This inverse relationship suggests how a subset $I^{(1)}$ may selectively activate its node $v^{(1)}$ rather than the node $v^{(2)}$ corresponding to a superset $I^{(2)}$. On the other hand, the superset $I^{(2)}$ must also be able to directly activate its node $v^{(2)}$ rather than the node $v^{(1)}$ of a subset $I^{(1)}$. To achieve subset access, the positive LTM traces of $v^{(1)}$ become larger than the positive LTM traces of $v^{(2)}$. Since presentation of $I^{(2)}$ activates the entire subset pattern $I^{(1)}$, a further property is needed to understand why the subset node $v^{(1)}$ is not activated by the superset $I^{(2)}$. This property—which we call the Associative Decay Rule—implies that some LTM traces decay toward zero during learning. Thus the associative learning laws considered herein violate Hebb's [35] learning postulate.

In particular, the relative sizes of the LTM traces projecting to an F_2 node reflect the internal structuring of the input patterns coded by that node. During learning of $I^{(1)}$, the LTM traces decay toward zero in pathways which project to $v^{(1)}$ from F_1 cells where $I^{(1)}$ equals zero (Fig. 10a). Simultaneously, the LTM traces become large in the pathways which project to $v^{(1)}$ from F_1 cells where $I^{(1)}$ is positive (Fig. 10a). In contrast, during learning of $I^{(2)}$, the LTM traces become large in all the pathways which project to $v^{(2)}$ from F_1 cells where $I^{(2)}$ is positive (Fig. 10b), including those cells where $I^{(1)}$ equals zero. Since $I^{(2)}$ is a superset of $I^{(1)}$, the Weber Law Rule implies that LTM traces in pathways to $v^{(2)}$ (Fig. 10b) do not grow as large as LTM traces in pathways to $v^{(1)}$ (Fig. 10a). On the other hand, after learning occurs, more positive LTM traces exist in pathways to $v^{(2)}$ than to $v^{(1)}$. Thus a trade-off exists between the individual sizes of LTM traces and the number of positive LTM traces which lead to each F_2 node. This trade-off enables $I^{(1)}$ to access $v^{(1)}$ (Fig. 10c) and $I^{(2)}$ to access $v^{(2)}$ (Fig. 10d).

14. WEBER LAW RULE AND ASSOCIATIVE DECAY RULE FOR BOTTOM-UP LTM TRACES

We now describe more precisely how the conjoint action of a Weber Law Rule and an Associative Decay Rule allow direct access to both subset and superset F_2 codes. To fix ideas, suppose that each input pattern I to F_1 is a pattern of 0's and 1's. Let $|I|$ denote the number of 1's in the input pattern I. The two rules can be summarized as follows.

Associative Decay Rule

As learning of I takes place, LTM traces in the bottom–up coding pathways and the top–down template pathways between an inactive F_1 node and an active F_2 node approach 0. Associative learning within the LTM traces can thus cause decreases as well as increases in the sizes of the traces. This is a non-Hebbian form of associative learning.

Weber Law Rule

As learning of I takes place, LTM traces in the bottom–up coding pathways which join active F_1 and F_2 nodes approach an asymptote of the form

$$\frac{\alpha}{\beta + |I|}, \tag{25}$$

where α and β are positive constants. By (25), larger $|I|$ values imply smaller positive LTM traces in the pathways encoding I.

Direct access by the subset $I^{(1)}$ and the superset $I^{(2)}$ can now be understood as follows. By (25), the positive LTM traces which code $I^{(1)}$ have size

$$\frac{\alpha}{\beta + |I^{(1)}|} \tag{26}$$

and the positive LTM traces which code $I^{(2)}$ have size

$$\frac{\alpha}{\beta + |I^{(2)}|}, \tag{27}$$

where $|I^{(1)}| < |I^{(2)}|$. When $I^{(1)}$ is presented at F_1, $|I^{(1)}|$ nodes in F_1 are suprathreshold. Thus the *total* input to $v^{(1)}$ is proportional to

$$T_{11} = \frac{\alpha |I^{(1)}|}{\beta + |I^{(1)}|} \tag{28}$$

and the *total* input to $v^{(2)}$ is proportional to

$$T_{12} = \frac{\alpha |I^{(1)}|}{\beta + |I^{(2)}|}. \tag{29}$$

Because (25) defines a *decreasing* function of $|I|$ and because $|I^{(1)}| < |I^{(2)}|$, it follows that $T_{11} > T_{12}$. Thus $I^{(1)}$ activates $v^{(1)}$ instead of $v^{(2)}$.

When $I^{(2)}$ is presented at F_1, $|I^{(2)}|$ nodes in F_1 are suprathreshold. Thus the *total* input to $v^{(2)}$ is proportional to

$$T_{22} = \frac{\alpha|I^{(2)}|}{\beta + |I^{(2)}|}. \tag{30}$$

We now invoke the Associative Decay Rule. Because $I^{(2)}$ is superset of $I^{(1)}$, only those F_1 nodes in $I^{(2)}$ that are also activated by $I^{(1)}$ project to positive LTM traces at $v^{(1)}$. Thus the *total* input to $v^{(1)}$ is proportional to

$$T_{21} = \frac{\alpha|I^{(1)}|}{\beta + |I^{(1)}|}. \tag{31}$$

Both T_{22} and T_{21} are expressed in terms of the Weber function

$$W(|I|) = \frac{\alpha|I|}{\beta + |I|}, \tag{32}$$

which is an *increasing* function of $|I|$. Since $|I^{(1)}| < |I^{(2)}|$, $T_{22} > T_{21}$. Thus the superset $I^{(2)}$ activates its node $v^{(2)}$ rather than the subset node $v^{(1)}$. In summary, direct access to subsets and supersets can be traced to the opposite monotonic behavior of the functions (25) and (32).

It remains to show how the Associative Decay Rule and the Weber Law Rule are generated by the STM and LTM laws (8)–(22). The Associative Decay Rule for bottom–up LTM traces follows from (22). When the F_1 node v_i is inactive, $h(x_i) = 0$. When the F_2 node v_j is active, $f(x_j) = 1$. Thus if z_{ij} is the LTM trace in a bottom–up pathway from an inactive F_1 node v_i to an active F_2 node v_j, (22) reduces to

$$\frac{d}{dt} z_{ij} = -K z_{ij} \sum_{k \neq i} h(x_k). \tag{33}$$

The signal function $h(x_k)$ is scaled to rise steeply from 0 to the constant 1 when x_k exceeds zero. For simplicity, suppose that

$$h(x_k) = \begin{cases} 1 & \text{if } x_k > 0 \\ 0 & \text{otherwise.} \end{cases} \tag{34}$$

Thus during a learning trial when v_i is inactive,

$$\sum_{k \neq i} h(x_k) = |X|, \tag{35}$$

where $|X|$ is the number of positive activities in the F_1 activity pattern X. By (33) and (35), when v_i is inactive and v_j is active,

$$\frac{d}{dt} z_{ij} = -K z_{ij} |X| \tag{36}$$

which shows that z_{ij} decays exponentially toward zero.

The Weber Law Rule for bottom–up LTM traces z_{ij} follows from (22), (24), and (34). Consider an input pattern I of 0's and 1's that activates $|I|$ nodes in F_1 and node v_j in F_2. Then, by (34),

$$\sum_{k=1}^{M} h(x_k) = |I|. \tag{37}$$

For each z_{ij} in a bottom–up pathway from an active F_1 node v_i to an active F_2 node v_j, $f(x_j) = 1$ and $h(x_i) = 1$, so

$$\frac{d}{dt} z_{ij} = K\left[(1 - z_{ij})L - z_{ij}(|I| - 1)\right]. \tag{38}$$

At equilibrium, $dz_{ij}/dt = 0$. It then follows from (38) that at equilibrium

$$z_{ij} = \frac{\alpha}{\beta + |I|} \tag{39}$$

as in (25), with $\alpha = L$ and $\beta = L - 1$. Both α and β must be positive, which is the case if $L > 1$. By (22), this means that each lateral inhibitory signal $-h(x_k)$, $k \neq i$, is weaker than the direct excitatory signal $Lh(x_i)$, other things being equal.

When top–down signals from F_2 to F_1 supplement a bottom–up input pattern I to F_1, the number $|X|$ of positive activities in X may become smaller than $|I|$ due to the $\frac{2}{3}$ Rule. If v_i remains active after the F_2 node v_j becomes active, (38) generalizes to

$$\frac{d}{dt} z_{ij} = K\left[(1 - z_{ij})L - z_{ij}(|X| - 1)\right]. \tag{40}$$

By combining (36) and (40), both the Associative Decay Rule and the Weber Law Rule for bottom–up LTM traces may be understood as consequences of the LTM equation

$$\frac{d}{dt} z_{ij} = \begin{cases} K\left[(1 - z_{ij})L - z_{ij}(|X| - 1)\right] & \text{if } v_i \text{ and } v_j \text{ are active} \\ -K|X|z_{ij} & \text{if } v_i \text{ is inactive and } v_j \text{ is active} \\ 0 & \text{if } v_j \text{ is inactive.} \end{cases} \tag{41}$$

Evaluation of term $|X|$ in (41) depends upon whether or not a top–down template perturbs F_1 when a bottom–up input pattern I is active.

15. TEMPLATE LEARNING RULE AND ASSOCIATIVE DECAY RULE FOR TOP–DOWN LTM TRACES

The Template Learning Rule and the Associative Decay Rule together imply that the top–down LTM traces in all the pathways from an F_2 node v_j encode the critical feature pattern of all input patterns which have activated v_j without triggering F_2 reset. To see this, as in Section 14, suppose that an input pattern I of 0's and 1's is being learned.

Template Learning Rule

As learning of I takes place, LTM traces in the top–down pathways from an active F_2 node to an active F_1 node approach 1.

The Template Learning Rule and the Associative Decay Rule for top–down LTM traces z_{ji} follow by combining (19) and (20) to obtain

$$\frac{d}{dt} z_{ji} = f(x_j)\left[-z_{ji} + h(x_i)\right]. \tag{42}$$

If the F_2 node v_j is active and the F_1 node v_i is inactive, then $h(x_i) = 0$ and $f(x_j) = 1$, so (42) reduces to

$$\frac{d}{dt} z_{ji} = -z_{ji}. \tag{43}$$

Thus z_{ji} decays exponentially toward zero and the Associative Decay Rule holds. On the other hand, if both v_i and v_j are active, then $f(x_j) = h(x_i) = 1$, so (42) reduces to

$$\frac{d}{dt} z_{ji} = -z_{ji} + 1. \tag{44}$$

Thus z_{ji} increases exponentially toward 1 and the Template Learning Rule holds.

Combining equations (42)–(44) leads to the learning rule governing the LTM traces z_{ji} in a top–down template

$$\frac{d}{dt} z_{ji} = \begin{cases} -z_{ji} + 1 & \text{if } v_i \text{ and } v_j \text{ are active} \\ -z_{ji} & \text{if } v_i \text{ is inactive and } v_j \text{ is active} \\ 0 & \text{if } v_j \text{ is inactive.} \end{cases} \tag{45}$$

Equation (45) says that the template of v_j tries to learn the activity pattern across F_1 when v_j is active.

The $\frac{2}{3}$ Rule controls which nodes v_i in (45) remain active in response to an input pattern I. The $\frac{2}{3}$ Rule implies that if the F_2 node v_j becomes active while the F_1 node v_i is receiving a large bottom–up input I_i, then v_i will remain active only if z_{ji} is sufficiently large. Hence there is some critical strength of the top–down LTM traces such that if z_{ji} falls below that strength, then v_i will never again be active when v_j is active, even if I_i is large. As long as z_{ji} remains above the critical LTM strength, it will increase when I_i is large and v_j is active, and decrease when I_i is small and v_j is active. Once z_{ji} falls below the critical LTM strength, it will decay toward 0 whenever v_j is active; that is, the feature represented by v_i drops out of the critical feature pattern encoded by v_j.

These and related properties of the network can be summarized compactly using the following notation.

Let $\mathbf{I}$ denote the set of indices of nodes v_i which receive a positive input from the pattern I. When I is a pattern of 0's and 1's, then

$$I_i = \begin{cases} 1 & \text{if } i \in \mathbf{I} \\ 0 & \text{otherwise,} \end{cases} \tag{46}$$

where $\mathbf{I}$ is a subset of the F_1 index set $\{1 \ldots M\}$. As in Section 12, let $V^{(j)} = D_1(z_{j1} \cdots z_{ji} \cdots z_{jM})$ denote the template pattern of top–down LTM traces in pathways leading from the F_2 node v_j. The index set $\mathbf{V}^{(j)} = \mathbf{V}^{(j)}(t)$ is defined as follows: $i \in \mathbf{V}^{(j)}$ iff z_{ji} is larger than the critical LTM strength required for v_i to be active when v_j is active and $i \in \mathbf{I}$. For fixed t, let $\mathbf{X}$ denote the subset of indices $\{1 \ldots M\}$ such that $i \in \mathbf{X}$ iff the F_1 node v_i is active at time t.

With this notation, the $\frac{2}{3}$ Rule can be summarized by stating that when a pattern I is presented,

$$\mathbf{X} = \begin{cases} \mathbf{I} & \text{if } F_2 \text{ is inactive} \\ \mathbf{I} \cap \mathbf{V}^{(j)} & \text{if the } F_2 \text{ node } v_j \text{ is active.} \end{cases} \tag{47}$$

The link between STM dynamics at F_1 and F_2 and LTM dynamics between F_1 and F_2 can now be succinctly expressed in terms of (47),

$$\frac{d}{dt} z_{ij} = \begin{cases} K\left[(1 - z_{ij})L - z_{ij}(|\mathbf{X}| - 1)\right] & \text{if } i \in \mathbf{X} \text{ and } f(x_j) = 1 \\ -K|\mathbf{X}|z_{ij} & \text{if } i \notin \mathbf{X} \text{ and } f(x_j) = 1 \\ 0 & \text{if } f(x_j) = 0 \end{cases} \tag{48}$$

and

$$\frac{d}{dt} z_{ji} = \begin{cases} -z_{ji} + 1 & \text{if } i \in \mathbf{X} \text{ and } f(x_j) = 1 \\ -z_{ji} & \text{if } i \notin \mathbf{X} \text{ and } f(x_j) = 1 \\ 0 & \text{if } f(x_j) = 0. \end{cases} \tag{49}$$

A number of definitions that were made intuitively in Sections 3–9 can now be summarized as follows.

Definitions

Coding

An active F_2 node v_J is said to *code* an input I on a given trial if no reset of v_J occurs after the template $V^{(J)}$ is read out at F_1.

Reset could, in principle, occur due to three different factors. The read-out of the template $V^{(J)}$ can change the activity pattern X across F_1. The new pattern X could conceivably generate a maximal input via the $F_1 \to F_2$ adaptive filter to an F_2 node other than v_J. The theorems below show how the $\frac{2}{3}$ Rule and the learning rules prevent template read-out from undermining the choice of v_J via the $F_1 \to F_2$ adaptive filter. Reset of v_J could also, in principle, occur due to the learning induced in the LTM traces z_{iJ} and z_{Ji} by the choice of v_J. In a real-time learning system whose choices are determined by a continuous flow of bottom-up and top-down signals, one cannot take for granted that the learning process, which alters the sizes of these signals, will maintain a choice within a single learning trial. The theorems in the next sections state conditions which prevent either template readout or learning from resetting the F_2 choice via the adaptive filter from F_1 to F_2.

Only the third possible reset mechanism—activation of the orienting subsystem A by a mismatch at F_1—is allowed to reset the F_2 choice. Equations (5) and (47) imply that if v_J becomes active during the presentation of I, then inequality

$$|\mathbf{I} \cap \mathbf{V}^{(J)}| \geq \rho|\mathbf{I}| \tag{50}$$

is a necessary condition to prevent reset of v_J by activation of A. Sufficient conditions are stated in the theorems below.

Direct Access

Pattern I is said to have *direct access* to an F_2 node v_J if presentation of I leads at once to activation of v_J and v_J codes I on that trial.

By Eqs. (13) and (34), input I chooses node v_J first if, for all $j \neq J$,

$$\sum_{i \in I} z_{iJ} > \sum_{i \in I} z_{ij}. \tag{51}$$

The conditions under which v_J then codes I are characterized in the theorems below.

Fast Learning

For the remainder of this article we consider the *fast learning case* in which learning rates enable LTM traces to approximately reach the asymptotes determined by the STM patterns on each trial. Given the fast learning assumption, at the end of a trial during which v_J was active, (48) implies that

$$z_{iJ} \cong \begin{cases} \dfrac{L}{L - 1 + |\mathbf{X}|} & \text{if } i \in \mathbf{X} \\ 0 & \text{if } i \notin \mathbf{X} \end{cases} \tag{52}$$

and (49) implies that

$$z_{Ji} \cong \begin{cases} 1 & \text{if } i \in \mathbf{X} \\ 0 & \text{if } i \notin \mathbf{X}. \end{cases} \tag{53}$$

Thus although $z_{ij} \neq z_{ji}$ in (52) and (53), z_{ij} is large iff z_{ji} is large and $z_{ij} = 0$ iff $z_{ji} = 0$. We can therefore introduce the following definition.

Asymptotic Learning

An F_2 node v_j has *asymptotically learned* the STM pattern X if its LTM traces z_{ij} and z_{ji} satisfy (52) and (53).

By (47), $\mathbf{X}$ in (52) and (53) equals either $\mathbf{I}$ or $\mathbf{I} \cap \mathbf{V}^{(j)}$. This observation motivates the following definition.

Perfect Learning

An F_2 node v_j has *perfectly learned* an input pattern I iff v_j has asymptotically learned the STM pattern $X = I$.

16. DIRECT ACCESS TO NODES CODING PERFECTLY LEARNED PATTERNS

We can now prove the following generalization of the fact that subset and superset nodes can be directly accessed (Sect. 13).

THEOREM 1 (Direct access by perfectly learned patterns). *An input pattern I has direct access to a node v_J which has perfectly learned I if $L > 1$ and all initial bottom–up* LTM *traces satisfy the*

$$\textit{Direct Access Inequality} \qquad 0 < z_{ij}(0) < \frac{L}{L - 1 + M}, \tag{54}$$

where M is the number of nodes in F_1.

Proof. In order to prove that I has direct access to v_J we need to show that: (i) v_J is the first F_2 node to be chosen; (ii) v_J remains the chosen node after its template $V^{(J)}$ is read out at F_1; (iii) read out of $V^{(J)}$ does not lead to F_2 reset by the orienting subsystem; and (iv) v_J remains active as fast learning occurs.

To prove property (i), we must establish that, at the start of the trial, $T_J > T_j$ for all $j \neq J$. When I is presented, $|\mathbf{I}|$ active pathways project to each F_2 node. In particular, by (13) and (34),

$$T_J = D_2 \sum_{i \in \mathbf{I}} z_{iJ} \tag{55}$$

and

$$T_j = D_2 \sum_{i \in \mathbf{I}} z_{ij}. \tag{56}$$

Because node v_J perfectly codes I at the start of the trial, it follows from (52) that

$$z_{iJ} = \begin{cases} \dfrac{L}{L - 1 + |\mathbf{I}|} & \text{if } i \in \mathbf{I} \\ 0 & \text{if } i \notin \mathbf{I}. \end{cases} \tag{57}$$

By (55) and (57),

$$T_J = \frac{D_2 L |\mathbf{I}|}{L - 1 + |\mathbf{I}|}. \tag{58}$$

In order to evaluate T_j in (56), we need to consider nodes v_j which have asymptotically learned a different pattern than I, as well as nodes v_j which are as yet uncommitted. Suppose that v_j, $j \neq J$, has asymptotically learned a pattern $V^{(j)} \neq I$.

Then by (52),

$$z_{ij} = \begin{cases} \dfrac{L}{L - 1 + |\mathbf{V}^{(j)}|} & \text{if } i \in \mathbf{V}^{(j)} \\ 0 & \text{if } i \notin \mathbf{V}^{(j)}. \end{cases} \tag{59}$$

By (59), the only positive LTM traces in the sum $\Sigma_{i \in \mathbf{I}} z_{ij}$ in (56) are the traces with indices $i \in \mathbf{I} \cap \mathbf{V}^{(j)}$. Moreover, all of these positive LTM traces have the same value. Thus (59) implies that

$$T_j = \frac{D_2 L |\mathbf{I} \cap \mathbf{V}^{(j)}|}{L - 1 + |\mathbf{V}^{(j)}|}. \tag{60}$$

We now prove that T_J in (58) is larger than T_j in (60) if $L > 1$; that is,

$$\frac{|\mathbf{I}|}{L - 1 + |\mathbf{I}|} > \frac{|\mathbf{I} \cap \mathbf{V}^{(j)}|}{L - 1 + |\mathbf{V}^{(j)}|}. \tag{61}$$

Suppose first that $|\mathbf{V}^{(j)}| > |\mathbf{I}|$.. Then $|\mathbf{I}| \geq |\mathbf{I} \cap \mathbf{V}^{(j)}|$ and $(L - 1 + |\mathbf{I}|) < (L - 1 + |\mathbf{V}^{(j)}|)$, which together imply (61).

Suppose next that $|\mathbf{V}^{(j)}| \leq |\mathbf{I}|$. Then, since $\mathbf{V}^{(j)} \neq \mathbf{I}$, it follows that $|\mathbf{I}| > |\mathbf{I} \cap \mathbf{V}^{(j)}|$. Thus, since the function $w/(L - 1 + w)$ is an increasing function of w,

$$\frac{|\mathbf{I}|}{L - 1 + |\mathbf{I}|} > \frac{|\mathbf{I} \cap \mathbf{V}^{(j)}|}{L - 1 + |\mathbf{I} \cap \mathbf{V}^{(j)}|}. \tag{62}$$

Finally, since $|\mathbf{V}^{(j)}| \leq |\mathbf{I} \cap \mathbf{V}^{(j)}|$,

$$\frac{|\mathbf{I} \cap \mathbf{V}^{(j)}|}{L - 1 + |\mathbf{I} \cap \mathbf{V}^{(j)}|} \geq \frac{|\mathbf{I} \cap \mathbf{V}^{(j)}|}{L - 1 + |\mathbf{V}^{(j)}|}. \tag{63}$$

Inequalities (62) and (63) together imply (61). This completes the proof that I first activates v_J rather than any other previously coded node v_j.

It remains to prove that I activates v_J rather than an uncommitted node v_j which has not yet been chosen to learn any category. The LTM traces of each uncommitted node v_j obey the Direct Access Inequality (54), which along with $|\mathbf{I}| \leq M$ implies that

$$T_J = \frac{D_2 L |\mathbf{I}|}{L - 1 + |\mathbf{I}|} \geq \frac{D_2 L |\mathbf{I}|}{L - 1 + M} > D_2 \sum_{i \in \mathbf{I}} z_{ij} = T_j. \tag{64}$$

This completes the proof of property (i).

The proof of property (ii), that v_J remains the chosen node after its template $V^{(J)}$ is read out, follows immediately from the fact that $\mathbf{V}^{(J)} = \mathbf{I}$. By (47), the set $\mathbf{X}$ of active nodes remains equal to $\mathbf{I}$ after $V^{(J)}$ is read-out. Thus T_J and T_j are unchanged by read-out of $V^{(J)}$, which completes the proof of property (ii).

Property (iii) also follows immediately from the fact that $\mathbf{I} \cap \mathbf{V}^{(J)} = \mathbf{I}$ in the inequality

$$|\mathbf{I} \cap \mathbf{V}^{(J)}| \geq \rho|\mathbf{I}|. \tag{50}$$

Property (iv) follows from the fact that, while v_J is active, no new learning occurs, since v_J had already perfectly learned input pattern I before the trial began. This completes the proof of Theorem 1.

17. INITIAL STRENGTHS OF LTM TRACES

A. *Direct Access Inequality: Initial Bottom–Up* LTM *Traces are Small*

Theorem 1 shows that the Direct Access Inequality (54) is needed to prevent uncommitted nodes from interfering with the direct activation of perfectly coded nodes. We now show that violation of the Direct Access Inequality may force all uncommitted nodes to code a single input pattern, and thus to drastically reduce the coding capacity of F_2.

To see this, suppose that for all v_j in F_2 and all $i \in \mathbf{I}$,

$$z_{ij}(0) > \frac{L}{L - 1 + |\mathbf{I}|}. \tag{65}$$

Suppose that on the first trial, v_{j_1} is the first F_2 node to be activated by input I. Thus $T_{j_1} > T_j$, where $j \neq j_1$, at the start of the trial. While activation of v_{j_1} persists, T_{j_1} decreases towards the value $D_2L|\mathbf{I}|(L - 1 + |\mathbf{I}|)^{-1}$ due to learning. However, for all $j \neq j_1$,

$$T_j = D_2 \sum_{i \in \mathbf{I}} z_{ij}(0) > \frac{D_2L|\mathbf{I}|}{L - 1 + |\mathbf{I}|}. \tag{66}$$

By (66), T_{j_1} eventually decreases so much that $T_{j_1} = T_{j_2}$ for some other node v_{j_2} in F_2. Thereafter, T_{j_1} and T_{j_2} both approach $D_2L|\mathbf{I}|(L - 1 + |\mathbf{I}|)^{-1}$ as activation alternates between v_{j_1} and v_{j_2}. Due to inequality (65), all F_2 nodes v_j eventually are activated and their T_j values decrease towards $D_2L|\mathbf{I}|(L - 1 + |\mathbf{I}|)^{-1}$. Thus *all* the F_2 nodes asymptotically learn the same input pattern I. The Direct Access Inequality (54) prevents these anomalies from occurring. It makes precise the idea that the initial values of the bottom–up LTM traces $z_{ij}(0)$ must not be too large.

B. *Template Learning Inequality: Initial Top–Down Traces are Large*

In contrast, the initial top–down LTM traces $z_{ji}(0)$ must not be too small. The $\frac{2}{3}$ Rule implies that if the initial top–down LTM traces $z_{ji}(0)$ were too small, then no uncommitted F_2 node could ever learn any input pattern, since all F_1 activity would be quenched as soon as F_2 became active.

To understand this issue more precisely, suppose that an input I is presented. While F_2 is inactive, $\mathbf{X} = \mathbf{I}$. Suppose that, with or without a search, the uncommitted F_2 node v_J becomes active on that trial. In order for v_J to be able to encode I given an arbitrary value of the vigilance parameter ρ, it is necessary that $\mathbf{X}$ remain equal to $\mathbf{I}$ after the template $V^{(J)}$ has been read out; that is,

$$\mathbf{I} \cap \mathbf{V}^{(J)}(0) = \mathbf{I} \qquad \text{for any } I. \tag{67}$$

Because I is arbitrary, the $\frac{2}{3}$ Rule requires that $\mathbf{V}^{(J)}$ initially be the entire set $\{1,\ldots,M\}$. In other words, the initial strengths of all the top–down LTM traces $z_{J1}\ldots z_{JM}$ must be greater than the critical LTM strength, denoted by $\bar{z}$, that is required to maintain suprathreshold STM activity in each F_1 node v_i such that $i \in \mathbf{I}$. Equation (49) and the $\frac{2}{3}$ Rule then imply that, as long as I persists and v_J remains active, $z_{Ji} \to 1$ for $i \in \mathbf{I}$ and $z_{Ji} \to 0$ for $i \notin \mathbf{I}$. Thus $\mathbf{V}^{(J)}$ contracts from $\{1,\ldots,M\}$ to $\mathbf{I}$ as the node v_J encodes the pattern I.

It is shown in the Appendix that the following inequalities imply the $\frac{2}{3}$ Rule

$\frac{2}{3}$ Rule Inequalities

$$\max\{1, D_1\} < B_1 < 1 + D_1; \tag{68}$$

and that the critical top–down LTM strength is

$$\bar{z} \equiv \frac{B_1 - 1}{D_1}. \tag{69}$$

Then the

Template Learning Inequality

$$1 \geq z_{ji}(0) > \bar{z} \tag{70}$$

implies that $\mathbf{V}^{(j)}(0) = \{1\ldots M\}$ for all j, so (67) holds.

C. *Activity-Dependent Nonspecific Tuning of Initial* LTM *Values*

Equations (52) and (53) suggest a simple developmental process by which the opposing constraints on $z_{ij}(0)$ and $z_{ji}(0)$ of Sections 17A and B can be achieved. Suppose that at a developmental stage prior to the category learning stage, all F_1 and F_2 nodes become endogenously active. Let this activity nonspecifically influence F_1 and F_2 nodes for a sufficiently long time interval to allow their LTM traces to approach their asymptotic values. The presence of noise in the system implies that the initial z_{ij} and z_{ji} values are randomly distributed close to these asymptotic values. At the end of this stage, then,

$$z_{ij}(0) \cong \frac{L}{L - 1 + M} \tag{71}$$

and

$$z_{ji}(0) \cong 1 \tag{72}$$

for all $i = 1\ldots M$ and $j = M + 1\ldots N$. The bottom–up LTM traces $z_{ij}(0)$ and the top–down LTM traces $z_{ji}(0)$ are then as large as possible, and still satisfy the Direct Access Inequality (54) and the Template Learning Inequality (70). Switching from this early developmental stage to the category learning stage could then be viewed as a switch from an endogenous source of broadly-distributed activity to an exogenous source of patterned activity.

18. SUMMARY OF THE MODEL

Below, we summarize the hypotheses that define the model. All subsequent theorems in the article assume that these hypotheses hold.

Binary Input Patterns

$$I_i = \begin{cases} 1 & \text{if } i \in \mathbf{I} \\ 0 & \text{otherwise.} \end{cases} \tag{46}$$

Automatic Bottom–Up Activation and $\frac{2}{3}$ Rule

$$\mathbf{X} = \begin{cases} \mathbf{I} & \text{if } F_2 \text{ is inactive} \\ \mathbf{I} \cap \mathbf{V}^{(j)} & \text{if the } F_2 \text{ node } v_j \text{ is active.} \end{cases} \tag{47}$$

Weber Law Rule and Bottom–Up Associative Decay Rule

$$\frac{d}{dt} z_{ij} = \begin{cases} K\left[(1 - z_{ij})L - z_{ij}(|\mathbf{X}| - 1)\right] & \text{if } i \in \mathbf{X} \text{ and } f(x_j) = 1 \\ -K|\mathbf{X}|z_{ij} & \text{if } i \notin \mathbf{X} \text{ and } f(x_j) = 1 \\ 0 & \text{if } f(x_j) = 0. \end{cases} \tag{48}$$

Template Learning Rule and Top–Down Associative Decay Rule

$$\frac{d}{dt} z_{ji} = \begin{cases} -z_{ji} + 1 & \text{if } i \in \mathbf{X} \text{ and } f(x_j) = 1 \\ -z_{ji} & \text{if } i \notin \mathbf{X} \text{ and } f(x_j) = 1 \\ 0 & \text{if } f(x_j) = 0. \end{cases} \tag{49}$$

Reset Rule

An active F_2 node v_j is reset if

$$\frac{|\mathbf{I} \cap \mathbf{V}^{(j)}|}{|\mathbf{I}|} < \rho \equiv \frac{P}{Q}. \tag{73}$$

Once a node is reset, it remains inactive for the duration of the trial.

F_2 Choice and Search

If $\mathbf{J}$ is the index set of F_2 nodes which have not yet been reset on the present learning trial, then

$$f(x_j) = \begin{cases} 1 & \text{if } T_j = \max\{T_k : k \in \mathbf{J}\} \\ 0 & \text{otherwise,} \end{cases} \tag{24}$$

where

$$T_j = D_2 \sum_{i \in \mathbf{X}} z_{ij}. \tag{74}$$

In addition, all STM activities x_i and x_j are reset to zero after each learning trial. The initial bottom-up LTM traces $z_{ij}(0)$ are chosen to satisfy the

Direct Access Inequality

$$0 < z_{ij}(0) < \frac{L}{L-1+M}. \tag{54}$$

The initial top-down LTM traces are chosen to satisfy the

Template Learning Inequality

$$1 \geq z_{ji}(0) > \bar{z} \equiv \frac{B_1 - 1}{D_1}. \tag{75}$$

Fast Learning

It is assumed that fast learning occurs so that, when v_j in F_2 is active, all LTM traces approach the asymptotes,

$$z_{ij} \cong \begin{cases} \dfrac{L}{L-1+|\mathbf{X}|} & \text{if } i \in \mathbf{X} \\ 0 & \text{if } i \notin \mathbf{X} \end{cases} \tag{52}$$

and

$$z_{ji} \cong \begin{cases} 1 & \text{if } i \in \mathbf{X} \\ 0 & \text{if } i \notin \mathbf{X}. \end{cases} \tag{53}$$

on each learning trial. A complete listing of parameter constraints is provided in Table 1.

TABLE 1
Parameter Constraints

$A_1 \geq 0$
$C_1 \geq 0$
$\max\{1, D_1\} < B_1 < 1 + D_1$
$0 < \varepsilon \ll 1$
$K = O(1)$
$L > 1$
$0 < \rho \leq 1$
$0 < z_{ij}(0) < \dfrac{L}{L-1+M}$
$1 \geq z_{ji}(0) > \bar{z} \equiv \dfrac{B_1 - 1}{D_1}$
$0 \leq I_i, f, g, h \leq 1$

19. ORDER OF SEARCH AND STABLE CHOICES IN SHORT-TERM MEMORY

We will now analyze further properties of the class of ART systems which satisfy the hypotheses in Section 18. We will begin by characterizing the order of search. This analysis provides a basis for proving that learning self-stabilizes and leads to recognition by direct access.

This discussion of search order does not analyse where the search ends. Other things being equal, a network with a higher level of vigilance will require better F_1 matches, and hence will search more deeply, in response to each input pattern. The set of learned filters and templates thus depends upon the prior levels of vigilance, and the same ordering of input patterns may generate different LTM encodings due to the settings of the nonspecific vigilance parameter. The present discussion considers the order in which search will occur in response to a single input pattern which is presented after an arbitrary set of prior inputs has been asymptotically learned.

We will prove that the values of the F_2 input functions T_j at the start of each trial determine the order in which F_2 nodes are searched, assuming that no F_2 nodes are active before the trial begins. To distinguish these initial T_j values from subsequent T_j values, let O_j denote the value of T_j at the start of a trial. We will show that, if these values are ordered by decreasing size, as in

$$O_{j_1} > O_{j_2} > O_{j_3} > \cdots, \tag{76}$$

then F_2 nodes are searched in the order $v_{j_1}, v_{j_2}, v_{j_3}, \ldots$ on that trial. To prove this result, we first derive a formula for O_j.

When an input I is first presented on a trial,

$$O_j = D_2 \sum_{i \in \mathbf{I}} z_{ij}, \tag{77}$$

where the z_{ij}'s are evaluated at the start of the trial. By the Associative Decay Rule, z_{ij} in (77) is positive only if $i \in \mathbf{V}^{(j)}$, where $\mathbf{V}^{(j)}$ is also evaluated at the start of the trial. Thus by (77),

$$O_j = D_2 \sum_{i \in \mathbf{I} \cap \mathbf{V}^{(j)}} z_{ij}. \tag{78}$$

If the LTM traces z_{ij} have undergone learning on a previous trial, then (52) implies

$$z_{ij} = \frac{L}{L - 1 + |\mathbf{V}^{(j)}|} \tag{79}$$

for all $i \in \mathbf{V}^{(j)}$. If v_j is an uncommitted node, then the Template Learning Inequality implies that $\mathbf{I} \cap \mathbf{V}^{(j)} = \mathbf{I}$. Combining these facts leads to the following formula for O_j.

Order Function

$$O_j = \begin{cases} \dfrac{D_2 L|\mathbf{I} \cap \mathbf{V}^{(j)}|}{L - 1 + |\mathbf{V}^{(j)}|} & \text{if } v_j \text{ has been chosen on a previous trial} \\ D_2 \Sigma_{i \in \mathbf{I}} z_{ij}(0) & \text{if } v_j \text{ is an uncommitted node.} \end{cases} \tag{80}$$

In response to input pattern I, (76) implies that node v_{j_1} is initially chosen by F_2. After v_{j_1} is chosen, it reads-out template $V^{(j_1)}$ to F_1. When $V^{(j_1)}$ and I both perturb F_1, a new activity pattern X is registered at F_1, as in Fig. 4b. By the $\frac{2}{3}$ Rule, $\mathbf{X} = \mathbf{I} \cap \mathbf{V}^{(j_1)}$. Consequently, a new bottom-up signal pattern from F_1 to F_2 will then be registered at F_2. How can we be sure that v_{j_1} will continue to receive the largest input from F_1 after its template is processed by F_1? In other words, does read-out of the top-down template $V^{(j_1)}$ confirm the choice due to the ordering of bottom-up signals O_j in (76)? Theorem 2 provides this guarantee. Then Theorem 3 shows that the ordering of initial T_j values determines the order of search on each trial despite the fact that the T_j values can fluctuate dramatically as different F_2 nodes get activated.

THEOREM 2 (Stable choices in STM). *Assume the model hypotheses of Section* 18. *Suppose that an F_2 node v_J is chosen for* STM *storage instead of another node v_j because $O_J > O_j$. Then read-out of the top-down template $V^{(J)}$ preserves the inequality $T_J > T_j$ and thus confirms the choice of v_J by the bottom-up filter.*

Proof. Suppose that a node v_J is activated due to the input pattern I, and that v_J is not an uncommitted node. When v_J reads out the template $V^{(J)}$ to F_1, $\mathbf{X} = \mathbf{I} \cap \mathbf{V}^{(J)}$ by the $\frac{2}{3}$ Rule. Then

$$T_j = D_2 \sum_{i \in \mathbf{I} \cap \mathbf{V}^{(J)}} z_{ij}. \tag{81}$$

Since $z_{ij} > 0$ only if $i \in \mathbf{V}^{(j)}$,

$$T_j = D_2 \sum_{i \in \mathbf{I} \cap \mathbf{V}^{(J)} \cap \mathbf{V}^{(j)}} z_{ij}. \tag{82}$$

By (79), if T_j is not an uncommitted node,

$$T_j = \frac{D_2 L |\mathbf{I} \cap \mathbf{V}^{(J)} \cap \mathbf{V}^{(j)}|}{L - 1 + |\mathbf{V}^{(j)}|}. \tag{83}$$

By (80) and (83),

$$T_j \leq O_j. \tag{84}$$

Similarly, if v_j is an uncommitted node, the sum T_j in (82) is less than or equal to the sum O_j in (80). Thus read-out of template $V^{(J)}$ can only cause the bottom-up signals T_j, other than T_J, to decrease. Signal T_J, on the other hand, remains unchanged after read-out of $V^{(J)}$. This can be seen by replacing $V^{(j)}$ in (83) by $V^{(J)}$. Then

$$T_J = \frac{D_2 L |\mathbf{I} \cap \mathbf{V}^{(J)}|}{L - 1 + |\mathbf{V}^{(J)}|}. \tag{85}$$

Hence, after $V^{(J)}$ is read-out

$$T_J = O_J. \tag{86}$$

Combining (84) and (86) shows that inequality $T_J > T_j$ continues to hold after $V^{(J)}$

is read out, thereby proving that top–down template read-out confirms the F_2 choice of the bottom–up filter.

The same is true if v_J is an uncommitted node. Here, the Template Learning Inequality shows that $\mathbf{X} = \mathbf{I}$ even after $v^{(J)}$ is read out. Thus *all* bottom–up signals T_j remain unchanged after template read-out in this case. This completes the proof of Theorem 2.

Were the $\frac{2}{3}$ Rule not operative, read-out of the template $V^{(j_1)}$ might activate many F_1 nodes that had not previously been activated by the input I alone. For example, a top–down template could, in principle, activate all the nodes of F_1, thereby preventing the input pattern, as a pattern, from being coded. Alternatively, disjoint input patterns could be coded by a single node, despite the fact that these two patterns do not share any features. The $\frac{2}{3}$ Rule prevents such coding anomalies from occurring.

THEOREM 3 (Initial filter values determine search order). *The Order Function O_j determines the order of search no matter how many times F_2 is reset during a trial.*

Proof. Since $O_{j_1} > O_{j_2} > \cdots$, node v_{j_1} is the first node to be activated on a given trial. After template $V^{(j_1)}$ is read out, Theorem 2 implies that

$$T_{j_1} = O_{j_1} > \max\{O_j: j \neq j_1\} \geq \max\{T_j: j \neq j_1\}, \tag{87}$$

even though the full ordering of the T_j's may be different from that defined by the O_j's. If v_{j_1} is reset by the orienting subsystem, then template $V^{(j_1)}$ is shut off for the remainder of the trial and subsequent values of T_{j_1} do not influence which F_2 nodes will be chosen.

As soon as v_{j_1} and $V^{(j_1)}$ are shut off, $T_j = O_j$ for all $j \neq j_1$. Since $O_{j_2} > O_{j_3} > \cdots$, node v_{j_2} is chosen next and template $V^{(j_2)}$ is read-out. Theorem 2 implies that

$$T_{j_2} = O_{j_2} > \max\{O_j: j \neq j_1, j_2\} \geq \max\{T_j: j \neq j_1, j_2\}. \tag{88}$$

Thus $V^{(j_2)}$ confirms the F_2 choice due to O_{j_2} even though the ordering of T_j values may differ both from the ordering of O_j values and from the ordering of T_j values when $V^{(j_1)}$ was active.

This argument can now be iterated to show that the values $O_{j_1} > O_{j_2} > \cdots$ of the Order Function determine the order of search. This completes the proof of Theorem 3.

20. STABLE CATEGORY LEARNING

Theorems 2 and 3 describe choice and search properties which occur on such a fast time scale that no new learning can occur. We now analyse properties of learning throughout an entire trial, and use these properties to show that code learning self-stabilizes across trials in response to an arbitrary list of binary input patterns. In Theorem 2, we proved that read-out of a top–down template confirms the F_2 choice made by the bottom–up filter. In Theorem 4, we will prove that learning also confirms the F_2 choice and does not trigger reset by the orienting subsystem. In addition, learning on a single trial causes monotonic changes in the LTM traces.

THEOREM 4 (Learning on a single trial). *Assume the model hypotheses of Section 18. Suppose that an F_2 node v_J is chosen for* STM *storage and that read-out of the template $V^{(J)}$ does not immediately lead to reset of node v_J by the orienting subsystem. Then the* LTM *traces z_{iJ} and z_{Ji} change monotonically in such a way that T_J increases and all other T_j remain constant, thereby confirming the choice of v_J by the adaptive filter. In addition, the set $\mathbf{I} \cap \mathbf{V}^{(J)}$ remains constant during learning, so that learning does not trigger reset of v_J by the orienting subsystem.*

Proof. We first show that the LTM traces $z_{Ji}(t)$ can only change monotonically and that the set $\mathbf{X}(t)$ does not change as long as v_J remains active. These conclusions follow from the learning rules for the top-down LTM traces z_{Ji}. Using these facts, we then show that the $z_{iJ}(t)$ change monotonically, that $T_J(t)$ can only increase, and that all other $T_j(t)$ must be constant while v_J remains active. These conclusions follow from the learning rules for the bottom-up LTM traces z_{iJ}. Together, these properties imply that learning confirms the choice of v_J and does not trigger reset of v_J by the orienting subsystem.

Suppose that read-out of $V^{(J)}$ is first registered by F_1 at time $t = t_0$. By the $\frac{2}{3}$ Rule, $\mathbf{X}(t_0) = \mathbf{I} \cap \mathbf{V}^{(J)}(t_0)$. By (49), $z_{Ji}(t)$ begins to increase towards 1 if $i \in \mathbf{X}(t_0)$, and begins to decrease towards 0 if $i \notin \mathbf{X}(t_0)$. The Appendix shows that when v_J is active at F_2, each activity x_i in F_2 obeys the equation

$$\varepsilon \frac{dx_i}{dt} = -x_i + (1 - A_1 x_i)(I_i + D_1 z_{Ji}) - (B_1 + C_1 x_i). \tag{89}$$

By (89), $x_i(t)$ increases if $z_{Ji}(t)$ increases, and $x_i(t)$ decreases if $z_{Ji}(t)$ decreases. Activities x_i which start out positive hereby become even larger, whereas activities x_i which start out non-positive become even smaller. In particular, $\mathbf{X}(t) = \mathbf{X}(t_0) = \mathbf{I} \cap \mathbf{V}^{(J)}(t_0)$ for all times $t \geq t_0$ at which v_J remains active.

We next prove that $T_J(t)$ increases, whereas all other $T_j(t)$ remain constant, while v_J is active. We suppose first that v_J is not an uncommitted node before considering the case in which v_J is an uncommitted node. While v_J remains active, the set $\mathbf{X}(t) = \mathbf{I} \cap \mathbf{V}^{(J)}(t_0)$. Thus

$$T_J(t) = D_2 \sum_{i \in \mathbf{I} \cap \mathbf{V}^{(J)}(t_0)} z_{iJ}(t). \tag{90}$$

At time $t = t_0$, each LTM trace in (90) satisfies

$$z_{iJ}(t_0) \cong \frac{L}{L - 1 + |\mathbf{V}^{(J)}(t_0)|} \tag{91}$$

due to (79). While v_J remains active, each of these LTM traces responds to the fact that $\mathbf{X}(t) = \mathbf{I} \cap \mathbf{V}^{(J)}(t_0)$. By (47) and (52), each $z_{iJ}(t)$ with $i \in \mathbf{I} \cap \mathbf{V}^{(J)}(t_0)$ increases towards

$$\frac{L}{L - 1 + |\mathbf{I} \cap \mathbf{V}^{(J)}(t_0)|}, \tag{92}$$

each $z_{iJ}(t)$ with $i \notin \mathbf{I} \cap \mathbf{V}^{(J)}(t_0)$ decreases towards 0, and all other bottom-up

LTM traces $z_{iJ}(t)$ remain constant. A comparison of (91) with (92) shows that $T_J(t)$ in (90) can only increase while v_J remains active. In contrast, all other $T_j(t)$ are constant while v_J remains active.

If v_J is an uncommitted node, then no LTM trace $z_{iJ}(t)$ changes before time $t = t_0$. Thus

$$z_{iJ}(t_0) = z_{iJ}(0), \qquad i = 1,2,\ldots, M. \tag{93}$$

By the Template Learning Inequality (75), $\mathbf{I} \cap \mathbf{V}^{(J)}(t_0) = \mathbf{I}$, so that (90) can be written as

$$T_J(t) = D_2 \sum_{i \in \mathbf{I}} z_{iJ}(t). \tag{94}$$

By (93) and the Direct Access Inequality (54),

$$z_{iJ}(t_0) < \frac{L}{L - 1 + M}, \qquad i = 1,2,\ldots, M. \tag{95}$$

While v_J remains active, $\mathbf{X}(t) = \mathbf{I} \cap \mathbf{V}^{(J)}(t_0) = \mathbf{I}$, so that each $z_{iJ}(t)$ in (94) approaches the value

$$\frac{L}{L - 1 + |\mathbf{I}|}. \tag{96}$$

Since $|\mathbf{I}| \leq M$ for any input pattern I, a comparison of (95) and (96) shows that each $z_{iJ}(t)$ with $i \in \mathbf{I}$ increases while v_J remains active. In contrast, each $z_{iJ}(t)$ with $i \notin \mathbf{I}$ decreases towards zero and all other $z_{ij}(t)$ remain constant. Consequently, by (94), $T_J(t)$ increases and all other $T_j(t)$ are constant while v_J remains active. Thus learning confirms the choice of v_J. Hence the set $\mathbf{X}(t)$ remains constant and equal to $\mathbf{I} \cap \mathbf{V}^{(J)}(t_0)$ while learning proceeds.

This last fact, along with the hypothesis that read-out of $V^{(J)}$ does not immediately cause reset of v_J, implies that learning cannot trigger reset of v_J. By the Reset Rule (73), the hypothesis that read-out of $V^{(J)}$ does not immediately cause reset of v_J implies that

$$|\mathbf{I} \cap \mathbf{V}^{(J)}(t_0)| = |\mathbf{X}(t_0)| \geq \rho |\mathbf{I}|. \tag{97}$$

The fact that $\mathbf{X}(t)$ does not change while v_J remains active implies that

$$|\mathbf{X}(t)| = |\mathbf{X}(t_0)| \geq \rho |\mathbf{I}| \tag{98}$$

and hence that learning does not trigger reset of v_J. Thus v_J remains active and learning in its LTM traces $z_{iJ}(t)$ and $z_{Ji}(t)$ can continue until the trial is ended. This completes the proof of Theorem 4.

Theorems 2–4 immediately imply the following important corollary, which illustrates how $\frac{2}{3}$ Rule matching, the learning laws, and the Reset Rule work together to prevent spurious reset events.

COROLLARY 1 (Reset by mismatch). *An active F_2 node v_J can be reset only by the orienting subsystem. Reset occurs when the template $V^{(J)}$ causes an F_1 mismatch such that*

$$|\mathbf{I} \cap \mathbf{V}^{(J)}| < \rho|\mathbf{I}|. \tag{99}$$

Reset cannot be caused within the attentional subsystem due to reordering of adaptive filter signals T_j by template read-out or due to learning.

Theorem 4 implies another important corollary which characterizes how a template changes due to learning on a given trial.

COROLLARY 2 (Subset recoding). *If an F_2 node v_J is activated due to an input I and if read-out of $V^{(J)}$ at time $t = t_0$ implies that*

$$\left|\mathbf{I} \cap \mathbf{V}^{(J)}(t_0)\right| \geq \rho|\mathbf{I}|, \tag{100}$$

then v_J remains active until I shuts off, and the template set $\mathbf{V}^{(J)}(t)$ contracts from $\mathbf{V}^{(J)}(t_0)$ to $\mathbf{I} \cap \mathbf{V}^{(J)}(t_0)$.

With these results in hand, we can now prove that the learning process self-stabilizes in response to an arbitrary list of binary input patterns.

THEOREM 5 (Stable category learning). *Assume the model hypotheses of Section* 18. *Then in response to an arbitrary list of binary input patterns, all* LTM *traces $z_{ij}(t)$ and $z_{ji}(t)$ approach limits after a finite number of learning trials. Each template set $\mathbf{V}^{(j)}$ remains constant except for at most $M - 1$ times $t_1^{(j)} < t_2^{(j)} < \cdots < t_{r_j}^{(j)}$ at which it progressively loses elements, leading to the*

Subset Recoding Property $$\mathbf{V}^{(j)}\left(t_1^{(j)}\right) \supset \mathbf{V}^{(j)}\left(t_2^{(j)}\right) \supset \cdots \supset \mathbf{V}^{(j)}\left(t_{r_j}^{(j)}\right). \tag{101}$$

All LTM *traces oscillate at most once due to learning. The* LTM *traces $z_{ij}(t)$ and $z_{ji}(t)$ such that $i \notin V^{(j)}(t_1^{(j)})$ decrease monotonically to zero. The* LTM *traces $z_{ij}(t)$ and $z_{ji}(t)$ such that $i \in \mathbf{V}^{(j)}(t_{r_j}^{(j)})$ are monotone increasing functions. The* LTM *traces $z_{ij}(t)$ and $z_{ji}(t)$ such that $i \in \mathbf{V}^{(j)}(t_k^{(j)})$ but $i \notin \mathbf{V}^{(j)}(t_{k+1}^{(j)})$ can increase at times $t \leq t_{k+1}^{(j)}$ but can only decrease towards zero at times $t > t_{k+1}^{(j)}$.*

Proof. Suppose that an input pattern I is presented on a given trial and the Order Function satisfies

$$O_{j_1} > O_{j_2} > O_{j_3} > \cdots. \tag{76}$$

Then no learning occurs while F_2 nodes are searched in the order $v_{j_1}, v_{j_2}, \ldots,$ by Theorem 3. If all F_2 nodes are reset by the search, then no learning occurs on that trial. If a node exists such that

$$|\mathbf{I} \cap \mathbf{V}^{(j)}| \geq \rho|\mathbf{I}|, \tag{102}$$

then search terminates at the first such node, v_{j_k}. Only the LTM traces z_{ij_k} and $z_{j_k i}$ can undergo learning on that trial, by Theorem 4. In particular, if an uncommitted node v_{j_k} is reached by the search, then the Template Learning Inequality implies

$$|\mathbf{I} \cap \mathbf{V}^{(j_k)}| = |\mathbf{I} \cap \mathbf{V}^{(j_k)}(0)| = |\mathbf{I}| \geq \rho|\mathbf{I}| \tag{103}$$

so that its LTM traces undergo learning on that trial. In summary, learning on a given trial can change only the LTM traces of the F_2 node v_{j_k} at which the search ends.

Corollary 2 shows that the template set $\mathbf{V}^{(j_k)}$ of the node v_{j_k} is either constant or contracts due to learning. A contraction can occur on only a finite number of trials, because there are only finitely many nodes in F_1. In addition, there are only finitely many nodes in F_2, hence only finitely many template sets $\mathbf{V}^{(j)}$ can contract. The Subset Recoding Property is hereby proved.

The monotonicity properties of the LTM traces follow from the Subset Recoding Property and Theorem 4. Suppose for definiteness that the search on a given trial terminates at a node v_J in response to an input pattern I. Suppose moreover that the template set $\mathbf{V}^{(J)}(t)$ contracts from $\mathbf{V}^{(J)}(t_k^{(J)})$ to $\mathbf{V}^{(J)}(t_{k+1}^{(J)}) = \mathbf{I} \cap \mathbf{V}^{(J)}(t_k^{(J)})$ due to read-out of the template $V^{(J)}(t_k^{(J)})$ on that trial. A comparison of (91) and (92) shows that each $z_{iJ}(t)$ with $i \in \mathbf{V}^{(J)}(t_{k+1}^{(J)})$ increases from

$$\frac{L}{L - 1 + |\mathbf{V}^{(J)}(t_k^{(J)})|} \tag{104}$$

to

$$\frac{L}{L - 1 + |\mathbf{V}^{(J)}(t_{k+1}^{(J)})|}, \tag{105}$$

that each $z_{iJ}(t)$ with $i \notin \mathbf{V}^{(J)}(t_{k+1}^{(J)})$ decreases towards zero, and that all other bottom-up LTM traces $z_{ij}(t)$ remain constant. In a similar fashion, each $z_{Ji}(t)$ with $i \in \mathbf{V}^{(J)}(t_{k+1}^{(J)})$ remains approximately equal to one, each $z_{Ji}(t)$ with $i \notin \mathbf{V}^{(J)}(t_{k+1}^{(J)})$ decreases towards zero, and all other top-down LTM traces $z_{ji}(t)$ remain constant.

Due to the Subset Recoding Property (101),

$$|\mathbf{V}^{(J)}(t_1^{(J)})| > |\mathbf{V}^{(J)}(t_2^{(J)})| > \cdots > |\mathbf{V}^{(J)}(t_{r_J}^{(J)})|. \tag{106}$$

Thus each LTM trace $z_{iJ}(t)$ with $i \in \mathbf{V}^{(J)}(t_{r_J}^{(J)})$ increases monotonically, as from (104) to (105), on the r_J trials where search ends at v_J and the template set $\mathbf{V}^{(J)}(t)$ contracts. On all other trials, these LTM traces remain constant. The other monotonicity properties are now also easily proved by combining the Subset Recoding Property (101) with the learning properties on a single trial. In particular, by the Subset Recoding Property, no LTM traces change after time

$$t = \max\left\{t_{r_j}^{(j)}: j = M + 1, M + 2, \ldots, N\right\}. \tag{107}$$

Thus all LTM traces approach their limits after a finite number of learning trials. This completes the proof of Theorem 5.

21. CRITICAL FEATURE PATTERNS AND PROTOTYPES

The property of stable category learning can be intuitively summarized using the following definitions.

The *critical feature pattern* at time t of a node v_j is the template $V^{(j)}(t)$. Theorem 5 shows that the critical feature pattern of each node v_j is progressively refined as the learning process discovers the set of features that can match all the input patterns which v_j codes. Theorem 5 also says that the network discovers a set of *self-stabilizing* critical feature patterns as learning proceeds. At any stage of learning, the set of all critical feature patterns determines the order in which previously coded nodes will be activated, via the Order Function

$$O_j = \frac{D_2 L|\mathbf{I} \cap \mathbf{V}^{(j)}|}{L - 1 + |\mathbf{V}^{(j)}|}. \tag{108}$$

The *Reset Function*

$$R_j = \frac{|\mathbf{I} \cap \mathbf{V}^{(j)}|}{|\mathbf{I}|} \tag{109}$$

determines how many of these nodes will actually be searched, and thus which node may be recoded on each trial. In particular, an unfamiliar input pattern which has never before been experienced by the network will directly access a node v_{j_1} if the

Direct Access Conditions

$$O_{j_1} > \max(O_j\colon j \neq j_1) \qquad \text{and} \qquad R_{j_1} \geq \rho. \tag{110}$$

are satisfied.

An important example of direct access occurs when the input pattern I^* satisfies $\mathbf{I}^* = \mathbf{V}^{(j)}$, for some $j = M + 1, M + 2, \ldots, N$. Such an input pattern is called a *prototype*. Due to the Subset Recoding Property (101), at any given time a prototype pattern includes all the features common to the input patterns which have previously been coded by node v_j. Such a prototype pattern may never have been experienced itself. When an unfamiliar prototype pattern is presented for the first time, it will directly access its category v_j and is thus recognized. This property follows from Theorem 1, since v_j has perfectly learned I^*. Moreover, because $\mathbf{I}^* = \mathbf{V}^{(j)}$, a prototype is optimally matched by read-out of the template $V^{(j)}$.

A prototype generates an optimal match in the bottom–up filter, in the top–down template, and at F_1, even though it is unfamiliar. This is also true in human recognition data [20, 22, 23]. Theorem 5 thus implies that an ART system can discover, learn, and recognize stable prototypes of an arbitrary list of input patterns. An ART system also supports direct access by unfamiliar input patterns which are not prototypes, but which share invariant properties with learned prototypes, in the sense that they satisfy the Direct Access Conditions.

22. DIRECT ACCESS AFTER LEARNING SELF-STABILIZES

We can now prove that all patterns directly access their categories after the recognition learning process self-stabilizes. In order to discuss this property precisely, we define three types of learned templates with respect to an input pattern I:

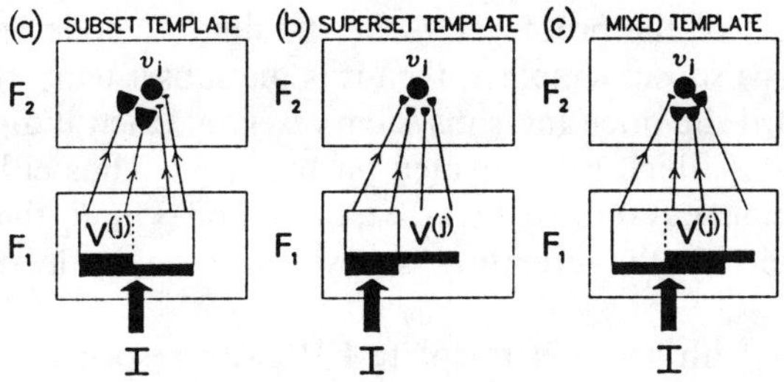

FIG. 11. Subset, superset, and mixed templates $V^{(j)}$ with respect to an input pattern I: In (a), (b), and (c), the lower black bar designates the set of F_1 nodes that receive positive bottom–up inputs due to I. The upper black bar designates the set of F_1 nodes that receive positive top–down inputs due to the template $V^{(j)}$. (a) denotes a subset template $V^{(j)}$ with respect to I. (b) denotes a superset template $V^{(j)}$ with respect to I. (c) denotes a mixed template $V^{(j)}$ with respect to I. When node v_j in F_2 is not an uncommitted node, the top–down LTM traces in the template $V^{(j)}$ are large if and only if the LTM traces in the corresponding bottom–up pathways are large (Sect. 15). The absolute bottom–up LTM trace size depends inversely upon the size $|\mathbf{V}^{(j)}|$ of $V^{(j)}$, due to the Weber Law Rule (Sect. 14). Larger LTM traces are drawn as larger endings on the bottom–up pathways. The arrow heads denote the pathways that are activated by I before any top–down template influences F_1.

subset templates, superset templates, and mixed templates. The LTM traces of a subset template V satisfy $\mathbf{V} \subseteq \mathbf{I}$: they are large only at a subset of the F_1 nodes which are activated by the input pattern I (Fig. 11a). The LTM traces of a superset template V satisfy $\mathbf{V} \supset \mathbf{I}$: they are large at all the F_1 nodes which are activated by the input pattern I, as well as at some F_1 nodes which are not activated by I (Fig. 11b). The LTM traces of a mixed template V are large at some, but not all, the F_1 nodes which are activated by the input pattern I, as well as at some F_1 nodes which are not activated by I: the set $\mathbf{I}$ is neither a subset nor a superset of $\mathbf{V}$ (Fig. 11c).

THEOREM 6 (Direct access after learning self-stabilizes). *Assume the model hypotheses of Section* 18. *After recognition learning has self-stabilized in response to an arbitrary list of binary input patterns, each input pattern I either has direct access to the node v_j which possesses the largest subset template with respect to I, or I cannot be coded by any node of F_2. In the latter case, F_2 contains no uncommitted nodes.*

Remark. The possibility that an input pattern cannot be coded by any node of F_2 is a consequence of the fact that an ART network self-stabilizes its learning in response to a list containing arbitrarily many input patterns no matter how many coding nodes exist in F_2. If a list contains many input patterns and F_2 contains only a few nodes, one does not expect F_2 to code all the inputs if the vigilance parameter ρ is close to 1.

Proof. Since learning has already stabilized, I can be coded only by a node v_j whose template $V^{(j)}$ is a subset template with respect to I. Otherwise, after template $V^{(j)} = V$ was read-out, the set $\mathbf{V}^{(j)}$ would contract from $\mathbf{V}$ to $\mathbf{I} \cap \mathbf{V}$ by Corollary 2 (Sect. 20), thereby contradicting the hypothesis that learning has already stabilized. In particular, input I cannot be coded by a node whose template is a superset template or a mixed template with respect to I. Nor can I be coded by an uncommitted node. Thus if I activates any node other than one with a subset template, that node must be reset by the orienting subsystem.

For the remainder of the proof, let v_J be the first F_2 node activated by I. We show that if $V^{(J)}$ is a subset template, then it is the subset template with the largest index set; and that if the orienting subsystem resets v_J, then it also resets all nodes with subset templates which get activated on that trial. Thus either the node with maximal subset template is directly accessed, or all nodes in F_2 that are activated by I are quickly reset by the orienting subsystem because learning has already self-stabilized.

If v_j is any node with a subset template $V^{(j)}$ with respect to I, then the Order Function

$$O_j = \frac{D_2 L|\mathbf{V}^{(j)}|}{L - 1 + |\mathbf{V}^{(j)}|}, \tag{111}$$

by (108). Function O_j in (111) is an increasing function of $|\mathbf{V}^{(j)}|$. Thus if the first chosen node v_J has a subset template, then $V^{(J)}$ is the subset template with the largest index set.

If v_j is any node with a subset template $V^{(j)}$ with respect to I, then the Reset Function

$$R_j = \frac{|\mathbf{I} \cap \mathbf{V}^{(j)}|}{|\mathbf{I}|} = \frac{|\mathbf{V}^{(j)}|}{|\mathbf{I}|}, \tag{112}$$

by (109). Once activated, such a node v_j will be reset if

$$R_j < \rho. \tag{113}$$

Thus if the node with the largest index set $\mathbf{V}^{(j)}$ is reset, (112) and (113) imply that all other nodes with subset templates will be reset.

Finally, suppose that v_J, the first node activated, does not have a subset template, but that some node v_j with a subset template is activated in the course of search. We need to show that $|\mathbf{I} \cap \mathbf{V}^{(j)}| = |\mathbf{V}^{(j)}| < \rho|\mathbf{I}|$, so that v_j is reset. Since v_j has a subset template,

$$O_j = \frac{D_2 L|\mathbf{V}^{(j)}|}{L - 1 + |\mathbf{V}^{(j)}|}. \tag{111}$$

Since $|\mathbf{I} \cap \mathbf{V}^{(J)}| \leq |\mathbf{V}^{(J)}|$,

$$O_J = \frac{D_2 L|\mathbf{I} \cap \mathbf{V}^{(J)}|}{L - 1 + |\mathbf{V}^{(J)}|} \leq \frac{D_2 L|\mathbf{V}^{(J)}|}{L - 1 + |\mathbf{V}^{(J)}|}. \tag{114}$$

Since v_J was chosen first, $O_J > O_j$. Comparison of (111) and (114) thus implies that $|\mathbf{V}^{(J)}| > |\mathbf{V}^{(j)}|$. Using the properties $O_j < O_J$, $|\mathbf{I} \cap \mathbf{V}^{(J)}| < \rho|\mathbf{I}|$, and $|\mathbf{V}^{(J)}| > |\mathbf{V}^{(j)}|$ in turn, we find

$$\frac{|\mathbf{V}^{(j)}|}{L - 1 + |\mathbf{V}^{(j)}|} < \frac{|\mathbf{I} \cap \mathbf{V}^{(J)}|}{L - 1 + |\mathbf{V}^{(J)}|} < \frac{\rho|\mathbf{I}|}{L - 1 + |\mathbf{V}^{(J)}|} < \frac{\rho|\mathbf{I}|}{L - 1 + |\mathbf{V}^{(j)}|}, \tag{115}$$

which implies that

$$|\mathbf{I} \cap \mathbf{V}^{(J)}| = |\mathbf{V}^{(J)}| < \rho|\mathbf{I}|. \tag{116}$$

Therefore all F_2 nodes are reset if v_J is reset. This completes the proof of Theorem 6.

Theorem 6 shows that, in response to any familiar input pattern I, the network knows how to directly access the node v_j whose template $V^{(j)}$ corresponds to the prototype $I^* = V^{(j)}$ which is closest to I among all prototypes learned by the network. Because direct access obviates the need for search, recognition of familiar input patterns and of unfamiliar patterns that share categorical invariants with familiar patterns is very rapid no matter how large or complex the learned recognition code may have become. Grossberg and Stone [12] have, moreover, shown that the variations in reaction times and error rates which occur during direct access due to prior priming events are consistent with data collected from human subjects in lexical decision experiments and word familiarity and recall experiments.

Theorems 5 and 6 do not specify how many list presentations and F_2 nodes are needed to learn and recognize an arbitrary list through direct access. We make the following conjecture: in the fast learning case, if F_2 has at least n nodes, then each member of a list of n input patterns which is presented cyclically will have direct access to an F_2 node after at most n list presentations.

Given arbitrary lists of input patterns, this is the best possible result. If the vigilance parameter ρ is close to 1 and if a nested set of n binary patterns is presented in order of decreasing size, then exactly n list presentations are required for the final code to be learned. On the other hand, if a nested set of n patterns is presented in order of increasing size, then only one list presentation is required for the final code to be learned. Thus the number of trials needed to stabilize learning in the fast learning case depends upon both the ordering and the internal structure of the input patterns, as well as upon the vigilance level.

23. ORDER OF SEARCH: MATHEMATICAL ANALYSIS

The Order Function

$$O_j = \frac{D_2 L|\mathbf{I} \cap \mathbf{V}^{(j)}|}{L - 1 + |\mathbf{V}^{(j)}|} \tag{108}$$

for previously coded nodes v_j shows that search order is determined by two opposing tendencies. A node v_j will be searched early if $|\mathbf{I} \cap \mathbf{V}^{(j)}|$ is large and if $|\mathbf{V}^{(j)}|$ is small. Term $|\mathbf{I} \cap \mathbf{V}^{(j)}|$ is maximized if $V^{(j)}$ is a superset template of I. Term $|\mathbf{V}^{(j)}|$ is small if $V^{(j)}$ codes only a few features. The relative importance of the template intersection $|\mathbf{I} \cap \mathbf{V}^{(j)}|$ and the template size $|\mathbf{V}^{(j)}|$ is determined by the size of $L - 1$ in (108). If $L - 1$ is small, both factors are important. If $L - 1$ is large, the template intersection term dominates search order. The next theorem completely characterizes the search order in the case that $L - 1$ is small.

THEOREM 7 (Search order). *Assume the model hypotheses of Section* 18. *Suppose that input pattern I satisfies*

$$L - 1 \leq \frac{1}{|\mathbf{I}|} \tag{117}$$

and

$$|\mathbf{I}| \leq M - 1. \tag{118}$$

Then F_2 nodes are searched in the following order, if they are reached at all.

Subset templates with respect to I are searched first, in order of decreasing size. If the largest subset template is reset, then all subset templates are reset. If all subset templates have been reset and if no other learned templates exist, then the first uncommitted node to be activated will code I. If all subset templates are searched and if there exist learned superset templates but no mixed templates, then the node with the smallest superset template will be activated next and will code I. If all subset templates are searched and if both superset templates $V^{(J)}$ and mixed templates $V^{(j)}$ exist, then v_j will be searched before v_J if and only if

$$|\mathbf{V}^{(j)}| < |\mathbf{V}^{(J)}| \quad \text{and} \quad \frac{|\mathbf{I}|}{|\mathbf{V}^{(J)}|} < \frac{|\mathbf{I} \cap \mathbf{V}^{(j)}|}{|\mathbf{V}^{(j)}|}. \tag{119}$$

If all subset templates are searched and if there exist mixed templates but no superset templates, then a node v_j with a mixed template will be searched before an uncommitted node v_J if and only if

$$\frac{L|\mathbf{I} \cap \mathbf{V}^{(j)}|}{L - 1 + |\mathbf{V}^{(j)}|} > \sum_{i \in \mathbf{I}} z_{iJ}(0). \tag{120}$$

The proof is based upon the following lemma.

LEMMA 1. *If (117) holds, then for any pair of F_2 nodes v_J and v_j with learned templates, $O_J > O_j$ if either*

$$\frac{|\mathbf{I} \cap \mathbf{V}^{(J)}|}{|\mathbf{V}^{(J)}|} > \frac{|\mathbf{I} \cap \mathbf{V}^{(j)}|}{|\mathbf{V}^{(j)}|} \tag{121}$$

or

$$\frac{|\mathbf{I} \cap \mathbf{V}^{(J)}|}{|\mathbf{V}^{(J)}|} = \frac{|\mathbf{I} \cap \mathbf{V}^{(j)}|}{|\mathbf{V}^{(j)}|} \quad \text{and} \quad |\mathbf{V}^{(J)}| > |\mathbf{V}^{(j)}|. \tag{122}$$

Proof of Lemma 1. We need to show that if either (121) or (122) holds, then $O_J > O_j$. By (108), $O_J > O_j$ is equivalent to

$$\begin{aligned} &|\mathbf{I} \cap \mathbf{V}^{(J)}| \cdot |\mathbf{V}^{(j)}| - |\mathbf{I} \cap \mathbf{V}^{(j)}| \cdot |\mathbf{V}^{(J)}| \\ &\quad + (L-1)[|\mathbf{I} \cap \mathbf{V}^{(J)}| - |\mathbf{I} \cap \mathbf{V}^{(j)}|] > 0. \end{aligned} \tag{123}$$

Suppose that (121) holds. Then:

$$|\mathbf{I} \cap \mathbf{V}^{(J)}| \cdot |\mathbf{V}^{(j)}| - |\mathbf{I} \cap \mathbf{V}^{(j)}| \cdot |\mathbf{V}^{(J)}| > 0. \tag{124}$$

Since $L > 1$, inequality (123) then follows at once if $[|\mathbf{I} \cap \mathbf{V}^{(J)}| - |\mathbf{I} \cap \mathbf{V}^{(j)}|] \geq 0$.

Suppose that $|\mathbf{I} \cap \mathbf{V}^{(j)}| > |\mathbf{I} \cap \mathbf{V}^{(J)}|$. Each term in (124) is an integer. The entire left-hand side of (124) is consequently a positive integer, so

$$|\mathbf{I} \cap \mathbf{V}^{(J)}| \cdot |\mathbf{V}^{(j)}| - |\mathbf{I} \cap \mathbf{V}^{(j)}| \cdot |\mathbf{V}^{(J)}| \geq 1 > \frac{|\mathbf{I}| - 1}{|\mathbf{I}|}. \tag{125}$$

Inequality (124) also implies that $|\mathbf{I} \cap \mathbf{V}^{(J)}| \geq 1$, and in general $|\mathbf{I}| \geq |\mathbf{I} \cap \mathbf{V}^{(j)}|$. Thus by (117) and (125),

$$\begin{aligned} |\mathbf{I} \cap \mathbf{V}^{(J)}| \cdot |\mathbf{V}^{(j)}| - |\mathbf{I} \cap \mathbf{V}^{(j)}| \cdot |\mathbf{V}^{(J)}| &> (L-1)(|\mathbf{I}| - 1) \\ &\geq (L-1)\left[|\mathbf{I} \cap \mathbf{V}^{(j)}| - |\mathbf{I} \cap \mathbf{V}^{(J)}|\right]. \end{aligned} \tag{126}$$

Inequality (126) implies (123), and hence $O_J > O_j$.

Suppose next that (122) holds. Then

$$|\mathbf{I} \cap \mathbf{V}^{(J)}| \cdot |\mathbf{V}^{(j)}| - |\mathbf{I} \cap \mathbf{V}^{(j)}| \cdot |\mathbf{V}^{(J)}| = 0. \tag{127}$$

Also, $|\mathbf{V}^{(J)}| > |\mathbf{V}^{(j)}|$, so

$$\frac{|\mathbf{I} \cap \mathbf{V}^{(J)}|}{|\mathbf{I} \cap \mathbf{V}^{(j)}|} = \frac{|\mathbf{V}^{(J)}|}{|\mathbf{V}^{(j)}|} > 1. \tag{128}$$

Equations (127) and (128) imply (123), thereby completing the proof of Lemma 1.

We can now prove the theorem.

Proof of Theorem 7. First we show that a node v_J with a subset template is searched before any node v_j with a mixed or superset template. Since $\mathbf{I} \cap \mathbf{V}^{(J)} = \mathbf{V}^{(J)}$ but $\mathbf{I} \cap \mathbf{V}^{(j)}$ is a proper subset of $\mathbf{V}^{(j)}$,

$$\frac{|\mathbf{I} \cap \mathbf{V}^{(J)}|}{|\mathbf{V}^{(J)}|} = \frac{|\mathbf{V}^{(J)}|}{|\mathbf{V}^{(J)}|} = 1 > \frac{|\mathbf{I} \cap \mathbf{V}^{(j)}|}{|\mathbf{V}^{(j)}|}. \tag{129}$$

By (121) in Lemma 1, $O_J > O_j$. Thus all subset templates are searched before mixed templates or learned superset templates.

We next show that a node v_J with a subset template is also searched before any uncommitted node v_j. Since

$$O_j = D_2 \sum_{i \in \mathbf{I}} z_{ij}, \tag{130}$$

the Direct Access Inequality (54) implies that

$$O_j < \frac{D_2 L |\mathbf{I}|}{L - 1 + M}. \tag{131}$$

The right-hand side of (131) is an increasing function of L. Thus by (117).

$$\frac{D_2 L |\mathbf{I}|}{L - 1 + M} \leq \frac{D_2\left(|\mathbf{I}|^{-1} + 1\right)|\mathbf{I}|}{|\mathbf{I}|^{-1} + M} = \frac{D_2(1 + |\mathbf{I}|)}{|\mathbf{I}|^{-1} + M}. \tag{132}$$

Inequality (118) implies that

$$\frac{D_2(1 + |\mathbf{I}|)}{|\mathbf{I}|^{-1} + M} \leq \frac{D_2 M}{|\mathbf{I}|^{-1} + M} < D_2. \tag{133}$$

On the other hand, since $|\mathbf{V}^{(J)}| \geq 1$,

$$O_J = \frac{D_2 L |\mathbf{V}^{(J)}|}{L - 1 + |\mathbf{V}^{(J)}|} \geq \frac{D_2 L \cdot 1}{L - 1 + 1} = D_2. \tag{134}$$

Inequalities (131)–(134) together imply $O_J > O_j$.

If v_J has a subset template, then $|\mathbf{I} \cap \mathbf{V}^{(J)}| = |\mathbf{V}^{(J)}|$. Thus all nodes with subset templates have the same ratio $|\mathbf{I} \cap \mathbf{V}^{(J)}|\, |\mathbf{V}^{(J)}|^{-1} = 1$. By (122) in Lemma 1, nodes with subset templates are searched in the order of decreasing template size.

If all subset templates are searched and if no other learned templates exist, then an uncommitted node will be activated. This node codes I because it possesses an unlearned superset template that does not lead to F_2 reset.

Suppose all subset templates have been searched and that there exist learned superset templates but no mixed templates. If node v_J has a superset template $V^{(J)}$, then

$$O_J = \frac{D_2 L |\mathbf{I}|}{L - 1 + |\mathbf{V}^{(J)}|}. \tag{135}$$

By (135), the first superset node to be activated is the node v_J whose template is smallest. Node v_J is chosen before any uncommitted node v_j because, by (54),

$$O_J \geq \frac{D_2 L |\mathbf{I}|}{L - 1 + M} > D_2 \sum_{i \in \mathbf{I}} z_{ij}(0) = O_j. \tag{136}$$

If v_J is activated, it codes I because its template satisfies

$$|\mathbf{I} \cap \mathbf{V}^{(J)}| = |\mathbf{I}| \geq \rho |\mathbf{I}|. \tag{137}$$

Suppose that all subset templates are searched and that a superset template $V^{(J)}$ and a mixed template $V^{(j)}$ exist. We prove that $O_j > O_J$ if and only if (119) holds. Suppose that (119) holds. Then also

$$\frac{|\mathbf{I} \cap \mathbf{V}^{(J)}|}{|\mathbf{V}^{(J)}|} = \frac{|\mathbf{I}|}{|\mathbf{V}^{(J)}|} < \frac{|\mathbf{I} \cap \mathbf{V}^{(j)}|}{|\mathbf{V}^{(j)}|}. \tag{138}$$

By condition (121) of Lemma 1, $O_j > O_J$. Conversely, suppose that $O_j > O_J$. Then

$$\frac{|\mathbf{I} \cap \mathbf{V}^{(j)}|}{L - 1 + |\mathbf{V}^{(j)}|} > \frac{|\mathbf{I} \cap \mathbf{V}^{(J)}|}{L - 1 + |\mathbf{V}^{(J)}|} = \frac{|\mathbf{I}|}{L - 1 + |\mathbf{V}^{(J)}|}. \tag{139}$$

Since $V^{(j)}$ is a mixed template with respect to I, $|\mathbf{I} \cap \mathbf{V}^{(j)}| < |\mathbf{I}|$. Thus (139) implies that $|\mathbf{V}^{(j)}| < |\mathbf{V}^{(J)}|$ as well as

$$|\mathbf{I} \cap \mathbf{V}^{(j)}| \cdot |\mathbf{V}^{(J)}| - |\mathbf{I}| \cdot |\mathbf{V}^{(j)}| > (L-1)\big[|\mathbf{I}| - |\mathbf{I} \cap \mathbf{V}^{(j)}|\big] > 0, \qquad (140)$$

from which (119) follows. This completes the proof of Theorem 7.

Note that Lemma 1 also specifies the order of search among mixed templates. If all the activated mixed template nodes are reset, then the node v_J with the minimal superset template will code I. Unless (120) holds, it is possible for an uncommitted node v_J to code I before a node with a mixed template v_j is activated. Inequality (120) does not automatically follow from the Direct Access Inequality (54) because $|\mathbf{I} \cap \mathbf{V}^{(j)}|$ may be much smaller than $|\mathbf{I}|$ when $V^{(j)}$ is a mixed template.

24. ORDER OF SEARCH: COMPUTER SIMULATIONS

Figures 12 and 13 depict coding sequences that illustrate the order of search specified by Theorem 7 when $(L-1)$ is small and when the vigilance parameter ρ is close to 1. In Fig. 12, each of nine input patterns was presented once. Consider the order of search that occurred in response to the final input pattern I that was presented on trial 9. By trial 8, nodes v_{M+1} and v_{M+2} had already encoded subset templates of this input pattern. On trial 9, these nodes were therefore searched in order of decreasing template size. Nodes v_{M+3}, v_{M+4}, v_{M+5}, and v_{M+6} had encoded mixed templates of the input pattern. These nodes were searched in the order $v_{M+3} \rightarrow v_{M+5} \rightarrow v_{M+4}$. This search order was not determined by template size *per se*, but was rather governed by the ratio $|\mathbf{I} \cap \mathbf{V}^{(j)}|\,|\mathbf{V}^{(j)}|^{-1}$ in (121) and (122). These ratios for nodes v_{M+3}, v_{M+5}, and v_{M+4} were $\frac{9}{10}$, $\frac{14}{16}$, and $\frac{7}{8}$, respectively. Since $\frac{14}{16} = \frac{7}{8}$, node v_{M+5} was searched before node v_{M+4} because $|\mathbf{V}^{(M+5)}| = 16 > 8 =$

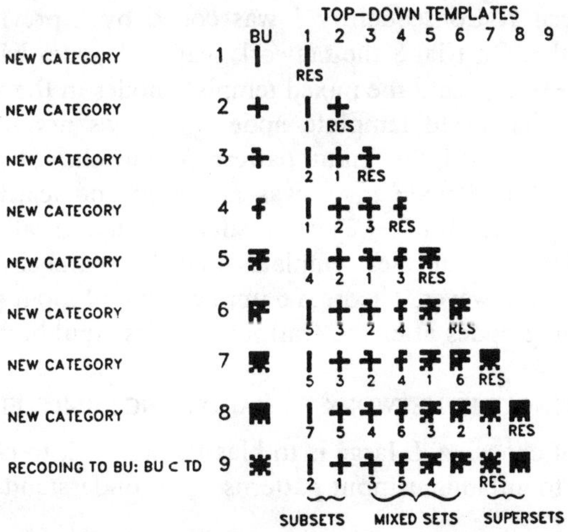

FIG. 12. Computer simulation to illustrate order of search: On trial 9, the system first searches subset templates, next searches some, but not all, mixed templates, and finally recodes the smallest superset template. A smaller choice of vigilance parameter could have terminated the search at a subset template or mixed template node.

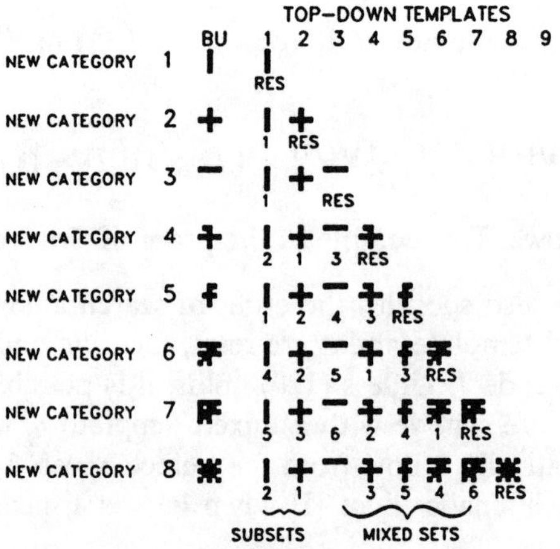

FIG. 13. Computer simulation to illustrate order of search: Unlike the search described in Fig. 12, no learned superset template exists when the search begins on trial 8. Consequently, the system first searches subset templates, next searches mixed templates, and finally terminates the search by coding a previously uncommitted node.

$|\mathbf{V}^{(M+4)}|$. The mixed template node v_{M+6} was not searched. After searching v_{M+5}, the network activated the node v_{M+7} which possessed the smallest superset template. A comparison of rows 8 and 9 in column 7 shows how the superset template of v_{M+7} was recoded to match the input pattern. By (119), the superset template node v_{M+7} was searched before the mixed template node v_{M+6} because the ratio $|\mathbf{I}|\,|\mathbf{V}^{(M+7)}|^{-1} = \frac{17}{21}$ was larger than $|\mathbf{I} \cap \mathbf{V}^{(M+6)}|\,|\mathbf{V}^{(M+6)}|^{-1} = \frac{14}{18}$.

The eight input patterns of Fig. 13 illustrate a search followed by coding of an uncommitted node. The last input pattern I in Fig. 13 is the same as the last input pattern in Fig. 12. In Fig. 13, however, there are no superset templates corresponding to input pattern I. Consequently I was coded by a previously uncommitted node v_{M+8} on trial 8. On trial 8 the network searched nodes with subset templates in the order $v_{M+2} \rightarrow v_{M+1}$ and the mixed template nodes in the order $v_{M+4} \rightarrow v_{M+6} \rightarrow v_{M+5} \rightarrow v_{M+7}$. The mixed template node v_{M+3} was not searched because its template badly mismatched the input pattern I and thus did not satisfy (120). Instead, the uncommitted node v_{M+8} was activated and learned a template that matched the input pattern. If $(L-1)$ is not small enough to satisfy inequality (117), then mixed templates or superset templates may be searched before subset templates. For all $L > 1$, however, Theorem 6 implies that all input patterns have direct access to their coding nodes after the learning process equilibrates.

25. BIASING THE NETWORK TOWARDS UNCOMMITTED NODES

Another effect of choosing L large is to bias the network to choose uncommitted nodes in response to unfamiliar input patterns I. To understand this effect, suppose that for all i and j,

$$z_{ij}(0) \cong \frac{L}{L-1+M}. \tag{71}$$

Then when I is presented, an uncommitted node is chosen before a coded node v_j if

$$\frac{|\mathbf{I} \cap \mathbf{V}^{(j)}|}{L - 1 + |\mathbf{V}^{(j)}|} < \frac{|\mathbf{I}|}{L - 1 + M}. \tag{141}$$

This inequality is equivalent to

$$\frac{|\mathbf{I} \cap \mathbf{V}^{(j)}|}{|\mathbf{I}|} < \frac{L - 1 + |\mathbf{V}^{(j)}|}{L - 1 + M}. \tag{142}$$

As L increases, the ratio

$$\frac{L - 1 + |\mathbf{V}^{(j)}|}{L - 1 + M} \rightarrow 1, \tag{143}$$

whereas the left-hand side of (142) is always less than or equal to 1. Thus for large values of L, the network tends to code unfamiliar input patterns into new categories, even if the vigilance parameter ρ is small. As L increases, the automatic scaling property (Sect. 2A) of the network also becomes weaker, as does the tendency to search subset templates first.

Recall that parameter L describes the relative strength of the bottom–up competition among LTM traces which gives rise to the Weber Law Rule (Sect. 12B), with smaller L corresponding to stronger LTM competition. Thus the structural process of LTM competition works with the state-dependent process of attentional vigilance to control how coarse the learned categories will be.

26. COMPUTER SIMULATION OF SELF-SCALING COMPUTATIONAL UNITS: WEIGHING THE EVIDENCE

We can now understand quantitatively how the network automatically rescales its matching and signal-to-noise criteria in the computer simulations of Fig. 7. On the first four presentations, the input patterns are presented in the order $ABAB$. By trial 2, learning is complete. Pattern A directly accesses node v_{M+1} on trial 3, and pattern B directly accesses node v_{M+2} on trial 4. Thus patterns A and B are coded within different categories. On trials 5–8, patterns C and D are presented in the order $CDCD$. Patterns C and D are constructed from patterns A and B, respectively, by adding identical upper halves to A and B. Thus, pattern C differs from pattern D at the same locations where pattern A differs from pattern B. However, because patterns C and D represent many more active features than patterns A and B, the difference between C and D is treated as noise and is deleted from the critical feature pattern of v_{M+3} which codes both C and D, whereas the difference between A and B is considered significant and is included within the critical feature patterns of v_{M+1} and v_{M+2}.

The core issue in the network's different categorization of patterns A and B versus patterns C and D is the following: Why on trial 2 does B reject the node v_{M+1} which has coded A, whereas D on trial 6 accepts the node v_{M+3} which has coded C? This occurs despite the fact that the mismatch between B and $V^{(M+1)}$ equals the mismatch between D and $V^{(M+3)}$:

$$|\mathbf{B}| - |\mathbf{B} \cap \mathbf{V}^{(M+1)}| = 3 = |\mathbf{D}| - |\mathbf{D} \cap \mathbf{V}^{(M+3)}|. \tag{144}$$

The reason is that

$$\frac{|\mathbf{B} \cap \mathbf{V}^{(M+1)}|}{|\mathbf{B}|} = \frac{8}{11}, \tag{145}$$

whereas

$$\frac{|\mathbf{D} \cap \mathbf{V}^{(M+3)}|}{|\mathbf{D}|} = \frac{14}{17}. \tag{146}$$

In this simulation, the vigilance parameter $\rho = 0.8$. Thus

$$\frac{|\mathbf{B} \cap \mathbf{V}^{(M+1)}|}{|\mathbf{B}|} < \rho < \frac{|\mathbf{D} \cap \mathbf{V}^{(M+3)}|}{|\mathbf{D}|}. \tag{147}$$

By (73), pattern B resets v_{M+1} on trial 2 but D does not reset v_{M+3} on trial 6. Consequently, B is coded by a different category than A, whereas D is coded by the same category as C.

27. CONCLUDING REMARKS: SELF-STABILIZATION AND UNITIZATION WITHIN ASSOCIATIVE NETWORKS

Two main conclusions of our work are especially salient. First, the code learning process is one of progressive refinement of distinctions. The distinctions that emerge are the resultant of all the input patterns which the network ever experiences, rather than of some preassigned features. Second, the matching process compares whole patterns, not just separate features. It may happen that two different input patterns to F_1 overlap a template at the same set of feature detectors, yet the network will reset the F_2 node in response to one input but not the other. The degree of mismatch of template pattern and input pattern *as a whole* determines whether coding or reset will occur. Thus the learning of categorical invariants resolves two opposing tendencies. As categories grow larger, and hence code increasingly global invariants, the templates which define them become smaller, as they discover and base the code on sets of critical feature patterns, or prototypes, rather than upon familiar pattern exemplars. This article shows how these two opposing tendencies can be resolved within a self-organizing system, leading to dynamic equilibration, or self-stabilization, of recognition categories in response to an arbitrary list of arbitrarily many binary input patterns. This self-stabilization property is of major importance for the further development of associative networks and the analysis of cognitive recognition processes.

Now that properties of self-organization, self-stabilization, and self-scaling are completely understood within the class of ART networks described herein, a number of generalizations also need to be studied. Within this article, an input pattern to level F_1 is globally grouped at F_2 when the F_2 population which receives the maximal input from the $F_1 \rightarrow F_2$ adaptive filter is chosen for short term memory (STM) storage. Within the total architecture of an ART system, even this simple type of F_2 reaction to the $F_1 \rightarrow F_2$ adaptive filter leads to powerful coding properties. On the other hand, a level F_2 which makes global choices must be viewed as a special case of a more general design for F_2.

If the second processing stage F_2 makes a choice, then later processing stages which are activated by F_2 alone could not further analyse the input pattern across F_1. The coding hierarchy for individual input patterns would end at the choice, or global grouping, stage. By contrast, a coding scheme wherein F_2 generates a spatially distributed representation of the F_1 activity pattern, rather than a choice, could support subsequent levels $F_3, F_4, \ldots, F_n$ for coding multiple groupings, or chunks, and thus more abstract invariants of an input pattern. This possibility raises many issues concerning the properties of these configurations and their invariants, and of the architectural constraints which enable a multilevel coding hierarchy to learn and recognize distributed invariants in a stable and globally self-consistent fashion.

A parallel neural architecture, called a *masking field* [9, 11, 12, 24–26, 36] is a type of circuit design from which F_2—and by extension higher levels $F_3, F_4, \ldots, F_n$ —may be fashioned to generate distributed representations of filtered input patterns. Masking field properties are of value for visual object recognition, speech recognition, and higher cognitive processes. Indeed, the same circuit design can be used for the development of general spatially distributed self-organizing recognition codes. The purpose of a masking field is to detect simultaneously, and weight properly in STM, all salient parts, or groupings, of an input pattern. The pattern as a whole is but one such grouping. A masking field generates a spatially distributed, yet unitized, representation of the input pattern in STM. Computer simulations of how a masking field can detect and learn unitized distributed representations of an input are found in Cohen and Grossberg [24–26]. Much further work needs to be done to understand the design of ART systems all of whose levels F_i are masking fields.

Other useful generalizations of the ART system analysed herein include systems whose learning rate is slow relative to the time scale of a single trial; systems in which forgetting of LTM values can occur; systems which process continuous as well as binary input and output patterns; and systems in which Weber Law processing is realized through competitive STM interactions among F_1 nodes rather than competitive LTM interactions among bottom-up LTM traces (Sect. 12B). All of these generalizations will be considered in our future articles of this series.

Preprocessing of the input patterns to an ART system is no less important than choosing levels F_i capable of supporting a hierarchy of unitized codes of parts and wholes. In applications to visual object recognition, neural circuits which generate pre-attentively completed segmentations of a visual image before these completed segmentations generate inputs to an ART network have recently been constructed [37–40]. In applications to adaptive speech recognition, inputs are encoded as STM patterns of temporal order information across item representations before these STM patterns generate inputs to an ART network [9, 11–13, 24, 26, 36]. Further work needs to be done to characterize these preprocessing stages and how they are joined to their ART coding networks. Although a great deal of work remains to be done, results such as those in the present article amply illustrate that the whole is much greater than the sum of its parts both in human experience and in self-organizing models thereof.

APPENDIX

Table 1 lists the constraints on the dimensionless model parameters for the system summarized in Section 18. We will now show that the $\frac{2}{3}$ Rule holds when these constraints are satisfied. Then we describe four alternative, but dynamically equivalent, systems for realizing the $\frac{2}{3}$ Rule and attentional gain control.

Recall that x_i ($i = 1 \ldots M$) denotes the STM activity of an F_1 node v_i; that x_j ($j = M + 1 \ldots N$) denotes the STM activity of an F_2 node v_j; that z_{ij} denotes the strength of the LTM trace in the bottom–up pathway from v_i to v_j; that z_{ji} denotes the strength of the LTM trace in the top–down pathway from v_j to v_i; that I_i denotes the bottom–up input to v_i; that $\mathbf{I}$ denotes the set of indices $i \in \{1 \ldots M\} v_i$ such that $I_i > 0$; that $\mathbf{X} = \mathbf{X}(t)$ denotes the set of indices i such that $x_i(t) > 0$; and that $\mathbf{V}^{(j)} = \mathbf{V}^{(j)}(t)$ denotes the set of indices i such that $z_{ji}(t) > \bar{z}$.

Combining equations (8), (10), (11), and (12), we find the following equation for the ith STM trace of F_1

$$\varepsilon \frac{dx_i}{dt} = -x_i + (1 - A_1 x_i)\Big(I_i + D_1 \sum_j f(x_j) z_{ji}\Big) - (B_1 + C_1 x_i) \sum_j f(x_j). \quad \text{(A1)}$$

When F_2 is inactive, all top–down signals $f(x_j) = 0$. Hence by (A1),

$$\varepsilon \frac{dx_i}{dt} = -x_i + (1 - A_1 x_i) I_i. \quad \text{(A2)}$$

When the F_2 node v_J is active, only the top–down signal $f(x_J)$ is nonzero. Since $f(x_J) = 1$,

$$\varepsilon \frac{dx_i}{dt} = -x_i + (1 - A_1 x_i)(I_i + D_1 z_{Ji}) - (B_1 + C_1 x_i). \quad \text{(A3)}$$

Since each x_i variable changes rapidly relative to the rate of change of the LTM trace z_{Ji} (since $0 < \varepsilon \ll 1$), then x_i is always close to its steady state, $dx_i/dt = 0$. By (A2), then

$$x_i \cong \frac{I_i}{1 + A_1 I_i} \quad \text{if } F_2 \text{ is inactive} \quad \text{(A4)}$$

and, by (A3),

$$x_i \cong \frac{I_i + D_1 z_{Ji} - B_1}{1 + A_1(I_i + D_1 z_{Ji}) + C_1} \quad \text{if the } F_2 \text{ node } v_J \text{ is active.} \quad \text{(A5)}$$

The $\frac{2}{3}$ Rule, as defined by

$$\mathbf{X} = \begin{cases} \mathbf{I} & \text{if } F_2 \text{ is inactive} \\ \mathbf{I} \cap \mathbf{V}^{(J)} & \text{if the } F_2 \text{ node } v_J \text{ is active,} \end{cases} \quad (47)$$

can be derived as follows. Note first that (A4) implies that, when F_2 is inactive, $x_i > 0$ iff $I_i > 0$; i.e., $\mathbf{X} = \mathbf{I}$. On the other hand, if v_J is active, (A5) implies that

$$x_i > 0 \quad \text{iff } z_{Ji} > \frac{B_1 - I_i}{D_1}. \quad \text{(A6)}$$

The $\frac{2}{3}$ Rule requires that x_i be positive when the F_1 node v_i is receiving large inputs, both top–down and bottom–up. Thus setting $z_{Ji} = 1$ And $I_i = 1$ (their maximal values) in (A6) implies the constraint:

$$1 > \frac{B_1 - 1}{D_1}. \tag{A7}$$

The $\frac{2}{3}$ Rule also requires that x_i be negative if v_i receives no top–down input, even if the bottom–up input is large. Thus setting $z_{Ji} = 0$ and $I_i = 1$ in (A6) implies the constraint:

$$0 < \frac{B_1 - 1}{D_1}. \tag{A8}$$

Finally, the $\frac{2}{3}$ Rule requires that x_i be negative if v_i receives no bottom–up input, even if the top–down input is large. Thus setting $I_i = 0$ and $z_{Ji} = 1$ in (A6) implies the constraint

$$1 < \frac{B_1}{D_1}. \tag{A9}$$

Inequalities (A7), (A8), and (A9) are summarized by the

$\frac{2}{3}$ Rule Inequalities

$$\max\{1, D_1\} < B_1 < 1 + D_1. \tag{68}$$

Since $0 \le I_i \le 1$, (A6) also shows that if v_J is active and if

$$z_{Ji}(t) \le \frac{B_1 - 1}{D_1}, \tag{A10}$$

then $x_i(t) \le 0$; i.e., $i \notin \mathbf{X}$. However if $i \notin \mathbf{X}$, z_{Ji} decays toward 0 whenever v_J is active. Thus if (A10) is true at some time $t = t_0$, it remains true for all $t \ge t_0$. Therefore

$$\bar{z} \equiv \frac{B_1 - 1}{D_1} \tag{69}$$

is the critical top–down LTM strength such that if $z_{Ji}(t_0) \le \bar{z}$, then $z_{Ji}(t) \le \bar{z}$ for all $t \ge t_0$. Whenever v_J is active and $t \ge t_0$, the F_1 node v_i will be inactive.

Figure 14 depicts four ways in which attentional gain control can distinguish bottom–up and top–down processing to implement the $\frac{2}{3}$ Rule. All of these systems generate the same asymptote (A5) when F_2 is active, and the same asymptotes, up to a minor change in parameters, when F_2 is inactive. The parameters in all four systems are defined to satisfy the constraints in Table 1.

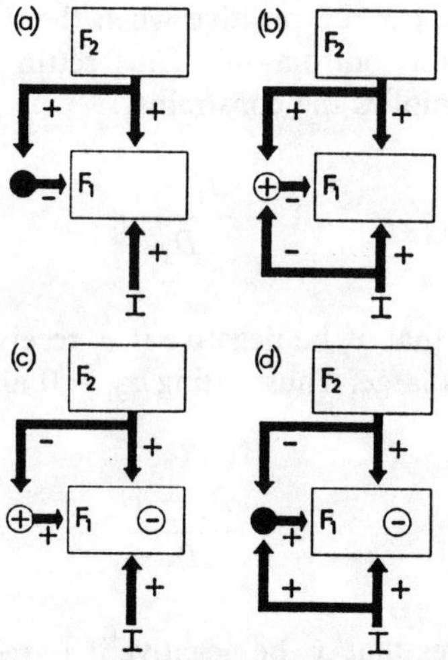

FIG. 14. Design variations for realizing $\frac{2}{3}$ Rule matching properties at F_1: In (a) and (b), F_2 excites the gain control channel, whereas in (c) and (d), F_2 inhibits the gain control channel. In (b), the input pattern I inhibits the gain control channel, whereas in (d), I excites the gain control channel. In (a) and (d), the gain control channel phasically reacts to its inputs (closed circles). Activation of the gain control channel in (a) nonspecifically inhibits F_1, and in (d) nonspecifically excites F_1. In (b) and (c), the gain control channel is tonically, or persistently, active in the absence of inputs (open circles surrounding plus signs). Activation of the gain control channel in (b) nonspecifically inhibits F_1, and in (c) nonspecifically excites F_1. In (c) and (d), the F_1 cells are maintained in a state of tonic hyperpolarization, or inhibition, in the absence of external inputs (open circles surrounding minus signs). All four cases lead to equivalent dynamics.

In Fig. 14a, F_2 can phasically excite the gain control channel, which thereupon nonspecifically inhibits the cells of F_1. Thus

$$\varepsilon \frac{dx_i}{dt} = -x_i + (1 - A_1 x_i)\left(I_i + D_1 \sum_j f(x_j) z_{ji}\right) - (B_1 + C_1 x_i) G_1, \quad \text{(A11)}$$

where

$$G_1 = \begin{cases} 0 & \text{if } I \text{ is active and } F_2 \text{ is inactive} \\ 1 & \text{if } I \text{ is inactive and } F_2 \text{ is active} \\ 1 & \text{if } I \text{ is active and } F_2 \text{ is active} \\ 0 & \text{if } I \text{ is inactive and } F_2 \text{ is inactive.} \end{cases} \quad \text{(A12)}$$

In other words $G_1 = \Sigma_j f(x_j)$. Thus (A11) is just (A1) in a slightly different notation.

In Fig. 14b, the plus sign within an open circle in the gain control channel designates that the gain control cells, in the absence of any bottom–up or top–down signals, are endogenously maintained at an equilibrium potential which exceeds their output threshold. Output signals from the gain control cells nonspecifically inhibit the cells of F_1. In short, the gain control channel tonically, or persistently, inhibits F_1 cells in the absence of bottom–up or top–down signals. Bottom–up and top–down signals phasically modulate the level of nonspecific inhibition. In particular, a bottom–up input alone totally inhibits the gain control channel, thereby disinhibiting the cells of F_1. A top–down signal alone maintains the inhibition from the gain control channel, because the inhibition is either on or off, and is thus not further increased by F_2. When both a bottom–up input and a top–down signal are active, their inputs to the gain control channel cancel, thereby again maintaining the same level of inhibition to F_1. The STM equations at F_1 are

$$\varepsilon \frac{dx_i}{dt} = -x_i + (1 - A_1 x_i)\Big(I_i + D_1 \sum_j f(x_j) z_{ji}\Big) - (B_1 + C_1 x_i) G_2. \quad \text{(A13)}$$

where

$$G_2 = \begin{cases} 0 & \text{if } I \text{ is active and } F_2 \text{ is inactive} \\ 1 & \text{if } I \text{ is inactive and } F_2 \text{ is active} \\ 1 & \text{if } I \text{ is active and } F_2 \text{ is active} \\ 1 & \text{if } I \text{ is inactive and } F_2 \text{ is inactive.} \end{cases} \quad \text{(A14)}$$

The equilibrium activities of x_i are as follows. If I is active and F_2 is inactive, then (A4) again holds. If I is inactive and F_2 is active, then (A5) again holds. Equation (A5) also holds if I is active and F_2 is active. If I is inactive and F_2 is inactive, then

$$x_i \cong \frac{-B_1}{1 + C_1}, \quad \text{(A15)}$$

which is negative; hence no output signals are generated.

In Fig. 14c, as in Fig. 14b, the gain control cells are tonically active (plus sign in open circle). In Fig. 14c, however, these cells nonspecifically excite the cells of F_1. In the absence of any external signals, F_1 cells are maintained in a state of tonic hyperpolarization, or negative activity (denoted by the minus sign in the open circle). The tonic excitation from the gain control cells balances the tonic inhibition due to hyperpolarization and thereby maintains the activity of F_2 cells near their output threshold of zero. A bottom–up input can thereby excite F_1 cells enough for them to generate output signals. When top–down signals are active, they inhibit the gain control cells. Consequently those F_1 cells which do not receive bottom–up or top–down signals become hyperpolarized. Due to tonic hyperpolarization, F_1 cells which receive a bottom–up signal or a top–down signal, but not both, cannot exeed their output threshold. Only F_1 cells at which large top–down and bottom–up signals converge can generate an output signal.

The STM equations at F_1 are

$$\varepsilon \frac{dx_i}{dt} = -x_i + (1 - A_1 x_i)\Big(I_i + D_1 \sum_j f(x_j) z_{ji} + B_1 G_3\Big) - (B_1 + C_1 x_i), \quad \text{(A16)}$$

where

$$G_3 = \begin{cases} 1 & \text{if } I \text{ is active and } F_2 \text{ is inactive} \\ 0 & \text{if } I \text{ is inactive and } F_2 \text{ is active} \\ 0 & \text{if } I \text{ is active and } F_2 \text{ is active} \\ 1 & \text{if } I \text{ is inactive and } F_2 \text{ is inactive.} \end{cases} \tag{A17}$$

The equilibrium activities of x_i are as follows. If I is active and F_2 is inactive, then

$$x_i \cong \frac{I_i}{1 + A_1 I_i + A_1 B_1 + C_1}. \tag{A18}$$

Thus $x_i > 0$ iff $I_i > 0$. If I is inactive and F_2 is active, then (A5) holds. If I is active and F_2 is active, then (A5) holds. If I is inactive and F_2 is inactive, then

$$x_i \cong \frac{B_1 - B_1}{1 + A_1 B_1 + C_1} = 0. \tag{A19}$$

Hence no output signals are generated from F_1. The coefficient B_1 in term $B_1 G_3$ of (A16) may be decreased somewhat without changing system dynamics.

In Fig. 14d, the gain control cells are phasically excited by bottom–up signals and inhibited by top–down signals. Once active, they nonspecifically excite F_1 cells. In the absence of any external signals, F_1 cells are maintained in a state of tonic hyperpolarization, or negativity. In response to a bottom–up input, the gain control channel balances the tonic hyperpolarization of F_1 cells, thereby allowing those cells which receive bottom–up inputs to fire. When a top–down signal is active, no gain control outputs occur. Hence top–down signals alone cannot overcome the tonic hyperpolarization enough to generate output signals from F_1. Simultaneous convergence of an excitatory bottom–up signal and an inhibitory top–down signal at the gain control cells prevents these cells from generating output signals to F_1. Consequently, only those F_1 cells at which a bottom–up input and top–down template signal converge can overcome the tonic hyperpolarization to generate output signals.

The STM equations of F_1 are

$$\varepsilon \frac{dx_i}{dt} = -x_i + (1 - A_1 x_i)\Big(I_i + D_1 \sum_j f(x_j) z_{ji} + B_1 G_4\Big) - (B_1 + C_1 x_i), \tag{A20}$$

where

$$G_4 = \begin{cases} 1 & \text{if } I \text{ is active and } F_2 \text{ is inactive} \\ 0 & \text{if } I \text{ is inactive and } F_2 \text{ is active} \\ 0 & \text{if } I \text{ is active and } F_2 \text{ is active} \\ 0 & \text{if } I \text{ is inactive and } F_2 \text{ is inactive.} \end{cases} \tag{A21}$$

The equilibrium activities of x_i are as follows. If I is active and F_2 is inactive, then

(A18) holds. If I is inactive and F_2 is active, then (A5) holds. Equation (A5) also holds if I is active and F_2 is active. If I is inactive and F_2 is inactive, then (A15) holds.

In all four cases, an F_1 cell fires only if the number of active excitatory pathways which converge upon the cell exceeds the number of active inhibitory pathways which converge upon the cell, where we count a source of tonic hyperpolarization as one input pathway. A similar rule governs the firing of the gain control channel in all cases.

ACKNOWLEDGMENTS

Thanks to Cynthia Suchta and Carol Yanakakis for their valuable assistance in the preparation of the manuscript.

REFERENCES

1. E. Basar, H. Flohr, H. Haken, and A. J. Mandell (Eds.), *Synergetics of the Brain*, Springer-Verlag, New York, 1983.
2. J. P. Banquet and S. Grossberg, Probing cognitive processes through the structure of event-related potentials during learning: An experimental and theoretical analysis, Submitted for publication, 1986.
3. G. A. Carpenter and S. Grossberg, Category learning and adaptive pattern recognition: A neural network model, Proceedings of the Third Army Conference on Applied Mathematics and Computing, ARO Report 86-1, 1985, 37–56.
4. G. A. Carpenter and S. Grossberg, Neural dynamics of adaptive pattern recognition: Priming, search, attention, and category formation, *Soc. Neurosci. Abstracts*, **11**, 1985, 1110.
5. G. A. Carpenter and S. Grossberg, Neural dynamics of category learning and recognition: Attention, memory consolidation, and amnesia, in *Brain Structure, Learning, and Memory* (J. Davis, R. Newburgh, and E. Wegman, Eds.), AAAS Symposium Series, 1986.
6. G. A. Carpenter and S. Grossberg, Neural dynamics of category learning and recognition: Structural invariants, reinforcement, and evoked potentials, in *Pattern Recognition and Concepts in Animals, People, and Machines* (M. L. Commons, S. M. Kosslyn, and R. J. Herrnstein, Eds.), Erlbaum, Hillsdale, NJ, 1986.
7. S. Grossberg, Adaptive pattern classification and universal recoding. I. Parallel development and coding of neural feature detectors, *Biol. Cybernet.* **23**, 1976, 121–134.
8. S. Grossberg, Adaptive pattern classification and universal recoding. II. Feedback, expectation, olfacation, and illusions, *Biol. Cybernet.* **23**, 1976, 187–202.
9. S. Grossberg, A theory of human memory: Self-organization and performance of sensory-motor codes, maps, and plans, in *Progress in Theoretical Biology* (R. Rosen and F. Snell, Eds.), Vol. 5, pp. 233–374, Academic Press, New York, 1978.
10. S. Grossberg, How does a brain build a cognitive code? *Psychol. Rev.*, **87**, 1980, 1–51.
11. S. Grossberg, The adaptive self-organization of serial order in behavior: Speech, language, and motor control, in *Pattern Recognition by Humans and Machines* (E. C. Schwab and H. C. Nusbaum, Eds.), Vol. 1, Academic Press, New York, 1986.
12. S. Grossberg and G. O. Stone, Neural dynamics of word recognition and recall: Attentional priming, learning, and resonance, *Psychol. Rev.* **93**, 1986, 46–74.
13. S. Grossberg and G. O. Stone, Neural dynamic of attention switching and temporal order information in short term memory, *Memory and Cognition*, in press, 1986.
14. S. Grossberg, Do all neural networks really look alike? A comment on Anderson, Silverstein, Ritz, and Jones, *Psychol. Rev.* **85**, 1978, 592–596.
15. J. A. Anderson, J. W. Silverstein, S. R. Ritz, and R. S. Jones, Distinctive features, categorical perception, and probability learning: some applications of a neural model, *Psychol. Rev.* **84**, 1977, 413–451.
16. K. Fukushima, Neocognitron: A self-organizing neural network model for a mechanism of pattern recognition unaffected by shift in position, *Biol. Cybernet.* **36**, 1980, 193–202.
17. J. J. Hopfield, Neural networks and physical systems with emergent collective computational abilities, *Proc. Nat. Acad. Sci. U.S.A.* **79**, 1982, 2554–2558.

18. T. Kohonen, *Associative Memory: A System-Theoretical Approach*, Springer-Verlag, New York, 1977.
19. J. I. McClelland and D. E. Rumelhart, Distributed memory and the representation of general and specific information, *J. Exp. Psychol. Gen.* **114**, 1985, 159–188.
20. M. I. Posner, *Cognition: An Introduction*, Scott, Foresman, Glenview, Ill., 1973.
21. E. E. Smith and D. L. Medin, *Categories and Concepts*, Harvard Univ. Press, Cambridge, Mass., 1981.
22. M. I. Posner and S. W. Keele, On the genesis of abstract ideas, *J. Exp. Psychol.* **77**, 1968, 353–363.
23. M. I. Posner and S. W. Keele, Retention of abstract ideas, *J. Exp. Psychol.* **83**, 1970, 304–308.
24. M. A. Cohen and S. Grossberg, Neural dynamics of speech and language coding: Developmental programs, perceptual grouping, and competition for short term memory, *Human Neurobiology*, 1986, **5**, 1–22.
25. M. A. Cohen and S. Grossberg, Unitized recognition codes for parts and wholes: The unique cue in configural discriminations, in *Pattern Recognition and Concepts in Animals, People, and Machines* (M. L. Commons, S. M. Kosslyn, and R. J. Herrnstein, Eds.), Erlbaum, Hillsdale, N.J., 1986.
26. M. A. Cohen and S. Grossberg, Masking fields: A massively parallel architecture for discovering, learning, and recognizing multiple groupings of patterned data. *Applied Optics*, in press, 1986.
27. S. Grossberg, Some psychophysiological and pharmacological correlates of a developmental, cognitive and motivational theory, in *Brain and Information: Event Related Potentials* (R. Karrer, J. Cohen, and P. Tueting, Eds.), New York Academy of Sciences, New York, 1984, pp. 58–151.
28. S. Grossberg, The quantized geometry of visual space: The coherent computation of depth, form, and lightness, *Behavioral Brain Sci.* **6**, 1983, 625–692.
29. C. C. Lin and L. A. Segal, *Mathematics Applied to Deterministic Problems in the Natural Sciences*, Macmillan, New York, 1974.
30. S. Ellias and S. Grossberg, Pattern formation, contrast control, and oscillations in the short term memory of shunting on-center off-surround networks, *Biol. Cybernet.* **20**, 1975, 69–98.
31. S. Grossberg, Contour enhancement, short-term memory, and constancies in reverberating neural networks, *Studies Appl. Math.*, **52**, 1973, 217–257.
32. S. Grossberg and D. Levine, Some developmental and attentional biases in the contrast enhancement and short term memory of recurrent neural networks, *J. Theoret. Biol.* **53**, 1975, 341–380.
33. G. A. Carpenter, and S. Grossberg, Self-organization of neural recognition codes: Nonlinear Weber Law modulation of associative learning, 1986, in preparation.
34. C. von der Malsburg and D. J. Willshaw, Differential equations for the development of topological nerve fibre projections, in *Mathematical Psychology and Psychophysiology* (S. Grossberg, Ed.), Amer. Math. Soc., Providence, R.I., 1981, pp. 39–47.
35. D. O. Hebb, *The Organization of Behavior*, Wiley, New York, 1949.
36. S. Grossberg, Unitization, automaticity, temporal order, and word recognition. *Cognition Brain Theory*, 7, 1984, 263–283.
37. S. Grossberg, Cortical dynamics of three-dimensional form, color, and brightness perception: Parts I and II. *Perception Psychophys.*, in press, 1986.
38. S. Grossberg, and E. Mingolla, Neural dynamics of form perception: Boundary completion, illusory figures, and neon color spreading, *Psychol. Rev.*, **92**, 1985, 173–211.
39. S. Grossberg and E. Mingolla, Neural dynamics of perceptual grouping: Textures, boundaries, and emergent segmentations. *Perception Psychophys.*, **38**, 1985, 141–171.
40. S. Grossberg and E. Mingolla, Neural dynamics of surface perception: Boundary webs, illuminants, and shape-from-shading, *Comput. Vision, Graphics, Image Process.*, **37**, (1987) 116–165.

Part 4
Analysis and Applications

Backpropagation Through Time: What It Does and How to Do It

PAUL J. WERBOS

Backpropagation is now the most widely used tool in the field of artificial neural networks. At the core of backpropagation is a method for calculating derivatives exactly and efficiently in any large system made up of elementary subsystems or calculations which are represented by known, differentiable functions; thus, backpropagation has many applications which do not involve neural networks as such.

This paper first reviews basic backpropagation, a simple method which is now being widely used in areas like pattern recognition and fault diagnosis. Next, it presents the basic equations for backpropagation through time, and discusses applications to areas like pattern recognition involving dynamic systems, systems identification, and control. Finally, it describes further extensions of this method, to deal with systems other than neural networks, systems involving simultaneous equations or true recurrent networks, and other practical issues which arise with this method. Pseudocode is provided to clarify the algorithms. The chain rule for ordered derivatives—the theorem which underlies backpropagation—is briefly discussed.

I. Introduction

Backpropagation through time is a very powerful tool, with applications to pattern recognition, dynamic modeling, sensitivity analysis, and the control of systems over time, among others. It can be applied to neural networks, to econometric models, to fuzzy logic structures, to fluid dynamics models, and to almost any system built up from elementary subsystems or calculations. The one serious constraint is that the elementary subsystems must be represented by functions known to the user, functions which are both continuous and differentiable (i.e., possess derivatives). For example, the first practical application of backpropagation was for estimating a dynamic model to predict nationalism and social communications in 1974 [1].

Unfortunately, the most general formulation of backpropagation can only be used by those who are willing to work out the mathematics of their particular application. This paper will mainly describe a simpler version of backpropagation, which can be translated into computer code and applied directly by neural network users.

Section II will review the simplest and most widely used form of backpropagation, which may be called "basic backpropagation." The concepts here will already be familiar to those who have read the paper by Rumelhart, Hinton, and Williams [2] in the seminal book *Parallel Distributed Processing,* which played a pivotal role in the development of the field. (That book also acknowledged the prior work of Parker [3] and Le Cun [4], and the pivotal role of Charles Smith of the Systems Development Foundation.) This section will use new notation which adds a bit of generality and makes it easier to go on to complex applications in a rigorous manner. (The need for new notation may seem unnecessary to some, but for those who have to *apply* backpropagation to complex systems, it is essential.)

Section III will use the same notation to describe backpropagation through time. Backpropagation through time has been applied to concrete problems by a number of authors, including, at least, Watrous and Shastri [5], Sawai and Waibel *et al.* [6], Nguyen and Widrow [7], Jordan [8], Kawato [9], Elman and Zipser, Narendra [10], and myself [1], [11], [12], [15]. Section IV will discuss what is missing in this simplified discussion, and how to do better.

At its core, backpropagation is simply an efficient and exact method for calculating all the derivatives of a single target quantity (such as pattern classification error) with respect to a large set of input quantities (such as the parameters or weights in a classification rule). Backpropagation through time extends this method so that it applies to dynamic systems. This allows one to calculate the derivatives needed when optimizing an iterative analysis procedure, a neural network with memory, or a control system which maximizes performance over time.

II. Basic Backpropagation

A. The Supervised Learning Problem

Basic backpropagation is current the most popular method for performing the supervised learning task, which is symbolized in Fig. 1.

In supervised learning, we try to adapt an artificial neural network so that its actual outputs ($\hat{\boldsymbol{Y}}$) come close to some target outputs ($\boldsymbol{Y}$) for a training set which contains T patterns. The goal is to adapt the parameters of the network so that it performs well for patterns from outside the training set.

The main use of supervised learning today lies in pattern

Manuscript received September 12, 1989; revised March 15, 1990.
The author is with the National Science Foundation, 1800 G St. NW, Washington, DC 20550.
IEEE Log Number 9039172.

Reprinted from *Proc. IEEE,* vol. 78, no. 10, Oct. 1990, pp. 1550–1560.

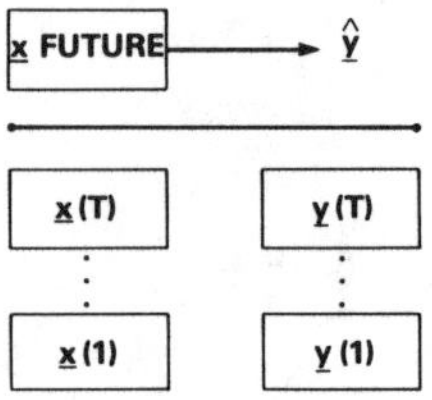

Fig. 1. Schematic of the supervised learning task.

recognition work. For example, suppose that we are trying to build a neural network which can learn to recognize handwritten ZIP codes. (AT&T has actually done this [13], although the details are beyond the scope of this paper.) We assume that we already have a camera and preprocessor which can digitize the image, locate the five digits, and provide a 19 × 20 grid of ones and zeros representing the image of each digit. We want the neural network to input the 19 × 20 image, and output a classification; for example, we might ask the network to output four binary digits which, taken together, identify which decimal digit is being observed.

Before adapting the parameters of the neural network, one must first obtain a training database of actual handwritten digits and correct classifications. Suppose, for example, that this database contains 2000 examples of handwritten digits. In that case, $T = 2000$. We may give each example a label t between 1 and 2000. For each sample t, we have a record of the input pattern and the correct classification. Each input pattern consists of 380 numbers, which may be viewed as a vector with 380 components; we may call this vector $\mathbf{X}(t)$. The desired classification consists of four numbers, which may be treated as a vector $\mathbf{Y}(t)$. The actual output of the network will be $\hat{\mathbf{Y}}(t)$, which may differ from the desired output $\mathbf{Y}(t)$, especially in the period *before* the network has been adapted. To solve the supervised learning problem, there are two steps:

- We must specify the "topology" (connections and equations) for a network which inputs $\mathbf{X}(t)$ and outputs a four-component vector $\hat{\mathbf{Y}}(t)$, an approximation to $\mathbf{Y}(t)$. The relation between the inputs and outputs must depend on a set of weights (parameters) $\mathbf{W}$ which can be adjusted.
- We must specify a "learning rule"—a procedure for adjusting the weights $\mathbf{W}$ so as to make the actual outputs $\hat{\mathbf{Y}}(t)$ approximate the desired outputs $\mathbf{Y}(t)$.

Basic backpropagation is currently the most popular learning rule used in supervised learning. It is generally used with a very simple network design—to be described in the next section—but the same approach can be used with *any* network of differentiable functions, as will be discussed in Section IV.

Even when we use a simple network design, the vectors $\mathbf{X}(t)$ and $\mathbf{Y}(t)$ need not be made of ones and zeros. They can be made up of any values which the network is capable of inputting and outputting. Let us denote the components of $\mathbf{X}(t)$ as $X_1(t) \cdots X_m(t)$ so that there are m inputs to the network. Let us denote the components of $\mathbf{Y}(t)$ as $Y_1(t) \cdots Y_n(t)$ so that we have n outputs. Throughout this paper, the components of a vector will be represented by the *same* letter as the vector itself, in the same case; this convention turns out to be convenient because $\mathbf{x}(t)$ will represent a different vector, very closely related to $\mathbf{X}(t)$.

Fig. 1 illustrates the supervised learning task in the general case. Given a history of $\mathbf{X}(1) \cdots \mathbf{X}(T)$ and $\mathbf{Y}(1) \cdots \mathbf{Y}(T)$, we want to find a mapping from $\mathbf{X}$ to $\mathbf{Y}$ which will perform well when we encounter *new* vectors $\mathbf{X}$ outside the training set. The index "t" may be interpreted either as a time index or as a pattern number index; however, this section will not assume that the order of patterns is meaningful.

B. Simple Feedforward Networks

Before we specify a learning rule, we have to define exactly how the outputs of a neural net depend on its inputs and weights. In basic backpropagation, we assume the following logic:

$$x_i = X_i, \qquad 1 \le i \le m \tag{1}$$

$$\text{net}_i = \sum_{j=1}^{i-1} W_{ij} x_j, \qquad m < i \le N + n \tag{2}$$

$$x_i = s(\text{net}_i), \qquad m < i \le N + n \tag{3}$$

$$Y_i = x_{i+N}, \qquad 1 \le i \le n \tag{4}$$

where the function s in (3) is usually the following sigmoidal function:

$$s(z) = 1/(1 + e^{-z}) \tag{5}$$

and where N is a constant which can be any integer you choose as long as it is no less than m. The value of $N + n$ decides how many neurons are in the network (if we include inputs as neurons). Intuitively, net_i represents the total level of voltage exciting a neuron, and x_i represents the intensity of the resulting output from the neuron. (x_i is sometimes called the "activation level" of the neuron.) It is conventional to assume that there is a threshold or constant weight W_{io} added to the right side of (2); however, we can achieve the same effect by assuming that one of the inputs (such as X_m) is always 1.

The significance of these equations is illustrated in Fig. 2. There are $N + n$ circles, representing all of the neurons

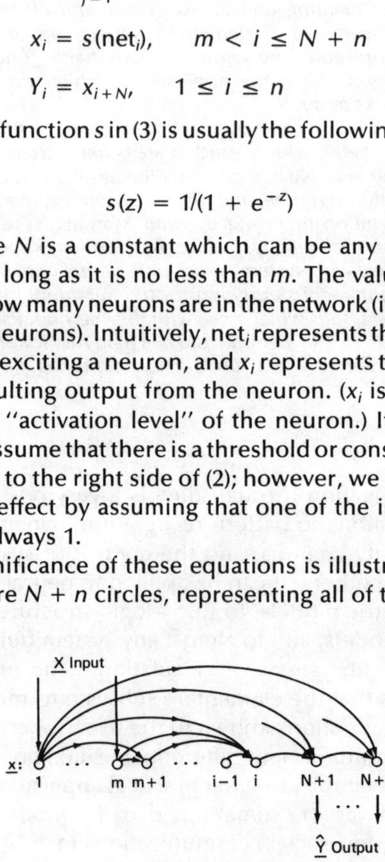

Fig. 2. Network design for basic backpropagation.

in the network, *including* the input neurons. The first m circles are really just copies of the inputs $X_1 \cdots X_m$; they are included as part of the vector $\mathbf{x}$ only as a way of simplifying the notation. *Every* other neuron in the network—such as neuron number i, which calculates net_i and x_i—takes input from *every* cell which precedes it in the network. Even the last output cell, which generates $\hat{Y}_n$, takes input from other output cells, such as the one which outputs $\hat{Y}_{n-1}$.

In neural network terminology, this network is "fully connected" in the extreme. As a practical matter, it is usually desirable to limit the connections between neurons. This can be done by simply fixing some of the weights W_{ij} to zero so that they drop out of all calculations. For example, most researchers prefer to use "layered" networks, in which all connection weights W_{ij} are zeroed out, *except* for those going from one "layer" (subset of neurons) to the next layer. In general, one may zero out as many or as few of the weights as one likes, based on one's understanding of individual applications. For those who first begin this work, it is conventional to define only three layers—an input layer, a "hidden" layer, and an output layer. This section will assume the full range of *allowed* connections, simply for the sake of generality.

In computer code, we could represent this network as a Fortran subroutine (assuming a Fortran which distinguishes upper case from lower case):

```
          SUBROUTINE NET(X, W, x, Yhat)
          REAL X(m),W(N+n,N+n),x(N+n),Yhat(n),net
          INTEGER, i,j,m,n,N
C   First insert the inputs, as per equation (1)
          DO 1 i = 1,m
        1 x(i) = X(i)
C   Next implement (2) and (3) together for each value
C     of i
          DO 1000 i = m+1,N+n
C         calculate net_i as a running sum, based on (2)
          net = 0
          DO 10 j = 1,i-1
   10           net = net + W(i,j)*x(j)
C               finally, calculate x_i based on (3) and (5)
 1000       x(i) = 1/(1+exp(-net))
C   Finally, copy over the outputs, as per (4)
          DO 2000 i = 1,n
 2000       Yhat(i) = x(i+N);
```

In the pseudocode, note that X and W are technically the inputs to the subroutine, while x and *Yhat* are the outputs. *Yhat* is usually regarded as "the" output of the network, but x may also have its uses outside of the subroutine proper, as will be seen in the next section.

C. Adapting the Network: Approach

In basic backpropagation, we choose the weights W_{ij} so as to minimize square error over the training set:

$$E = \sum_{t=1}^{T} E(t) = \sum_{t=1}^{T} \sum_{i=1}^{n} (1/2)(\hat{Y}_i(t) - Y_i(t))^2. \tag{6}$$

This is simply a special case of the well-known method of least squares, used very often in statistics, econometrics, and engineering; the uniqueness of backpropagation lies in *how* this expression is minimized. The approach used here is illustrated in Fig. 3.

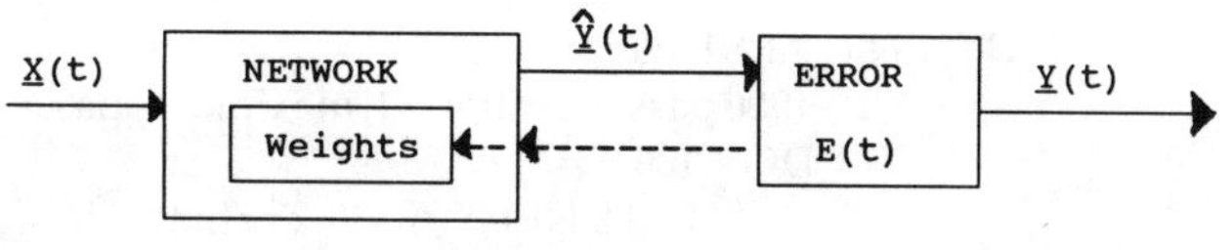

Fig. 3. Basic backpropagation (in pattern learning).

In basic backpropagation, we start with arbitrary values for the weights $\mathbf{W}$. (It is usual to choose random numbers in the range from -0.1 to 0.1, but it may be better to guess the weights based on prior information, in cases where prior information is available.) Next, we calculate the outputs $\hat{Y}(t)$ and the errors $E(t)$ for that set of weights. Then we calculate the derivatives of E with respect to all of the weights; this is indicated by the dotted lines in Fig. 3. If increasing a given weight would lead to more error, we adjust that weight downwards. If increasing a weight leads to less error, we adjust it upwards. After adjusting all the weights up or down, we start all over, and keep on going through this process until the weights and the error settle down. (Some researchers iterate until the error is close to zero; however, if the number of training patterns exceeds the number of weights in the network—as recommended by studies on generalization—it may not be possible for the error to reach zero.) The uniqueness of backpropagation lies in the method used to calculate the derivatives exactly for all of the weights in only one pass through the system.

D. Calculating Derivatives: Theoretical Background

Many papers on backpropagation suggest that we need only use the conventional chain rule for partial derivatives to calculate the derivatives of E with respect to all of the weights. Under certain conditions, this can be a rigorous approach, but its generality is limited, and it requires great care with the side conditions (which are rarely spelled out); calculations of this sort can easily become confused and erroneous when networks and applications grow complex. Even when using (7) below, it is a good idea to test one's gradient calculations using explicit perturbations in order to be sure that there is no bug in one's code.

When the idea of backpropagation was first presented to the Harvard faculty in 1972, they expressed legitimate concern about the validity of the rather complex calculations involved. To deal with this problem, I proved a new chain rule for *ordered* derivatives:

$$\frac{\partial^+ \text{TARGET}}{\partial z_i} = \frac{\partial\, \text{TARGET}}{\partial z_i} + \sum_{j>i} \frac{\partial^+ \text{TARGET}}{\partial z_j} * \frac{\partial z_j}{\partial z_i} \tag{7}$$

where the derivatives with the superscript represent *ordered* derivatives, and the derivatives without subscripts represent ordinary partial derivatives. This chain rule is valid only for *ordered* systems where the values to be calculated can be calculated one by one (if necessary) in the order z_1, $z_2, \cdots, z_n$, TARGET. The simple partial derivatives represent the *direct* impact of z_i on z_j *through the system equation* which determines z_j. The ordered derivative represents the *total* impact of z_i on TARGET, accounting for both the *direct* and *indirect* effects. For example, suppose that we had a simple system governed by the following two equations, in order:

$$z_2 = 4 * z_1$$

$$z_3 = 3 * z_1 + 5 * z_2.$$

The "simple" partial derivative of z_3 with respect to z_1 (the *direct* effect) is 3; to calculate the simple effect, we *only* look at the equation which determines z_3. However, the ordered derivative of z_3 with respect to z_1 is 23 because of the indirect impact by way of z_2. The simple partial derivative measures what happens when we increase z_1 (e.g., by 1, in this example) and assume that everything else (like z_2) in the equation which determines z_3 remains constant. The ordered derivative measures what happens when we increase z_1, *and also* recalculate all other quantities—like

z_2—which are later than z_1 in the causal ordering we impose on the system.

This chain rule provides a straightforward, plodding, "linear" recipe for how to calculate the derivatives of a given TARGET variable with respect to *all* of the inputs (and parameters) of an ordered differentiable system *in only one pass through the system*. This paper will not explain this chain rule in detail since lengthy tutorials have been published elsewhere [1], [11]. But there is one point worth noting: because we are calculating ordered derivatives of *one* target variable, we can use a simpler notation, a notation which works out to be easier to use in complex practical examples [11]. We can write the ordered derivative of the TARGET with respect to z_i as "F_z_i," which may be described as "the feedback to z_i." In basic backpropagation, the TARGET variable of interest is the error E. This changes the appearance of our chain rule in that case to

$$F\_z_i = \frac{\partial E}{\partial z_i} + \sum_{j>i} F\_z_j * \frac{\partial z_j}{\partial z_i}. \quad (8)$$

For purposes of debugging, one can calculate the true value of any ordered derivative simply by perturbing z_i at the point in the program where z_i is calculated; this is particularly useful when applying backpropagation to a complex network of functions other than neural networks.

E. Adapting the Network: Equations

For a given set of weights $\boldsymbol{W}$, it is easy to use (1)-(6) to calculate $\boldsymbol{Y}(t)$ and $E(t)$ for each pattern t. The trick is in how we then calculate the derivatives.

Let us use the prefix "F_" to indicate the ordered derivative of E with respect to whatever variable the "F_" precedes. Thus, for example,

$$F\_\hat{Y}(t) = \frac{\partial E}{\partial \hat{Y}_i(t)} = \hat{Y}_i(t) - Y_i(t), \quad (9)$$

which follows simply by differentiating (6). By the chain rule for ordered derivatives as expressed in (8),

$$F\_x_i(t) = F\_\hat{Y}_{i-N}(t) + \sum_{j=i+1}^{N+n} W_{ji} * F\_net_j(t),$$

$$i = N + n, \cdots, m + 1 \quad (10)$$

$$F\_net_i(t) = s'(net_i) * F\_x_i(t), \qquad i = N + n, \cdots, m + 1 \quad (11)$$

$$F\_W_{ij} = \sum_{t=1}^{T} F\_net_i(t) * x_j(t) \quad (12)$$

where s' is the derivative of $s(z)$ as defined in (5) and F_Y_k is assumed to be zero for $k \leq 0$. Note how (10) requires us to run *backwards* through the network in order to calculate the derivatives, as illustrated in Fig. 4; this backwards propagation of information is what gives backpropagation its name. A little calculus and algebra, starting from (5), shows us that

$$s'(z) = s(z) * (1 - s(z)), \quad (13)$$

which we can use when we implement (11). Finally, to adapt the weights, the usual method is to set

$$\text{New } W_{ij} = W_{ij} - \text{learning\_rate} * F\_W_{ij} \quad (14)$$

where the learning_rate is some small constant chosen on an ad hoc basis. (The usual procedure is to make it as large as possible, up to 1, until the error starts to diverge; however, there are more analytic procedures available [11].)

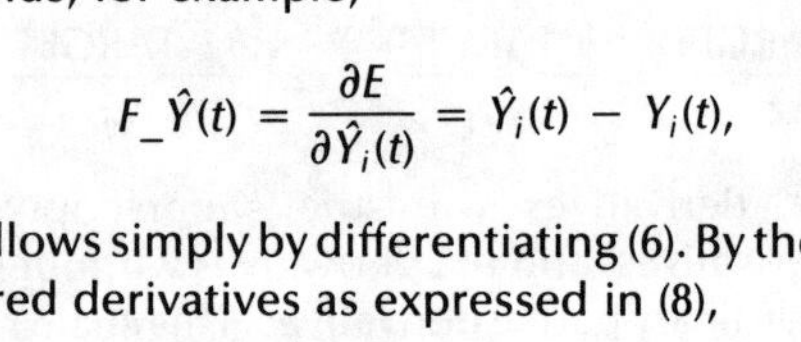

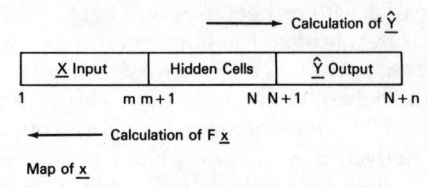

Fig. 4. Backwards flow of derivative calculation.

F. Adapting the Network: Code

The key part of basic backpropagation—(10)-(13)—may be coded up into a "dual" subroutine, as follows.

```
      SUBROUTINE F_NET(F_Yhat, W, x, F_W)
      REAL F_Yhat(n),W(N+n,N+n),x(N+n),
        F_W(N+n,N+n),F_net(N+n),F_x(N+n)
      INTEGER i,j,n,m,N
C  Initialize equation (10)
      DO 1 i = 1,N
 1       F_x(i) = 0
      DO 2 i = 1,n
 2       F_x(i+N)=F_Yhat(i)
C  RUN THROUGH (10)-(12) AS A SET,
C     FOR i RUNNING BACKWARDS
      DO 1000 i=N+n,m+1,-1
C          complete (10) for the current value of i */
           DO 10 j = i+1,N+n
C          modify "DO 10" if needed to be sure
C             nothing is done if i=N+n
 10           F_x(i) = F_x(i)+W(j,i)*F_net(j)
C          next implement (11), exploiting (13)
           F_net(i) = F_x(i)*x(i)*(1.-x(i))
C          then implement (12) for the current
C             value of i
           DO 12 j = 1,i-1
 12           F_W(i,j)=F_net(i)*x(j)
 1000 CONTINUE
```

Note that the array F_W is the only output of this subroutine.

Equation (14) represented "batch learning," in which weights are adjusted only after *all T* patterns are processed. It is more common to use pattern learning, in which the weights are continually updated after each observation. Pattern learning may be represented as follows:

```
C  PATTERN LEARNING
         DO  1000 pass_number=1, maximum_passes
             DO   100 t =1,T
                  CALL NET(X(t), W, x, Yhat)
C                 Next Implement equation (9)
                  DO   9 i = 1,n
 9                    F_Yhat(i)=Yhat(i)-Y(t,i)
C                 Next Implement (10)-(12)
                  CALL F_NET(F_Yhat, W, x, F_W)
C                 Next Implement (14)
C                 Note how weights are updated
C                   within the "DO 100" loop.
```

```
      DO  14 i = m+1,N+n
          DO  14 j = 1,i-1
14            W(i,j)=W(i,j)-
              learning_rate*
              F_W(i,j)
100   CONTINUE
1000  CONTINUE
```

The key point here is that the weights W are adjusted in response to the *current* vector F_W, which only depends on the current pattern t; the weights are adjusted after each pattern is processed. (In batch learning, by contrast, the weights are adjusted only *after* the "DO 100" loop is completed.)

In practice, maximum_passes is usually set to an enormous number; the loop is exited only when a test of convergence is passed, a test of error size or weight change which can be injected easily into the loop. True real-time learning is like pattern learning, but with only one pass through the data and no memory of earlier times t. (The equations above could be implemented easily enough as a real-time learning scheme; however, this will not be true for backpropagation through time.) The term "on-line learning" is sometimes used to represent a situation which *could* be pattern learning or *could* be real-time learning. Most people using basic backpropagation now use pattern learning rather than real-time learning because, with their data sets, many passes through the data are needed to ensure convergence of the weights.

The reader should be warned that I have not actually tested the code here. It is presented simply as a way of explaining more precisely the preceding ideas. The C implementations which I have worked with have been less transparent, and harder to debug, in part because of the absence of range checking in that language. It is often argued that people "who know what they are doing" do not need range checking and the like; however, people who think they never make mistakes should probably not be writing this kind of code. With neural network code, especially, good diagnostics and tests are very important because bugs can lead to slow convergence and oscillation—problems which are hard to track down, and are easily misattributed to the algorithm in use. If one *must* use a language without range checking, it is extremely important to maintain a version of the code which is highly transparent and safe, however inefficient it may be, for diagnostic purposes.

III. Backpropagation Through Time

A. Background

Backpropagation through time—like basic backpropagation—is used most often in pattern recognition today. Therefore, this section will focus on such applications, using notation like that of the previous section. See Section IV for other applications.

In some applications—such as speech recognition or submarine detection—our classification at time t will be more accurate if we can account for what we saw at earlier times. *Even though* the training set still fits the same format as above, we want to use a more powerful class of networks to do the classification; we want the output of the network at time t to account for variables at earlier times (as in Fig. 5).

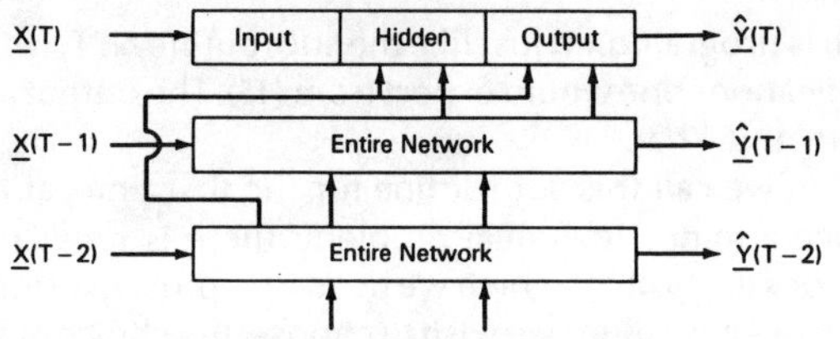

Fig. 5. Generalized network design with time lags.

The Introduction cited a number of examples where such "memory" of previous time periods is very important. For example, it is easier to recognize moving objects if our network accounts for *changes* in the scene from the time $t - 1$ to time t, which requires memory of time $t - 1$. Many of the best pattern recognition algorithms involve a kind of "relaxation" approach where the representation of the world at time t is based on an *adjustment* of the representation at time $t - 1$; this requires memory of the *internal* network variables for time $t - 1$. (Even Kalman filtering requires such a representation.)

B. Example of a Recurrent Network

Backpropagation can be applied to any system with a well-defined order of calculations, even if those calculations depend on past calculations within the network itself. For the sake of generality, I will show how this works for the network design shown in Fig. 5 where *every* neuron is potentially allowed to input values from *any* of the neurons at the two previous time periods (including, of course, the input neurons). To avoid excess clutter, Fig. 5 shows the hidden and output sections of the network (parallel to Fig. 2) only for time T, but they are present at other times as well. To translate this network into a mathematical system, we can simply replace (2) above by

$$\text{net}_i(t) = \sum_{j=1}^{i-1} W_{ij}x_j(t) + \sum_{j=1}^{N+n} W'_{ij}x_j(t-1) + \sum_{j=1}^{N+n} W''_{ij}x_j(t-2). \tag{15}$$

Again, we can simply fix some of the weights to be zero, if we so choose, in order to simplify the network. In most applications today, the W'' weights are fixed to zero (i.e., erased from all formulas), and all the W' weights are fixed to zero as well, except for W'_{ii}. This is done in part for the sake of parsimony, and in part for historical reasons. (The "time-delay neural networks" of Watrous and Shastri [5] assumed that special case.) Here, I deliberately include extra terms for the sake of generality. I allow for the fact that *all* active neurons (neurons other than input neurons) can be allowed to input the outputs of *any* other neurons if there is a time lag in the connection. The weights W' and W'' are the weights on those time-lagged connections between neurons. [Lags of more than two periods are also easy to manage; they are treated just as one would expect from seeing how we handle lag-two terms, as a special case of (7).]

These equations could be embodied in a subroutine:

SUBROUTINE NET2($X(t)$, W', W'', $x(t-2)$,

$x(t-1)$, $x(t)$, Yhat),

which is programmed just like the subroutine NET, with the modifications one would expect from (15). The output arrays are $x(t)$ and $Yhat$.

When we call this subroutine for the first time, at $t = 1$, we face a minor technical problem: there is no value for $x(-1)$ or $x(0)$, both of which we need as inputs. In principle, we can use any values we wish to choose; the choice of $x(-1)$ and $x(0)$ is essentially part of the definition of our network. Most people simply set these vectors to zero, and argue that their network will start out with a blank slate in classifying whatever dynamic pattern is at hand, both in the training set and in later applications. (Statisticians have been known to treat these vectors as weights, in effect, to be adapted along with the other weights in the network. This works fine in the training set, but opens up questions of what to do when one applies the network to new data.)

In this section, I will assume that the data run from an initial time $t = 1$ through to a final time $t = T$, which plays a crucial role in the derivative calculations. Section IV will show how this assumption can be relaxed somewhat.

C. Adapting the Network: Equations

To calculate the derivatives of F_W_{ij}, we use the same equations as before, *except* that (10) is replaced by

$$F\_x_i(t) = F\_\hat{Y}_{i-N}(t) + \sum_{j=i+1}^{N+n} W_{ji} * F\_net_j(t) + \sum_{j=m+1}^{N+n} W'_{ji} * F\_net_j(t+1) + \sum_{j=m+1}^{N+n} W''_{ji} * F\_net_j(t+2). \qquad (16)$$

Once again, if one wants to fix the W'' terms to zero, one can simply delete the rightmost term.

Notice that this equation makes it impossible for us to calculate $F\_x_i(t)$ and $F\_net_i(t)$ until *after* $F\_net_j(t+1)$ and $F\_net_j(t+2)$ are already known; therefore, we can only use this equation by proceeding *backwards in time*, calculating F_net for time T, and then working our way backwards to time 1.

To adapt this network, of course, we need to calculate $F\_W'_{ij}$ and $F\_W''_{ij}$ as well as F_W_{ij}:

$$F\_W'_{ij} = \sum_{t=1}^{T} F\_net_i(t+1) * x_j(t) \qquad (17)$$

$$F\_W''_{ij} = \sum_{t=1}^{T} F\_net_i(t+2) * x_j(t). \qquad (18)$$

In all of these calculations, $F\_net(T+1)$ and $F\_net(T+2)$ should be treated as zero. For programming convenience, I will later define quantities like $F\_net'_i(t) = F\_net_i(t+1)$, but this is purely a convenience; the subscript "i" and the time argument are enough to identify which derivative is being represented. (In other words, $net_i(t)$ represents a specific quantity z_i as in (8), and $F\_net_i(t)$ represents the ordered derivative of E with respect to that quantity.)

D. Adapting the Network: Code

To fully understand the meaning and implications of these equations, it may help to run through a simple (hypothetical) implementation.

First, to calculate the derivatives, we need a new subroutine, dual to NET2.

```
      SUBROUTINE F_NET2(F_Yhat, W, W', W", x, F_net,
     F_net', F_net", F_W, F_W', F_W")
         REAL F_Yhat(n), W(N+n,N+n),
           W'(N+n,N+n), W"(N+n,N+n)
         REAL x(N+n), F_net(N+n), F_net'(N+n),
           F_net"(N+n)
         REAL F_W(N+n,N+n), F_W'(N+n,N+n),
           F_W"(N+n,N+n), F_x(N+n)
         INTEGER i, j, n, m, N
C  Initialize equation (16)
         DO 1 i = 1,N
 1          F_x(i)=0.
         DO 2 i = 1,n
 2          F_x(i+N)=F_Yhat(i)
C  RUN THROUGH (16), (11), AND (12) AS A SET,
C    RUNNING BACKWARDS
         DO 1000 i=N+n,m+1,−1
C           first complete (16)
            DO 161 j = i+1,N+n
 161           F_x(i)=F_x(i)+W(j,i)*F_net(j)
            DO 162 j = m+1,N+n
 162           F_x(i)=F_x(i)+W'(j,i)*F_net'(j)
                 +W"(j,i)*F_net"(j)
C           next implement (11)
            F_net(i)=F_x(i)*x(i)*(1−x(i))
C           implement (12), (17), and (18)
             (as running sums)
            DO 12 j = 1,i−1
 12            F_W(i,j)=F_W(i,j)
                 +F_net(i)*x(j)
            DO 1718 j =1,N+n
               F_W'(i,j)=F_W'(i,j)
                 +F_net'(i)*x(j)
 1718          F_W"(i,j)=F_W"(i,j)
                 +F_net"(i)*x(j)
 1000    CONTINUE
```

Notice that the last two DO loops have been set up to perform running sums, to simplify what follows.

Finally, we may adapt the weights as follows, by batch learning, where I use the abbreviation $x(i,)$, to represent the vector formed by $x(i,j)$ across all j.

```
      REAL x(−1:T,N+n), Yhat(T,n)
      DATA x(0,),x(−1,) / (2*(N+n)) * 0.0/
      DO  1000 pass_number=1,maximum_passes
C        First calculate outputs and errors in
C          a forward pass
         DO 100 t=1,T
 100        CALL NET2(X(t),W,W',W",x(t−2),
              x(t−1),x(t,),Yhat(t,))
C        Initialize the running sums to 0 and
C          set F_net(T), F_net(T+1) to 0
         DO 200 i = m+1,N+n
            F_net'(i)=0.
            F_net"(i)=0.
            DO 199 j = 1,N+n
               F_W(i,j)=0.
               F_W'(i,j)=0.
 199           F_W"(i,j)=0.
 200     CONTINUE
```

```
C  NEXT CALCULATE THE DERIVATIVES IN A SWEEP
   BACKWARDS THROUGH TIME
          DO  500 t = T,1,-1
C                 First, calculate the errors at the
C                   current time t
                DO  410 i = 1,n
  410                F_Yhat(i)=Yhat(t,i)-Y(t,i)
C             Next, calculate F_net(t) for time t and
C               update the F_W running sums
              call F_NET2(F_Yhat,W,W',W",x(t,),
                F_net,F_net',F_net",F_W,
                F_W',F_W")
C             Move F_net(t+1) to F_net(t), in effect,
C               to prepare for a new t value
                DO  420 i = m+1,N+n
                     F_net"(i)=F_net'(i)
  420                F_net'(i)=F_net(i)
  500           CONTINUE
C  FINALLY, UPDATE THE WEIGHTS BY
   STEEPEST DESCENT
          DO  999 i = m+1,N+n
                DO  998 j = 1,N+n
                     W(i,j)=W(i,j)-
                        learning_rate*F_W(i,j)
                     W'(i,j)=W'(i,j)-
                        learning_rate*F_W'(i,j)
  998                W"(i,j)-learning_rate*
                        F_W"(i,j);
  999           CONTINUE
 1000     CONTINUE
```

Once again, note that we have to go backwards in time in order to get the required derivatives. (There are ways to do these calculations in forward time, but exact results require the calculation of an entire *Jacobian* matrix, which is far more expensive with large networks.) For backpropagation through time, the natural way to adapt the network is in one big batch. Also note that we need to store a lot of intermediate information (which is inconsistent with real-time adaptation). This storage can be reduced by clever programming if W' and W'' are sparse, but it cannot be eliminated altogether.

In using backpropagation through time, we usually need to use much smaller learning rates than we do in basic backpropagation if we use steepest descent at all. In my experience [20], it may also help to start out by fixing the W' weights to zero (or to 1 when we want to force memory) in an initial phase of adaptation, and slowly free them up.

In some applications, we may not really care about errors in classification at all times t. In speech recognition, for example, we may only care about errors at the *end* of a word or phoneme; we usually do output a preliminary classification before the phoneme has been finished, but we usually do not care about the accuracy of that preliminary classification. In such cases, we may simply set *F_Yhat* to zero in the times we do not care about. To be more sophisticated, we may replace (6) by a more precise model of what we *do* care about; whatever we choose, it should be simple to replace (9) and the *F_Yhat* loop accordingly.

IV. Extensions of the Method

Backpropagation through time is a very general method, with many extensions. This section will try to describe the most important of these extensions.

A. Use of Other Networks

The network shown in (1)–(5) is a very simple, basic network. Backpropagation can be used to adapt a wide variety of other networks, including networks representing econometric models, systems of simultaneous equations, etc. Naturally, when one writes computer programs to implement a different kind of network, one must either describe *which* alternative network one chooses or *else* put options into the program to give the user this choice.

In the neural network field, users are often given a choice of network "topology." This simply means that they are asked to declare which *subset* of the possible weights/connections will actually be used. Every weight removed from (15) should be removed from (16) as well, along with (12) and (14) (or whichever apply to that weight); therefore, simplifying the network by removing weights simplifies all the other calculations as well. (Mathematically, this is the same as fixing these weights to zero.) Typically, people will remove an entire block of weights, such that the limits of the sums in our equations are all shrunk.

In a truly brain-like network, each neuron [in (15)] will only receive input from a small number of other cells. Neuroscientists do not agree on how many inputs are typical; some cite numbers on the order of 100 inputs per cell, while others quote 10 000. In any case, all of these estimates are small compared to the billions of cells present. To implement this kind of network efficiently on a conventional computer, one would use a linked list or a list of offsets to represent the connections actually implemented for each cell; the same strategy can be used to implement the backwards calculations and keep the connection costs low. Similar tricks are possible in parallel computers of all types. Many researchers are interested in devising ways to *automatically* make and break connections so that users will not have to specify all this information in advance [20]. The research on topology is hard to summarize since it is a mixture of normal science, sophisticated epistemology, and extensive ad hoc experimentation; however, the paper by Guyon *et al.* [13] is an excellent example of what works in practice.

Even in the neural network field, many programmers try to avoid the calculation of the exponential in (5). Depending on what kind of processor one has available, this calculation can multiply run times by a significant factor.

In the first published paper which discussed backpropagation at length as a way to adapt neural networks [14], I proposed the use of an artificial neuron ("continuous logic unit," CLU) based on

$$s(z) = 0, \quad z < 0$$

$$s(z) = z, \quad 0 < z < 1$$

$$s(z) = 1, \quad z > 1.$$

This leads to a very simple derivative as well. Unfortunately, the *second* derivatives of this function are not well behaved, which can affect the efficiency of some applications. Still, many programmers are now using piecewise linear approximations to (5), along with lookup tables, which can work relatively well in some applications. In earlier experiments, I have also found good uses for a Taylor series approximation:

$$s(z) = 1/(1 - z + 0.5 * z^2), \qquad z < 0$$

$$s(z) = 1 - 1/(1 + z + 0.5 * z^2), \qquad z > 0.$$

In a similar spirit, it is common to speed up learning by "stretching out" $s(z)$ so that it goes from -1 to 1 instead of 0 to 1.

Backpropagation can also be used without using neural networks at all. For example, it can be used to adapt a network consisting entirely of user-specified functions, representing something like an econometric model. In that case, the way one proceeds depends on who one is programming for and what kind of model one has.

If one is programming for oneself and the model consists of a sequence of equations which can be invoked one after the other, then one should consider the tutorial paper [11], which also contains a more rigorous definition of what these "F_x_i" derivatives really mean and a proof of the chain rule for ordered derivatives. If one is developing a tool for others, then one might set it up to look like a standard econometric package (like SAS or Troll) where the user of the system types in the equations of his or her model; the backpropagation would go *inside* the package as a way to speed up these calculations, and would mostly be transparent to the user. If one's model consists of a set of simultaneous equations which need to be solved at each time, then one must use more complicated procedures [15]; in neural network terms, one would call this a "doubly recurrent network." (The methods of Pineda [16] and Almeida [17] are special cases of this situation.)

Pearlmutter [18] and Williams [19] have described alternative methods, designed to achieve results similar to those of backpropagation through time, using a different computational strategy. For example, the Williams–Zipser method is a special case of the "conventional perturbation" equation cited in [14], which rejected this as a neural network method on the grounds that its computational costs scale as the square of the network size; however, the method does yield exact derivatives with a time-forward calculation.

Supervised learning problems or forecasting problems which involve memory can also be translated into control problems [15, p. 352], [20], which allows the use of adaptive critic methods, to be discussed in the next section. Normally, this would yield only an approximate solution (or approximate derivatives), but it would also allow time-forward real-time learning. If the network itself contains calculation noise (due to hardware limitations), the adaptive critic approach might even be more robust than backpropagation through time because it is based on mathematics which allow for the presence of noise.

B. Applications Other Than Supervised Learning

Backpropagation through time can also be used in two other major applications: neuroidentification and neurocontrol. (For applications to sensitivity analysis, see [14] and [15].)

In neuroidentification, we try to do with neural nets what econometricians do with forecasting models. (Engineers would call this the identification problem or the problem of identifying dynamic systems. Statisticians refer to it as the problem of estimating stochastic time-series models.) Our training set consists of vectors $\boldsymbol{X}(t)$ and $\boldsymbol{u}(t)$, not $\boldsymbol{X}(t)$ and $\boldsymbol{Y}(t)$. Usually, $\boldsymbol{X}(t)$ represents a set of observations of the eXternal (sic) world, and $\boldsymbol{u}(t)$ represents a set of actions that we had control over (such as the settings of motors or actuators). The *combination* of $\boldsymbol{X}(t)$ and $\boldsymbol{u}(t)$ is input to the network at each time t. Our target, at time t, is the vector $\boldsymbol{X}(t + 1)$.

We could easily build a network to input these inputs, and aim at these targets. We could simply collect the inputs and targets into the format of Section II, and then use basic backpropagation. But basic backpropagation contains no "memory." The forecast of $\boldsymbol{X}(t + 1)$ would depend on $\boldsymbol{X}(t)$, but *not* on previous time periods. If human beings worked like this, then they would be unable to predict that a ball might roll out the far side of a table after rolling down under the near side; as soon as the ball disappeared from sight [from the current vector $\boldsymbol{X}(t)$], they would have no way of accounting for its existence. (Harold Szu has presented a more interesting example of this same effect: if a tiger chased after such a memoryless person, the person would forget about the tiger after first turning to run away. Natural selection has eliminated such people.) Backpropagation through time permits more powerful networks, which do have a "memory," for use in the same setup.

Even this approach to the neuroidentification problem has its limitations. Like the usual methods of econometrics [15], it may lead to forecasts which hold up poorly over multiple time periods. It does not properly identify where the noise comes from. It does not permit real-time adaptation. In an earlier paper [20], I have described some ideas for overcoming these limitations, but more research is needed. The first phase of Kawato's cascade method [9] for controlling a robot arm is an identification phase, which is more robust over time, and which uses backpropagation through time in a different way; it is a special case of the "pure robust method," which also worked well in the earliest applications which I studied [1], [20].

After we have solved the problem of identifying a dynamic system, we are then ready to move on to controlling that system.

In neurocontrol, we often *start out* with a model or network which describes the system or plant we are trying to control. Our problem is to adapt a *second* network, the *action* network, which inputs $\boldsymbol{X}(t)$ and outputs the control $\boldsymbol{u}(t)$. (In actuality, we can allow the action network to "see" or input the *entire* vector $\boldsymbol{x}(t)$ calculated by the model network; this allows it to *account* for memories such as the recent appearance of a tiger.) Usually, we want to adapt the action network so as to maximize some measure of performance or utility $U(\boldsymbol{X}, t)$ summed over time. Performance measures used in past applications have included everything from the energy used to move a robot arm [8], [9] through to net profits received by the gas industry [11]. Typically, we are given a set of possible initial states $\boldsymbol{x}(1)$, and asked to train the action network so as to maximize the sum of utility from time 1 to a final time T.

To solve this problem using backpropagation through time, we simply calculate the derivatives of our performance measure with respect to all of the weights in the action network. "Backpropagation" refers to how we calculate the derivatives, not to anything involving pattern recognition or error. We then adapt the weights according to these derivatives, as in (12), except that the sign of the adjustment term is now positive (because we are *maximizing* rather than *minimizing*).

The easiest way to implement this approach is to merge

the utility function, the model network, and the action network into one big network. We can then construct the dual to this entire network, as described in 1974 [1] and illustrated in my recent tutorial [11]. However, if we wish to keep the three component networks distinct, then the bookkeeping becomes more complicated. The basic idea is illustrated in Fig. 6, which maps exactly into the approach used by Nguyen and Widrow [7] and by Jordan [8].

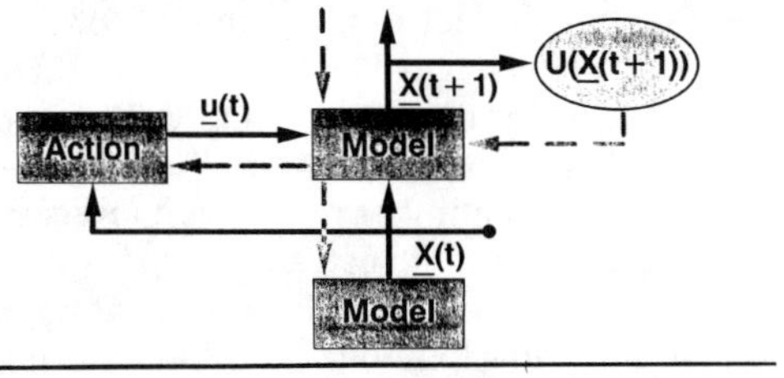

Fig. 6. Backpropagating utility through time. (Dashed lines represent derivative calculations.)

Instead of working with a *single* subroutine, NET, we now need *three* subroutines:

UTILITY($\boldsymbol{X}$; t; $\boldsymbol{x}''$; U)

MODEL($\boldsymbol{X}(t)$, $\boldsymbol{u}(t)$; $\boldsymbol{x}(t)$; $\boldsymbol{X}(t+1)$)

ACTION($\boldsymbol{x}(t)$; $\boldsymbol{W}$; $\boldsymbol{x}'(t)$; $\boldsymbol{u}(t)$).

In each of these subroutines, the two arguments on the right are technically outputs, and the argument on the far right is what we usually think of as the output of the network. We need to know the full vector $\boldsymbol{x}$ produced inside the model network so that the action network can "see" important memories. The action network does not need to have its own internal memory, but we need to save its internal state ($\boldsymbol{x}'$) so that we can later calculate derivatives. For simplicity, I will assume that MODEL does not contain any lag-two memory terms (i.e., W'' weights). The primes after the x's indicate that we are looking at the internal states of different networks; they are unrelated to the primes representing lagged values, discussed in Section III, which we will also need in what follows.

To use backpropagation through time, we need to construct dual subroutines for *all* three of these subroutines:

F_UTILITY($\boldsymbol{x}''$; t; F_X)

F_MODEL(F_net′, F_X($t+1$); $\boldsymbol{x}(t)$; F_net, F_u)

F_ACTION(F_u; $\boldsymbol{x}'(t)$; F_W).

The outputs of these subroutines are the arguments on the far right (including F_net), which are represented by the broken lines in Fig. 4. The subroutine F_UTILITY simply reports out the derivatives of $U(\boldsymbol{x}, t)$ with respect to the variables X_i. The subroutine F_MODEL is like the earlier subroutine F_NET2, except that we need to output F_u instead of derivatives to weights. (Again, we are adapting only the action network here.) The subroutine F_ACTION is virtually identical to the old subroutine F_NET, except that we need to calculate F_W as a running sum (as we did in F_NET2).

Of these three subroutines, F_MODEL is by far the most complex. Therefore, it may help to consider some possible code.

```
      SUBROUTINE F_MODEL(F_net', F_X', x, F_net, F_u)
C     The weights inside this subroutine are those
C     used in MODEL, analogous to those in NET2, and are
C     unrelated to the weights in ACTION
      REAL F_net'(N+n),F_X'(n),x(N+n),
     F_net(N+n),F_u(p),F_x(N+n)
      INTEGER i,j,n,m,N,p
      DO 1 i=1,N
1       F_x(i)=0.
      DO 2 i = 1,n
2       F_x(i+N)=F_X(i)
      DO 1000 i = N+n,1,-1
        DO 910 j = i+1,N+n
910       F_x(i)=F_x(i)+W(j,i)*F_net(j)
        DO 920 j = m+1,N+n
920       F_x(i)=F_x(i)+W'(j,i)*F_net'(j)
1000    F_net(i)=F_x(i)*x(i)*(1-x(i));
      DO 2000 i = 1,p
2000    F_u(i)=F_x(n+i)
```

The last small DO loop here assumes that $\boldsymbol{u}(t)$ was part of the input vector to the original subroutine MODEL, inserted into the slots between $\boldsymbol{x}(n+1)$ and $\boldsymbol{x}(m)$. Again, a good programmer could easily compress all this; my goal here is only to illustrate the mathematics.

Finally, in order to adapt the action network, we go through multiple passes, each starting from one of the starting values of $\boldsymbol{x}(1)$. In each pass, we call ACTION and then MODEL, one after the other, until we have built up a stream of forecasts from time 1 up to time T. Then, for each time t going backwards from T to 1, we call the UTILITY subroutine, then F_UTILITY, then F_MODEL, and then F_ACTION. At the end of the pass, we have the correct array of derivatives F_W, which we can then use to adjust the weights of the action network.

In general, backpropagation through time has the advantage of being relatively quick and exact. That is why I chose it for my natural gas application [11]. However, it cannot account for noise in the process to the controlled. To account for noise in maximizing an arbitrary utility function, we must rely on adaptive critic methods [21]. Adaptive critic methods do *not* require backpropagation through time in any form, and are therefore suitable for true real-time learning. There are other forms of neurocontrol as well [21] which are not based on maximizing a utility function.

C. Handling Strings of Data

In most of the examples above, I assumed that the training data form one lone time series, from t equals 1 to t equals T. Thus, in adapting the weights, I always assumed batch learning (except in the code in Section II); the weights were always adapted *after* a complete set of derivatives was calculated, based on a complete pass through all the data. Mechanically, one could use pattern learning in the backwards pass through time; however, this would lead to a host of problems, and it is difficult to see what it would gain.

Data in the real world are often somewhere between the two extremes represented by Sections II and III. Instead of having a set of unrelated patterns or one continuous time series, we often have a *set* of time series or strings. For example, in speech recognition, our training set may consist of a set of strings, each consisting of one word or one sentence. In robotics, our training set may consist of a set of strings, where each string represents one experiment with a robot.

In these situations, we can apply backpropagation through time to a *single string* of data at a time. For each string, we can calculate complete derivatives and update the weights. Then we can go on to the next string. This is like pattern learning, in that the weights are updated incrementally before the entire data set is studied. It requires intermediate storage for only one string at a time. To speed things up even further, we might adapt the net in stages, initially fixing certain weights (like W_{ii}) to zero or one.

Nevertheless, string learning is not the same thing as real-time learning. To solve problems in neuroidentification and supervised learning, the only consistent way to have internal memory terms *and* to avoid backpropagation through time is to use adaptive critics in a supporting role [15]. That alternative is complex, inexact, and relatively expensive for these applications; it may be unavoidable for true real-time systems like the human brain, but it would probably be better to live with string learning and focus on *other* challenges in neuroidentification for the time being.

D. Speeding Up Convergence

For those who are familiar with numerical analysis and optimization, it goes without saying that steepest descent—as in (12)—is a very inefficient method.

There is a huge literature in the neural network field on how to speed up backpropagation. For example, Fahlman and Touretzky of Carnegie-Mellon have compiled and tested a variety of intuitive insights which can speed up convergence a hundredfold. Their benchmark problems may be very useful in evaluating other methods which claim to do the same. A few authors have copied simple methods from the field of numerical analysis, such as quasi-Newton methods (BFGS) and Polak-Ribiere conjugate gradients; however, the former works only on small problems (a hundred or so weights) [22], while the latter works well only with batch learning and very careful line searches. The need for careful line searches is discussed in the literature [23], but I have found it to be unusually important when working with large problems, including simulated linear mappings.

In my own work, I have used Shanno's more recent conjugate gradient method with batch learning; for a *dense* training set—made up of distinctly different patterns—this method worked better than anything else I tried, including pattern learning methods [12]. Many researchers have used *approximate* Newton's methods, without saying that they are using an approximation; however an *exact* Newton's method can also be implemented in $O(N)$ storage, and has worked reasonably well in early tests [12]. Shanno has reported new breakthroughs in function minimization which may perform still better [24]. Still, there is clearly a lot of room for improvement through further research.

Needless to say, it can be much easier to converge to a set of weights which do not minimize error or which assume a simpler network; methods of that sort are also popular, but are useful only when they clearly fit the application at hand for identifiable reasons.

E. Miscellaneous Issues

Minimizing square error and maximizing likelihood are often taken for granted as fundamental principles in large parts of engineering; however, there is a large literature on alternative approaches [12], both in neural network theory and in robust statistics.

These literatures are beyond the scope of this paper, but a few related points may be worth noting. For example, instead of minimizing square error, we could minimize the 1.5 power of error; all of the operations above still go through. We can minimize E of (5) *plus* some constant k times the sum of squares of the weights; as k goes to infinity and the network is made linear, this converges to Kohonen's pseudoinverse method, a common form of associative memory. Statisticians like Dempster and Efron have argued that the linear form of this approach can be better than the usual least squares methods; their arguments capture the essential insight that people can forecast by analogy to historical precedent, instead of forecasting by a comprehensive model or network. Presumably, an ideal network would bring together both kinds of forecasting [12], [20].

Many authors worry a lot about local minima. In using backpropagation through time in robust estimation, I found it important to keep the "memory" weights near zero at first, and free them up gradually in order to minimize problems. When T is much larger than m—as statisticians recommend for good generalization—local minima are probably a lot less serious than rumor has it. Still, with T larger than m, it is very easy to construct local minima. Consider the example with $m = 2$ shown in Table I.

Table 1 Training Set for Local Minima

t	$\mathbf{X}(t)$	$Y(t)$
1	0 1	.1
2	1 0	.1
3	1 1	.9

The error for each of the patterns can be plotted as a contour map as a function of the two weights w_1 and w_2. (For this simple example, no threshold term is assumed.) Each map is made up of straight contours, defining a fairly sharp trough about a central line. The three central lines for the three patterns form a triangle, the vertices of which correspond roughly to the local minima. Even when T is much larger than m, conflicts like this can exist within the training set. Again, however, this may not be an overwhelming problem in practical applications [19].

V. Summary

Backpropagation through time can be applied to many different categories of dynamical systems—neural networks, feedforward systems of equations, systems with time lags, systems with instantaneous feedback between variables (as in ordinary differential equations or simultaneous equation models), and so on. The derivatives which it calculates can be used in pattern recognition, in systems identification, and in stochastic and deterministic control. This paper has presented the key equations of backpropagation, as applied to neural networks of varying degrees of complexity. It has also discussed other papers which elaborate on the extensions of this method to more general applications and some of the tradeoffs involved.

REFERENCES

[1] P. Werbos, "Beyond regression: New tools for prediction and analysis in the behavioral sciences," Ph.D. dissertation, Committee on Appl. Math., Harvard Univ., Cambridge, MA, Nov. 1974.
[2] D. Rumelhart, D. Hinton, and G. Williams, "Learning internal representations by error propagation," in D. Rumelhart and F. McClelland, eds., *Parallel Distributed Processing, Vol. 1.* Cambridge, MA: M.I.T. Press, 1986.
[3] D. B. Parker, "Learning-logic," M.I.T. Cen. Computational Res. Economics Management Sci., Cambridge, MA, TR-47, 1985.
[4] Y. Le Cun, "Une procedure d'apprentissage pour reseau a seuil assymetrique," in *Proc. Cognitiva '85*, Paris, France, June 1985, pp. 599–604.
[5] R. Watrous and L. Shastri, "Learning phonetic features using connectionist networks: an experiment in speech recognition," in *Proc. 1st IEEE Int. Conf. Neural Networks*, June 1987.
[6] H. Sawai, A. Waibel, P. Haffner, M. Miyatake, and K. Shikano, "Parallelism, hierarchy, scaling in time-delay neural networks for spotting Japanese phonemes/CV-syllables," in *Proc. IEEE Int. Joint Conf. Neural Networks*, June 1989.
[7] D. Nguyen and B. Widrow, "The truck backer-upper: An example of self-learning in neural networks," in W. T. Miller, R. Sutton, and P. Werbos, Eds., *Neural Networks for Robotics and Control.* Cambridge, MA: M.I.T. Press, 1990.
[8] M. Jordan, "Generic constraints on underspecified target trajectories," in *Proc. IEEE Int. Joint Conf. Neural Networks*, June 1989.
[9] M. Kawato, "Computational schemes and neural network models for formation and control of multijoint arm trajectory," in W. T. Miller, R. Sutton, and P. Werbos, Eds., *Neural Networks for Robotics and Control.* Cambridge, MA: M.I.T. Press, 1990.
[10] R. Narendra, "Adaptive control using neural networks," in W. T. Miller, R. Sutton, and P. Werbos, Eds., *Neural Networks for Robotics and Control.* Cambridge, MA: M.I.T. Press, 1990.
[11] P. Werbos, "Maximizing long-term gas industry profits in two minutes in Lotus using neural network methods," *IEEE Trans. Syst., Man, Cybern.*, Mar./Apr. 1989.
[12] —, "Backpropagation: Past and future," in *Proc. 2nd IEEE Int. Conf. Neural Networks*, June 1988. The transcript of the talk and slides, available from the author, are more introductory in nature and more comprehensive in some respects.
[13] I. Guyon, I. Poujaud, L. Personnaz, G. Dreyfus, J. Denker, and Y. Le Cun, "Comparing different neural network architectures for classifying handwritten digits," in *Proc. IEEE Int. Joint Conf. Neural Networks*, June 1989.
[14] P. Werbos, "Applications of advances in nonlinear sensitivity analysis," in R. Drenick and F. Kozin, Eds., *Systems Modeling and Optimization: Proc. 10th IFIP Conf. (1981).* New York: Springer-Verlag, 1982.
[15] —, "Generalization of backpropagation with application to a recurrent gas market model," *Neural Networks*, Oct. 1988.
[16] F. J. Pineda, "Generalization of backpropagation to recurrent and higher order networks," in *Proc. IEEE Conf. Neural Inform. Processing Syst.*, 1987.
[17] L. B. Almeida, "A learning rule for asynchronous perceptrons with feedback in a combinatorial environment," in *Proc. 1st IEEE Int. Conf. Neural Networks*, 1987.
[18] B. A. Pearlmutter, "Learning state space trajectories in recurrent neural networks," in *Proc. Int. Joint Conf. Neural Networks*, June 1989.
[19] R. Williams, "Adaptive state representation and estimation using recurrent connectionist networks," in W. T. Miller, R. Sutton, and P. Werbos, Eds., *Neural Networks for Robotics and Control.* Cambridge, MA: M.I.T. Press, 1990.
[20] P. Werbos, "Learning how the world works: Specifications for predictive networks in robots and brains," in *Proc. 1987 IEEE Int. Conf. Syst., Man, Cybern.*, 1987.
[21] —, "Consistency of HDP applied to a simple reinforcement learning problem," *Neural Networks*, Mar. 1990.
[22] J. Dennis and R. Schnabel, *Numerical Methods for Unconstrained Optimization and Nonlinear Equations.* Englewood Cliffs, NJ: Prentice-Hall, 1983.
[23] D. Shanno, "Conjugate-gradient methods with inexact searches," *Math. Oper. Res.*, vol. 3, Aug. 1978.
[24] —, "Recent advances in numerical techniques for large-scale optimization," in W. T. Miller, R. Sutton, and P. Werbos, Eds., *Neural Networks for Robotics and Control.* Cambridge, MA: M.I.T. Press, 1990.

A Neural Network for Visual Pattern Recognition

Kunihiko Fukushima
NHK Science and Technical Research Laboratories

This model of the neural network offers insight into the brain's complex mechanisms as well as design principles for new information processors.

Visual pattern recognition such as reading characters or distinguishing shapes—a task easily accomplished by human beings—presents significant difficulties to those attempting to design information processors that can do the same thing. The solution to this design dilemma apparently resides in the brain itself.

The human brain has more than 10 billion neural cells, which have complicated interconnections and constitute a large-scale network. Hence, uncovering the neural mechanisms of the higher functions of the brain is not easy. In the conventional neurophysiological approach, for example, a microelectrode is used to record the response of these cells. However, the recording can be made from, at most, a few cells simultaneously. Although we can obtain fragmentary knowledge thus, understanding the mechanism of the network as a whole proves difficult.

A modeling approach, which is a synthetic approach using neural network models, therefore continues to gain importance. In the modeling approach, we study how to interconnect neurons to synthesize a *brain model*, which is a network with the same functions and abilities as the brain.

When synthesizing a model, we try to follow physiological evidence as faithfully as possible. For parts not yet clear, however, we construct a hypothesis and synthesize a model that follows the hypothesis. We then analyze or simulate the behavior of the model and compare it with that of the brain. If we find any discrepancy in the behavior between the model and the brain, we change the initial hypothesis and modify the model following a new hypothesis. We then test the behavior of the model again. We repeat this procedure until the model behaves in the same way as the brain. Although we must still verify the validity of the model by physiological experiment, it is probable that the brain uses the same mechanism as the model, because both respond in the same way. Hence, modeling neural networks promises to help us uncover the mechanism of the brain.

The relationship between modeling neural networks and neurophysiology resembles that between theoretical physics and experimental physics. Modeling takes a synthetic approach, while neurophysiology or psychology takes an analytical approach.

Once we complete a model, its simplification makes it easy to see the essential algorithm of information processing in the brain. We can use the algorithm directly as a design principle for new information processors.

Modeling neural networks is useful in explaining the brain and also in engineering applications. It brings the results of neurophysiological and psychological research to engineering applications in the most direct way possible.

This article discusses a neural network model thus obtained, a model with selective attention in visual pattern recognition.[1,2]

Researchers have reported various models capable of visual pattern recognition, models that have the function of self-organization and can learn to recognize patterns. Many are hierarchical networks consisting of layers of neuron-like cells. The ability to process information increases in proportion to the number of layers in the network. Various studies have attempted to find effective learning procedures for the self-organization of multilayered networks. An example of *learning-with-a-teacher* (supervised learning) useful for training multilayered networks is the back-propagating errors

Reprinted from *IEEE Computer*, vol. 21, no. 3, pp. 65–75, March 1988.

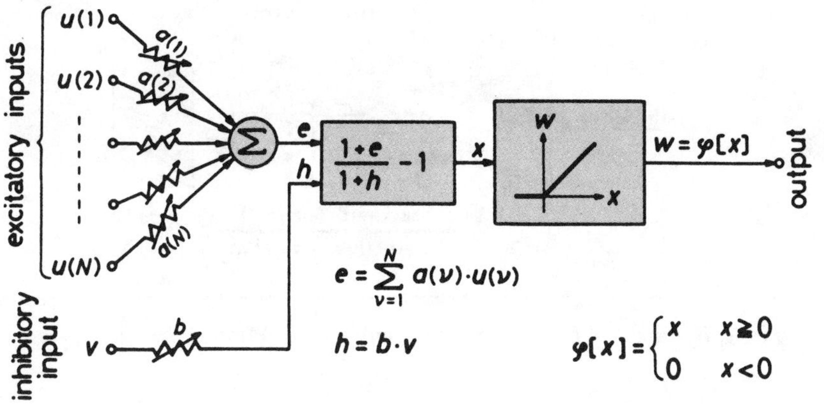

Figure 1. Input-to-output characteristics of a u_S cell: a typical example of the cells employed in the neural network model.[7] The strength of the input connections (or weights), a(1), a(2), ... , and b, is variable and reinforced during the process of self-organization of the network. The excitatory effect e, which is the weighted sum of all the excitatory inputs, is suppressed by the inhibitory effect h in a shunting manner. When the inhibition is stronger than the excitation, the output of the cell becomes zero. Some of the cells in the network have fixed input connections formed from the beginning and not variable. In some kinds of cells, a nonlinear summation of excitatory inputs is performed.

procedure.[3] The *cognitron*[4] model, which I proposed in 1975, uses *learning-without-a-teacher* (unsupervised learning). The procedure used in the cognitron has been classified under the competitive-learning paradigm.[5]

The cognitron, like many other models, does not have the ability to correctly recognize position-shifted or shape-distorted patterns. The conventional cognitron usually recognizes the same pattern presented at a different position as a different pattern. I proposed the *neocognitron*[6,7] to eliminate this defect. The neocognitron has the ability to recognize stimulus patterns correctly, even if the patterns are shifted in position or distorted in shape.

When two or more patterns are presented simultaneously, however, the neocognitron does not always correctly recognize them. To improve the function of the neocognitron, backward connections were added to the conventional neocognitron, which had only forward connections. The new model thus obtained acquired the function of selective attention in visual pattern recognition. This model, discussed in this article, can automatically segment and recognize individual patterns presented simultaneously. The model can also restore imperfect patterns and eliminate noise from contaminated patterns.

Although various models of associative memory have reportedly been able to recall complete patterns from imperfect ones,[8] most do not work well unless the stimulus pattern is identical in size, shape, and position to a training pattern. In contrast to such earlier models, the new model works well even for deformed stimulus patterns, regardless of their position.

Physiology

In the visual area of the cerebrum, neurons respond selectively to local features of a visual pattern, such as lines and edges in particular orientations.[9] In the area higher than the visual cortex, cells exist that respond selectively to certain figures like circles, triangles, squares, or even human faces.[10] Accordingly, the visual system seems to have a hierarchical structure, in which simple features are first extracted from a stimulus pattern, then integrated into more complicated ones. In this hierarchy, a cell in a higher stage generally receives signals from a wider area of the retina and is more insensitive to the position of the stimulus.

Within the hierarchical structure of the visual system are forward (afferent, or bottom-up) and backward (efferent, or top-down) signal flows. For example, anatomical observations show that the major visual areas of the cerebrum interconnect in a precise topographical and reciprocal fashion.

Such neural networks in the brain are not always complete at birth. They develop gradually, neurons extending branches and making connections with many other neurons, adapting flexibly to circumstances after birth.

This kind of physiological evidence suggests a network structure for the model.

Outline of the model

The model is a network consisting of neuron-like cells of the *analog* type; that is, their inputs and outputs take non-negative analog values, corresponding to the instantaneous firing frequencies of biological neurons. Figure 1 shows a typical example of the cells employed in the network.

The network has a hierarchical multilayered structure consisting of a cascade of many layers of cells, as shown in Figure 2. The network has forward and backward connections between cells. In this hierarchy, the forward signals manage the function of pattern recognition, while the backward signals manage the function of selective attention, pattern segmentation, and associative recall.

Some of the connections between cells are variable, and the network can acquire the ability to recognize patterns by learning-without-a-teacher. The network can be trained to recognize any set of patterns. During the process of learning, variable connections grow gradually in accordance with the stimuli given the network. The repeated presentation of a set of training patterns is sufficient for the self-organization of the network; it does not need information about the categories into which these patterns should be classified.

When a composite figure consisting of two or more patterns is presented to the model that has finished learning, the model selectively focuses its attention on one pattern after another, segments the pattern from the others, and recognizes it separately. Even if noise or defects affect the pattern, the model can recognize it and recall the complete pattern in which the noise has been eliminated and the defects corrected. Perfect recall does not require that the stimulus pattern be identical in shape to the training pattern the model learned. A pattern distorted in shape or changed in size can be correctly recognized and the missing portions restored.

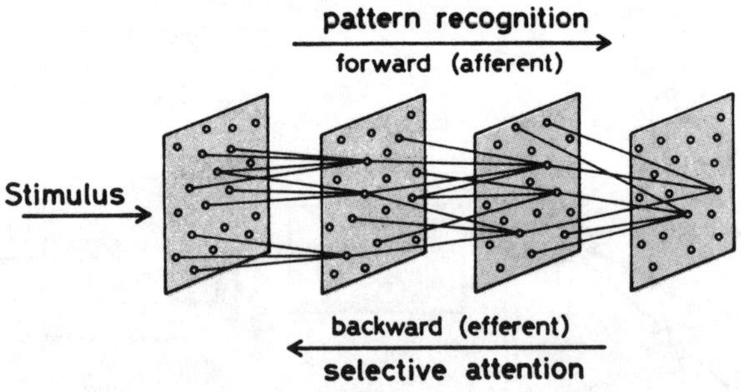

Figure 2. Hierarchical network structure and the signal flow in the network.

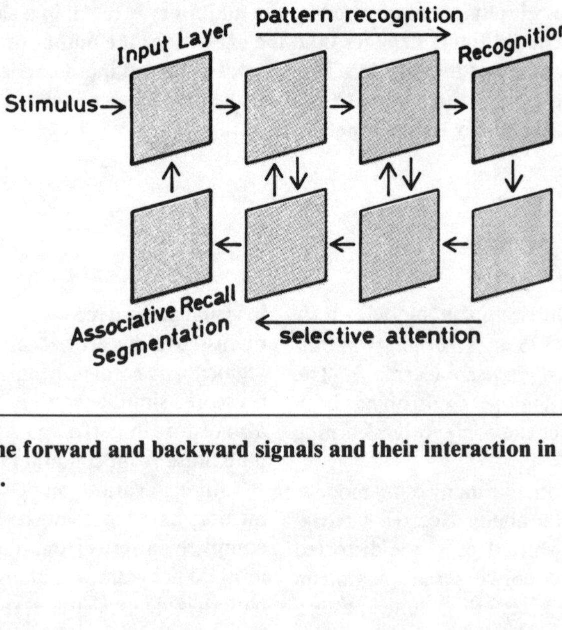

Figure 3. The forward and backward signals and their interaction in the hierarchical network.

Figure 3 schematically illustrates the signal flow in the network. In this diagram, layers of cells in the forward paths and the backward paths are drawn separately.

A stimulus pattern is presented to the lowest stage of the forward paths, the *input layer*, which consists of a two-dimensional array of receptor cells. The highest stage of the forward paths is the *recognition layer*. After the process of learning ends, the final result of the pattern recognition shows in the response of the cells of the highest stage. In other words, cells of the recognition layer work as *gnostic cells* (or *grandmother cells*); usually one cell is activated, corresponding to the category of the specific stimulus pattern. Pattern recognition by the network occurs on the basis of similarity in shape among patterns, unaffected by deformation, changes in size, and shifts in the position of the input patterns.

The output of the recognition layer is sent to lower stages through the backward paths. The forward and the backward signals interact with each other in the hierarchical network. The backward signals facilitate the forward signals and, at the same time, the forward signals gate the backward signal flow.*

The result of associative recall appears in the lowest stage of the backward paths, the *recall layer*. We can also interpret the output of the recall layer as the result of segmentation. The response of the recall layer is fed back to the input layer.

At each stage of the hierarchical network, several kinds of cells exist. Notation such as u_S, u_C, w_S, and x_C denotes cells, where letters u and w indicate the cells in the forward paths and backward paths, respectively. Figure 4 illustrates how the different cells, represented by circles, are connected to each other. Although the figure shows only one of each kind of cell in each stage, numerous cells actually exist arranged in a two-dimensional array. For example, the notation u_{Cl} denotes a u_C cell in the l-th stage of the hierarchical network. The L-th stage is the highest stage. In Figure 4, L=3. The notation U_{Cl} denotes the layer of u_{Cl} cells. In Figure 4, layer U_{C0} is the input layer, layer U_{C3} is the recognition layer, and layer W_{C0} is the recall layer.

Between the cells in Figure 4 are connections denoted by single lines or by double lines. A single line indicates one-to-one connections between the two groups of cells; a double line indicates converging or diverging connections between them.

A more detailed illustration of the spatial interconnections between neighboring cells appears in Figure 5. The functions of these cells will be considered next.

Forward paths in the network

If we consider the forward paths in the network only, the model has almost the same structure and function as the neocognitron[6,7] neural network model. In

*This process resembles that of the adaptive resonance theory[11] in the sense that the forward and backward signals interact with each other, but the method of interaction differs.

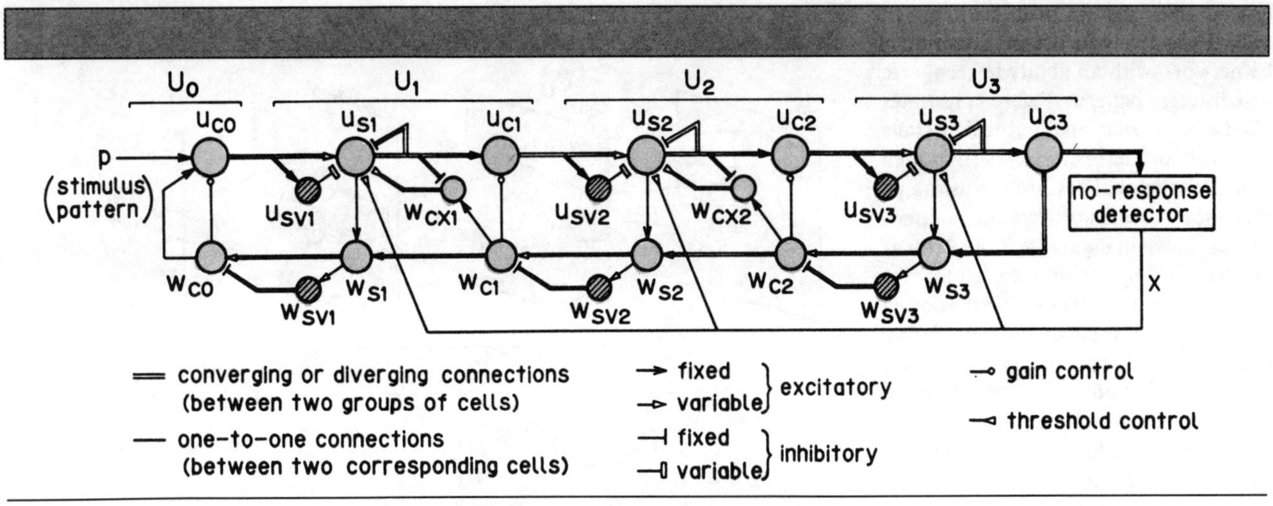

Figure 4. Hierarchical structure of the interconnections between different kinds of cells.[2]

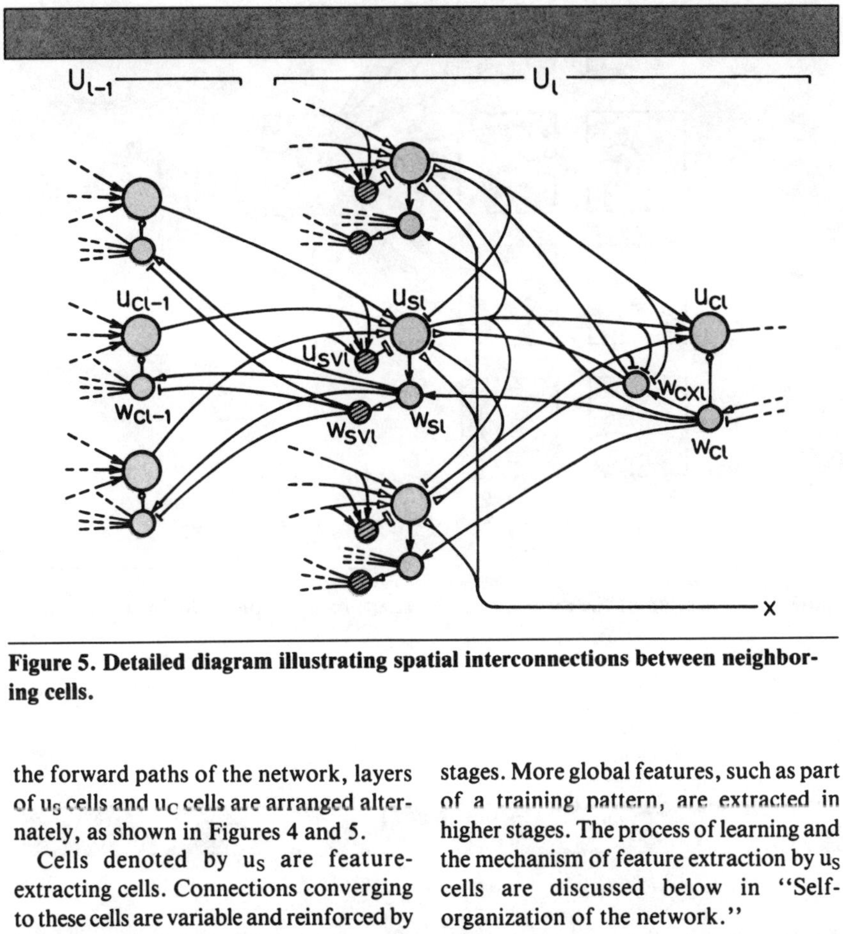

Figure 5. Detailed diagram illustrating spatial interconnections between neighboring cells.

the forward paths of the network, layers of u_S cells and u_C cells are arranged alternately, as shown in Figures 4 and 5.

Cells denoted by u_S are feature-extracting cells. Connections converging to these cells are variable and reinforced by learning (or training). After finishing the learning, u_S cells can extract features from the input pattern. In other words, a u_S cell is activated only when a particular feature is presented at a certain position in the input layer. The features extracted by the u_S cells are determined during the learning process. Generally speaking, local features, such as a line at a particular orientation, are extracted in the lower stages. More global features, such as part of a training pattern, are extracted in higher stages. The process of learning and the mechanism of feature extraction by u_S cells are discussed below in "Self-organization of the network."

The u_C cells are inserted in the network to allow for positional errors in the features of the stimulus. Connections from u_S cells to u_C cells are fixed and invariable.

The lower part of Figure 6 shows a detailed structure between layers of u_S cells and u_C cells. Each layer of u_S cells or u_C cells is divided into subgroups according to the features to which they respond. The cells in each subgroup are arranged in a two-dimensional array. The connections converging to the cells in a subgroup are homogeneous: All the cells in a subgroup receive input connections of the same spatial distribution, where only the positions of the preceding cells shift in parallel with the position of the cells in the subgroup. This condition of homogeneity holds for fixed connections and for variable connections. As discussed in "Self-organization of the network," the reinforcement of the variable connections is always performed under this condition.

Each u_C cell receives signals from a group of u_S cells that extract the same feature, but from slightly different positions. The u_C cell is activated if at least one of these u_S cells is active. Even if the stimulus feature shifts position and another u_S cell is activated instead of the first one, the same u_C cell keeps responding. Hence, the u_C cell's response is less sensitive to shifts in position of the input pattern.

In the whole network, with its alternate layers of u_S cells and u_C cells, the process of feature extraction by u_S cells and toleration of positional shift by u_C cells repeats. During this process, local features extracted in a lower stage are gradually integrated into more global features. Figure 6 illustrates this situation.

Finally, each u_C cell of the recognition layer U_{CL} at the highest stage (denoted by u_{CL}) integrates all the information of the input pattern; each cell responds only to one specific pattern. In other words, only one u_{CL} cell, corresponding to the category of the input pattern, is activated. Other cells respond to the patterns of other categories.

Tolerating positional error a little at a

time at each stage, rather than all in one step, plays an important role in endowing the network with an ability to recognize even distorted patterns. Figure 7 illustrates this. Let a u_S cell in an intermediate stage of the network have already been trained to extract a global feature consisting of three local features of a training pattern "A" as shown in Figure 7a. The cell tolerates the positional error of each local feature, if its deviation falls within the dotted circle. Hence, this u_S cell responds to any of the deformed patterns shown in Figure 7b. The toleration of positional errors should not be too large at this stage. If too large errors are tolerated at one step, the network may come to respond erroneously, such as recognizing a stimulus like Figure 7c as an "A" pattern.

Since errors in the relative position of local features are tolerated in the process of extracting and integrating features, the same u_{CL} cell responds in the highest stage, even if the input pattern is deformed, changed in size, or shifted in position.* The network recognizes the "shape" of the pattern independent of its size and position.

When two or more patterns are simultaneously presented to the input layer U_{C0}, two or more u_{CL} cells may be activated at first. However, all of these cells but one soon stop responding. Usually only one u_{CL} cell continues to respond because of competition by lateral inhibition between feature-extracting u_S cells.[2] Lateral inhibition works in the highest stage and in the intermediate stages.

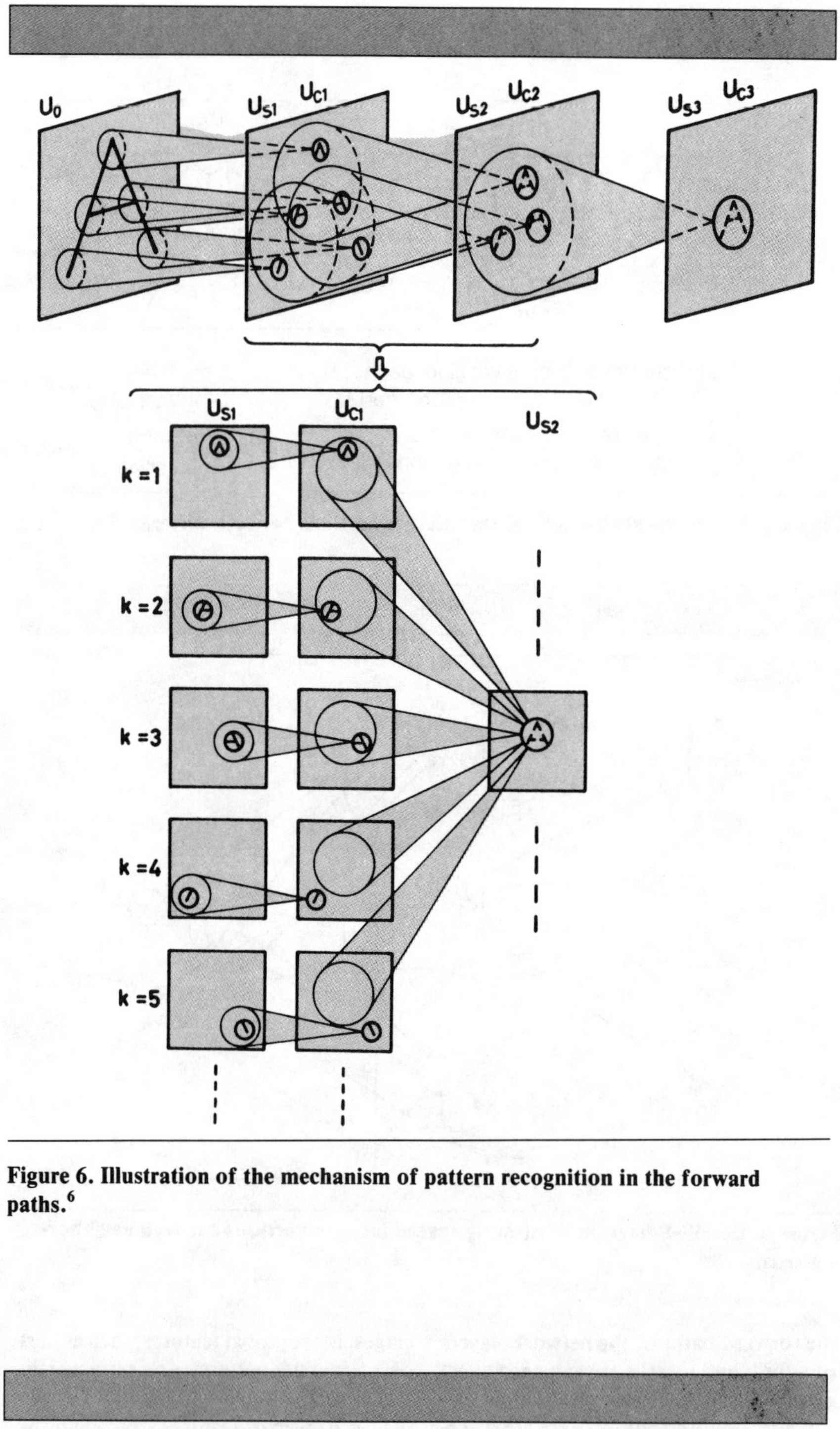

Figure 6. Illustration of the mechanism of pattern recognition in the forward paths.[6]

Self-organization of the network

The self-organization of the network results from learning-without-a-teacher. The network by itself acquires the ability to classify and to recognize patterns correctly on the basis of similarity in shape.

In the initial state before learning, all the variable connections in the network have

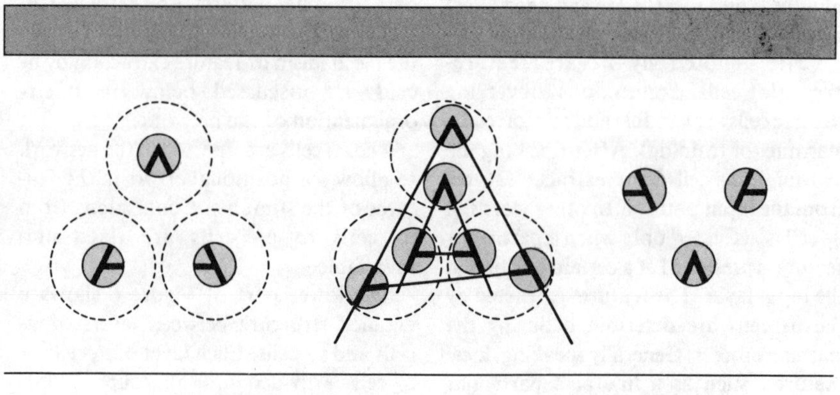

Figure 7. Illustration of the principle for recognizing deformed patterns.

*It is difficult to state quantitatively to what degree the network can cope with deformation in patterns, because we do not have an appropriate mathematical measure to correctly express the psychological feeling of the deformation. We can get a rough idea of the degree of deformation that can be tolerated. For example, in an article to be published in April 1988,[12] Figure 14 shows some examples of deformed patterns that the neocognitron recognized correctly. These examples were obtained by a neocognitron trained by learning-with-a-teacher. Generally, the results obtained by learning-without-a-teacher are somewhat worse.

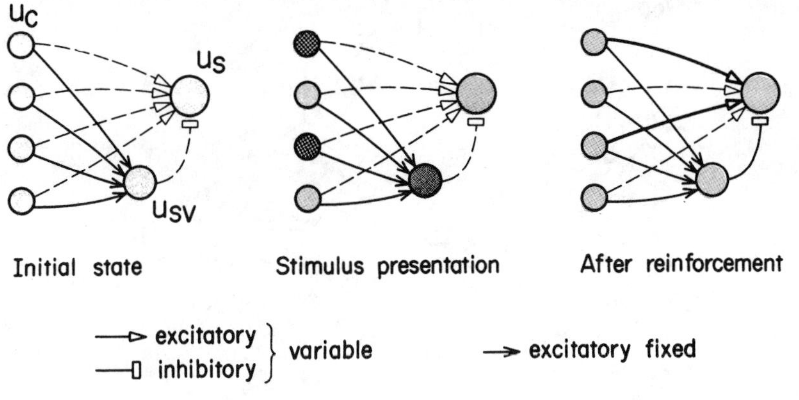

Figure 8. The process of reinforcement of the forward connections converging to a feature-extracting u_S cell. The density of the shadow in a circle represents the intensity of the response of the cell. (a) shows the initial state before training. (b) shows stimulus presentation during the training. (c) shows the connections after reinforcement.

a strength of zero. In the network, reinforcement of the forward connections comes first; the backward connections are reinforced later. Hence, during the process of reinforcement of the forward connections, no backward signal flows in the network. The variable forward connections are reinforced in a manner similar to that in the neocognitron.[6,7] After finishing the reinforcement of the forward connections, the network reinforces the backward connections by the same amount as the forward connections with which they form pairs.

The reinforcement of the forward connections is performed according to two principles. The first was introduced for the self-organization of the cognitron[4] model. Specifically, among the cells situated in a certain small area, only the one responding most strongly has its input connections reinforced. The amount of reinforcement of each input connection to this maximum-output cell is proportional to the intensity of the response of the cell from which the relevant connection leads.

This principle is applied to the variable input connections converging to feature-extracting u_S cells. Both excitatory and inhibitory connections are reinforced following this principle.

Figure 8 illustrates this process of reinforcement, showing only the forward connections converging to a u_S cell. As shown in Figure 8a, the u_S cell receives variable excitatory connections from a group of u_C cells in the preceding layer. The cell also receives a variable inhibitory connection from a subsidiary inhibitory cell, called a u_{SV} cell. The u_{SV} cell receives fixed excitatory connections from the same group of u_C cells as does this u_S cell, and always responds with the average intensity of the output of the u_C cells. The initial strength of these variable connections is nearly zero.*

Suppose this u_S cell responds most strongly of the u_S cells in its vicinity when a training stimulus is presented (see Figure 8b). According to the first principle, variable connections leading from activated u_C and u_{SV} cells are reinforced as shown in Figure 8c. The variable excitatory connections to the u_S cell grow into a "template" that exactly matches the spatial distribution of the response of the cells in the preceding layer. The inhibitory variable connections from the u_{SV} cell are reinforced at the same time, but not as strongly because the output of the u_{SV} cell is not as large.

After completion of the training, the u_S cell acquires the ability to extract the feature of the stimulus presented during the training period. Through the excitatory connections, the u_S cell receives signals indicating the existence of the relevant feature to be extracted. If an irrelevant feature is presented, the inhibitory signal from the u_{SV} cell becomes stronger than the direct excitatory signals from the u_C cells, and the response of the u_S cell is suppressed. The u_S cell is activated only when the relevant feature is presented. We could say that the u_{SV} cell watches for the existence of irrelevant features. Thus, inhibitory u_{SV} cells play an important role in endowing the feature-extracting u_S cells with the ability to differentiate irrelevant features, and in increasing the selectivity of feature extraction.

According to this principle, among the u_S cells in a certain small area, only the one cell that yields the maximum output has its input connections reinforced. Because of the "winner-takes-all" nature of this principle, duplicate formation of cells that extract the same feature does not occur, and the formation of a redundant network can be prevented. Only the one cell giving the best response to a training stimulus is selected, and only that cell is reinforced so as to respond more appropriately to the stimulus.

Once a cell is selected and reinforced to respond to a feature, the cell usually loses its responsiveness to other features. When a different feature is presented, usually a different cell yields the maximum output and has its input connections reinforced. Thus, "division of labor" among the cells occurs automatically.

With this principle, the network also develops a self-repairing function. If a cell that has responded strongly to a stimulus is damaged and ceases to respond, another cell, which happens to respond more strongly than others, starts to grow and substitutes for the damaged cell. Until then, the larger response of the first cell had prevented the growth of a second cell.

The second principle introduced for the self-organization of the network states that the maximum-output cell not only grows, but also controls the growth of neighboring cells, working, so to speak, like a seed in crystal growth. Neighboring cells have their input connections reinforced in the same way as the seed cell.

When a seed cell is selected from a subgroup of u_S cells, all the other u_S cells in the subgroup grow to have input connections of the same spatial distribution as the seed cell. As a result, all the u_S cells in a subgroup grow to receive input connec-

*Each u_S cell has very weak and diffused excitatory connections only during the initial period of self-organization. Once a reinforcement of the input connections begins, these weak and diffuse initial connections disappear.[12]

tions of identical spatial distribution where only the positions of the preceding u_C cells have shifted in parallel with the positions of the u_S cells. Because connections develop iteratively in a subgroup, all the u_S cells in the subgroup come to respond selectively to a particular feature. Differences among these cells arise only from differences in position of the feature to be extracted.

Backward paths

The output of the recognition layer U_{CL} is sent back to lower stages through backward paths. It reaches the recall layer W_{C0} at the lowest stage of the backward paths. The backward signals are transmitted retracing the same route as the forward signals, because the cells in the backward paths receive gate signals from the cells in the forward paths. Guided by the forward signal flow, the backward signals reach exactly the same positions at which the input pattern is presented.

Since the backward signals are sent back only from the activated u_{CL} cell, only the signal components corresponding to the recognized pattern reach the recall layer W_{C0}. Therefore, we can interpret the output of the recall layer as the result of segmentation, where only components relevant to a single pattern are selected from the stimulus. Even if the stimulus pattern now recognized is a deformed version of a training pattern, the deformed pattern is segmented and emerges with its deformed shape.

Let us consider this process in more detail. First, look at the backward signals from an arbitrary w_S cell to the w_C cells of the preceding stage (see Figure 5). The network is designed so that the strength of the variable backward connections is automatically controlled in the following manner: After finishing the reinforcement of the forward connections (refer to Figure 8), the backward connections descending from a w_S cell are automatically reinforced to have a strength proportional to the forward connections ascending to the u_S cell paired with the w_S cell. Consequently, if an excitatory forward path forms to a u_S cell from a u_C cell, an excitatory backward path forms automatically from the corresponding w_S cell to the corresponding w_C cell. This also holds for the inhibitory backward path via the subsidiary w_{SV} cell, which corresponds to the u_{SV} cell in the forward paths. Hence, depending on whether a u_S cell receives an overall excitatory or inhibitory effect from a u_C cell through forward connections, the corresponding w_C cell also receives an overall excitatory or inhibitory effect from the corresponding w_S cell through backward connections.

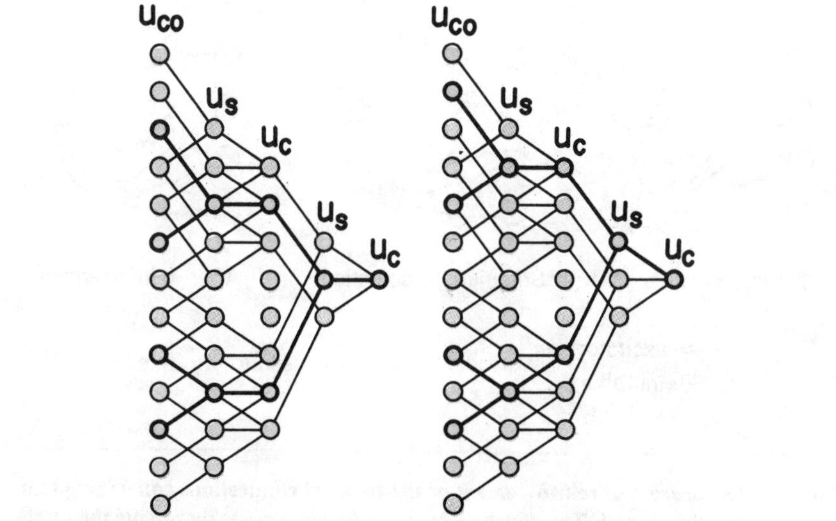

Figure 9. A simplified illustration of the forward signal flow in the network. Deformed stimuli (a) and (b) presented at different positions on the input layer (u_{C0}) elicit the same response from the u_C cell at the highest stage. The backward signals are controlled to retrace the same route as the forward signals, in the opposite direction.

Corresponding to the fixed forward connections that converge to a u_C cell from a number of u_S cells, many backward connections diverge from a w_C cell towards w_S cells (see Figure 5). However, we do not want all the w_S cells receiving excitatory backward signals from the w_C cell to be activated for the following reason: To activate a u_C cell in the forward path, the activation of at least one preceding u_S cell is sufficient. Usually only a small number of preceding u_S cells actually are activated, as shown in Figure 9. To elicit a similar response from the w_S cells in the backward paths, the network is synthesized in such a way that each w_S cell receives excitatory backward signals from w_C cells and a gate signal from the corresponding u_S cell. The w_S cell is activated only when it receives a signal both from u_S and w_C cells. Because of this network architecture, in the backward paths from w_C cells to w_S cells, the signals retrace the same route as the forward signals from u_S cells to u_C cells.

Gain control

Interaction between forward and backward signals is not unilateral. Forward cells receive gain-control signals from the corresponding backward cells, and the forward signal flow is facilitated by the backward signals. The gain of each u_C cell in forward paths is controlled by a signal from a corresponding w_C cell (Figures 4 and 5). When the w_C cell is silent, the gain between the inputs and the output of the u_C cell gradually attenuates from its initial value of 1.0 with the passage of time. When the w_C cell is activated, however, the attenuated gain recovers. Thus, only the forward signals are facilitated in the paths in which backward signals flow.

Now let's consider a case in which a stimulus consisting of two or more patterns is presented. Let one of the u_{CL} cells in the recognition layer be activated and one of the patterns in the stimulus recognized. Only the forward paths relevant to this pattern are facilitated by the action of backward signals from the u_{CL} cell. The forward paths corresponding to other patterns gradually lose their responsiveness because they receive no facilitation. Attention focuses selectively on only one of the patterns in the stimulus.

Threshold control

When some part of the input pattern is missing and the feature that should exist there fails to be extracted in the forward paths, the backward signal flow stops at that point. In such a case, the threshold for extraction of that feature automatically lowers and the model tries to extract even vague traces of the undetected feature. The w_{CX} cells detect the failure to extract a feature when the cells in the backward paths are active but the corresponding cells in the forward paths are not (Figures 4 and 5). The signal from w_{CX} cells weakens the efficiency of inhibition by u_{SV} cells and virtually lowers the threshold for feature extraction by u_S cells. (The signal from w_{CX} cells works like a neuromodulator in biological systems.) Thus, u_S cells are made to respond even to incomplete features to which they would not, in the normal state, respond.

Once a feature is thus extracted in the forward paths, the backward signal can be further transmitted to lower stages through the path unlocked by the newly activated forward cell. Hence, a complete pattern, including defective parts, emerges in the recall layer. Noise and blemishes have been eliminated from this pattern, because no backward signals return to their components. Thus, we can interpret the output of the recall layer W_{C0} as an auto-associative recall from associative memory.

Sometimes all the u_{CL} cells in the recognition layer are silent. The no-response state of the u_{CL} cells may occur, for instance, if the stimulus pattern differs greatly in shape from the original pattern, or if too many patterns are simultaneously presented to the input layer. If all the u_{CL} cells in the recognition layer are silent, information processing of the network goes no further because no backward signal flows in the network.

The no-response detector shown at the far right in Figure 4 always monitors the response of the u_{CL} cells. If all the u_{CL} cells are silent, the no-response detector sends another threshold-control signal through path x (shown in Figure 4) to all the u_S cells of all stages and lowers their threshold for feature extraction. The longer the silent state of the u_{CL} cells continues, the higher the value of the threshold-control signal. Hence, at least one u_{CL} cell is activated after a certain time.

Switching attention

Suppose one pattern in a composite stimulus is being attended to and recognized. A momentary interruption of the backward signal-flow suffices to switch attention to another pattern.

The gain of u_C cells is designed to be controlled as follows when switching attention: After the disappearance of the facilitating signal from the corresponding w_C cell in the backward path, each u_C cell has its gain lowered if the gain was previously kept high by facilitation. A decrease in gain occurs like fatigue, depending on the degree of the forced increase of the gain until then. On the other hand, the u_C cell will recover its gain if the gain was previously attenuated.

Because of this method of controlling the gain of the u_C cells, signals corresponding to the previous pattern have difficulty flowing through the forward paths. Usually another u_{CL} cell, hitherto silent, will be activated. (If no u_{CL} cell is activated, the no-response detector works until at least one u_{CL} cell is activated.) Consequently, the backward signals from the newly activated u_{CL} cell ease the flow of the forward signals for the new pattern. A repetition of this process switches attention to each of the patterns in the stimulus figure in turn, and they are recognized and recalled one after another.

Computer simulation

Let's look at the behavior of the model as simulated on a MicroVAX II minicomputer, with a program written in Fortran. The simulated network has three stages of hierarchy (L = 3). The input layer U_{C0} has 19×19 cells. The number of cells in the network totals about 41,399.*

The variable connections in the network were reinforced by learning-without-a-teacher. Figure 10 shows the five training patterns presented to the network during the learning period. Each of these patterns was presented only 11 times, enough to complete the self-organization.** During the learning period, these patterns were repeatedly presented only in this shape; deformed versions were not presented at all. After completing the learning cycle, all the variable connections were fixed.

Figures 11 through 14 show the behavior of a network that has finished learning. In these figures, the response of the cells in the input layer U_{C0} and the recall layer W_{C0} is shown in time sequence. The numeral to the upper left of each pattern represents time t after the start of stimulus presentation.*** The stimulus pattern given to this network is identical to the response of the input layer at $t = 0$, shown in the upper left of each figure. (Note that the input pattern p appears directly in layer U_{C0} at $t = 0$, because no response is elicited from layer W_{C0} at $t < 0$.)

Figure 11 shows the response to a stimulus consisting of two juxtaposed patterns, "2" and "3." In the recognition layer, not shown in this figure, the u_{CL} cell corresponding to pattern "2" happens to be activated first. The signal is fed back to the recall layer through backward paths, but the middle part of the segmented pattern "2" is missing because of the interference from the closely adjacent "3." However, the missing part soon recovers because the components of pattern "3," which is not being attended to, are gradually attenuated by the decrease of gain of the forward cells.

At $t = 5$, the backward signal flow is interrupted for a moment to switch attention. The mark ▼ denotes the execution of this operation. Since the facilitating signals from backward cells stop, forward cells whose responsiveness has been kept high by facilitation will now lose some of their responsiveness. On the other hand, cells whose responsiveness has been decreased will recover their responsiveness. Thus, the forward paths for pattern "2," which have so far been facilitated, now lose their conductivity and the u_{CL} cell for pattern "3" is activated in the recognition layer. Since the backward signals are fed back from this newly activated u_{CL} cell, pattern "3" emerges in the recall layer.

Figure 12 shows an example of the response to a stimulus consisting of superimposed patterns. The pattern "4" is isolated first, the pattern "2" next, and finally pattern "1" is extracted.

---

*The number of cells actually used in the network depends on the set of training patterns presented during the training cycle. Because it is difficult to estimate in advance, this computer simulation series had a surplus. The total of 41,399, which excluded the cells in the non-response detector, included 19×19 u_{C0} and w_{C0}; $19 \times 19 \times 21$ u_{S1} and w_{S1}; 19×19 u_{SV1} and w_{SV1}; $11 \times 11 \times 21$ u_{C1}, w_{C1}, and w_{CX1}; $11 \times 11 \times 27$ u_{S2}, w_{S2}, u_{C2}, w_{C2}, and w_{CX2}; 11×11 u_{SV2} and w_{SV2}; $7 \times 7 \times 5$ u_{S3} and w_{S3}; 7×7 u_{SV3} and w_{SV3}; and $1 \times 1 \times 5$ u_{C3}.

**The reinforcement of the variable connections to cells of a higher stage was delayed until completion of the learning of the preceding stages. So, each of the training patterns was presented three, four, and four times for training stages 1, 2, and 3, respectively.

***Simulating the process of one step of t takes several seconds on a MicroVAX II, but computer time varies considerably depending on the presented stimulus.

Segmentation of individual patterns can be successful even if input patterns are deformed in shape or shifted in position. For example, "2" patterns in Figures 11 and 12 differ in shape from the training pattern (Figure 10), but the segmented patterns appearing in the recall layer are identical in shape to the stimulus patterns now presented.

Pattern segmentation can be successful even for a stimulus consisting of two patterns from the same category. Figure 13 shows such an example, in which the smaller "4" is segmented first, followed by the larger "4."

Figure 14 shows the response to a greatly deformed pattern with several parts missing and contaminated by noise. Because of the large difference between the stimulus and the training pattern, no response is elicited from the recognition layer (not shown in the figure) at first. Accordingly, no feedback signal appears at the recall layer W_{C0}. The no-response detector detects this situation, and the threshold-control signal is sent to all feature-extracting cells in the network, which makes them respond more easily even to incomplete features. Thus, at time $t=2$, the u_{CL} cell for "2" is activated in the recognition layer, and backward signals are fed back from it. In the pattern now sent back to the recall layer W_{C0}, noise has been completely eliminated, and some of the missing parts have begun to be interpolated. This partly interpolated signal, namely the output of the recall layer W_{C0}, is again fed back positively to the input layer U_{C0}. The interpolation continues gradually while the signal circulates through the feedback loop, and finally the missing part of the stimulus is completely filled in. The missing part is interpolated quite naturally, despite the considerable difference in shape between the stimulus and the training pattern.

In the pattern for which interpolation has already finished, the horizontal bar at the bottom of the "2" is shorter than in the training pattern. But no matter how short the horizontal bar, the pattern is a perfect character "2." Hence, this component of the pattern is left intact and is reproduced like the stimulus pattern. The deformation of the stimulus pattern is tolerated, and only indispensable missing parts are naturally interpolated, without strain. It is also important to note that noise has been completely eliminated, because attention is not focused on the components of the noise.

As we can see from these experiments,

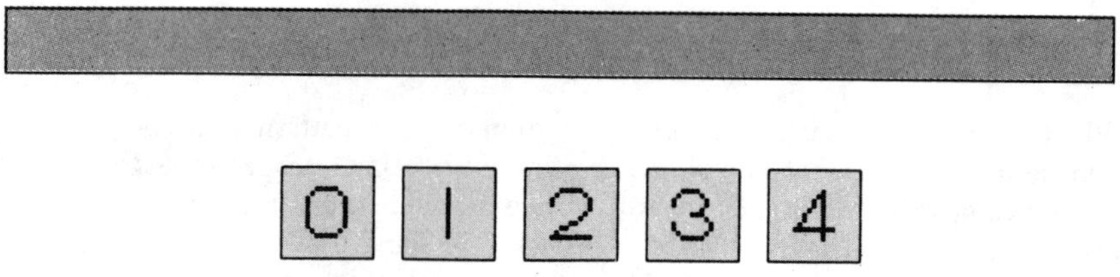

Figure 10. Five training patterns used for learning.

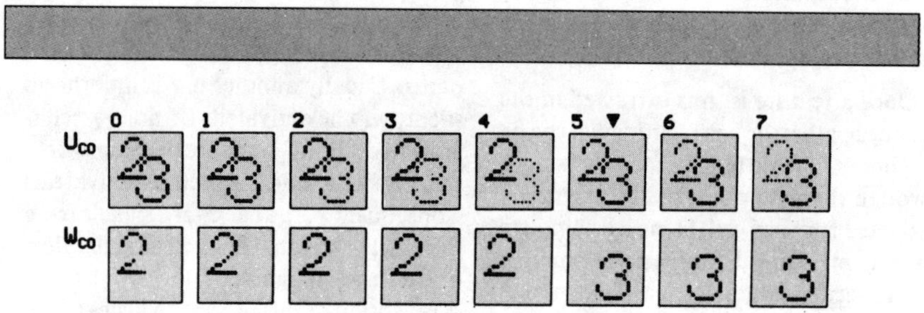

Figure 11. An example of the response to juxtaposed patterns.

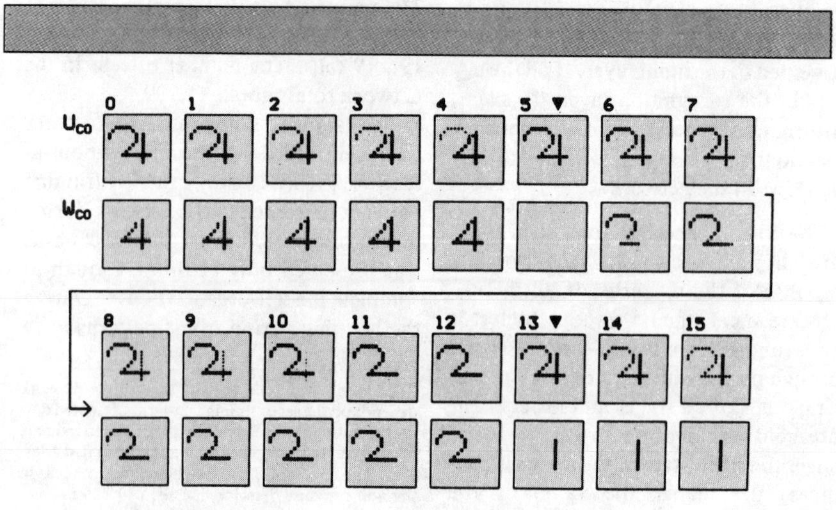

Figure 12. An example of the response to superimposed patterns.

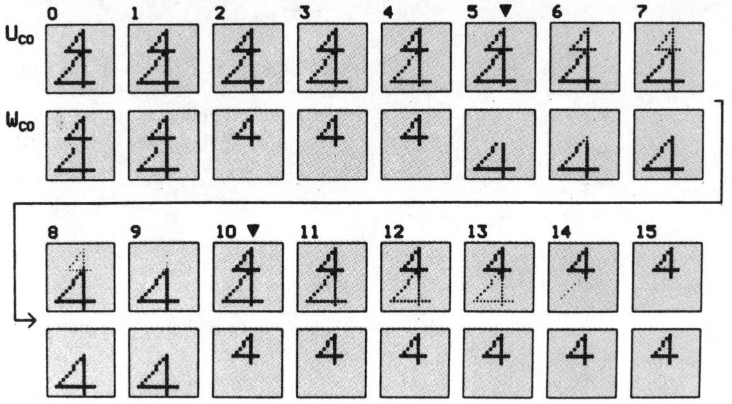

Figure 13. An example of the response to a stimulus consisting of two patterns of the same category.

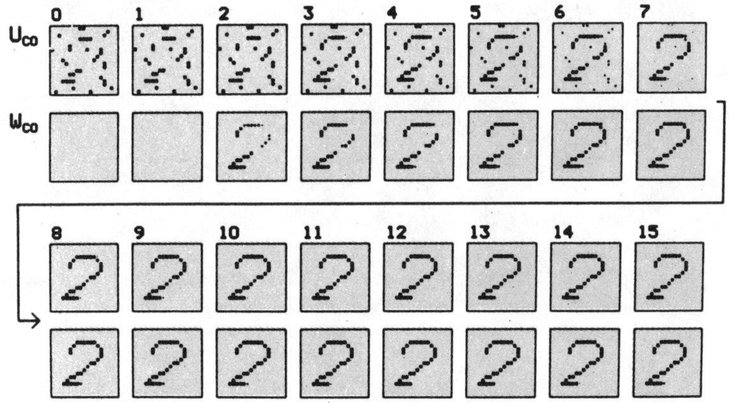

Figure 14. An example of the response to an incomplete distorted pattern with noise.

the model works well for most of the stimuli. However, the model has difficulty processing some stimuli, such as a pattern like "11" when drawn with an extremely narrow space between the two "1"s. Wide enough spacing poses no problem, but if the spacing is so narrow that the two parallel lines fall together into the receptive field of a single u_C cell of the first stage, the gain control of u_C cells may not work effectively to separate them.

The model discussed in this article has properties and abilities that most modern computers and pattern recognizers do not possess: pattern recognition, selective attention, segmentation, and associative recall. When a composite stimulus consisting of two or more patterns is presented, the model pays selective attention to each of the patterns one after the other, segments a pattern from the rest, and recognizes it separately.

We can also consider this model one of associative memory, with the ability to repair imperfect patterns. In contrast to earlier models, this model has perfect associative recall, even for deformed patterns, without regard to their positions.

Finally, the model can learn. We can train it to recognize any set of patterns. Hence, we can design a universal system that we can use, after training, for an individual purpose. □

Acknowledgments

The author would like to thank Takayuki Ito and Sei Miyake for their help on various aspects of this work.

References

1. K. Fukushima, "A Neural Network Model for Selective Attention in Visual Pattern Recognition," *Biological Cybernetics*, Vol. 55, No. 1, Oct. 1986, pp. 5-15.

2. K. Fukushima, "A Neural Network Model for Selective Attention in Visual Pattern Recognition and Associative Recall," *Applied Optics*, Vol. 26, No. 23, Nov. 1987, pp. 4985-4992.

3. D.E. Rumelhart, G.E. Hinton, and R.J. Williams, "Learning Representations by Back-Propagating Errors," *Nature*, Vol. 322, No. 6008, Oct. 1986, pp. 533-536.

4. K. Fukushima, "Cognitron: A Self-Organizing Multilayered Neural Network," *Biological Cybernetics*, Vol. 20, No. 3/4, Nov. 1975, pp. 121-136.

5. D.E. Rumelhart, and D. Zipser, "Feature Discovery by Competitive Learning," *Cognitive Science*, Vol. 9, 1985, pp. 75-112.

6. K. Fukushima, "Neocognitron: A Self-Organizing Neural Network Model for a Mechanism of Pattern Recognition Unaffected by Shift in Position," *Biological Cybernetics*, Vol. 36, No. 4, April 1980, pp. 193-202.

7. K. Fukushima and S. Miyake, "Neocognitron: A New Algorithm for Pattern Recognition Tolerant of Deformation and Shifts in Position," *Pattern Recognition*, Vol. 15, No. 6, 1982, pp. 455-469.

8. T. Kohonen, *Associative Memory: A System-Theoretical Approach*, Springer-Verlag, Berlin, 1977.

9. D.H. Hubel and T.N. Wiesel, "Receptive Fields, Binocular Interaction, and Functional Architecture in the Cat's Visual Cor-

tex," *J. Physiology*, Vol. 160, No. 1, London, 1962, pp. 106-154.

10. C. Bruce, R. Desimone, and C.G. Gross, "Visual Properties of Neurons in a Polysensory Area in the Superior Temporal Sulcus of the Macaque," *J. Neurophysiology*, Vol. 46, No. 2, Aug. 1981, pp. 369-384.

11. G.A. Carpenter and S. Grossberg, "A Massively Parallel Architecture for a Self-Organizing Neural Pattern Recognition Machine," *Computer Vision, Graphics and Image Processing*, Vol. 37, No. 1, Jan. 1987, pp. 54-115.

12. K. Fukushima, "Neocognitron: A Hierarchical Neural Network Capable of Visual Pattern Recognition," to appear in *Neural Networks*, Vol. 1, No. 2, April 1988.

CMAC: An Associative Neural Network Alternative to Backpropagation

W. THOMAS MILLER, III, MEMBER, IEEE, FILSON H. GLANZ, MEMBER, IEEE, AND L. GORDON KRAFT, III

The CMAC neural network, an alternative to backpropagated multilayer networks, is described. CMAC has the advantages of the following properties: local generalization, rapid algorithmic computation based on LMS training, incremental training, functional representation, output superposition, and a fast practical hardware realization, all of which are discussed. A geometrical explanation of how CMAC works is provided, and brief descriptions of applications in robot control, pattern recognition, and signal processing are given. Possible disadvantages of CMAC are that it does not have global generalization and that it can have noise due to hash coding. Care must be exercised, as with all neural networks, to assure that a low error solution will be learned.

I. Introduction and Background

Within the last eight years there has been increased interest in systems that learn, using models of biological neurons. As technology has developed in diverse application areas, there has been an increased need for controlling complex systems, with nonlinearities and many degrees of freedom, leading to a search for new ways of handling the large amounts of computation and numbers of variables found in these problems. Many of these systems are so complex that the physical principles and/or the overwhelming size makes writing meaningful model equations impossible.

In this paper we describe a neural network called CMAC (Cerebellar Model Arithmetic Computer) [1], [2]. At the University of New Hampshire, we have been using CMAC in real-time control of an industrial robot and in other applications, typically employing neural networks with hundreds of thousands of adjustable weights that can be trained to approximate nonlinearities which are not explicitly written out or even known. CMAC can learn nonlinear relationships from a very broad category of functions. Furthermore, the learning algorithm generally converges in a small number of iterations.

Manuscript received September 14, 1989; revised March 16, 1990. The work summarized in this manuscript was supported in part by the National Science Foundation under grant IRI-8813225, by the Office of Naval Research and the National Institute of Standards and Technology under ONR grant N00014-89-J-1686, and by the Defense Advanced Research Projects Agency under ONR grant N00014-89-J-3100.

The authors are with Department of Electrical and Computer Engineering, University of New Hampshire, Durham, New Hampshire 03824, USA.

IEEE Log Number 9039173.

Neural networks of one form or another have been "modeled" for a number of decades. Some of the better known models are the Perceptron of Rosenblatt [3], the adaline of Widrow [4], [5], and the recurrent networks of Hopfield [6], [7]. Much of the past effort was devoted to systems with binary inputs and outputs. Because it was recognized in the 1960s that not all binary functions can be realized with a single "linear" threshold element, there has been considerable interest in multilayer networks and the question of how to train them. In the last decade backpropagation has been developed as a method of training multilayer networks, and most recent application papers use this approach. Nonbinary inputs and outputs have also been considered.

The CMAC neural network described in this paper is an alternative to the well known backpropagation-trained analog multilayer neural network. An alternative is useful since backpropagation has the disadvantages of: requiring many iterations to converge and therefore inappropriate for online real-time learning (this imposes the need to use small networks, and therefore many difficult problems of current interest cannot be solved); requiring an large number of computations per iteration so that the algorithm runs slowly unless implemented in expensive custom hardware; having an error surface which can have relative minima, a hazard to backpropagation training which is based on gradient search techniques; not allowing successful incremental learning (if one has finite time to train) in the sense that to achieve reasonable convergence all inputs must be seen before any weight change can take place.

In the 1970s James Albus reported the work he had been doing on CMAC [1], [2], [8], [9]. Albus used CMAC to do rote learning of movements of an artificial arm. After a number of years of being referred to in the robot control literature as being impractical, it was demonstrated that CMAC was not only practical, but that it could be used to learn general state space dependent control responses [10]. Since then the Robotics Laboratory at the University of New Hampshire has been investigating and using CMAC with considerable success [10]–[22]. Other groups working with CMAC include Ersu *et al.* [23]–[26], and Moody at Yale [27]. We are

Reprinted from *Proc. IEEE*, vol. 78, no. 10, Oct. 1990, pp. 1561–1567.

also aware of several industrial research groups using CMAC.

CMAC is an associative neural network in that only a small subset of the network influences any instantaneous output, and that subset is determined by the input to the network. The associative mapping built into CMAC assures local generalization: similar inputs produce similar outputs while distant inputs produce nearly independent outputs. As the result of the built-in associative properties, we have found that the number of training passes required for network convergence is orders of magnitude smaller with CMAC than with backpropagation on real problems.

II. Description of CMAC

In this section we describe CMAC in a mostly geometrical way: the input space, the outputs, and the mechanism of generalization.

Figure 1 shows a set-oriented overview of CMAC. An input vector is the collection of *N* appropriate sensors of the real

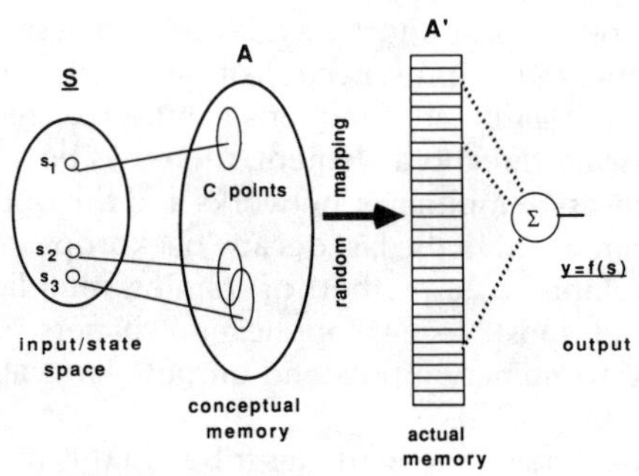

Fig. 1. Set-oriented block diagram of CMAC. The input/state space and the conceptual memory *A* are *N*-dimensional. The actual memory *A'* has as many dimensions as there are output components.

world and/or measures of the desired goal. The input space consists of the set of all possible input vectors. The number *N* of input vector components and the number of outputs is arbitrary within some practical limits. The CMAC algorithm maps any input it receives into a set of *C* points in a large "conceptual" memory (*A* in Fig. 1) in such a way that two inputs that are "close" in input space will have their *C* points overlap in the *A* memory, with more overlap for closer inputs. If two inputs are far apart in the input space there will be no overlap in their *C*-element sets in the *A* memory, and therefore no generalization.

For practical systems the input space is extremely large. For example, a system with 10 inputs, each of which can take on 100 different values, would have $100^{10} = 10^{20}$ points in its input space, requiring a correspondingly large number of locations in the memory *A*. Since most learning problems do not involve all of the input space, the memory requirement is reduced by mapping the *A* memory onto a much smaller physical memory *A'*. As a result, any input presented to CMAC will generate *C* real memory locations, the contents of which will be added in order to obtain an output. Notice that the nonlinearity that all neural networks must have is in the associative input mapping, not in the sigmoid/threshold function normally at the output of each neuron.

Figure 2 is a network diagram of a two-input CMAC as implemented in our laboratory. Each variable in the input

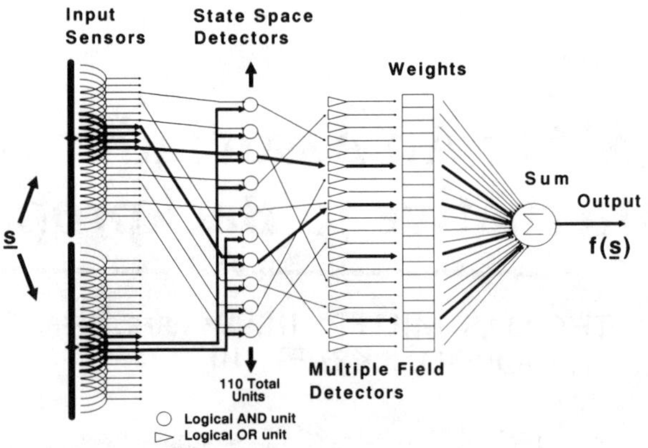

Fig. 2. A simple example of a CMAC neural network with two inputs and one output. The generalization parameter *C* has the value 4. Note that only a partial set of the state space detectors is shown.

state vector *s* is fed to a series of input sensors with overlapping receptive fields. Each input sensor produces a binary output which is ON if the input falls within its receptive field and is OFF otherwise. The width of the receptive field of each sensor produces input generalization, while the offset of the adjacent fields produces input quantization. Each input variable excites exactly *C* input sensors, where *C* is the ratio of generalization width to quantization width ($C = 4$ in Fig. 2, $C = 32$ to 256 in typical implementations).

The binary outputs of the input sensors are combined in a series of threshold logic units (called state-space detectors) with thresholds adjusted to produce logical AND functions (the output is ON only if all inputs are ON). Each of these units receives one input from the group of sensors for each input variable, and thus its input receptive field is the interior of a hypercube in the input hyperspace (the interior of a square in the two-dimensional input space of Fig. 2). The state space detectors of Fig. 2 correspond logically to the individual memory locations of the *A* memory in Fig. 1.

If the input sensors were fully interconnected, there would be a very large number of state-space detectors, and a large subset of these detectors would be excited for each possible input. The input sensors are interconnected in a sparse and regular fashion, however, in such a way that each input vector excites exactly *C* state-space detectors. Figure 3 depicts the organization of the receptive fields in the input space. The total collection of state-space detectors is divided into *C* subsets. The receptive fields of the units in each of the subsets are organized so as to span the input space without overlap. Each input vector excites one state-space detector from each subset, for a total of *C* excited detectors for any input. There are many ways to organize the receptive fields of the individual subsets which produce similar results. In our implementation, each of the subsets of state-space detectors is identical in organization, but each subset is offset relative to the others along hyperdiagonals in the input hyperspace (adjacent subsets are offset by the quantization level of each input variable).

The organization of the receptive fields of the state-space detectors guarantees that a fixed number *C* of detectors is excited by any input. However, the total number of state-space detectors can still be large for many practical problems. On the other hand, it is unlikely that the entire input state-space of a large system would be visited in solving a

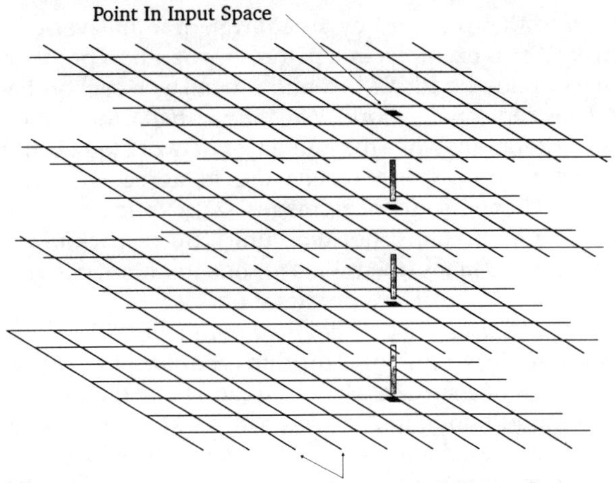

Fig. 3. The organization of the receptive fields for the simple two-input CMAC in Fig. 2, with $C = 4$. The state space detectors are organized into four subsets, offset relative to each other in the input space. The boundaries of the receptive fields are shown for each subset. The dark square in each plane indicates the same region of the input space projected onto the receptive fields of each of the four subsets.

specific problem (most of the possible input vectors would never be experienced). Thus it is not necessary to store unique information for each receptive field. Following this logic, the outputs of the state-space detectors are connected randomly to a smaller set of threshold logic units (called multiple field detectors in Fig. 2) with thresholds adjusted such that the output will be ON if any input is ON (a logical OR function). The receptive field of each of these units is thus the union of the fields of many of the state-space detectors. Since exactly C state-space detectors are excited by any input, at most C multiple field detectors will be excited by any input. The converging connections between the large set of state-space detectors and the smaller set of multiple field detectors are referred to as "collisions." In practice, the converging connections are implemented by assigning a virtual address to each of the state-space detectors, and passing the addresses of the active state-space detectors through a random hashing function.

Finally, the output of each multiple field detector is connected, through an adjustable weight, to an output summing unit. The output for a given input is thus the sum of the weights selected by the excited multiple field detectors. The set of all weights in Fig. 2 corresponds to the A' memory of Fig. 1. Note that while the number of input sensors and state-space detectors is determined by the number of inputs, their dynamic ranges, the level of quantization, and the degree of generalization, the number of multiple field detectors and adjustable weights is an independent design parameter. The necessary size of the weight memory is related to the size of the subset of the input space that is likely to be visited in solving a particular problem, rather than to the total size of the input space. Thus, simple problems in a many dimensional input space require only small weight memories, even though the size of the input space may be huge.

Ideally, the associative mapping within the CMAC network assures that nearby points in the input space generalize while distant points do not generalize. The effect of the converging connections between the state-space detectors and the multiple field detectors, however, is to create randomly distributed low-magnitude generalization with distant points in the space. Figure 4 illustrates this effect

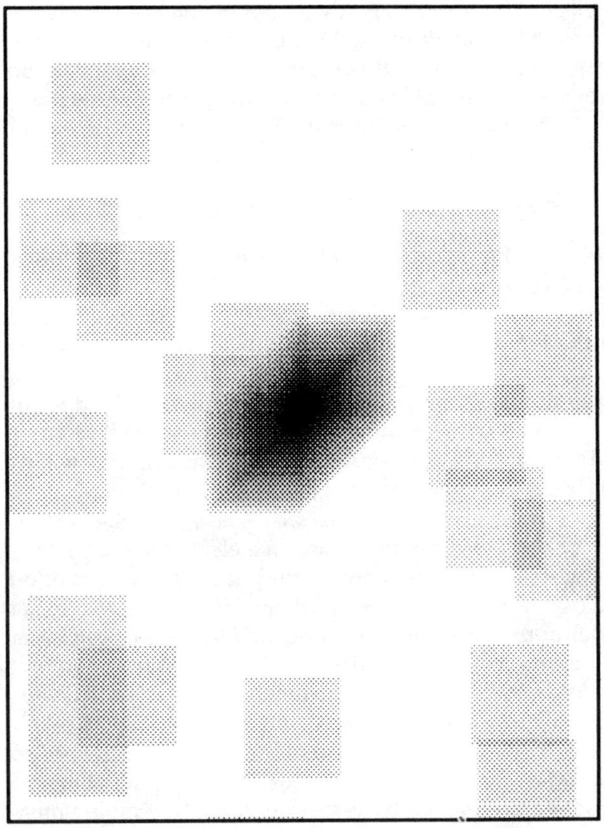

Fig. 4. Generalization of a single point within a 128×96 input space, using a CMAC with $C = 16$ and 1000 memory locations. Greater generalization is indicated by darker shading.

for a simple two-input CMAC. The size of the input space in this example is 128 points along the horizontal axis and 96 points along the vertical axis, for a total of 12 288 points in the input space. The figure shows the degree to which a central point in the space generalizes with all other points in the space, for a CMAC with 1000 adjustable weights and $c = 16$. Note that even when using this small memory (relative to the size of the input space), the characteristic of local generalization in the space is largely preserved. Note also that the generalization region is not symmetrical about the horizontal or vertical axes. The asymmetry is related to the distribution of the state-space detector receptive fields in the input space (Fig. 3) and varies somewhat for different points within the input space. Other distributions for the detectors are possible, which would preserve the associative mapping characteristics of CMAC but would modify the shapes of the generalization regions. The effects of receptive field distribution on CMAC performance has not yet been systematically studied.

Network training is typically based on observed training data pairs $\mathbf{s}_o$ and f_o (supervised learning), where f_o is the desired network output in response to the input $\mathbf{s}_o$, using the least mean square (LMS) training rule [28]. Although the CMAC network can be trained to represent arbitrary nonlinear relationships between the input vector **s** and the output $f(\mathbf{s})$, convergence of the weights during training can be demonstrated by comparing the CMAC structure with well-known linear adaptive elements [4], [5]. Let **x** represent the vector of binary outputs of the multiple field detectors in Fig. 2, and let **w** represent the vector of adjustable weights. For each training input $\mathbf{s}_0$ there is a corresponding pattern of multiple field detector outputs $\mathbf{x}_0$ which is dependent on the fixed pattern of the CMAC network interconnections, but is independent of the values of the weights. The weight update described above can then be written as

$$d\mathbf{w} = (\beta/C)(f_o - \mathbf{w}^T\mathbf{x}_0)\mathbf{x}_0$$

which is the well-known LMS adaptation rule for linear adaptive elements.

The nonlinear nature of the CMAC network is embodied in the interconnections of the input sensors, state-space detectors, and multiple field detectors, which perform a fixed nonlinear mapping of the continuous valued input vector **s** to a many-dimensional binary valued vector x (which has tens or hundreds of thousands of dimensions in typical implementations). the adaptation problem is linear in this many-dimensional space, and all of the convergence theorems for linear adaptive elements apply [16].

Because CMAC uses a linear output stage, superposition holds in the weight domain. For example, if the weight set $\mathbf{W}_1$ produces the nonlinear function $f_1(\mathbf{s})$ and the weight set $\mathbf{W}_2$ produces the nonlinear function $f_2(\mathbf{s})$, then the weight set $\mathbf{W}_1 + \mathbf{W}_2$ will produce the function $f_1(\mathbf{s}) + f_2(\mathbf{s})$. It is thus possible to characterize the ability of a CMAC network of given dimension, quantization, and generalization to reproduce arbitrary functions by examining its ability to produce orthogonal basis functions, such as multidimensional sinusoids.

III. Properties of CMAC

This section summarizes the main properties of CMAC and thus serves as a basis for understanding the concepts and details introduced in the previous section.

1) CMAC accepts real inputs and gives real outputs. The input components are quantized, but the number of levels can be as large as desired so that any degree of accuracy is achievable.

2) CMAC has a built-in local generalization, meaning that input vectors that are "close" in the input (state) space will give outputs that are close, even if the input has not be trained on, as long as there has been training in that region of the state-space. The measure of "closeness" is not Euclidean distance but "city block distance," a generalization of Hamming distance where the distance is the sum, over all components, of the absolute value of the differences of each component. Locally generalizing networks have less learning interference than globally generalizing networks such as a multilayer perceptron.

3) CMAC has the property that large networks can be used and trained in practical time, even with the software version of the system. This is because there is a small number of calculations per output even though there is a large number of weights. In our CMAC realizations at UNH we typically have tens or hundreds of thousands of weights and 10 to 128 additions per output; in both hardware and software this is a small amount of computation in comparison to that required by an equivalent multilayer perceptron. As an example, in a pattern recognition problem we have trained both CMAC and a two-layer backpropagated perceptron network. We found that CMAC took about 50 iterations while the multilayer network took about 12,000 iterations. These results are in agreement with Moody's chaotic sequences results [27]. Notice that the results were iterations, not time units. Since backpropagation takes so many operations for one iteration, it is very much slower than CMAC per iteration.

4) CMAC uses the LMS adaptation rule of Widrow and Hoff [4]. This least squares algorithm is equivalent to a gradient search of a surface which is quadratic and therefore has a unique minimum. In contrast, backpropagation is known to be a gradient search of a surface which may have relative minima. Of course, when using LMS training, the well-known precautions should be observed [28].

5) CMAC can learn a wide variety of functions. It is easy to show, for example, that a one-input CMAC can learn any discrete one-dimensional single-valued function, given a few mild conditions on the parameters of the CMAC.

6) CMAC obeys superposition in the output space, which means that a multidimensional discrete Fourier series can be used to show what functions can be learned. For example, if multidimensional sinusoids of various spatial frequencies (harmonics) can be learned, a whole class of functions is also learnable. Notice that the functions learned are still nonlinear, since the superposition is in the output space only. Notice also that in spite of the spatial frequency constraints implied by the superposition discussed above, there is no such constraint in time response if consecutive inputs to CMAC are not neighbors in the state-space as would be the case when learning a function whose input is the state of a shift register.

7) CMAC has a practical hardware realization using logic cell arrays [29]. VLSI versions are possible with learning cycles in the microsecond region.

IV. Example Applications of CMAC

One of the advantages of CMAC at this stage of neural network development is that its realization in software is sufficiently fast and efficient for large networks that many applications are possible. We have used CMAC in a number of real-time robotic [10]–[15], [22], pattern recognition [17], [21], signal processing [18], [19], and speech processing demonstrations.

In this section we briefly describe three applications in which we have used CMAC. Readers who would like more information on a particular application are referred to the appropriate papers in the literature. We describe a robot control application, a character recognition application, and a deconvolution/inverse filtering application.

A. Robot Control

One robot tracking problem which we have used to demonstrate neural network control involved the control of a five-axis industrial robot with a video camera attached to the fifth axis in the place of a gripper [16]. The camera looked at an object on a conveyor belt and the control problem was to move the robot in such a way as to keep the object at a fixed orientation and size on the video monitor screen, and simultaneously have the centroid of the object follow a trajectory defined in the video image space rectangular coordinate system. No kinematics of the robot were known to the system, no height measurements other than the length of the object were found by the image processing, and no camera–screen calibrations were given to the system. All of these had to be learned by the neural network system. Figure 5 shows the physical setup of the system. The object in this case was a white disposable razor.

Because of the slowness of the image processing, updates of the object image were too infrequent. A second CMAC was used to predict the object position in between image processing results. This CMAC learned to do its prediction with no initial knowledge of the system. The acquisition and orientation of the object and the trajectory following of the object centroid were all done as the object passed along the five-foot-long conveyor belt, having been placed (within limits) at a random orientation and position on the belt. The trajectories to be followed were either repeated or random, and were described by specifying both video image X and Y coordinate velocities and accelerations.

Training was done at the end of each control cycle based on the error between the desired position and the actual position of the object in the image. In order to initiate training, a simple fixed gain control loop was included in parallel in the system in order to keep the camera close enough to the object initially that the image could be found and the error determined for training. As the system learned more, the fixed gain controller had less and less influence on the control and the learning had more and more. The input vector had 12 components which describe the robot joint positions, the predicted image parameters, and the desired image parameter changes. There were four outputs from the inverse model, one to drive each of the four robot joint motors. The fifth motor was not driven in order to keep the camera vertical. The image prediction CMAC has as inputs the latest image parameters, the latest joint angles, and the latest motor voltages. The outputs of this CMAC were the predicted changes in image parameters. Each network consisted of 16 384 × 4 16-bit weights, and the generalization parameter was $C = 64$.

The RMS control error for each of the four image parameters decreased each trial and generally converged to the sensor sensitivity of one pixel within 15 trials in the repeated trajectory case and about 50 trials in the random trajectory case. The average error was always below the error of the fixed gain controller without learning.

B. Pattern Recognition

A second application of CMAC shows its use in pattern recognition. In this example the first five letters of the alphabet, each in lower case and upper case, and each in 72 rotations 5° apart around the circle, were trained into CMAC. The images were obtained by putting each letter on a calibrated rotating platform in front of a camera which was interfaced through a frame buffer to an 80386-based personal computer. In order to obtain a reasonably sized feature vector, the computer averaged all pixels in each box of an 8 × 8 array centered on the letters. The rows of these averages were summed, as were the columns, giving the 16

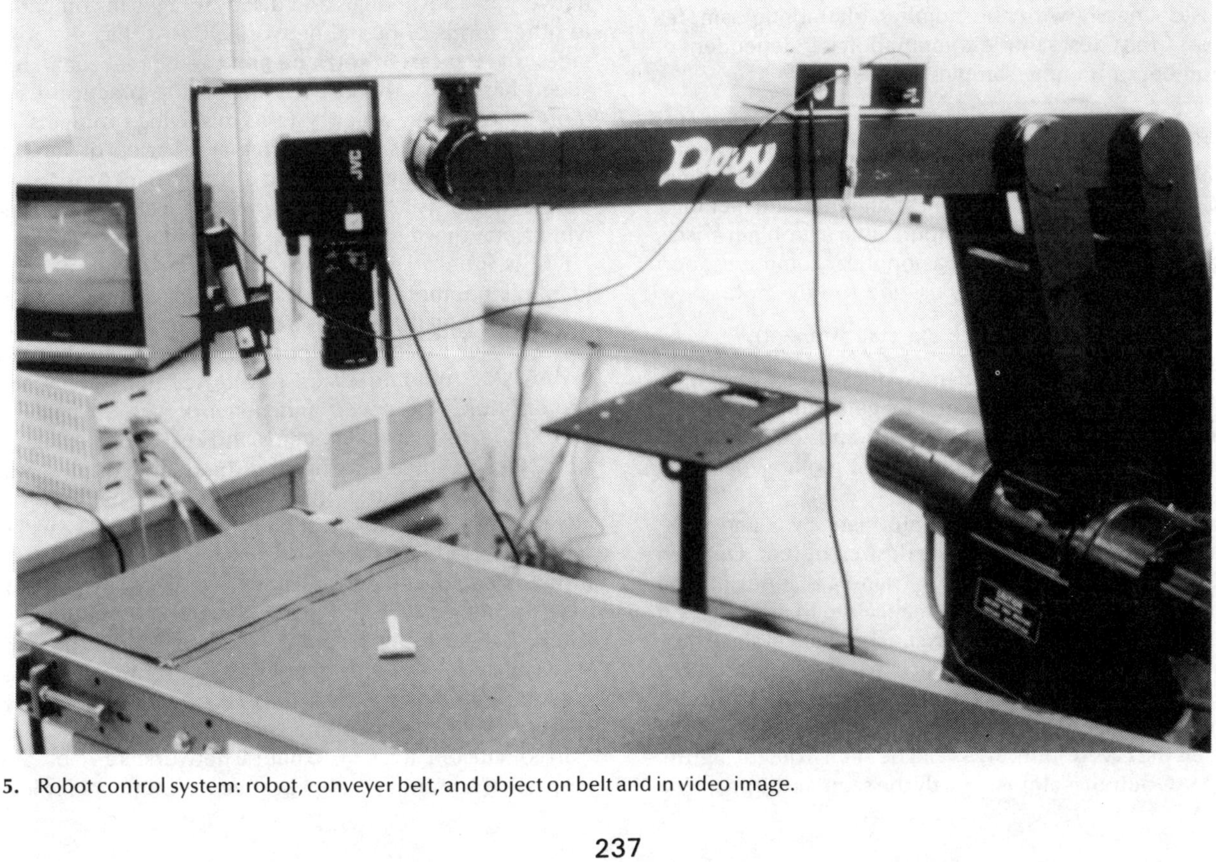

Fig. 5. Robot control system: robot, conveyer belt, and object on belt and in video image.

features used in the pattern recognition. Files of these features for each letter (case and rotation) were made to use in the training. A separate file was made of new images to act as a test set after training.

Table 1 summarizes the results. Five other classifiers were included in order to compare the CMAC results with standard techniques. The table briefly lists these and also gives the notation used. The "random" letters were placed at purely random rotations with no attention paid to the 5° increments used for the training data. Note that, although the nearest neighbor technique did as well as CMAC, test sample computation for the nearest neighbor approach increases linearly with the number of training samples whereas CMAC test sample computation is independent of the number of training samples.

Table 1 Character Recognition Results

	Percent Correct on Test Set[a]					
EXPT[b]	CMAC	Temp	F-WT	R-Coord	Hyper	NNBR
U/U	100.0	78.3	75.0	100.0	82.8	100.0
U/RU	100.0	71.1	68.3	99.4	77.8	100.0
UL/U	100.0	56.4	63.3	93.3	70.3	100.0
UL/RU	100.0	47.2	57.8	93.3	71.7	100.0
L/L	100.0	85.3	60.0	99.2	73.6	100.0
L/RL	100.0	83.9	61.1	100.0	73.9	100.0
UL/L	100.0	38.6	46.9	83.3	36.1	100.0
UL/RL	100.0	38.3	50.0	83.3	35.6	100.0

[a]Classification techniques shown:

CMAC: A CMAC based classifier.
Temp: Standard template matching.
F-Wt: Feature weighting method.
R-Coord: Rotated coordinate method.
Hyper: "Optimal" hyperplane separation.
NNBR: Nearest neighbor method.

[b]Experiments indicated by *Train/Test* where:

U: 72 upper case examples, 5° rotations.
RU: 36 random upper case examples, random rotations.
L: 72 lower case examples, 5° rotations.
RL: 36 random lower case examples, random rotations.

C. *Signal Processing*

A third application involves a signal processing problem [19]: Given the output of a nonlinear channel with memory, learn to generate the original input. Such a problem arises, for example, in equalization of a nonlinear communication channel [30]. The nonlinearity used in this example is

$$y(n) = \arctan [x(n)] + B \arctan [x(n-1)]$$

where $B = 0.1$. The memory of the system in this case is one. In this simulation, $y(n)$ is created by generating uniformly distributed pseudorandom noise $x(n)$ and feeding it into the equation above, along with the last input value $x(n-1)$.

The input to CMAC has two components: $y(n)$ and $y(n-1)$. The value of $x(n)$ is used as the desired output. On each presentation of the input 2-vector, training is done until the squared error is appropriately small. Note that there is no repeating of the input vectors (except by chance) since they are generated from the $x(n)$s which are not repeated, that is, there is no fixed training set. Figure 6 shows the input sequence $y(n)$ to CMAC, the desired output (goal) sequence $x(n)$, and the CMAC output. As can be seen from the figure, the CMAC output is almost exactly the same as the goal; that is, CMAC has learned to invert the nonlinear output in order to obtain the input sequence (the goal) $x(n)$. If a new random number sequence is used to generate a test sequence, which is run through the trained CMAC, the output is of similar high quality.

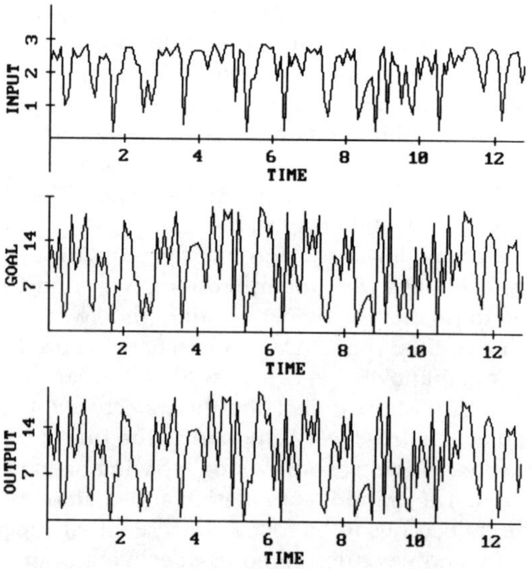

Fig. 6. Nonlinear inverse filtering showing CMAC output time series and the time series it has learned. The input time series is generated from the goal time series by the arctangent nonlinearity given in the text equation.

V. Conclusions

In the foregoing we have explained the properties of a neural network called CMAC, described the mechanism of CMAC, and given several examples of how we have applied CMAC to solve a variety of problems. This form of neural network has advantages and disadvantages in comparison to other forms of neural networks. CMAC has the advantages that it is fast in software and can be realized in high-speed hardware, thereby leading to the practical use of more weights and larger systems in solving problems. Furthermore, CMAC is able to learn a large variety of nonlinear functions, reducing the need to use slow backpropagation-based networks. And CMAC has a local generalization which may have advantages over global generalization: There is little or no learning interference due to recent learning in remote parts of the input space, and local generalization usually requires a smaller number of additions, therefore giving fast computation speeds. Furthermore, CMAC/LMS training takes fewer iterations than backpropagation. The speed and network size advantage of CMAC means that real systems and real problems can be undertaken with results beyond the quality of other standard methods. On the other hand, CMAC has some disadvantages: The generalization is not global, so we will not find mysterious properties "emerging" from the training, if that is an advantage; collisions due to the hash coding necessary to reduce the memory size to something realizable can cause a noise or interference if care is not taken in design to prevent that happening; and some design care must be exercised in order to be assured that a low error solution will be learned in a specific application.

In conclusion, the CMAC neural network is a viable alternative to the multilayer backpropagated network for learning situations with analog inputs and outputs, especially where speed of convergence and speed of computation are important, and where large numbers of weights are needed. CMAC has proven able to learn unknown nonlinear functions quickly and generalize on inputs it has never seen.

References

[1] J. S. Albus, "A theory of cerebellar functions," Mathematical Biosciences, vol. 10, pp. 25–61, 1971.

[2] ——, "Theoretical and experimental aspects of a cerebellar model," Ph.D. dissertation, Univ. of Maryland, 1972.

[3] F. Rosenblatt, *The Principles of Neurodynamics.* New York: Spartan, 1962.

[4] B. Widrow and M. E. Hoff, "Adaptive switching circuits," *Proc. IRE Western Electronic Show and Conv.*, vol. 4, pp. 96–104, 1960.

[5] B. Widrow, "Generalization and information storage in networks of adaline 'neurons,' " *Self-Organizing Systems*, M. C. Yovits, Ed. Wash., DC: Spartan, 1962, pp. 435–461.

[6] J. J. Hopfield, "Neurons with graded response have collective computational properties like those of two-state neurons," *Proc. Natl. Acad. Sci. USA*, vol. 81, pp. 3088–3092, May 1984.

[7] ——, "Neural networks and physical systems with emergent collective computational abilities," *Proc. Natl. Acad. Sci. USA*, vol. 79, pp. 2554–2558, Apr. 1982.

[8] J. S. Albus, "Data storage in the cerebellar model articulation controller," *J. Dynamic systems, Measurement and Control*, pp. 228–233, Sept. 1975.

[9] ——, "A new approach to manipulator control: the cerebellar model articulation controller (CMAC)," pp. 220–227, Sept. 1975.

[10] W. T. Miller, "A nonlinear learning controller for robotic manipulators," *Proc. SPIE, Intelligent Robots and Computer Vision*, vol. 726, pp. 416–423, Oct. 1986.

[11] ——, "A learning controller for nonrepetitive robotic operations," *Proc. Workshop on Space Telerobotics*, publication 87-13, vol. II, Pasadena, CA, pp. 273–281, Jan. 10–22, 1987.

[12] ——, "Sensor based control of robotic manipulators using a general learning algorithm," *IEEE Trans. Robotics Automat.*, vol. RA-3, pp. 157–165, Apr. 1987.

[13] W. T. Miller, F. H. Glanz, and L. G. Kraft, "Application of a general learning algorithm to the control of robotic manipulators," *Internat. J. Robotics Research*, vol. 6, pp. 84–98, Summer 1987.

[14] W. T. Miller and R. P. Hewes, "Real time experiments in neural network based learning during high speed nonrepetitive robotic operations," *Proc. 3rd IEEE Int. Symp. on Intelligent Control*, pp. 513–518, Aug. 24–26, 1988.

[15] W. T. Miller, "Real time learned sensor processing and motor control for a robot with vision," *1st Annual Conf. of the Intl. Neural Network Society*, p. 347, Sept. 1988.

[16] ——, "Real time application of neural networks for sensor-based control of robots with vision," *IEEE SMC*, vol. 19, pp. 825–831, July–Aug. 1989.

[17] F. H. Glanz and W. T. Miller, "Shape recognition using a CMAC based learning system," *Proc. SPIE Conf. on Robotics and Intelligent Systems*, vol. 848, pp. 294–298, Nov. 1987.

[18] ——, "Deconvolution using a CMAC neural network," *Proc. 1st Annual Conf. of the Intl. Neural Network Society*, p. 440, Sept. 1988.

[19] ——, "Deconvolution and nonlinear inverse filtering using a neural network," *Intl. Conf. on Acoustics and Signal Processing*, vol. 4, pp. 2349–2352, May 23–29, 1989.

[20] L. G. Kraft and D. P. Campagna, "A comparison of CMAC neural network and traditional adaptive control systems," *Proc. 1989 American Control Conf.*, vol. 1, pp. 884–889, June 21–23, 1989.

[21] D. Herold, W. T. Miller, L. G. Kraft, and F. H. Glanz, "Pattern recognition using a CMAC based learning system," *Proc. SPIE, Automated Inspection and High Speed Vision Architectures II*, vol. 1004, pp. 84–90, Nov. 10–11, 1989.

[22] W. T. Miller, R. P. Hewes, F. H. Glanz, and L. G. Kraft, "Real-time dynamic control of an industrial manipulator using a neural-network-based learning controller," *IEEE Trans. Robotics Automat.*, vol. 6, pp. 1–9, Feb. 1990.

[23] E. Ersu and H. Tolle, "Hierarchical learning control—An approach with neuron-like associative memories," *Proc. IEEE Conf. on Neural Information Processing Systems*, Nov. 1988.

[24] ——, "A new concept for learning control inspired by brain theory," *Proc. FAC 9th World Congress*, July 2–6, 1984.

[25] E. Ersu and J. Militzer, "Real-time implementation of an associative memory-based learning control scheme for non-linear multivariable processes," *Proc. 1st Measurements and Control Symp. on Applications of Multivariable Systems Techniques*, pp. 109–119, 1984.

[26] E. Ersu and X. Mao, "Control of pH using a self-organizing control concept with associative memories," *Proc. Intl. IASTED Conf. on Applied Control and Identification*, 1983.

[27] J. Moody, "Fast learning in multi-resolution hierarchies," in *Advances in Neural Information Processing*, D. Touretzky, Ed. Morgan Kaufmann, 1989.

[28] B. Widrow and S. D. Stearns, *Adaptive Signal Processing.* Englewood Cliffs, NJ: Prentice-Hall, 1985.

[29] W. T. Miller, B. A. Box, and E. C. Whitney, "Design and implementation of a high speed CMAC neural network using programmable CMOS logic cell arrays," Univ. of New Hampshire, Rept. no. ECE.IS.90.01, Feb. 6, 1990.

[30] K. Hardwicke, "On the applicability of piecewise affine models in nonlinear adaptive equalization," MS thesis, University of Texas at Austin, 1987.

A Statistical Approach to Learning and Generalization in Layered Neural Networks

ESTHER LEVIN, NAFTALI TISHBY, AND SARA A. SOLLA

A general statistical description of the problem of learning from examples is presented. Our focus is on learning in layered networks, which is posed as a search in the network parameter space for a network that minimizes an additive error function of statistically independent examples. By imposing the equivalence of the minimum error and the maximum likelihood criteria for training the network, we arrive at the Gibbs distribution on the ensemble of networks with a fixed architecture. Using this ensemble, the probability of correct prediction of a novel example can be expressed, serving as a measure of the network's generalization ability. The entropy of the prediction distribution is shown to be a consistent measure of the network's performance. This quantity is directly derived from the ensemble statistical properties and is identical to the stochastic complexity of the training data. Our approach is a link between the information-theoretic model-order-estimation techniques, particularly minimum description length, and the statistical mechanics of neural networks. The proposed formalism is applied to the problems of selecting an optimal architecture and the prediction of learning curves.

I. Introduction

Layered neural networks are nonlinear parametric models that can approximate any continuous input–output relation [1], [2]. The quality of the approximation depends on the architecture of the network used, as well as on the complexity of the target relation. The problem of finding a suitable set of parameters that approximate an unknown relation F is usually solved using supervised learning algorithms. Supervised learning requires a training set, that is, a set of input–output examples related through the relation F, as formalized by Valiant [3]. Learning the training set is often posed as an optimization problem by introducing an error measure. This error is a function of the training examples as well as of the network parameters, and it measures the quality of the network's approximation to the relation F on the restricted domain covered by the training set. The minimization of this error over the network's parameter space is called the training process. The task of learning, however, is to minimize that error for all possible examples related through F, namely, to generalize.

In this work we focus on a statistical description of the learning process by dealing with the ensemble of all networks with the same parameter space. The common method of parameter estimation is the maximum likelihood (ML) approach. By imposing the equivalence of the error minimization and the likelihood maximization we arrive at the Gibbs distribution on the parameter space for a canonical ensemble (see, for example, [4]) of networks with the given architecture. This distribution is interpreted as the post-training distribution, where the probability of arriving at a specific network decreases exponentially with the error of the network on the training examples. The imposed equivalence condition leaves only one free parameter for the training process: the ensemble temperature, which determines the level of acceptable training error as well as the level of stochasticity in the training algorithm. The normalization integral of the Gibbs distribution (that is, the partition function) measures the weighted volume of the configuration space of trained networks, and its functional form determines the average training error as well as the information gained (entropy) during training.

The training process selects network configurations that perform well on the restricted domain defined by the training examples. It is well known, however, that there can be little connection between the training error, restricted to the training set, and the network's ability to generalize outside of that set [5]–[7]. It is generally possible to get increasingly better performance on the training examples by increasing the complexity of the model, but such a procedure does not necessarily lead to a better generalization ability. Using the Gibbs posttraining distribution and the likelihood that results from the equivalence condition, we are able to express the probability of predicting a novel independent example. We show that this prediction probability induces a consistent measure of generalization, which can be viewed as an application to layered networks of the predictive minimum description length method (MDL) as proposed by Rissanen [8].

The problem of estimating the sufficient training set size for learning with layered networks has been previously discussed [9] in a distribution-free, worst case analysis. Our work is a step toward a typical case theory of generalization with layered networks. Though the general principles described can be applied to a wider class of parametric models, they are of special interest in the context of statistical mechanics of "neural networks."

Manuscript received September 25, 1989; revised March 21, 1990.
E. Levin and N. Tishby are with AT&T Bell Laboratories, Murray Hill, NJ 07974, USA.
S. A. Solla is with AT&T Bell Laboratories, Holmdel, NJ 07733, USA.
IEEE Log Number 9039174.

Reprinted from *Proc. IEEE*, vol. 78, no. 10, Oct. 1990, pp. 1568–1574.

A. Layered Networks

We would like to "learn," or model, an input-output relation F by a feedforward layered network, consisting of L layers of processing. The architecture is fixed and determined by the number $\{N_l, 0 \le l \le L\}$ of processing elements per layer and by their connectivity. The elements of the $(l+1)$th layer are connected to the previous layer and their state is determined through the recursion relation

$$\begin{cases} u_i^{(l+1)} = \sum_{j=1}^{N_l} w_{ij}^{(l+1)} v_j^{(l)} + w_i^{(l+1)} \\ v_i^{(l+1)} = h(u_i^{(l+1)}), \qquad 1 \le i \le N_{l+1}. \end{cases} \tag{1}$$

The input to the ith element of the lth layer $u_i^{(l)}$ determines the state $v_i^{(l)}$ of the element through a sigmoid nonlinearity, such as $h(x) = 1/(1 + \exp(-x))$. The parameters of the network are the connections $\{w_{ij}^{(l)}, 1 \le j \le N_{l-1}, 1 \le i \le N_l, 1 \le l \le L\}$ and the biases $\{w_i^{(l)}, 1 \le i \le N_l, 1 \le l \le L\}$, corresponding to a point ω in the $D = \Sigma_{l=1}^{L} N_l(N_{l-1} + 1)$ dimensional Euclidean space $\boldsymbol{R}^D$. For every point ω in the *network configuration space* $\boldsymbol{W} \subset \boldsymbol{R}^D$, the network (1) is a realization of a deterministic mapping from an input $x \in X \subset \boldsymbol{R}^p$ to an output $y \in Y \subset \boldsymbol{R}^q$, provided that $N_0 = p$ and $N_L = q$. We denote this mapping by $y = F_\omega(x)$, $F_\omega: \boldsymbol{R}^p \times \boldsymbol{W} \to \boldsymbol{R}^q$. In what follows we discuss the ensemble of all networks in the configuration space $\boldsymbol{W}$.

We focus on the problem of learning an unknown input-output relation F from examples: a training set of m input-output pairs, related through the unknown relation F, $\xi^{(m)} \equiv \{\xi_i, 1 \le i \le m\}$, where $\xi \equiv (x, y)$, $x \in X \subset \boldsymbol{R}^p$, and $y \in Y \subset \boldsymbol{R}^q$. The relation F can be generally described by the probability density function defined over the space of input-output pairs $X \otimes Y \subset \boldsymbol{R}^{p+q}$: $P_F(\xi) = P_F(x)P_F(y\,|\,x)$, where $P_F(x)$ defines the region of interest in the input space and $P_F(y\,|\,x)$ describes the functional or the statistical relation between the inputs and the outputs. The training set consists of examples drawn independently according to this probability density function. Learning the training set by a layered network is posed as an optimization problem by introducing a measure of quality of the approximation of the desired relation F by the mapping F_ω realized by the network. The additive error function

$$\boldsymbol{E}^{(m)}(\omega) \equiv \boldsymbol{E}(\xi^{(m)}\,|\,\omega) = \sum_{i=1}^{m} \mathbf{e}(y_i\,|\,x_i, \omega) \tag{2}$$

measures the dissimilarity between F and F_ω on the restricted domain covered by the training set. The error function $\mathbf{e}(y\,|\,x, \omega)$ is a distance measure on $\boldsymbol{R}^q$ between the target output y and the output of the network on the given input x, that is, $\mathbf{e}(y\,|\,x, \omega) = \boldsymbol{d}(y, F_\omega(x))$.

II. Probability Inference in the Network Space

A. Error Minimization as a ML Approach

Our first goal is to introduce a statistical description of the training process. The statistical modeling problem is usually posed as one of finding a set of parameters ω that maximizes the likelihood of the training set of m independent examples

$$\operatorname*{Max}_{\omega \in \boldsymbol{W}} P(\xi^{(m)}\,|\,\omega) = \prod_{i=1}^{m} P_F(x_i) \cdot \operatorname*{Max}_{\omega \in \boldsymbol{W}} \prod_{i=1}^{m} p(y_i\,|\,x_i, \omega), \tag{3}$$

where the conditional probability $p(y\,|\,x, \omega)$ should be considered as a measure of the "reasonable expectation" of the *compatibility* of the pair (x, y) to the network ω, rather than relative frequency in some sample space [10].

Our primary requirement is that the maximization of the likelihood (3) be equivalent to the minimization of the additive error (2), for *every* set of independent training examples $\xi^{(m)}$. These two optimization criteria can be equivalent only if they are directly related through an arbitrary monotonic and smooth function ϕ, namely,

$$\prod_{i=1}^{m} p(y_i\,|\,x_i, \omega) = \phi\left(\sum_{i=1}^{m} \mathbf{e}(y_i\,|\,x_i, \omega)\right), \tag{4}$$

assuming that the derivatives w.r.t. ω vanish at the extreme points of both the likelihood and the error. The only solution to the functional equation (4) is given by [11], [12]

$$p(y\,|\,x, \omega) = \frac{1}{z(\beta)} \exp[-\beta \mathbf{e}(y\,|\,x, \omega)]$$

$$z(\beta) = \int_Y \exp[-\beta \mathbf{e}(y\,|\,x, \omega)]\, dy \tag{5}$$

where β is a positive integration constant which determines the sensitivity of the probability $p(y\,|\,x, \omega)$ to the error value. The mean error $\bar{\mathbf{e}} = \int \mathbf{e}(y\,|\,x, \omega) p(y\,|\,x, \omega)\, dy$, is a measure of the *acceptable error level*, and is related to β through

$$\bar{\mathbf{e}} = -\frac{\partial \log z}{\partial \beta}; \qquad \frac{\partial \bar{\mathbf{e}}}{\partial \beta} < 0. \tag{6}$$

We assume that the normalization constant $z(\beta)$ or, equivalently, the mean error $\bar{\mathbf{e}}$, is not an explicit function of the specific network ω or the input x. This assumption is justified considering that the integration in (5) is performed over all possible output values, and is rigorously correct if the error is invariant under translations in the range Y.

An important example is the quadratic error function $\mathbf{e}(y\,|\,x, \omega) = (y - F_\omega(x))^2$. The resulting $p(y\,|\,x, \omega)$ in this case is the Gaussian distribution

$$p(y\,|\,x, \omega) = (2\pi\sigma^2)^{-1/2} \exp[-(y - F_\omega(x))^2/(2\sigma^2)] \tag{7}$$

with $\beta = 1/(2\sigma^2)$. Then $z(\beta) = \sqrt{(\pi/\beta)}$, and $\bar{\mathbf{e}} = \sigma^2$, both independent of the network ω and the input x.

B. The Gibbs Distribution

The conditional likelihood (3) can now be inverted using the Bayes formula to induce a distribution on the network configuration space $\boldsymbol{W}$ given the set of input-output pairs $\xi^{(m)}$

$$\rho^{(m)}(\omega) \equiv P(\omega\,|\,\xi^{(m)}) = \frac{\rho^{(0)}(\omega) \prod_{i=1}^{m} p(y_i\,|\,x_i, \omega)}{\int_W \rho^{(0)}(\omega) \prod_{i=1}^{m} p(y_i\,|\,x_i, \omega)\, d\omega}, \tag{8}$$

where $\rho^{(0)}$ is a nonsingular *prior* distribution on the configuration space.

Writing (8) directly in terms of the training error $\boldsymbol{E}(\xi^{(m)}\,|\,\omega)$, we arrive at the "Gibbs canonical distribution" on the ensemble of networks

$$\rho^{(m)}(\omega) = \frac{1}{\boldsymbol{Z}^{(m)}} \rho^{(0)}(\omega) \exp[-\beta \boldsymbol{E}^{(m)}(\omega)], \tag{9a}$$

where the normalization integral

$$Z^{(m)}(\beta) = \int_W \rho^{(0)}(\omega) \exp\left[-\beta E^{(m)}(\omega)\right] d\omega \tag{9b}$$

is the error moment generating function, known in statistical mechanics as the partition function, and it measures the weighted accessible volume in configuration space. Equation (9) has a clear intuitive meaning as the *posttraining* distribution in $\mathbf{W}$: The probability of each point ω is reduced exponentially with the error of the network on the training set $\xi^{(m)}$. Though this distribution may appear unlikely for some training methods, it arises naturally for stochastic algorithms, such as simulated annealing, [13] which essentially implement the Gibbs distribution in configuration space. It is the only distribution that corresponds directly to the error minimization, it is the most probable distribution for large networks, and it is well utilized in statistical mechanics (see, for example, [4]).

Learning the training examples results in a modification of the probability distribution over the network's parameters space. In the Gibbs formulation, training on an additional independent example ξ_{m+1} is equivalent to multiplying the distribution $\rho^{(m)}$ by the factor $\exp(-\beta \mathbf{e}(y_{m+} | x_{m+1}, \omega))$ and renormalizing, that is,

$$Z^{(m+1)} = \int_W \rho^{(0)}(\omega) \exp\left[-\beta E^{(m)}(\omega) - \beta \mathbf{e}(y_{m+1} | x_{m+1}, \omega)\right] d\omega$$

$$\leq \int_W \rho^{(0)}(\omega) \exp\left[-\beta E^{(m)}(\omega)\right] d\omega = Z^{(m)}. \tag{10}$$

Training thus results in a reduction of the weighted volume in configuration space or, equivalently, in a monotonic increase of the *ensemble free energy* $\beta \mathbf{f} \equiv -\log Z^{(m)}$ with the size m of the training set. It is this free energy, as a function of the parameter β, which determines the average training error

$$\langle E^{(m)} \rangle = \int_W \rho^{(m)}(\omega) E^{(m)}(\omega)\, d\omega = -\frac{\partial \log Z^{(m)}}{\partial \beta} \geq 0, \tag{11}$$

as well as the ensemble fluctuations around this error

$$\frac{\partial \langle E \rangle}{\partial \beta} = -\frac{\partial^2 \log Z}{\partial \beta^2} = -\langle (E - \langle E \rangle)^2 \rangle < 0. \tag{12}$$

The average training error is thus a decreasing function of the sensitivity parameter β, as expected.

C. Information Gain and Entropy

An important characterization of the learning process is the amount of information gained during training. A common way of quantifying this information gain is by the statistical distance between the pre- and posttraining distributions, given by the relative entropy of the ensemble with respect to the prior distribution (Kullback–Leibler distance [14]), that is,

$$S^{(m)} \equiv D[\rho^{(m)} | \rho^{(0)}] = \int_W \rho^{(m)}(\omega) \log \frac{\rho^{(m)}(\omega)}{\rho^{(0)}(\omega)}\, d\omega \geq 0. \tag{13}$$

The familiar thermodynamic relation

$$S^{(m)} = -\log Z^{(m)} - \beta \langle E^{(m)} \rangle \tag{14}$$

identifies this quantity as the thermodynamic entropy, which decreases by reducing the weighted configuration volume $Z^{(m)}$, as well as by decreasing the training error $\langle E^{(m)} \rangle$. Equation (14) provides another meaning for the parameter β, namely the Lagrange multiplier for the constrained average training error $\langle E^{(m)} \rangle$ during minimization of the relative entropy (13), and the inverse of β plays the role of the ensemble temperature, as in statistical mechanics.[1]

D. Training Without Errors

The interesting case of error-free learning can now be recovered by taking the limit $\beta \to \infty$, that is, the zero temperature limit. The Gibbs measure in this limit is simply the prior distribution restricted to the zero error region in $\mathbf{W}$, namely,

$$\rho^{(m)}(\omega) = \frac{\rho^{(0)}(\omega) \prod_{i=1}^{m} \theta(\omega, \xi_i)}{Z^{(m)}} \tag{15}$$

where $\theta(\omega, \xi)$ is a "masking function" that is equal to 1 when the error $\mathbf{e}(y | x, \omega)$ is zero, and which vanishes elsewhere. Equation (15) becomes meaningless when the number of examples increases beyond the capacity [5], [9], [18], [19] of the network, that is, when the training set cannot be learned without errors due to noisy examples or a nonlearnable input-output relation F. In such cases, reaching the capacity is not an indication of the best generalization, which generally can be improved by training with finite error on additional examples. In this sense our formalism generalizes the work of Denker *et al.* [15] to the more common case of finite average training error [16].

The conditional probability (5) in this case is given by

$$p(y | x, \omega) = z^{-1} \theta(\omega, \xi) \tag{16}$$

suggesting another interpretation regarding the probability that the pair ξ was included in a training set leading to the network ω.

III. Generalization and the Stochastic Complexity

A. The Prediction Probability

The learning process selects network configurations that have small error on the restricted domain defined by the training examples. Whether the learning process leads to successful rule extraction—in that the resulting network configurations ω implement the desired relation F—can only be tested through performance on *novel* patterns not belonging to the training set. It is generally possible to get increasingly better performance of the models on the training set, but such a procedure does not necessarily lead to better generalization.

The generalization ability can be measured by the probability that networks trained on m examples, given an input x, will correctly predict the output y, where the pair (x, y) is an independent sample from P_F. The quantity of interest is the conditional probability

$$P(y | x, \xi^{(m)}) \equiv p^{(m)}(y | x) = \int_W \rho^{(m)}(\omega) p(y | x, \omega)\, d\omega$$

$$= \frac{Z^{(m+1)}(\xi)}{Z^{(m)} z} \tag{17}$$

[1]The usual entropy $S = -\int_W \rho(\omega) \log \rho(\omega)\, d\omega$ is maximized by the Gibbs distribution, subject to the $\langle E^{(m)} \rangle$ constraint.

where $\rho^{(m)}(\omega) = P(\omega \mid \xi^{(m)})$ of Eq. (9) is the posttraining probability of network ω, and $p(y \mid x, \omega)$ of Eq. (5) is the probability that the new pair ξ is compatible with the network ω. The prediction probability has a clear intuitive meaning, since the ratio $(Z^{(m+1)}/Z^{(m)})$ describes the relative volume of networks that are compatible with all $m + 1$ examples among those that are compatible with the m training examples.

Since $Z^{(m)}$ is a monotonic function of m, the statistical prediction error [8] $-\log p^{(m)}(\xi)$ follows from Eq. (17) and can be expressed as a free energy derivative

$$-\log p^{(m)} \approx -\frac{\partial \log Z^{(m)}}{\partial m} + \log z. \tag{18}$$

A reliable estimate of the generalization ability requires the prediction of a large number of independent points $\xi^{(T)}$, distributed according to the underlying probability function $P_F(\xi)$. The average statistical prediction error can be shown to be a consistent measure of the generalization ability using the Gibbs inequality, that is,

$$\begin{aligned} \frac{-1}{T} \log \prod_{t=1}^{T} p^{(m)}(y_t \mid x_t) &= \frac{-1}{T} \sum_{t=1}^{T} \log p^{(m)}(y_t \mid x_t) \underset{T\to\infty}{\to} \langle -\log p^{(m)} \rangle \\ &\equiv -\int P_F(\xi) \log p^{(m)}(y \mid x)\, d\xi \\ &\geq -\int P_F(\xi) \log P_F(y \mid x)\, d\xi. \end{aligned} \tag{19}$$

This measure is called the *stochastic complexity* [8] and it was introduced by Rissanen for the purpose of estimating the generalization in statistical models. The maximal statistical generalization ability, or minimal stochastic complexity, is obtained if and only if the prediction probability $p^{(m)}(y \mid x)$ of the trained networks equals $P_F(y \mid x)$. In that case the trained networks implement the underlying relation F.

Another important property of the statistical prediction error $-\log p^{(m)}$ is that it is bounded by the generalization and training errors on the example ξ. Using the positivity of the relative entropies

$$\int_W \rho^{(m+1)}(\omega) \log \frac{\rho^{(m+1)}(\omega)}{\rho^{(m)}(\omega)}\, d\omega \geq 0;$$

$$\int_W \rho^{(m)}(\omega) \log \frac{\rho^{(m)}(\omega)}{\rho^{(m+1)}(\omega)}\, d\omega \geq 0$$

we obtain

$$\beta \langle \mathbf{e}(y \mid x) \rangle_{\rho^{(m+1)}} \leq -\log p^{(m)}(y \mid x) - \log z \leq \beta \langle \mathbf{e}(y \mid x) \rangle_{\rho^{(m)}} \tag{20}$$

with equalities if, and only if, the two errors are equal. Thus $-1/\beta \log p^{(m)}$ is bounded by the more natural measure of generalization: the average error on examples not in the training set, that is, *the generalization error.* Note that minimizing the statistical prediction error amounts to minimizing the distance between the ensemble posttraining prediction distribution and the *true* distribution of the data. From (20) it is clear that this is a weaker form of generalization than minimizing the pretraining or the generalization error directly.

The stochastic complexity $\langle -\log p^{(m)} \rangle$ has an additional meaning as the average number of bits required to encode a novel example, given a system trained on the m examples. The network with minimal prediction error is thus the one that provides maximal average compression of the data. The training of networks that minimize the statistical prediction error is an application to layered networks of the principle of minimum stochastic complexity, also known as the minimum description length principle (MDL) [8].

B. Sample and Ensemble Averages

The partition function and all the quantities derived from it are functions of the random choice of a specific training set, and as such are still random variables. The typical performance of the network must be estimated by averaging these random variables over all possible training sets of the given size m. This averaging, denoted by $\langle\langle\ \rangle\rangle$, should be done at the end with respect to the *external* measure $P_F(\xi)$ and is different from the ensemble average over the Gibbs measure. As is evident from Eqs. (11), (12), and (18), the important function from which the interesting quantities are derived is the free energy $-\log Z^{(m)}(\beta)$. Due to the external nature of $P_F(\xi)$—it is independent of β or m—we can interchange partial derivatives with sample averaging, and the basic problem is reduced to the calculation of the *quenched* free energy $\langle\langle \log Z(m, \beta) \rangle\rangle$. This generally very difficult problem can be solved in special cases using the "replica method" [17]–[19], which has become an almost standard tool in the study of random systems in statistical physics. The basic equations of our theoretical framework are thus summarized by

$$\langle\langle \log Z(m, \beta) \rangle\rangle = \int P_F(\xi^{(m)}) \log Z(\xi^{(m)}, \beta)\, d\xi^{(m)} \tag{21a}$$

$$\langle\langle \langle E^{(m)} \rangle \rangle\rangle = -\frac{\partial \langle\langle \log Z(m, \beta) \rangle\rangle}{\partial \beta} \tag{21b}$$

$$\langle\langle -\log p^{(m)} \rangle\rangle \approx -\frac{\partial \langle\langle \log Z(m, \beta) \rangle\rangle}{\partial m} + \log z(\beta) \tag{21c}$$

with

$$P_F(\xi^{(m)})\, d\xi^{(m)} = \prod_{i=1}^{m} P_F(\xi_i)\, d\xi_i.$$

C. The Role of β

The parameter β plays an important role in our framework. It is the ensemble inverse temperature and it controls the amount of stochasticity in the training algorithm. In addition, the presence of finite β regularizes the error-free case and allows the formal derivation of the training and prediction errors from the ensemble-free energy. The most significant benefit of keeping the parameter β finite is that it can be optimized to obtain the best generalization ability. Indeed, as has been recently shown [18]–[20], a variable β strategy gives superior generalization for various learning problems. A simple linear learning problem illustrates this effect in the next section.

IV. Applications

A. Learning in the Noisy Linear Map

The ideas are now illustrated by analyzing a simple example: the linear learning problem. Consider a linear network: the output of the network is given by $F_\omega(x) = \omega^T x$, where x and ω are D-dimensional real column vectors and ω^T denotes the transpose of ω. The prior on the network configuration space is taken to be a D-dimensional symmetric Gaussian distribution $\rho^{(0)}(\omega) = N(0, R_\omega)$, with $R_\omega = \sigma_\omega^2 \cdot \boldsymbol{I}_D$, $\sigma_\omega >> 1$, and $\boldsymbol{I}_D$ is the D-dimensional unit matrix.

The examples are generated by a similar linear map corrupted by additive white Gaussian noise: $y = \omega_0^T x + \eta$, where the noise $\eta \sim N(0, \sigma_\eta^2)$. The distribution over the domain X is taken to be also a D-dimensional Gaussian $x \sim N(0, R_x)$; $R_x = \sigma_x^2 \cdot \boldsymbol{I}_D$. These two distributions determine the underlying probability distribution of the examples $P_F(\xi)$. Learning proceeds using a quadratic error function: $\mathbf{e}(y|x, \omega) = (y - \omega^T x)^2 = ((\omega - \omega_0)^T x - \eta)^2$.

The average free energy can be calculated [21] for $m > D$ and $\sigma_\omega >> 1$, and is

$$\langle\langle \log \boldsymbol{Z}(m, \beta) \rangle\rangle = -D \log \sigma_\omega - \frac{\omega_0^T \omega_0}{2\sigma_\omega^2} - \frac{1}{2} D \log (2\beta\sigma_x^2 m) - \beta m \sigma_\eta^2 + \beta D \sigma_\eta^2 + O\left(\frac{1}{m}\right). \quad (22)$$

The training and generalization errors follow from (21)

$$\langle\langle \langle E^{(m)} \rangle \rangle\rangle = \frac{D}{2\beta} + (m - D)\sigma_\eta^2 \quad (23a)$$

$$\langle\langle -\log p^{(m)} \rangle\rangle \approx \frac{D}{2m} + \beta\sigma_\eta^2 + \log \sqrt{\frac{\pi}{\beta}} + O\left(\frac{1}{m^2}\right). \quad (23b)$$

It is interesting to note that the optimal β, that is, the one that gives minimal prediction error, can be easily determined from Eq. (23b) to be $\beta_o = 1/2\sigma_\eta^2$, and is just the β corresponding to the level of noise in the examples. For this value of β the average prediction error reaches asymptotically its lowest possible value (Eq. (19)), which is the entropy of the noise in the examples. The optimal value β_o corresponds to a training error which is simply a constant per training example (Eq. (23a)), but not minimal! Reducing the training error by increasing the value of β beyond β_o *increases* the prediction error, due to an *overfitting* of the model to the noisy data. The asymptotic $D/2m$ decrease of the prediction error is of the form obtained for other learning problems by various authors [18]–[20], [22].

B. Architecture Selection in the Contiguity Problem

The sum over the generalization errors during the training process

$$\frac{1}{T}\sum_{i=1}^{T} \langle \mathbf{e}(y_t|x_t) \rangle_{\rho^{(t-1)}} \geq \frac{1}{T}\sum_t \frac{-1}{\beta} \log p^{(t)}(y|x)z \quad (24)$$

is an upper bound on the statistical prediction error and can be used as the practical generalization measure. By exchanging the averaging over the network ensemble with the summation over the training set we get an effective estimate $\hat{\boldsymbol{G}}^{(T)}$ of the generalization measure from the training samples $\xi^{(T)}$ alone

$$\hat{\boldsymbol{G}}^{(T)} = \frac{1}{T}\sum_{m=0}^{T-1} \frac{1}{T-m} \sum_{t=m+1}^{T} \mathbf{e}(y_t|x_t, \omega_m) \approx \frac{1}{T}\sum_t \langle \mathbf{e}(y_t|x_t) \rangle_{\rho^{(t-1)}} \quad (25)$$

where the ensemble averaging is approximated by randomly selecting the initial training points ω_m for each $0 \leq m \leq T - 1$ [23].

To demonstrate the utility of this generalization measure ((Eq. 25)) for determining a sufficient size of the training set, as well as selecting the optimal architecture of the network, we focus on a simple Boolean mapping known as the "clumps" or contiguity problem [24]. For binary patterns of 10 bits, 792 of the 1024 patterns contain two or three continuous blocks of ones, or "clumps" separated by zeros. The Boolean function that separates this set into the subsets of two and three clumps cannot be implemented by a single-layer perceptron [25] and two layers of units are needed. There are, however, several two-layer networks that can implement the mapping, varying only in the connectivity between the first and second layer, the receptive width, as depicted in Fig. 1.

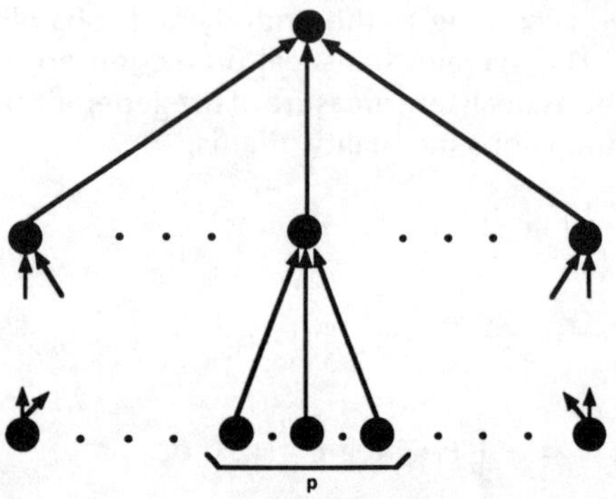

Fig. 1. The network architecture used for the contiguity problem. The receptive field width p is the size of the input field connected to each hidden unit. By varying the receptive field we observe a significant change in the generalization ability of the network.

Though the training error can be reduced on a small training set of 150 patterns for almost all the different architectures, these networks have a very different generalization ability at the end of the training process. To illustrate this point, the network was trained on increasing subsets of the training set, starting with 10 patterns, and increasing the number of patterns by 10 after convergence of the training algorithm on the previous subset. Using the generalization measure—as given by Eq. (25)—estimated within the training set, we were able to evaluate the generalization ability of the network and determine the optimal architecture. A more detailed description of these experiments can be found in Tishby *et al.* [23]. In Fig. 2 we plot the generalization

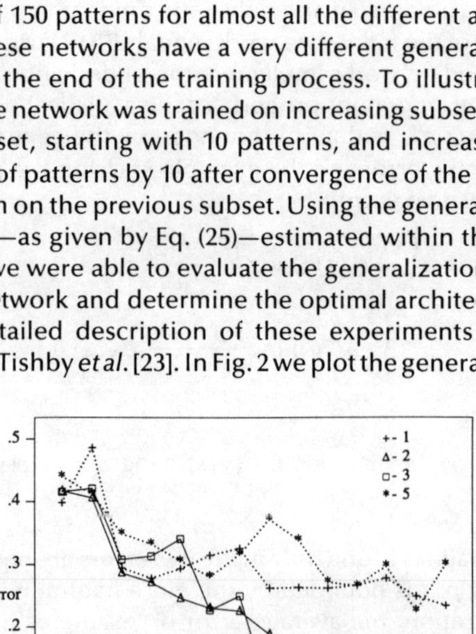

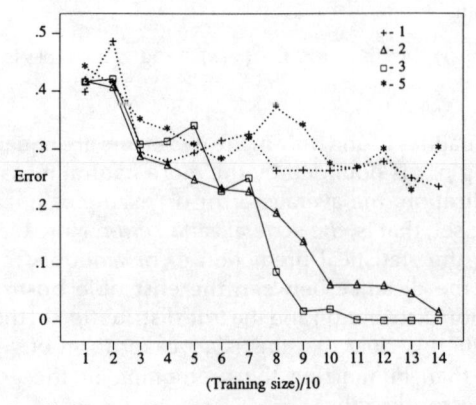

Fig. 2. Prediction errors at the end of training as a function of the training size, for various receptive fields. The difference in generalization ability is evident.

measure, estimated from the training set alone, and the average generalization error, calculated from all 792 patterns, as a function of the current training size, for the various receptive widths given in Fig. 1. We observe that, although for receptive widths of 1 and 5 the prediction error remains high throughout the training set, it drops sharply after about half of the patterns for the receptive widths of 2 and 3, indicating the superior generalization ability of these networks. The method described here is similar to the cross-validation techniques commonly used in pattern recognition [26].

C. Learning Curves in the Annealed Approximation

The calculation of the sample average free energy for the general layered network is a very hard problem. A useful approximation, introduced by Schwartz *et al.* [27], becomes valid when the partition function itself is a "self-averaging" quantity, namely, when the random $\mathbf{Z}^{(m)}(\beta)$ converges for large m to a deterministic function and an "annealed" average can be used. In this case the partition function is asymptotically independent of the specific training set $\xi^{(m)}$ and can be evaluated directly by the average

$$\langle\langle \mathbf{Z}^{(m)}(\beta)\rangle\rangle = \int_W d\omega \rho^{(0)}(\omega) \prod_{i=1}^{m} \int_{X\otimes Y} P_F(\xi) \cdot \exp\left[-\beta e(y \mid x, \omega)\right] d\xi$$

$$\equiv z^m \cdot \int_W \rho^{(0)}(\omega) g^m(\omega, \beta)\, d\omega \tag{26}$$

where

$$g(\omega, \beta) \equiv \int_{X\otimes Y} P_F(\xi) \frac{\exp\left[-\beta \mathbf{e}(y \mid x, \omega)\right]}{z} d\xi = \langle\langle p(y \mid x, \omega)\rangle\rangle$$

is the sample average of the likelihood (5), and is a measure of the compatibility of the network ω to the modeled relation F.

Within the annealed approximation, the average prediction probability after training on m examples can be written as a ratio of two successive moments of a well-defined prior distribution.

$$\langle\langle p^{(m)}\rangle\rangle \approx \frac{\langle\langle \mathbf{Z}^{(m+1)}(\beta)\rangle\rangle}{\langle\langle \mathbf{Z}^{(m)}(\beta)\rangle\rangle z} = \frac{\langle g^{m+1}\rangle_{\rho^{(0)}(g)}}{\langle g^{m}\rangle_{\rho^{(0)}(g)}}. \tag{27}$$

The density $\rho^{(0)}(g) \equiv \int \rho^{(0)}(\omega)\delta(g(\omega) - g)\, d\omega$, where $\delta(x)$ is the Dirac delta function, is the prior $\rho^{(0)}(\omega)$ expressed as a function of the single variable $g(\omega, \beta)$, and contains all the information about the configuration space $\mathbf{W}$ and about the task (the desired relation F) through the definition of $g(\omega, \beta)$. Learning curves, $\langle -\log p^{(m)}\rangle$ versus m, can now be obtained simply by calculating the moments of such prior densities [23], [27].

The asymptotic behavior of the moments ratio (27) is determined solely by the functional form of $\rho^{(0)}(g)$ near $g = 1$. If, for example, $\rho^{(0)}(g) \sim (1 - g)^d$ as $g \to 1$, for some exponent $d \geq 0$

$$p^{(m)} \approx 1 - \frac{d+1}{m}; \qquad -\log p^{(m)} \approx \frac{d+1}{m} \tag{28}$$

for large m. The asymptotic form (28) is in agreement with the $1/m$ decrease of the generalization error found earlier [18]–[20], [22]. This annealed approximation suggests an interesting possible relation between the value of the exponent d and the VC-dimension [9], [28] of the learning system.

V. Summary

By using a few simple and plausible assumptions we show that the Gibbs formulation of statistical mechanics is well suited for the typical case analysis of the problem of learning from examples in layered networks. We propose a statistical measure of generalization that can be derived directly from the free energy of the network's ensemble, and which is shown to be equivalent to the stochastic complexity of the training data. By doing this we link the statistical mechanics of neural networks with the modern methods of statistical estimation theory. The formalism can be applied to analytic and numerical evaluation of learning curves, as well as be a practical method for training networks that generalize well.

Acknowledgment

The authors give special thanks to Neri Merhav for many illuminating discussions, for his help in the calculations of the linear example, and for critically reading the manuscript. Useful discussions with Géza Györgyi, Dan Schwartz, Andrew Ogielski, and John Denker are greatly appreciated.

References

[1] R. P. Lippmann, "An introduction to computing with neural nets," *ASSP Magazine*, vol. 4, no. 2, pp. 4–22, 1987.
[2] G. Cybenko, "Continuous valued neural networks with two hidden layers are sufficient," Tufts University preprint, 1988.
[3] L. G. Valiant, "A theory of the learnable," *Comm. ACM*, vol. 27, no. 11, pp. 1134–1142, 1984.
[4] L. D. Landau and E. M. Lifshitz, *Course of theoretical physics*, vol. 5, 3rd ed. Pergamon, 1980.
[5] T. Cover, "Geometrical and statistical properties of systems of linear inequalities with applications to patterns recognition," *IEEE Trans. Electron. Comput.*, vol. 14, pp. 326–334, 1965.
[6] E. B. Baum, "On the capabilities of multilayer perceptrons," *J. Complexity*, 1989.
[7] H. White, "Learning in artificial neural networks: A statistical perspective," *Neural Computation*, vol. 1, pp. 425–464, 1989.
[8] J. Rissanen, "Stochastic complexity and modeling," *Ann. Statist.*, vol. 14, pp. 1080–1100, 1986.
[9] E. B. Baum and D. Haussler, "What size net gives valid generalization," *Neural Computation*, vol. 1, pp. 151–160, 1989.
[10] R. T. Cox, "Probability, frequency and reasonable expectation," *Amer. J. Phys.*, vol. 14, pp. 1–26, 1946.
[11] J. Aczél and Z. Daróczy, *On Measures of Information and Their Characterizations*. Academic Press, 1975, p. 16.
[12] Y. Tikochinsky, N. Tishby, and R. D. Levine, "Alternative approach to maximum entropy inference," *Phys. Rev. A*, vol. 30, pp. 2638–2644, 1984.
[13] S. Kirkpatrick, C. D. Gelatt, and M. P. Vecchi, "Optimization by simulated annealing," *Science*, vol. 220, pp. 671–680, 1983.
[14] S. Kullback, *Information Theory and Statistics*. New York: Wiley, 1959.
[15] J. Denker *et al.*, "Large automatic learning, rule extraction, and generalization," *Complex Systems*, vol. 1, pp. 877–922, 1987.
[16] P. Carnevali and S. Patranello, "Learning networks of neurons with Boolean logic," *Europhys. Lett.*, vol. 4, pp. 503–508, 1199–1204, 1987.
[17] E. Gardner, "The space of interactions of neural networks models," *J. Phys. A*, vol. 21, pp. 257–270, 1988; E. Gardner and B. Derrida, *J. Phys. A*, vol. 21, pp. 271–284, 1988.
[18] D. Hansel and H. Sompolinsky, "Learning from examples in a single-layer neural network," *Europhys. Lett.*, 1990.
[19] G. Györgyi and N. Tishby, "Statistical theory of learning a rule," in *Neural Networks and Spin Glasses*. W. Theumann and R. Kobrele Eds. New Jersey: World Scientific, 1990.

[20] H. Sompolinsky, S. Seung, and N. Tishby, "Learning from examples in large neural networks," to be published.

[21] E. Levin, N. Tishby, and S. A. Solla, in *Proc. 2nd Ann. Workshop on Computational Learning Theory* (COLT'89), R. Rivest, D. Haussler, and M. K. Warmuth, Eds. San Mateo, CA: Morgan Kaufmann, 1989, pp. 245–260.

[22] D. Haussler, N. Littlestone, and M. K. Warmuth, "Predicting {0, 1} Functions on Randomly Drawn Points," in *Proc. COLT'88* San Mateo, CA: Morgan Kaufmann, 1988, pp. 280–295.

[23] N. Tishby, E. Levin, and S. A. Solla, "Consistent inference of probabilities in layered networks: Predictions and generalization," in *Proc. Int. Joint Conf. on Neural Networks* (IJCNN), vol. 2, pp. 403–409, IEEE Press, Washington DC, June 1989. New York: IEEE Press, 1989.

[24] T. Maxwell, C. L. Giles, and Y. C. Lee, "Generalization in neural networks, the contiguity problem," in *Proc. IEEE 1st Int. Conf. con Neural Networks*, San Diego, 1987; T. Grossman, R. Meir, and E. Domany, "Learning by choice of internal representations," *Complex Systems*, vol. 2, pp. 555–563, 1988.

[25] M. Minsky, and S. Papert, *Perceptrons*. Cambridge, MA: M.I.T. Press, 1969.

[26] M. Stone, "Cross-validatory choice and assessment of statistical predictions," *J. R. Stat. Soc. Ser. B*, vol. 36, pp. 111–133, 1974.

[27] D. B. Schwartz, V. K. Samalam, J. S. Denker, and S. A. Solla, "Exhaustive learning," *Neural. Comp.*, 1990.

[28] A. Blumer, A. Ehrenfeucht, D. Haussler, and M. K. Warmuth, "Learnability and the Vapnik-Chervonenkis dimension," UCSC-CRL 87-20 and *J. ACM*, 1988

On the Convergence Properties of the Hopfield Model

JEHOSHUA BRUCK

The main contribution is showing that the known convergence properties of the Hopfield model can be reduced to a very simple case, for which we have an elementary proof. The convergence properties of the Hopfield model are dependent on the structure of the interconnections matrix W and the method by which the nodes are updated. Three cases are known: (1) convergence to a stable state when operating in a serial mode with symmetric W, (2) convergence to a cycle of length at most 2 when operating in a fully parallel mode with symmetric W, and (3) convergence to a cycle of length 4 when operating in a fully parallel mode with anti-symmetric W. We review the three known results and prove that the fully parallel mode of operation is a special case of the serial mode of operation, for which we present an elementary proof. The elementary proof (one which does not involve the concept of an energy function) follows from the relations between the model and cuts in the graph. We also prove that the three known cases are the only interesting ones by exhibiting exponential lower bounds on the length of the cycles in the other cases.

I. Introduction

A. What is a (Neural) Network?

The neural network model considered is the one suggested by Hopfield in 1982 [1]. It is a discrete-time system that can be represented by a weighted graph. A weight is attached to each edge of the graph and a threshold value is attached to each node (neuron) of the graph. The *order* of the network is the number of nodes in the corresponding graph. Let N be a neural network of order n; then N is uniquely defined by (W, T) where:

- W is an $n \times n$ matrix, with element w_{ij} equal to the weight attached to edge (i, j)
- T is a vector of dimension n, where element t_i denotes the threshold attached to node i.

Every node (neuron) can be in one of two possible states, either 1 or -1. The state of node i at time t denoted by $v_i(t)$. The *state* of the neural network at time t is the vector $V(t) = (v_1(t), v_2(t), \cdots, v_n(t))$.

The state of a node at time $(t + 1)$ is computed by

$$v_i(t+1) = \operatorname{sgn}(H_i(t)) = \begin{cases} 1 & \text{if } H_i(t) \geq 0 \\ -1 & \text{otherwise} \end{cases} \quad (1)$$

where

$$H_i(t) = \sum_{j=1}^{n} w_{j,i} v_j(t) - t_i.$$

Note that every node in the network is actually a linear threshold (LT) element with the states of the other nodes being its inputs and the threshold being t_i.

The next state of the network, that is, $V(t + 1)$, is computed from the current state by performing the evaluation (1) at a subset of the nodes of the network, to be denoted by S. The modes of operation are determined by the method by which the set S is selected in each time interval. If the computation is performed at a single node in any time interval, that is, $|S| = 1$ ($|S|$ denotes the number of nodes in the set S), then we will say that the network is operating in a *serial* mode, and if the computation is performed in all nodes in the same time, that is, $|S| = n$, then we will say that the network is operating in a *fully parallel* mode. All the other cases, that is, $1 < |S| < n$, will be called *parallel* modes of operation. The set S can be chosen at random or according to some deterministic rule.

A state $V(t)$ is called *stable* iff $V(t) = \operatorname{sgn}(WV(t) - T)$, that is, there is no change in the state of the network no matter what the mode of operation is. The set of stable states of a network N is denoted by M_N. A set of distinct states $\{V_1, \cdots, V_k\}$ is a *cycle* of length k if a sequence of evaluations results in the sequence of states: $V_1, \cdots, V_k, V_1, \cdots$ repeating forever.

B. Three Simple Examples

To make the foregoing definitions clear, we consider three simple examples. The networks considered in these examples consist of two nodes only, like the one in Fig. 1.

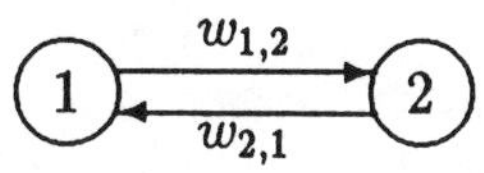

Fig. 1. A network with two nodes.

Example 1: serial operation, symmetric W: Consider the network $N = (W, T)$ with

$$W = \begin{pmatrix} 0 & -1 \\ -1 & 0 \end{pmatrix}$$

Manuscript received July 17, 1989; revised February 21, 1990.

J. Bruck is with the IBM Research Division, Almaden Research Center, 650 Harry Road, San Jose, CA 95120-6099, USA.

IEEE Log Number 9037383.

Reprinted from *Proc. IEEE*, vol. 78, no. 10, Oct. 1990, pp. 1579–1585.

and T being the 0 vector. It can be verified that when N is operating in a serial mode $M_N = \{(-1, 1), (1, -1)\}$.

Example 2: fully-parallel operation, symmetric W: Consider the network $N = (W, T)$, with

$$W = \begin{pmatrix} 0 & -1 \\ -1 & 0 \end{pmatrix}$$

and T being the 0 vector. It can be verified that when N is operating in a fully parallel mode $M_N = \{(-1, 1)(1, -1)\}$ and that $\{(1, 1), (-1, -1)\}$ is a cycle of length 2.

Example 3: fully-parallel operation, antisymmetric W: Consider the network $N = (W, T)$ with

$$W = \begin{pmatrix} 0 & 1 \\ -1 & 0 \end{pmatrix}$$

and T being the 0 vector. It can be verified that when N is operating in a fully parallel mode there are no stable states and the set of states

$$\{(1, 1), (-1, 1), (-1, -1), (1, -1)\}$$

is a cycle of length 4.

One of the fascinating properties of the network model is the fact that these three examples are special cases of a general property—the convergence property. Note that since the state-space of a network is finite, the network will always converge to the stable states/cycles in the state-space.

C. Convergence Properties

The convergence properties are dependent on the structure of W and the method by which the nodes are updated. The three foregoing examples are special cases of the following three known results:

1) Convergence to a stable state when operating in a serial mode with symmetric nonnegative diagonal W [1].
2) Convergence to a cycle of length at most 2 when operating in a fully-parallel mode with symmetric W [2].
3) Convergence to a cycle of length 4 when operating in a fully-parallel mode with antisymmetric W [3].

The main idea in the proof of the convergence properties is to define a so-called *energy function* and to show that this energy function is nondecreasing when the state of the network changes as a result of computation. Since the energy function is bounded from above it follows that it will converge to some value. Our approach here is to get a proof that does not involve the concept of an energy function.

In Section II it is shown that finding the global maximum of the energy function associated with the network operating in a serial mode is *equivalent* to finding the minimum cut in the *undirected* graph associated with the network. We then use this relation to derive an elementary proof (one that does not involve the concept of an energy function) for convergence in the serial mode (see the Appendix for a proof of this result that uses the concept of an energy function). Getting an elementary proof using the relation to cuts in a graph led to the following question:

Is the convergence property unique? Three convergence properties were described in Section I-C. The idea in the proofs of those results is to use the concept of an energy function. Two different energy functions were used for those three results. The question is whether the three convergence properties are inherently different. The answer is no. In Section III it is shown that the two properties of convergence in a fully parallel mode are special cases of the convergence in a serial mode for which we have an elementary proof. Also we prove that those are the only three interesting cases by proving exponential lower bounds on the length of the cycles in the other cases.

II. The Model and Cuts in a Graph

The idea in this section is to establish the relation between the method of computation performed by the network to a particular problem in graph theory, namely, the problem of finding a minimum cut (MC) in an undirected graph. In fact, it is shown that finding a global maximum of the energy function associated with a network operating in a serial model is *equivalent* to find a minimum cut in the undirected graph associated with the network. We use this relation to get a very elementary proof for convergence in a network operating in a serial mode. It also possible to consider directed graphs and show how to program a network to perform a local random search for the MC [4].

A. The Equivalence with the Undirected Case

The neural network model, when operating in a serial mode, is actually performing a local search for a maximum of the energy function denoted by E_1:

$$E_1(t) = V^T(t)WV(t) - 2V^T(t)T. \tag{2}$$

Theorem 8 (see the Appendix) implies that a network, when operating in a serial mode, will always get to a stable state which corresponds to a local maximum in the energy function E_1. This property suggests the use of the network as a device for performing a local search algorithm in order to find a local maximal value of the energy function E_1 [5]. The value of E_1 that corresponds to the initial state is improved by performing a sequence of random serial iterations until the network reaches a local maximum. The local search algorithm performed by the neural network model is imposed by the way the network is operating. Consider a network N operating in a serial mode, and let L_N denote the local search algorithm performed by the network N.

Algorithm L_N for max $(E_1(V))$ is:

1) Start with a random assignment $V \in \{-1, 1\}^n$.
2) Choose a node $i \in \{1 \cdots n\}$ at random.
3) Try to improve E_1 by performing the evaluation

$$v_i = \text{sgn}\left(\sum_{j=1}^{n} w_{j,i}v_j - t_i\right).$$

4) Go to step 2.

The class of optimization problems that can be represented by quadratic functions is very rich [6]. One problem, which is not only representable by a quadratic function but actually is equivalent, is the problem of finding an MC in a graph [6]–[8]. To make the above statements clear, let us start by defining the term "cut in a graph."

Definition: Let $G = (V, E)$ be a weighted and undirected graph, with W being an $n \times n$ symmetric matrix of weights of the edges of G. Let V_1 be a subset of V, and let $V_{-1} = V - V_1$. The *set of edges* incident at one node in V_1 and at one node in V_{-1} is called a *cut* of the graph G. A *minimum cut* in a graph is a cut for which the sum of the corresponding edge weights is minimal over all V_1.

Theorem 1: [6], [8] Let $G = (V, E)$ be a weighted and undirected graph, with W being the matrix of its edge weights. Then the MC problem in G is equivalent to $\max Q_G(X)$, where $X \in \{-1, 1\}^n$, and:

$$Q_G(X) \overset{\text{def}}{=} \sum_{i=1}^{n} \sum_{j=1}^{n} w_{i,j} x_i x_j.$$

Proof: Assign a variable x_i to every node $i \in V$. Let W^{++} denote the sum of the weights of edges in G with both end points equal to 1, and let W^{--} and W^{+-} denote the corresponding sums of the other two cases. Thus,

$$Q_G = 2(W^{++} + W^{--} - W^{+-})$$

which also can be written as

$$Q_G = 2(W^{++} + W^{--} + W^{+-}) - 4W^{+-}$$

$$= \sum_{i=1}^{n} \sum_{j=1}^{n} w_{i,j} - 4W^{+-}. \tag{3}$$

The first term in (3) above is constant (equals the sum of weights of edges in G); hence, maximization of Q_G is equivalent to minimization of W^{+-} is actually a weight of a cut in G with V_1 being the set of nodes in G that correspond to variables that are equal to 1. □

The above theorem can be applied to get the equivalence with the energy associated with the network.

Theorem 2: Let $N = (W, T)$ be a network with W being an $n \times n$ symmetric zero diagonal matrix. Let G be a weighted graph with $(n + 1)$ nodes, with its weight matrix W_G being

$$W_G = \begin{pmatrix} W & T \\ T^T & 0 \end{pmatrix}.$$

The problem of finding a state V in N for which E_1 is a global maximum is equivalent to the MC problem in the corresponding graph G.

Proof: Note that the graph G is built out of N by adding one node to N and connecting it to the other n nodes, with the edge connected to node i having a weight t_i (the corresponding threshold). Clearly, if the state of the added node is constrained to -1, then for all $X \in \{-1, 1\}^n$

$$Q_G(X, -1) = E_1(X).$$

Hence, the equivalence follows from Theorem 1. Note that the state of node $(n + 1)$ need not be constrained to -1. There is a symmetry in the cut; that is $Q_G(X) = Q_G(-X)$ for all $X \in \{-1, 1\}^{n+1}$. Thus, if a minimum cut is achieved with the state of node $(n + 1)$ being 1, then a minimum is also achieved by the cut obtained by interchanging V_1 and V_{-1} (resulting in $x_{n+1} = -1$). □

B. A Simple Proof for Convergence

The relation between neural networks and the MC problem leads to the following nice interpretation of the algorithm L_N performed by the model.

Algorithm L_N for the MC problem is:

1) Start with a random cut.
2) Choose a node k at random.
3) Compare the sum of weights of the edges which belong to the cut and incident at node k with the sum of weights of the other edges which are incident at node k. Move node k to the side of the cut which will result in a decrease in the weight of the cut. Ties (the case of equality) are broken by placing node k in V_1.
4) Go to step 2.

Hence, we have an elementary proof for convergence:

Theorem 3: Let $N = (W, T)$ be a network with $T = 0$ and W be a symmetric zero-diagonal matrix. If N is operating in a serial mode then it will always converge to a stable state.

Proof: By the foregoing derivation we can consider the operation of N as the running of algorithm L_N for the minimum cut in N. In each iteration the value of the cut is nonincreasing (ties are broken as described above); thus, the algorithm will always stop resulting in a cut whose weight is a local minimum. □

Clearly, the proof above is for a special case of a network (that is why it is simple). In Section III we show that *all* the other general cases can be reduced to the foregoing simple case.

III. A Unified Approach to Convergence

Convergence to a stable state/cycle of a certain length is one of the most important properties of the neural network model. The convergence properties are dependent on the structure of the interconnection matrix W and the method by which the nodes are updated. The three known cases are mentioned in the Section I-B. Those results were proved by using the concept of an energy function. In this section we answer the three following questions: (i) Is the convergence property unique? (ii) Is there an elementary proof for convergence (one that does not involve the concept of an energy function)? (iii) Are there any interesting cases besides the three known cases?

The answer to the first question is yes; in fact we prove that convergence in a fully parallel mode is a special case of convergence in a serial mode. In Section II we presented a proof (see Theorem 3) for convergence in a very simple network based on the relations between networks and cuts in a graph. In this section we show that all the other cases are special cases of this simple network; hence, we have an elementary proof for the convergence properties (a positive answer to (ii)). We also consider other cases and exhibit exponentially (in the number of nodes) long cycles in networks that are not of the three known cases; hence we have a negative answer to (iii).

A. Convergence Theorems

One of the most important properties of the model is the fact that in certain cases it always converges, as summarized by the following theorem. Notice that these three cases correspond to the three simple examples in the Section I-B.

Theorem 4: Let $N = (W, T)$ be a neural network, then:

1) Assume N is operating in a serial mode and W is a symmetric matrix with the elements of the diagonal being nonnegative. Then the network will always converge to a stable state, that is, there are no cycles in the state space [1].
2) Assume N is operating in a fully parallel mode and W is a symmetric matrix. Then the network will always converge to a stable state or to a cycle of

length 2, that is, the cycles in the state space are of length ≤ 2 [2].

3) Assume N is operating in a fully parallel mode and W is an antisymmetric matrix with zero diagonal and let $T = 0$. Then the network will always converge to a cycle of length 4 [3].

The main idea in the proof of the three parts of the theorem is to define a so-called *energy function* and to show that this energy function is nondecreasing when the state of the network changes. Since the energy function is bounded from above it follows that the energy will converge to some value. An important note is that originally the energy function was defined by others such that it is nonincreasing [1]–[3]; we changed it to be nondecreasing such that the value of the energy will comply with some known graph problems (for example, MC, see Section II). The second step in the proof is to show that constant energy implies in the first case a stable state, in the second a cycle of length ≤ 2, and in the third a cycle of length 4 (see the Appendix for a proof of part 1 of the theorem that involves the concept of an energy function). Two different energy functions were defined:

$$E_1(t) = V^T(t)WV(t) - (V(t) + V(t))^T T$$

$$E_2(t) = V^T(t)WV(t-1) - (V(t) + V(t-1))^T T. \tag{4}$$

The energy function $E_1(t)$ was used to prove the first part of the theorem and $E_2(t)$ was used to prove the second and third parts of the theorem. In the next section we reveal the relation between the three cases.

B. A Unified Theorem via Reductions

In this section we prove that the three cases of Theorem 4 are special cases of a network operating in a serial mode with W being a symmetric zero-diagonal matrix. Notice that the reduction is in the sense that it is possible to derive the state of one network given the state of the other network. The first lemma presents the two reductions associated with W being a symmetric matrix [4].

Lemma 1: Let $N = (W, T)$ be a neural network where W is a symmetric matrix. Let $\hat{N} = (\hat{W}, \hat{T})$ be obtained from N as follows: $\hat{N}$ is a bipartite graph, with

$$\hat{W} = \begin{pmatrix} 0 & W \\ W & 0 \end{pmatrix}$$

and

$$\hat{T} = \begin{pmatrix} T \\ T \end{pmatrix}.$$

(a) For any serial mode of operation in N there exists an equivalent serial mode of operation in $\hat{N}$, provided W has a nonnegative diagonal.

(b) There exists a serial mode of operation in $\hat{N}$ which is equivalent to a fully parallel mode of operation in N.

Proof: The new network $\hat{N}$ is a bipartite graph with $2n$ nodes. The set of nodes of $\hat{N}$ can be subdivided into two sets: let P_1 and P_2 denote the set of the first and the last n nodes, respectively. Clearly, no two nodes of P_1 (and also P_2) are connected by an edge; that is, both P_1 and P_2 are independent sets of nodes in $\hat{N}$. Another observation is that P_1 and P_2 are symmetric in the sense that a node $i \in P_1$ has an edge set similar to that of a node $(i + n) \in P_2$.

Proof of (a): Let V_0 be an initial state of N, and let $(i_1, i_2 \cdots)$ be the order by which the states of the nodes are evaluated in a serial mode in N. We will show that starting from the initial state (V_0, V_0) in $\hat{N}$ (the state of both P_1 and P_2 is V_0) and using the order $(i_1, (i_1 + n), i_2, (i_2 + n), \cdots)$ for the evaluation of states will result in:

1) The state of P_1 will be equal to the state of P_2 in $\hat{N}$ after an arbitrary even number of evaluations.
2) The state of N at time k is equal to the state of P_1 at time $2k$, for an arbitrary k.

The proof of (1) is by induction. Given that at some arbitrary time k the state of P_1 is equal to the state of P_2, it will be shown that after performing the evaluation at node i and then at node $(n + i)$ the states of P_1 and P_2 remain equal.

There are two cases:

- If the state of node i does not change as a result of evaluation, then by the symmetry of $\hat{N}$ there will be no change in the state of node $(n + i)$.
- If there is a change in the state of node i, then because $\hat{W}_{i,n+i}$ is nonnegative it follows that there will be a change in the state of node $(n + i)$ (the proof is straightforward and won't be presented).

The proof of (2) follows from (1): by (1) the state of P_1 is equal to the state of P_2 right before the evaluation at a node of P_1. The proof is by induction: assume that the current state of N is the same as the state of P_1 in $\hat{N}$. Then an evaluation performed at a node $i \in P_1$ will have the same result as an evaluation performed at node $i \in N$. □

Proof of (b): Let's assume as in part (a) that $\hat{N}$ has the initial state (V_0, V_0). Clearly, performing the evaluation at all nodes belonging to P_1 (in parallel) and then at all nodes belonging to P_2, and continuing with this alternating order is equivalent to a fully parallel mode of operation in N. The equivalence is in the sense that the state of N is equal to the state of the subset of nodes (either P_1 or P_2) of $\hat{N}$ at which the last evaluation was performed. A key observation is that P_1 and P_2 are independent sets of nodes, and a parallel evaluation at an independent set of nodes is equivalent to a serial evaluation of all the nodes in the set. Thus, the fully parallel mode of operation in N is equivalent to a serial mode of operation in $\hat{N}$. □

The second lemma presents the reduction associated with W being an antisymmetric matrix.

Lemma 2: Let $N = (W, T)$ be a neural network where W is an antisymmetric matrix with zero diagonal and $T = 0$. Assume that WV has no zero for all $V \in \{1, -1\}^n$. Let $\tilde{N} = (\hat{W}, \hat{T})$ be obtained from N as follows: $\tilde{N}$ is a bipartite graph, with

$$\tilde{W} = \begin{pmatrix} 0 & 0 & 0 & -W \\ 0 & 0 & W & 0 \\ 0 & -W & 0 & 0 \\ W & 0 & 0 & 0 \end{pmatrix}$$

and $\tilde{T} = 0$. There exists a serial mode of operation in $\tilde{N}$ which is equivalent to a fully parallel mode of operation in N.

Proof: The new network $\tilde{N}$ is a bipartite graph with $4n$ nodes. The set of nodes of $\tilde{N}$ can be subdivided into four sets, to be denoted by P_1, P_2, P_3, and P_4, that correspond to the first, second, third, and fourth sets of n nodes of $\tilde{N}$, respectively. Note that P_1 is connected only to P_4 and that

P_2 is connected only to P_3. Another observation is that $\tilde{W}$ is a symmetric matrix. This follows from the assumption that $W^T = -W$. We consider fully parallel iterations in the network N and denote that state of N after k iterations by V_k. In the network $\tilde{N}$ we consider parallel iterations at the sets P_i (which are in fact serial iterations), and denote the state of $\tilde{N}$ by a vector which is a concatenation of the states of the P_is.

Let us assume that the initial state of N is V_0. We show that if the initial state of $\tilde{N}$ is $(-V_0, V_0, V_0, -V_0)$ and the order of evaluation is $P_1, P_2, P_3, P_4, P_1, P_2, \cdots$, then the network $\tilde{N}$ simulates the network N. Note that after an even number of iterations in $\tilde{N}$, the state of P_1 is the complement of the state of P_2 and the state of P_3 is the complement of the state of P_4.

Now we claim that: (i) After $8k$ iterations at $\tilde{N}$ the state of P_3 is equal to the state of N after $4k$ evaluations and the state of P_1 is equal to the state of N after $4k - 1$ evaluations. (ii) After $8k + 4$ iterations the state of P_4 is equal to the state of N after $4k + 2$ evaluations and the state of P_2 is equal to the state of N after $4k + 1$ evaluations. The proof of those two claims is by induction on k. Clearly, after 4 iterations in $\tilde{N}$ we have that the state of the network is $(-V_1, V_1, -V_2, V_2)$, which establishes the basis of the induction (one can consider the next 4 iterations and get the basis for (i)). We assume that (i) and (ii) are true for k and prove (i) and (ii) for $k + 1$. Here we present only the proof of (i). By the assumption, after $8k + 4$ iterations the state of $\tilde{N}$ is $(-V_{4k+1}, V_{4k+1}, -V_{4k+2}, V_{4k+2})$. Hence, after $8(k + 1)$ iterations the state of $\tilde{N}$ is $(V_{4k+3}, -V_{4k+3}, V_{4(k+1)}, -V_{4(k+1)})$, which established (i).

Note that evaluation at a set P_i, $1 \leq i \leq 4$, is equivalent to a serial evaluation of the nodes in the set, since the sets are independent sets of nodes. Hence, the network $\tilde{N}$ operating in a serial mode can simulate the network N operating in a fully parallel mode. □

Using the transformations suggested by the above lemmas we show that the three known convergence properties are special cases of convergence in a network operating in a serial mode with W being a symmetric zero-diagonal matrix.

Theorem 5: Let $N = (W, T)$ be a neural network. Given (1), then (2), (3), and (4) below hold.

1) If N is operating in a serial mode and W is a symmetric matrix with zero diagonal, then the network will always converge to a stable state.
2) If N is operating in a serial mode and W is a symmetric matrix with nonnegative elements on the diagonal, then the network will always converge to a stable state.
3) If N is operating in a fully parallel mode then, for an arbitrary symmetric matrix W, the network will always converge to a stable state or a cycle of length 2; that is, the cycles in the state-space are length ≤ 2.
4) If N is operating in a fully parallel mode then, for an antisymmetric matrix W with zero diagonal, with $T = 0$, the network will always converge to a cycle of length 4.

Proof: The proof is based on Lemma 1 and Lemma 2.

(2) is implied by (1): By Lemma 1 part (*a*), every network with nonnegative diagonal symmetric matrix W which is operating in a serial mode can be transformed to an equivalent network to be denoted by $\hat{N}$, which is operating in a serial mode with $\hat{W}$ being a symmetric zero-diagonal symmetric matrix. $\hat{N}$ will converge to a stable state (by (1)); hence, N will also converge to a stable state which will be equal to the state of P_1. Note that trivially (1) is implied by (2).

(3) is implied by (1): By Lemma 1 part (*b*), every network operating in a fully parallel mode can be transformed to an equivalent network to be denoted by $\hat{N}$, which is operating in a serial mode with $\hat{W}$, being a symmetric zero-diagonal matrix. $\hat{N}$ will converge to a stable state (by (1)). When $\hat{N}$ reaches a stable state there are two cases:

1. The state of P_1 is equal to the state of P_2; in this case N will converge to a stable state which is equal to the state of P_1.
2. The states of P_1 and P_2 are distinct; in this case N will oscillate between the two states defined by P_1 and P_2, that is, N will converge to a cycle of length 2.

(4) is implied by (1): By Lemma 2 every network operating in a fully parallel mode can be transformed to an equivalent network, to be denoted by $\tilde{N}$, which is operating in a serial mode, with $\hat{W}$ being a symmetric zero-diagonal matrix. $\tilde{N}$ will converge to a stable state (by (1)). We denote this stable state by (U_1, U_2, U_3, U_4) with U_i corresponding to the state of P_i. We claim that the U_i are distinct, hence, the stable state in $\tilde{N}$ corresponds to a cycle of length 4 in N.

To prove that the U_i are distinct observe that, by Lemma 2, $U_1 = -U_2$ and $U_3 = -U_4$. Also, in a stable state $U_1 = \text{sgn}(WU_4)$ and $U_4 = \text{sgn}(-WU_1)$. Assume that $U_1 = U_4$; then sgn $(WU_1 = \text{sgn}(-WU_1)$. This is a contradiction. Also, when we assume that $U_1 = -U_4$, we reach a contradiction. Hence at a stable state the U_i are distinct. From Lemma 2 it follows that in the network N we have a cycle of length 4: U_2, U_4, U_1, U_3. □

An Elementary Proof for Convergence: To show that we have an elementary proof for all the cases, we have to reduce case 1 in Theorem 5 to the simple case considered in Theorem 3. Namely, we have to show that, the case where the network is operating in a serial mode with W a zero-diagonal symmetric matrix and T is an arbitrary vector, can be reduced to that in which $T = 0$. This reduction follows from Theorem 2.

To summarize, we showed that the three known cases of convergence can be reduced to a very simple case: a network operating in a serial mode with W a symmetric zero-diagonal matrix and $T = 0$. For this special case we have an elementary proof that uses the equivalence with cuts in a graph (see Section II). Next we show that, indeed, the three known cases are the only interesting ones.

C. Big Cycles

In the previous section we considered the convergence properties in three cases that can be characterized by the mode of operation and the structure of W: (i) serial mode of operation, symmetric W, (ii) fully parallel mode of operation, symmetric W, and (iii) fully parallel mode of operation, antisymmetric W. Using this characterization, there are three more cases that can be considered: (iv) serial mode of operation, antisymmetric W, (v) serial mode of operation, arbitrary W and (vi) fully parallel mode of operation, arbitrary W. In this section we prove that cases (iv)–(vi) are not interesting by showing that networks of these types can have exponentially (in the number of nodes) long cycles in their state space. First we show that cases (iv) and (v) can have an exponentially long cycle by considering a network with antisymmetric W.

Theorem 6: Let $n \geq 2$ be an even integer. There exists a network $N = (W, T)$ of order n with W antisymmetric which, when operating in a serial mode, has a cycle of length 2^n.

Proof: Consider the network $\hat{N} = (\hat{W}, \hat{T})$ defined by

$$\hat{W} = \begin{pmatrix} 0 & 1 \\ -1 & 0 \end{pmatrix}$$

and $\hat{T} = (0, 0)$. This is the same network as the one in Example 3 in Section I-B. When we consider serial mode of operation in $\hat{N}$ we find that there is a cycle of length 4: $\{(1, 1), (-1, 1), (-1, -1), (1, -1)\}$. This cycle corresponds to the following order of evaluation: $1, 2, 1, 2 \cdots$.

To get the result we construct a network of order $2n$, to be denoted by N, simply taking n networks like $\hat{N}$. In N we can generate a cycle of length 2^{2n} by going through all the possible states. The idea is to consider the state of every one of the n subnetworks as a symbol over $GF(4)$ and to go through the possible states lexicographically. □

Next we show that there is an exponentially long cycle also in case (vi):

Theorem 7: Let n be a positive integer. There exists a network $N = (W, T)$ of order $3n$, which when operating in a fully parallel mode has a cycle of length 2^n.

Proof: The idea in the proof is to construct a linear shift register [9] using linear threshold elements. A linear shift register device is simply a shift register in which the input of a cell is the output of the previous cell. The input to the first cell is a sum mod 2 of a certain subset of the cells. There is a way to select the subset of cells that sum up to be the input to the first cell in such a way that the shift register will go through all the possible states (2 to the number of cells). For more details on this subject see [9]. To construct a linear shift register using linear threshold elements we need to implement two basic operations: (i) IDENTITY—to implement the function of a single cell in a shift register, (ii) XOR—to implement the sum mod 2. Clearly, only the XOR is a problem. But XOR can be implemented by a depth 2 circuit of linear threshold elements (see [10]). For XOR of n variables we need n linear threshold elements. Since we have a depth 2 circuit we need to introduce a delay between any two cells in the shift register. For that we need n more elements. To summarize, we can implement a linear shift register device with n cells using $3n$ linear threshold elements. Hence, for every n, we have a network of linear threshold elements of order $3n$ which, when operating in a fully parallel mode, goes through a cycle of length 2^n. □

IV. Concluding Remarks

We have presented a unified approach for proving convergence in the Hopfield model. The idea in our approach is to reduce all the known cases to a very simple case of convergence for which the proof is elementary. We also proved that those cases are the only interesting cases by proving exponential lower bounds on the size of cycles in the other cases.

V. Appendix: Proof of Convergence Using the Energy Function

We consider the first convergence property (serial mode), and prove it using the concept of the energy function.

Theorem 8: Let $N = (W, T)$ be a neural network operating in a serial mode. Let W be a symmetric matrix with nonnegative diagonal. Then the network will always converge to a stable state, i.e., there are no cycles in the state–space [1].

Proof: The energy function is defined as follows:

$$E_1(t) = V^T(t)WV(t) - 2V(t)^T T \tag{5}$$

where a superscript T indicates a matrix transpose. Let $\Delta E = E_1(t+1) - E_1(t)$ be the difference between the energies associated with two consecutive states, and let ΔV_k denote the difference between the next state and the current state of node k at some arbitrary time t. H_k is defined in (1). From (1) it follows that

$$\Delta V_k = \begin{cases} 0 & \text{if } V_k(t) = \operatorname{sgn}(H_k(t)) \\ -2 & \text{if } V_k(t) = 1 \text{ and } \operatorname{sgn}(H_k(t)) = -1 \\ 2 & \text{if } V_k(t) = -1 \text{ and } \operatorname{sgn}(H_k(t)) = 1. \end{cases} \tag{6}$$

By the assumption (serial mode of operation) the computation is performed only at a single node at any given time. Suppose this computation is performed at an arbitrary node k; then the energy difference resulting from this computation is

$$\Delta E = \Delta V_k\left(\sum_{j=1}^{n} W_{k,j}V_j + \sum_{i=1}^{n} W_{i,k}V_i\right) + W_{k,k}\Delta V_k^2 - 2\Delta V_k T_k. \tag{7}$$

From the symmetry of W and the definition of H_k it follows that

$$\Delta E = 2\Delta V_k H_k + W_{k,k}\Delta V_k^2. \tag{8}$$

Hence, since $\Delta V_k H_k \geq 0$ and $W_{k,k} \geq 0$ it follows that $\Delta E \geq 0$ for every k. Since E_1 is bounded from above, the value of the energy will converge.

The second step in the proof is to show that convergence of the value of the energy implies convergence to a stable state. The following two simple facts are helpful for this step:

1) If $\Delta V_k = 0$ then $\Delta E = 0$.
2) If $\Delta V_k \neq 0$ then $\Delta E = 0$ only if the change in V_k is from -1 to 1, with $H_k = 0$.

Hence, once the energy in the network has converged, it is clear from the preceding facts that the network will reach a stable state after at most n^2 time intervals. □

References

[1] J. J. Hopfield, "Neural networks and physical systems with emergent collective computational abilities," *Proc. Nat. Acad. Sci. USA*, vol. 79, pp. 2554–2558, 1982.
[2] E. Goles, F. Fogelman, and D. Pellegrin, "Decreasing energy functions as a tool for studying threshold networks," *Discrete Appl. Math.*, vol. 12, pp. 261–277, 1985.
[3] E. Goles, "Antisymmetrical neural networks," *Discrete Appl. Math.*, vol. 13, pp. 97–100, 1986.
[4] J. Bruck and J. W. Goodman, "A generalized convergence theorem for neural networks," *IEEE Trans. Inform. Theory*, vol. 34, pp. 1089–1092, Sept. 1988.

[5] J. J. Hopfield and D. W. Tank, "Neural computations of decisions in optimization problems," *Biolog. Cybern.*, vol. 52, pp. 141–152, 1985.
[6] P. L. Hammer and S. Rudeanu, *Boolean Methods in Operations Research*. New York: Springer-Verlag, 1968.
[7] C. H. Papadimitriou and K. Steiglitz, *Combinatorial Optimization: Algorithms and Complexity*. Englewood Cliffs, NJ: Prentice-Hall, 1982.
[8] J. C. Picard and H. D. Ratliff, "Minimum cuts and related problems," *Networks*, vol. 5, pp. 357–370, 1974.
[9] S. W. Golomb, *Shift Register Sequences*. CA: Aegean Park Press, 1982.
[10] J. Bruck, "Harmonic analysis of polynomial threshold functions," *SIAM J. Dis. Math.*, vol. 3, no. 2, pp. 168–177, May 1990.

Constructive Approximations for Neural Networks by Sigmoidal Functions

LEE K. JONES, MEMBER, IEEE

Invited Paper

A constructive algorithm is given for uniformly approximating real continuous mappings by linear combinations of bounded sigmoidal functions.

I. Introduction and Summary

An important problem in the theory of single layer neural networks is that of efficiently approximating a given real continuous function $f(X)$ on the unit cube $\boldsymbol{I}^n$ in $\boldsymbol{R}^n$ by a finite linear combination of functions of the form $\sigma(\Phi^t X + \theta)$ for sigmoidal σ. Sigmoidal functions are those for which $\lim_{x \to +\infty} \sigma(x) = 1$, $\lim_{x \to -\infty} \sigma(x) = 0$. This describes the situation when identical neurons receive affinely varying inputs with a linear combination of their outputs as a network output.

In [1] Cybenko has demonstrated the existence of uniform approximations to any continuous f provided that σ is continuous. His proof is nonconstructive, relying on the Hahn-Banach Theorem and the dual characterization of $C(\boldsymbol{I}^n)$. (An earlier nonconstructive proof, for the case of nondecreasing σ, was given by Hornik, Stinchcombe, and White [2].) In this note we extend Cybenko's result to include any bounded sigmoidal σ (even nonmeasurable ones). The approximating functions are explicitly constructed. In fact the number of terms in the linear combination is minimal (in a sense to be specified) for n = 1.

II. Constructive Approximation to a Given $f(X)$ by a Sum of Ridge Functions

It is well known that any continuous function on $\boldsymbol{I}^n$ can be uniformly approximated by a finite Fourier cosine series with terms of the form $\cos(\Phi^t X)$. This follows, for example, by first approximating f by a function h on $\boldsymbol{I}^n$ with continuous partials $\partial^{2n} h / \partial x_1^2 \partial x_2^2 \cdots \partial x_n^2$. Then h has a uniformly convergent cosine series in $\boldsymbol{I}^n$ which may be truncated to approximate f. Hence we can uniformly approximate by a finite sum of continuous ridge functions, i.e., univariate functions with arguments of the form $\Phi^t X$.

The cosine series approach may be adequate for functions f which are sufficently band limited; but, if f has energy at high frequencies, the number of terms in the truncated cosine series approximation may be prohibitive. This might be remedied by projection pursuit: approximate f by a sum of ridge functions $\Sigma_1^N g_i(\Phi_i^t X)$ where the g_i, Φ_i are sequentially chosen so as to include all energy in an optimal direction Φ_i. If we are only interested in approximation in $L_2(\boldsymbol{I}^n)$, there is a relaxed projection pursuit algorithm [3] (which could be implemented with a finite sample of noisy values of a sufficiently smooth f), yielding an $O(1/\sqrt{N})$ approximation (in the infinite sample case) which is a sum of N ridge functions.

We summarize this algorithm as follows: we are given noisy values of f on a finite set. We start with $f_0 = 0$ and at stage $\bar{n} + 1$ construct

$$f_{\bar{n}+1}(X) = (1 - \alpha_{\bar{n}}) f_{\bar{n}}(X) + g_{\bar{n}+1}(\Phi_{\bar{n}+1}^t X)$$

where $0 \le \alpha_{\bar{n}} \le 1$ and $\Phi_{\bar{n}+1}$ is a unit vector in $\boldsymbol{R}^n$. The univariate function $g_{\bar{n}+1}$, $\alpha_{\bar{n}}$, and $\Phi_{\bar{n}+1}$ are optimally determined (using a given statistical routine for each $\alpha_{\bar{n}}$, $\Phi_{\bar{n}+1}$ and numerical minimization routine over $\alpha_{\bar{n}}$, $\Phi_{\bar{n}+1}$) to find the best fit of the form $g_{\bar{n}+1}(\Phi_{\bar{n}+1}^t X)$ to the noisy values of $f - (1 - \alpha_{\bar{n}}) f_{\bar{n}}$.

III. Constructive Approximation to a Given $f(x)$ on [0,1]

So we need only give the sigmoidal approximation for $n = 1$, the general construction then following by composition with a favorite ridge expansion. First we provide the construction in R^1 for a special $\bar{\sigma}$ called the hard limiter: $\bar{\sigma}(x) = 1$, $x \ge 0$; $\bar{\sigma}(x) = 0$, $x < 0$. Suppose for the moment that $f(x)$ is strictly increasing in [0, 1] with $f(0) = 0$, $f(1) = 1$. For any even integer $l = 2k$ we find an approximation with error at most $1/l$: Define $a_i (i = 0, 1, 2, \cdots l)$ by $a_i = f^{-1}(i/l)$ and let

$$g_l = \frac{1}{k} (\bar{\sigma}(x - a_1) + \bar{\sigma}(x - a_3) + \cdots \bar{\sigma}(x - a_{l-1})) \quad (1)$$

If the reader sketches the staircase function g_l he sees immediately that $|g_l(x) - f(x)| \le 1/l$ for $x \in [0, 1]$. In fact no sigmoidal linear combination with fewer than k terms could

Manuscript received August 17, 1989; revised March 16, 1990.

The author is with the Institute for Visualization and Perception Research and the Department of Mathematics, University of Lowell, Lowell, MA 01854, USA.

Reprinted from *Proc. IEEE*, vol. 78, no. 10, Oct. 1990, pp. 1586–1589.

approximate f on [0, 1] to this degree of accuracy: For then such a combination $\tilde{g}$ would be a function with $k - 1$ or fewer jumps. Since $\tilde{g}(-\infty) = 0$ we may modify $\tilde{g}$ to $\tilde{\tilde{g}}$ by changing $\tilde{g}$ to 0 for $x \leq 0$ and leaving $\tilde{g}$ otherwise unchanged. Then $\tilde{\tilde{g}}$ would again have $k - 1$ or fewer jumps and still approximate f to within $1/l$ in [0, 1]. Clearly each jump of $\tilde{\tilde{g}}$ in [0, 1] cannot be greater than $2/l$ in absolute value. But then $\tilde{\tilde{g}}(1) \leq 2(k-1)/l < 1 - 1/l$; a clear contradiction.

So any strictly increasing function $f(x)$ on [0, 1] may be so approximated by normalization and this is best possible using hard limiters. Since any continuous f may be arbitrarily well approximated by the difference of two strictly increasing continuous functions, we have a simple construction using $\bar{\sigma}$ consisting of a linear combination of 2 functions of the form (1).

Finally we extend the construction to the case of an arbitrary sigmoidal $\sigma(x)$ bounded in absolute value by a real number $B > 0$. We need only take $f(x)$ to be strictly increasing as the previous paragraph. For a given $\epsilon > 0$ we find $m > 0$ such that $|\sigma(mx) - 1| < \epsilon$ for $x > \epsilon/2$ and $|\sigma(mx)| < \epsilon$ for $x < -\epsilon/2$. Hence we may write

$$\sigma(mx) = \bar{\sigma}(x) + \eta(x) + \gamma(x)$$
$$\text{with } |\eta(x)| \leq B + 1,\ |\gamma(x)| \leq \epsilon \text{ and}$$
$$\eta(x) = 0 \quad \text{for } |x| > \frac{\epsilon}{2} \tag{2}$$

Suppose we picked $\epsilon < \min_{i=1,2,\ldots,l}(a_i - a_{i-1})$. Then for $x \in [0, 1]$

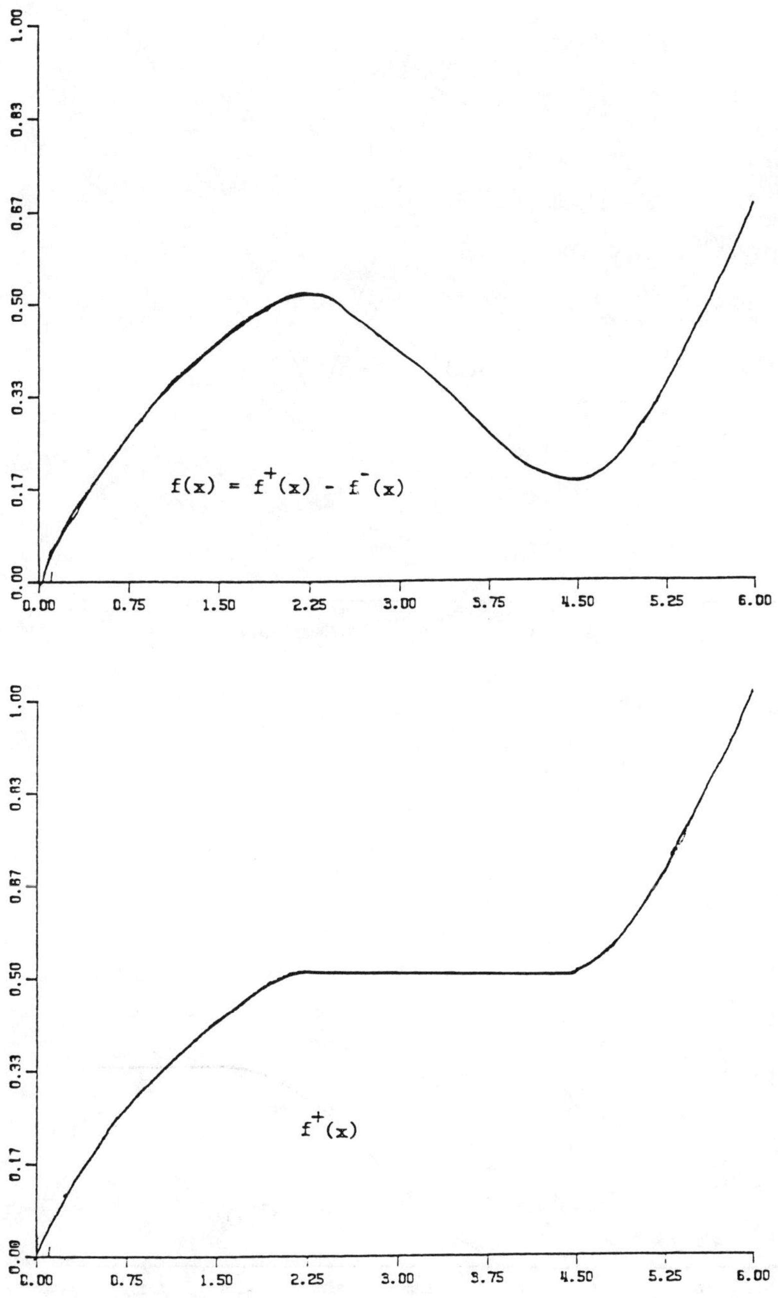

Fig. 1. $f(x)$, $f^+(x)$

$$\left|\frac{1}{k}(\sigma(m(x - a_1)) + \sigma(m(x - a_3)) + \cdots \sigma(m(x - a_{l-1}))) - f(x)\right| \leq |g_l(x) - f(x)| + \epsilon + \left|\frac{1}{k}(\eta(x - a_1) + \eta(x - a_3) + \cdots \eta(x - a_{l-1}))\right| \leq \frac{1}{l} + \frac{B + 1}{k} + \epsilon \tag{3}$$

which follows easily by noting that the above function sequence $\eta(x - a_{l-i})$ has disjoint supports. By taking l sufficiently large and ϵ sufficiently small the construction may be made sufficiently accurate.

For practical applications in one dimension with smooth functions, f can easily be resolved as the difference of two nondecreasing functions f^+ and f^- by taking antiderivatives of the positive and negative parts of f', respectively. The above a_i's (say for f^+) are chosen in the set $f^{+^{-1}}(i/l)$. An example is presented in Figs. 1–3.

References

[1] G. Cybenko, "Approximations by superposition of a sigmoidal function," *Math. Control Systems Signals*, vol. 2, no. 4, 1989.

[2] K. Hornik, M. Stinchcombe, and H. White, "Multilayer feedforward networks are universal approximators," *Neural Networks*, vol. 2, 1989.

[3] L. Jones, "A simple lemma on iterative sequences in Hilbert space and convergence rates for projection pursuit regression." University of Lowell Technical Reports Series, no. 16, Lowell, MA, Nov. 1989; submitted to *Annals of Statistics*.

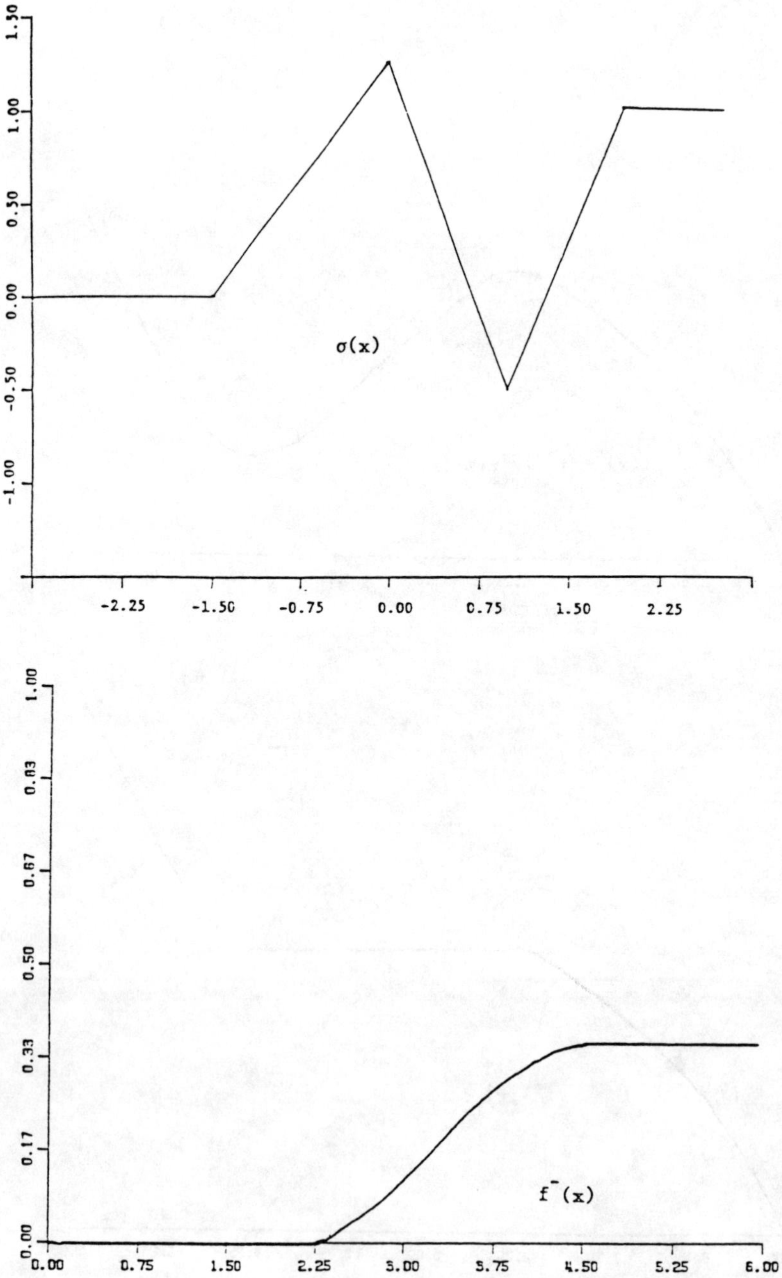

Fig. 2. $\sigma(x)$, $f^-(x)$

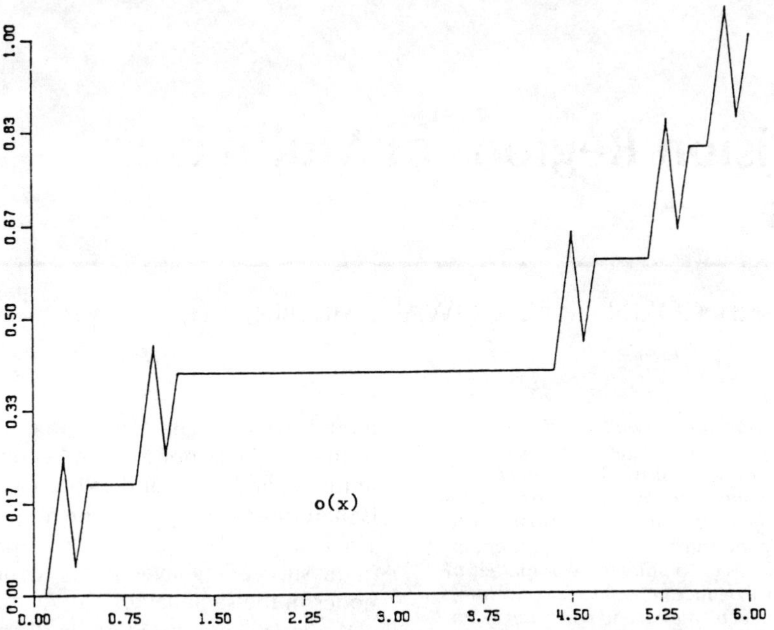

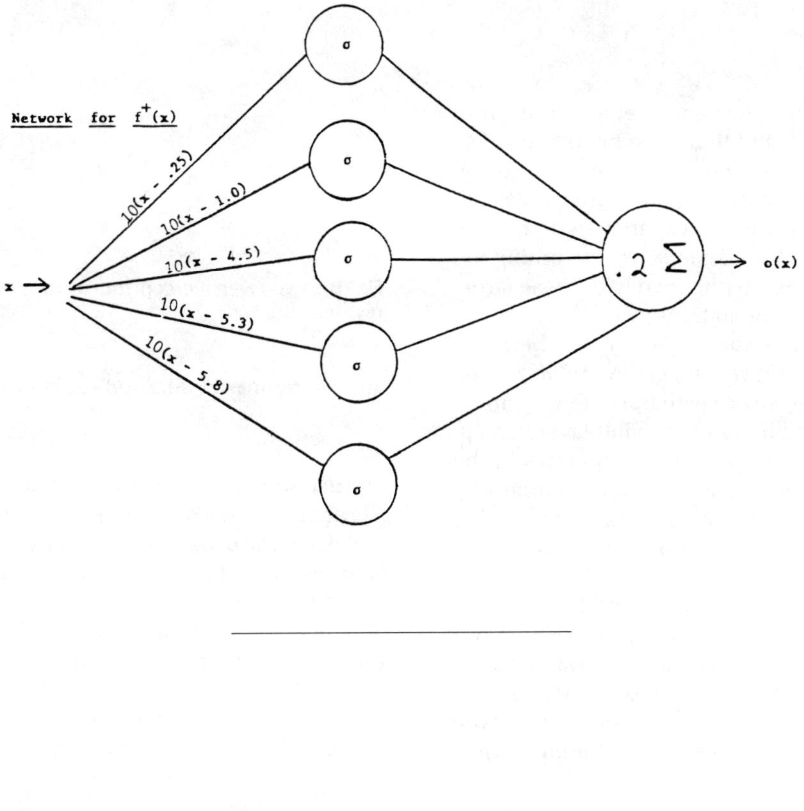

Fig. 3. Network for $f^+(x)$

On the Decision Regions of Multilayer Perceptrons

GAVIN J. GIBSON AND COLIN F. N. COWAN, MEMBER, IEEE

This paper examines the capabilities of two-layer Perceptrons with respect to the geometric properties of the decision regions they are able to form. It is now known that two-layer Perceptrons can form decision regions which are nonconvex and even disconnected, though the extent of their capabilities in comparison to three-layer structures is not well understood. By relating the geometry of arrangements of hyperplanes to combinatorial properties of subsets of hypercube vertices, we deduce certain facts concerning the decision regions of two-layer Perceptrons and construct examples of decision regions, which can be realized by three-layer Perceptrons but not by a two-layer structure. This indicates that the gradation in ability between two- and three-layer architectures is strict.

I. Introduction

In recent years there has been considerable interest in multilayer Perceptrons [1], and they have been applied to a variety of problems in image processing, pattern recognition, and signal processing, among other areas. We concern ourselves in particular with the capabilities of the two-layer Perceptrons, and deduce some facts concerning the decision regions which can be obtained with these structures. We begin with some definitions.

Throughout, R will denote the set of real numbers and N will denote the set of positive integers. A *multilayer Perceptron* is a computational device with the following architecture. The basic building block of the multilayer Perceptron is the single neuron or node, which operates in the following manner. A node receives a number of inputs $x_1, \cdots, x_n$, say, which are then multiplied by a set of weights $w_1, \cdots, w_n$ and the resultant values are summed. To this weighted sum of inputs is added a constant θ, known as the node bias, and the output of the node is obtained by evaluating a nonlinear function f of the total. We restrict our attention to Perceptrons where the node activation function f is defined by $f(x) = 1$, if $x \geq 0$, and 0 otherwise.

In the multilayer structure a number of nodes of the type described above are arranged in layers. A multidimensional input is passed to each node in the first layer. The outputs of the first layer nodes then become inputs to the nodes in the second layer, and so on. The output of the network is therefore the outputs of the nodes lying in the final layer. Thus, weighted connections exist from a node to every node in the succeeding layer, but no connections exist between nodes in the same layer.

We restrict our attention, in the main, to Perceptrons of only two layers, with a single node in the output layer (Fig. 1). Such a Perceptron specifies a function $g: R^n \rightarrow \{0, 1\}$,

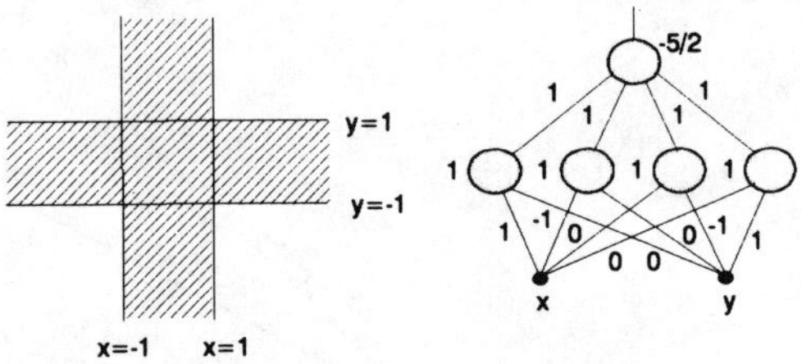

Fig. 1. Two-layer Perceptron with nonconvex decision region.

and we define its *decision region* to be

$$S = \{x \in R^n \mid g(x) = 1\}.$$

The *decision boundary* of a Perceptron with decision region S is defined to be $B(S)$, where $B(S)$ is the topological boundary of S in the usual topology on R^n. It is clear that the decision region and boundary of a Perceptron composed of a single node are, respectively, the half-space $\boldsymbol{w}.\boldsymbol{x} + \theta \geq 0$, and the hyperplane $\boldsymbol{w}.\boldsymbol{x} + \theta = 0$, where $\boldsymbol{w}$ and θ represent the weight vector and bias of the node, respectively.

In addition, we shall require the following definitions. A *polyhedral subset* of R^n is a finite intersection of closed half-spaces. The n-dimensional hypercube H_n is defined by

$$H_n = \{(x_1, \cdots, x_n) \in R^n \mid x_i \in [0, 1], 1 \leq i \leq n\}.$$

The *vertices* of H_n are the extreme points of H_n, that is all points, $\boldsymbol{x}$, in H_n with $x_i \in \{0, 1\}$, for all i. An *edge* of H_n is the closed line segment joining two vertices of H_n whose coordinates differ in a single component only. A *hyperplane cut* of the vertices of H_n is a subset of vertices V such that there exists some linear functional $h: R^n \rightarrow R$ and a real constant

Manuscript received April 17, 1989; revised March 14, 1990.

G. J. Gibson was with the Dept. of Electrical Engineering, University of Edinburgh, Edinburgh EH9 3JL, Scotland. He is now with Roke Manor Research Ltd., Romsey, Hants, SO51 OZN, England.

C. F. N. Cowan is with the Dept. of Electrical Engineering, University of Edinburgh, EH9, Scotland.

IEEE Log Number 9039176.

Reprinted from *Proc. IEEE*, vol. 78, no. 10, Oct. 1990, pp. 1590–1594.

c, with the property that $h(\boldsymbol{v}) > c$, where $\boldsymbol{v}$ is a hypercube vertex, if and only if $\boldsymbol{v} \in V$. Equivalently, a hyperplane cut is a subset of the hypercube vertices, which can be separated from the remaining vertices by a hyperplane.

Finally, if $X \subset R^n$, we define the *affine hull* of X, denoted aff (X) to be the subset of R^n

$$\text{aff}\,(X) = \left\{ y \in R^n \,\middle|\, y = \sum_1^s \lambda_i x_i,\ x_i \in X,\ s \in N,\ \sum_1^s \lambda_i = 1 \right\}.$$

Thus, if X consists of two distinct points, aff (X) is the line which contains them; if X consists of three non-collinear points, aff (X) is the plane which they generate, and so on.

It has been stated in the literature [2] that two-layer Perceptrons are capable of forming decision regions which must be (or else be complementary to) a polyhedral set in R^n. It has been demonstrated since, however, that this is not so [3], [4], and this can be seen from the simple example (Fig. 1) of a two-layer Perceptron with a decision region which is certainly not convex. Indeed, examples of Perceptrons which result in disjoint decision regions can also be constructed [4] (see later, Fig. 3), which suggests that two-layer Perceptrons are more versatile than was originally believed. Now it is a simple matter to show [2] that a three-layer Perceptron can create any decision region which can be expressed as a finite union of polyhedral sets. We demonstrate that the same can be said of the two-layer architecture if and only if $n = 1$, giving examples of higher dimensional regions which can never be realized as the decision regions of two-layer Perceptrons.

II. Two-Layer Perceptron Decision Regions

Before proceeding with our analysis we make some simplifications which will prove useful. We define a relation $\sim$ on all Lebesque measurable subsets of R^n as follows. For sets $S_1, S_2 \subset R^n$ let $S_1 \sim S_2$ precisely when

$$\int_{S_1 \cap S_2'} d\mu = 0$$

and

$$\int_{S_1' \cap S_2} d\mu = 0$$

where μ denotes the Lebesque measure and S' denotes the complement of S in R^n. It is clear that $\sim$ is an equivalence relation which identifies sets identical except for regions of zero (n-dimensional) volume, a reasonable strategy to adopt when considering Perceptron decision regions. We are now able to make the following observations.

Proposition 1: The decision region of a two-layer Perceptron is a union of polyhedral sets.

Proof: Let m denote the number of first layer nodes. It follows from the choice of node activation function f that for any input to the net, the vector of first-layer node outputs $y = (y_1, \cdots, y_m)$ must be a vertex of the hypercube H_m. For any given hypercube vertex y let $X(\boldsymbol{y}) \subset R^n$ be the set of all inputs which result in $\boldsymbol{y}$ being output from the first layer. It is clear that $X(\boldsymbol{y})$ is the representation of an intersection (possibly empty) of half-spaces whose boundaries are the decision boundaries of the first layer nodes. By the above equivalence, we can consider these half-spaces to be closed, so that $X(\boldsymbol{y})$ is a polyhedral set. The decision region of the Perceptron is therefore given by the union of those $X(\boldsymbol{y})$ where $\boldsymbol{y}$ is a hypercube vertex which, when presented as input to the second-layer node, results in an output of 1, and is therefore a finite union of polyhedral sets.

Proposition 2: Let $S \subset R^n$ be the decision region of a two-layer Perceptron. Then S can be realized as the decision region of a two-layer Perceptron in which no pair of first-layer nodes have the same decision boundary.

Proof: Clearly it suffices to show that any two first-layer nodes with a common boundary can be replaced by a single node. Let us then suppose that nodes N_1 and N_2 have decision boundary L. In addition, we suppose that the connections from nodes N_1 and N_2 to the output nodes have weights w_1 and w_2 respectively, and that the output node has bias θ. If $\boldsymbol{x} \in L'$ is an input to the net, then either N_1 and N_2 give the same output, or else they give opposite outputs. In the former case the combination of N_1 and N_2 can be replaced by N_1 alone with a connection weight of $w_1 + w_2$ to the output node, without affecting the output of the network for inputs $\boldsymbol{x} \in L'$. In the latter case the combination can be replaced by N_1 alone with output connection weight $w_1 - w_2$, and output node bias θ replaced by $\theta + w_2$. In either case the resultant decision region is equivalent to that of the original.

Proposition 3: Let $S \subset R^n$ be the decision region of a two-layer Perceptron and let $L_1, \cdots, L_m$ denote the hyperplanes which constitute the decision boundaries of the first-layer nodes. If $\boldsymbol{x} \in B(S)$ then $\boldsymbol{x} \in L_i$ for some i, $1 \le i \le m$.

Proof: If we assume the contrary, then it follows that there exists some open neighborhood of $\boldsymbol{x}$, $N(\boldsymbol{x})$, such that $N(\boldsymbol{x}) \cap L_i = \phi$, for all i. It is clear that for all $\boldsymbol{y} \in N(\boldsymbol{x})$, $g(\boldsymbol{y}) = g(\boldsymbol{x})$, where g denotes the function produced by the network. Therefore $\boldsymbol{x}$ cannot lie in $B(S)$ and a contradiction is obtained.

We now give some consideration to conditions on the first-layer nodes which are necessary for a network to produce a desired decision region.

Proposition 4: Let S be the decision region of a two-layer Perceptron with boundary $B(S)$ and let $L \subset R^n$ be a hyperplane. Suppose there exists $\boldsymbol{x} \in B(S)$ such that $N(\boldsymbol{x}) \subset L$, where $N(\boldsymbol{x}) \subset B(S)$ is a neighborhood of $\boldsymbol{x}$ (in the subspace topology on $B(S)$), then there is a first-layer node with decision boundary L.

Proof: Let m denote the number of first-layer nodes. Choose points $\boldsymbol{y}_i \in N(\boldsymbol{x})$, $1 \le i \le mn$, with the property that $\boldsymbol{y}_i \notin \text{aff}\,(\{\boldsymbol{y}_{k_1}, \cdots, \boldsymbol{y}_{k_t}\})$, where $t \le n - 1$, $k_1 < k_2 \cdots < k_t < i$. The reader can easily verify that such a sequence can be chosen. By Proposition 3, every $\boldsymbol{y}_i$ must lie on the decision boundary of some first layer node, and a simple counting argument shows that there is a first-layer node which has n of the points y_i on its decision boundary. It follows from the choice of the points y_i that the decision boundary of this node must coincide with the hyperplane L.

At this point we remark that Propositions 1–4 can be extended, with only minor modifications to the proofs, to include Perceptrons with three or more layers, although we do not consider such structures in this paper. Now Proposition 4 demonstrates that certain first-layer nodes are necessary for the formation of a given decision region. A natural question to consider is that of whether these nodes are also sufficient. That is, if $S \subset R^n$ can be realized as the decision region of a two-layer Perceptron, and $L_1, \cdots, L_m$ constitute the set of all hyperplanes satisfying the condition of the statement of Proposition 4, can S be realized, in general, as the decision region of a two-layer Perceptron with only m first layer nodes, with decision boundaries $L_1, \cdots, L_m$? As we shall demonstrate in Example 9, this question must be answered in the negative, except in the situation where $n = 1$ (see Proposition 6).

We now describe in more detail the connection between the geometry of the hypercube and that of the decision regions that can be formed by a two-layer Perceptron. Suppose P is a two-layer Perceptron with an n-dimensional input and m first-layer nodes (with of course a single output node), and let $L_1, \cdots, L_m$ denote the hyperplane decision boundaries of the first-layer nodes. As in Proposition 1, any region of space expressible as an intersection of m half-spaces with boundaries $L_1, \cdots, L_m$ can be identified with a vertex of H_m, where the ith coordinate of the vertex signifies which of the two half-spaces defined by L_i contains the particular region. Notice that, in general, some hypercube vertices will correspond to empty intersections. This correspondence is illustrated in Fig. 2, for a particular case when $n = 2$ and $m = 3$ [6].

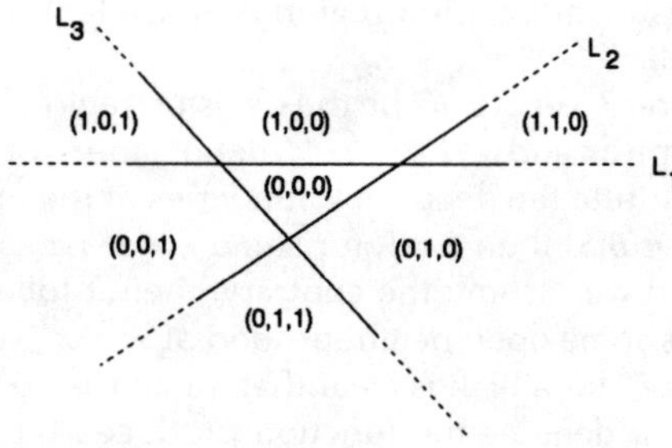

Fig. 2. Polyhedral regions with one possible correspondence with hypercube vertices.

With this in mind, we can write down necessary and sufficient conditions for a given union of the polyhedral sets defined by $L_1, \cdots, L_m$ to be realizable as the decision region of P.

Proposition 5: Let P, $L_1, \cdots, L_m$, and S be as described above and let $\mathbf{v}_1, \cdots, \mathbf{v}_k$ be the hypercube vertices which correspond to the polyhedral sets in the union which constitutes S. Then S can be realized as the decision region of P if and only if there exist a (possibly empty) set of hypercube vertices, $\mathbf{v}_{k+1}, \cdots, \mathbf{v}_{k+r}$, such that

(a) $\mathbf{v}_1, \cdots, \mathbf{v}_{k+r}$ constitute a hyperplane cut of H_m, and
(b) the hypercube vertices $\mathbf{v}_{k+1}, \cdots, \mathbf{v}_{k+r}$ correspond to empty intersections of the half-spaces defined by $L_1, \cdots, L_m$.

Proof: This is obvious since the inputs to the output node must necessarily be vertices of H_m, and the vertices of H_m which, when presented as inputs to the output node result in a positive output, must constitute a hyperplane cut of H_m.

In order to illustrate Proposition 5, consider the regions (1, 0, 1) and (0, 1, 1) in Fig. 2. Now these two vertices do not in themselves constitute a hyperplane cut of H_3, but the addition of (1, 1, 1), whose associated polyhedral set is empty, remedies this. Thus we can realize the union of the two regions corresponding to (1, 0, 1) and (0, 1, 1) as the decision region of a two-layer Perceptron. We remark that this decision region consists of two disjoint subregions. Figure 3 illustrates another decision region which can be created by a two-layer Perceptron, which has six first-layer nodes. The reader can verify that, when regions are identified with vertices as in Fig. 3, an output node with decision boundary $3\,\Sigma_1^3 x_i + \Sigma_4^6 x_i = 5/2$ will produce a hyperplane cut which satisfies condition (b) in the statement of Proposition 5.

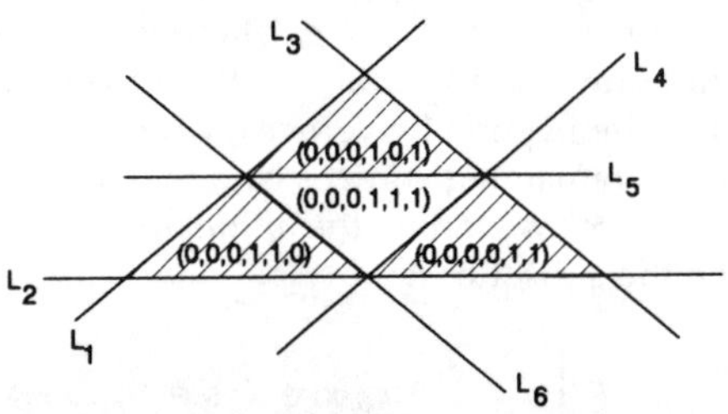

Fig. 3. Two-layer Perceptron decision region with corresponding hypercube vertices.

The next result deals with the capabilities of the two-layer Perceptron when the input dimension $n = 1$, and demonstrates that two layers are sufficient for the formation of any decision region in this situation.

Proposition 6: Let $S \subset R$ be any finite union of disjoint, closed intervals. Then S can be realized as the decision region of a two-layer perceptron.

Proof: Without loss of generality it suffices to consider the situations

(a) $S = [a_1, a_2] \cup [a_3, a_4] \cdots \cup [a_k, \infty]$, and
(b) $S = [a_1, a_2] \cup [a_3, a_4] \cdots \cup [a_{k-1}, a_k]$, where $a_1 < a_2 < \cdots < a_k$, and $[a_i, a_{i+1}]$ denotes the interval $a_i \leq x \leq a_{i+1}$. In either case consider the network which has k first-layer nodes whose decision boundaries are the points $a_1, \cdots, a_k$. Further assume that the first layer nodes are constructed so that node i will yield a positive output whenever the input x lies in the closed interval which has a_i as a boundary point. Then the set S can be realized by setting all connection weights to the output node to the value 1 and the output node bias to $-k/2$, for case (a), and $-(k+1)/2$ for (b).

It is now clear, at least so far as the complexity of decision regions is concerned, that two-layer Perceptrons have the same capabilities as multilayer structures when the input dimension $n = 1$. However, as we shall demonstrate, this is not so for higher values of n. We require the following result concerning hyperplane sections of the hypercube, the proof of which is obvious and is therefore omitted.

Lemma 7 [5]: Let L be a hyperplane which partitions the set of vertices of the hypercube H_m into two sets V_1 and V_2. Let $\mathbf{e}_1$ and $\mathbf{e}_2$ be two parallel edges of H_m, with end points $\mathbf{v}_1$, $\mathbf{w}_1$ and $\mathbf{v}_2$, $\mathbf{w}_2$, respectively. Suppose $\mathbf{v}_1, \mathbf{v}_2 \in V_1$ and $\mathbf{w}_1, \mathbf{w}_2 \in V_2$. Then

$$\mathbf{w}_1 - \mathbf{v}_1 = \mathbf{w}_2 - \mathbf{v}_2.$$

In summary, Lemma 7 states that any two parallel edges which cross a hyperplane must do so in the same direction. We can now use Lemma 7 to construct an example of a two-dimensional union of polyhedral sets which cannot be realized as the decision region of a two-layer Perceptron, thereby demonstrating that the result of Proposition 6 does not hold for $n > 1$.

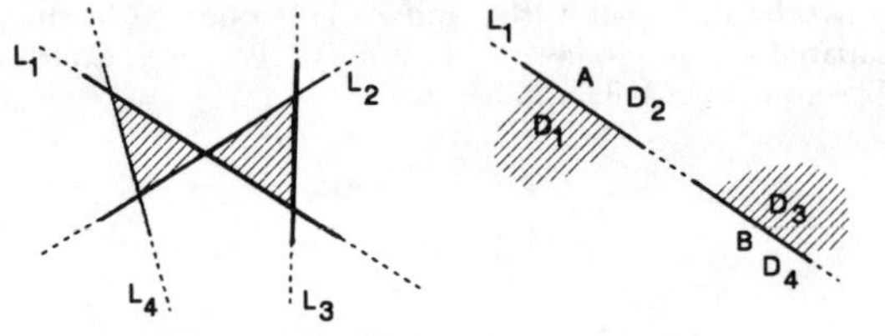

(a) (b)

Fig. 4 (a) Decision region unrealizable by two-layer Perceptron. (b) Relevant detail of Fig. 4(a).

Let S denote the shaded region bounded by lines L_1, L_2, L_3, and L_4, as depicted in Fig. 4(a).

Proposition 8: S cannot be realized as the decision region of a two-layer Perceptron.

Proof: We assume the contrary and obtain a contradiction. Suppose, then, that S can be realized as the decision region of a two-layer Perceptron. By Proposition 4 it follows that there must be first-layer nodes $N_1, \cdots, N_4$ with decision boundaries $L_1, \cdots, L_4$ respectively. Let $L_5, \cdots, L_m$ denote the decision boundaries of the remaining first-layer nodes (if any exist). By Proposition 2 we can assume that all the lines L_i are distinct from each other and hence intersect pairwise in only finitely many points. We can therefore find points A and B, as illustrated in Fig. 4(b), which lie on L_1 only. Now some neighborhood of A on L_1 constitutes part of the common boundary of two polyhedral sets D_1 and D_2 where $D_1 \subset S$ and $D_2 \subset S'$. Likewise $D_3 \subset S$ and $D_4 \subset S'$ have a similar relationship to the point B. It is clear that the hypercube vertices corresponding to D_1 and D_2, denoted $\boldsymbol{v}_1$ and $\boldsymbol{v}_2$ respectively, differ only in the first component (corresponding to position with respect to L_1). Without loss of generality, we can assume

$$\boldsymbol{v}_2 = \boldsymbol{v}_1 + (1, 0, \cdots, 0). \tag{1}$$

If $\boldsymbol{v}_3$ and $\boldsymbol{v}_4$ are the hypercube vertices corresponding to D_3 and D_4, then

$$\boldsymbol{v}_3 = \boldsymbol{v}_4 + (1, 0, \cdots, 0). \tag{2}$$

Now in order to create the decision region S, the decision boundary of the output node must be a hyperplane in R^m which partitions the vertices of H_m into sets V_1 and V_2 such that $\boldsymbol{v}_1, \boldsymbol{v}_3 \in V_1$ and $\boldsymbol{v}_2, \boldsymbol{v}_4 \in V_2$. By considering (1) and (2) we can now obtain an immediate contradiction to Lemma 7. It follows that S cannot be realized as the decision region of a two-layer Perceptron.

We remark that the example used in Proposition 8 can easily be modified to produce an example of a region in R^n, for any $n > 2$, which cannot be realized as the decision region of a two-layer Perceptron.

The following provides a counterexample to the converse of Proposition 4.

Example 9: Consider the shaded region $S_1 \subset S_2$ (Fig. 5). By Proposition 4, any two-layer Perceptron which has decision region $S_1 \cup S_2$ must include in its architecture eight first-layer nodes with decision boundaries $L_1, \cdots, L_8$, these being the hyperplanes essential for the creation of the desired boundary. We can demonstrate however, by a straightforward adaptation of the ideas of Lemma 7, that any two-layer Perceptron which incorporates only these eight nodes in its first layer cannot create a decision region which includes S_1 and S_2 but excludes both S_3 and S_4. This is left

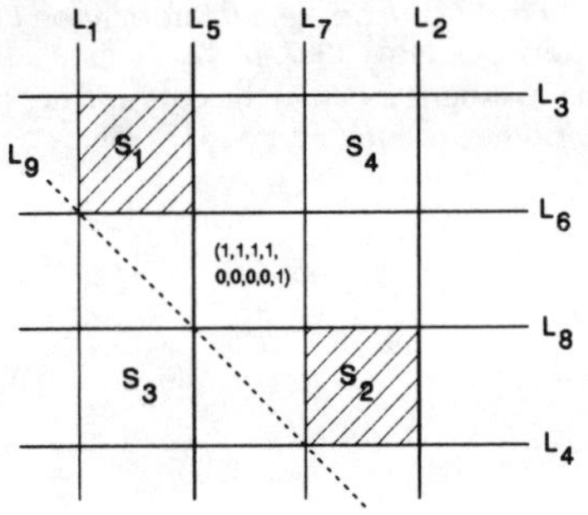

Fig. 5. Counterexample to converse of Proposition 4.

for the reader to verify. The addition of a first-layer node with decision boundary L_9, a hyperplane which is not essential for the creation of the desired boundary, yields a Perceptron which can create the decision region $S_1 \cup S_2$. When the correspondence with hypercube vertices is that defined by the labeling of the central region in Fig. 5, it can be verified that an output node with decision boundary

$$\sum_{i=1}^{4} 3x_i + 2x_5 + x_6 + x_7 + 2x_8 + 3x_9 = 35/2$$

will result in the desired decision region. The converse of Proposition 4 is therefore false.

III. Conclusions

The characterization of the spatial regions which can be realized as the decision regions of two-layer Perceptrons is a difficult mathematical problem, and one which is related to certain problems of combinatorics and convex set theory. In particular, the understanding of this problem would be facilitated by an understanding of the hyperplane cuts of the hypercube and the combinatorial properties of arrangements of hyperplanes, both of which areas of mathematics are far from completely understood. However, by making use of existing knowledge it is possible to deduce certain facts concerning the decision regions of two-layer Perceptrons. Specifically, it can be shown that the two-layer Perceptron has the same capabilities as higher order structures when the input space is one-dimensional, but is limited in its ability to form decision regions in comparison to three-layer Perceptrons, if the input space is of higher dimension. As yet, however, the extent of this limitation is not completely understood and, indeed, the examples of nonconvex and disconnected decision regions included in this paper and others illustrate clearly that the two layer Perceptron is a more capable structure than was once supposed. We surmise that this problem, which demonstrates the strong connections between the study of neural networks and combinatorial geometry, is certainly worthy of further investigation.

References

[1] B. Widrow, R. G. Winter, and R. A. Baxter, "Layered neural nets for pattern recognition," *IEEE Trans. ASSP*, vol. 36, pp. 1109–1118, July 1988.

[2] R. Lippmann, "Computing with neural nets," *IEEE ASSP Mag.*, vol. 4, no. 2, Apr. 1987.

[3] A. Wieland and R. Leighton, "Geometric analysis of neural network capabilities," *Proc. 1st Int. Conf. on Neural Nets*, IEEE, San Diego, CA, June 1987, vol. 2, pp. 754–756.

[4] W. H. Huang and R. P. Lippmann, "Neural net and traditional

classifiers," *Proc. Conf. on Neural Information Processing Systems*, Denver, CO, Nov. 1987, p. 42.

[5] M. R. Emmamy-Khansary, "On the cuts and cut number of the 4-cube," *J. Comb. Theory*, Ser. A, 41, 1986.

[6] J. Makhoul, R. Schwartz, and A. El-Jaroudi, "Classification capabilities of two-layer neural nets," *Proc. Int. Conf. ASSP*, Glasgow, May 1989, pp. 653–638.

Nearest Neighbor Pattern Classification Perceptrons

OWEN J. MURPHY

A three-layer Perceptron that employs the nearest neighbor pattern classification rule is presented. This neural network is of interest because it is designed specifically for the set of training patterns, and the incorporation of the training of the network into the design eliminates the need for the use of training algorithms. The entire design and training process can be completed in polynomial time in terms of the number of training patterns.

I. Introduction

Feedforward neural networks have been used successfully as pattern classifiers in many applications. A pattern P is represented in terms of d features or properties and can be viewed as a point in d-dimensional space. A typical pattern classification problem deals with assigning a given pattern to one of m categories $c_1, c_2, \cdots, c_m$ based on its feature values $(p_1, p_2, \cdots, p_d)$. Given samples (training patterns) from the various classes, the objective is to establish decision regions in the space to distinguish patterns belonging to different classes.

A neural network for pattern classification (i.e., a Perceptron) is typically designed by first constructing the network and then applying training procedures that compute the boundaries of the decision regions. (See Lippmann [1] for a survey of this area.) Recent work has indicated that this design strategy has serious limitations. Brady *et al.* [2] have shown that the widely used *backpropagation algorithm* [3], when applied to a single-layer perceptron, fails to classify some linearly separable families. Although the *perceptron learning procedure* [4], [5] would find a separating solution, the procedure can be applied only to single-layer networks. The result of Mirchandani and Cao [6] further suggests that this design technique is precarious at best since any algorithm can only work if a sufficient number of hidden nodes have been built into the network where this number is determined by the training patterns. If the network is not sufficiently large, the training techniques will never converge. Alternatively, one may choose the number of hidden nodes to be unnecessarily high, in which case there may be an insufficient number of patterns to reliably train the network. Recently, it has also been shown that training a neural network is NP complete [7]. This suggests that even the best training algorithms may require computation time that is prohibitive for other than small networks.

Manuscript received July 16, 1989; revised March 6, 1990.
The author is with the Department of Computer Science, University of Vermont, Burlington, VT 05405.
IEEE Log Number 9039177.

The main contribution of this paper is to propose an alternative technique for designing multilayer neural networks for pattern classification. The strategy employs the nearest neighbor classification rule [8] where every pattern is assigned the same category as its closest training pattern. The design of the network is based on the training patterns, and is of interest since the procedure is algorithmic (guaranteed to halt). Futhermore, it runs in polynomial time where the polynomial is a function of the number of training patterns.

II. Nearest Neighbor Classification

The Voronoi tessellation is a collection of disjoint polytopes that assigns to each training pattern a territory with the property that each point in that territory (polytope) is closer to that pattern than to any other. The tessellation is best described with a constructive algorithm. For a given training pattern X, its accompanying Voronoi polytope can be computed as follows. Construct a line segment from X to every other training pattern, and compute the hyperplane that bisects each line segment. (The equation of the hyperplane that bisects the line segment joining X_1 and X_2 is

$$g(X) = (X_1 - X_2) \cdot X + 1/2|X_2|^2 - 1/2|X_2|^2.) \qquad (1)$$

After eliminating the portions of space on the sides of the hyperplanes opposite X, the space remaining is the Voronoi polytope for X. The union of all the Voronoi polytopes in the set is the Voronoi tessellation. An example of the Voronoi tessellation for a collection of points in the plane (represented by "x"'s) is given in Fig. 1.

Definition: Let $\mathcal{P}$ *be a finite set of points in d-dimensional space* $\mathcal{S}$. *Define* $\mathcal{H}_{XY} = \{Z \in \mathcal{S} : |Z - X| < |Z - Y|\}$ *for* $X, Y \in \mathcal{P}$ and $\mathcal{R}_X = \bigcap_{Y \neq X} \mathcal{H}_{XY}$. $\mathcal{R} = \{\mathcal{R}_X : X \in \mathcal{P}\}$ is the Voronoi tessellation.

Shamos and Hoey [9] have given an algorithm for computing the Voronoi tessellation in the plane in $O(n \log n)$ time and $O(n)$ storage where n is the number of training patterns. For higher dimensions, Edelsbrunner and Seidel [10] have presented an algorithm that computes the Voronoi

Reprinted from *Proc. IEEE*, vol. 78, no. 10, Oct. 1990, pp. 1595–1598.

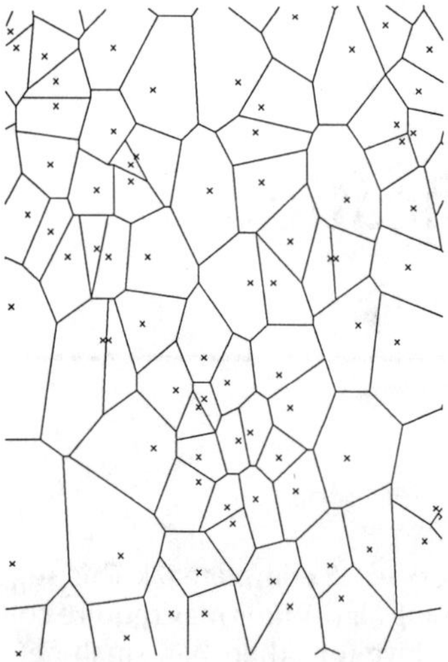

Fig. 1. Voronoi tessellation in the plane.

tessellation in d-dimensional space in $O(n^{\lceil (d+1)/2 \rceil})$ time and $O(n^{\lceil d/2 \rceil})$ storage.

Nearest neighbor classification is made easy with the Voronoi tessellation. Each polytope is assigned the class of the training pattern contained in the polytope, and when a pattern falls in the polytope, it is assigned to that class. It is straightforward to build a three-layer perceptron for nearest neighbor classification once the facets of the Voronoi tessellation have been computed from the training patterns. The input to the nodes of the first layer of the net is the pattern (i.e., a point in d-dimensional space). All other inputs and outputs throughout the net are 0 and 1. Each polytope requires a node in the first layer for each facet (hyperplane) of the polytope, and a single node in the second layer which takes the logical AND of the output from the first-layer nodes. The nodes of the first layer compute linear threshold functions corresponding to the facets of the polytone as given in (1). The outputs of these nodes in the first layer are 1 only for inputs that fall on the side of the facet occupied by the training pattern. Therefore, the second-layer node will output 1 if and only if the input pattern lies within the polytope. The third layer consists of output nodes, one for each of the m classes. Each polytope is assigned the proper classification by connecting the output from the second-layer node to the output node corresponding to the polytope's classification. A logical OR operation is then performed at each of the third-layer nodes, which gives the output from the network. An example of part of the neural net corresponding to the polytope of Fig. 2 is given in Fig. 3.

The design costs of the network are dependent on the number of training patterns and on the dimensionality of

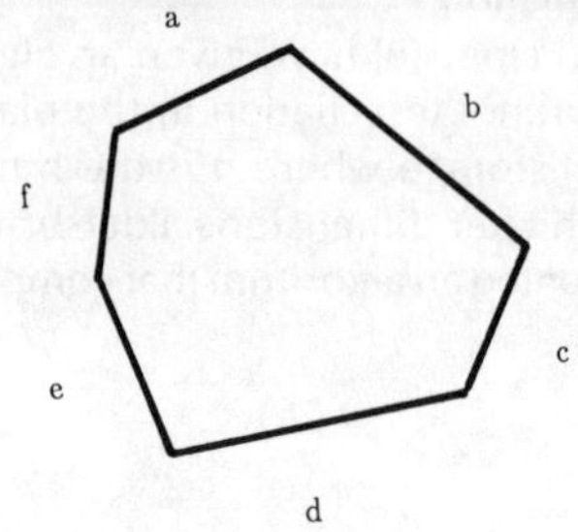

Fig. 2. Example polytope.

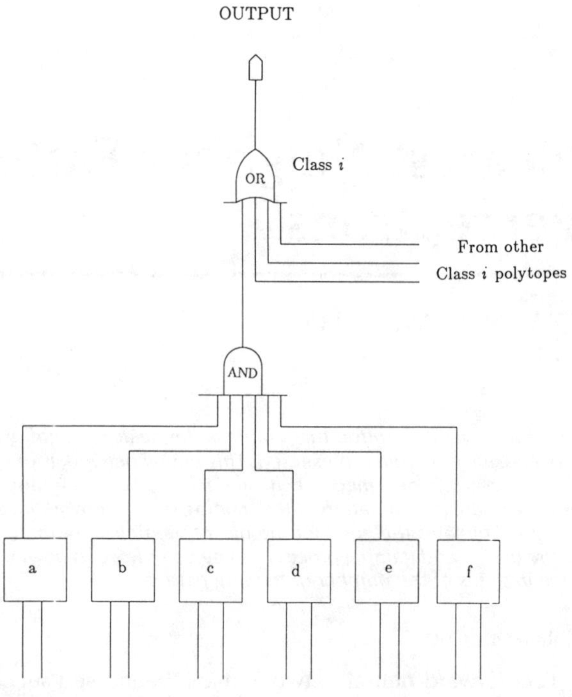

Fig. 3. Network components for polytope of Fig. 2.

the feature space. The number of facets of the Voronoi tessellation in the planar case cannot exceed $3n - 6$, and as mentioned earlier, these can be computed in $O(n \log n)$ time. Therefore, the network requires $O(n)$ nodes, and it can be constructed within $O(n \log n)$ time and $O(n)$ storage. In the general d-dimensional case, the Voronoi tessellation has $O(n^2)$ facets which can be constructed in $O(n^{\lceil (d+1)/2 \rceil})$ time and $O(n^{\lceil d/2 \rceil})$ storage.

If the design time is prohibitive, an alternative network can be designed in $O(n^2)$ time with $O(n^2)$ nodes by using the procedure discussed when defining the tessellation. For this network, every training pattern will have exactly $n - 1$ first-layer nodes, one for each of the bisecting hyperplanes that separate this training pattern from the others. Many of the hyperplanes associated with these nodes may not belong to the tessellation. Although this means that this network may require more first-level nodes than the network built directly from the tessellation, this difference tends to decrease as the dimensionality (and the cost of computing the tessellation) increases.

III. Experimental Results

The multilayer neural network has been tested on a variety of two-dimensional two-class pattern classification problems. In each experiment, a collection of training patterns was computed from a uniform distribution over the unit square. The patterns that fell within the boundaries of some geometric object [e.g., the "2" of Fig. 4(a)] were assigned to class 2, and all other points were assigned to class 1. (Admittedly, superior results can be obtained by using more sophisticated procedures for selecting training patterns. See [11] for examples of such techniques.) The Voronoi tessellation was then computed, and each polytope was assigned the classification of the pattern contained within the polytope.

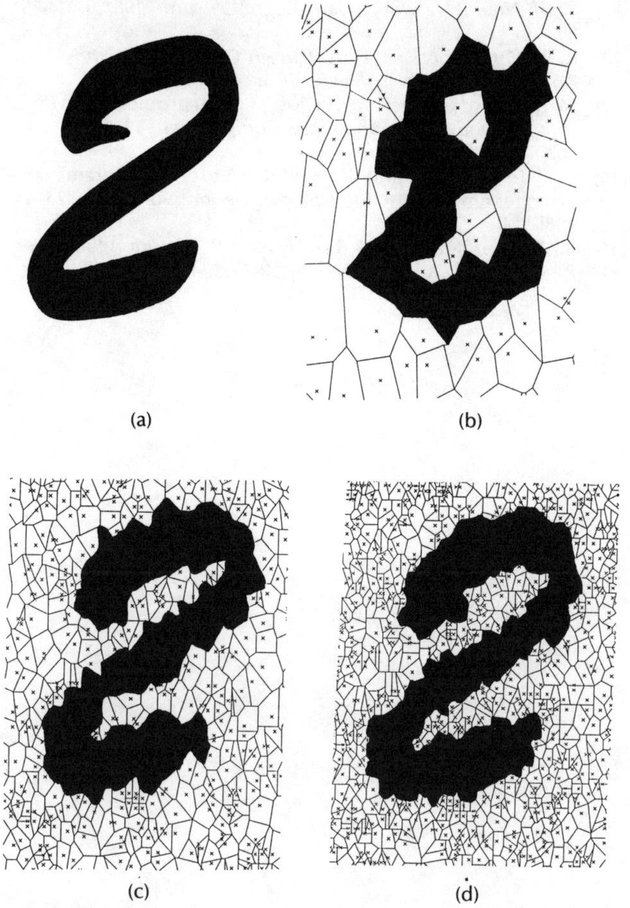

Fig. 4. (a) Example 1 feature space. (b) Example 1 decision regions (100 training patterns). (c) Example 1 decision regions (400 training patterns). (d) Example 1 decision regions (800 training patterns).

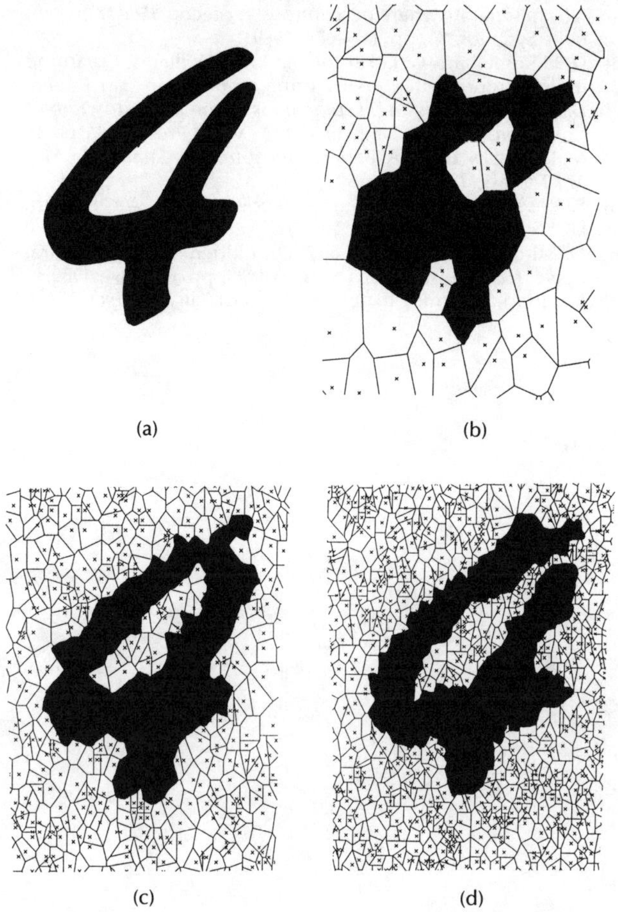

Fig. 5. (a) Example 2 feature space. (b) Example 2 decision regions (100 training patterns). (c) Example 2 decision regions (400 training patterns). (d) Example 2 decision regions (800 training patterns).

Each experiment was repeated three times, each time with additional training patterns included. Some typical results of these experiments are given in Figs. 4 and 5. Part (a) of each figure indicates the desired decision regions. Parts (b),(c), and (d) indicate the decision regions achieved for experiments using 100, 400, and 800 training patterns, respectively. The training patterns belonging to class 1 in these figures are designated by the "x"'s in the figures; the line segments indicate the boundaries of the Voronoi polygons for the class 1 patterns, and the shaded areas are the polygons that are assigned to class 2. Although the number of training patterns may appear to be unreasonable, note that fewer training patterns appropriately chosen from boundary locations would yield equivalent results.

As one might expect and as indicated by the experimental results, the probability of misclassification decreases as the number of training patterns increased. This can easily be explained on an informal basis. Under uniform conditions on the unit hypercube, the probability of misclassification is less than the sum of the volumes of the polytopes which intersect the boundaries of decision regions. As the number of training patterns is increased, the collective volume of these polytopes decreases. Therefore, the probability of misclassification asymptotically appraoches 0 as the number of training patterns increases.

IV. Conclusions

An alternative approach to neural network design for pattern classification has been presented. The advantages of this technique are outlined as follows.

1) The technique provides an alternative to the limitations and unpredictability of the known training techniques.

2) Since the nearest neighbor classification rule is employed, the network is capable of forming arbitrarily complex decision regions.

3) The network is designed specifically for the set of training patterns, and the training of the network is incorporated into the design. This eliminates the problems that arise from having too many, too few, or inappropriate training patterns.

4) The design and training of the network can be completed in polynomial time, whereas it has been shown that training a neural network is an NP-complete problem.

References

[1] R. P. Lippmann, "An introduction to computing with neural nets," *IEEE ASSP Mag.*, pp. 4–22, Apr. 1987.

[2] M. L. Brady, R. Raghavan, and J. Slawny, "Back progpagation

fails to separate where perceptrons succeed," *IEEE Trans. Circuits Sys.*, vol. 36, pp. 665-674, 1989.
[3] D. E. Rumelhart, G. E. Hinton, and R. J. Williams, "Learning internal representations by error propagation," in *Parallel Distributed Processing: Explorations in the Microstructure of Cognition*, Vol. 1. Cambridge, MA: M.I.T. Press, 1986, ch. 8.
[4] M. L. Minsky and S. A. Papert, *Perceptrons. Cambridge, MA: M.I.T. Press, 1969.*
[5] F. Rosenblatt, *Principles of Neurodynamics*. Washington, DC: Spartan, 1959.
[6] G. Mirchandani and W. Cao, "On hidden nodes for neural nets," *IEEE Trans. Circuits Syst.*, vol. 36, pp. 661-664, 1989.
[7] J. S. Judd, "Learning in networks is hard," in *Proc. 1st IEEE Int. Conf. Neural Networks*, San Diego, CA, June 1987, pp. 685-692.
[8] R. O. Duda and P. E. Hart, *Pattern Classification and Scene Analysis*. New York: Wiley, 1973.
[9] M. I. Shamos and D. Hoey, "Closest-point problems," in *Proc. 16th Annu. Symp. Foundations Comput. Sci.*, 1975, pp. 151-162.
[10] H. Edelsbrunner and R. Seidel, "Voronoi diagrams and arrangements," *Discrete Comput Geom.*, vol. 1, pp. 25-44, 1986.
[11] R. C. Gonzalez and J. T. Tou, *Pattern Recognition Principles*. Reading, MA: Addison-Wesley, 1974.

Convergence Properties and Stationary Points of a Perceptron Learning Algorithm

JOHN J. SHYNK, MEMBER, IEEE AND SUMIT ROY

The Perceptron is an adaptive linear combiner that has its output quantized to one of two possible discrete values, and it is the basic component of multilayer, feedforward neural networks. The least-mean-square (LMS) adaptive algorithm adjusts the internal weights to train the network to perform some desired function, such as pattern recognition. In this paper, we present an analysis of the stationary points of a single-layer Perceptron that is based on the momentum LMS algorithm, and we illustrate some of its convergence properties. When the input of the perceptron is a Gaussian random vector, the stationary points of the algorithm are not unique and the behavior of the algorithm near convergence depends on the step size μ and the momentum constant α.

I. Introduction

A single-layer Perceptron [1], or adaptive linear neuron (ADALINE) [2], consists of one summing node and N adaptive weights $\{w_k(n)\}$ as shown in Fig. 1. It is the simplest feedforward neural network structure, and it corresponds to a single "neuron" element. This basic component may be combined in parallel with many similar components to produce a multilayer Perceptron that has greater learning and computing capabilities [3]. The output $y(n)$ of the summer is filtered by a hard limiter[1] to produce a binary output $y_q(n)$ (denoted by +1 and −1). This output is compared to another binary signal, which corresponds to some desired response $d_q(n)$, and an error signal $e(n)$ is generated. An adaptive learning algorithm [4] then uses this error to make adjustments to the Perceptron weights so as to match $y_q(n)$ and $d_q(n)$ in a statistically meaningful way. The input signals $\{x_k(n)\}$ can be binary valued (± 1) or they can be drawn from a continuous distribution. In our analysis, we assume that they form a Gaussian random vector whose components may or may not be correlated.

The Perceptron in Fig. 1 can be used as a pattern classifier whereby the N-dimensional vector space represented by the input signals is partitioned into two subspaces, corresponding to the two classes (denoted by A and B). It is well known, however, that the partition in this case is a hyperplane [2]; more complex partitions can be achieved only by adding "hidden" layers to the Perceptron [1]. Figure 2 shows

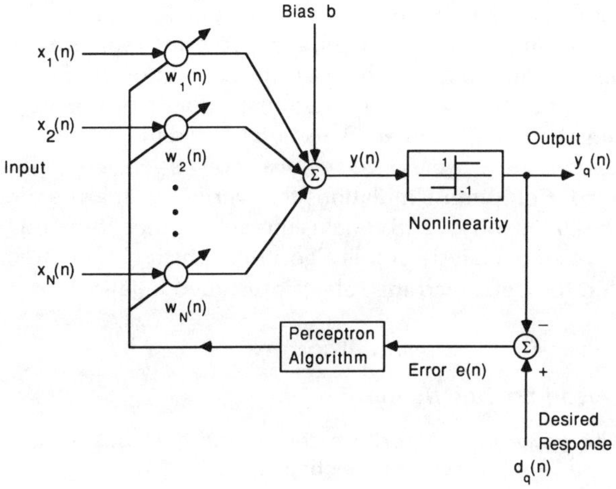

Fig. 1. Single-layer Perceptron with hard limiter.

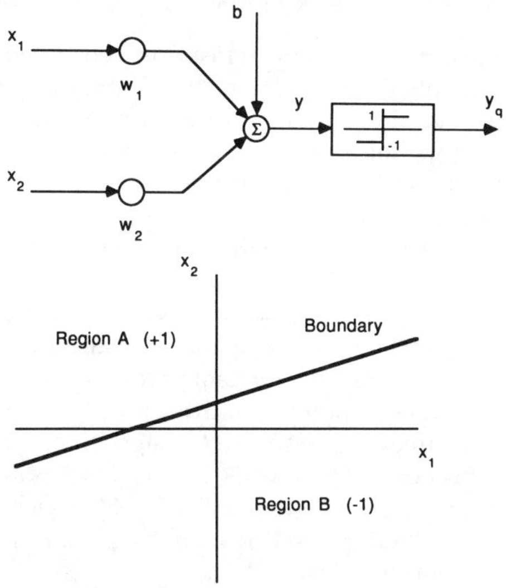

Fig. 2. Perceptron decision regions for two weights.

Manuscript received September 6, 1989; revised March 25, 1990. This work was supported by Rockwell, Inc., with matching support from the University of California MICRO Program, and by the University of Pennsylvania.

J. J. Shynk is with the Center for Information Processing Research, Department of Electrical and Computer Engineering, University of California, Santa Barbara, CA 93106, USA.

S. Roy is with the Department of Electrical Engineering, University of Pennsylvania, Philadelphia, PA 19104, USA.

[1]In some cases, the hard limiter is replaced by a smooth nonlinearity such as the sigmoid function [1].

IEEE Log Number 9039178.

Reprinted from *Proc. IEEE*, vol. 78, no. 10, Oct. 1990, pp. 1599–1604.

an example of the partition for the case of two input signals ($N = 2$); observe that the decision boundary is defined by the line $x_2 = -(w_1/w_2)x_1 - (b/w_2)$, where b represents a bias factor. The perceptron can be trained to identify this decision boundary so that for a given input, it will correctly decide to which class the sample pair belongs.

In this paper, we present an analysis of the stationary (convergence) points of an adaptive algorithm that adjusts the perceptron weights [5]. This algorithm is identical in form to the least-mean-square (LMS) algorithm [4], except that a hard limiter is incorporated at the output of the summer as shown in Fig. 1. We include a momentum term in the weight update [3]; this modified algorithm is similar to the momentum LMS (MLMS) algorithm [6], [7], except again it contains the output nonlinearity. Section II describes the perceptron algorithm in detail, and it presents a simple two-input example that will be used for illustration purposes throughout the paper. The stationary points of the algorithm are then presented in Section III, and the properties of the adaptive weight vector near convergence are discussed. Computer simulations that verify the analysis are given in Section IV, and conclusions are outlined in Section V. A related analysis of this algorithm, which is also often called the delta learning rule, is presented in [8].

II. Perceptron Learning Algorithm

A. Algorithm Description

The perceptron algorithm considered here has the following weight updating mechanism:

$$W(n+1) = W(n) + 2\mu e(n)X(n) + \alpha[W(n) - W(n-1)] \tag{1}$$

where $W(n)$ and $X(n)$ are the N-dimensional weight and signal vectors, respectively:

$$W(n) = [w_1(n), \cdots, w_N(n)]^T \tag{2a}$$

and

$$X(n) = [x_1(n), \cdots, x_N(n)]^T. \tag{2b}$$

The superscript T is vector transpose, and n denotes the present sample time. Equation (1) is a second-order algorithm that requires storage of the present and previous weight vectors before the new weight vector can be computed. The step size μ and the momentum constant α, where $\mu > 0$ and $|\alpha| < 1$, determine the convergence rate and steady-state performance of the algorithm. The component given by $\alpha[W(n) - W(n-1)]$ is the so-called momentum term [3]. Intuitively, if the previous weight change is large, then adding a fraction of this amount to the current weight update will accelerate the descent process toward the algorithm convergence point. However, it can be shown that the misadjustment [4] of the MLMS algorithm is increased in direct proportion to α [6], [7].

The output error $e(n)$ is derived as the difference between the (binary-valued) desired response $d_q(n)$ and the quantized filter output $y_q(n)$:

$$e(n) = d_q(n) - y_q(n) = d_q(n) - \operatorname{sgn}(y(n)) \tag{3}$$

where sgn (g) is the sign function defined as

$$\operatorname{sgn}(g) = \begin{cases} +1, & g \geq 0 \\ -1, & g < 0. \end{cases} \tag{4}$$

Observe in Fig. 1 that there are N input signals which are weighted and then summed to produce the *unquantized* output $y(n)$; this part of the perceptron is simply a linear combiner. The intermediate output $y(n)$ is thus given by the following inner product:

$$y(n) = W^T(n)X(n) = X^T(n)W(n). \tag{5}$$

Note that $y(n)$ is always quantized to produce $y_q(n)$. The desired response $d_q(n)$ is also constrained to be ± 1, so we can view it as being a quantized version of some *underlying* process $d(n)$, that is

$$d_q(n) = \operatorname{sgn}(d(n)). \tag{6}$$

In general, $d(n)$ will be correlated with $X(n)$, and it can often be represented as a function (possibly nonlinear) of the elements of $X(n)$. One interesting case that will be examined later is when $d(n)$ is a linear function of $X(n)$ according to

$$d(n) = F^T(n)X(n) = X^T(n)F(n) \tag{7}$$

where $F(n)$ is an unknown weight vector defined in a manner similar to $W(n)$. In our analysis, we assume that $F(n)$ is constant such that $F(n) = F$.

B. Two-Weight Example

For illustration purposes, we consider a simple example for $N = 2$, corresponding to a special case of the decision regions shown in Fig. 2. Assume that the bias term is zero ($b = 0$) so that the boundary passes through the origin, and let the data be generated such that the boundary lies at a 45° angle with respect to the signal axes. Region A (above and on the line) is denoted by $+1$, and region B (below the line) is denoted by -1.

The network is trained as follows. The input signals $x_1(n)$ and $x_2(n)$ are independently assigned values from a zero-mean, Gaussian distribution having a variance of 1. If the corresponding point on the plane lies in region A, [that is, $x_2(n) \geq x_1(n)$], $d_q(n)$ will be set equal to $+1$; otherwise, $d_q(n) = -1$. The input samples and the associated desired sample will be presented to the network, and the perceptron algorithm will adjust the weights according to the update in (1). Clearly, a stationary point should be of the form $w_1(n) = -w_2(n)$, since this is the way the data were generated.

For this simple example, it is straightforward to model the underlying desired process as the following linear combination of the input signals: $d(n) = x_2(n) - x_1(n)$. As such, the vector F in (7) is[2] $F = [-1 \quad 1]^T$. Since the input samples are assumed to form a Gaussian vector, then $d(n)$ is necessarily a Gaussian process. This property will lead to some convenient analytical expressions for the stationary points, as discussed in the next section.

III. Stationary Points of the Algorithm

A. Mean Weight Vector

In order to determine the stationary points of the Perceptron algorithm, we examine the expected value of (1):

$$E[W(n+1)] = E[W(n)] + 2\mu E[e(n)X(n)] + \alpha(E[W(n)] - E[W(n-1)]). \tag{8}$$

[2]As another example, if the boundary was chosen to lie along the x_2 axis, then $F = [-1 \quad 0]^T$.

At convergence, assuming that μ has been chosen "sufficiently small," we have $E[W(n+1)] = E[W(n)] = E[W(n-1)] = W_*$, where W_* represents a stationary point. Alternatively, we may view (1) as a gradient-descent algorithm, and we are interested in finding weight values such that the gradient is zero. As a result, (8) reduces to the following *orthogonality condition* [4]:

$$E[e_*(n)X(n)] = 0. \quad (9)$$

The subscript * indicates that the error is generated when the weights are at the stationary point W_*. Equation (9) states that the error and the input signal are statistically orthogonal at convergence. This result is identical to that of the standard (linear) LMS algorithm, and it can be used to find W_*. If we substitute (3), then (9) can be rearranged as

$$E[X(n)d_q(n)] = E[X(n)\ \mathrm{sgn}\ (y_*(n))] \quad (10)$$

where $y_*(n)$ is the unquantized output at convergence. Define the cross-correlation between $X(n)$ and $d_q(n)$ as $P_q = E[X(n)d_q(n)]$. Note that the actual form of this vector depends on the statistics of the underlying process $d(n)$; later we consider the linear example described previously for $d(n)$, but for now we leave P_q in this more general form. Assuming that $X(n)$ is a zero-mean, Gaussian vector with correlation matrix $R = E[X(n)X^T(n)]$, then the right-hand side of (10) becomes [9]

$$E[X(n)\ \mathrm{sgn}\ (y_*(n))] = \frac{1}{c\sigma_{y_*}} E[X(n)y_*(n)] \quad (11)$$

where the constant $c = \sqrt{\pi/2}$ and $\sigma^2_{y_*}$ is the variance of $y_*(n)$, given by

$$\sigma^2_{y_*} = E[y^2_*(n)] = E[W^T_* X(n)X^T(n)W_*] = W^T_* R W_*. \quad (12)$$

Equation (5) was used to derive (12) and, because W_* is fixed, we have brought it outside the expectation. The expectation on the right-hand side of (11) can be expanded in a similar way, as follows:

$$E[X(n)y_*(n)] = RW_*. \quad (13)$$

Substituting (11) and (13) into (10), we have the following equivalent expression for (9):

$$W_* = c\sigma_{y_*} R^{-1} P_q \quad (14)$$

which, after substituting (12), becomes

$$W_* = c\sqrt{W^T_* R W_*}\ R^{-1} P_q. \quad (15)$$

The square root is well defined because the variance in (12) is always nonnegative, and we assume that R is positive definite so that the inverse exists. This expression defines the stationary points of the perceptron algorithm. Observe that it is a *nonlinear* function of W_*; because of this form, there may be infinitely many solutions. However, if for fixed values of μ and α the convergence point $\sigma^2_{y_*}$ of $\sigma^2_y(n) = E[y^2(n)]$ is unique, then the weight vector W_* will also be unique according to (14). Note that the output variance $\sigma^2_y(n)$ is nonstationary and dependent on n because the perceptron weights are time-varying.

It is interesting to consider when $d(n)$ is also a Gaussian process. In this case, we have from (6) that

$$P_q = \frac{1}{c\sigma_d} E[X(n)d(n)] \quad (16)$$

where σ^2_d is the variance of $d(n)$, which is independent of n when $d(n)$ is stationary. Substituting (16) into (14) and defining the cross-correlation between $X(n)$ and $d(n)$ as $P = E[X(n)d(n)]$, we have

$$W_* = \frac{\sigma_{y_*}}{\sigma_d} R^{-1} P. \quad (17)$$

If $\sigma_{y_*} = \sigma_d$, then the optimal solution here is identical in form to the Wiener solution of the standard (linear) MLMS algorithm [6], [7], that is

$$W_* = R^{-1}P. \quad (18)$$

In general, however, σ_{y_*} does not equal σ_d so that a *scaled* version of (18) would be obtained, as given in (17). Finally, if we assume that $d(n)$ is generated according to (7) for a fixed value of F, then $P = RF$, $\sigma^2_d = F^TRF$, and

$$W_* = \frac{\sigma_{y_*}}{\sigma_d} F, \quad (19)$$

that is, the optimal weights are directly proportional to F, where the proportionality constant is a nonnegative scalar. This result is consistent with our intuition; if W_* and F are related as in (19), then $y(n)$ and $d(n)$ will have the same sign for any $X(n)$, and the error will necessarily be zero, corresponding to a stationary point. To continue further, we need to examine the convergence properties of the output variance $\sigma^2_y(n)$ of the linear combiner.

B. Steady-State Output Variance

The output variance of the linear combiner can be written as

$$\sigma^2_y(n, n) = E[W^T(n)X(n)X^T(n)W(n)] \quad (20)$$

where we have substituted (5). For notational clarity, we have added a second time argument; together these arguments correspond to those of the weight vector and the input signal vector, respectively, under the expectation. After the weights are updated, the *a posteriori* variance can be expressed as

$$\sigma^2_y(n+1, n) = E[W^T(n+1)X(n)X^T(n)W(n+1)]. \quad (21)$$

Substituting the weight recursion from (1), we have that

$$\begin{aligned}\sigma^2_y(n+1, n) = {} & (1+\alpha)^2 E[W^T(n)X(n)X^T(n)W(n)] \\ & + 4\mu(1+\alpha)E[X^T(n)X(n)X^T(n)W(n)e(n)] \\ & + 4\mu^2 E[X^T(n)X(n)X^T(n)X(n)e^2(n)] \\ & - 2\alpha(1+\alpha)E[W^T(n)X(n)X^T(n)W(n-1)] \\ & - 4\mu\alpha E[X^T(n)X(n)X^T(n)W(n-1)e(n)] \\ & + \alpha^2 E[W^T(n-1)X(n)X^T(n)W(n-1)]\end{aligned} \quad (22)$$

which can be written more compactly as

$$\begin{aligned}\sigma^2_y(n+1, n) = {} & (1+\alpha)^2\sigma^2_y(n, n) + 4\mu(1+\alpha)a(n) + 4\mu^2 b(n) \\ & - 2\alpha(1+\alpha)\gamma(n, n-1) - 4\mu\alpha a(n-1) \\ & + \alpha^2\sigma^2_y(n-1, n)\end{aligned} \quad (23)$$

where, for convenience, we have defined the following scalar quantities:

$$\gamma(n, n-1) = E[W^T(n)X(n)X^T(n)W(n-1)] \quad (24a)$$

$$a(n) = E[X^T(n)X(n)X^T(n)W(n)e(n)] \quad (24b)$$

and

$$b(n) = E[X^T(n)X(n)X^T(n)X(n)e^2(n)]. \quad (24c)$$

In contrast to that in (20) and (21), the arguments of γ and a are defined only according to those of W under the expectation, and the argument of b is determined by that of e. To continue, we also need a recursion for $\gamma(n+1, n)$, as follows:

$$\begin{aligned}\gamma(n+1, n) &= E[W^T(n+1)X(n)X^T(n)W(n)]\\ &= (1+\alpha)E[W^T(n)X(n)X^T(n)W(n)]\\ &\quad + 2\mu E[X^T(n)X(n)X^T(n)W(n)e(n)]\\ &\quad -\alpha E[W^T(n)X(n)X^T(n)W(n-1)]\\ &= (1+\alpha)\sigma_y^2(n, n) + 2\mu a(n) - \alpha\gamma(n, n-1)\end{aligned} \quad (25)$$

where again (1) has been substituted.

Near convergence the weights approach W_*, a stationary point, and we have for "small"[3] μ that $\sigma_y^2(n+1, n) \approx \sigma_y^2(n, n) \approx \sigma_y^2(n-1, n) \to \sigma_{y.}^2$, $\gamma(n+1, n) \approx \gamma(n, n-1) \to \gamma$, $a(n) \approx a(n-1) \to a$, and $b(n) \to b$, which are all independent of time. Therefore, we can replace (23) and (25) by the following coupled pair of *deterministic* equations:

$$\sigma_{y.}^2 \approx (1 + 2\alpha + 2\alpha^2)\sigma_{y.}^2 + 4\mu a - 2\alpha(1+\alpha)\gamma + 4\mu^2 b \quad (26a)$$

and

$$\gamma \approx (1+\alpha)\sigma_{y.}^2 + 2\mu a - \alpha\gamma. \quad (26b)$$

By eliminating the common terms from these two expressions, we have the following condition that defines the output variance *near convergence:*

$$(1-\alpha)a + \mu b \approx 0. \quad (27)$$

Notice that this condition depends on the parameters μ and α. By examining a near convergence, we can approximate it as follows:

$$a \approx W_*^T E[X(n)X^T(n)X(n)e_*(n)] = W_*^T S \quad (28)$$

where W_* is the weight vector in (14), which has been factored from the expectation because we are assuming that the weight fluctuations near convergence are negligible. The vector S is given by $S = E[X(n)X^T(n)X(n)e_*(n)]$. By substituting (14) and (28) into (27) and solving for $\sigma_{y.}$, we find that

$$\sigma_{y.} \approx \frac{-b\mu}{c(1-\alpha)\,P_q^T R^{-1} S} = \frac{\mu}{c(1-\alpha)} k \quad (29)$$

where we have defined the positive scalar $k = -b/(P_q^T R^{-1} S)$. Substituting (29) into (14), the following expression is obtained, which represents the properties of the perceptron weight vector near convergence:

$$W_* \approx k\left(\frac{\mu}{1-\alpha}\right) R^{-1} P_q. \quad (30)$$

In general, it is difficult to determine closed-form expressions for P_q, S, b, and thus k. However, we are not so much interested in evaluating (30) as we are in the asymptotic relationship (i.e., near convergence) between the weights and the parameters μ and α. Notice that W_* is a *linear* function of μ; if μ is increased by a factor of 10, for example, then the weight values are also scaled by a factor of 10. On the other hand, W_* depends on α in a *nonlinear* way. Furthermore, it behaves differently for positive and negative values of α. If $\alpha > 0$, then the weights increase as $\alpha \to 1$, becoming extremely large as α approaches 1. However, for $\alpha < 0$, the weights decrease as $\alpha \to -1$, remaining relatively small.

Finally, if we assume that $d(n)$ is generated according to (6) and (7), then (30) simplifies to

$$W_* \approx k'\left(\frac{\mu}{1-\alpha}\right) F \quad (31)$$

where (19) has been used and $k' = -b/(F^T S)$ is a positive scalar. Thus, the weights near convergence are proportional to F.

IV. Computer Simulations

In the simulations presented here, a two-weight perceptron ($N = 2$) was examined with $b = 0$, $R = I$ (the identity matrix), and $F = [-1 \;\; 1]^T$. As such, the boundary passes through the origin at an angle of 45° with respect to the signal axes, $P = [-1 \;\; 1]^T$, and $\sigma_d^2 = 2$. The perceptron was trained to "learn" the location of this boundary starting from the zero weight vector. In all simulations, the weight trajectories were averaged over 100 independent computer runs to generate relatively smooth curves. We considered two cases: (a) one weight was fixed and the other was allowed to adapt, and (b) both weights were allowed to adapt.

Figure 3 shows the weight trajectories of $w_2(n)$ for four values of μ with $\alpha = 0$ and $w_1(n)$ fixed at -1. Since one weight

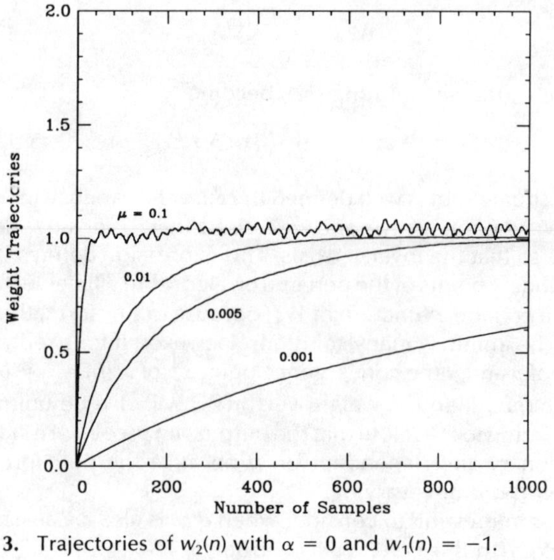

Fig. 3. Trajectories of $w_2(n)$ with $\alpha = 0$ and $w_1(n) = -1$.

[3]As a result, the weight fluctuations about W_* will be negligible and we can ignore them.

is fixed, the stationary points are unique in this case, corresponding to $w_2(n) \rightarrow 1$ [recall that we must have $w_2(n) = -w_1(n)$]. Observe that $w_2(n)$ converges to 1 as expected, and that the rate of convergence increases as μ is increased. The steady-state weight variance is greater for larger values of μ; this result is similar to that observed for the standard LMS algorithm, and it is a form of misadjustment [4]. Figure 4

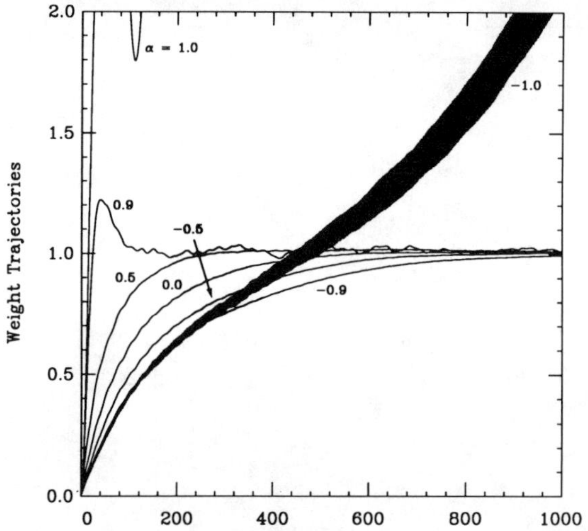

Fig. 4. Trajectories of $w_2(n)$ with $\mu = 0.01$ and $w_1(n) = -1$.

shows similar weight trajectories, except μ was kept fixed at 0.01 and α was varied for several positive and negative values. Observe that the rate of convergence increases as α is increased until it becomes unstable at $\alpha = 1$. On the other hand, the rate of convergence decreases as α becomes negative and it is again unstable when $\alpha = -1$. These results suggest that negative values of α would not be used even though the algorithm is stable.

Figures 5 and 6 show several weight trajectories of $w_2(n)$ for various values of μ and α, where $w_1(n)$ was also adapted. We show only the trajectories of $w_2(n)$ because we have found that $w_1(n) \approx -w_2(n)$ when we initialize them both to zero. In Fig. 5, observe that the weight trajectories are

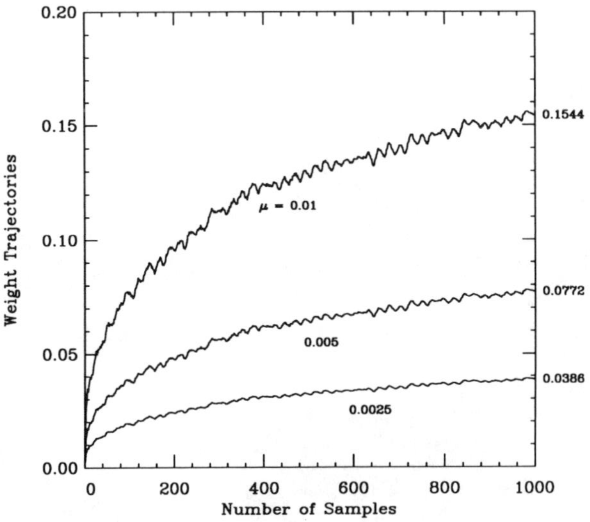

Fig. 5. Trajectories of $w_2(n)$ with $\alpha = 0$.

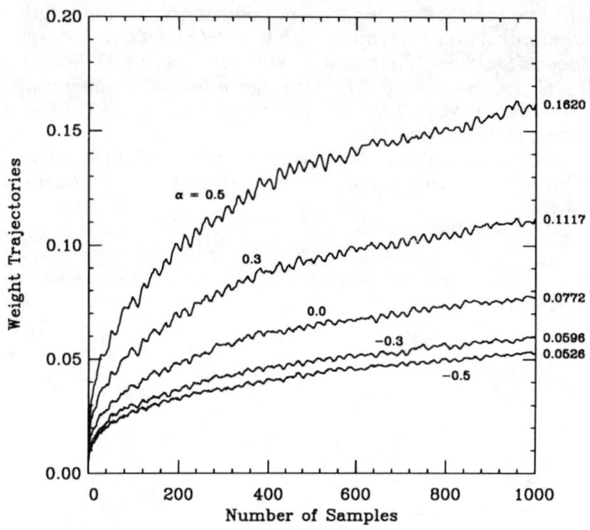

Fig. 6. Trajectories of $w_2(n)$ with $\mu = 0.005$.

directly proportional to changes in the step size μ, as predicted by the analysis in Section III and (31), and observe in Fig. 6 that they depend on α in a nonlinear way. (The weight value at iteration 1000 for each curve is shown to the right of the figures.) For a value of $\alpha = 0.5$, $w_2(n)$ should be scaled up by a factor of 2, and this result is verified by the simulation. On the other hand, the weights should be scaled down by a factor of 0.667 for $\alpha = -0.5$; this result is also verified in the simulation. A similar property is evident for $\alpha = \pm 0.3$, and we have observed the relationship predicted by (30) and (31) for other values of μ and α.

V. Conclusion

The stationary points and weight trajectories near convergence of a perceptron learning algorithm with momentum updating have been examined for a Gaussian input vector. It was demonstrated that the stationary points are not unique, and that the behavior of the algorithm near convergence depends on the step size μ and the momentum factor α, as well as the statistics of the underlying process $d(n)$. As μ is increased, the weight trajectories increase in direct proportion to changes in μ. On the other hand, the algorithm convergence properties depend on α in a nonlinear way, and it is unstable for $|\alpha| = 1$, as demonstrated by computer simulations.

Acknowledgment

The authors thank Neil Bershad for his helpful comments concerning the analysis of the steady-state output variance.

References

[1] R. P. Lippmann, "An introduction to computing with neural nets," *IEEE ASSP Mag.*, vol. 4, pp. 4–22, Apr. 1987.
[2] B. Widrow, R. G. Winter, and R. A. Baxter, "Layered neural nets for pattern recognition," *IEEE Trans. Acoust., Speech, Sig. Proc.*, vol. 36, pp. 1109–1118, July 1988.
[3] D. E. Rumelhart, G. E. Hinton, and R. J. Williams, "Learning internal representations by error propagation," *Parallel Distributed Processing: Explorations in the Microstructure of Cognition*, pp. 318–362, D. E. Rumelhart and J. L. McClelland, Eds. Cambridge, MA: M.I.T. Press, 1986.
[4] B. Widrow and S. D. Stearns, *Adaptive Signal Processing.* Englewood Cliffs, NJ: Prentice-Hall, 1985.

[5] J. J. Shynk and S. Roy, "Analysis of a perceptron learning algorithm with momentum updating," *Proc. IEEE Int. Conf. Acoust., Speech, Sig. Proc.*, Albuquerque, NM, Apr. 1990, pp. 1377–1380.
[6] J. J. Shynk and S. Roy, "The LMS algorithm with momentum updating," *Proc. IEEE Int. Symp. Circuits Syst.*, pp. 2651–2654, Espoo, Finland, June 1988.
[7] S. Roy and J. J. Shynk, "Analysis of the momentum LMS algorithm," *IEEE Trans. Acoust., Speech, Sig. Proc.*, to be published.
[8] G. O. Stone, "An analysis of the delta rule and the learning of statistical associations," *Parallel Distributed Processing: Explorations in the Microstructure of Cognition*, pp. 444–459, D. E. Rumelhart and J. L. McClelland, Eds. Cambridge, MA: M.I.T. Press, 1986.
[9] R. Price, "A useful theorem for nonlinear devices having Gaussian inputs," *IRE Trans. Inform. Theory*, vol. IT-4, pp. 69–72, June 1958.

Part 5
Related Techniques

Entropy Nets: From Decision Trees to Neural Networks

ISHWAR K. SETHI, SENIOR MEMBER, IEEE

*A multiple-layer artificial network (ANN) structure is capable of implementing arbitrary input–output mappings. Similarly, hierarchical classifiers, more commonly known as decision trees, possess the capabilites of generating arbitrarily complex decision boundaries in an n-*dimensional space. Given a decision tree, it is possible to restructure it as a multilayered neural network. The objective of this paper is to show how this mapping of decision trees into a multilayer neural network structure can be exploited for the systematic design of a class of layered neural networks, called *entropy nets,* that have far fewer connections. Several important issues such as the automatic tree generation, incorporation of incremental learning, and the generalization of knowledge acquired during the tree design phase are discussed. Finally, a two-step methodology for designing entropy networks is presented. The advantages of this methodology are that it specifies the number of neurons needed in each layer, along with the desired output. This leads to a faster progressive training procedure that allows each layer to be trained separately. Two examples are presented to show the success of neural network design through decision tree mapping.

I. Introduction

Artificial neural networks offer an exciting computational paradigm for cognitive machines. The main attribute of the ANN paradigm is the distributed representation of the knowledge in the form of connections between a very large number of simple computing elements, called neurons. These neurons are arranged in several distinct layers. The interfacing layer on the input side of the network is called the sensory layer; the one on the output side is the output layer or the motor control layer. All the intermediate layers are called hidden layers. All the computing elements may perform the same type of input–output operation, or different layers of computing elements may realize different kinds of input–output transfer functions. The reason for all the excitement about ANN's lies in their capability to generalize input–output mapping from a limited set of training examples.

One important application area for ANN's is pattern recognition. A pattern, in general, could be a segment of time-sampled speech, a moving target, or the profile of a prospective graduate student seeking admission. Pattern recognition implies initiating certain actions based on the observation of input data. The input data representing a pattern are called the measurement or feature vector. The function performed by a pattern recognition system is the mapping of the input feature vector into one of the various decision classes. The mapping performed by a pattern recognition system can be represented in many cases by writing the equations of the decision boundaries in the feature space. A linear input–output mapping realized by a particular pattern recognition system then implies that the decision boundaries have a linear form. However, most of the pattern recognition problems of practical interest need a nonlinear mapping between the input and output. Although a single neuron is capable of only a linear mapping, a layered network of neurons with multiple hidden layers provides any desired mapping. It is this capability of the layered networks that has resulted in the renewed interest in the ANN field.

An example of a multiple hidden layer network is shown in Fig. 1(a). Generally, all neurons in a layer are connected

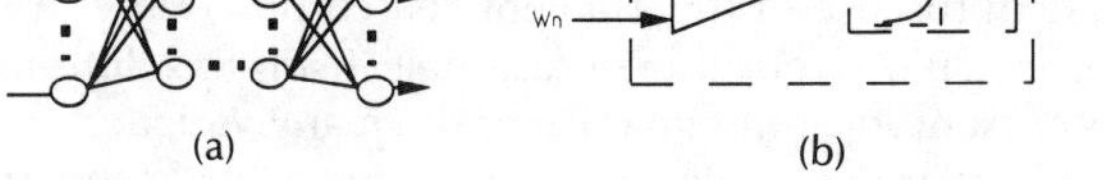

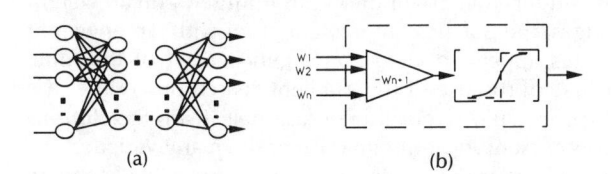

Fig. 1. (a) An example of a multiple hidden layer neural network. (b) A typical neuron model. The triangular shape represents the summation. The inner dotted box represents the sigmoid activation function.

to all the neurons in the adjacent layers. The connection strength between two neurons from adjacent layers is represented in the form of a weight value. The significance of this weight value is that it acts as a signal multiplier on the corresponding connection link. Each neuron in the layered network is typically modeled as shown in Fig. 1(b). As indicated in the figure, the input to a neuron is the linear summation of all the incoming signals on the various connection links. This net summation is compared to a threshold value, often called bias. The difference arising due to the comparison drives an output function, usually called an activation function, to produce a signal at the output line of the neuron. The two most common choices for the activation function are sigmoid and hyperbolic tangent func-

Manuscript received July 28, 1989; revised March 13, 1990.
The author is with the Department of Computer Science, Wayne State University, Detroit, MI 48202.
IEEE Log Number 9039179.

Reprinted from *Proc. IEEE*, vol. 78, no. 10, Oct. 1990, pp. 1605–1613.

tions. In the context of pattern recognition, such layered networks are also called multilayer perceptron (MLP) networks. It can be easily shown that two hidden layers are sufficient to form piecewise linear decision boundaries of any complexity [1], [2]. However, it must be noted that two layers are not necessary for arbitrary decision regions [3]. The first hidden layer is the *partitioning* layer that divides the entire feature space into several regions. The second hidden layer is the *ANDing* layer that performs *ANDing* of partitioned regions to yield convex decision regions for each class. The output layer can be considered as the *ORing* layer that logically combines the results of the previous layer to produce disjoint decision regions of arbitrary shape with holes and concavities if needed.

The most common training paradigm for layered networks is the paradigm of supervised learning. In this mode of learning, the network is presented with examples of input–output mapping pairs. During the learning process, the network continuously modifies its connection strengths or weights to achieve the mapping present in the examples. While the single-layer neuron training procedures have been around for 30–40 years, the extension of these training procedures to multilayer neuron networks proved to be a difficult task because of the so-called *credit assignment* problem, i.e., what should be the desired output of the neurons in the hidden layers during the training phase?

One of the solutions to the credit assignment problem that has gained prominence is to propagate back the error at the output layer to the internal layers. The resulting backpropagation algorithm [4] is the most frequently used training procedure for layered networks. It is a gradient descent procedure that minimizes the error at the output layer. Although the convergence of the algorithm has been proved only under the assumption of infinitely small weight changes, the practical implementations with larger weight changes appear to yield convergence most of the time. Because of the use of the gradient search procedure, the backpropagation algorithm occasionally leads to solutions that represent local minima. Recently, many variations of the backpropagation algorithm have been proposed to speed up the network learning time. Some other examples of layered network training procedures are Boltzmann learning [5], counterpropagation [6], and Madaline Rule-II [7]. These training procedures, including the backpropagation algorithm, however, are generally slow. Additionally, these training procedures *do not specify in any way the number of neurons needed in the hidden layers.* This number is an important parameter that can significantly affect the learning rate as well as the overall classification performance, as indicated by the experimental studies of several researchers [1], [8].

There exists a class of conventional pattern classifiers that has many similarities with the layered networks. This class of classifiers is called hierarchical or decision tree classifiers. As the name implies, these classifiers arrive at a decision through a heirarchy of stages. Unlike many conventional pattern recognition techniques, the decision tree classifiers also do not impose any restriction on the underlying distribution of the input data. These classifiers are capable of producing arbitrarily complex decision boundaries that can be learned from a set of training vectors. While the tree-based learning is noniterative or single step, the neural net learning is incremental. The incremental learning mode is more akin to human learning where the hypotheses are continually refined in response to more and more training examples. However, the advantage of single-step learning is that all the training examples are considered simultaneously to form hypotheses, thus leading to faster learning. The two significant differences between the decision tree classifiers and the layered networks are: 1) the sequential nature of the tree classifiers as opposed to the massive parallelism of the neural networks, and 2) the limited generalization capabilities of the tree classifiers as the learning mechanism in comparison to layered networks. The aim of this paper is to show how the similarities between the tree classifiers and the layered networks can be used for developing a pragmatic approach to the design and training of neural networks for classification. The motivation for this work is to provide a systematic layered network design methodology that has built-in solutions to the credit assignment problem and the network topology.

The organization of the rest of the paper is as follows. In Section II, I introduce decision trees and their mapping in the form of layered networks. A recursive tree design procedure is introduced in Section III to acquire knowledge from the input data. Section IV discusses the issues related to incremental learning and the generalization of the captured knowledge. This is followed by a two-step layered network design procedure that allows the training of all the layers by progressively propagating the acquired knowledge. In Section V, I present experimental results that demonstrate the speed of learning, as well as the extent of generalization possible through the present design approach. Section VI contains the summary of the paper.

II. Decision Tree Classifiers

The decision trees offer a structured way of decision making in pattern recognition. The rationale for decision tree-based partitioning of the decision space has been well summarized by Kanal [9]. A decision tree is characterized by an order of set nodes. Each of the internal nodes is associated with a decision function of one or more features. The terminal nodes or leaf nodes of the decision tree are associated with actions or decisions that the system is expected to make. In an *m*-ary decision tree, there are *m* descendants for every node. Binary decision tree form is the most commonly used tree form. An equivalent binary tree exists for any *m*-ary decision tree. Henceforth in this paper, a decision tree will imply a binary tree.

A decision tree induces a hierarchical partitioning over the decision space. Starting with the root node, each of the successive internal nodes partitions its associated decision region into two half spaces, with the node decision function defining the dividing hyperplane. An example of a decision tree and the corresponding hierarchical partitioning induced by the tree are shown in Fig. 2. It is easy to see that as the depth of the tree increases, the resulting partitioning becomes more and more complex.

Classification using decision tree is performed by traversing the tree from the root node to one of the leaf nodes using the unknown pattern vector. The response elicited by the unknown pattern is the class or decision label attached to the leaf node that is reached by the unknown vector. It is obvious that all the conditions along any particular path from the root to the leaf node of the decision tree must be satisfied in order to reach that particular leaf

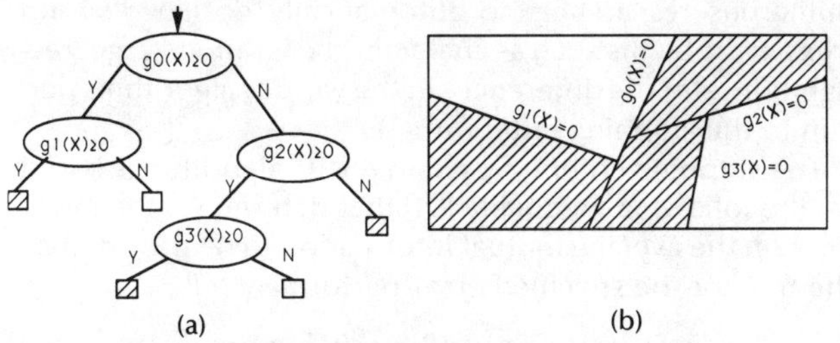

Fig. 2. (a) An example of a decision tree. Square boxes represent terminal nodes. (b) Hierarchical partitioning of the two-dimensional space induced by the decision tree of (a).

node. Thus, each path of a decision tree implements an AND operation on a set of half spaces. If two or more leaf nodes result in the same action or decision, then the corresponding paths are in an OR relationship. Since a layered neural network for classification also implements *ANDing* of hyperplanes followed by *ORing* in the output layer, it is obvious that a decision tree and a layered network are equivalent in terms of input–output mapping. Not only that, a decision tree can be restructured as a layered network by following certain rules. These rules can be informally stated as follows.

- The number of neurons in the first layer of the layered network equals the number of internal nodes of the decision tree. Each of these neurons implements one of the decision functions of internal nodes. This layer is the *partitioning* layer.
- All leaf nodes have a corresponding neuron in the second hidden layer where the *ANDing* is implemented. This layer is the *ANDing* layer.
- The number of neurons in the output layer equals the number of distinct classes or actions. This layer implements the *ORing* of those tree paths that lead to the same action.
- The connections between the neurons from the partitioning layer and the neurons from the *ANDing* layer implement the hierarchy of the tree.

An example of tree restructuring following the above rules is shown in Fig. 3 for the decision tree of Fig. 2. As this

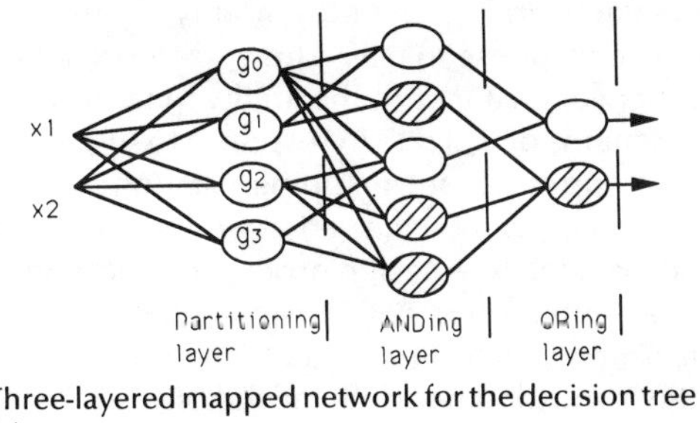

Fig. 3. Three-layered mapped network for the decision tree of Fig. 2(a).

example shows, it is fairly straightforward to map a decision tree into a layered network of neurons. It should be noted that the mapping rules given above do not attempt to optimize the number of neurons in the partitioning layer. However, a better mapping can be achieved incorporating checks in the mapping rules for replications of the node decision functions in different parts of the tree to avoid the duplication of the neurons in the partitioning layer. It can be further enhanced by using algorithms [10] that produce an optimal tree from the partitioning specified by a given decision tree.

The most important consequence of the tree-to-network mapping is that it defines *exactly the number of neurons needed* in each of the three layers of neural network, as well as a way of *specifying the desired response* for each of these neurons, as I shall show later. Hitherto, this number of neurons has been determined by empirical means, and the credit assignment problem has been tackled with backpropagation. In comparison to the standard feedforward layered networks that are fully connected, the mapped network has far fewer connections. Except for one neuron in the partitioning layer that corresponds to the root node of the decision tree, the remaining neurons do not have connections with all the neurons in the adjacent layers. A fewer number of connections is an important advantage from the VLSI implementation point of view [11] given the present state of technology. To emphasize this difference in the architecture, I shall henceforth refer to the mapped network as the *entropy net* due to the mutual information-based data-driven tree generation methodology that is discussed in the next section. Such a methodology is a must if the tree-to-network mapping is to be exploited.

While the above mapping rules transform a sequential decision making process into a parallel process, the resulting network, however, has the same limitations that were exhibited by the MADALINE [7] type of early multilayer ANN models; there is no adaptability beyond the first hidden layer. In terms of the decision trees, this limitation is best described by saying that once a wrong path is taken at an internal node, there is no way of recovering from the mistake. The layered networks of neurons avoid this pitfall because of their adaptability beyond the partitioning layer that allows some corrective actions after the first hidden layer. As I shall show later, it is possible to have the same adaptability capabilities in the entropy network as those of neural networks obtained through the backpropagation training. This becomes possible by combining the dual concepts of soft decision making and incremental learning that are described after the next section or recursive tree design procedure.

III. Mutual Information and Recursive Tree Design

Several automatic tree generation algorithms exist in the pattern recognition literature where the problem of tree generation has been dealt with in two distinct ways. Some of the early approaches break the tree design process into two stages. The first stage yields a set of prototypes for each pattern class. These prototypes are viewed as entries in a decision table which is later converted into a decision tree using some optimal criterion. Examples of this type of tree design approaches can be found in [12], [13]. The problem of finding prototypes from binary or discrete-valued patterns is considered in [14], [15]. The other tree design approaches try to obtain the tree directly from the given set of labeled pattern vectors. These direct approaches can be considered as a generalization of decision table conversion approaches, with all the available pattern vectors for the design forming the decision table entries. Examples of these direct tree design approaches can be found in [16]–[19].

There are three basic tasks that need to be solved during the tree design process: 1) defining the hierarchical ordering and choice of the node decision functions, 2) deciding when to declare a node as terminal node, and 3) setting up a decision rule at each terminal node. The last task is the easiest part of the tree design process. It is usually solved by following the majority rule. In its complete generality, the decision tree design problem is a difficult problem, and no optimal tree design procedure exists [20]. Some of the tree design difficulties are simplified in practice by enforcing a binary decision based on a single feature at each of the nonterminal nodes. This results in the decision space partitioning with the hyperplanes that are orthogonal to the feature axes. While the use of a single feature decision function at every nonterminal node reduces the computational burden at the tree design time, it usually leads to larger trees.

One popular approach for ordering and locating the partitioning hyperplanes is based on defining a *goodness measure of partitioning* in terms of mutual information. Consider a two-class problem with only one measurement x. Let $x = t$ define the partitioning of the one-dimensional feature space. If we view the measurement x taking on values greater or less than threshold t as two outcomes x_1 and x_2 of an event X, then the amount of average mutual information obtained about the pattern classes from the observation of even X can be written as

$$I(C; X) = \sum_{i=1}^{2} \sum_{j=1}^{2} p(c_i, x_j) \log_2 [p(c_i|x_j) \mid p(c_i)] \tag{1}$$

where C represents the set of pattern classes and the $p(\cdot)$'s are the various probabilities. Clearly, for better recognition, the choice of the threshold t should be such that we get as much information as possible from the event X. This means that the value which maximizes (1) should be selected over all possible values of t. Average mutual information gain (AMIG) thus provides a basis for measuring the goodness of a partitioning.

Another popular criterion for partitioning is the Gini index of diversity [19]. In this criterion, the impurity of a set of observations as a partitioning stage s is defined as

$$I(s) = \sum_{i \neq j} p(c_i|s)\, p(c_j|s) \tag{2}$$

where $p(c_i|s)$ denotes the conditional probability. The further split in the data is made by selecting a partitioning that yields the greatest reduction in the average data impurity. The advantage of this criterion is its simpler arithmetic.

The above or similar partitioning measures immediately suggest a top-down recursive procedure for the tree design. The AMIG (average mutual information gain) algorithm [17] is one such example of the recursive tree design procedure that seeks to maximize the amount of mutual information gain at every stage of tree development. Unlike many other algorithms that either operate on discrete features or two classes, the AMIG algorithm is capable of generating decision trees for continuous-valued multifeature, multiclass pattern recognition problems from a set of labeled pattern vectors. The AMIG algorithm at any stage of tree development essentially employs a brute force search technique to determine the best feature for that stage, along with its best threshold value to define an *event* for the corresponding node. Since the orientation of dividing hyperplanes is restricted, i.e., only one feature is used at any internal node, the search space for maximizing the average mutual information gain is small. The search is made efficient by ordering the labeled patterns along different feature axes to obtain a small set of possible candidate locations along each axis. The AMIG algorithm or its variants have been used by numerous researchers to automatically design decision trees in problems such as character recognition, target recognition, etc. The differences in the various algorithms pertain to the stopping criterion.

The stopping criterion used in AMIG algorithm is based on the following inequality [21] that determines the lower limit on the average mutual information to be provided by the tree for the specified error performance P_e:

$$I(C; T) \geq H(C) - H(P_e) - P_e \log_2 (m - 1) \tag{3}$$

where $H(C)$ and $H(P_e)$, respectively, represent the pattern class and the error entropy. The criterion used in [18] is to test the statistical significance of the mutual information gain that results from further splitting a node. Recently, Goodman and Smyth [22] have derived several fundamental bounds for mutual information-based recursive tree design procedures, and have suggested a new stopping criterion which is claimed to be more robust in the presence of noise.

Instead of using a stopping criterion to terminate the recursive partitioning, Breiman *et al.* [19] use a pruning approach with the Gini criterion to design decision trees. In their approach, the recursive partitioning continues until the tree becomes very large. This tree is then selectively pruned upwards to find a best subtree having the lowest error estimate. Trees obtained using pruning are typically less biased towards the design samples.

Summarizing the above discussion, it is clear that there exist several automatic tree generation procedures that are driven by the example pattern vectors. Any of these procedures in conjunction with the decision tree-to-network mapping discussed earlier can be used to design an entropy network for a given pattern recognition problem. While the design of layered networks through decision tree mapping eliminates the guesswork about the number of neurons in different layers and provides a direct method of obtaining connection strengths, the problem of adaptability of the entropy network beyond the partitioning layer still remains. The solution to this is discussed in the next section.

IV. Incremental Learning and Generalization

Incremental learning implies modifying the existing knowledge in response to new data or facts. In the context of neural networks, it means the ability to modify the connection strengths or weights in response to sequential presentation of input-output mapping examples. While the tree design phase can be viewed as an inductive learning phase and even the tree design process can be made incremental in a limited sense [23], it is essential to have incremental learning capability in the mapped networks. Such a capability is needed not only for the obvious reasons of adaptability and compatibility with networks designed through other approaches, but also for reducing the storage demands on the batch-oriented recursive tree design procedures. With the incremental learning capability in the entropy network, it is possible to divide the task of knowledge acquisition over the processes of tree building and mapped network training. Using only a small representative subset of the available input-output mapping examples, a decision tree can be designed without putting too much storage demands during the recursive tree generation phase. After the mapping has been done, the remaining examples can be used to further train the network in an incremental fashion.

To have the ability to modify weights in response to training examples, it is essential *to solve the credit assignment problem* for the intermediate layers, i.e., the partitioning layer and the ANDing layer. Fortunately, *in the entropy network, this problem is automatically solved during the tree design stage* when different paths are assigned class labels. As can be noticed from the tree-to-network mapping, there exists a group of neurons for every pattern class in the ANDing layer of the network. The membership in this group is known from the tree-to-network mapping. Thus, given an example pattern from class c, it is known that only one neuron from the group c of the ANDing layer neuron should produce an output of "1," while the remaining neurons from that group as well as those from the other groups should produce a "0" response. Therefore, the solution to the credit assignment problem for the ANDing layer is very simple: enhance the response of the neuron producing the highest output among the neurons from group c, and suppress the response of the remaining neurons in the ANDing layer for a pattern from class c. This is similar to the *winner-take-all* approach followed for the neural net training in the self-organizing mode [24]. The reason that this simple approach works in the entropy network is that the network has a built-in hierarchy of the decision tree which is not present in the other layered networks. Once the identity of the firing neuron is the ANDing layer is established for a given example pattern, the desired response from the partitioning layer neurons is also established because of tree-to-network mapping. Hence, the tree-to-network mapping not only provides the architecture of the multilayer net, but it also solves the credit assignment problem, thus giving rise to an incremental learning capability for the entropy network. Since the initial network configuration itself provides a reasonably good starting solution to the various network parameters, the incremental learning can be very fast, leading to drastically reduced training time on the whole.

One very important characteristic of learning, whether incremental or not, is that it should lead to generalization capability on the part of the network. The amount of generalization achieved is reflected in the network response to those patterns that did not form part of the input–output mapping examples. To put it in other words, how well the network interpolates among the examples shown determines the degree of generalization achieved. In a typical neural net, the generalization is achieved by incorporating nonlinearities in the neurons. This is done by choosing a nonlinear activation function for the neuron model. While the choice of a particular nonlinearity is not crucial for learning a specific set of input–output mapping examples, it does determine the amount of generalization that the network will achieve [25]. The soft nonlinearities, such as the sigmoid function, provide much better generalization compared to the relay type of hard nonlinearities. An intuitive understanding of why the soft nonlinearities provide better generalization in a parallel environment like the multilayer neural networks can be had by saying that these types of nonlinearities allows the decision making to be delayed as far as possible in the hope that at the later layers, more information will be available to make a better decision. Hard nonlinearities, on the other hand, do not provide this privilege of postponing decisions, and consequently do not lead to much generalization in the network.

Since each node of the decision tree produces a binary decision, the activation function associated with the neurons in the entropy network can be considered as a relay function. Obviously, it is not good for generalization, and must be replaced by sigmoid or some other soft nonlinear function. The signal level effect of having sigmoid nonlinearity in place of relay nonlinearity is that it changes all the internal signals from binary to analog. Consequently, small changes in the features do not affect the response of the neurons in different layers as much as compared to the binary signal case where a small change can result in a complete reversal of the signal state. This enhances the capability of the entropy network to deal with problems having noise and variability in the patterns, thus leading to better generalization. Another consequence of sigmoid nonlinearity is that it altogether eliminates or minimizes the need for training the partitioning layer in the incremental learning mode. With the relay type of hard nonlinearity, it may not be possible to converge to the proper weights in the ANDing layer for the desired response if the threshold values in the partitioning layer, determined during the tree design phase, are not proper. In such cases, the partitioning layer training must adjust these threshold weights. However, with sigmoid activation function, the thresholds in the partitioning layers can be off to a reasonable extent without affecting the convergence of the weight values for the ANDing layer. This is very important as it *eliminates altogether any reference to the previous layers during the learning process and provides a direct layer-by-layer progressive propagation method for learning.*

Another way of looking at the use of a sigmoid function is that it allows the actual feature values to be carried across different layers in a coded form, while the hard nonlinearities lose the actual feature value at the partitioning layer itself. In addition to the generality or the better decision making that results from carrying through the actual feature values in coded form, the other very important consequence of carrying through the coded information is that the final decision boundaries need not be piecewise linear, as would be the case with hard nonlinearities. Moreover, for the linear boundaries, the orientation need not be parallel to different feature axes. Thus, while the partitioning layer neurons get information about single features only, the neurons in the successive layers do receive information on many features, thereby producing boundaries of desired shape and orientation.

Based on the discussion thus far, the following steps are suggested for designing entropy nets of pattern recognition tasks.

- Divide the available set of input–output mapping examples in two parts: tree design set and network training set. This should be done when a large number of input–output examples is available. Otherwise, the complete set of examples should be used for tree design and network training.
- Using AMIG or a similar recursive tree design procedure, develop a decision tree for the given problem.
- Map the tree into a three-layer neural net structure following the rules given earlier.
- Associate the sigmoid or some other soft nonlinearity with every neuron. Train the ANDing and ORing layers of the entropy network using the network training subset of the input–output mapping examples and the following procedure for determing the weight change.

Let $x(p)$ with category label $L(x(p))$ be the input pattern to the entropy network at the pth presentation during the training. Let $R_j(x(p))$ denote the response of the jth neuron from the ANDing/ORing layer. Let $G(j)$ represent the group membership of the jth neuron and w_{ij} the connection strength between the jth neuron and the ith neuron of the previous layer. Then

$$w_{ij}(p+1) = m_{ij} \cdot (w_{ij}(p) + \Delta w_{ij}(p)), \quad \text{if } R_j(x(p)) \geq R_k(x(p)) \text{ for all } k \text{ such that } G(k) = L(x(p)) = G(j)$$

and

$$w_{ik}(p+1) = m_{ik} \cdot (w_{ik}(p) - \Delta w_{ik}(p)), \quad \text{for all } k \neq j$$

where the amount of change in the weights is determined by the Window–Hoff procedure [26] or the LMS rule, as it is called many times. The term m_{ij} is either "1" or "0," indicating whether a connection exists to the jth neuron from the ith neuron or not. It should be noted that the presence or the absence of the connections is determined at the time of tree-to-network mapping. The suggested training procedure is such that it is possible to train each layer separately or simultaneously.

The above process of layered network design can be considered as a two-stage learning process. In the first stage, major aspects of the given problem are learned by simultaneously considering a large number of input–output mapping examples. Next, the refinement of the learned knowledge as well as its generalization are achieved by looking at the same or additional examples in isolation.

V. Design Examples

Following the above design approach for the layered networks, I present in this section two design examples. The first example is for a two-category pattern recognition task with only two features. The second example is for a multicategory, multifeature pattern recognition task involving waveform classification. The purpose of the first example is to bring out the generalization capability of the entropy network. The second example is presented to demonstrate and compare the efficacy of the methodology for multicategory problems in higher dimensional space.

There are three important parameters in the entropy net training. One of these is called the generalization constant α that determines the generalization capability of the entropy network. The parameter α controls the linear part of the sigmoid nonlinearity. Fig. 4 shows several plots of the sigmoid function for different values of α. Since a very large α value brings the sigmoid nonlinearity very close to the relay nonlinearity, the amount of generalization provided by α is inversely proportional to its value. The second parameter ρ is called the learning factor that may or may not remain fixed over the entire training. It controls the amount of correction that is applied to determine new weight values. The third parameter ϵ specifies the termination of the training procedure. The training is terminated if none of the weight components differs from its previous value by an amount greater than ϵ.

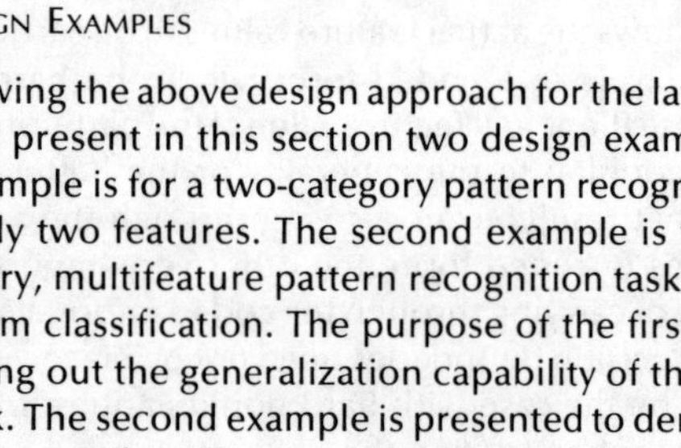

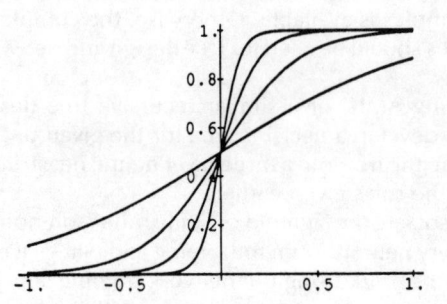

Fig. 4. Sigmoid function $1|(1 + \exp(-\alpha x))$ plots for different α values.

The first design example is an analog version of the EX-OR problem. Fig. 5(a) shows two pattern classes in the form of two different tones in a two-dimensional feature space, with the corresponding decision tree in Fig. 5(b). The tonal boundary is the decision boundary that the neural net is expected to learn. Entropy network mapping the tree of Fig. 5(b) is shown in Fig. 6. The threshold values of all the internal nodes of the tree of Fig. 5(b) were intentionally offset by an amount of 0.05 in the mapping process to determine the adatability of the entropy network. Using a uniform random number of generator, 60 input–output mapping examples for this problem were generated. The dots in Fig. 5(a) represent these randomly generated input–output map-

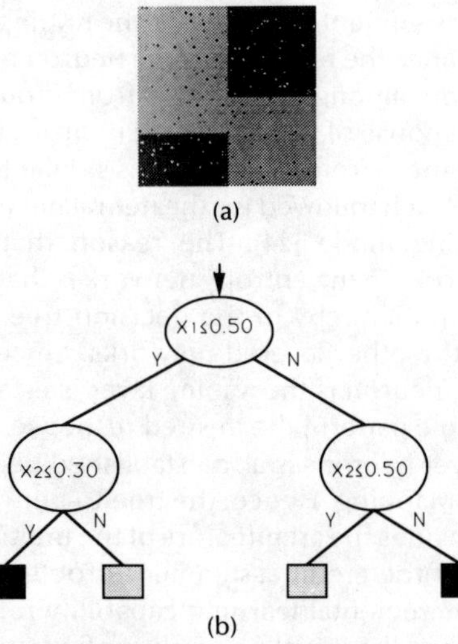

Fig. 5. (a) An analog version of EN-OR problem in a two-dimensional space. Two different tones represent two different class regions that a neural network is expected to learn. The dots correspond to input–output examples used for network training. (b) Decision tree for the analog EX-OR problem.

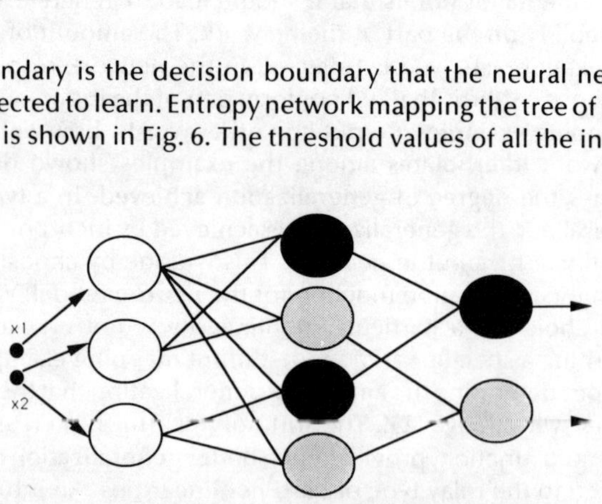

Fig. 6. Entropy network for the decision tree of Fig. 5(b). Tones in the network represent the class responsible for the corresponding neuron firing.

ping examples that were used to train the entropy network. While it is possible to train the ANDing and ORing layers simultaneously, each layer was trained separately to determine the progressive generalization capability of the entropy network. The parameters ρ and ϵ were set to 1.0 and 0.001, respectively, and different values for the generalization parameter α were used. The learning factor was made to decrease in inverse proportion to the iteration number. Results for two cases of training are shown in Figs. 7 and 8. The upper left image in each of these figures represents

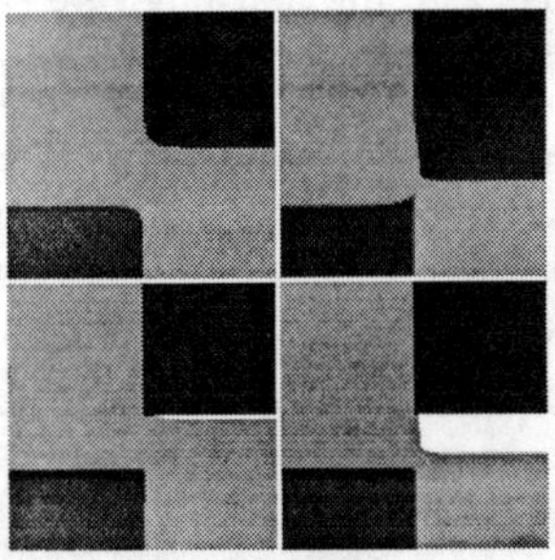

Fig. 7. Mapping learned by the entropy net for $\alpha = 20$. The upper left image is the mapping learned at the output layer. The upper right image is the mapping learned at the ANDing layer. The lower left and right images show the difference in the desired mapping and the learned mapping.

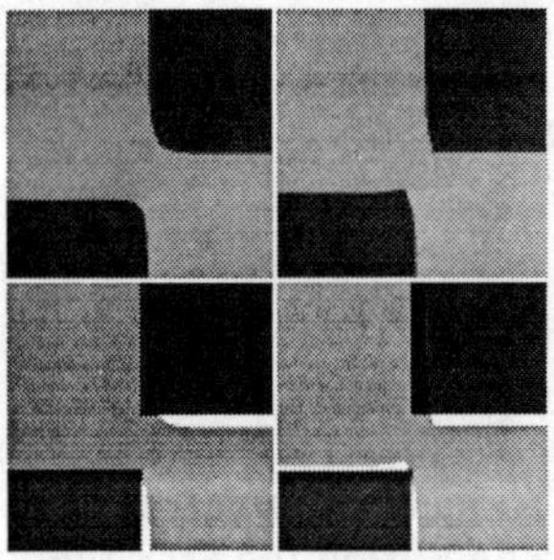

Fig. 8. Same as in Fig. 7, except $\alpha = 10$.

the decision boundary as learned by the net at its output layer. The lower left image shows the difference in the actual decision boundary and the learned boundary. The right-hand column represents the same for the ANDing layer. The decision boundary at the partitioning layer, of course, corresponds to the boundary represented by the decision tree. Fig. 7 represents the generalization performed by the net for an α value of 20.0, while Fig. 8 corresponds to a value of 10.0. Since the threshold values in the decision tree were offset by a small amount, the generalization needed is not large. This explains the better learning exhibited in Fig. 7 compared to Fig. 8. This experiment has been repeated many times with different seed values for the random generator program. In all of the cases, results obtained were almost similar to the above. The number of iterations for the ANDing layer averaged about 37. The corresponding number for the ORing layer is about 156. The notable feature of the entire training procedure was that only one neuron in the ANDing layer always responded for the pattern class represented by the lighter shade, although two neurons were put in the ANDing layer for each class as a result of the tree mapping. This indicates that the entropy network just does not mimic the decision tree, but has its own generalization capability.

In order to further test the generalization capability of the network, the class labels of the training examples were changed to correspond to the decision boundary of Fig. 9,

Fig. 9. Another decision boundary for learning by the entropy net of Fig. 6.

and the same network was trained with these modified examples. Training results for this case are shown in Figs. 10 and 11 for two values of α, 1, and 5, respectively. Since

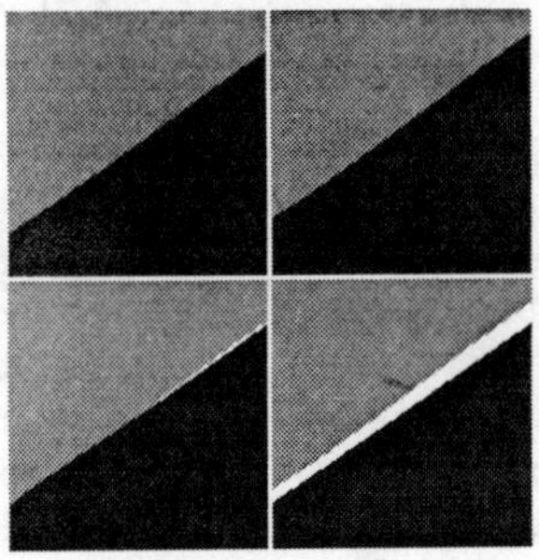

Fig. 10. Mapping learned by the entropy net with modified input–output examples. $\alpha = 1$.

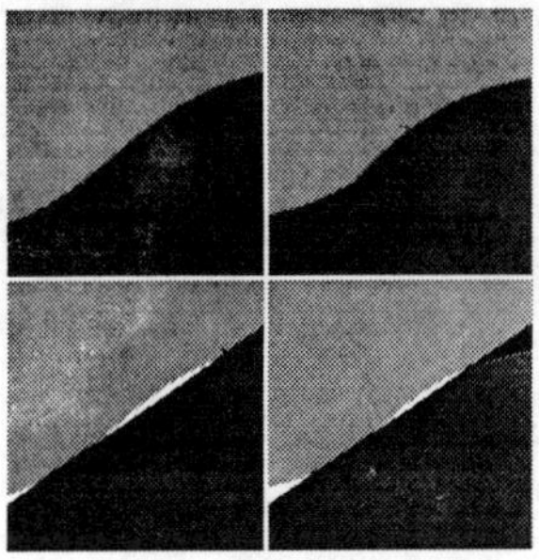

Fig. 11. Same as Fig. 10, except $\alpha = 5$.

there is large error in the decision tree boundary of Fig. 5(b) and Fig. 9, a large amount of generalization is needed in this particular case to let the entropy net adapt, as is evident in Figs. 10 and 11. It is important to note here that the final decision boundary in this case has an orientation other than the horizontal or vertical. This indicates that while the decision tree, designed with a single feature per node, has constraints on the orientation of the decision boundary, the entropy network has no such limitation due to the sigmoid function. While examining the output of the ANDing layer neurons, once again, the build up of the internal representation by the entropy network was observed; only one neuron per class was found to participate in the learning process. The remaining two neurons, one from each category, were found in the nonfiring state all the time. The pairing of firing and nonfiring neurons was not fixed; it was found to depend on the starting random weight values. The average number of iterations for the ANDing layer over the different runs was 193. The corresponding number for the ORing layer was 42. The larger number of iterations for the ANDing layer in this case is due to the great difference in the starting boundary that corresponds to the tree of Fig. 5(b) and the desired boundary of Fig. 9.

The second example uses a synthetic data set to simulate a well-known waveform recognition problem from the classification tree literature [19]. This was done to compare the classification performance of the entropy net to several other classifiers. The WAVE data consist of 21-dimensional continuous-valued feature vectors coming from three classes with equal *a priori* probability. Each class of data is generated by combining it with noise two of the three waveforms of Fig. 12 at 21 sampled positions (see [19] for details).

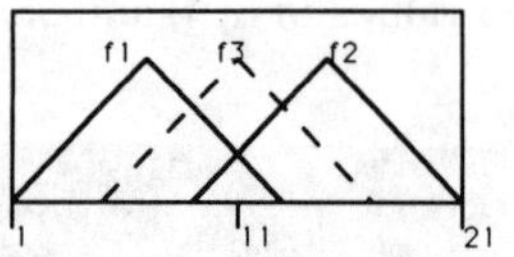

Fig. 12. Three basic functions to generate waveform data.

The training data set consists of 300 examples that were used to design the tree. The same set of examples was then used to train the entropy net. The test data have 5000 vectors. Using the training vectors, the AMIG algorithm produced the decision tree of Fig. 13 for waveform classification. The

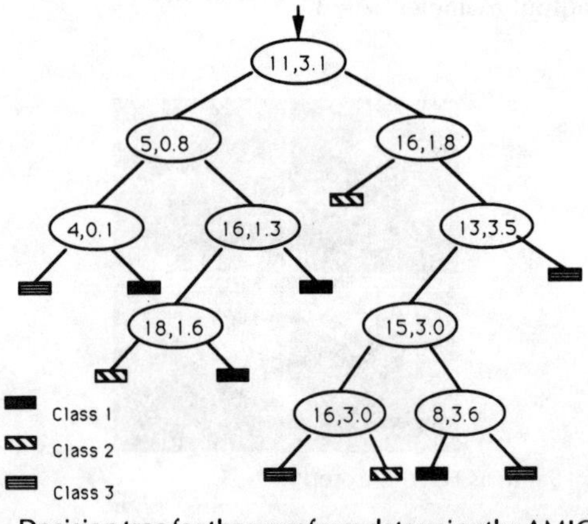

Fig. 13. Decision tree for the waveform data using the AMIG algorithm. The first number at each internal node represents a feature axis, and the second number corresponds to a threshold value on that axis.

two numbers within each internal node of the tree respectively represent the feature axis and the threshold value on that axis. There are only 8 features out of 21 features that are presented in the tree. This indicates that the tree has already acquired the ability to discriminate between the important and nonimportant features of the problem as far as the classification task is concerned.

To determine the learning progress of the entropy net, it was decided to perform classification on the test data after every ten iterations of weight adjustment with the training data and use the error rate on the test data as a measure of learning. Both of the layers were trained simultaneously. The initial choice for the weights was made randomly. The training procedure was repeated many times with different initial weight values. No significant differences, either in terms of the number of iterations or the error rate, were noticed due to initial weight selection. In all of the cases, stable classification performance was attained within 40 iterations. The best classification performance was obtained for an α value of 2.0. Next, a number of classification experiments were performed to gauge the effectiveness of the entropy net. These experiments include entropy net training using the backpropagation program of the PDP software [27]. In this case, the learning rate of 0.5 was found unsuitable in terms of the number of iterations and classification performance. However, using the learning rate of 0.1 resulted in stable performance with 40 iterations. Another entropy net mapping the decision tree given in [19] for the same problem was also realized and trained.

Fig. 14 summarizes the classification performance of several classifiers and the entropy net for different cases. These classifiers include the decison tree of Fig. 13, the decision tree from [19], and a nearest neighbor classifier that uses the training set as its database. It is seen that the entropy net, whether trained using the LMS rule or backpropagation, provides an improvement over the tree classifier performance because of the adaptability arising due to the use of sigmoid nonlinearity. In all three realizations of the entropy net, the performance is either better than the nearest neighbor performance or it is almost the same. The relative performance levels attained by different classifiers are similar to other studies for different classification tasks [8]. The shorter training time for the entropy net using the LMS rule or backpropagation also confirms the findings of other researchers that matching the network structure to the problem leads to less training time [1], [8].

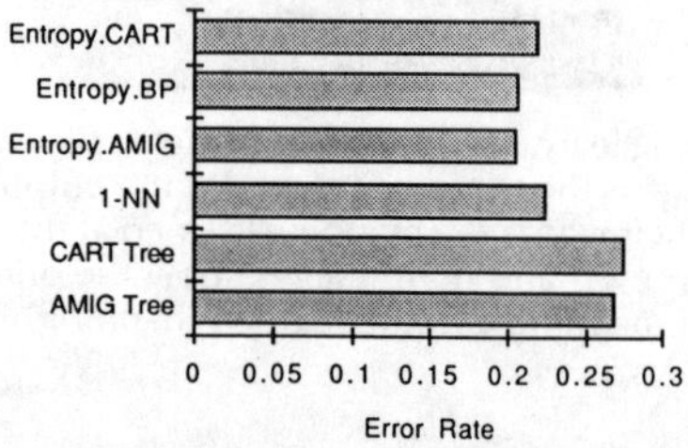

Fig. 14. Error rate for different classifiers for the waveform recognition problem. Entropy.BP represents the results when the entropy net for the AMIG tree was trained using backpropagation.

VI. Summary and Conclusions

A new neural network design methodology has been presented in this paper. This methodology has been developed by exploiting the similarities between the hierarchical classifiers of the traditional pattern recognition literature and the multiple-layer neural networks. It has been shown that the decision trees can be restructured as three-layer neural networks, called entropy networks. The entropy network architecture has the advantage of relatively fewer neural connections, which is an attractive feature from the VLSI fabrication point of view. Since it is possible to automatically generate decison trees using data-driven procedures, the tree-to-layered-network mapping rules provide a systematic tool to obtain layered network architecture. One very important property of the entropy network architecture is that the problem of credit assignment does not exist for these networks as it is automatically solved during the tree learning stage. The issues of incremental learning and generalization have been discussed, and the importance of soft nonlinearities has been stressed. Finally, a two-stage procedure has been given where the dominant aspects of the problem are learned during the tree development phase and the generalization of the learned knowledge takes place via the entropy network training. The effectiveness of the proposed methodology has been shown through two examples.

It needs to be mentioned that the tree-to-network mapping approach is not without any flaws. Because of the use of a single feature at each node during the tree design, it is possible in many cases, the EX-OR problem for one, to end up with very large trees. One possible solution to avoid very large trees is to apply the Hotelling or principal component transformation [28] to the data first. In terms of the entropy network, it is equivalent to adding an extra representation stage giving rise to a network which can be appropriately called a *hoteling-entropy* net. Such networks are currently under study, along with a study on the limitations of partially connected networks in comparison to fully connected feedforward networks with respect to missing data and broken connections.

ACKNOWLEDGMENT

I gratefully acknowledge the assistance of N. Ramesh, M. Otten, and G. Yu in running some experiments for me. I also thank Prof. A. Jain for many useful discussions.

REFERENCES

[1] D. J. Burr, "Experiments on neural net recognition of spoken and written text," *IEEE Trans. Acoust, Speech, Signal Processing*, vol. 36, pp. 1162–1168, July 1988.
[2] R. P. Lippmann, "An introduction to computing with neural nets," *IEEE ASSP Mag.*, pp. 4–22, Apr. 1987.
[3] A. Wieland and R. Leighton, "Geometric analysis of neural network capabilities," in *Proc. IEEE Int. Conf. Neural Networks, Vol. III*, San Diego, CA, June 1987, pp. 385–392.
[4] D. E. Rumelhart, G. E. Hinton, and R. J. Williams, "Learning internal representation by error propagation," in D. E. Rumelhart and J. L. McClelland, Eds., *Parallel Distributed Processing: Explorations in the Microstructure of Cognition. Vol. 1: Foundations.* Cambridge, MA: M.I.T. Press, 1986.
[5] D. H. Ackley, G. E. Hinton, and T. J. Sejnowski, "A learning algorithm for Boltzmann machines," *Cognitive Sci.*, vol. 9, pp. 147–169, 1985.
[6] R. Hecht-Nielsen, "Counterpropagation networks," *Appl. Opt.*, vol. 26, pp. 4979–4984, Dec. 1987.
[7] B. Widrow, R. G. Winter, and R. A. Baxter, "Layered neural nets for pattern recognition," *IEEE Trans. Acoust., Speech, Signal Processing*, vol. 36, pp. 1109–1118, July 1988.
[8] W. Y. Huang and R. P. Lippmann, "Comparison between neural net and conventional classifers," in *Proc. IEEE 1st Int. Conf. Neural Networks, Vol. IV*, San Diego, CA, June 1987, pp. 485–493.
[9] L. N. Kanal, "Problem-solving models and search strategies for pattern recognition," *IEEE Trans. Pattern Anal. Machine Intell.*, vol. PAMI-1, pp. 194–201, Apr. 1979.
[10] H. J. Payne and W. S. Meisel, "An algorithm for constructing optimal binary decision trees," *IEEE Trans. Comput.*, vol. C-25, pp. 905–916, Sept. 1977.
[11] L. A. Akers, M. R. Walker, D. K. Ferry, and R. O. Grodin, "Limited interconnectivity in synthetic neural systems," in R. Eckmiller and C. v.d. Malsburg, Eds., *Neural Computers.* New York: Springer-Verlag, 1988.
[12] C. R. P. Hartmann, P. K. Varshney, K. G. Mehrotra, and C. L. Gerberich, "Application of information theory to the construction of efficient decision trees," *IEEE Trans. Inform. Theory*, vol. IT-28, pp. 565–577, July 1982.
[13] I. K. Sethi and B. Chaterjee, "Efficient decision tree design for discrete variable pattern recognition problems," *Pattern Recognition*, vol. 9, pp. 197–206, 1978.
[14] ——, "A learning classifier scheme for discrete variable pattern recognition problems," *IEEE Trans. Syst., Man, Cybern.*, vol. SMC-8, pp. 49–52, Jan. 1978.
[15] J. C. Stoffel, "A classifer design technique for discrete variable pattern recognition problems," *IEEE Trans. Comput.*, vol. C-23, pp. 428–441, 1974.
[16] E. G. Henrichon and K. S. Fu, "A nonparametric partitioning procedure for pattern classification," *IEEE Trans. Comput.*, vol. C-18, pp. 614–624, July 1962.
[17] I. K. Sethi and G. P. R. Sarvarayudu, "Hierarchical classifier design using mutual information," *IEEE Trans. Pattern Anal. Machine Intell.*, vol. PAMI-4, pp. 441–445, July 1982.
[18] J. L. Talmon, "A multiclass nonparametric partitioning algorithm," in E. S. Gelsema and L. N. Kanal, Eds., *Pattern Recognition in Practice II.* Amsterdam: Elsevier Science Pub. B. V. (North-Holland), 1986.
[19] L. Breiman, J. Friedman, R. Olshen, and C. J. Stone, *Classification and Regression Trees.* Belmont, CA: Wadsworth Int. Group, 1984.
[20] L. Hyafil and R. L. Rivest, "Constructing optimal binary decision trees is NP-complete," *Inform. Processing Lett.*, vol. 5, pp. 15–17, 1976.
[21] R. M. Fano, *Transmission of Information.* New York: Wiley, 1963.
[22] R. M. Goodman and P. Smyth, "Decision tree design from a communication theory standpoint," *IEEE Trans. Inform. Theory*, vol. 34, pp. 979–994, Sept. 1988.
[23] J. R. Quinlan, "Induction of decision trees," *Machine Learning*, vol. 1, pp. 81–106, 1986.
[24] T. Kohonen, *Self-Organization and Associative Memory.* Berlin: Springer-Verlag, 1984.
[25] C. J. Matheus and W. E. Hohensee, "Learning in artifical neural systems," Univ. of Illnois, Urbana, Tech. Rep. TR-87-1394, 1987.
[26] B. Widrow and M. E. Hoff, "Adaptive switching circuits," in *1960 IRE WESCON Conv. Rec.*, part 4, 1960, pp. 96–104.
[27] J. L. McClelland and D. E. Rumelhart, *Explorations in Parallel Distributed Processing.* Cambridge, MA: M.I.T. Press, 1988.
[28] R. O. Duda and P. E. Hart, *Pattern Classification and Scene Analysis.* New York: Wiley, 1973.

A Performance Comparison of Trained Multilayer Perceptrons and Trained Classification Trees

LES ATLAS, MEMBER, IEEE, RONALD COLE, YESHWANT MUTHUSAMY, STUDENT MEMBER, IEEE, ALAN LIPPMAN, JEROME CONNOR, DONG PARK, MOHAMED EL-SHARKAWI, SENIOR MEMBER, IEEE, AND ROBERT J. MARKS II, SENIOR MEMBER, IEEE

Multilayer Perceptrons and trained classification trees are two very different techniques which have recently become popular. Given enough data and time, both methods are capable of performing arbitrary nonlinear classification. We first consider the important differences between multilayer Perceptrons and classification trees and conclude that there is not enough theoretical basis for the clear-cut superiority of one technique over the other. For this reason, we performed a number of empirical tests on three real-world problems in power system load forecasting, power system security prediction, and speaker-independent vowel recognition. In all cases, even for piecewise-linear trees, the multilayer Perceptron performed as well as or better than the trained classification trees.

I. Introduction

We use and compare two types of regression and classification systems. A regression system generates an output Y for an input X, where both X and Y are continuous and perhaps multidimensional. A classification system generates an output class C for an input X, where X is continuous and multidimensional and C is a member of a finite alphabet.

The use of trained classification and regression systems has been studied by many researchers in the past (see, for example, [1]–[4]). However, there has been a recent surge of interest in trainable systems such as artificial neural networks (ANNs). In particular it has been shown that the multilayer Perceptron (MLP) can be trained by example to solve the nonlinearly separable exclusive-OR problem [5], and this architecture has been linked to previous neural-like processors [6], [7]. Less known to the engineering community is the statistical technique of classification and regression trees (CART) which was developed during the years 1973 through 1984 [8], [9].

CART, like the MLP, can be trained to solve the exclusive-OR problem, the solution it provides is extremely easy to interpret, and both CART and MLPs are able to approximate arbitrary nonlinear decision boundaries. Although there have been no links made between CART and biological neural networks, the possible applications and paradigms used for MLP and CART are very similar.

The authors of this paper represent diverse interests in problems which have the commonality of being important and potentially well suited for trainable classifiers. The *load forecasting* problem, which is partially a regression problem, uses past load trends to predict the critical needs of future power generation. The *power security* problem uses the classifier as an interpolator of previously known states of the system. The *vowel recognition* problem is representative of the difficulties in automatic speech recognition caused by variability across speakers and phonetic context.

In each problem area, large amounts of real data were used for training and disjoint data sets were used for testing. We were careful to ensure that the experimental conditions were identical for the MLP and CART. We concentrated only on performance as measured in error on the test set and did no formal studies of training or testing time. (CART was, in general, quite a bit faster in training and testing.)

In all cases, even with various sizes of training sets, the multilayer Perceptron performed as well as or better than the trained classification trees. We also believe that integration of many of CART's well-designed attributes into MLP architectures could only improve the already promising performance of MLPs.

Manuscript received September 1, 1989; revised March 16, 1990. This work was supported by a National Science Foundation Presidential Young Investigator Award for L. Atlas and by separate grants from the National Science Foundation, Washington Technology Center, U.S. West Advanced Technologies, and Puget Sound Power and Light Co.

L. Atlas, J. Connor, D. Park, M. El-Sharkawi and R. J. Marks II are with the Dept. of Electrical Engineering, University of Washington, Seattle, WA 98195, USA.

R. Cole and Y. Muthusamy are with the Dept. of Computer Science and Engineering, Oregon Graduate Center, Beaverton, Oregon 97006-1999 USA.

A. Lippman is with the School of Oceanography, University of Washington, Seattle, WA 98195, USA.

IEEE Log Number 9037385.

Reprinted from *Proc. IEEE*, vol. 78, no. 10, Oct. 1990, pp. 1614–1619.

II. Background

A. Multilayer Perceptrons

The name "artificial neural networks" has in some communities become almost synonymous with MLPs trained by backpropagation. Our power studies made use of this standard algorithm [5] and our vowel studies made use of a conjugate gradient version [10] of backpropagation. In all cases the training data consisted of ordered pairs $\{(X, Y)\}$ for regression, or $\{(X, C)\}$ for classification. The input to the network is X and the output is, after training, hopefully very close to Y or C.

When MLPs are used for regression, the output Y can take on real values between 0 and 1. This normalized scale was used as the prediction value in the power forecasting problem. For MLP classifiers the output is formed by taking the (0, 1) range of the output neurons and either thresholding or finding a peak. For example, in the vowel study we chose the maximum of the 12 output neurons to indicate the vowel class.

B. Classification and Regression Trees (CART)

CART has already proven to be useful in diverse applications such as radar signal classification, medical diagnosis, and mass spectra classification. Given a set of training examples $\{(X, C)\}$, a binary tree is constructed by sequentially partitioning the p-dimensional input space, which may consist of quantitative and/or qualitative data, into p-dimensional polygons. The trained classification tree divides the domain of the data into nonoverlapping regions, each of which is assigned a class label C. For regression, the estimated function is piecewise constant over these regions.

The first split of the data space is made to obtain the best global separation of the classes. The next step in CART is to consider the partitioned training examples as two completely unrelated sets—those examples on the left of the selected hyperplane, and those on the right. CART then proceeds as in the first step, treating each subject of the training examples independently. A question that had long plagued the use of such sequential schemes was: when should the splitting stop? CART implements a novel, and very clever approach; splits continue until every training example is separated from every other, then a pruning criterion is used to sequentially remove less important splits.

The CART system was trained using two separate computer routines. One was the CART program from California Statistical Software; the other was a routine we designed ourselves. We produced our own routine to ensure a careful and independent test of the CART concepts described in [9].

C. Relative Expectations of MLP and CART

The nonlinearly separable exclusive-OR problem is an example of one that both MLP and CART can solve with zero error. In Fig. 1(a)—a trained MLP solution to this problem—the values along the arrows represent trained multiplicative weights and the values. In Fig. 1(b)—the very simple trained CART solution—y and n represent yes or no answers to the trained threshold and the values in the circles represent the output Y. It is interesting that CART did not train correctly for equal numbers of the four different input cases and that

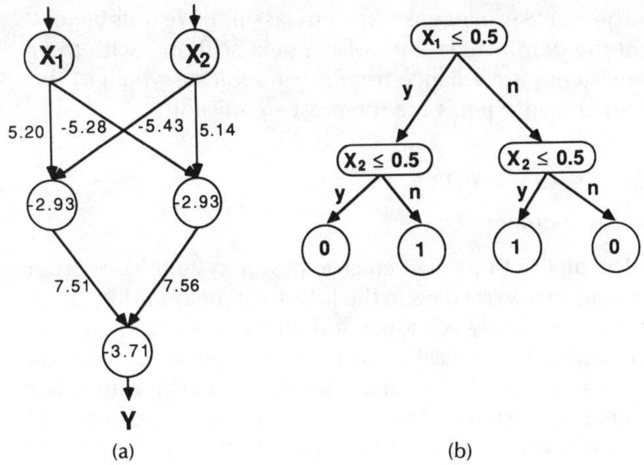

Fig. 1. (a) A multilayer perceptron (MLP) and (b) a classification tree. Both were trained to perfectly solve the exclusive-OR problem.

one extra example of one of the input cases was sufficient to break the symmetry and allow CART to train correctly. (Note the similarity to the well-known requirement of random and different initial weights for the MLP.)

CART trains on the exclusive-OR very easily since a piecewise-linear partition in the input space is a perfect solution. In general, the MLP will construct classification regions with smooth boundaries, whereas CART will construct regions with "sharp" corners (each region being, as described previously, an intersection of half planes.) We would thus expect MLP to have an advantage when classification boundaries tend to be smooth and CART to have an advantage when they are sharper.

Other important differences between MLP and CART include:

1) For an MLP the number of hidden units can be selected to avoid overfitting or underfitting the data. CART fits the complexity by using an automatic pruning technique to adjust the size of the tree. The selection of the number of hidden units or the tree size was implemented in our experiments by using data from a second training set (independent of the first).

2) An MLP becomes a classifier through an ad hoc application of thresholds or peak-picking to the output value(s). Great care has gone into the CART splitting rules while the usual MLP approach is rather arbitrary.

3) A trained MLP represents an approximate solution to an optimization problem. The solution may depend on initial choice of weights and on the optimization technique used. For complex MLPs many of the units are independently and simultaneously adjusting their weights to best minimize output error.

4) MLP is a distributed topology where a single point in the input space can have an effect across all units or analogously, one weight, acting alone, will have minimal effect on the outputs. CART is very different in that each split value can be mapped onto one segment in the input space. The behavior of CART makes it much more useful for data interpretation. A trained tree may be useful for understanding the structure of the data. The usefulness of MLPs for data interpretation is much less clear.

The above points, when taken in combination, do not make a clear case for either MLP or CART to be superior for the best performance as a trained classifier. We thus believe that the empirical studies of the next sections, with their consistent performance trends, will indicate which of the comparative aspects are the most significant.

III. Load Forecasting

A. The Problem

The ability to predict electric power system loads from an hour to several days in the future can help a utility operator to efficiently schedule and utilize power generation. This ability to forecast loads can also provide information that can be used to strategically trade energy with other generating systems. In order for these forecasts to be useful to an operator, they must be accurate and computationally efficient.

B. Methods

Hourly temperature and load data for the Seattle/Tacoma area were provided for us by the Puget Sound Power and Light Company. Forecasting for weekdays is a more critical problem for the power industry than for weekends and we selected the hourly data for all Tuesdays through Fridays in the interval of November 1, 1988 through January 31, 1989. These data consisted of 1368 hourly measurements from a total of 57 days.

These data were presented to both the MLP and the CART systems as a 6-dimensional input with a single, real-valued output. The MLP required that all values be normalized to the range (0, 1). These same normalized values were used with the CART technique. Our training and testing process consisted of training the classifiers on 523 days of the data and testing on the 4 days left over at the end of January 1989. Our training set consisted of 1272 hourly measurements and our test set contained 96 different hourly readings.

Several techniques of input and output pairing were tried; after some investigation we found that a good choice of data organization for our trainable classifier was

$$(X, Y) = (k, L_{k-2}, L_{k-1}, T_{k-2}, T_{k-1}, T_k, L_k)$$

where k was the hour (1–24) of the day and L_i and T_j signified the load and temperature at the ith and jth hour, respectively. The input thus consists of the hour, two previous load and temperature readings, and the current temperature. The actual current temperature was used during training and the predicted temperature was used during testing, thus representing the actual technique of relying upon weather reports. The output part is the predicted load L_k.

The MLP we used in these experiments had 6 inputs (plus the trained constant bias term), 10 units in one hidden layer, and one output. This topology was chosen by making use of data outside the training and test sets.

C. Results

We used an l_1 norm for the calculation of error rates and found that both techniques worked quite well. The average error rate was 1.39% for the MLP and 2.86% for CART. Although this difference (given the number of testing points) is not statistically significant, it is worth noting that the trained MLP offers performance at least as good as the current techniques used by the Puget Sound Power and Light Company and is currently being verified for application to future load prediction.

Figure 2 shows a detail of the comparative forecasting performance for three days. The daily periodicity in hourly loads was followed quite well by both techniques, and the MLP performed somewhat better than CART around the peaks in load.

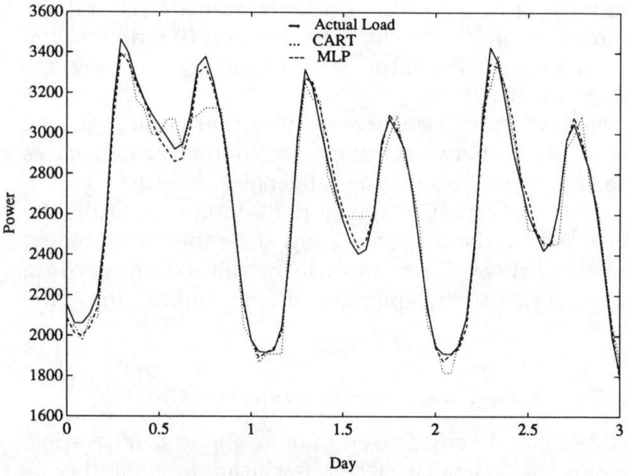

Fig. 2. A comparison of the performance of an MLP and CART (with linear combinations) in predicting three days of hourly power loads in megawatts.

IV. Power System Security

The assessment of security in a power system is an ongoing problem for the efficient and reliable generation of electric power. Static security addresses whether, after a disturbance such as a line break or other rapid load change, the system will reach a steady-state operating condition that does not violate any operating constraint and cause a "brownout" or "blackout."

The most efficient generation of power is achieved when the power system is operating near its insecurity boundary. In fact, the ideal case for efficiency would be the full knowledge of the absolute boundaries of the secure regions. The complexity of the power systems makes this full knowledge impossible. Load flow algorithms, which are based on iterative solutions of nonlinearly constrained equations, are conventionally used to slowly and accurately determine points of security or insecurity. In real systems the trajectories through the regions are not predictable in fine detail. Also, these changes can happen too fast to compute new results from the accurate load-flow equations.

We thus propose to use the sparsely known solutions of the load flow equations as a training set. The test set consists of points of unknown security. The error of the test set can then be computed by comparing the result of the trained classifier to load flow equation solutions.

Our technique for converting this problem to a problem for a trainable classifier involves defining a training set $\{(X, C)\}$ where X is composed of real power, reactive power, and apparent power at another bus. This three-dimensional input vector is paired with the corresponding security status ($C = 1$ for secure and $C = 0$ for insecure). Since the system was small, we were able to generate a large number of data points for training and testing. In fact, well over 20 000 total data points were available for the (disjoint) training and test sets.

A. Results

We observed that for any choice of training data set size, the error rate for the MLP was always lower than the rate for the CART classifier. This performance difference is illustrated in Fig. 3. For 10 000 points of training data, the MLP

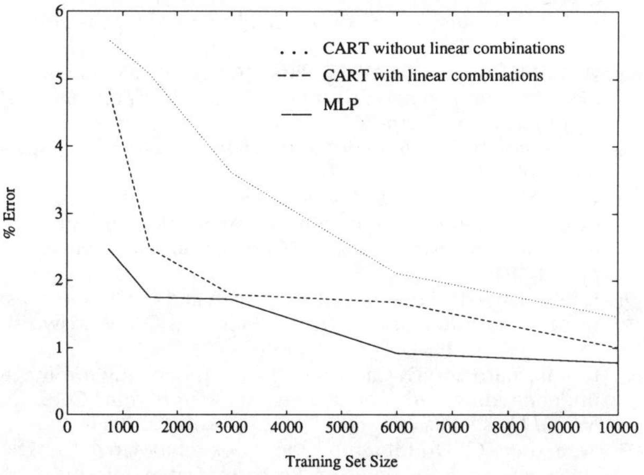

Fig. 3. The error rate in security prediction for the MLP and two versions of CART.

had an error rate of 0.78% and CART (using linear combinations) had an error rate of 1.46%. Although both of these results are impressive, the difference was statistically significant ($p > 0.99$).

In order to gain insight into the reasons for differences in importance, we looked at classifier decisions for two-dimensional slices of the input space. While the CART boundary sometimes was a better match, certain pathological difficulties made CART more error-prone than the MLP. Our other studies also showed that there were worse interpolation characteristics for CART, especially for sparse data. Apparently, starting with nonlinear combinations of inputs, which is what the MLP does, reduced error better than the piecewise linear fit of CART.

V. Speaker-Independent Vowel Classification

Speaker-independent classification of vowels excised from continuous speech is a most difficult task because of the many sources of variability that influence the physical realization of a given vowel. These sources of variability include the length of the speaker's vocal tract, phonetic context in which the vowel occurs, speech rate, and syllable stress.

To make the task even more difficult, the classifiers were presented only with information from a single spectral slice. The spectral slice, represented by 64 DFT coefficients (0–4 kHz), was taken from the center of the vowel, where the effects of coarticulation with surrounding phonemes are least apparent.

The training and test sets for the experiments consisted of featural descriptions X paired with an associated class C for each vowel sample. The 12 monophthongal vowels of English were used for the classes, as heard in the following words: b*ea*t, b*i*t, b*e*t, b*a*t, ros*e*s, th*e*, b*u*t, b*oo*t, b*oo*k, b*ou*ght, c*o*t, b*ir*d. The vowels were excised from a wide variety of phonetic contexts in utterances of the TIMIT database, a standard acoustic phonetic corpus of continuous speech, displaying a wide range of American dialectical variation [11], [12]. The training set consisted of 4104 vowels from 320 speakers. The test set consisted of 1644 vowels (137 occurrences of each vowel) from a different set of 100 speakers.

The MLP consisted of 64 inputs (the DFT coefficients, each normalized between zero and one), a single hidden layer of 40 units, and 12 output units (one for each vowel category). The networks were trained using backpropagation with conjugate gradient optimization [10]. The procedure for training and testing a network proceeded as follows: The network was trained on 100 iterations through the 4104 training vectors. The trained network was then evaluated on the training set and a different set of 1644 test vectors (the test set). The network was then trained for an additional 100 iterations and again evaluated on the training and test sets. This process was continued until the network had converged; convergence was observed as a consistent decrease or leveling off of the classification percentage on the test data over successive sets of iterations.

A. Results

In order to better interpret the vowel classification results, we performed listening experiments on a subset of the vowels used in these experiments. The vowels were excised from their sentence context and presented in isolation. Five listeners first received training in the task by classifying 900 vowel tokens and receiving feedback about the correct answer on each trial. During testing, each listener classified 600 vowels from the test set (50 from each category) without feedback. The average classification performance on the test set was 51% correct, compared to chance performance of 8.3%. Details of this experiment are presented in [13]. When using the scaled spectral coefficients to train both techniques, the MLP correctly classified 47.4% of the test set while CART without linear combinations performed at only 38.2%.

One reason for the poor performance of CART without linear combinations may be that each coefficient (corresponding to energy in a narrow frequency band) contains little information when considered independently of the other coefficients. For example, reduced energy in the 1-kHz band may be difficult to detect if the energy in the 1.06-kHz band is increased by an appropriate amount. The CART classifier described in the preceding operates by making a series of inquiries about one frequency band at a time, an intuitively inappropriate approach.

We achieved our best CART results, 46.4%, on the test set by making use of arbitrary hyperplanes (linear combinations). This search-based approach gave results within 1% of the MLP results.

VI. Conclusions

In all cases the performance of the MLP was, in terms of percent error, better than CART. However, the difference in performance between the two classifiers was only significant (at the $p > 0.99$ level) for the power security problem.

There are several possible reasons for the sometimes

superior performance of the MLP technique, all of which we are currently investigating. One advantage may stem from the ability of MLP to easily find correlations between large numbers of variables. Although it is possible for CART to form arbitrary nonlinear decision boundaries, the efficiency of the recursive splitting process may be inferior to MLP's nonlinear fit. Another relative disadvantage of CART may be caused by the successive nature of node growth. For example, if the first split that is made for a problem turns out to be suboptimal given the successive splits, it becomes very inefficient to change the first split to be more suitable.

We feel that the careful statistics used in CART could also be advantageously applied to MLP. The superior performance of MLP is not yet indicative of best performance and it may turn out that careful application of statistics may allow further advancements in the MLP technique. Other input representations also might produce better performance for CART than for MLP.

New developments have been made in trained statistical classifiers since the development of CART. More recent techniques, such as projection pursuit [14], may prove as good as or superior to MLP. This continued interplay between MLP techniques and advanced statistics is a key part of our ongoing research.

Acknowledgment

The authors wish to thank Professor R. D. Martin of the University of Washington Department of Statistics and Professors Aggoune, Damborg, and Hwang of the University of Washington Department of Electrical Engineering for their helpful discussions. David Cohn and Carlos Rivera assisted with many of the experiments.

We would also like to thank Milan Casey Brace of Puget Power and Light for providing the load forecasting data.

References

[1] N. J. Nilsson, *Learning Machines*. New York: McGraw-Hill, 1965.

[2] A. G. Arkadev and E. M. Braverman, *Computers and Pattern Recognition*. Washington, D.C.: Thompson, 1966.

[3] W. S. Meisel, *Computer-Oriented Approache to Pattern Recognition*. New York: Academic Press, 1972.

[4] R. O. Duda and P. E. Hart, *Pattern Classification and Scene Analysis*. New York: Wiley, 1973.

[5] D. E. Rumelhart, G. E. Hinton, and R. J. Williams, "Learning internal representations by error propagation," ch. 2 in *Parallel Distributed Processing*, D. E. Rumelhart, J. L. McClelland, and the PDP Research Group. Cambridge, MA: M.I.T. Press, 1986.

[6] W. S. McCuloch and W. H. Pitts, "A logical calculus of the ideas imminent in nervous activity," *Bulletin of Mathematical Biophysics*, vol. 5, pp. 115–133, 1943.

[7] E. Rosenblatt, *Principles of Neurodynamics*. New York: Spartan Books, 1962.

[8] W. S. Meisel and D. A. Michalpoulos, "A partitioning algorithm with application in pattern classification and the optimization of decision trees," *IEEE Trans. Computers*, vol. C-22, pp. 93–103, 1973.

[9] L. Breiman, J. H. Friedman, R. A. Olshen and C. J. Stone, *Classification and Regression Trees*. Belmont, CA: Wadsworth International, 1984.

[10] P. E. Barnard and D. Casasent, "Image processing for image understanding with neural nets," *Proc. Intl. Joint Conf. on Neural Nets*. Washington, D. C., June 18–22, 1989.

[11] W. Fisher, G. Doddington, and K. Goudie-Marshall, "The DARPA Speech Recognition Research Database: Specification and Status," *Proc. of the Darpa Speech Recognition Workshop*, pp. 993–1000, Feb. 1986.

[12] L. Lamel, R. Kassel, and S. Seneff, "Speech database development: design and analysis of the acoustic-phonetic corpus," *Proc. of the DARPA Speech Recognition Workshop*, pp. 100–110, Feb. 1986.

[13] Y. Muthusamy, R. Cole, and M. Slaney, "Vowel information in a single spectral slice: Cochleagrams versus spectral slice: Cochleagrams versus spectrograms," *Proc. ICASSP '90*, Apr. 3–6, 1990 (to appear).

[14] J. H. Friedman and W. Stuetzle, "Projection pursuit regression," *J. Amer. Stat. Assoc.*, vol. 79, pp. 599–608, 1984.

Maximum *A Posteriori* Decision and Evaluation of Class Probabilities by Boltzmann Perceptron Classifiers

EYAL YAIR AND ALLEN GERSHO, FELLOW, IEEE

Invited Paper

Neural networks offer a valuable alternative to Bayesian classifiers in evaluating a posteriori class probabilities for classifying stochastic patterns. In contrast to the Bayesian classifier, the "neural" classifier makes no assumptions on the probabilistic nature of the problem, and is thus universal in the sense that it is not restricted to an underlying probabilistic model. Instead, it adjusts itself to a given training set by a learning algorithm, and thus, can learn the stochastic properties of the specific problem. Evaluation of the a posteriori probabilities can be computed, in principle, by stochastic networks such as the Boltzmann machine. However, these networks are computationally extremely inefficient. In this paper we show that the a posteriori class probabilities can be efficiently computed by a deterministic feedforward network which we call the Boltzmann Perceptron Classifier (BPC). Maximum a posteriori (MAP) classifiers are also constructed as a special case of the BPC. Structural relationship between the BPC and a conventional multilayer Perceptron (MLP) are given, and it is demonstrated that rather intricate boundaries between classes can be formed even with a relatively modest number of network units. Simulation results show that the BPC is comparable in performance to a Bayesian classifier although no assumptions on the probabilistic model of the problem are assumed for the BPC.

I. Introduction

Classification of stochastic patterns is a decision problem in which an observation $\mathbf{x}$, a random vector in the N-dimensional Euclidean space, is to be assigned to one of M possible decision categories of interest. The observation can be regarded as having been generated by a probabilistic model in which there are M sources (or classes), each is described by a *probability distribution function* (PDF), $Pr(\mathbf{x}|m)$, and an *a priori* probability (or prior) $Pr(m)$. At each time instant, a source $m \in \{1, \cdots, M\}$ is selected stochastically according to the *a priori* probability $Pr(m)$. Once chosen, the mth source generates a pattern vector $\mathbf{x}$ according to its own PDF $Pr(\mathbf{x}|m)$. The random vector $\mathbf{x}$ is the observed information available to the classifier, which has to select the best class for $\mathbf{x}$.

Traditionally, such a classification is performed by a *Bayesian classifier* which assigns the most probable class m^* to the observed data $\mathbf{x}$. Defining by $Pr(m|\mathbf{x})$ the probability of class m given that $\mathbf{x}$ was observed, the Bayesian classifier evaluates the following maximization scheme:

$$m^* = \underset{1 \le m \le M}{\text{argmax}} \{Pr(m|\mathbf{x})\}. \tag{1.1}$$

The quantities $Pr(m|\mathbf{x})$ are known as the *a posteriori* (or class) probabilities, and the Bayesian classifier thus supplies the *maximum a posteriori* (MAP) decision. To evaluate the *a posteriori* probabilities, Bayes' Rule can be used as follows:

$$Pr(m|\mathbf{x}) = \frac{Pr(m)\ Pr(\mathbf{x}|m)}{Pr(\mathbf{x})} \tag{1.2}$$

and since the denominator is independent of m, it is generally omitted in applying the maximization formula of (1.1).

The evaluation of the *a posteriori* probabilities using Bayes' Rule requires an *a priori* knowledge about the probability distribution functions of the sources and their priors. In most practical cases, this information is not available and thus, a probabilistic model is assumed. An assumption that is commonly made about the priors, when no information about them is available, is that they are all equal (i.e., no preference is made in choosing which source to use). The classifier then maximizes $Pr(\mathbf{x}|m)$, also called the likelihood of class m given $\mathbf{x}$, and is called a *maximum likelihood* classifier.

The need to have a specific probabilistic model is a major limitation of the Bayesian approach, and poor performance might be obtained if the true PDFs are different than those assumed by the model. The Bayesian classifier is thus severely restricted by the probabilistic model that was assumed.

In this paper, we show that neural network architectures may offer a valuable alternative to the Bayesian classifier,

Manuscript received August 19, 1989; revised March 15, 1990. This work was supported by the Weizmann Foundation for scientific research, the University of California MICRO program, Bell Communications Research, Bell-Northern Research, and Rockwell International Corporation.
E. Yair is with the IBM Scientific Center, Haifa, 32000, Israel.
A. Gersho is with the Center for Information Processing Research, Department of Electrical and Computer Engineering, University of California, Santa Barbara, CA 93106, USA.
IEEE Log Number 9039180.

Reprinted from *Proc. IEEE*, vol. 78, no. 10, Oct. 1990, pp. 1620–1628.

in which the *a posteriori* probabilities are computed with no *a priori* assumptions about the PDFs that generate the data. Rather than assuming certain types of PDFs for the input data, the "neural" classifier employs a general type of input–output mapping which is then designed to optimally comply with a given set of examples called the *training set*. The classifier is thus universal in the sense that it is not restricted by any set of *a priori* assumptions about the "world," and instead it learns the specific properties of the problem at hand from the training set.

One approach to obtain such a classifier is to define a stochastic network which, for a given data vector $\boldsymbol{x}$, chooses the classes stochastically in such a way that the probability of choosing each class will be that of the desired class probability. The network can be described by an irreducible finite-state Markov chain model which makes transitions between its states according to some prescribed stochastic transition rule. The classification is obtained by associating M subsets of states with the M classes and assessing the probabilities of attaining these states by observing the network at equilibrium and measuring their relative frequency of occurrence. These probabilities then serve as the actual class probabilities. The classifier is designed by shaping the equilibrium distribution of the Markov chain according to the training data by a learning algorithm which maximizes the similarity between the actual class probabilities and the desired ones. This approach overcomes the limitation of the Bayesian classifier since the network is not subject to *a priori* assumptions, and the learning is carried out by adjusting a general model to the specific details of the given problem.

Assuming that the stationary (or equilibrium) probability distribution function of the states is strictly positive (i.e., there is a nonzero probability of reaching any state from any other state), it can be written in exponential form as the Gibbs distribution

$$Pr(\boldsymbol{s}|\boldsymbol{x}) = \frac{1}{Z} e^{\beta H(\boldsymbol{s}|\boldsymbol{x})} \tag{1.3}$$

where $Pr(\boldsymbol{s}|\boldsymbol{x})$ denotes the probability of attaining a state vector $\boldsymbol{s}$ given that $\boldsymbol{x}$ was observed, $H(\boldsymbol{s}|\boldsymbol{x})$ is an arbitrary function of $\boldsymbol{s}$ and $\boldsymbol{x}$ called the *Hamiltonian* of the network, β is a nonnegative number called, for reasons to be discussed later, the *gain* parameter of the classifier, and Z is a normalization factor given by

$$Z = \sum_{\boldsymbol{s}} e^{\beta H(\boldsymbol{s}|\boldsymbol{x})} \tag{1.4}$$

where the sum is taken over all possible states. Hence, in the representation of (1.3), designing the equilibrium distribution $Pr(\boldsymbol{s}|\boldsymbol{x})$ is equivalent to the design of the Hamiltonian function.

Several methods to define the network (and its transition rules) such that the desired equilibrium Gibbs distribution is achieved were suggested recently. A general method (for a general Hamiltonian function), known as the Metropolis algorithm, was proposed in [1]. This algorithm is widely used in simulated annealing optimization procedures for which a Gibbs distribution is required [2]. Another technique to achieve the Gibbs distribution for a network of a binary state vector $\boldsymbol{s}$ and a quadratic Hamiltonian given by

$$H(\boldsymbol{s}|\boldsymbol{x}) = \tfrac{1}{2}\boldsymbol{s}'\boldsymbol{W}\boldsymbol{s} + \boldsymbol{s}'\boldsymbol{\delta} \tag{1.5}$$

for any symmetric zero-diagonal matrix $\boldsymbol{W}$ and any vector $\boldsymbol{\delta}$ (where $\boldsymbol{s}'$ denotes the transpose of $\boldsymbol{s}$), was proposed by Hinton *et al.* [3] and the network was called the *Boltzmann machine*. Choosing a quadratic Hamiltonian as above is especially suited to neural network architectures since it yields a network in which the computation can be performed in parallel by individual units. A Monte Carlo type learning algorithm was also proposed in [3] to design the network parameters ($\boldsymbol{W}$ and $\boldsymbol{\delta}$) based on a gradient descent technique for the Kullback–Leibler distortion function [4]. Finally, another algorithm, generalizing the approach of the Boltzmann machine for nonbinary units was given by Geman and Geman [5] under the name of the Gibbs Sampler. In this case, the units asynchronously evaluate local probabilities and make unconditional transitions according to these local distributions.

Several methods are therefore available to implement a stochastic network for pattern classification. Stochastic networks appear to offer a powerful alternative to Bayesian classifiers for cases in which the probabilistic nature of the problem is not known and any *a priori* assumptions should be avoided. However, no matter which technique is used to construct a Markov chain with the Gibbs equilibrium distribution, the computational complexity of the above techniques are extremely high. The use of Monte Carlo type learning, the complexity of achieving an equilibrium for the network, and the necessity to assess the state probabilities by observing random variables are major drawbacks for using such a stochastic scheme as a classifier in practical applications.

In the next section we present a significant improvement to the stochastic classifier by developing a deterministic scheme which has the same capabilities while being computationally manageable. We elaborate here on a previous study [6] and propose a deterministic network for the classifier which essentially evaluates the class probabilities of an underlying stochastic Markov model by a feedforward network. We call this scheme the *Boltzmann Perceptron Classifier* (BPC) since it is based on the same principles of the Boltzmann machine while its feedforward deterministic structure is similar to that of a multi-layer Perceptron. The derivation of the BPC from the stochastic Markov chain is accomplished by modifying the Hamiltonian function of (1.5) such that the class probabilities are analytically obtained from the Gibbs distribution. The BPC is computationally much simpler than its underlying stochastic Markov model, but yet is capable of generating the desired *a posteriori* probabilities and forming rather intricate class boundaries (when necessary) even with a relatively small number of units.

The outline of the paper is as follows. In Section II the BPC is derived from the Gibbs distribution as a layered feedforward network and its structural relation to a conventional multi-layer Perceptron (MLP) (such as described in [7]) is discussed. In Section III the high gain limit ($\beta \rightarrow \infty$) is discussed, and it is shown that the classifier then supplies a *maximum a posteriori* (MAP) decision for the input pattern. The class boundaries and the way in which they are formed are discussed in Section IV and it is demonstrated that the BPC is capable of forming rather intricate class boundaries even with a relatively small number of units. Experimental results with simulated data discussed in Section V show that the BPC is comparable in performance with a Bayesian classifier although no assumptions on the probabilistic model of the problem are assumed for the BPC.

II. The Multi-Class BPC

In this section, we develop a deterministic classifier which evaluates the class probabilities in a feedforward fashion. Suppose that the binary state vector s of a stochastic Markov chain is partitioned into two binary subvectors: v, y with dimensions J and M respectively, where M is the number of classes or decision categories of interest. Suppose also that the network has been brought to equilibrium (by any of the methods discussed in the previous section) with the Gibbs stationary joint distribution given by

$$Pr(v, y|x) = \frac{1}{Z} e^{\beta H(v,y|x)}. \quad (2.1)$$

The specific method used to achieve an equilibrium with the above distribution is irrelevant for the derivation of the BPC. We only use the fact that such a method exists, and analyze the equilibrium properties of the network.

The Hamiltonian of the network is defined, similarly to the one of the Boltzmann machine, by the following quadratic form

$$H(v, y|x) = v'Rx + y'Ax + v'Qy + v'c + y't \quad (2.2)$$

where the matrices A, R and Q are of dimensions $M \times N$, $J \times N$ and $J \times M$ respectively, and c and t are vectors of length J and M, respectively. The components of these quantities are the parameters specifying the classifier. In the following derivation we assume that these parameters have been supplied by a design (or learning) procedure that optimally estimates them so that the network achieves the best performance for some application of interest. An efficient learning algorithm suitable for the BPC was introduced in [6].

We are now interested in obtaining an efficient closed-form formula for the desired class probabilities $Pr(m|x)$ as a function of x using the above Hamiltonian function. Denote the natural basis of the M-dimensional Euclidean space by the set $E_M = \{e_1, \cdots, e_M\}$, where e_m is a vector of dimension M whose components are all zero except for the mth component which is equal to one. Let B_J denote the set of all binary vectors of length J. The probability of class m given a measurement vector x, $Pr(m|x)$, is defined to be the probability of attaining a state vector $s = (v, y)$ with $y = e_m$ and any $v \in B_J$. We may therefore restrict attention to the marginal distribution $Pr(s|x, y \in E_M)$, given by Bayes' Rule as

$$Pr(v, y|x, y \in E_M) = \frac{Pr(v, y \in E_M|x)}{\sum_{m=1}^{M} \sum_{v \in B_J} Pr(v, y = e_m|x)}. \quad (2.3)$$

The probability of class m given a pattern x is then given by

$$Pr(m|x) = Pr(y = e_m|x, y \in E_M)$$
$$= \sum_{v \in B_J} Pr(v, y = e_m|x, y \in E_M) \quad (2.4)$$

which, according to (2.3) and (2.1), can be expressed as

$$Pr(m|x) = \frac{1}{Z_x} \sum_{v \in B_J} e^{\beta H(v,m|x)} \quad (2.5)$$

where $H(v, m|x)$ is the Hamiltonian function evaluated with $y = e_m$, and

$$Z_x = \sum_{m=1}^{M} \sum_{v \in B_J} e^{\beta H(v,m|x)}. \quad (2.6)$$

Eq. (2.5), accompanied by (2.6), is a closed-form expression for the class probabilities as a function of the observation x. However, this expression is far from being efficient. The complexity of evaluating the summation over all possible $v \in B_J$ is $O(2^J)$, i.e., it grows exponentially with the number of network units, and this is practically unacceptable. We now show a simplification of (2.5) that evaluates $Pr(m|x)$ with a complexity of $O(J)$, which is linear with the number of units and will therefore be efficient for practical use.

Defining $L_m(x)$ to be

$$L_m(x) = \ln \left[\sum_{v \in B_J} e^{\beta H(v,m|x)} \right], \quad \text{for } m = 1, \cdots, M \quad (2.7)$$

the class probabilities can be written as

$$Pr(m|x) = \frac{e^{L_m(x)}}{\sum_{n=1}^{M} e^{L_n(x)}}, \quad \text{for } m = 1, \cdots, M. \quad (2.8)$$

By substituting the expression of the Hamiltonian from (2.2) with $y = e_m$ into (2.7), the quantities $L_m(x)$ can be expressed by

$$L_m(x) = \beta(a'_m x + t_m)$$
$$+ \ln \left[\sum_{v_1=0}^{1} \cdots \sum_{v_J=0}^{1} e^{\beta v'(Rx + q_m + c)} \right] \quad (2.9)$$

where a_m is the mth row of A, t_m is the mth component of t, q_m is the mth column of Q, and $v_1, \cdots, v_J$ are the components of the binary vector v. The second term in (2.9) can be simplified by using the separability of the exponent with respect to the J components $v_1, \cdots, v_J$ yielding

$$L_m(x) = \beta(a'_m x + t_m) + \sum_{j=1}^{J} \ln [1 + e^{\beta(r'_j x + c_j + q_{jm})}] \quad (2.10)$$

where r_j is the jth row of R, c_j is the jth component of c, and q_{jm} is the jmth entry of Q. Note that by using the particular form of the Hamiltonian given in (2.2) and the separability of the summation in (2.9) into the different components of the J-dimensional binary vector v, the complexity of evaluating $L_m(x)$ defined in (2.7) was reduced from exponential, $O(2^J)$, to linear, $O(J)$. This will result in the necessary reduction of complexity for $Pr(m|x)$ as well. If for any pair n, $m \in [1, M]$ we define

$$L_{nm}(x) \triangleq [L_n(x) - L_m(x)]/\beta \quad (2.11)$$

the desired class probabilities can then be expressed as

$$Pr(m|x) = \frac{1}{1 + \sum_{\substack{n=1 \\ n \neq m}}^{M} e^{-\beta L_{mn}(x)}}, \quad m = 1, \cdots, M. \quad (2.12)$$

To better understand the expression given for the class probabilities in (2.12) we can think of a classification of a pattern to one class in a set of possible classes as a *competition* between the classes, in which the pattern is classified to the *winning* class. In our case, the computation of the *a posteriori* probabilities via (2.12), a generalization of the logistic function

$$g_\beta(x) = \frac{1}{1 + e^{-\beta x}} \tag{2.13}$$

to M variables, represents a *soft competition* between the M classes, which results in a graded "scoring" for the different classes. Instead of having a sole winner, the classes share the total amount of unit probability, with $Pr(m|\mathbf{x})$ satisfying

$$\sum_{m=1}^{M} Pr(m|\mathbf{x}) = 1. \tag{2.14}$$

The BPC classifier is thus composed of two successive stages. In the first stage, which will be shown to be carried out by a two-layer Perceptron type network, the functions $L_{nm}(\mathbf{x})$, which we call the *decision functions*, are evaluated. In the second stage, a soft competition is carried out between the decision functions as depicted schematically in Fig. 1.

A *winner-take-all* competition, in which *only* one class, the most probable one, wins the competition, can be easily obtained by increasing the gain β. Note that if the gain is sufficiently large, the output probability distribution of (2.12) as a function of m is peaked around the most probable class, while the probabilities of all the other classes approach zero. In the limit as $\beta \to \infty$ there is only *one* winner since then $Pr(m|\mathbf{x})$ becomes a delta function around the most probable class. To realize this note that if $\beta \to \infty$, the class probability $Pr(m|\mathbf{x})$ is then either equal to one when $L_{mn}(\mathbf{x}) > 0$ for all $n = 1, \cdots, M$ and $n \neq m$, or to zero when not all the $L_{mn}(\mathbf{x})$ are positive. Note that from (2.14) only one of the $Pr(m|\mathbf{x})$ value can be unity. This means that the winning class m^* is the class for which $L_{m^*,n}(\mathbf{x}) > 0$ for all $n \neq m^*$, or, according to (2.11), $L_{m^*}(\mathbf{x}) > L_n(\mathbf{x})$ for all $n \neq m^*$. Hence, for an infinite value of the gain, the competition becomes a *winner-take-all* competition and the classifier supplies a *maximum a posteriori* (MAP) decision. In practice, due to the exponential dependency of the class probabilities upon the gain, a relatively moderate gain value (e.g., $\beta \approx$ 10–20) can be used to practically achieve the effect of an infinite gain.

A. Structural Properties of the BPC

As mentioned earlier, the decision functions $L_{nm}(\mathbf{x})$ can be evaluated by a layered Perceptron with sigmoid (S-shaped) nonlinearities. To demonstrate this structure we express (2.11) using (2.10) as

$$L_{nm}(\mathbf{x}) = \mathbf{a}'_{nm}\mathbf{x} + t_{nm} + \frac{1}{\beta}\sum_{j=1}^{J} \cdot \ln\left[\frac{1 + e^{\beta(\mathbf{r}_j'\mathbf{x} + c_j + q_{jn})}}{1 + e^{\beta(\mathbf{r}_j'\mathbf{x} + c_j + q_{jm})}}\right] \tag{2.15}$$

where $\mathbf{a}_{nm} = \mathbf{a}_n - \mathbf{a}_m$, and $t_{nm} = t_n - t_m$.

Let us define the following function, which will be the activation nonlinearity of the feedforward network:

$$f_q(x) \triangleq \frac{1}{\beta q}\ln\left[\frac{1 + e^{\beta q[x + (1/2)]}}{1 + e^{\beta q[x - (1/2)]}}\right] \tag{2.16}$$

for which it can be verified that

$$f_q(-x) = f_{-q}(x) = 1 - f_q(x). \tag{2.17}$$

The function $f_q(x)$ is a sigmoid function whose slope is governed by the weight q and the gain β. For low values of $|\beta q|$ the slope of $f_q(x)$ is moderate and it increases with $|\beta q|$. When $\beta \to \infty$, a situation which we call the *high gain limit*, the function $f_q(x)$ converges to an asymptotic function $\bar{f}(x)$ for $q > 0$ and to $\bar{f}(-x)$ for $q < 0$ where

$$\bar{f}(x) = \begin{cases} 0 & \text{for } x \leq -\frac{1}{2} \\ x + \frac{1}{2} & \text{for } -\frac{1}{2} < x < \frac{1}{2} \\ 1 & \text{for } x \geq \frac{1}{2}. \end{cases} \tag{2.18}$$

A function of the type of $\bar{f}(x)$ is called a linear-limiter (or a threshold-logic function [8]). An illustration of the function $f_q(x)$, which will be used as the activation nonlinearity of the BPC units, is given in Fig. 2 for several values of the gain $|\beta q|$.

By defining $q_{jnm} = q_{jn} - q_{jm}$ and making the following transformation of the network weights:

$$\mathbf{u}_{jnm} = \frac{1}{|q_{jnm}|}\mathbf{r}_j,$$
$$l_{jnm} = \frac{1}{|q_{jnm}|}\left(c_j + \frac{q_{jn} + q_{jm}}{2}\right) \tag{2.19}$$

it can be verified, using the odd-symmetry property in (2.17), that the decision function $L_{nm}(\mathbf{x})$ can be computed for any $n \neq m$ by the following two-layer sigmoidal Perceptron[1]

[1]Sigmoidal Perceptron is an MLP whose nonlinear activation functions are sigmoid (i.e., S-shaped) functions such as depicted in Fig. 2.

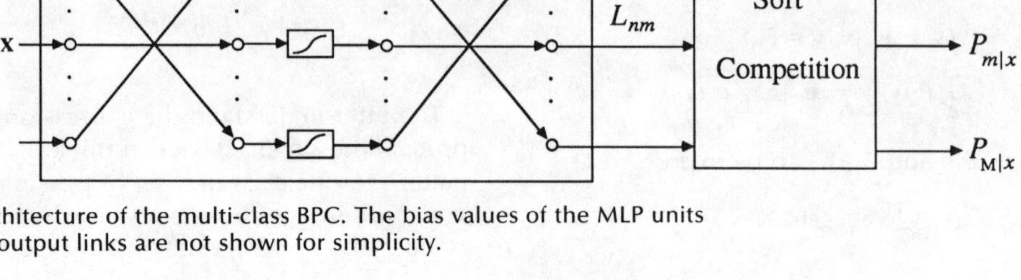

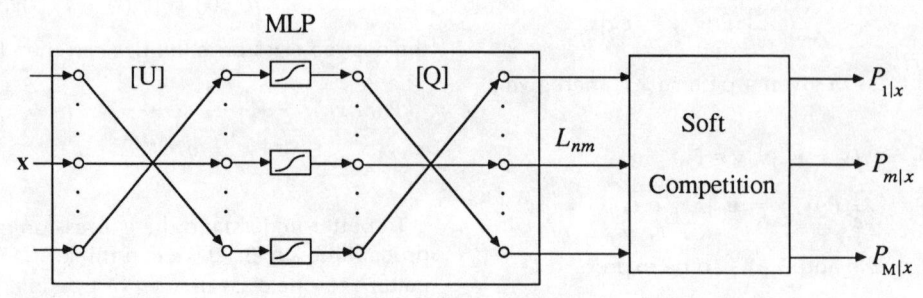

Fig. 1. Schematic architecture of the multi-class BPC. The bias values of the MLP units and the direct input–output links are not shown for simplicity.

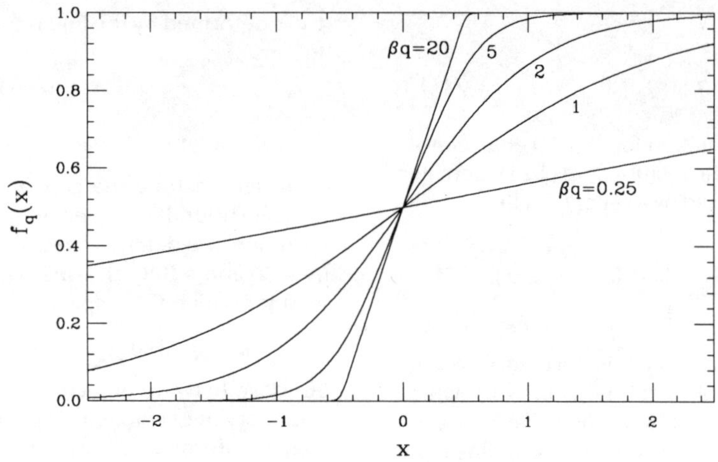

Fig. 2. The BPC nonlinearity, $f_q(x)$, for several values of βq. For $|\beta q| > 20$, $f_q(x)$ becomes, practically, equal to its asymptote, $\bar{f}(x)$.

$$y_{0nm} = \boldsymbol{a}'_{nm}\boldsymbol{x} + t_{nm},$$

$$y_{jnm} = \boldsymbol{u}'_{jnm}\boldsymbol{x} + l_{jnm}, \quad j = 1, \cdots, J \tag{2.20a}$$

$$L_{nm}(\boldsymbol{x}) = y_{0nm} + \sum_{j=1}^{J} q_{jnm} f_{|q_{jnm}|}(y_{jnm}). \tag{2.20b}$$

The first layer is comprised of $JM(M-1)$ hidden units with weights $\boldsymbol{u}_{jnm}$, bias values l_{jnm}, and the nonlinearity $f_q(\cdot)$, and the second layer has $M(M-1)$ units with weights q_{jnm}, bias values t_{nm}, and a direct input–output connection links $\boldsymbol{a}_{nm}$. The multi-class BPC, depicted in Fig. 1, is thus comprised of a two-layer sigmoidal MLP (2.20) followed by a soft-competition scheme (2.12).

III. The MAP-BPC

If a hard, rather than soft, decision is desired, in which only the most probable class for the input pattern is of interest rather than the exact class probabilities, the high gain limit can be used. We call this classifier the MAP-BPC because it supplies the *maximum a posteriori* decision for $\boldsymbol{x}$. When $\beta \to \infty$ the activation nonlinearities of the first layer become linear-limiter functions since $f_q(x)$ then approach their asymptotes $\bar{f}(x)$ (see (2.18)). The soft competition of (2.12) becomes a winner-take-all competition for which only the winning class is assigned a nonzero probability value according to

$$Pr(m|\boldsymbol{x}) = \begin{cases} 1 & \text{if } L_{mn}(\boldsymbol{x}) > 0 \text{ for all } n = 1, \cdots, M \\ & \quad \text{and } n \neq m \\ 0 & \text{otherwise.} \end{cases} \tag{3.1}$$

This scheme can be easily implemented by taking the logical AND of the signs of the quantities $L_{nm}(\boldsymbol{x})$ using hard-limiting nonlinearities. Denoting by $\bar{g}(x)$ the hard-limiting nonlinearity defined by: $\bar{g}(x) = 0$ for $x < 0$, and $\bar{g}(x) = 1$ otherwise, which is the asymptote of the logistic function $g_\beta(x)$ for the high gain limit, the MAP-BPC can thus be expressed by the following scheme:

$$y_{jnm}(\boldsymbol{x}) = \boldsymbol{u}'_{jnm}\boldsymbol{x} + l_{jnm}$$

$$L_{nm}(\boldsymbol{x}) = \boldsymbol{a}'_{nm}\boldsymbol{x} + t_{nm} + \sum_{j=1}^{J} q_{jnm}\bar{f}(y_{jnm}(\boldsymbol{x}))$$

$$Pr(m|\boldsymbol{x}) = \bar{g}\left[\tfrac{1}{2} - M + \sum_{n=1}^{M} \bar{g}(L_{mn}(\boldsymbol{x}))\right] \tag{3.2}$$

for which, for the simplicity of the notations, we assumed to have M^2 units in the second layer, including the trivial $L_{mm}(\boldsymbol{x}) = 0$. The above scheme is a three-layer Perceptron with linear-limiter nonlinearities in the first layer and hard-limiter nonlinearities in the last two layers. A schematic diagram of the MAP-BPC is given in Fig. 3.

IV. Class Boundaries Formed by the BPC

The boundary between any two classes n and m is given by the set of all $\boldsymbol{x} \in R^N$ that satisfy the implicit equation $L_{nm}(\boldsymbol{x}) = 0$, which is a subspace of dimension $N-1$ in the N-dimensional input space. Hereafter we refer to the *y-space* as the $(J+1)$-dimensional space described by the vector $\boldsymbol{y} = (y_0, \cdots, y_J)'$ whose components y_j are given by (2.20a) and the subscripts nm are omitted for simplicity. From (2.20b), the

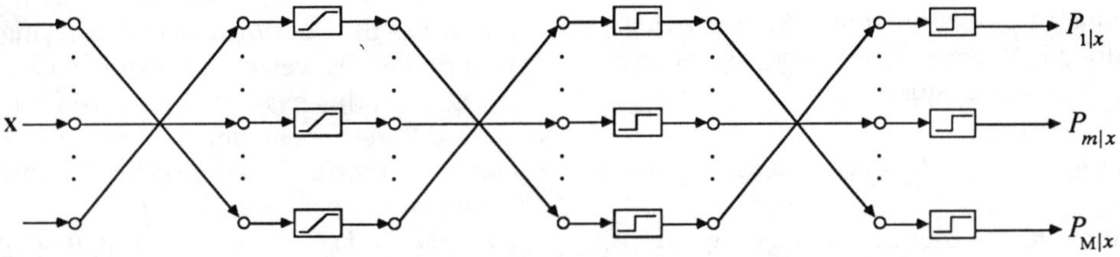

Fig. 3. Schematic diagram of the MAP-BPC classifier. Only one output is equal to one indicating the maximum *a posteriori* decision, while the rest of the outputs are equal to zero.

y-space boundary is given by

$$y_0 + \sum_{j=1}^{J} q_j f_j(y_j) = 0 \tag{4.1}$$

where $f_j(\cdot)$ is a shorthand notation for $f_{|q_j|}(\cdot)$. Let us denote by $\boldsymbol{u}_0 = \boldsymbol{a}$ and $l_0 = t$. Due to the relationship (2.20a) between $\boldsymbol{y}$ and $\boldsymbol{x}$ which can be expressed by a set of $J + 1$ linear equations

$$\boldsymbol{U}\boldsymbol{x} = \boldsymbol{y} - \boldsymbol{t} \quad \text{where: } \begin{array}{l} \boldsymbol{U} = [\boldsymbol{u}_0, \cdots, \boldsymbol{u}_J]' \\ \boldsymbol{t} = (l_0, \cdots, l_J)' \end{array} \tag{4.2}$$

not any $\boldsymbol{y}$ which is a solution to (4.1) is necessarily a valid solution for the boundary. Only solutions for $\boldsymbol{y}$ for which the set of linear equations of (4.2) can be solved for $\boldsymbol{x}$ are feasible. The three possible cases for the above linear set of equations are $J + 1 < N$, $J + 1 = N$, and $J + 1 > N$ which depend solely on the network structure. Obviously, the latter case is the most useful for most practical problems since the capability of the network to perform a desired classification increases with the number of hidden units. The following discussion thus concentrates on demonstrating how the boundary is formed in this case.

Let us assume that rank($\boldsymbol{U}$) = N where the first N rows of $\boldsymbol{U}$ are linearly independent, and denote these rows by the full-rank $N \times N$ matrix $\boldsymbol{U}_1$. The $J + 1 - N$ bottom rows of $\boldsymbol{U}$ are denoted by the $(J + 1 - N) \times N$ matrix $\boldsymbol{U}_2$. The rows of $\boldsymbol{U}_2$ can be represented by a linear combination of the rows of $\boldsymbol{U}_1$ as follows:

$$\boldsymbol{u}_k = \sum_{i=0}^{N-1} b_k(i)\boldsymbol{u}_i = \boldsymbol{U}_1'\boldsymbol{b}_k, \qquad k = N, \cdots, J \tag{4.3}$$

where $\boldsymbol{b}_k = (b_k(0), \cdots, b_k(N-1))'$ are quantities of the network, i.e., they depend only on the network weights, and thus are implicitly being designed in the learning phase. Eq. (4.3) can be also written in a compact form as $\boldsymbol{U}_2 = \boldsymbol{B}\boldsymbol{U}_1$ where $\boldsymbol{B} = [\boldsymbol{b}_N, \cdots, \boldsymbol{b}_J]'$. The coefficients $b_k(i)$ can thus be explicitly computed from the connection weights $\boldsymbol{U}$ of the first layer via

$$\boldsymbol{B} = \boldsymbol{U}_2\boldsymbol{U}_1^{-1}. \tag{4.4}$$

In order to allow a solution for $\boldsymbol{x}$, the same linear combination should be imposed on $\boldsymbol{y}$. Denoting by $\tilde{\boldsymbol{y}} = (y_0, \cdots, y_{N-1})'$, and by $\tilde{\boldsymbol{t}} = (l_0, \cdots, l_{N-1})'$, any solution $\boldsymbol{y}$ should satisfy

$$y_k = l_k + \boldsymbol{b}_k'(\tilde{\boldsymbol{y}} - \tilde{\boldsymbol{t}}), \qquad k = N, \cdots, J \tag{4.5}$$

which means that every y_k for $k = N, \cdots, J$ must be a linear combination of $y_0, \cdots, y_{N-1}$. Any feasible solution in the y-space must satisfy (4.1) and (4.5) which can be combined into one condition. Denoting by

$$\gamma_k = l_k - \boldsymbol{b}_k'\tilde{\boldsymbol{t}} = l_k - \boldsymbol{u}_k'\boldsymbol{U}_1^{-1}\tilde{\boldsymbol{t}}, \qquad k = N, \cdots, J \tag{4.6}$$

which are also quantities of the network, the y-space boundary in a reduced (N-dimensional) space is obtained by the set of solutions of the equation

$$y_0 + \sum_{j=1}^{N-1} q_j f_j(y_j) = -\sum_{j=N}^{J} q_j f_j(\gamma_j + \boldsymbol{b}_j'\tilde{\boldsymbol{y}}). \tag{4.7}$$

The boundary of the BPC can thus be formed in two steps, both of them are in the N-dimensional input space. First step is to form the y-boundary from all the solutions $\tilde{\boldsymbol{y}} \in R^N$ of (4.7). In the second step, this y-boundary is translated by $\tilde{\boldsymbol{t}}$ and deformed by the linear transformation $\boldsymbol{U}_1^{-1}$ according to

$$\boldsymbol{x} = \boldsymbol{U}_1^{-1}(\tilde{\boldsymbol{y}} - \tilde{\boldsymbol{t}}). \tag{4.8}$$

A. Example in a 2D Space

To demonstrate the capabilities of the BPC in forming intricate boundaries even with a small network we examine in some more details a specific example of a 2D input space ($N = 2$) and a BPC classifier with two hidden units ($J + 1 = 3$) for which the y-space boundary is given by

$$y_0 + q_1 f_1(y_1) = -q_2 f_2(\gamma_2 + b_2(0)y_0 + b_2(1)y_1). \tag{4.9}$$

Suppose that the objective of the classifier is to find the boundary between two 2D sources: (1) $\boldsymbol{x} \sim U[(0, 0), (10, 10)]$ (i.e., a uniform distribution on the square) and (2) $\boldsymbol{x} \sim N(\boldsymbol{\mu}, \Lambda)$ (i.e., a Gaussian distribution) with $\boldsymbol{\mu} = (4, 5)$ and $\Lambda_{11} = 1$, $\Lambda_{12} = \Lambda_{21} = 0.8$, $\Lambda_{22} = 3$. The Bayesian boundary is an ellipse in the 2D space as given in Fig. 5(a). We shall now see how this boundary can be formed by a BPC network with only two hidden units. Obviously many hidden units would have been required if this boundary were to be constructed by a union of many portions of hyperplanes (or lines in our 2D example) as in the case of a linear classifier. A BPC was designed for this problem by training the network using the learning algorithm given in [6] for 36 training patterns. Equations (2.19), (4.4), and (4.6) were used to obtain the pertinent variables $\boldsymbol{B}$, γ_k and $\boldsymbol{t}$ from the network weights. The left hand side of (4.9) is a linear function of y_0 "centered" at $y_0 = -q_1 f_1(y_1)$ while the right hand side is an increasing sigmoid function of y_0 centered at: $y_0 = -[b_2(1)y_1 + \gamma_2]/b_2(0)$. Hence, when y_1 is increased, these two curves are shifted along the y_0 axis. Regarding y_1 as a time variable, the sigmoid curve is shifted along the y_0 axis with a constant velocity $-b_2(1)/b_2(0)$, while the linear function is shifted with velocity $-q_1 f_1'(y_1)$ (where $f'(\cdot)$ is the derivative of $f(\cdot)$). In our example a closed ellipsoidal boundary is formed as illustrated in Figs. 4 and 5. The y-space boundary is then translated and rotated to its final position according to (4.8). The final result is given in Fig. 5(d) and is compared to the Bayesian boundary. Note that with *only* two hidden units and 36 training patterns the theoretical (Bayesian) boundary could have been approximated with a great deal of accuracy (Fig. 5(d)). The significance of such a property is that a compact network might be sufficient to solve complicated problems which, besides its computational efficiency, requires also a smaller amount of training data since the number of parameters to design is small.

V. Simulation Results

Simulation testing of the BPC with Gaussian, Laplacian and uniform sources showed that the BPC is comparable in performance with the Bayesian classifier. A typical example of the BPC performance in carrying out a soft classification task as well as supplying a MAP decision is given in Fig. 6. In this example there are four Gaussian sources (with different mean and variance values) which are associated with two classes. The PDFs $Pr(\boldsymbol{x}|m)$ of the four sources are given in Fig. 6(a), and the prior $Pr(m)$ of the sources are all equal. In Fig. 6(b) the performance in estimating the *a posteriori* class probability of class 1 by a BPC classifier having only four hidden units (marked by $\beta = 1$) is compared to the optimal (Bayesian) *a posteriori* probability (labeled by

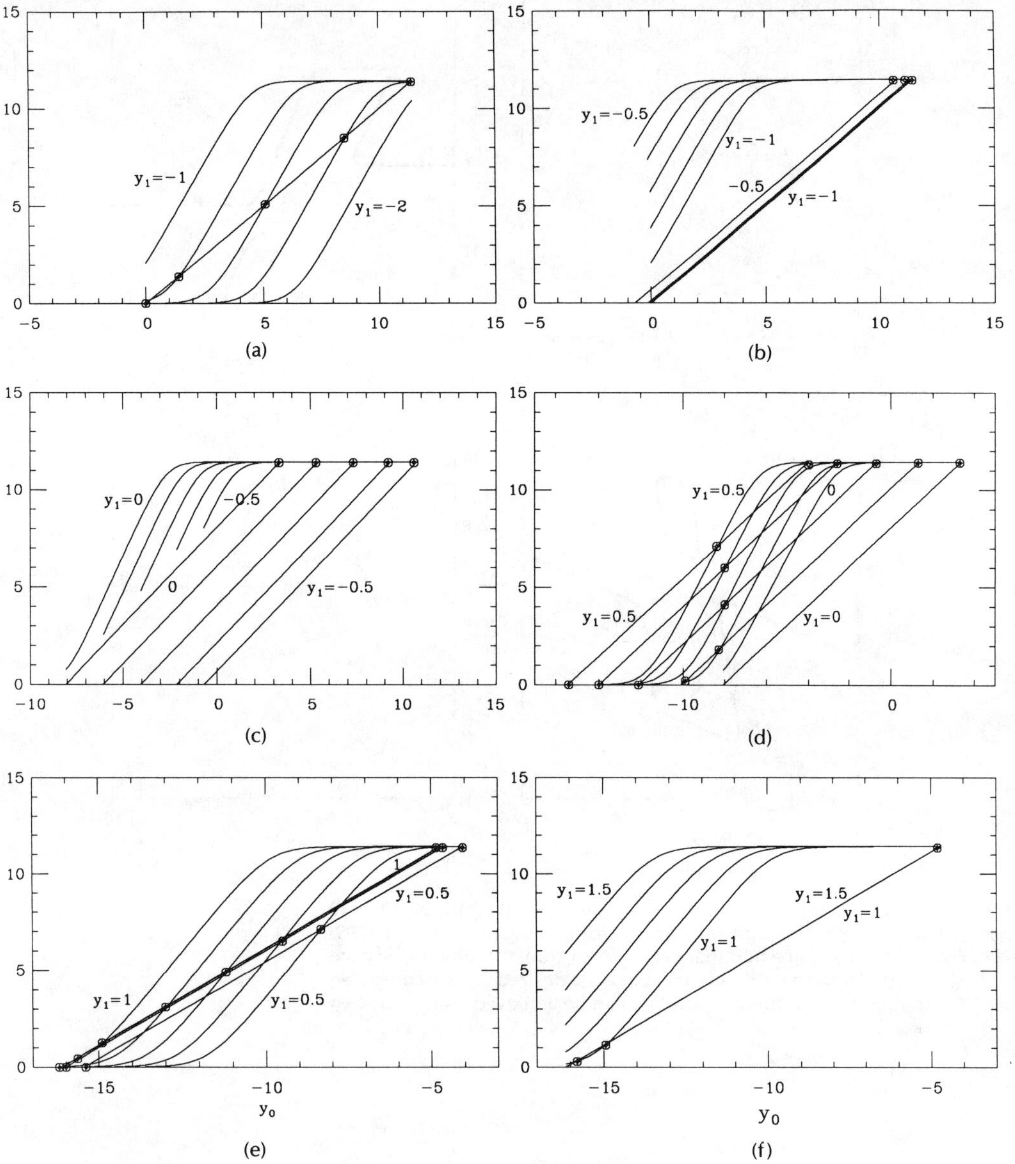

Fig. 4. Formation of the y-space boundary in the 2D example. In (a) through (f) y_1 is increased from $y_1 = -2$ to $y_1 = 1.5$ and the instantaneous relative positions of the two curves, the line and the sigmoid, are illustrated. In (a) y_1 is increased from -2 to -1. While the sigmoid is moving downward along the y_0 axis, the line is still not moving. The solutions (i.e., intersection points) for each value of y_1 are marked by the bullets. The movement of the line starts when $y_1 \approx 0.5$ (b) for which the sigmoid have already passed it. Then, the line starts accelerating (c) and intersects with the sigmoid again when $y_1 \approx 0$. In (d) we can observe the beginning of the construction of a closed region, as required by the given problem. This is completed in (e) when the line decelerates. Finally, in (f) the line "freezes" again, and from there on only one solution point remains. The trajectory of the boundary formed in the y-space is given in Fig. 5(b).

the letter B). The Bayesian probabilities were computed by (1.2) with the true Gaussian PDFs, while the BPC was designed from a training set of 30 samples drawn from the given problem. The results show that the BPC output is comparable to the Bayesian *a posteriori* probability although no assumptions on the probabilistic model of the problem were assumed. The curve marked by $\beta = 10$ demonstrates the high gain MAP decision provided by the BPC for a gain of $\beta = 10$ for which the input range is divided in accordance with the four sources of Fig. 6(a) into two disconnected subregions for the two classes. This typical example shows the power of the BPC in estimating the class probabilities without specifying a probabilistic model for the problem. Other simulations, comparing the BPC performance with the optimal Bayesian classifier for problems involving various combinations of Gaussian, Laplacian, and uniform sources, gave similar results to those presented in Figs. 5(d) and (6).

VI. Conclusions

The Boltzmann Perceptron classifier has capabilities of carrying out soft classification tasks or supplying MAP decisions. It has the power of stochastic networks such as the

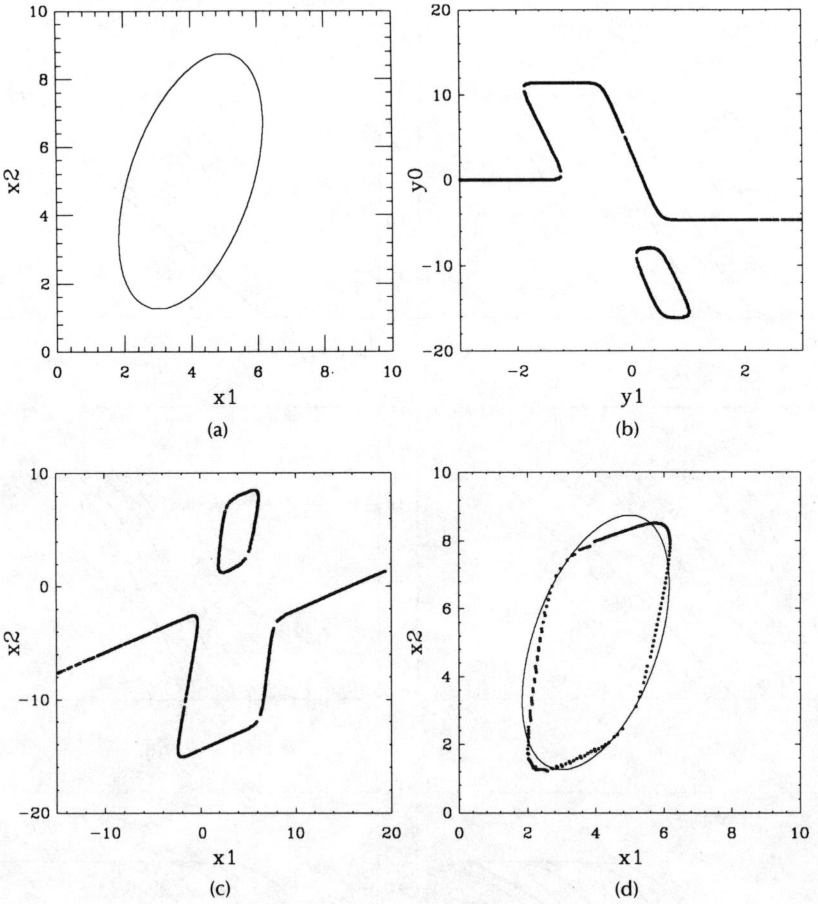

Fig. 5. Boundaries for the 2D example. (a) The true (Bayesian) boundary in the 10 × 10 square for the specified problem. (b) The *y*-space boundary formed by the solution of (4.9) as was illustrated in Fig. 4. (c) The *x*-space boundary after linear transforming the *y*-space boundary according to (4.8). (d) The *x*-space boundary inside the desired square compared with the true one. Note that quite an accurate boundary can be achieved using *only* two hidden units.

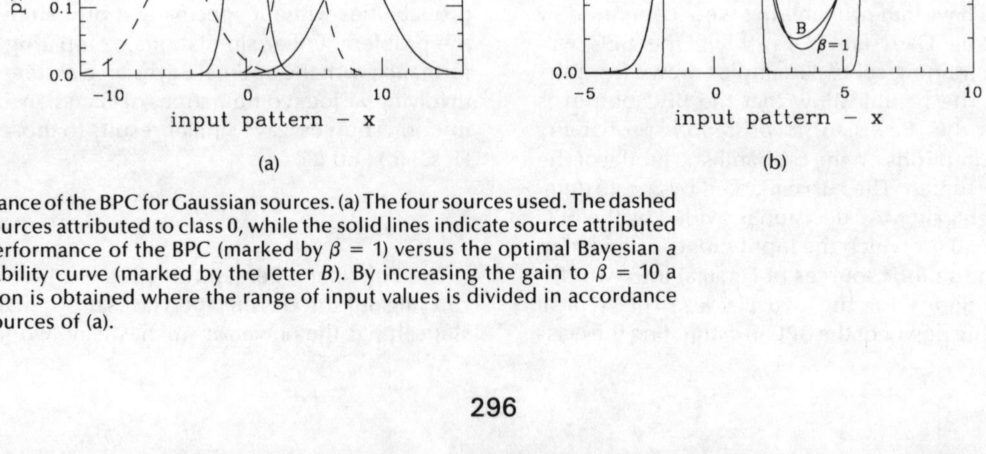

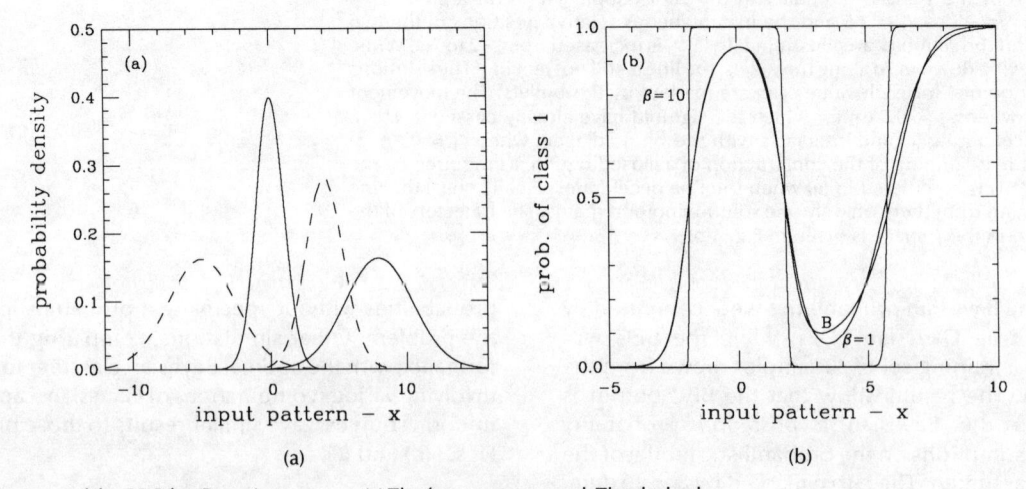

Fig. 6. Performance of the BPC for Gaussian sources. (a) The four sources used. The dashed lines indicate sources attributed to class 0, while the solid lines indicate source attributed to class 1. (b) Performance of the BPC (marked by $\beta = 1$) versus the optimal Bayesian a *posteriori* probability curve (marked by the letter *B*). By increasing the gain to $\beta = 10$ a MAP classification is obtained where the range of input values is divided in accordance with the four sources of (a).

Boltzmann machine to provide *a posteriori* probabilities but yet has a feedforward structure similar to that of a multilayer Perceptron and hence has a simple and computationally efficient implementation. It has powerful capabilities in tracking intricate boundaries between the classes even with a relatively small number of units. Overall, the BPC is a valuable alternative for the traditional Bayesian classifier for stochastic classification and decision problems. It requires no *a priori* assumptions about the probabilistic model of the problem at hand, but yet offers a low complexity network which is comparable in performance to the Bayesian classifier.

References

[1] N. Metropolis, A. W. Rosenbluth, M. N. Rosenbluth, A. H. Teller, and E. Teller, "Equations of state calculations by fast computing machines," *J. Chem. Phys.*, vol. 21, pp. 1087–1091, 1953.

[2] S. Kirkpatrick, C. D. Gelatt, and M. P. Vecchi, "Optimization by simulated annealing," *Science*, vol. 220, pp. 671–680, 1983.

[3] G. E. Hinton, T. R. Sejnowski, and D. H. Ackley, "Boltzmann machines: constraint satisfaction networks that learn," Carnegie-Mellon Technical Report, CMU-CS-84-119, 1984.

[4] S. Kullback, *Information Theory and Statistics*. New York: Wiley, 1959.

[5] S. Geman and D. Geman, "Stochastic relaxation, Gibbs distributions, and the Bayesian restoration of images," *IEEE Trans. on PAMI*, vol. 6, pp. 721–741, 1984.

[6] E. Yair and A. Gersho, "The Boltzmann Perceptron Network—a soft classifier, *Journal of Neural Networks*, March 1990.

[7] D. E. Rumelhart, G. E. Hinton, and R. J. Williams, "Learning internal representations by error propagation," in D. E. Rumelhart and J. L. McClelland (Eds.), *Parallel Distributed Processing: Explorations in the Microstructure of Cognition*. (Vol. 1, Chap. 8), MIT Press/Bradford Books, 1986.

[8] R. P. Lippmann, "An introduction to computing with neural networks," *IEEE Acoustic Speech and Signal Proc. Magazine*, April 4–22, 1987.

Part 6
Applications

Radar Signal Categorization Using a Neural Network

JAMES A. ANDERSON, MICHAEL T. GATELY, MEMBER, IEEE,
P. ANDREW PENZ, SENIOR MEMBER, IEEE, AND DEAN R. COLLINS, SENIOR MEMBER, IEEE

Invited Paper

Neural networks were used to analyze a complex simulated radar environment which contains noisy radar pulses generated by many different emitters. The neural network used is an energy minimizing network (the BSB model) which forms energy minima—attractors in the network dynamical system—based on learned input data. The system first determines how many emitters are present (the deinterleaving problem). Pulses from individual simulated emitters give rise to separate stable attractors in the network. Once individual emitters are characterized, it is possible to make tentative identifications of them based on their observed parameters. As a test of this idea, a neural network was used to form a small data base that potentially could make emitter identification.

We have used neural networks to cluster, characterize and identify radar signals from different emitters. The approach assumes the ability to monitor a region of the microwave spectrum and to detect and measure properties of received radar pulses. The microwave environment is assumed to be complex, so there are pulses from a number of different emitters present, and pulses from the same emitter are noisy or their properties are not measured with great accuracy.

For several practical applications, it is important to be able to tell *quickly*, first, how many emitters are present and, second, what their properties are. In other words time average prototypes must be derived from time dependent data without a tutor. Finally the system must tentatively identify the prototypes as members of previously seen classes of emitters.

Stages of Processing

We accomplish this task in several stages. Figure 1 shows a block diagram of the resulting system, which contains several neural networks. The system as a whole is referred to as the Adaptive Network Sensor Processor (ANSP).

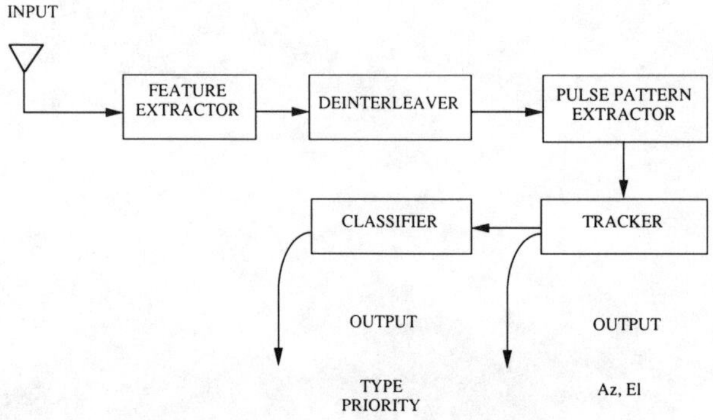

Fig. 1. Block diagram of the radar clustering and categorizing system.

In the block diagram given in Fig. 1, the first block is a *feature extractor*. We start by assuming a microwave radar receiver of some sophistication at the input to the system. This receiver is capable of processing each pulse into feature values, i.e., azimuth, elevation, signal to noise ratio (normalized intensity), frequency, and pulse width. This data is then listed in a *pulse buffer* and tagged with time of arrival of the pulse. In a complex radar environment, hundreds or thousands of pulses can arrive in fractions of seconds, so there is no lack of data. The problem, as in many data rich environments, is making sense of it.

The second block in Fig. 1 is the *deinterleaver* which clusters incoming radar pulses into groups, each group formed by pulses from a single emitter. A number of pulses are observed, and a neural network computes, off line, how many emitters are present, based on the sample, and estimates their properties. That is, it solves the so-called deinterleaving problem by identifying pulses as being produced by a particular emitter. This block also produces and passes forward measures of each cluster's azimuth, elevation, SNR, frequency, and pulse width.

The third block, the *pulse pattern extractor*, uses the deinterleaved information to compute the pulse repetition pattern of an emitter by using the times of arrival for the pulses

Manuscript received October 4, 1989; revised March 14, 1990. This research was initially supported by Texas Instruments, the Office of Naval Research (Contract N00014-86-K-0600 to J. A.), the National Science Foundation (Grant BNS-85-18675 to J. A.), and the Avionics Laboratory, Wright Research and Development Center, Aeronautical Systems Division (Contract F33615-87-C1454).

J. A. Anderson is with the Department of Cognitive and Linguistic Sciences, Box 1978, Brown University, Providence, RI 02912, USA.
M. T. Gately, P. A. Penz, and D. R. Collins are with Central Research Laboratories, Texas Instruments, Dallas, TX 75265, USA.

IEEE Log Number 9037384.

Reprinted from *Proc. IEEE*, vol. 78, no. 10, Oct. 1990, pp. 1646–1657.

that are contained in a given cluster. This information will be used for emitter classification.

The fourth block, the *tracker*, acts as a long term memory for the clusters found by the second block, storing the average azimuth, elevation, SNR, frequency, and pulse width. Since the diagram in Fig. 1 is organized via initial computational functionality, the tracking module follows the deinterleaver so as to store its outputs. In an operationally organized diagram, the tracker is the first block to receive pulse data from the feature extractor. It must identify most of the pulses in real time as previously learned by the deinterleaver module and only pass a small number of unknown pulses back to the deinterleaver module for further learning. The tracker also updates the cluster averages. Their properties can change with time because of emitter or receiver motion, for example.

The fourth and fifth blocks, the tracker and the *classifier* operate as a unit to classify the observed emitters, based on information stored in a data base of emitter types. Intrinsic emitter properties stored in these blocks are frequency, pulse width and pulse repetition pattern.

The most important question for the ANSP to answer is what the emitters might be and what can they do. That is, "who is looking at me, should I be concerned, and should I (or can I) do something about it?"

Emitter Clustering

Most of the initial theoretical and simulation effort in this project was focused on the deinterleaving problem. This is because the ANSP is being asked to form a conception of the emitter environment from the data itself. A teacher does not exist for most interesting situations.

In the simplest case, each emitter emits with constant properties, i.e., no noise is present. Then, determining how many emitters were present would be trivial: simply count the number of unique pulses via a look up table. Unfortunately, data is often moderately noisy because of receiver, environmental and emitter variability, and, sometimes, because of change of one or another emitter property at the emitter. Therefore, simple identity checks will not work. It is these cases which this paper will address.

Many neural networks are supervised algorithms, that is, they are trained by seeing correctly classified examples of training data and, when new data is presented will identify it according to their past experience. Emitter identification does not fall into this category because the correct answers are not known ahead of time. That, after all, is the purpose of this system. The basic problem of a self-organizing clustering system has many historical precedents in cognitive science. For example, William James, in a quotation well known to developmental psychologists, wrote around 1894,

> . . . the numerous inpouring currents of the baby bring to his consciousness . . . one big blooming buzzing Confusion. That Confusion is the baby's universe; and the universe of all of us is still to a great extent such a Confusion, potentially resolvable, and demanding to be resolved, but not yet actually resolved into parts.
>
> William James [15, p. 29]

We now know that the newborn baby is a very competent organism, and the outlines of adult perceptual preprocessing are already in place. The baby is designed to hear human speech in the appropriate way and to see a world like ours: that is, a baby is tuned to the environment in which he will live. The same is true of the ANSP, which must process pulses which will have feature values that fall within certain parameter ranges. That is, an effective feature analysis has been done for us by the receiver designer, and we do not have to organize a system from zero. This means that we can use a less general approach than we might have to in a less constrained problem. The result of both evolution and good engineering design is to build so much structure into the system that a problem, very difficult in its general form, becomes quite tractable.

At this point, neural networks are familiar to many and useful introductions are available ([7], [14], [20], [25]).

The Linear Associator

Let us begin our discussion of the network we shall use for the radar problem with the "outer product" associator, also called the "linear associator," as a starting point ([1], [17]–[19]). We assume a single computing unit, a simple model neuron, acts as a linear summer of its inputs. There are many such computing units. The set of activities of a group of units is the system state vector. Our notation has matrices represented by capital letters (A), vectors by lower case letters (f, g), and the elements of vectors as $f(i)$ or $g(j)$. A vector from a set of vectors is subscripted, for example, $f_1, f_2 \cdots$.

The ith unit in a set of units will display activity $g(i)$ when a pattern $f(j)$ is presented to its inputs, according to the rule,

$$g(i) = \sum_j A(i, j) f(j).$$

where $A(i, j)$ are the connections between the ith unit in an output set of units and the jth unit in an input set. We can then write the output pattern, g, as the matrix multiplication

$$g = Af.$$

During learning, the connection strengths are modified according to a generalized Hebb rule, that is, the change in an element of A, $\delta A(i, j)$, is given by

$$\delta A(i, j) \propto f_k(j) g_k(i)$$

where f_k and g_k are vectors associated with the kth learning example. Then we can write the matrix A as a sum of outer products,

$$A = \eta \sum_{k=1}^{n} g_k f_k^T$$

where η is a learning constant.

Prototype Formation

The linear model forms prototypes as part of the storage process, a property we will draw on. Suppose a category contains many similar items associated with the same response. Consider a set of correlated vectors, $\{f_k\}$, with mean p and distortion d.

$$f_k = p + d_k.$$

The final connectivity matrix will be

$$A = \eta \sum_{k=1}^{n} g f_k^T$$

$$= \eta g \left(n p^T + \sum_{k=1}^{n} d_k^T \right)$$

If the sum of the d_k is small, the connectivity matrix is approximated by

$$A = \eta n g p^T.$$

The system behaves as if it had repeatedly learned only one pattern, p, and responds best to it, even though p, in fact, may never have been learned.

Concept Forming Systems

This model has been applied directly to the formation of simple psychological "concepts" formed of nine randomly placed dots [16]. A "concept" in cognitive science describes the common and important situation where a number of different objects are classed together by some rule or similarity relationship. Much of the power of language, for example, arises from the ability to see that physically different objects are really "the same" and can be named and responded to in a similar fashion, for example, tables or lions. A great deal of experimentation and theory in cognitive science concerns itself with concept formation and use.

There are two related but distinct ways of explaining simple concepts in neural network models. First, there are prototype forming systems, which often involve taking a kind of average during the act of storage, and, second, there are models which explain concepts as related to attractors in a dynamical system. In the radar ANSP system to be described we use both ideas: we want to construct a system where the average of a category *becomes* the attractor in a dynamical system, and an attractor and its surrounding basin represent an individual emitter. (For a further discussion of concept formation in simple neural networks, see [2], [6], [16]).

Error Correction

By using an error correcting technique, the Widrow-Hoff procedure, we can force the simple associative system to give more accurate associations. Let us assume we are working with an autoassociative system. Suppose information is represented by associated vectors $f_1 \Rightarrow f_1, f_2 \Rightarrow f_2 \cdots$. A vector, f_k, is selected at random. Then the matrix, A, is incremented according to the rule

$$\Delta A = \eta (f_k - A f_k) f_k^T$$

where ΔA is the change in the matrix A. In the radar application, there is no "correct answer" in the general sense of a supervised algorithm. However every input pattern can be its own "teacher" in the error correction algorithm in that the network will try to better reconstruct that particular input pattern. The goal of learning a set of stimuli $\{f\}$ is to have the system behave as

$$A f_k = f_k$$

The error correcting learning rule will approximate this result with a least mean squares approximation, hence the alternative name for the Widrow-Hoff rule: the LMS (least mean squares) algorithm. The autoassociative system combined with error correction, when working perfectly, is forcing the system to develop a particular set of eigenvectors with eigenvalue 1.

The eigenvectors of the connection matrix are also of interest when simple Hebbian learning is used in an autoassociative system. Then, the simple outer product associator has the form

$$\Delta A = \eta f_k f_k^T.$$

There is now an obvious connection between the eigenvectors of the resulting outer product connectivity matrix and the principal components of statistics, because the form of this matrix is the covariance matrix. In fact, there is growing evidence that many neural networks are doing something like principal component analysis ([9], [12]).

BSB: A Dynamical System

We shall use for radar clustering a non-linear model that takes the basic linear associator, uses error correction to construct the connection matrix, and uses units containing a simple limiting nonlinearity. Consider an autoassociative feedback system, where the vector output from the matrix is fed back into the input. Because feedback systems can become unstable, we incorporate a simple limiting nonlinearity to prevent unit activity from getting too large or too small. Let $f[i]$ be the current state vector describing the system. $f[0]$ is the vector at step 0. At the $i + 1$st step, $f[i + 1]$, the next state vector, is given by the iterative equation,

$$f[i+1] = \text{LIMIT}\,[\alpha A f[i] + \gamma f[i] + \delta f[0]].$$

We stabilize the system by bounding the element activities within limits.

The first term, $\alpha A f[i]$, passes the current system state through the matrix and adds information reconstructed from the autoassociative cross connections. The second term, $\gamma f[i]$, causes the current state to decay slightly. This term has the qualitative effect of causing errors to eventually decay to zero as long as γ is less than 1. The third term, $\delta f[0]$, can keep the initial information constantly present and has the effect of limiting the flexibility of the possible states of the dynamical system since some vector elements are strongly biased by the initial input.

Once the element values for $f[i + 1]$ are calculated, the element values are "limited," that is, not allowed to be greater than a positive limit or less than a negative limit. This is a particularly simple form of the sigmoidal nonlinearity assumed by most neural network models. The limiting process contains the state vector within a set of limits, and we have previously called this model the "brain state in a box" or BSB model ([5], [8]). The system is in a positive feedback loop but is amplitude limited. After many iterations, the system state becomes stable and will not change: these points are attractors in the dynamical system described by the BSB equation. This final state will be the output of the system. In the fully connected case with a symmetric connection matrix the dynamics of the BSB system can be shown to be minimizing an energy function. The location of the attractors is controlled by the learning algorithm [13]. Aspects of the dynamics of this system are related to the "power" method of eigenvector extraction, since repeated iteration will lead to activity dominated by the eigenvectors with the largest positive eigenvalues. The signal processing abilities of such a network occur because eigenvectors arising from learning uncorrelated noise will tend to have small eigenvalues, while signal related eigenvectors will be large, will be enhanced by feedback, and will dominate the system state after a number of iterations.

We might conjecture that a category or a concept derived from many noisy examples would become identified with an attractor associated with a region in state space and that all examples of the concept would map into the point attractor. This is the behavior we want for radar pulse clustering.

Neural Network Clustering Algorithms

We know there will be many radar pulses, but we do not know the detailed descriptions of each emitter involved. We want to develop the structure of the microwave environment, based on input information. A number of models have been proposed for this type of task, including various competitive learning algorithms ([11], [26]).

Each pulse is different because of noise, but there are only a small number of emitters present relative to the number of pulses. We take the input data representing each pulse and form a state vector with it. A sample of several hundred pulses are stored in a "pulse buffer." We take a pulse at random and learn it, using the Widrow-Hoff error correcting algorithm with a small learning constant. Since there is no teacher, the desired output is assumed to be the input pulse data.

Learning rules for this class of dynamical system, Hebbian learning in general, and the Widrow-Hoff rule in particular, are effective at "digging holes in the energy landscape" so they fall where the vectors that are learned are. That is, the final low energy attractor states of the dynamical system when BSB dynamics are applied will tend to lie near or on stored information. Suppose we learn each pulse as it comes in, using Widrow Hoff error correction, but with a small learning constant. Metaphorically, we "dig a little hole" at the location of the pulse. But each pulse is different. So, after a while, we have dug a hole for each pulse, and *if the state vectors coding the pulses from a single emitter are not too far apart in state space*, we have formed an attractor that contains all the pulses from a single emitter, as well as new pulses from the same emitter. Figure 2 presents a (somewhat fanciful) picture of the behavior that we hope to obtain, where many nearby data points combine to give a single broad network energy minimum that contains them all.

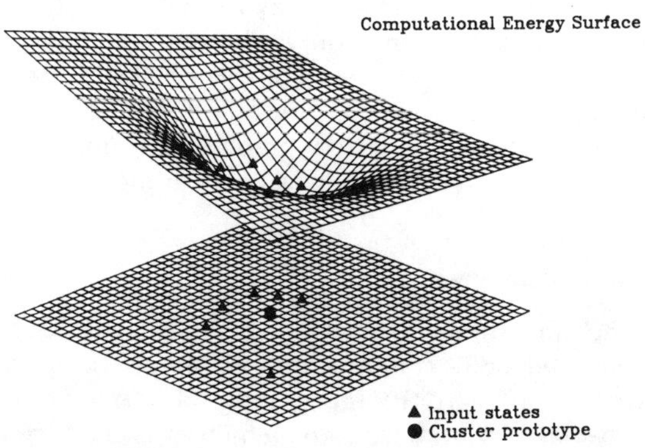

Fig. 2. Landscape surface of system energy. Several learned examples may contribute to the formation of a single energy minimum which will correspond to a single emitter. This drawing is only for illustrative purposes and is not meant to represent the very high dimensional simulations actually used.

We can see why this behavior will occur from an informal argument. Call the average emitter state vector of a particular emitter p. Then, every observed pulse, f_k, will be

$$f_k = p + d_k$$

where d_k is a distortion, which will be assumed to be different for every individual pulse, that is, different d_k are uncorrelated, and are relatively small compared to p. With a small learning constant, and with the connection matrix A starting from zero, the magnitude of the output vector, Af, will also be small after only a few pulses are learned. This means that the error vector will point outward, toward f_k, that is, toward $p + d_k$, as shown in Fig. 3.

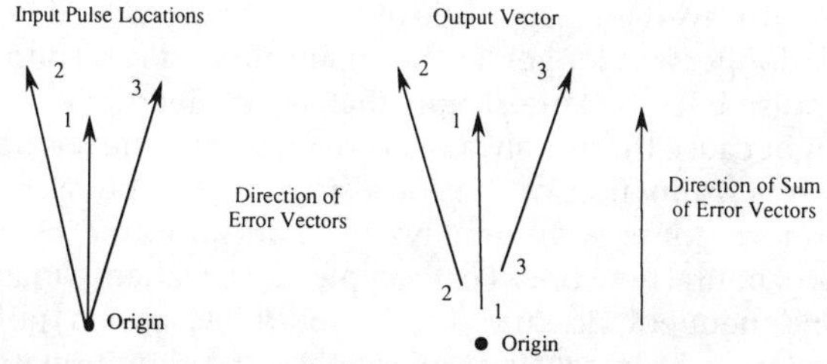

Fig. 3. Early in learning process: a situation with small learning constant, and many examples. The Widrow-Hoff procedure learns the error vector. The error vectors early in learning with a small learning constant point toward examples, and the average of the error vectors will point toward the category mean, that is, all the examples of a single emitter.

Early in the learning process with a small learning constant for a particular cluster, the error vectors (input minus output) all will point toward the cluster of input pulses. Widrow-Hoff learning can be described as using a simple associator to learn the error vector. Since every d_k is different and uncorrelated, the error vectors from different pulses will have the average direction of p. The matrix will act as if it is repeatedly learning p, the average of the vectors. It is easy to show that if the centers of different emitter clusters are spaced far apart, in particular, if the cluster centers are orthogonal, then p will be close to an eigenvector of A. In more interesting and difficult cases, where clusters are close together or the data is very noisy, it is necessary to resort to numerical simulation to see how well the network works in practice. As we hope to show, this technique does work quite well.

After the matrix has learned so many pulses that the input and output vectors are of comparable magnitude, the output of the matrix when $p + d_k$ is presented will be near p. (See Fig. 4) Then,

$$p \simeq Ap.$$

Over a number of learned examples,

$$\text{total error} \simeq \sum (p + d_k - A(p + d_k)$$

$$\simeq \sum (d_k - Ad_k)$$

The maximum values of the eigenvalues of A are 1 or below, the ds are uncorrelated, and this error term will average to zero.

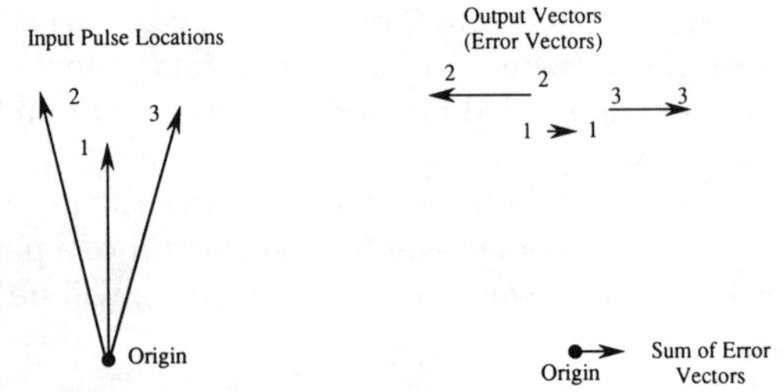

Fig. 4. Assume an eigenvector is close to a category mean, as will be the result after extensive error-correcting, autoassociative learning. The error terms from many learned examples, with a small learning constant, will average to zero and the system attractor structure will not change markedly. (There are very long-term "senility" mechanisms with continued learning, but they are not of practical importance for this application.)

However, as the system learns more and more random noise, the average magnitude of the error vector will tend to get longer and longer, as the eigenvalues of A related to the noise become larger. Note that system learning never stops because there is always an error vector to be learned, which is a function of the intrinsic noise in the system. Therefore, there is a "senility" mechanism found in this class of neural networks. For example, the covariance matrix of independent, identically distributed Gaussian noise added to each element is proportional to the identity matrix, then every vector becomes an eigenvector with the same eigenvalue, and this matrix is the matrix toward which A will evolve, if it continues to learn random noise indefinitely. When the BSB dynamics are applied to matrices resulting from learning *very* large numbers of noisy pulses, the attractor basins become fragmented, so that the clusters break up. However, the period of stable cluster formation is very long and it is easy to avoid cluster breakup in practice [4].

In BSB clustering the desired output is a particular stable state. Ideally, all pulses from one emitter will be attracted to that final state. Therefore a simple identity check is *now* sufficient to check for clusters. This check is performed by resubmitting the original noisy pulses to the network that has learned them and forming a list of the stable states that result. The list is then compared with itself to find which pulses came from the same emitter. For example, a symbol could be associated with the pulses from the same final state, i.e., the pulses have been deinterleaved or identified.

Once the emitters have been identified, the average characteristics of the features describing the pulse (frequency, pulse width and pulse repetition pattern) can be computed. These features are used to classify the emitters with respect to known emitter types in order to "understand" the microwave environment. A two stage system, which first clusters and then counts clusters is easy to implement, and, practically, allows convenient "hooks" to use traditional digital techniques in conjunction with the neural networks.

Stimulus Coding and Representation

The fundamental representation assumption of almost all neural networks is that information is carried by the pattern or set of activities of many neurons in a group of neurons. This set of activities carries the meaning of whatever the nervous system is doing and these sets of activities are represented as state vectors. The conversion of input data into a state vector, that is, the representation of the data in the network, is *the single most important engineering problem faced in network design.* In our opinion, choice of a good input and output representation is usually more important for the ultimate success of the system than the choice of a particular network algorithm or learning rule.

We now suggest an explicit representation of the radar data. From the radar receiver, we have a number of continuous valued features to represent: frequency, elevation, azimuth, pulse width, and signal strength. Our approach is to code continuous information as locations on a topographic map, i.e., a bar graph or a moving meter pointer. We represent each continuous parameter value by location of a block of activation on a linear set of elements. Increase in a parameter value moves the block of activity to the right, say, and a decrease, moves the activity to the left. We have used a more complex topographic representation in several other contexts, with success ([24], [27], [28]).

We represent the block/bar of activity value with a block of (three or four) "=", equal, symbols placed in a region of ".", period, symbols. Single characters are coded by eight bit ASCII bytes. The ASCII 1's and 0's are further transformed to +1's and −1's, so that the magnitude of any feature vector is the same regardless of the feature value. Input vectors are therefore purely binary. On recall, if the vector elements coding a character do not rise above a threshold size, the system is not "sure" of the output. Then that character is represented as the underline, "_", character. Being "not sure" can be valuable information relative to the confidence of a particular output state relative to an input. Related work has developed a more numeric, topographic representation for this task, called a "closeness code" [22] which has also been successfully used for clustering of simulated radar data.

Neural networks can incorporate new information about the signal and make good use of it. This is one version of what is called the *data fusion* or *sensor fusion* problem. To code the various radar features, we simply concatenate the topographic vectors of individual feature into a single long state vector. Bars in different fields code the different quantities. Figure 5 shows these fields.

Below we will gradually add information to the same network to show the utility of this fusion methodology. The conjecture is that adding more information about the pulse will produce more accurate clustering. Note that we can insert "symbolic" information (say word identifications or other appropriate information) in the state vector as character strings, forming a hybrid code. For instance the state vector can contain almost unprocessed spectral data together with the symbolic bar graph data combined with character strings representing symbols at the same time.

A Demonstration

For the simulations of the radar problem that we describe next, we used a BSB system with the following properties. The system used 480 units, representing 60 characters. Connectivity was 25%, that is, each element was connected at random to 120 others. There were a total of 10 simulated emitters with considerable added intrinsic noise. A pulse buffer of 510 different pulses was used for learning and, after learning, 100 new pulses, 10 from each emitter were used to test the system. There were about 2000 total learn-

```
              Radar Pulse Fields: Coding of Input Information
            Position of the bar of '=' codes an analog quanitity


Azimuth   Elevation  Frequency     Pulse Width  Pseudo-spectra
I<------->I<------->I<----------->I<---------->I<--------->I

...====.....====.........====.............===..=.=.=.=.=...


In any field:  A move to the left decreases the quantity
               A move to the right increases the quantity
```

Fig. 5. Input representation of analog input data uses bar codes. The state vector is partitioned into fields corresponding to azimuth, elevation, frequency, and pulse width, and a field corresponding to additional information that might become available with advances in receiver technology.

ing trials, that is, about four presentations per example. Parameter values were $\alpha = 0.5$, $\gamma = 0.9$, and $\delta = 0$. The limits for thresholding were $+2$ and -2. None of these parameters were critical, in that moderate variations of the parameters had little effect on the resulting classifications of the network.

Suppose we simply learn *frequency information*. Figure 6 shows the total number of attractors formed when ten new examples of each of ten emitters were passed through the BSB dynamics, using the matrix formed from learning the pulses in the pulse buffer. In a system that clustered perfectly, exactly 10 final states would exist, one different final state for each of the ten emitters. However, with only frequency information learned, all the 100 different inputs mapped into only two attractors.

Figure 6 and others like it below are graphical indications of the similarity between recalled clusters or states with computational energy minima. The states shown in the figures are ordered via a priori knowledge of the emitters, although this information was obviously not given to the network. One can visually interpret the outputs for equality of two emitters (*lumping* of *different* emitters) or separation of outputs for a single emitter (*splitting* of the *same* emitter) in the outputs. This display method is for the reader's benefit. The ANSP system determines the number and state vector of separate minima by a dot product search of the entire output list, as discussed above. Position of the bar of "="s codes the frequency in the frequency field which is the only field learned in this example.

Let us now give the system additional information about pulse *azimuth* and *elevation*. Clustering performance improves markedly, as shown in Fig. 7. We get nine different attractors. There is still uncertainty in the system, however, since few corners are fully saturated, as indicated by the underline symbols on the corners of some bar's. States 1 and 3 are in the same attractor, an example of incor-

```
                   Clustering by Frequency Information Only

Emitter                        Final Output State
Number

        Azimuth   Elevation  Frequency        Pulse Width Pseudo-spectra
        I<------->I<------->I<--------------->I<------>I<--------->I

 1      .......................====...............................
 2      ...............................====.......................
 3      .......................====...............................
 4      ...............................====.......................
 5      .......................====...............................
 6      .......................====...............................
 7      ...............................====.......................
 8      .......................====...............................
 9      .......................====...............................
10      .......................====...............................
```

Fig. 6. Final attractor states when only frequency information is learned. Ten different emitters are present, but only two different output states are found.

```
          Clustering Using Azimuth, Elevation and Frequency Information

Emitter                        Final Output State
Number

        Azimuth   Elevation  Frequency        Pulse Width Pseudo-spectra
        I<------->I<------->I<--------------->I<------>I<--------->I

 1      .====......====......====_................................
 2      ....====......====...............====.....................
 3      .====......====......====_................................
 4      ====_....====..................====.......................
 5      ._===......====......====_................................
 6      .....====......====....====...............................
 7      ...====.....====...................==_=...................
 8      .__===_....====_._....___=__..............................
 9      .__===_....====.._....___=__..............................
10      =__=..........====.......=__=.............................
```

Fig. 7. When azimuth, elevation, and frequency are provided for each data point, performance is better. However, two emitters are lumped together, and three others have very close final states.

```
a)  ......=......   Monochromatic pulse.

b)  ..=.=.=.=.=..   Subpulses with distinct frequencies.
                    (Or some kinds of FM or phase modulation)

c)  ..=========..   Continuous frequency sweep during the pulse.
                    i.e. pulse compression)
```

Fig. 8. Suppose we can assume that advances in receiver technology will allow us to incorporate a crude "cartoon" of the spectrum of an individual pulse into the coding of the state vector representing an example. The spectral information can be included in the state vector in only slightly processed form.

rect "lumping" as a result of insufficient information. Two other final states (8 and 9) are very close to each other in Hamming distance.

Let us assume that future advances in receivers will allow a quick estimation of the microstructure of each radar pulse. We have used, as shown in Fig. 8, a coding which is a crude graphical version of a Fourier analysis of an individual pulse, with the center frequency located at the middle of the field. Emitter pulse spectra were assigned arbitrarily.

Note that the spectral information can be included in the state vector in only slightly processed form: we have included almost a caricature of the actual spectrum.

Addition of *spectral information* improved performance somewhat. There were nine distinct attractors, though still many unsaturated states. Two emitters were still "lumped," 8 and 9. Figure 9 shows the results.

Suppose we add information about *pulse width* to azimuth, elevation, and frequency. The simulated pulse width information is very poor. It actually degrades performance, though it does allow separation of a couple of nearby emitters. The results are given in Fig. 10.

The reason pulse width data is of poor quality and hurts discrimination is because of a common artifact due to the way that pulse width is measured. When two pulses occur close together in time a very long pulse width is measured by the receiver circuitry. This can give rise in unfavorable cases to a spurious bimodal distribution of pulse widths for a single emitter. Therefore, a single emitter seems to have some short pulse widths and some very long pulse widths and this can split the category. Bimodal distributions of an emitter parameter, when the peaks are widely separated, is a hard problem for any clustering algorithm. A couple of difficult discriminations in this simulation, however, are aided by the additional data.

We now combine *all* this information about pulse properties together. None of the subsets of information could perfectly cluster the emitters. Pulse width, in particular, actually hurt performance. Figure 11 shows that, after learn-

```
                   Spectrum, Azimuth, Elevation, Frequency

Emitter                  Final Output State
Number

      Azimuth   Elevation Frequency             Pulse Width Pseudo-spectra
      I<------->I<------->I<--------------->I<------>I<--------->I

  1   .====.......====....__=_..........................=======....
  2   ....====.......====...............====...............=.=.=.=.=...
  3   ._===........====......====.......................=.......
  4   ====......====....................====............=======....
  5   ...====_.....===_._.....__=___....................=.=.=.=.=...
  6   .....====.....====....====.......................=.......
  7   ...====.....====....................====.........=======....
  8   ...====....====._......_.=___.....................=.=.=.=.=...
  9   ...====....====._......_.=___.....................=.=.=.=.=...
 10   ==_=...........===_........==_=...................=======....
```

Fig. 9. Including pseudo-spectral information helped performance considerably. Only two emitters are lumped together and the others are well separated.

```
                 Pulse Width, Azimuth, Elevation and Frequency

Emitter                  Final Output State
Number

      Azimuth   Elevation Frequency             Pulse Width Pseudo-spectra
      I<------->I<        >I<               >I<      >I<         >I

  1   .====.......====.......====...........===...................
  2   ....====.......====..............====....===...................
  3   .====.......====.......====...........===...................
  4   ====_.....====...................====..===...................
  5   .====.......====.......====_..........===...................
  6   .....====.....====....====..............===...................
  7   ...====.....====...................==_=..==_...................
Emitter 8 split
  8   ...====.....====._.................=____..==_...................
  8   ...====....====..........====..........._===...................

  9   ...====.....====...................==_=..==_...................
 10   ==_=..........====.........=__=.........===...................
```

Fig. 10. Suppose we add pulse width information to our other information. Pulse width data is of poor quality because when two pulses occur close together, a very long pulse width is measured by the receiver circuitry. This gives rise to a bimodal distribution of pulse widths, and the system splits one category.

```
                    Clustering With All Information

Emitter                          Final Output State
Number

        Azimuth  Elevation  Frequency          Pulse Width Pseudo-spectra
        I<------->I<------->I<---------------->I<------>I<--------->I

  1     .====.......====....__=_................===......=======....
  2     ....====.......====..............====....===....=.=.=.=.=...
  3     .====.......====......====................===........=.......
  4     ====......====......................====..===.....=======....
  5     .._===_....._====......_===_..............===....._.=.=.=._...
  6     .....====......====....====...............===..........=.......
  7     ...====.....====....................====..==_.....=======....
  8     ...====....====..........====...............===..=.=.=.=.=...
  9     .._====__..._===_._....._===_............._==_.........=.......
 10     ==_=..............===_..........==_=..........===.....=======....
```

Fig. 11. When all available information is used, ten stable, well-separated attractors are formed. This shows that such a network computation can make good use of additional information.

ing, using all the information, we now get ten well separated attractors, i.e., the correct number of emitters relative to the data set. The conclusion is that the additional information, even if it was noisy, could be used effectively. Poor information could be combined with other poor information to give good results.

Processing After Deinterleaving

Having used the ANSP system to deinterleave and cluster data, we also have a way of producing an accurate picture of each emitter. We now have an estimate of the frequency and pulse width and can derive other emitter properties [23], for example, the emitter pulse repetition pattern. One method to learn this pattern is to learn pulse repetition interval (PRI) pairs autoassociatively. Another is to autocorrelate the PRIs of a string. This technique probably provides more information than any other for characterizing emitters, because the resulting correlation functions are very useful for characterizing a particular emitter type.

Classification Problem and Neural Network Data Bases

The next task is to classify the observed emitters based on our previous experience with emitters of various types. We continue with the neural network approach because of the ability of networks to incorporate a great deal of information from different sensors, their ability to generalize (i.e., "guess") based on noisy or incomplete information, and their ability to handle ambiguity. Known disadvantages of neural networks used as data bases are their slow computation using traditional computer architectures, erroneous generalizations (i.e., "bad guesses"), their unpredictability, and the difficulty of adding new information to them, which may require time consuming relearning.

Information, in traditional expert systems, is often represented as collections of atomic facts, relating pairs or small sets of items together. Expert systems often assume "IF (*x*) THEN (*y*)" kinds of information representation. For example, such a rule in radar might look like:

IF (Frequency is 10 gHz)
AND (Pulse Width is 1 microsecond)
AND (PRI is constant at 1 kHz)
THEN (Emitter is a Klingon air traffic control radar).

Problems with this approach are that rules usually have many exceptions, data may be erroneous or noisy, and emitter parameters may be changed because of local conditions. Expert systems may be exceptionally prone to confusion when emitter properties change because of the rigidity of their data representation. Neural networks allow a different strategy: Always try to use as much information as you have, because, in most cases, the more information you have, the better performance will be.

As William James commented in the nineteenth century,

> . . . *the more other facts a fact is associated with in the mind, the better possession of it our memory retains.* Each of its associates becomes a hook to which it hangs, a mean to fish it up by when sunk beneath the surface. Together, they form a network of attachments by which it is woven into the entire tissue of our thought.
>
> William James [15, p. 301]

Perhaps, as William James suggests, information is best represented as large sets of correlated information. We could represent this in a neural network by a large, multimodal state vector [3]. Each state vector contains a large number of "atomic facts" together with their cross correlations. Our clustering demonstration showed that more information could be added and used efficiently and that identification depends on a cluster of information cooccurring.

Ultimately, we would like a system that would tentatively identify emitters based on measured properties and previously known information. Since we know, in operation, that parameters can and often do change, we can never be *sure* of the answers.

As a specific important example, radar systems can shift parameters in ways consistent with their physical design, that is, waveguide sizes, power supply size, and so on, for a number of reasons, for example, weather conditions. If an emitter is characterized by only one parameter, and that parameter is changed, then identification becomes very unlikely. Therefore, accuracy of measurement of a particular parameter may not be as useful for classification as one might expect. However, using a whole set of co-occurring properties, each at low precision, may prove a much more efficient strategy for identification. For further discussion of how humans often seem to use such a strategy in perception, consult George Miller's classic 1956 paper, "The magic number seven, plus or minus two" [21].

Classification Problem for Shifted Emitters

Our first neural net classification simulation is specifically designed to study sensitivity to shifts in parameters. Two data sets were generated. One set has "normal" emitter properties and the other set had all the emitter properties changed about 10 percent. The two sets each contained about 500 data points. The names used are totally arbitrary. The state vector was constructed of a name string (the first 10 characters) and bar codes for frequency, pulse width, and pulse repetition interval. For the classification function, the position of "+" symbols indicates the feature magnitude while the blank symbol fills the rest of the feature field. Again the "_" symbol indicates an undecided node.

Figures 12 and 13 show the resulting attractor interpretations. Figure 12 shows the vectors to be learned autoassociatively by the BSB model. The first field is the emitter name. The last three fields represent the numerical information produced by the deinterleaver and pulse repetition interval modules. An input consists of leaving the identification blank and filling in the analog information for the emitter which one wants to identify. The autoassociative connections fill in the missing identification information.

```
            Learn normal set, Test normal set

         Name      Frequency   P W      PRI
        I--------->I---------->I------>I-------->

   1    SAM Target+++          ++           ++
   2    Airborn In  +++             ++ ++
   3    AA FC       +++        ++          ++
   4    Airborn In   +++       ++          ++
   5    Airborn In   +++       ++          ++
   6    Airborn In    +++         ++    ++
   7    SAM Target    +++         ++     ++
   8    SAM Target      +++          ++ ++
   9    SAM Target       +++      ++                ++
  10    SAM Target       +++ ++                ++
```

Fig. 12. We can attach identification labels to emitters along with representations of their analog parameters. The names and values used here are random and were chosen arbitrarily.

Figure 12 shows the identification produced when the normal set is provided to the matrix: all the names are produced correctly and in a small number of iterations through the BSB algorithm. Figure 13 uses the same matrix, but the input data is now derived from sources whose mean values are shifted about 10%, to emulate this parameter shift.

There were three errors of classification. Emitter 3 was classified as "Airborn In" instead of "AA FC." Emitter 4 was classified as "SAM target" instead of "Airborn In." Emitter 7 was classified as "Airborn In" rather than the correct "SAM Target" name. Note that the recalled analog information is also not exactly the correct analog information even for the correctly identified emitters. At a finer scale, the number of iterations required to reach an attractor state was very long. This is a direct measure of the uncertainty of the neural network about the shifted data. Some of the final states were not fully limited, another indication of uncertainty.

Large Classification Data Bases

It would be of interest to see how the system worked with a larger data base. Some information about radar systems is published in *Jane's Weapon Systems* [10]. We can use this data as a starting point to see if a neural network might scale to larger systems. Figure 14 shows the kind of data available

```
Three Radars from Jane's:

China, JY-9, Search
Frequency     : 2.0 - 3.0 gHz
Pulse Width : 20 microseconds
PRF           : 0.850 kHz
PRF Variance: Constant frequency

Sweden, UAR1021, Surveillance
Frequency     : 8.6 - 9.5 gHz
Pulse Width : 1.5 microseconds
PRF           : 4.8 - 8.1 kHz
PRF Variance: 3 frequency staggered

USA, APQ113, FireControl
Frequency     : 16 - 16.4 gHz
Pulse Width : 1.1 microseconds
PRF           : 0.674 kHz
PRF Variance: None (Constant frequency)
```

Fig. 14. Sample data on radar transmitters taken from *Jane's Weapon Systems* [10].

from Jane's. Some radars have constant pulse repetition frequency (PRF) and others have highly variable PRFs. (Jane's lists Pulse Repetition Frequency (PRF) in its tables instead of Pulse Repetition Interval (PRI). We have used their term for their data in this simulation.) We represented PRF variability in the state vector coding by increasing the last bar width (Field 7, Fig. 15) for highly variable PRFs (see the Swedish radar, for an example.) Also, when a parameter is out of range (the average PRF of the Swedish radar) it is not represented.

We perform the usual partitioning of the state vector into fields, as shown in Fig. 15. For this simulation, the frequency scale is so coarse that even enormous changes in frequency would not change the bar coding significantly. We are more interested here in whether the system can handle large amounts of Jane's data. We taught the network 47 different kinds of radar transmitters. Some transmitter names were represented by more than one state vector because they

```
          Learn Normal Set, Test Set with Shifted Parameters

         Name      Frequency   P W      PRI
        I--------->I---------->I------>I-------->

   1    SAM Target+++        _+_          ++_
   2    Airborn In   +++                ++
   3    Airborn In  +++      _+_         +_            x error
   4    SAM Target    +++    _+           ++           x error
   5    Airborn In   +++       ++           ___
   6    Airborn In    +++         _+_    ++
   7    Airborn In    +++       __       ++            x error
   8    SAM Target      +++             +++_
   9    SAM Target     _++_   _  __         ++
  10    SAM Target       +++ ++             ___
```

Fig. 13. Even if the emitter parameters shift slightly, it is still possible to make some tentative emitter identifications. Three errors of identification were made. Neural networks are able to generalize to some degree, if the representations are chosen properly. The names and values used here are random and were chosen arbitrarily.

```
Coding into Partitioned State Vector:

Symbolic Fields:                            Continuous Fields:

Field 1    Country                    Field 4        Frequency
Field 2    Designation                Field 5        Pulse Width
Field 3    Purpose                    Field 6        PRF
                                      Field 7        PRF Variation

            1    2    3           4                  5       6    7
       I--->I--->I--->I-------------------->I-------->I------>I--->

       ChinaRY-9 Searc...==.........................=.=.......=....
       SwedeUAR10Surve.........==...........=......=..........==...
       USA..APQ11FireC................=.....=.......=.=.......=....

       Analog Bar Code Ranges:

       Frequency:     0 - 14 gHz
       Pulse Width:   0 - 10 microseconds
       PRF:           0 - 4 kHz
       PRF Variance:  0 - 200% of average PRF
```

Fig. 15. Bar code representation of *Jane's* data. Note the presence of both symbolic information such as country name and transmitter designation, and analog, bar-coded information such as frequency, pulse width, and so on.

can have several, quite different modes of operation, that is, the parameter part of the code can differ significantly from mode to mode. (The clustering algorithms would almost surely pick up different modes as different clusters.) After learning, we provided the measured properties to the transmitter to see if it could regenerate the name of the country that the radar belonged to. There were only three errors of retrieval from 47 sets of input data, corresponding to 94 percent accurate country identification. This experiment was basically coding a lookup table, using low precision representations of the parameters. Figure 16 shows a sample of the output, with reconstructions of the country, designations, and functions.

Conclusions

We have presented a system using neural networks which is capable of clustering and identifying radar emitters, given as input data large numbers of received radar pulses and with some knowledge of previously characterized emitter types.

Good features of this system are its robustness, its ability to integrate information from co-occurance of many features, and its ability to integrate information from individual data samples.

We might point out that the radar problem is similar to data analysis problems in other areas. For example, it is very similar to a problem in experimental neurophysiology, where action potentials from multiple neurons are recorded with a single electrode. Applications of the neural network techniques described here may not be limited to radar signal processing.

References

[1] J. A. Anderson, "A simple neural network generating an interactive memory," *Mathematical Biosciences*, vol. 14, pp. 197–220, 1972.

[2] J. A. Anderson, "Neural models for cognitive computation,"

```
                Final output states: 3 errors in reconstructed country

                  1    2    3           4                  5       6    7
             I--->I--->I--->I-------------------->I-------->I------>I--->

             ChinaRY-9 Searc...==.........................=.=.......=....
X            USA..FPS24Searc=.............................=.........=....
             China571..Surve.==.....................=.......=.......=....
             China581..Warni.=......................=.....=.........=....
             China311-AFireC.........===........=..................==....
             FrancTRS20Surve......=................=......=.........=....
             IndiaPSM-3Searc...===....................=....=........=....
             EnglaAS3-_FireC..=...........................=.........=....
             EnglaMAREC̄Marin.........=.............=......=.........=....
             ...
             USA..FPS24Searc=.............................=.........=....
             USA..PAR_0Appro.........=..........=...................==...
X            IsraeELM2̄2Marin...=.................=...........=......=....
             USA.._PR20Appro.........=...........=..................==...
             ...
             USA..TPS43FireC...=.......................=............=====
             USA..APQ11FireC................=...=................=..=....
             USA..APS12Surve.........=...........=..............===.==...
             IsraeELM22Marin...=................=..............===..==...
             IsraeELM20FireC.=...........................==.........=....
             SwedeGirafSearc....===................=..........=====.===..
             SwedeUAR10Surve.........==..........=.......=..........==...
             USSR.BarloSearc...==.................==.......=........=....
X            IsraeELM20FireC=............................==.........=....
             USSR.FireCFireC...=.................==.............=...=....
             USSR.HenSeWarni..=...........................===========....
             USSR.KnifeWarni=...........................=========...==...
             USSR.JayBiAirbo.............=.......==...............=====..
```

Fig. 16. Data retrieval: data from *Jane's Weapon Systems*—only part of the data. When only analog data is provided at the input, the network will fill in the most appropriate country name. In this trial simulation, a network learned 47 different transmitters and was able to correctly retrieve the associated country in 44 of them.

IEEE Transactions: Syst., Man, and Cybern., vol. SMC-13, pp. 799–815, 1983.

[3] J. A. Anderson, "Cognitive Capabilities of a Parallel System," In E. Bienenstock, F. Foglemann-Soulié, and G. Weisbuch, Eds. *Disordered Systems and Biological Organization*, Berlin: Springer, 1986, pp. 209–226.

[4] J. A. Anderson, "Concept formation in neural networks: Implications for evolution of cognitive functions," *Human Evolution*, vol. 2, pp. 81–97, 1987.

[5] J. A. Anderson, and M. C. Mozer, "Categorization and selective neurons," In G. E. Hinton and J. A. Anderson, Eds. *Parallel Models of Associative Memory* (Rev. Ed.), Hillsdale, NJ: Erlbaum, 1989, Ch. 8, pp. 251–276.

[6] J. A. Anderson, and G. L. Murphy, "Psychological Concepts in a Parallel System," *Physica*, vol. 22-D, pp. 318–336, 1986.

[7] J. A. Anderson and E. Rosenfeld, Eds. *Neurocomputing: Foundations of Research*, Cambridge, MA: MIT Press, 1988.

[8] J. A. Anderson, J. W. Silverstein, S. A. Ritz, and R. S. Jones, "Distinctive features, categorical perception, and probability learning: Some applications of a neural model," *Psychological Review*, vol. 84, pp. 413–451, 1977.

[9] P. Baldi, and K. Hornik, "Neural networks and principal component analysis: Learning from examples without local minima," *Neural Networks*, vol. 2, pp. 53–56, 1989.

[10] B. Blake, Ed. *Jane's Weapon Systems* (19th Edition), Surrey, UK: Jane's Information Group, 1988.

[11] G. Carpenter, and S. Grossberg, "ART 2: self organization of stable category recognition codes for analog input patterns," *Appl. Optics*, vol. 26, pp. 4919–4942, 1987.

[12] G. W. Cottrell, P. W. Munro, and D. Zipser, "Image compression by back propagation: A demonstration of extensional programming," In N. E. Sharkey, Ed., *Advances in Cognitive Science*, Vol. 3, Norwood, NJ: Ablex, 1988.

[13] R. M. Golden, "The 'Brain state in a box' neural model is a gradient descent algorithm," *Journal of Mathematical Psychology*, vol.30, pp. 73–80, 1986.

[14] G. E. Hinton, and J. A. Anderson, Eds., *Parallel Models of Associative Memory* (Rev. Ed.), Hillsdale, NJ: Erlbaum, 1989.

[15] W. James, *Briefer Psychology*. New York: Collier, 1894/1961.

[16] A. G. Knapp and J. A. Anderson, "A theory of categorization based on distributed memory storage," *Journal of Experimental Psychology: Learning, Memory and Cognition*, vol. 9, pp. 610–622, 1984.

[17] T. Kohonen, "Correlation matrix memories," *IEEE Transactions on Computers*, vol. C-21, pp. 353–359, 1972.

[18] ——, *Associative Memory*. Berlin: Springer, 1972.

[19] ——, *Self Organization and Associative Memory*. Berlin: Springer, 1984.

[20] J. L. McClelland, and D. E. Rumelhart, Eds., *Parallel, Distributed Processing*, Vol. 2, Cambridge, MA: MIT Press, 1986.

[21] G. A. Miller, "The magic number seven, plus or minus two: Some limits on our capacity for processing information," *Psychological Review*, vol. 63, pp. 81–97, 1956.

[22] P. A. Penz, "The closeness code," *Proc. IEEE Int. Conf. Neural Networks*, IEEE Catalog 87th0191-7, 1987, pp. III-515-523.

[23] P. A. Penz, A. J. Katz, M. I. Gately, D. R. Collins, and J. A. Anderson, "Analog capabilities of the BSB model as applied to the anti-radiation homing missile problem," *Proc. Int. Joint Conf. Neural Nets*, pp. II-7–11.

[24] M. L. Rossen, *Speech Syllable Recognition with a Neural Network*, Ph.D. Thesis, Department of Psychology, Brown University, Providence, RI 02912, May, 1989.

[25] D. E. Rumelhart, and J. L. McClelland, J. L., Eds., *Parallel, Distributed Processing*, Vol. 1, Cambridge, MA: MIT Press, 1986.

[26] D. E. Rumelhart, and D. Zipser, "Feature discovery by competitive learning," In. D. E. Rumelhart, and J. L. McClelland, Eds., *Parallel, Distributed Processing*, Vol. 1, Cambridge, MA: MIT Press, 1986, Ch. 5, pp. 151–193.

[27] M. E. Sereno, *A Neural Network Model of Visual Motion Processing*, Ph.D. Thesis, Department of Psychology, Brown University, Providence, RI, May, 1989.

[28] S. R. Viscuso, J. A. Anderson, and K. T. Spoehr, "Representing simple arithmetic in neural networks," In G. Tiberghien, Ed., *Advanced Cognitive Science: Theory and Applications*, London: Horwoods, 1989, Ch. 7, pp. 141–164.

Neural Network Models of Sensory Integration for Improved Vowel Recognition

BEN P. YUHAS STUDENT MEMBER, IEEE, MOISE H. GOLDSTEIN, JR., SENIOR MEMBER, IEEE, TERRENCE J. SEJNOWSKI, MEMBER, IEEE, AND ROBERT E. JENKINS, MEMBER, IEEE

Automatic speech recognizers currently perform poorly in the presence of noise. Humans, on the other hand, often compensate for noise degradation by extracting speech information from alternative sources and then integrating this information with the acoustical signal. Visual signals from the speaker's face are one source of supplemental speech information. We demonstrate that multiple sources of speech information can be integrated at a subsymbolic level to improve vowel recognition. Feedforward and recurrent neural networks are trained to estimate the acoustic characteristics of the vocal tract from images of the speaker's mouth. These estimates are then combined with the noise-degraded acoustic information, effectively increasing the signal-to-noise ratio and improving the recognition of these noise-degraded signals. Alternative symbolic strategies, such as direct categorization of the visual signals into vowels, are also presented. The performances of these neural networks compared favorably with human performance and with other pattern-matching and estimation techniques.

I. Introduction

We usually can communicate by using the acoustic speech signal alone, but often communication also involves visible gestures from the speaker's face and body. In situations where environmental noise is present or the listener is hearing impaired, these visual sources of information become crucial to understanding what has been said. Our ability to comprehend speech with relative ease under a wide range of environmental circumstances is due largely to our ability to fuse multiple sources of information in real time. Loss of information in the acoustic signal can be compensated for by using information about speech articulation from the movements around the mouth, or by using semantic information conveyed by facial expressions and other gestures. At the same time, the listener can use knowledge of linguistic constraints to further compensate for ambiguities remaining in the received speech signals.

Speech perception can be improved greatly by watching the face of the speaker [1], [2]. Normal hearing subjects tested on isolated word recognition in noise for a limited vocabulary were able to improve their performance from an initial 13% correct to a 90% performance level when given visual access to the speakers in addition to the noise-degraded acoustic speech signal [3]. This produced an effective gain of 15 dB in the signal-to-noise ratio (S/N). Even when the acoustic signal is completely absent, as in the profoundly deaf, the visual signal alone is able to provide significant speech information through lipreading [4], [5]. Multimodal sensory integration can occur during speech recognition, but it is not clear how or at what level of processing this integration takes place [6].

In contrast to human performance, the performance of automatic speech recognition systems are not as robust and tend to degrade rapidly in noisy environments [7]. Efforts have been made to reduce the noise in the acoustic signal [8] and much work has been done to formalize linguistic constraints [9], but few have attempted to use additional external information sources. One notable exception is a system built by Eric Petajan [10] for isolated digit recognition that used vector-quantized binary images of the speaker's mouth. In this system, the acoustic and visual speech information were independently encoded into symbol strings, and a set of rules was used to reconcile conflicting interpretations. They symbolic intermediates were needed to perform the necessary processing and integration in real time on the serial digital computers available.

The massively parallel architecture of artificial neural networks make it feasible to explore subsymbolic alternatives to Petajan's system. The use of many-dimensional representations allows information from several sources to be combined "softly," before being reduced to discrete symbols. In addition, learning algorithms provide a means of training networks to fuse these signals without explicit rules or restrictive *a priori* models.

In this paper, visual speech signals are preprocessed with a neural network to improve automatic speech recognition.

Manuscript received October 16, 1989; revised March 15, 1990. This work was supported by the Air Force Office of Scientific Research under grant AFOSR-86-0246 and by Internal Research and Development of the Applied Physics Laboratory of Johns Hopkins University.

B. P. Yuhas is with Bell Communications Research (BELLCORE), 445 South Street, Morristown, NJ 07962, USA.

M. H. Goldstein is with the Speech Processing Laboratory, Dept. of Electrical and Computer Engineering, Johns Hopkins University, Baltimore, MD 21218, USA.

T. J. Sejnowski is with the Computational Neurobiology Laboratory, the Salk Institute and with the Dept. of Biology, University of California at San Diego, La Jolla, CA 92037 USA.

R. E. Jenkins is with the Applied Physics Laboratory, Johns Hopkins University, Laurel, MD 20707, USA.

IEEE Log Number 9039183.

Reprinted from *Proc. IEEE*, vol. 78, no. 10, Oct. 1990, pp. 1658–1668.

The approach taken here is to use the visual speech signals to clean up the acoustic signal. In effect, we are building a better microphone. Neural networks are trained to estimate the associated acoustic structure from the concurrent visual speech signal. This acoustic estimate is then fused with the noise-degraded acoustic information. By combining the visual and acoustic sources of speech information, we demonstrate that the visual signal can be used to improve the performance of automatic vowel recognition in the presence of noise. This approach does not require categorical preprocessing or explicit rules. The results described here are based on vowels spoken by a single speaker.

II. Speech

There are many ways to characterize speech. At one level, there are linguistic descriptions using abstract symbols. These representations are highly compact and efficiently represented on digital computers. At another level, there are acoustic descriptions of speech based on continuous, analog signals. They make minimal assumptions about the structure of speech, but require extensive storage and are difficult to work with on serial digital computers. Within the speech research community, the degree to which speech contains symbolic and subsymbolic structures remains controversial [11].

The speech representation that is appropriate depends on many factors, including the tools one has available. Neural network models have aspects that allow for symbolic and subsymbolic representations. Information can be represented locally by associating a concept with a single unit. While the individual unit may represent a discrete category, its level of activation can be continuous. At the same time, information can also be distributed across a whole set of units, with a concept being represented by the joint activation of a group of units. These characteristics allow network models for speech processing to have representations that extend across acoustic and linguistic levels.

A. Speech as Symbols

In a linguistic description, the *phoneme* is the shortest distinguishing unit of a given language. For example, the words *beet* and *neat* are distinguished by the phonemes /b/ and /n/, and *boot* and *beet* are distinguished by the phonemes /u/ and /i/. While the phonemes /u/ and /i/ are linguistic abstractions, the speech sounds themselves are identified as *phones* and represented in brackets, [u] and [i]. Phones are descriptive of a set of speech sounds [12], whereas phonemes are functional characterizations that can distinguish one word from another. When the same word is pronounced differently by two individuals, then the same phoneme in that work may be represented by two different phones.

The visual correlate of the phoneme is the *viseme*: the smallest visibly distinguishing unit of a given language [13]. The mapping between the phonemes and visemes is generally many to one; for example, the phonemes /p/, /b/, and /m/ are usually visibly indistinguishable and treated as a single viseme [14].

The physical realities of speech signals are often difficult to reconcile with these linguistic units, and consequently it is often impossible to find invariant features that define these speech segments. To provide a transition between these levels, a hierarchy of descriptive languages has evolved. Phonemes can be represented as sets of binary distinctive features [15]. For example, the difference between the sounds [z] and [s] is the absence or presence of the feature voicing. At an even lower level, the binary distinctive features can be represented by the continuously changing locations, movements and relative timing of the speech articulators [16]. Here the description of speech becomes closely related to the acoustic signal itself.

B. Speech as Signals

Acoustic speech signals are often represented by the magnitude of their short-term power spectrum. This representation assumes that the signals are approximately stationary over a short time and that the phase information is not essential. Early experiments in machine synthesis indicated that the phase component of the spectrum does not play an important role is speech recognition [17]. It has also been found that phase information contributes little to speech intelligibility [8]. The ability to read spectrograms has been used as further evidence that the short-term power spectrum carries the necessary information to convey speech information [18]. Today, some form of the short-term power spectrum serves as a basic unit for most automatic speech recognition systems [9], [19].

The acoustic speech signal emitted from the mouth can be modeled as the response of the vocal-tract filter to a switchable sound source [20], [21]. In a first-order vocal-tract model, the configuration of the articulators (such as the mouth opening, lips, teeth, tongue, velum, and glottis) defines the shape of the vocal-tract filter, which then determines the filter's frequency response. The resonances of the vocal-tract filter appear as peaks in the envelope of the short-term power spectrum of the acoustic signal and are called formants.

A simplified model of the vocal tract for non-nasalized speech consists of a series of tubes of uniform length with different diameters. The acoustic characteristics of this model can be represented as an all-pole filter using linear predictive coding (LPC) [22], which allows for a compact representation of the vocal-tract filter using only a few time-varying coefficients. Speech signals are routinely encoded, stored, and resynthesized by using LPC coefficients along with a characterization of the driving source.

C. The Audio–Visual Interaction

Although some of the articulatory features are often visible (for example, the lips, the teeth, and sometimes the tongue), other components of the articulatory system, such as the glottis and velum, are not. Those articulators that are visible tend to modify the acoustic signal in ways that are more susceptible to acoustic distortion than are those effects due to the hidden articulators [6], [10]. For example, the quasi-periodic sound produced by the glottis is rather resistant to noise degradation. The information in the visual speech signal tends to complement the information in the acoustic signal. Consequently, phonemes, such as /b/ and /k/, that are produced in visibly distinct manners, have acoustic correlates that are among the first pairs to be confused in the presence of noise. Conversely, phonetic segments that are visibly indistinguishable, such as /p/, /b/, and

/m/, are among the most resistant to confusion when presented acoustically [23], [14]. This complementary structure demonstrates how these two speech signals can interact to improve the perception of speech in noise.

The visible and acoustic speech signals combine using a common representation that lies somewhere between the abstract linguistic segment and the continuous analog signal. At one end, the two signals can be symbolically interpreted and the visual signal provides a linguistic-level constraint. At the other, the visual signal can provide an independent estimate of the vocal-tract transfer function and serve as a low-level acoustic constraint. Neural networks provide a computational framework within which one can explore this full range of representations.

III. Neural Networks

The architecture of artificial neural networks is motivated by the computational style found in biological nervous systems. The key features are a large number of relatively simple nonlinear processing units and high degree of connectivity between these units. A unit performs a nonlinear transformation on the sum of its inputs to produce an output signal. When this output signal travels across a connection to another unit, the signal is attenuated or amplified by the weight associated with that connection. Computation is performed by the interaction of these units and signals. Rather than having an explicit program, the computation is defined by the properties of the individual units and their interconnects.

In terms of architectural abstraction, these models differ from actual neural networks found in the nervous systems. For example, the processing units used in this study simply add their weighted inputs and have a static sigmoidal nonlinear output function, while neurons in real nervous systems have more complex spatiotemporal nonlinearities and are capable of much more complex discriminations [24]. Nevertheless, in terms of architecture, these networks provide alternative approaches to difficult computational problems. The architecture and weights needed to solve a particular problem can be either predefined or found using learning algorithms [25], [26]. These algorithms iteratively adjust the weights to reduce some error measure defined on a set of training examples. Neural networks have been constructed to solve a variety of problems, such as optimization problems, mapping text to speech, associative memories, and pattern classification [27]–[30].

A. Architecture

Feedforward network architectures were used in this study. The units in a feedforward network are arranged in layers, with connections only allowed between layers, and only in one direction. The units that receive inputs from outside the network are referred to as input units, and those that are observed from outside the network are output units. The remaining units are referred to as hidden, because they only exchange signals with other parts of the network. The units themselves use a nonlinear sigmoid squashing function to transform the sum of their inputs. The standard multilayered feedforward networks with arbitrary squashing functions are a class of universal approximators [31]. Moreover, any nonlinear mapping can be learned by a network if there are sufficient data to characterize the mapping and if the number of parameters in the network matches the information content of the data [32], [33].

B. Training

A modified backpropagation algorithm was used to train feedforward networks [26]. The gradient was calculated in the standard manner, but instead of using steepest descent, a conjugate-gradient algorithm was used to update the weights. In addition, the fixed-step size and momentum term associated with backpropagation were replaced with a line-search minimization [34].[1]

The number of adjustable weights in a neural network can often exceed the number of training patterns. In these cases, the networks have too many free parameters and are subject to the problem of overfitting or overlearning the training data. The effects of overlearning can be minimized by increasing the size of the training data set, by reducing the number of hidden units, or by stopping the training before the network has completely converged.

IV. The Speech Signals

The speech signals used in this study were obtained from video recordings of a seated speaker facing a camera under well-lit conditions. The visual and acoustic signals were stored on a laser disc [35] where the individual frames and their corresponding speech segments were indexed. The NTSC video standard of 30 frames/s was used and each frame had 33 ms of speech associated with it. Phonemes usually are shortened or dropped altogether during fluent speech, so single video frames often span more than one phoneme. To avoid this problem, we selected speech samples such as stressed vowels in isolated words or consonant-vowel-consonant (CVC) nonsense syllables that change relatively slowly. In these contexts, the vowels often were steady state over periods of 50–100 ms.

For a given phoneme, a preliminary list of candidate words was identified from a transcription of the laser disc. Each word was then played acoustically to confirm the suspected pronunciation. A representative frame for the vowel was then isolated by alternately dropping a frame and then listening until the surrounding consonants were removed. The number of frames that remained after this process depended upon the degree to which that particular vowel was stressed. Stressed vowels, for example, can last up to 132 ms or 4 frames, while an unstressed vowel in continuous speech will often not last the full 33 ms of a single frame. The acoustic signals of the remaining frames were digitized and visually examined to ensure that each signal was approximately in steady state. From this set, a single frame was selected only if the periodic waveform appeared relatively stable, neither increasing nor decreasing in amplitude.

This paper describes results obtained using data from a single male speaker. A data set was constructed of 108 images of 9 different vowels in 12 sets. The vowels were

[1] Our neural networks were simulated on a MIPS M/120 computer and an ANALOGIC AP5000 array processor. Because of the conjugate-gradient learning algorithm, the time it took to perform on backpropagation step varied depending upon the number of evaluations required in the line-minimization search. For a network with 2559 weights it took the MIPS M/120 approximately 35 msec to perform one evaluation.

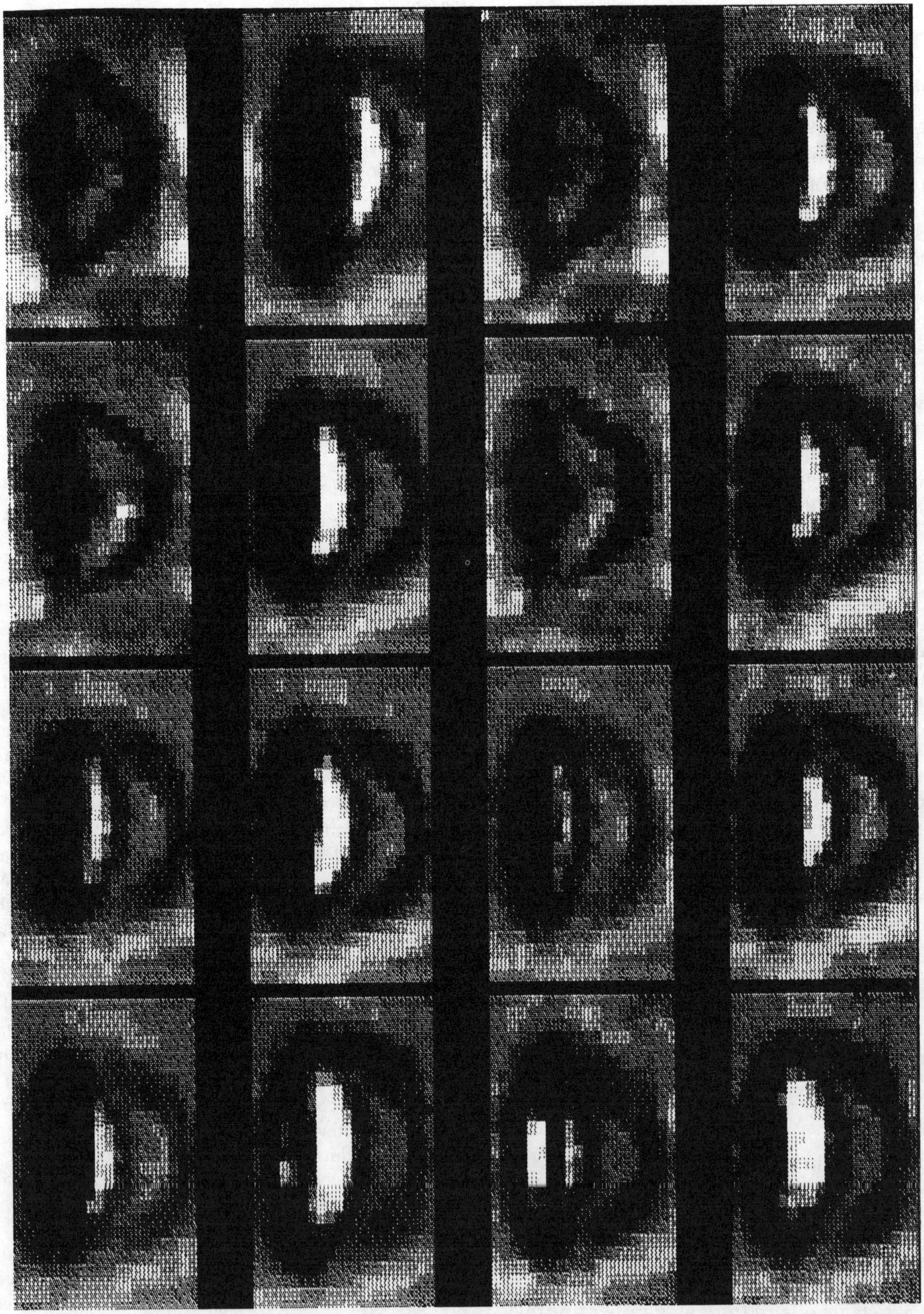

Fig. 1. Typical images used to train the neural networks.

taken from words and CVCs. Because these words and syllables were spoken deliberately and in isolation, these vowels were isolated easily. In other experiments not presented here data from a female speaker were also studied [36].

A. Preprocessing the Images

Instead of searching for an optimal encoding of the input images, we chose a simple representation that seemed to contain the relevant information. A rectangular area-of-interest was automatically defined and centered about the mouth. The image was further reduced to produce an image that could be comfortably handled by out network simulations. Within the rectangle, the average value of each 4 × 4 pixel squares was computed to produce a topographically accurate gray-scale image of 20 × 25 pixels (Fig. 1). Rather than attempting to extract special features, this encoding represented a form that could be obtained easily through an array of analog photoreceptors.

Two methods of processing these images of the speaker's mouth were explored. In the first approach, we treated the images categorically and attempted to make hard phonemic decisions directly from the images. Such linguistic identifications can be used to constrain the linguistic interpretation of a noise-degraded acoustic signal. In the second approach, we obtained acoustic information directly from the images by estimating the transfer function of the vocal tract. These independent estimates were then used to constrain the acoustic interpretation of the noise-degraded acoustic signal directly.

V. Categorization

Neural networks were trained to identify the vowel directly from the image. The images were presented across 500 input units, and the output consisted of 9 output units, each representing one of the nine vowels in the data. An input image was correctly categorized when the activation value of the correct vowel unit was larger than all the other output units. The data set of 108 images was split into a test set and a training set of 54 images, each containing a balanced set of vowels. The number of hidden units varied.

A network was trained until the categorization of all 54 images in the training set was perfect. Overtraining was minimized by immediately terminating the training at this point, before the output units were driven to saturation. In a few cases, the network would learn all but one or two tokens and then take an excessive amount of time to learn the last few cases. Often this additional training would result in poorer performance on the test set. The training was therefore stopped at 500 epochs whether or not all the training data were categorized correctly. After the network was trained, it then was tested on the second set of 54 images from the same speaker.

A. Results

The results reported here are based on networks with five hidden units; fewer than five hidden units produced worse results. Performance levels were averaged across eight networks initialized with different random weights. The networks were trained on 54 patterns. For half of the networks, the training and test sets were reversed. The eight networks trained on the male data obtained an average performance of 76% correct categorizations for the images in the test set.

This performance compared favorably with the traditional categorization technique of nearest neighbor. A nearest-neighbor classifier (NN) was constructed using the training data as the set of stored templates. The individual images from the test set were correlated with the stored templates, and the image was classified according to its closest match. The process was repeated, but with the test and training sets reversed. The NN classifier correctly classified and male data set with an average accuracy of 79%.

The performance of the network also compared favorably with two human subjects tested and trained on the same data. After 5 training sessions, the two subjects obtained an average of 70% on the images in the test set, with performances in some follow-up sessions approaching 80%. In Fig. 2, the types of errors made by the human subjects in these experiments are compared to those made by the network.

NETWORK RESPONSE

STIMULI	i	I	e	ɛ	æ	α	Λ	o	u
i	100.0								
I	16.7	66.7					12.5		
e			54.2	45.8					
ɛ			16.7	79.2					
æ				8.3	79.2				
α			12.5			45.8	37.5		
Λ				8.3		8.3	83.3		
o								91.7	8.3
u									100.0

(a)

HUMAN RESPONSE

STIMULI	i	I	e	ɛ	æ	α	Λ	o	u
i	79.2	20.8							
I	25.0	58.3		12.5					
e			37.5	58.3					
ɛ			37.5	62.5					
æ			12.5		83.3				
α						79.2	20.8		
Λ							95.8		
o								87.5	12.5
u									100.0

(b)

Fig. 2. Confusion matrices for a) networks trained to categorize individual images by vowel and b) well-trained human subjects categorizing the same images. The networks results are accumulated from four different networks. The human responses are accumulated from four trials by two subjects. Percentages less than 4.3% were omitted in order to simplify the matrix.

B. Discussion

Since steady-state vowels are relatively easy to identify acoustically, why is the performance less than perfect on the test images? Was it the lack of information in the images, or was it the lack of clear categories? To address the second part of this question, the short-term spectra of the corresponding acoustic data were examined. Networks were trained to categorize the acoustic spectra using the same procedures as used for the visual speech signals. The performance on the acoustic signals was almost identical to that of the visual signals, with the network obtaining 82% on the testing set. This suggests that some of the discrepancy between the performance on the training and test sets can be attributed to inherent ambiguity of the categories.

It is difficult, if not impossible, to correctly identify isolated speech segments out of context. The particular pronunciation of a given vowel varies depending upon the particular context in which it is produced. This phenomena, called *coarticulation*, produces large variations in the production of a given vowel. For example, the same vowel takes on quite different physical realizations depending upon the surrounding phonemic context. In automatic speech recognition, the best performances have been obtained when commitment to a categorical decision is delayed to a higher level of processing that takes into account more contextual information [7], [9]. This allows additional constraints from both internal and external sources to be introduced and to assist in the decision making.

The problem becomes more acute when the speech segments are taken from continuous speech. When a vowel is in a stressed position within an isolated word, the coarticulation is significantly less dramatic than when the vowel is extracted from the middle of continuous discourse. The effect of these differences is seen in machine recognition, where unstressed words are harder to recognize than are stressed words [9]. To demonstrate this, we constructed a second data set of 108 images taken from continuous speech spoken by a second speaker. The data had the same distribution of vowels and the networks were trained in the same manner as before. On this data, the networks were able to achieve only 40% on the test set.[2]

VI. Subsymbolic Processing

Summerfield has proposed and evaluated a variety of ways in which information in the acoustic and visual signals might merge [6]. He concluded from psychoacoustic experiments that information from the two modalities must be integrated before phonetic or lexical categorization takes place. One striking observation was that an auditorially presented larynx-frequency pulse can be used to improve lipreading even though there is not enough information in the pulse alone to phonetically segment the signal.

The assumption made is that the acoustic and visual signal streams share a common representation at their conflux [6]. In this section, we propose that the vocal tract transfer function can serve as this common representation, and we show that networks can be designed for integrating visual and acoustic speech signals using this representation. An estimate of the vocal tract's acoustic characteristics are obtained directly from images of the speaker's mouth. This estimate then serves as an independent source of acoustic information and is used to constrain the interpretation of the acoustic signal.

A. The Corresponding Acoustic Signal

The acoustic speech signal is produced by a source signal that passes through the vocal tract and is emitted from the mouth [20]. For voiced speech, the driving signal is a quasi-periodic pulse train convolved with the glottal waveform. This driving signal's contribution to the short-term acoustic spectrum is a series of harmonics reducing in amplitude by −12 dB per octave. This reduction is partially compensated by the radiation of the acoustic signal from the lips, which produces an effective gain of +6 dB per octave. The spectral envelope of the short-term spectrum that remains after these two effects are removed is the frequency response of the vocal-tract filter. The transfer function of the vocal tract can be estimated by measuring the short-term spectral amplitude envelope (STSAE) of the acoustic signal.

There is not enough information in the visual speech signal to completely specify the vocal-tract transfer function. Many different acoustic signals can be produced by vocal-tract configurations that correspond to the same visual signal. Thus, the visual signals can provide only a partial description of the vocal-tract filter. Nonetheless, it may be possible to obtain a *good* estimate of the vocal-tract transfer function if additional constraints are considered. Neural networks with the architecture shown in Fig. 3 were trained

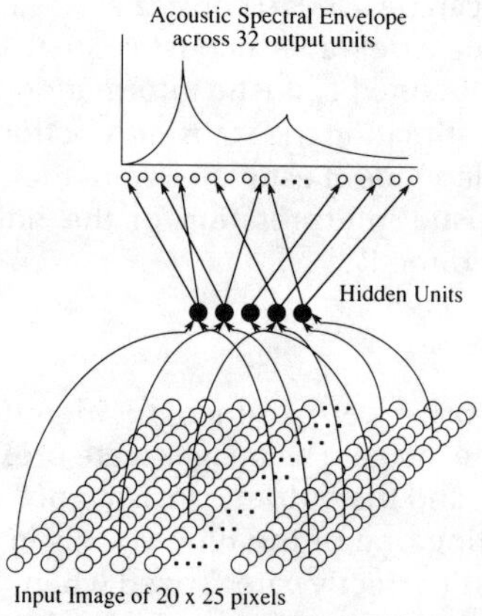

Fig. 3. Network architecture for estimating acoustic structure from visual speech signals. This feedforward network has all units in layer *i* connected to all units in layer *i* + 1. The output layer consisted of 32 units, each of which represented the amplitude of the vocal tract transfer function at a particular frequency and bandwidth.

to estimate the STSAE of the acoustic signal directly from the visual signals around the mouth. The estimate of the STSAE was then combined with estimates from acoustic information to improve the S/N ratio prior to recognition.

The same images of the male speaker used in the categorization experiments were used in these experiments. Each video frame had 33 ms of acoustic speech associated with it. The short-term power spectra of the corresponding acoustic data were calculated and the spectral envelopes were obtained using cepstral analysis [22.]. Each smoothed envelope was sampled at 32 frequencies to produce a vector of scalar values. These vectors were used to represent the vocal-tract transfer functions corresponding to the images.

B. Training

The network shown in Fig. 3 was trained to produce the STSAE across its 32 output units when a visual signal was

[2]Differences in experimental design make it difficult to compare our results with the performance of human lip-readers measured in other studies. In most experiments, human subjects are usually exposed to dynamic information as vowels are presented within a larger context. Berger *et al.* tested the identification of twelve vowels in CV and VC syllables within a context, using live presentation [37]. His data show that lipreaders without training performed at a 53% accuracy level. Jackson *et al.* used 15 vowels and diphthongs in an /h/-V-/g/ context, and found that the average performance level across 10 viewers to be 54% correct [38]. Montgomery and Jackson repeated these experiments and found a mean performance level of 54.2% [4].

presented to the network across the input units. The network had five hidden units as in the categorization experiment. However, there were now 32 output units, each representing the linearly spaced samples of the short-term spectrum's envelope.

One of the consequences of training a network on a continuous mapping, rather than on a discrete categorization, was the problem of deciding when to stop training. We attempted to identify the point at which overlearning began by dividing the test set into two subsets. One subset was used to *track* the error during training by testing the subset after each training epoch as a measure of generalization. When the error of the tracking set started to increase, the training was stopped and the weights in the network were saved. This procedure was unnecessary when the training was simply stopped at 500 iterations.

C. Evaluation

Vowels are largely identified by their spectral shape, and in particular by the location of their spectral peaks, or formants [39], [40]. Nevertheless, evaluating the quality of these spectral estimates is significantly more difficult than judging the accuracy of a categorization because the perceptual processes involved in processing the spectral peaks are not well understood. To assay our spectral estimates, a simple vowel-recognition system was constructed (Fig. 4). The

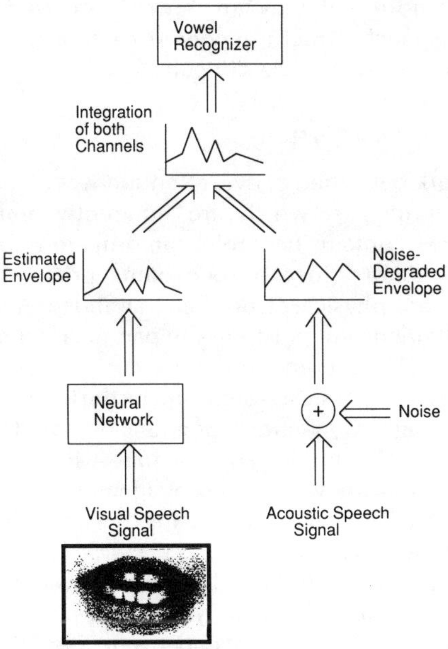

Fig. 4. System used to combine visual and acoustic speech information. A simple vowel recognizer was constructed to receive speech signals from the two modalities. Independent estimates of the vocal tract transfer function were produced and then combined with a weighted average before being passed to the recognizer. A neural network was trained to perform the mapping of the image into the estimated envelope of the acoustic spectra. Noise was introduced into the acoustic speech signal and the improvement due to the visual information was assessed.

vowel recognizer at the top of Fig. 4 was constructed using a simple feedforward network trained to recognize nine vowels from their STSAEs. The network was trained on 6 examples each of 9 different vowels until its performance was 100% on the training data. This network served as a *perfect* recognizer of the noise-free training data and was used to assess the benefit of the visually estimated spectra when combined with the noise-degraded acoustic spectra.

The vowel recognizer was presented with a STSAE through two channels. The path shown on the right in Fig. 4 was for information obtained from the acoustic signal, while the path on the left provided spectral estimates obtained independently from the corresponding visual speech signal.

The first step was to test the performance of the recognizer when the acoustic spectral envelopes were degraded by noise. Zero-mean random vectors were normalized and added to the training STSAEs to produce signals with S/N ratios ranging from −12 dB to 24 dB. Noise-corrupted vectors were produced at 3 dB intervals from −12 dB to 24 dB. At each noise level, 12 different vectors were produced for each of the STSAE in the set. At each level, the performances of the recognizer on the degraded signals were averaged. The overall performance on the training data fell with decreased S/N ratios. At − 12 dB, the recognizer operated at the chance level, which was 11% with nine vowels in the data set (Fig. 5).

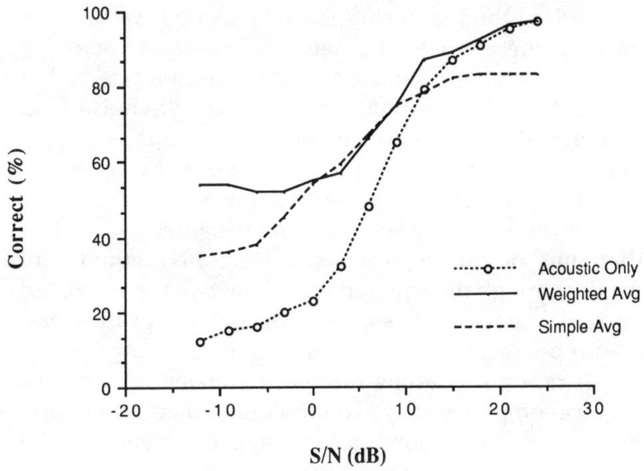

Fig. 5. Intelligibility of noise-degraded speech as a function of speech-to-noise ratio in dB. The lower curve shows the performance of the recognizer under varying signal-to-noise conditions using only the acoustic channel. The intermediate dashed curve shows the performance when the two independent estimates are equally weighted. The top curve shows the improved performance by using a weighting function based on the signal-to-noise. When the visual signal is used alone, the percent correct is 55% across all S/N levels.

The next step was to compensate for the noise degradation by providing an independent estimate of the STSAE from the visual signal, as shown on the left side of Fig. 4. The network on this pathway was trained to estimate the spectral envelopes corresponding to the input images. The data used to train this network were different from the data used to train the recognizer. The noise-degraded acoustic signal was then combined with the output from the network processing the images to provide a single estimate which is then passed on to the recognizer. When the two estimates were simply averaged together, the recognition rates were improved, as shown by the dashed curve in Fig.

5. At a S/N ratio of − 12 dB the recognizer performed at 35% compared to 11% without the visual signal.

However, averaging the two independent sources of information was far less than optimal at the extremes. Using the STSAE estimated from the visual signal alone, the recognizer was capable of a 55% recognition level. When these estimates were combined with the noise-degraded acoustic signal, the performance fell to as low as 35% at −12 dB S/N. Similarly, at very high S/N ratios, the fused inputs produced poorer results than the acoustic signal presented alone. Clearly, the acoustic and visual signals needed to be weighted according to their relative information content to compensate for the degraded performance at the S/N ratio extremes.

The two estimates of the spectral estimates of the vocal tract transfer function, $S_{\text{visually estimated}}$ and S_{acoustic} were combined with a weighting factor α that depends on the S/N ratio:

$$S_{\text{combined}} = \alpha S_{\text{visually estimated}} + (1 - \alpha) S_{\text{acoustic}} \quad (1)$$

At each S/N ratio, α was varied to optimize performance. The optimal α was found empirically to vary approximately linearly with the S/N ratio to 0 to 24 dB. The improved performance is evident in Fig. 5.

A third method of fusing the two spectra was accomplished using a σ–π neural network. These second-order networks took the estimated STSAE, the noise-degraded acoustic STSAE and a measure of the signal-to-noise ratio as input, and tried to produce a noise-free STSAE as output. In contrast to the simple weighted sum used by first-order units, the units in these second-order networks determine the activation level by summing the weighted product or other units' output [26]. The results from this method were mixed: although the squared-error between the estimated and actual spectra was significantly lower, its categorization was poorer. These results suggest that the vowel recognizer is doing something more complicated than simply making a comparison based upon a squared-error measure. They also raise questions as to the appropriateness of the squared-error measure used for training.

D. Comparing Performance

The quality of the networks' estimates were compared to a combination of two optimal linear-estimation techniques. The first step was to encode the images using a Hotelling or Karhunen-Loeve transform [41]. The images were encoded as five-dimensional vectors defined by the largest principal components of the covariance matrix of the images in the training set. This is an optimal encoding of the images with respect to a least-squared-error (LSE) measure. The next step was to find a mapping from these encoded image vectors to their corresponding short-term spectral amplitude envelopes (STSAEs). The fit was found using a linear least-squares fit.

The estimates obtained by this two-stage process were significantly poorer in overall mean-squared error. The mean-squared error of the estimates made by the networks was 46% better on the training set and 12% better on the test set. The main objective of this comparison was to show that arbitrary encoding of the images may result in a loss of relevant information. In contrast, the network learning algorithm allows the network to produce its own encoding at the hidden layer based upon relevant features. The activation levels of the five hidden units served to encode the image as did the five-dimensional vectors obtained using principal components. The primary difference is that the encoding found by the network optimized the desired output, whereas the principal components optimized the LSE reconstruction of the images.

E. Discussion

The recognition rates of noise-degraded acoustic signals were improved by introducing speech information extracted from the visual speech correlates. The relative improvement provided by fusing these signals varied with the S/N ratio, agreeing with the experimental data presented by Sumby and Pollack in their seminal 1954 paper [3]. This was accomplished without making hard decisions on the separate acoustic and visual sensory channels, and no explicit rules were needed to combine the information. In general, the psychoacoustic evidence suggests that the visual and acoustic speech signals interact in the human perceptual systems even before categorical cognitive processes are activated [42]–[45], [6].

In acoustic speech recognition, significant improvements can be made with existing systems by improving the quality of the signal at the earliest levels [9]. The approach described above provides a means of improving the input to existing speech recognition systems. The strength of this approach is more evident when networks are used on nonsegmental speech structures where categorical identification becomes even more difficult.

VII. Dynamics and Speech

In the work described above, attention was restricted to static visual images, which are inherently ambiguous because they contain incomplete information about the speech articulators. Speech is a dynamic process and the articulators are physical structures that move. As a given moment, their current positions are part of larger dynamic trajectories. These trajectories are constrained by the mechanics of the physical system and by the linguistic rules of the language. Dynamic dependencies could provide additional constraints that can serve to restrict the acoustic interpretation of the visual speech signal. In this section, we outline an approach to introducing dynamic constraints in neural network models.

One way to include temporal constraints is to map time into space, as in NETtalk [28]. In NETalk, consecutive letters were translated into a string of concurrent stimuli and presented to the network in groups of seven. The network was given a sequence of letters and asked to provide a phonetic transcription of the centrally located letter. A similar approach, called a time-delay neural network model, has been effective in acoustic speech-recognition systems [46], [47].

A different way to introduce dynamic constraints is to use feedback connections that provide temporal memory. One approach is to have projections from the output units to the input layer [48]. A second approach is to have projections from hidden units to the input layer [49]. These architectures are based on feedforward networks with a subset of the input units, called *state units*, receiving information from previous time steps. Thus, at time t, the network receives inputs $I(t)$ and a subset of activations from the upper layers at previous time $t - 1$.

When working with static images, it was possible to use a simple vowel recognizer to test the quality and utility of the acoustic spectra estimated from static images. The success of the vowel recognizer depended on the careful selection of vowels from isolated words or syllables. For continuous speech, however, it is difficult and often impossible to make these definitive identifications of short speech segments taken out of context, so alternative assessments are necessary.

Networks with feedback were used to estimate the STSAE from images within a larger context. The performance of the network on continuous speech was evaluated on its ability to preserve the salient features of the spectral sequences, such as the resonances, or formants, of the estimated vocal-tract filter. The perception of vowels by humans depend upon the location and amplitude of these formants [39], with some of the highest quality machine speech being produced using formant-based synthesizers [50]. To see how well these formats were identified by the network, the sequences of spectra were arranged in a visual display similar to a spectrogram. The spectrogram shown in Fig. 6 was

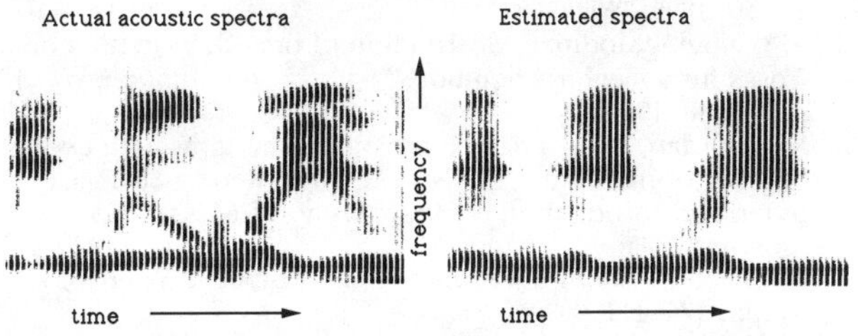

Fig. 6. Spectrograms created from the actual acoustic spectra are compared to visually estimated spectra for the sentence: "We will weigh you." Individual spectral estimates were converted to a grey scale and then aligned by frequency as a function of time. Actual acoustic data from the test set are shown on the left and estimates produced by the feedback neural network model are shown on the right.

created from spectra estimated from a sequence of images not in the training set. In this form, we can observe the changes of energy in the different frequency bands as a function of time. Clearly, much of the acoustic structure was being estimated in these sequences. The ultimate test will be to either resynthesize the acoustic speech signal from these estimated acoustic parameters, or to feed the fused spectra into a full-scale speech recognizer.

VIII. Conclusions

Under noisy conditions, speech recognition can be aided by extracting information from the visual speech signals and combining it with residual acoustic information. In this article we have examined two representations for the speech information in the visual signal, both of which can be combined with information from the acoustic signal. In the first case the visual signal was treated symbolically, while in the second it was used to provide subsymbolic information about the corresponding acoustic signal. These two cases are two points on a continuum of speech descriptions. Other descriptions, such as description of the articulators themselves [51] could also have been used.

A better understanding of the visual and acoustic sensory systems in humans and other animals will lead to better artificial sensors and their effective integration. Acoustic speech recognition systems, by using models of the human cochlea as a preprocessor, are already benefitting from what is known about the human auditory system [19], [52]. Synthetic cochleas that can process massive amounts of sensory data is real time already have been fabricated in analog VLSI [53]. The output of these chips is a highly distilled, parallel and distributed representation of the acoustic signal. Our results are an encouraging first step toward solving the problem of fusing multiple sources of distributed sensory data. Massively parallel network models could provide the means by which distributed representation can be integrated in real time for producing rapid recognition and decisive actions for automated systems.

IX. Acknowledgment

We would like to thank Nancy Giacobbe for her work on the human subject experiments.

References

[1] H. W. Ewersten, and H. Birk-Nielsen, "A comparative analysis of the audiovisual, auditive and visual perception of speech," *Acta Oto-Larynsol.*, vol. 72, pp. 201–205, 1971.

[2] N. P. Erber, "Auditory-visual perception of speech," *J. Speech Hearing Disorders*, vol. 40, pp. 481–492, 1975.

[3] W. H. Sumby and I. Pollack, "Visual contribution to speech intelligibility in noise," *J. Acoust. Soc. Am.*, vol. 26, pp. 212–215, 1954.

[4] A. Montgomery and P. L. Jackson, "Physical characteristics of the lips underlying vowel lipreading," *J. Acoust. Soc. Am.*, vol. 73, pp. 2134–2144, 1983.

[5] L. E., Bernstein, S. P. Eberhardt, and M. E. Demorest, "Single-channel vibrotactile supplements to visual perception of intonation and stress," *J. Acoust. Soc. Am.*, vol. 85, pp. 397–405, 1989.

[6] Q. Summerfield, "Some preliminaries to a comprehensive account of audio-visual speech perception," in *Hearing by Eye: The Psychology of Lip-Reading*. B. Dodd and R. Campbell, Eds. Hillsdale, NJ: Lawrence Erlbaum Assoc. Publishers, 1987.

[7] J. Allen, "A perspective on man-machine communication by speech," *Proc. IEEE*, vol. 73, pp. 1537–1696, 1985.

[8] CHABA (Committee on Hearing, Bioacoustics, and Biomechanics), *Removal of Noise From Noise-Degraded Speech Signals*. Washington, D.C.: National Research Council, National Academy Press, 1989.

[9] K. F. Lee, *Automatic Speech Recognition: The Development of the SPHINX System*. Boston: Kluwer Academic Press, 1989.

[10] E. D. Petajan, *An Improved Automatic Lipreading System to Enhance Speech Recognition*, AT&T Bell Laboratories Technical Report No. 11251-071012-111TM, Murray Hill, NJ, 1987.

[11] B. Lindblom, "Phonetic invariance and the adaptive nature of speech," in *Working Models of Human Perception*, B. Elsendoorn and H. Bouma, Eds. London, England: Academic Press, 1989, pp. 139–173.

[12] J. Lyons, *Introduction to Theoretical Linguistics*. Cambridge, England: Cambridge University Press, 1971.

[13] C. G. Fisher, "Confusions among visually perceived consonants," *J. Speech Hearing Res.*, vol. 11, pp. 796–803, 1968.

[14] B. E. Walden, R. A. Prosek, A. Montgomery, C. K. Scherr, and J. J. Jones, "Effects of training on the visual recognition of consonants," *J. Speech Hearing Res.*, vol. 20, pp. 130–145, 1977.

[15] R. Jacobson and M. Halle, *Fundamentals of Language*. The Hague, Netherlands: Mouton & Co., Publishers, 1956.

[16] O. Fujimura, "Relative invariance of articulatory movements: An iceberg model," in *Invariance and Variability in Speech Processes*, J. Perkell and D. H. Klatt, Eds. Hillsdale, NJ: Lawrence Erlbaum Assoc. Publishers, 1986.

[17] H. K. Dunn, "The calculation of vowel resonances, and an

electric vocal tract," *J. Acoust. Soc. Am.*, vol. 22, pp. 740–753, 1950.

[18] R. A. Cole, A. I. Rudnicky, V. W. Zue, and D. R. Reddy, "Speech as patterns on paper," in *Perception and Production of Fluent Speech*, R. A. Cole, Ed. Hillsdale, NJ: Lawrence Erlbaum Assoc. Publishers, 1980.

[19] F. Jelinek, "The development of an experimental discrete dictation recognizer," *Proc. IEEE*, vol. 73, pp. 1616–1624, 1985.

[20] G. Fant, *Acoustic Theory of Speech Production.* The Hague, Netherlands: Mouton & Co., Publishers, 1960.

[21] J. L. Flanagan, *Speech Analysis, Synthesis and Perception.* Berlin: Springer-Verlag, 1972.

[22] J. D. Markel, and A. H. Gray, Jr., *Linear Prediction of Speech.* Berlin: Springer-Verlag, 1976.

[23] G. A. Miller, and P. E. Nicely, "An analysis of perceptual confusions among some English consonants, *J. Acoust. Soc. Am.*, vol. 27, pp. 338–352, 1955.

[24] T. J. Sejnowski, "Open questions about computation in cerebral cortex," *Parallel Distributed Processing in the Microstructure of Cognition.* Vol. 1, *Foundations.* J. McClelland and D. Rumelhart, Eds. Cambridge, MA: M.I.T. Press, 1986.

[25] F. J. Pineda, "Generalization of back-propagation to recurrent neural networks," *Phys. Rev. Lett.*, vol. 59, pp. 2229–2232, 1987.

[26] D. E. Rumelhart, J. L. McClelland, and the PDP Research Group, *Parallel Distributed Processing: Explorations in the Microstructures of Cognition.* Cambridge, MA: M.I.T. Press, 1986, vol. 1.

[27] J. J. Hopfield, and D. W. Tank, "Neural computation of decisions in optimizations problems," *Biol. Cybern.*, vol. 52, pp. 141–152, 1985.

[28] T. J. Sejnowski, and C. R. Rosenberg, "Parallel networks that learn to pronounce English text," *Complex Systems*, vol. 1, pp. 145–168, 1987.

[29] T. Kohonen, *Self-Organization and Associative Memory.* Berlin: Springer-Verlag, 1984.

[30] G. A. Carpenter, "Neural network models for pattern recognition and associative memory," *Neural Networks*, vol. 2, pp. 243–258, 1989.

[31] K. Hornik, M. Stinchcombe, H. White, "Multilayer feedforward networks are universal approximators," *Neural Networks*, vol. 2, pp. 359–366, 1989.

[32] Y. S. Abu-Mostafa, "The Vapnik-Chervonenkis dimension: Information versus complexity in learning," *Neural Computation*, vol. 1, pp. 312–317, 1989.

[33] H. White, "Learning in artificial neural networks: A statistical perspective," *Neural Computation*, vol. 1, pp. 425–464, 1989.

[34] W. H. Press, B. P. Flannery, S. A. Teukolsky, and W. T. Vetterling, *Numerical Recipes in C.* Cambridge, England: Cambridge University Press, 1988.

[35] L. E. Bernstein, and S. P. Eberhardt, *Johns Hopkins Lipreading Corpus I-II*, Johns Hopkins University, Baltimore, MD, 1986.

[36] B. P. Yuhas, *The Processing of Visual Speech Signals Using Parallel Distributed Processing.* Ph.D. dissertation, Department of Electrical and Computer Engineering, Johns Hopkins University, Baltimore, MD, 1990.

[37] K. W. Berger, "Vowel confusions in speechreading," *Ohio J. Speech and Hearing*, vol. 5, pp. 123–128, 1970.

[38] P. L. Jackson, A. A. Montgomery, and C. A. Binnie, "Perceptual dimensions underlying vowel lipreading performance," *J. Speech Hearing Res.*, vol. 19, pp. 796–812, 1976.

[39] G. E. Peterson, and H. L. Barney, "Control methods used in a study of the vowels," *J. Acoust. Soc. Am.*, vol. 24, pp. 175–184, 1952.

[40] R. L. Miller, "Auditory tests with synthetic vowels," *J. Acoust. Soc. Am.*, vol. 25, pp. 114–121, 1953.

[41] R. C. Gonzalez, and P. Wintz, *Digital Image Processing.* Reading, MA: Addison-Wesley, 1977, pp. 104–108.

[42] H. McGurk, and J. MacDonald, "Hearing lips and seeing voices," *Nature*, vol. 264, pp. 746–748, 1976.

[43] H. McGurk, and J. MacDonald, "Visual influences on speech processes," *Perception & Psychophysics*, vol. 24, pp. 253–257, 1978.

[44] P. K. Kuhl, and A. N. Meltzoff, "The bimodal perceptions of speech in infancy," *Science*, vol. 218, pp. 1138–1141, 1982.

[45] E. Spelke, "Infants' intermodal perception of speech events," *Cog. Psychol.*, vol. 8, pp.. 553–560, 1976.

[46] D. W. Tank, J. J. Hopfield, "Neural computation by concentrating information in time," *Proc. Nat. Acad. Sci. USA*, vol. 94, pp. 1896–1900, 1987.

[47] A. Waibel, "Modular construction of time-delay neural networks for speech recognition," *Neural Computation*, vol. 1, pp. 39–46, 1989.

[48] M. I. Jordan, "Supervised learning and systems with excess degrees of freedom," COINS Technical Report 88-27, Computer and Information Science, Univ. of Massachusetts at Amherst, 1988.

[49] J. L. Elman, *Finding structure in time, Cognitive Science*, vol. 14, pp. 179–211, 1990.

[50] D. H. Klatt, "Speech perception: A model of acoustic-phonetic analysis and lexical access," in *Perception and Production of Fluent Speech*, R. A. Cole, Ed. Hillsdale, NJ: Lawrence Erlbaum Assoc. Publishers, 1980.

[51] O. Rioul, and B. S. Atal, personal communication, 1990.

[52] S. Seneff, *Pitch and Spectral Analysis of Speech Based on an Auditory Synchrony Model*, M.I.T. Research Laboratory of Electronics Technical Report 504, Massachusetts Institute of Technology, Cambridge, MA, 1985.

[53] C. Mead, *Analog VLSI and Neural Systems.* New York, NY: Addison-Wesley, 1989.

Author Index

Subject Index

Editor's Biography

Clifford G. Y. Lau (Senior Member, IEEE) received the B.S. and M.S. degrees from the University of California at Berkeley, and the Ph.D. degree from the University of California at Santa Barbara in 1978, all in electrical engineering and computer science.

Prior to 1978, he was employed as an electronics engineer at the Pacific Missile Test Center, Point Mugu, and worked on electronic countermeasure techniques, missile navigation, guidance, and control. From 1978 to 1980, he was on the faculty of the Division of Head and Neck Surgery, University of California at Los Angeles, and did research on the vestibular and oculomotor systems. From 1980 to 1988 he was with the ONR Western Regional Office, and was involved in microelectronic circuits, VLSI systems, and signal processing. He was the chairman of the Design, Architecture, Software, and Testing Committee for the DoD Very High Speed Integrated Circuits program. He has published technical papers on a wide range of topics, including equivalent networks, control system instability, wafer scale integration, VLSI reliability, vestibulo-ocular system models, and neural networks.

Dr. Lau is presently a Scientific Officer at the Electronics Division, Office of Naval Research, and is responsible for the management of basic research programs in VLSI algorithms and architectures for signal processing, VLSI reliability, ultra-dependable multiprocessor computers, and electronic neural networks. He is an Associate Editor of the *IEEE Transactions on Circuits and Systems*, and is the organizing chairman of the first Government Neural Network Applications Workshop. He is the co-editor of a recently introduced book, *An Introduction to Neural and Electronic Networks*.